BLUES
RHYTHM & BLUES
SOUL

•

by Jerry Osborne
and
Bruce Hamilton

Distributed by

O'SULLIVAN
WOODSIDE
& CO.
Phoenix, Arizona

Published in the United States of America

First Edition.

Manufactured in the United States of America.

ISBN: 0-89019-071-2

ACKNOWLEDGEMENTS

Jellyroll Productions dedicates this book to Victor Pearlin, Dick Haggett and Nay Nasser, whose support and assistance in the research and development of this book never wavered over the years.

Especial credit must be given as well to Darryl Stolper and Ferdie Gonzalez. We also want to thank the following for their efforts: Alligator Productions, Dave Antrell, Frank Black, Blues Unlimited, Bob Cattaneo, Ken Clee, Len Eisenstein, Robert Ferlingere, Tom Koehler, Rip Lay, Geri-Anne Osborne, High Nelson, Val Shively, Dean Silverstone, Jeff Stolper, Mike Valle and Joel Whitburn.

—Jerry and Bruce, 1980

CONTENTS

HOW TO USE THIS RECORD GUIDE

It is the intent of this price guide to present an in-depth listing of collectible records in blues and rhythm and blues in a manner that has never been attempted before—exhaustively comprehensive and cross-referenced—so that anything can be found easily that's in the book and when located, will be grouped with other material by the same artist or artists.

The unique usefulness of this book will become more and more apparent the more anyone uses it.

Six years in the price guide business has taught us a lot about collectors and the general public (that massive populace out there, teeming with hundreds of thousands—if not millions—of potential record collectors) and what they want and are looking for in a price guide.

WHAT'S NOT HERE

We're beginning to feel like a miniaturized Encyclopaedia Britannica, whose problem (like ours) is ***too much*** information. Our real job is to decide what to put in versus what to leave out. Most people—especially serious collectors—are not really interested in listings of thousands of records by people they've never heard of that have no collector value. The main redeeming feature, a negative one, in favor of listing a $2 record is to be able to look it up as a reassurance that it is ***not*** valuable.

THE SIZE IS RIGHT

We've listed all of what we believe to be the significant names of singles and groups in both rhythm and blues and blues, whether they have money records or not, but we chose to cut the cost of what would have made this an expensive $15, $20 or $25 book by eliminating many thousands of records that are worth $5 or less on the collector's market. This meant leaving out ***all*** records by many performers, though their names remain in! This will be of little concern, though, to most serious collectors.

The mind-blower is that this book documents many hundreds of singles that are worth from $100 to over $1,000 each!

ARTISTS WITH NO RECORDS

We have listed all significant artists' names, even though none of their records may be worth over $5, because the uninitiated—the non-collector—would find it frustrating to look up his favorite R & B or soul records and not find anything at all. The listings of these artists' names means that in future editions, as their records come of value, they will be added to our computer banks and will be in our guide.

Even when earlier works have reached or far-surpassed that $5 plateau, their later recordings may not have. A case in point: if you were to look up the first record The Clovers ever released (on Rainbow), you'd find it to be worth as much as $360 in mint condition. Even their first record on Atlantic (a much more common label) is still a respectable $60 collector's item, but as the group's fame spread and their records sold more and more copies, ones released on Atlantic just a year later will bring only $16, two years later $10, and three years later only $6. By the time "Love, Love, Love" and "Devil Or Angel" came out, enough have survived today that they're considered only of minimal value and we've not listed them.

COMPLETE DISCOGRAPHIES?

Looking ahead to the second edition, we can see that there are certain artists whose entire discographies would have collector interest, and we plan to add an entire section to list everything done by them (Fats Domino, perhaps, for one) in the chronological order they were released, but with no values attributed. Then, in our regular A-Z listings, as in this book, we'll alphabetically repeat only the records by those artists with collector value. We openly solicit reader input as to who those artists should be!

TELLING GROUPS APART

If two different groups have exactly the same name (a very common occurrence in rhythm and blues) but neither has any records worth over $5—The Challengers, for instance—we list the name only once and no records by either group. We list the same name more than once only if two or more groups with the same name ***each*** have records worth over $5. It is not our purpose to list how many groups or individuals recorded under the same name; what is important is to be able to distinguish between those with the same names that ***do*** have collectible records. Even then there are some interesting problems with changing personnel. When does a group cease being the same group as, one by one, all personnel change?

OUR FIRST INTENT

The structure of this book has changed several times as its purposes clarified over a period of four years. Its intent was first to be an all-inclusive book of the music of blacks, excluding only jazz and gospel. It didn't take long before our research showed us the impossibility of that task for one mere book. Blues

78s prior to World War II could take a full book by themselves.

THE DIVIDING LINE

Even though the roots of rhythm and blues have been with us since recorded music began, the art in its defined form really came into being in the 40s. Partially because of a much-maligned Petrillo musicians-union strike in the early 40s, many anthologies and discographies have chosen that blank period of inactivity as the dividing line between early and "contemporary" blues. World War II and its aftermath changed tastes, too, as wars always do, and that, combined with the history that was about to be made with the advent of the long play album and the revolutionary, compact 45, all combined to make the division a logical, clean one.

PERMANENCY OF THE 45

The little seven-inch records with the big holes soon took over and have become the most "in" of all recorded collectibles. In the future the long play album will relegate the 45 to second place, a trend that is already making itself felt. But that's another matter, and not one for concern here, because collecting singles will be around longer than anyone reading this. Collector interest in the 45 was inevitable because of its small, thin size and durability compared to the larger, breakable 78.

R & B IS BIG!

Collecting rhythm and blues has blossomed into the biggest area in the hobby in terms of money records. There are possibly as many as 600 R & B singles that are worth $100 or more!

WHAT THE BOOK COULDN'T BE

We seriously entertained including popular music by blacks because of the cross-over by some performers, but that, too, had to be ruled out, even to the extent of our having at times to make what will assuredly seem to be arbitrary decisions as to whether records belong in this book, the ***Popular And Rock*** singles book, the ***Big Bands*** book, or where. It became obvious that this guide should not—could not, in fact—be a book on ***all*** the music of blacks, or all music ***by*** blacks. The form needed to be zeroed in on.

WHAT IS A BLACK RECORD?

Blacks developed the sounds of blues and rhythm and blues, and they so heavily dominate them, were we to exclude white performers entirely, they'd scarely be missed! More of a problem would have been to absolutely determine just what constituted a "black" record in the first place. Would the records have to have been on an all-black, black-owned label? Many groups were mixed, that is, comprising of two, three or four members of different color, race or background. Too, many of the most popular all-black rhythm and blues records of the 50s were written by whites.

A MANDATORY CHANGE

It became increasingly clear that the genre was what counted and despite the dominance of the blacks, one of the beauties of the form was the lack of color barriers. The blues, and then eventually, the extension of adding "rhythm" to the blues, in its origins, in its simplest form an expression of unhappiness, was usually associated with the poor of the ghettos or of the south. As whites had also fallen victim to the poverty that oppressed the blacks, they, too, inevitably shared "the blues." No book like this could have excluded the blues music of the white man, Harmonica Frank. He was one of the first "exceptions" that we discovered we must include. When our direction changed, we realized our original title for the book, "Blacks And Blues," was no longer appropriate.

Despite our changes in focus, this book remains essentially 98% documentation of the music of blacks. Our second edition will undoubtedly integrate many more white and "mixed" groups, possibly even some of British origin.

THE EARLY RECORDS

Most material documented prior to WWII is for special purpose, such as the acknowledgment that the Dinwiddie Colored Quartet, who recorded for Monarch in 1902 (the same records were released later on the old Victor label), are recognized as the first black group records. Then there's Joe Turner, whose discography in these pages begins in 1939. Anything short of a comprehensive listing of his records would have been unthinkable in a book that is 75% rhythm and blues.

THE 78 VERSUS THE 45

All records listed in this book are 45s unless indicated otherwise and the prices shown are for first pressings (please refer to the ***very important*** article on first pressings). We have listed a few 33 1/3 singles, rare and short-lived dinosaurs that never got off the ground in sales and public acceptance. Though many collectors will buy an occasional or rare 78,there are few who don't prefer the 45 if it is also available. Even when there are no 45 counterparts, 78s usually will never command the prices 45s would have. The exceptions are very rare. The most notable, of course, is the 78 of "Stormy Weather" by The Five Sharps. The exceptionally-high value attributed to it comes from the notoriety that's been attached to it, the legends surrounding it and the long-standing focus of attention on it.

A BIG CONTROVERSY

Many collectors insist that they would never pay $5,000 for a mint copy of "Stormy Weather," and that no record should ever be worth more than a few hundred dollars.

While it's true that most collectors would not pay that kind of money for "Stormy Weather," it's also true that most collectors couldn't ***afford*** to pay that kind of money for ***any*** record.

It's equally true that these same collectors don't ***have*** a copy in their collections.

And lastly, it's true that there are a few collectors who would ***gladly*** pay that price to be in possession of such a sought-after, infamous item. Supply and demand is what the game is all about. And, while most collectors maintain in absolute sincerity that they'd never ***pay*** such outrageous prices, if they ever came into possession of a copy and circumstances dictated that they must sell, they ***always*** change their minds about its value. That's not a reflection on the hobby, it's just human nature.

RELATIVE VALUES

We do not list both 78s and 45s of the same record. When a 78 is listed it means that a 45 does not exist, to the best of our knowledge. You can depend with 99%+ assurance that if we state a record was issued on 45, it was. However, conversely, there are times when we've indicated a price for a 78 when we think there possibly may have been a 45, but we can't verify it. Generally, 78s are less collectible because of their fragility, their size, their lesser quality, and the difficulty of playing them easily on modern-day equipment. If you should find a 78 and see we've only priced the 45 version of the same record, you can safely assume that the record you have is worth about a third or less. The more expensive and the earlier a 45, the greater the supply of 78s and the wider the discrepancy between values. A rare 1950 rhythm and blues 45 may be worth ten times as much as its common counterpart 78. 78s from 1958 or 1959, on the other hand, just before they were discontinued, can often bring nearly as much as the more common 45 (and sometimes even more).

IS IT A FAKE?

If you should have a 45 and note that we've listed it only as a 78, you may have a valuable item (see The Orioles). We must issue the warning, however, that very often illegitimate 45 ***copies*** of these records have been put out, illegally taken from original 78s, so one should not automatically rejoice upon finding one, till its authenticity is checked out by an expert. Be particularly suspicious of the $5, $10 or $25 "bargains" that show up at swap meets. However, if what seems to be a valuable find appears in a box marked at $1 or under, you'd better pick it up, as most fake records cost that much to produce.

REPEATING OURSELVES

In most cases where a listing is repeated in this price guide, it is because of two initial releases with different second sides or some other early change, including second issues on a different label. The differences in price in such cases are unpredictable, so the multiple listings are important. The most common duplication of titles are for 45s released simultaneously on black and colored plastic. The latter are usually in higher collector demand and more valuable, though not always rarer.

THE EARLY BLUES? NO!

This is essentially a book of post-war blues and rhythm and blues 45s, though the chronology of 78s represented go back as far as 1902. There are some valuable early 45s that are merely re-issues of 78s that were recorded several years before. The dates in the far right column are when those records were originally recorded, if the later release dates are not known. If we have no substantiated information on either date, we've made no attempt to guess.

Even though we've traced some roots of rhythm and blues back into the 1930s and before, the era of pre-war blues, as we've mentioned, is too formidable and would require a price guide of its own. The determination of values would be arbitrary to some extent, since it's known, for instance, that some depression-era blues records, particularly in the south, were released by labels that pressed 50 or fewer copies to circulate through local outlets. Obviously, no collector could ever hope, no matter how much money he was willing to spend, to get a complete collection of that kind of material. There are probably no copies in existence today of many of those records. When such a record does surface and is auctioned off, the price it is likely to bring seems to be geared more than anything to the pocketbooks of the collectors at that moment who want it most. A single sale under such circumstances would hardly be indicative of the record's true worth, since it may never be offered again. Some of the people who auction that sort of material—and, even some of the collectors themselves—tend to be close-mouthed about what prices are realized. The dealers don't want the inevitable competition that would come from others if they knew how much they were making, and the collectors fear investors who may jump into the market and drive the prices even higher than they are already.

WHAT WE MAY DO

Were Jellyroll to expand this book to cover sections of pre-war blues in future editions, it may be necessary only to document prices on those records that turn up in quantities commensurate with the numbers pressed and only to give rough estimations on those that are ***impossible*** to price. We would like to open serious dialog on this subject with blues collectors and we invite their comments.

HOW TO LOOK UP R & B

Our solutions to cross-referencing had to consider both collectors and non-collectors. If John "non-collector" Doe had a copy of "Darling, Listen To The Words Of This Song," by Ruth McFadden And The Supremes, we reason he'd be most likely to look it up under "M." So we've listed "McFadden" as a cross-reference to The Supremes, which we wanted to keep together. We've tried to cross-reference all possibilities, including possible confusing situations, such as having three "John Lee's," one artist whose last name is Lee and two whose given first names were John Lee, but all of whom recorded as John Lee!

HOW TO LOOK UP BLUES

Groups offer the most sought-after sound in rhythm and blues, but not in the case of the blues. A headline blues performer may have gone by several names, or may have had different groups or backing instrumentalists accompanying him. These names are all of interest and are noted, but are still secondary to the star. We felt that no matter how many different names a blues artist used, the collector would want all of his records to be listed together in the guide, and that's why whenever possible we've used his real name. To have done so in any other manner would have opened up a zoo of contradictions. Even though we didn't know the artist's real name in many cases, these are usually secondary performers or ones who used only one stage name. These listings seldom serve as complete discographies, but then, they are not ***intended*** to be.

WHEN SIDE "A" IS SIDE "B"

The alphabetical listing of records in a book such as this presents the problem of which ***side*** of each record to list first. "Snake Walk, Part 1," and "Snake Walk, Part 2," would be obvious, but few others are. If we were to adhere to a strict technical formula as designated on the records themselves, we would go by a pre-determined "A" and "B" side on each release, which is sometimes actually labelled "A" or "B," but most often indicated by a side number that is different from the larger record numbers that we use in the guide. The accepted industry designation is that the smaller of these two master numbers is the "A" side. For instance, if the side number on "Rosemarie" by The Five Chimes we were to see as 1301 and the number on the other side's song, "Never Love Another," as 1302, we would know the smaller number indicated "Rosemarie" as the first side that we should alphabetize, with "Never Love Another" as the "flip." As a practicality, however, it doesn't always work. The "A" side of a record isn't always the hit side. The master number on "Money Honey," by Clyde McPhatter and The Drifters was higher than "The Way I Feel," but it's still the side most people would look up, so that's the side we list first.

A reference in parenthesis concerning who performed a featured vocal, or if the song is an instrumental, always follows the side being referred to, even if that information happens by chance to be on a line by itself. References to both sides of any record are indented in paragraphs by themselves, without parentheses, ending with a period.

Another consideration in alphabetization is that most rhythm and blues records that are real money items today weren't hits when they came out, and it's the ballad side that collector's tend to prefer today. More often than not, the "jump" side tended to be the side with the lower master number. Confused? Well, in short, we've tried to list the records alphabetically by the side most likely to be looked up, with all other considerations set aside. Good luck!

MECHANICALS

Computer logic in our alphabetization will be easy to determine once it's understood that spaces and punctuation preceed the letter "A." Thus, Mello-Moods appear in our book with five other groups listed before the "computer logic" inserted Mello-Moods. "I Will" appears before "I'll," and "I'll appears before "Ida."

If you see the line, "Acklin, Barbara, Gene Chandler &" it means that Gene Chandler's name appeared before Barbara Acklin's on their record or records.

A WARNING!

The two columns of good to very good and near mint each represent the average selling price for records in that condition (see the page on Scarcity, Demand and Grading). ***It must be understood that a price approximately halfway between these two columns is the top price for the average best condi-***

tion available on the older records. A record that shows any signs of wear whatsoever does not qualify for the price in the right-hand column!

NO SWAP MEET BARGAINS?

We would like to make a ***special appeal*** to readers of this introduction who are in the businesses of running thrift shops, antique stores, or are habitues of swap meets and may find themselves in the occasional position of peddling old records to the public. We receive ***constant*** complaints from collectors who run into these people claiming they misuse our guides.

Everyone who goes to swap meets is looking for bargains, and the record collector is no exception. It seems, however, that anyone who has one of our guides no longer sells anything for a bargain, even at the swap meet. In fact, the prices asked, regardless of condition, are usually across-the-board from the right-hand near mint column. The simple point is: no dealer at a swap has any right to ask or expect to receive the prices in this book for any of these records he may wish to sell. First, he does not know how to grade, and if he happens to have been lucky enough to come across a record we list as having a value of $20 to $80, his idea of a bargain is to price it at $65 or $70. In actual fact, most all records found at swap meets qualify no better than good to very good, which would mean $20 to $35 for the record he's trying to squeeze $65 or $70 for. This is the ***best*** condition usually found. The average condition ***usually found*** is good or less. On the same scale, such a record would be valued at $10 to $20. When a collector buys this kind of item from an established dealer, he has this dealer's ***guarantee of authenticity*** and he can exchange it for a full refund if he ever finds the dealer was in error. He gets no such guarantees from the swap meet table. Finally, even if the stranger at the meet sells the record the collector wants at a fair price—the same price a dealer would ask—why should the collector buy from him? He still gets no guarantee and he's still not getting a ***bargain***, which is what the swap meet is supposed to be all about.

OUR POINT IS MADE

Obviously, in a free enterprise society any merchant can charge what he wishes for anything he thinks he can sell. Our whole point in bringing the subject up is to introduce some objectivity into an arena where there has been little meeting of minds.

CONDITION COUNTS

A last comment on condition: this book documents values for conditions varying from the extremes of used, but still playable "good," to the enigmatic "mint," or what we refer to as being as close to that ultimate, unreachable state of perfection as one can reach, "near mint." Mint, if one insists on using the term, is mint regardless of age, and it is a mistake to set a different set of standards for grading depending on age. Quality can only be measured against any product, including records, by how it was when it was new. (Naturally, no unplayed, untouched 78 is going to be as free of surface noise as a modern-day 45.) Condition counts not only for the record's surface, but its label as well.

PLEAS, PLEASE!

As always, we welcome comments or criticisms, but more than either, we welcome direction and input as asked for in this introduction to verify listings in this book either to amplify information known, or to correct errors. Here are some of the things we'd appreciate from our collector-friends:

(1) Clear, glossy photos of any rare records you do not see pictured in this book.

(2) Unpublished, or rare photos of any of the stars that you would loan us for reproduction in our second edition. We will take care of them and return them, of course.

(3) Substantiated dates of release on any that are missing from our listings.

(4) Early records ***only*** that may have been overlooked by any of the artists who have already been established in the guide. We would prefer, as first choice, to have Xeroxed copies of both sides of any records you feel we should document. If you do not have access to a duplicator, please include ***all*** pertinent information, including the ***exact*** titles and credits, even down to parentheses and punctuation.

(5) Correction of errors. We're not expecting much here, since we've really done our homework on this book and have proofed it with excruciating care. Nonetheless, we'd appreciate your input. In many cases, we'll warn you that what you may have read elsewhere is in error and the information is correct here for the first time!

Please address all correspondence on any of the above directly to:

Jellyroll Productions, Inc.
Box 3017
Scottsdale, Arizona 85257

CONDITION: YOU NEED TO KNOW WHAT SHAPE YOUR RECORDS ARE IN

Just because a record is old does not necessarily make it valuable. There *has* to be a demand for it. For the value to continue to rise, the demand must always be greater than the supply. Another factor is condition. The most accurate grading system and the easiest one to explain and understand is as follows:

M - MINT

Mint means the record must be in perfect condition. There can be no compromise. If you have two mint records, but can tell a slight difference between the two, one is not mint. It is for this reason that the term "near mint" appears as the highest grade listed in our books. Label defects—such as stickers, writing, rubbing, fading, or warping and wrinkling—will detract from its value. If a record is, indeed, perfect in every way, it will bring somewhat more than the near mint listing.

VG - VERY GOOD

The halfway mark between good and near mint. The disc should have only a minimum amount of foreign, or surface noise and it should not detract at all from the recorded sound. A VG record may show some label wear, but as with audio, it would be minimal.

G - GOOD

The most misunderstood of all grades. Good should not mean bad! A record in good condition will show signs of wear, with an audible amount of foreign noises. There may be scratches and it may be obvious it was never properly cared for (such as being stacked with other records not in sleeves). Nevertheless, it still plays "good" enough to enjoy.

F - FAIR

Fair is the beginning of bad. A fair record will play all the way through without skips, but will contain a distracting amount of noises.

P-POOR

Stepped on by an elephant and it sells for peanuts.

The more this system is used, the more widespread will be the satisfaction between buyers and sellers. More and more dealers are subscribing to it.

All reputable dealers offer a money-back guarantee if the record is not in the condition described.

YOUR NAME SHOULD BE IN NEXT YEAR'S GUIDES

Do you plan to stay in record collecting? If so, next year you'll be glad that you sent us your name, address and interests **this** year for **next** year's collector's directory that appears in our popular and rock singles and albums guides.

IMPORTANT NOTICE: If your name is in this year's directory, it will not appear again unless you send us the information again. People's addresses and interests change, and we want our lists to be accurate and up-to-date.

Don't put it off, or you'll forget! Take a few minutes now and jot down the information we request and sign your name. Send us your name, address or box number, city, state, zip code (and country if other than the U.S.), telephone number (optional), and your interests (in 20 words or less). Don't forget to sign your letter to authorize us to include your name in our next Directory Series.

Collector's Directory
Jellyroll Productions, Inc.
Box 3017
Scottsdale, Arizona 85257

THE VITAL IMPORTANCE OF FIRST PRESSINGS

By Victor Pearlin

Editor's note: The values stated for the records listed in this book are ONLY for first pressings. Second pressings should not be confused with re-issues, which will have different record numbers. In some cases re-issues (and their different values) are listed in the guide, but the prices shown for them, too, are for first pressings only.

A second pressing, simply defined, is like a second printing of a rare book, whether easily identifiable or not. It is of less value and in less demand than that which came first. A second pressing, or any later pressing (sometimes years later), may have different colored plastic, an entirely different label design, or a different colored label—but it will still retain the original record number!

Many labels that list records in this book are not included in the following article. In most cases this is because the label was small and didn't change its design, or it didn't have any records that sold well enough to have a second pressing.

The following information on how to identify first pressings of 45 r.p.m. records on the various labels listed in based upon my observations and experience. Hence, the record numbers listed at which the record labels change in design and/or color are approximate, but are mostly reliable.

Please keep in mind that these guidelines are for the very first pressings on the record labels listed. In almost all cases, there are exceptions, usually regional. The reader should bear in mind that records were pressed, often simultaneously, in various parts of the country. Often on West Coast pressings, older label designs continued to be used on later numbers after the label change occurred in East Coast pressings.

A few of the examples I have seen include: Decca in the 30000 range with the flat black label and the lines at the side; Ember after #1065 with the Log label; End with the white label well past #1045 (and even approaching #1100!).

We will be continuing to document variations and additional information for future editions of this guide, so if anyone has any contributions they will be welcomed. Readers may write and/or send photos or duplicated copies of the labels to Jellyroll Productions or directly to me (my address is in the back of the book).

Label	Numbers	Description
ACE	500 - 505(?)	Black label
	505 - 527	Yellow label
	528 on	White label
ALADDIN	3068 - 3259	Blue label (colored plastic: green on 3097, opaque red on 3144)
	3260 - 3399	Maroon label
	3400 on	Black label
ARGO	5250 - 5281	"Ship" label
	5282 - 5360	Black with vertical "Argo"
	5361 on	Same as above or on tan label
ATCO	6050 - 6090	Brown label
	6091 on	Yellow and white label
ATLANTIC	931 - 1083	Yellow and black label, no fan
	1084 - 2134	Red and black label, no fan
BACKBEAT	501 - 530	White label
	531 on	Red label
BRUCE	All	All first pressings have "Mfg. by Nu-Way Enterprises, Inc." under the label; saw-tooth (or wavey lines are second pressings)
BRUNSWICK	55000 - 55166	Brown label
	55167 - 55250	Orange label
	55251 on	Black and multi-color label
CAPITOL	791 - 4290	Purple label, "Capitol" on top
	4291 - 4663	Purple label, "Capitol" on side
	4680 on	Orange and yellow "pinwheel" label
CHECKER	750 - 800	Maroon and silver "web" top, no Record Co. (colored plastic occurs 768 - 800)
	801 - 876	Maroon and silver "web" top, add Record Co.
	877 - 1050	Maroon label with vertical "Checker"
	1050 - 1100	Light blue label with checkers across top (approximately through 1100)
	1101 on	Light blue label without checkers
CHESS	1425 - 1670	Blue and silver with chess pieces
	1671 - 1798	Blue with vertical "Chess"
	1799 - 1840	Multi-color *or* same as above
	1841 - 1950	Black label
	1951 on	*Light* blue label
COMBO	1 - 100	Shiny red label
	101 on	Purple label, "Combo" in large print
DECCA	23000 - 29400	Flat black label with lines at each side of "Decca"
	29401 - 31100	Flat black label with lines underneath "Decca"
	31101 on	Shiny black multi-color label
DELUXE	3300 - 3323	Flat black and "AA" after number, no "Hi-Fidelity" (colored plastic: clear blue and red occurs in 3300s)
	6000 - 6090	Flat black, no "Hi-Fidelity"
	6091 - 6190	Flat black, "Hi-Fidelity" on label
	6191 - 6200	Yellow label
DOOTONE	300 - 413	Solid color label, usually maroon, but also shiny red, blue or black (shiny maroon, yellow or multi-color labels are re-issues)

Label	Numbers	Description
DOOTO	414 - 450	Yellow label
DOT	1000 - 1100	Shiny brown label with gold print
	1101 - 1150	Yellow label with black print
	1151 - 1288	Flat brown label with silver print
	15000 - 15500	Flat brown label with silver print
	15501 on	Black label (through a few numbers above 15500 are on brown)
DUKE	101 - 342	Yellow and purple label
	343 on	Orange label
EMBER	1001 - 1038	Red or orange label
	1039 - 1064	Multi-color label with Logs
	1065 on	Black label
END	1000 - 1010	Black label
	1011 - 1045	White or gray label
	1046 on	White or multi-color label
EXCELLO	2001 - 2057	Yellow label
	2058 - 2209	Orange label
	2210 on	White and blue label
FEDERAL	12001 - 12129	Gold top label (colored plastic: clear blue on 12064)
	12130 - 12196	Some with gold top label, but mostly silver top label
	12197 - 12244	Green label, no "Hi-Fidelity"
	12245 - 12369	Green label, small "Hi-Fidelity"
	12370 on	Green label, large "Hi-Fidelity"
FEE BEE	201 - 221	Orange with Bee on label
FLASH	101 - 103	Red label
	104 - 113	Brown label
	114 - 127	Blue label
	128 - 133	Black label
FLIP	301 - 394	Brown label
	305 on	Blue label (re-issues through approximately 350 have the matrix number (FL-) on the label in parentheses
FURY	1000 - 1019	Maroon label
	1020 - 1023	Yellow label, no horse's head
	1024 - 1032	Yellow label, with horse's head
	1033 - 1039	Multi-color label
	1040 on	Yellow label, with horse's head, or multi-color
GEE	1 - 12	Yellow and green label
	1000 - 1021	Red label, without "trade mark" and "reg. U.S. Pat. Off."
	1022 - 1025	Red label, with "trade mark" on left and "reg. U.S. Pat. Off." on right
	1026 - 1038	Same as 1000 - 1021
	1039 - 1052	Same as 1022 - 1025
	1053 on	Gray label
GONE	5001 - 5003	Black label, with shadow print
	5004 - 5056	Black label, not shadow print
	5057 on	Multi-color label
GOTHAM	100 - 288	Blue label
	289 - 304	Red label; 304 also on blue label and yellow label (colored plastic: opaque red, occurs around 289 - 293)
GRAND	All	All on thick vinyl with small lettering on the label.
HERALD	401 - 409	Black label
	410 - 415	Yellow label, block print, no flag(colored plastic: clear red)
	416 - 528	Yellow label, script print inside flag (colored plastic: clear red, through about 421; 432 and some later numbers pressed in block print style)
	529 - 550	Multi-color label (many later numbers were pressed in a variety of styles)
	551 on	Yellow label, block print inside flag (and other styles)
HOLIDAY	2601 - 2603	Flat black label
	2604 - 2611	Shiny red label
HULL	711 - 712	Pink label
	713 - 715	Black label, no outise ring
	716 - 721	Red label or black label with silver ring outside
	722 - 742	Red label, no outside ring
	743 on	Tan label
IMPERIAL	5000 - 5290	Blue script label (colored plastic: opaque red occurs between 5220 - 5234); there is much overlapping in styles throughout the series
	5291 - 5357	Red script label
	5358 - 5460	Red block label
	5461 on	Black label
JAMIE	1000 - 1100	Black label
	1101 - 1124	Yellow label
	1125 on	White and mustard label
JOSIE	760 - 829	Tan label, brown print, "Joz" design
	830 - 845	Tan label, red print, "Joz" design
	846 on	Tan label, "Josie" design
JOYCE	101 - 105	Blue label, large "Y" in "Joyce"
JUBILEE	5000 - 5092	Blue script label (colored plastic: clear red beginning with 5055)
	5093 - 5340	Blue script variation, line under "Jubilee" (colored plastic: clear red through 5120)
	5341 on	Black label

Label	Numbers	Description
KING	500 - 1470	Maroon label (colored plastic: clear blue, purple, green or red occurs between 1000 - 1150)
	1471 - 1502	Blue label
	4449 - 4544	Blue label, "AA" after number, no "Hi-Fidelity" (colored plastic: clear blue, purple, green or red occurs between 4450 - 4520)
	4545 - 4834	Blue label, no "AA", no "Hi-Fidelity"
	4835 - 5266	Blue label, small "Hi-Fidelity"
	5267 on	Blue label, large "Hi-Fidelity"
MERCURY	5000s and 8000s	Maroon label
	70000 - 71039	Maroon label on many up through 71080, or head of Mercury with square on maroon, black, pink or green label
	71040 - 72320	Maroon or black label with oval Mercury design
	72321 on	Red label
MGM	55000s	Yellow label
	10000 - 12828	Yellow label
	12829 on	Black label
METEOR	5000 - 5001	Yellow label
	5002 - 5030	Red label
	5031 - 5046	Black label
MODERN	830 - 980	Shiny red or black label
	981 - 1028	Flat black label
MOTOWN	1000 - 1010	Pink label
	1011 on	Blue label
MUSIC CITY	730 - 792	Maroon label
	793 - 800	Flat black label
	800 on	Shiny black multi-colored label
OKEH	6800 - 7092	Purple label, small "Okeh"
	7093 - 7140	Yellow label, some purple label overlap
	7141 on	Purple label, large "Okeh"
OLD TOWN	700s	Yellow label with green print block
	1000 - 1012	Yellow label, old English script with brown print
	1013 - 1028	Yellow label, block print with ropes
	1029 - 1051	Yellow label, block print without ropes
	1052 - 1130	Blue label
ONYX	501 - 514	Shiny black label
	515 - 520	Flat black and orange, or flat black and green label
PARADISE	101 - 109	Maroon label with ropes
	110 on	Purple label, without ropes
PEACOCK	1500 - 1604	Flat maroon label
	1605 - 1675	Shiny red label
	1676 - 1900	White label
	1901 on	White label
RAINBOW	100 - 250	Blue label (approximately through 250) (colored plastic: occurs in 200s)
	251 on	Yellow label
RAMA	1 - 196	Blue label
	197 - 222	Red label, without "Reg. U.S. Pat. Off."
	223 - 233	Red label, with "Reg. U.S. Pat. Off." on left side of label instead of words "45 RPM"
RCA VICTOR	50-0000 - 50-0105	Gray label, gold print (colored plastic: red)
	50-0106 - 50-0141	Gray label, silver print
	47-2800 - 47-4572	Blue green label
	47-4573 - 47-8574	Black label, dog on top
	47-8575 - 47-9650	Black label, dog on side (change-over is approximate)
RED TOP	100 - 111	Light blue label
	112 on	Red label
RPM	300 - 360	Red, maroon, black or blue label, "RPM" in script
	361 - 452	Shiny red-black or blue label, "RPM" in block letters
	453 - 502	Flat black, or a few on shiny red or blue, "RPM" in block letters
SPARK	101 - 108	Red label with silver top
	109	Blue label
	110 - 119	Red label
	120 - 122	Yellow and black label
SPECIALTY	300 - 607	Wavey horizontal yellow lines on label (colored plastic: red and clear occur in mid-400s)
	608 on	Without wavey horizontal yellow lines on label
TAMLA	54025 - 54043	Yellow label with horizontal lines
	54044 - 54175	Yellow label with logo/globes at top (approximately through 54175)
	54176 on	Yellow label with logo in a box
VEE JAY	100 - 285	Brown label, thin silver circle, no "Trademark Reg." under "Vee" (colored plastic: red occurs in low 100s)
	286 - 353	Brown label, thick silver circle and "Trademark Reg." under "Vee"
	354 on	Black label
WINLEY	212	Blue label
	213 - 230	Orange label, 3/16" print (approximately through 230)
	231 on	Orange label, "Winley" is in 1/4" print

DO YOU KNOW IF YOUR RECORD COLLECTION IS ADEQUATELY PROTECTED AGAINST LOSS?

LIST YOUR RECORD COLLECTION UNDER A GENERAL HOMEOWNERS POLICY

If you do not have your record collection listed separately in your general homeowners policy, in the event of a loss, you would be paid only a fraction of your collection's actual value.

For example, if your Elvis Presley, Milkcow Blues Boogie, (Sun 215) worth $275.00 in mint condition, is destroyed in a fire, the insurance company would only be able to give you 10% of the ORIGINAL COST of the record. Since this record was released in 1955 and sold for 89¢, you would receive 9¢ for your record!

OBTAIN COMPLETE COVERAGE FOR YOUR COLLECTION

Getting FULL coverage for your record valuables is SIMPLE. It can be accomplished in two easy steps:

1. Make a list of your records. Using the Osborne/Hamilton Price Guide for Collectible Records, write down:

1. Name of artist
2. Title of record
3. Label and number
4. Price value

2. Call your insurance agent and tell him you have an itemized list of records that you want protected with your household goods on your homeowners or renters policy or highlight your record collection in the Osborne/Hamilton Guide and turn the guide in to your agent.

* If you do not have all the information listed above, simply inform your insurance agent that you have records which need to be listed with your general household goods. Many insurance companies are currently using the Record Collector's Price Guides to appraise collections.

Be The Expert! Order the Complete

RECORD COLLECTOR'S PRICE GUIDE SERIES

A Guide to RECORD COLLECTING

Lists the World's 50 Most Valuable Records

The guide is the complete introduction to the highly profitable explosive hobby of collecting records.

This book will tell how to start record collecting today, where to buy the records in demand, and who will pay top dollars for old records. Listed are the most collectible recordings in the fields of Popular & Rock, Movie Soundtracks, the Big Bands, Country/Western, Disco, and Rhythm & Blues. Special feature is the Worlds's 50 Most Valuable records shown in a second color throughout the book.

5½" x 8½"   160 pages $5.95

RECORD ALBUMS 1948-1978

Official Price Guide for Collectible Records

Now out in a greatly expanded 2nd edition, ***Record Albums 1948-1978*** is bursting with helpful information for the record collector. Over 28,000 listings that chronicle the values on today's market of the "big records with the little holes" — the 10" and 12" long play albums. Listings cover Popular artists, Rock, Country/Western, Rockabilly, Rhythm & Blues and a special, "easy reference" section of Original Cast and Movie Soundtrack albums.

8½" x 11"   264 pages $7.95

POPULAR & ROCK RECORDS 1948-1978

The second edition of the ***Popular & Rock Records 1948-1978,*** spans the entire history of the "little record with the big hole" - from Elvis, the Bealtes, and Bill Haley's Comets on up to Fleetwood Mac. The current collector prices and year of release are listed on over 30,000 45s and selected 78s. Special notations are made on prized collectible picture sleeves.

8½" x 11"   264 pages $7.95

Each of our price guides includes a special ***Dealers and Collectors Directory*** of over 1,300 buyers and sellers of collectible records!

55 YEARS OF RECORDED COUNTRY/WESTERN MUSIC

This popular price guide has listed recordings dating back to 1921. It traces the history of country/western music from those early days into the revolutionary "Rockabilly" explosion of the early '50s and on up to now. The values of these many thousands of old 78s and newer 45s are documented between its covers. Special feature is an exclusive interview of Gene Autry.

8½" x 11"   208 pages $6.95

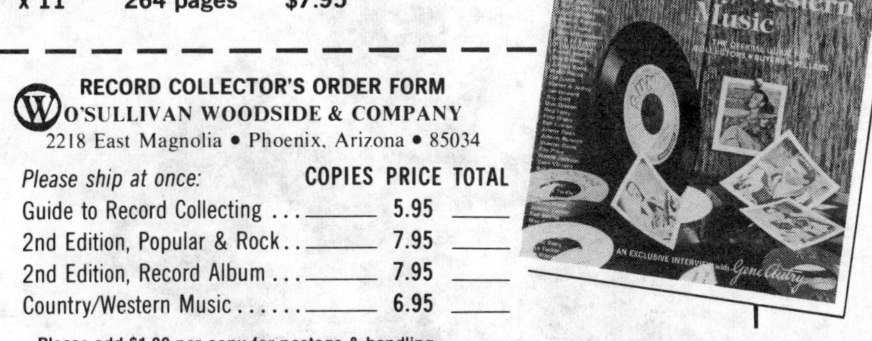

RECORD COLLECTOR'S ORDER FORM
O'SULLIVAN WOODSIDE & COMPANY
2218 East Magnolia • Phoenix, Arizona • 85034

Please ship at once:	COPIES	PRICE	TOTAL
Guide to Record Collecting	____	5.95	____
2nd Edition, Popular & Rock	____	7.95	____
2nd Edition, Record Album	____	7.95	____
Country/Western Music	____	6.95	____

Please add $1.00 per copy for postage & handling. ____
Enclosed is my ☐ check ☐ money order for. . ____

Name: ____
Address: ____
City: ____ State: ____ Zip: ____
Signature: ____

(prices subject to change without notice)

Buy from book and record stores or Fill in order form and MAIL

TODAY

Johnny Ace

Faye Adams

A-TONES, Roger & The:
see Bailon, Roger as Roger & The A-Tones

ABBOTT, Billy & The Jewels

ACCENTS, The

ACE, Buddy

ACE, Johnny

TITLE/FLIP	LABEL & NO.	GOOD TO VERY GOOD	NEAR MINT	YR.
ANYMORE/How Can You Be So Mean?	Duke 144	1.50	6.00	55
CLOCK, THE/Aces Wild	Duke 112	2.00	8.00	53
CROSS MY HEART/Angel	Duke 107	2.00	8.00	53
MIDNIGHT HOURS JOURNEY/ Trouble And Me (by Earl Forrest)	Flair 1015	8.00	32.00	53
MY SONG/Follow The Rule	Duke 102	2.50	10.00	52
NEVER LET ME GO/Burly Cutie	Duke 136	1.50	6.00	54
PLEASE FORGIVE ME/Gone So Long	Duke 128	1.50	6.00	54
PLEDGING MY LOVE/No Money	Duke 136	1.50	6.00	55
SAVING MY LOVE FOR YOU/Yes Baby	Duke 118	2.00	8.00	54
SO LONELY/I'm Crazy Baby	Duke 148	1.50	6.00	55
STILL I LOVE YOU SO/Don't You Know?	Duke 154	1.50	6.00	55

ACKLIN, Barbara

ACKLIN, Barbara, Gene Chandler &

ACTORS, The

AD LIBS, The

ADAMS, Alberta

TITLE/FLIP	LABEL & NO.	GOOD TO VERY GOOD	NEAR MINT	YR.
MESSIN' AROUND WITH THE BLUES/This Morning	Chess 1551	2.50	10.00	54

ADAMS, Faye:
see Scruggs, Faye as Faye Adams

ADAMS, Jo-Jo

TITLE/FLIP	LABEL & NO.	GOOD TO VERY GOOD	NEAR MINT	YR.
CALL MY BABY/Rebecca	Parrot 788	8.00	32.00	53

ADAMS, Jo-Jo as Dr. Jo-Jo Adams

TITLE/FLIP	LABEL & NO.	GOOD TO VERY GOOD	NEAR MINT	YR.
DIDN'T I TELL YOU?/I've Got A Crazy Baby	Chance 1127	10.00	40.00	52

ADAMS, Johnny

ADAMS, Johnny & The Gondoliers:
see Gondoliers, Johnny Adams & The

ADAMS, Marie

TITLE/FLIP	LABEL & NO.	GOOD TO VERY GOOD	NEAR MINT	YR.
HE'S MY MAN/Alone	Peacock 1604	1.50	6.00	52
I'M GONNA PLAY THE HONKY TONKS/My Search Is Over	Peacock 1583	2.00	8.00	52
I'M THE BLUEST GAL IN TOWN/Ain't Car Crazy	Peacock 1614	1.50	6.00	53
SWEET TALKIN' DADDY/My Song	Peacock 1610	1.50	6.00	53

ADAMS, Woodrow & The Boogie Blues Blasters

TITLE/FLIP	LABEL & NO.	GOOD TO VERY GOOD	NEAR MINT	YR.
WINE HEAD WOMAN/Baby You Just Don't Know	Meteor 5018	10.00	40.00	55

ADAMS, Woodrow & The Three B's

TITLE/FLIP	LABEL & NO.	GOOD TO VERY GOOD	NEAR MINT	YR.
PRETTY BABY BLUES/She's Done Come And Gone (78)	Checker 757	9.00	36.00	52

ADMIRALS, The

TITLE/FLIP	LABEL & NO.	GOOD TO VERY GOOD	NEAR MINT	YR.
CLOSE YOUR EYES/Give Me Your Love	King 4782	10.00	40.00	55
IT'S A SAD, SAD FEELING/Ow With Cathy Ryan.	King 4792	4.00	16.00	55
OH YES/Left With A Broken Heart	King 4772	15.00	60.00	55
TWENTY FOUR HOURS A DAY/With You With Cathy Ryan.	King 1495	2.50	10.00	55

ADMIRATIONS, Norven Baskerville & The

TITLE/FLIP	LABEL & NO.	GOOD TO VERY GOOD	NEAR MINT	YR.
GONNA FIND MY PRETTY BABY/Li'l Li'l Lulu	X-tra 100	4.00	16.00	—

ADVENTURERS, The

TITLE/FLIP	LABEL & NO.	GOOD TO VERY GOOD	NEAR MINT	YR.
ROCK & ROLL UPRISING/My Mama Done Tole Me (33 single)	Columbia 42227	10.00	40.00	61
ROCK & ROLL UPRISING/My Mama Done Tole Me	Columbia 42227	5.00	20.00	61

AGEE, Ray

TITLE/FLIP	LABEL & NO.	GOOD TO VERY GOOD	NEAR MINT	YR.
FLIRTIN' BLUES/It's Bedtime, Baby	Modern 883	3.00	12.00	52
MY LONESOME DAYS ARE GONE/No More Blue Shadows Fallin'	Modern 891	3.00	12.00	52
ONE I LOVE, THE/Deep Trouble	Aladdin 3161	2.50	10.00	52
TROUBLES BRING ME DOWN/ My Poor Heart	Recorded In Hollywood 240	2.00	8.00	52
WOBBLE LOO/Another Fool Sings The Blues	Spark 119	2.00	8.00	55

AGEE, Ray as Isom Ray

TITLE/FLIP	LABEL & NO.	GOOD TO VERY GOOD	NEAR MINT	YR.
ROCK HARD/	RGA 114	5.00	20.00	—

AGENTS, Mask-Men & The (with "Wailing" Harmon Bethea)

AGENTS, Masked Man & The (with "Wailing" Harmon Bethea)

AGENTS, Maskman & The (with "Wailing" Harmon Bethea)

AH-MOORS, The

TITLE/FLIP	LABEL & NO.	GOOD TO VERY GOOD	NEAR MINT	YR.
HONEY, HONEY, HONEY/The Answer To Write Me A Letter (78)	Rainbow 10060	3.00	12.00	—

AHSLEY, Tyrone

AKENS, Jewel

ALABAMA SLIM:
see Willis, Ralph as Alabama Slim

ALADDINS, The

TITLE/FLIP	LABEL & NO.	GOOD TO VERY GOOD	NEAR MINT	YR.
ALL OF MY LIFE/So Long, Farewell, Bye Bye	Aladdin 3314	12.50	50.00	56
CRY, CRY, BABY/Remember	Aladdin 3275	12.50	50.00	55
GET OFF MY FEET/I Had A Dream Last Nite	Aladdin 3298	12.50	50.00	55
HELP ME/Lord Show Me	Aladdin 3358	10.00	40.00	56

ALADDINS, The

TITLE/FLIP	LABEL & NO.	GOOD TO VERY GOOD	NEAR MINT	YR.
OUR LOVE WILL BE/Simple Simon	Witch 111	1.50	6.00	62

ALBERT & CHARLES

TITLE/FLIP	LABEL & NO.	GOOD TO VERY GOOD	NEAR MINT	YR.
WEIRD/	Pioneer 1005	12.50	50.00	—

ALCOVES, The

TITLE/FLIP	LABEL & NO.	GOOD TO VERY GOOD	NEAR MINT	YR.
HEAVEN/The Ballad Of Cassius Clay	Carlton 602	1.50	6.00	—

ALEXANDER, Alger as Texas Alexander with Benton's Busy Bees

TITLE/FLIP	LABEL & NO.	GOOD TO VERY GOOD	NEAR MINT	YR.
BOTTOM'S BLUES/Crossroads (78)	Freedom 1538	6.25	25.00	50

ALEXANDER, Arthur

ALICE JEAN & THE MONDELLOS:
see Mondellos, Alice Jean & The

ALLEN TRIO, The

TITLE/FLIP	LABEL & NO.	GOOD TO VERY GOOD	NEAR MINT	YR.
THAT'S WHAT I LIKE/Teach Me Tonight (by The Five Dips)	Original 1005	40.00	160.00	55

ALLEN, Annisteen

TITLE/FLIP	LABEL & NO.	GOOD TO VERY GOOD	NEAR MINT	YR.
I DON'T WANT NO SUBSTITUTE/Down By The River	King 4691	1.50	6.00	53
TRYING TO LIVE WITHOUT YOU/My Baby Keeps Rollin'	King 4622	1.50	6.00	53
WANTED/My Brand Of Lovin'	King 4642	1.50	6.00	53
YES, I KNOW/Baby, I'm Doin' It	King 4608	1.50	6.00	53

ALLEN, Big Clyde & The Movin' Masters Band

ALLEN, Blinky & His Orchestra

TITLE/FLIP	LABEL & NO.	GOOD TO VERY GOOD	NEAR MINT	YR.
BLOW ROBBIE BLOW/Say When	Flair 1032	2.50	10.00	54
CHOP HOUSE/High Gear	Flair 1043	2.50	10.00	54
I'M A FOOL TO CARE/An Angel Child	Flair 1047	2.50	10.00	54
MY BABY LOVES ME/Take Me Back	Swing Time 327	3.00	12.00	53

ALLEN, George:
see Smith, George as George Allen

TITLE/FLIP	LABEL & NO.	GOOD TO VERY GOOD	NEAR MINT	YR.
ALLEN, Jesse				
GOTTA CALL THAT NUMBER/Gonna Tell My Mama	Imperial 5256	3.00	12.00	53
I WONDER WHAT'S THE MATTER?/Sittin' And Wonderin'	Imperial 5185	3.00	12.00	53
MY SUFFERING/Let's Party	Coral 65078	4.00	16.00	51
ROCK THIS MORNING/Gonna Move Away From Town	Aladdin 3129	4.00	16.00	52
ROCKIN' AND ROLLIN'/I Love You So	Imperial 5315	2.00	8.00	53
THINGS I'M GONNA DO, THE/What A Party	Imperial 5303	2.00	8.00	53
ALLEN, Lee				
SHIMMY/Rockin' At Cosmo's	Aladdin 3334	1.50	6.00	56
ALLEN, Ricky				
ALLEN, Sue: see Black, Oscar & Sue Allen				
see Four Students, Sue Allen & The				
ALLEN, Tony & The Champs				
NITE OWL/I	Specialty 560	4.00	16.00	55
ALLEN, Tony & The Chimes				
CHECK YOURSELF, BABY/Especially	Specialty 570	2.00	8.00	56
ALLEN, Tony & The Originals				
ALLEN, Tony & The Twilighters				
IT HURTS ME SO/The Trakey-Doo	Bethlehem 3004	1.50	6.00	62
JUST LIKE BEFORE/Come-a, Come-a, Baby	Bethlehem 3002	1.50	6.00	61
ALLEN, Tony & The Wanderers				
EVERYBODY'S SOMEBODY'S FOOL/If Love Was Money	Kent 356	2.00	8.00	61
ALLEN, Tony & The Wonders				
ALLEN TRIO, The: see Five Dips, The				
ALLEY CATS, The				
ALLISON, Gene				
ALPACAS, Willie Walker & The				
THREE HUNDRED AND SIXTY-FIVE/Money And Man	Freedom 44006	2.50	10.00	58
ALTAIRS, The				
IF YOU LOVE ME/Groovie Time	Amy 803	2.00	8.00	60
ALTEERS, The				
WORDS CAN'T EXPLAIN/Keep Laughin'	Laurie 3097	1.50	6.00	61
AMBASSADORS, The				
DARLING I'M SORRY/Willa-Bea	Timely 1001	125.00	500.00	54
AMBERS, The				
ALL OF MY DARLING/So Glad	Todd 1042	1.50	6.00	59
NEVER LET YOU GO/I'll Make A Bet With Ralph Mathis.	Ebb 142	2.00	8.00	58
AMBERTONES, The				
I NEED SOME/If I Do	Dottie 1130	1.50	6.00	—
AMMONS, Gene				
AMOS, Ira				
WHAT HAVE YOU BEEN DOING TO ME?/ Blue And Disgusted (78)	Modern 20-817	2.00	8.00	50
AMY, Curtis				
REALIZATION BLUES/Sleeping Blues (78) Vocals by Hubert Robinson	Gold Star 618	2.00	8.00	47
ANDERSON, Bubba				
WHERE HAS MY LOVER GONE?/Please Don't Leave Me	Ace 662	6.25	25.00	62
ANDERSON, Elton				
SHED SO MANY TEARS/Roll On Train	Vin 1001	3.00	12.00	—
ANDERSON, Jimmy & His Joy Jumpers				

TITLE/FLIP	LABEL & NO.	GOOD TO VERY GOOD	NEAR MINT	YR.
ANDERSON, Milton as Little Milton				
Anderson should not be confused with Milton Campbell, who also uses the name Little Milton.				
LITTLE MILTON'S BOOGIE (instrumental)/ Boogie Woogie Baby (78)	Delta 403	3.00	12.00	53
ANDREWS, Lee & The Hearts: see Hearts, Lee Andrews & The				
ANDREWS, Ruby				
ANGEL FACE				
KEEP YOUR HEAD UP HIGH/What's The Stuff Joe's Got?	Gem 210	2.50	10.00	54
WHEN THE SAINTS GO MARCHIN' IN/ Don't Ever Leave Me Again	Big Town 114	2.00	8.00	55
ANGEL, Johnny				
I BELIEVE/Baby I'm Confessin'	Excello 2077	1.50	6.00	56
ANGELETTES, The (female group)				
ANGELINOS, The				
ANGELOS, The				
ANGELOS, The (female group)				
ANGELS, Gabriel & The				
ANGELS, Hannibal & The				
ANGELS, Little Betty & The				
ANGELS, The (female group)				
LEAVING YOU BABY/Sha-Wa-Wa	Irma 105	8.00	32.00	56
ANGELS, The (male group)				
GLORY OF LOVE/It's You I Love Best	Gee 1024	5.00	20.00	56
LOVELY WAY TO SPEND AN EVENING/You're Still My Baby	Grand 121	20.00	80.00	55
WEDDING BELLS ARE RINGING IN MY EARS/ Times Have Changed With Sonny Gordon.	Grand 115	20.00	80.00	54
ANGLOS, Linda Martell & The				
ANGLOS, The				
SINCE YOU'VE BEEN GONE/Small Town Boy	Scepter 12204	1.50	6.00	67
ANNUALS, The				
ONCE IN A LIFETIME/Hungry, I'm Hungry	Marconn 1	4.00	16.00	—
ANSWERS, The				
HAVE NO FEAR/Keeps Me Worried All The Time	United 212	7.00	28.00	57
ANTHONY & THE IMPERIALS				
APOLLOS, The				
I LOVE YOU DARLING/Bandstand Baby	Harvard 803	15.00	60.00	59
AQUA-NITES, The				
LOVER DON'T YOU WEEP/Carioca	Astra 1000	3.00	12.00	65
LOVER DON'T YOU WEEP/Christy	Astra 2001	2.50	10.00	—
ARABIANS, The				
HEAVEN SENT YOU/The Shack	Jam 3738	4.00	16.00	60
HEAVEN SENT YOU/The Shack	Twin Star 1018	1.50	6.00	60
MY HEART BEATS OVER AND OVER AGAIN/ Crazy Little Fever	Magnificant 102	2.50	10.00	60
MY HEART BEATS OVER AND OVER AGAIN/ Crazy Little Fever Re-issue with the label name re-spelled.	Magnificent 102	2.00	8.00	—
TEARDROPS IN THE NIGHT/Take Me	Magnificent 114	2.50	10.00	60
ARCADES, The				
FINE LITTLE GIRL/My Love	Johnson 320	6.25	25.00	—
ARCHIBALD: see Gross, Leon T. as Archibald				
ARGYLES, The				
MOONBEAM/Every Time You Smile	Bally 1030	1.50	6.00	57

TITLE/FLIP	LABEL & NO.	GOOD TO VERY GOOD	NEAR MINT	YR.
ARIST-O-KATS, The				
I DON'T SEE ME IN YOUR EYES ANYMORE/Chasin' The Blues	Vita 168	4.00	16.00	57
ARISTO-KATS, The				
ARISTOCRATS, The				
ARMONDA & THE JAYS: see Jays, Armonda & The				
ARMSTEAD, Jo				
ARNOLD, Bee				
DEEDLE DEE, DEEDLE DEE/Plant You Now Dig You Later	Goldband 1032	3.00	12.00	54
LITTLE GIRL OF MINE/Way Down Under	Goldband 1029	3.00	12.00	54
ARNOLD, Calvin				
ARNOLD, William as Billy Boy				
DON'T STAY OUT ALL NIGHT/I Ain't Got You	Vee Jay 171	1.50	6.00	55
HERE'S MY PICTURE/You've Got Me Wrong	Vee Jay 192	1.50	6.00	55
I WAS FOOLED/I Wish You Would	Vee Jay 146	1.50	6.00	55
MY HEART IS CRYING/Kissing At Midnight	Vee Jay 238	1.50	6.00	56
PRISONER'S PLEA/Rockinitis	Vee Jay 260	1.50	6.00	57
ARNOLD, William as Billy Boy Arnold				
I AIN'T GOT NO MONEY/Hello Stranger (78)	Cool 103	3.00	12.00	53
ARPEGGIOS, The				
MARY/I'll Be Singing	Aries 001	3.00	12.00	63
ARROWS, Big Bo & The				
ARROWS, Joe Lyons & The				
HONEY CHILE/What's New With You	Hollywood 1065	8.00	32.00	56
NO END TO TRUE LOVE/One Too Many Times	Hollywood 1071	8.00	32.00	56
SHUFFLIN' JIVE/Bob-A-Loop	Hit Maker 600	5.00	20.00	—
ARROWS, The				
ANNIE MAE/Indian Bop Hop	Flash 132	4.00	16.00	58
I'M CHECKING ON YOU BABY/No Other Arms	Hugo 11171/11172	4.00	16.00	—
ARTISTICS, The				
LIFE BEGINS AT SIXTEEN/One Way	S & G 302	2.50	10.00	—
ARVETTES, The (female group)				
ASCOTS, The				
PERFECT LOVE/I'm Touched	Ace 650	3.00	12.00	62
ASTORS, The				
ASTROS, Pepe & The				
NOW, AIN'T THAT A SHAME/Judy, My Love	Swami 553/554	2.00	8.00	—
ATLANTICS, The				
REMEMBER THE NIGHT/Flame Of Love	Linda 107	1.50	6.00	61
ATTRACTIONS, The				
AUDIOS, Cell Foster & The				
HONEST I DO/I Prayed For You	Ultra 105	15.00	60.00	56
AUGUST, Joseph "Google Eyes"				
CRYIN' FOR YOU/Rock My Soul (78)	Domino 350	1.50	6.00	50
MY OLD LOVE/Whose Little Who Are You? (78)	Lee 209	1.50	6.00	51
OH HO, DOODLE LU/Lead Us On	Duke 156	3.00	12.00	56
OH WHAT A FOOL/Play The Game	Duke 117	4.00	16.00	54
ROUGH AND ROCKY ROAD, A/No Wine, No Woman (78)	Coleman 123	2.50	10.00	49
ROUGH AND ROCKY ROAD, A/No Wine, No Woman	Okeh 6820	7.00	28.00	51
AUSTIN, Augie & The Chromatics: see Chromatics, Augie Austin & The				
AUSTIN, Billy & The Hearts: see Hearts, Billy Austin & The				
AUSTIN, Patti				
AUSTIN, Sil				
AUTOMATIONS, The				
AVALONS, The (female group)				
LOUELLA/You Broke Our Hearts	Dice 90/91	1.50	6.00	58
AVALONS, The				
CHAINS AROUND MY HEART/Ooh! She Flew	Groove 0141	12.50	50.00	56
HEART'S DESIRE/Ebbtide	Unart 2007	7.00	28.00	58
IT'S FUNNY BUT IT'S TRUE/Sugar, Sugar	Groove 0174	12.50	50.00	56
YOU DO SOMETHING TO ME/You Can Count On Me	Casino 108	5.00	20.00	59
AVALONS, The				
BEGIN THE BEGUINE/Malanese	NPC 302	1.50	6.00	—
AVERNE DOZEN, Harvey & The				
AVERY, Nettie Dady with The Florida Gators				
REALITY BLUES/Got Nobody (78)	Asco 1009	5.00	20.00	—
AVONS, The				
BABY/Bonnie	Hull 722	4.00	16.00	57
GIRL TO CALL MY OWN, A/The Grass Is Greener On The Other Side	Hull 754	2.50	10.00	62
OUR LOVE WILL NEVER END/I'm Sending S.O.S. (red label)	Hull 717	4.00	16.00	56
OUR LOVE WILL NEVER END/I'm Sending S.O.S. (black label)	Hull 717	5.00	20.00	56
WHAT LOVE CAN DO/On The Island	Hull 731	3.00	12.00	59
WHAT WILL I DO?/Please Come Back To Me	Hull 728	3.00	12.00	58
WHISPER/If I Just	Hull 744	1.50	6.00	61
YOU ARE SO CLOSE TO ME/Gonna Catch You Nappin'	Hull 726	3.00	12.00	58

B

TITLE/FLIP	LABEL & NO.	GOOD TO VERY GOOD	NEAR MINT	YR.
BABY BOY WARREN: see Warren, Robert as Baby Boy Warren				
BABY CORTEZ: see Cortez, Dave as Baby Cortez				
BABY DOLLS, The				
THANKS, MR. DEE-JAY/What a Wonderful Love	Maske	1.50	6.00	61
BABY DOLLS, The (with Bill Baker)				
IS THIS THE END?/Boy Friend	Elgin 021	1.50	6.00	—
BABY FACE & THE SUNNYLAND TRIO: see Foster, Leroy as Baby Face				
BABY FACE LEROY: see Foster, Leroy as Baby Face Leroy				
BABY FACE: see Foster, Leroy as Baby Face				
BABY JANE & THE ROCK-A-BYES (female group)				
BACHELORS, The				
AFTER/You Know! You Know!	Poplar 101	1.50	6.00	57
CAN'T HELP LOVING YOU/Pretty Baby	Aladdin 3210	75.00	300.00	53
YOU'VE LIED/I Found Love	Royal Roost 620	12.50	50.00	56
BACHELORS, The (with Dean Barlow)				
BABY/Tell Me Now	Earl 102	8.00	32.00	57
DELORES/I Want To Know About Love	Earl 101	8.00	32.00	57
BACHELORS, The (with Joe Van Loan)				
YESTERDAY'S ROSES/Hereafter	Mercury 8159	15.00	60.00	49
BACK PORCH BOYS, The: see Seward, Alec (with Louis Hayes) as The Back Porch Boys				

TITLE/FLIP	LABEL & NO.	GOOD TO VERY GOOD	NEAR MINT	YR.
BAD BOYS, The				
BAGDADS, The				
BAILEY, J. R.				
BAILEY, Little Marie				
BROWNSKIN WOMAN BLUES/Tear Drops Are Falling	Excello 2007	7.00	28.00	53
MY BABY'S BLUES/Drive, Soldier, Drive	Excello 2016	7.00	28.00	53
BAILEY, Morris & The Thomas Boys				
CALENDAR HANGING ON THE WALL/Tell Me Why	Bailey 500	5.00	20.00	—
BAILON, Roger as Roger & The A-Tones				
WHY?/Look A Who	Nike 002	1.50	6.00	—
BAINES, Houston: see Boines, Houston as Houston Baines				
BAKER, Bill				
THANK HEAVEN/The Price Of Love	Vim 515	5.00	20.00	—
BAKER, Bill: see Baby Dolls, The; see Chestnuts, Bill Baker & The				
BAKER, C. B.				
SKIN TO SKIN/Goin' Back Home (78)	Sittin' In With 625	2.00	8.00	51
BAKER, Jeanette: see Dots, The (with Jeanette Baker)				
BAKER, Lavern				
LIVING MY LIFE FOR YOU/I Can't Hold Out Any Longer	Atlantic 1020	2.50	10.00	54
SOUL ON FIRE/How Can You Leave A Man Like This?	Atlantic 1004	3.00	12.00	53
BAKER, Lavern & The Gliders				
BAKER, Lavern, Jackie Wilson &				
BAKER, Lavern: see Rhodes, Todd				
BAKER, Mickey as Big Red McHouston				
I'M TIRED/Where Is My Honey?	Groove 0020	2.00	8.00	54
BAKER, Mickey: see Mickey & Sylvia				
BAKER, Rodney & The Chantiers: see Chantiers, Rodney Baker & The				
BAKER, Ronnie & The Deltones: see Deltones, Ronnie Baker & The				
BAKER, Sam				
BAKER, Willie				
Baker should not be confused with an artist by the same name who recorded before WWII.				
BEFORE SHE LEAVES TOWN/Goin' Back Home Today	DeLuxe 6023	10.00	40.00	53
BEFORE SHE LEAVES TOWN/Goin' Back Home Today	Rockin' 527	20.00	80.00	53
BAKER, Yvonne (recorded earlier as Yvonne Mills) & The Sensations				
BALLADEERS, Billy Mathews & The				
I LOVE YOU, YES I DO/Smooth Sailing (78)	Mercury 8073	3.00	12.00	48
I NEVER KNEW I LOVED YOU/If You Only Knew	Jubilee 5024	25.00	100.00	50
RED SAILS IN THE SUNSET/It Ain't Right	Jubilee 5021	25.00	100.00	50
BALLADIERS, Bill Mathews & The				
PLEASE GIVE MY HEART A BREAK/Rock And Roll (78)	Arlington 201	2.50	10.00	49
BALLADIERS, The				
FORGET ME NOT/What Will I Tell My Heart	Aladdin 3123	15.00	60.00	52
Both sides were recorded in 1947.				
KEEP ME WITH YOU/Please Don't Deceive My Heart	Aladdin 3008	15.00	60.00	49
Both sides were recorded in 1947.				
BALLARD, Hank & The Dapps				
BALLARD, Hank & The Midnighters				
BALLOU, Classie & His Tempo Kings Orchestra				
DIRTY DEAL/Lovin', Huggin', Kissin' My Baby	Goldband 1037	3.00	12.00	—
BALTINEERS, The				
MOMENTS LIKE THIS/New Love	Teenage 1000	12.50	50.00	56
TEARS IN MY EYES/Joe's Calypso	Teenage 1002	12.50	50.00	56
BAN LONS , The				
I LIKE IT/	Fidelity 4056	2.50	10.00	—
BANDITS, The				
BANISTER, James & His Combo				
GOLD DIGGER/Blues And Trouble	States 141	11.00	44.00	54
BANKS, Darrell				
BANKS, Eddie & The Five Dreamers: see Five Dreamers, Eddie Banks & The				
BANKS, Toni: see Four Fellows, The				
BARBARA & THE BROWNS				
BARBARA & THE UNIQUES				
BARDS, The				
AVALON/Gravy	Dawn 209	15.00	60.00	55
I'M A WINE DRINKER/Easy Going Baby	Dawn 208	15.00	60.00	55
BARKER, Blue Lu				
BOW-LEGGED DADDY/Love That Man	Capitol 807	3.00	12.00	49
'ROUND AND 'ROUND THE VALLEY/That's How I Got My Man	Capitol 977	3.00	12.00	49
BARLOW, Dean & The Crickets: see Crickets, Dean Barlow & the				
BARLOW, Dean & The Montereys: see Montereys, Dean Barlow & The				
BARLOW, DEAN: see Bachelors, The				
BARNER, Juky Boy: see Bonner, Weldon as Juke Boy Barner				
BARNES, J. J.				
BARNES, Jimmy				
BARNES, Jimmy & The Gibralters				
BARNEY & THE GOOGLES: see Googles, Barney & The				
BARONS, The				
EXACTLY LIKE YOU/Forget About Me	Decca 29293	9.00	36.00	54
YEAR AND A DAY, A/My Baby's Gone	Decca 48323	9.00	36.00	54
BARONS, The				
I MISS YOU SO/Money Don't Grow On Trees	Spartan 402	1.50	6.00	61
WILLOW WEEP FOR ME/I've Been Hurt	Spartan 400	1.50	6.00	61
The label indicates the group was "Formerly the Peppermints."				
BARONS, The				
CRYIN' FOR YOU BABY/So Long, My Darling	Imperial 5383	1.50	6.00	56
DON'T WALK OUT/Once In A Lifetime	Imperial 5397	2.00	8.00	56
ETERNALLY YOURS/Boom Boom	Imperial 5343	7.00	28.00	55
MY DREAM, MY LOVE/I Know I Was Wrong	Imperial 5359	2.00	8.00	55
SEARCHING FOR LOVE/Cold Kisses	Imperial 5370	1.50	6.00	55
BARONS, The				
FOREVER/Believe In Me (78)	Modern 818	1.50	6.00	51
BARONS, Walter Miller & The				
MY LAST MILE/Standing On The Highway	Meteor 5037	7.00	28.00	56

BARRAGE, Harold:
see Burrage, Harold as Harold Barrage

BARRELHOUSE SAMMY:
see McTell, Willie Samuel as Barrelhouse Sammy

BARRELL HOUSE BLOTT

TITLE/FLIP	LABEL & NO.	GOOD TO VERY GOOD	NEAR MINT	YR.
BRAND NEW MAN (AND LEE)/Chicks, Going Crazy	Chance 1136	8.00	32.00	53

BARRETT, Richard:
see Chantels, Richard Barrett & The
see Sevilles, Richard Barrett & The

BARTHOLOMEW, Dave

TITLE/FLIP	LABEL & NO.	GOOD TO VERY GOOD	NEAR MINT	YR.
AIN'T GONNA DO IT/Country Boy Goes Home (78)	Imperial 5069	2.00	8.00	50
ANOTHER MULE/I Want To Be With Her	Imperial 5322	3.00	12.00	54
CARNIVAL DAY/That's How You Got Killed Before (78)	Imperial 5064	2.00	8.00	49
COUNTRY GAL/Snatchin' Back (78)	Bayou 005	1.50	6.00	49
DAVE'S BOOGIE WOOGIE/Bum Mae (78)	DeLuxe 1114	1.50	6.00	47
DAVE'S BOOGIE WOOGIE/Bum Mae (78)	DeLuxe 2224	1.50	6.00	47
EVERY NIGHT, EVERY DAY/Four Winds	Imperial 5350	2.50	10.00	54
GOLDEN RULE, THE/Mother Knows Best	King 4559	5.00	20.00	51
GOOD JAX BOOGIE/Tijim (78)	Jax 1-2	2.00	8.00	50
This record, "Good Jax Boogie," was a musical tribute to Jax Beer.				
HIGH FLYING WOMAN/Stormy Weather	King 4585	5.00	20.00	51
HIGH SOCIETY BLUES/Girl Town (78)	DeLuxe 3217	1.50	6.00	49
I'LL NEVER BE THE SAME/In The Alley	King 4508	5.00	20.00	51
JUMP CHILDREN/Cat Music	Imperial 5308	4.00	16.00	54
LAWDY LAWDY LARD, Part 1/Lawdy Lawdy Lard, Part 2	King 4523	5.00	20.00	52
LOVIN' YOU/Three Times Loser	Imperial 5408	1.50	6.00	56
MR. FOOL/Country Boy (78)	DeLuxe 3223	1.50	6.00	49
MY DING-A-LING/Bad Habit	King 4544	10.00	40.00	52
NO MORE BLACK NIGHTS/Air Tight	Imperial 5249	5.00	20.00	52
OH CUBANAS/Going to Town (78)	Imperial 5096	2.00	8.00	50
OLD COW HAND FROM A BLUES BAND, AN/ Shrimp And Gumbo	Imperial 5373	1.50	6.00	56
STAR DUST/She's Got Great Big Eyes (78)	DeLuxe 1104	1.50	6.00	47
SWEET HOME BLUES/Twins	King 4482	5.00	20.00	51
TEXAS HOP/When the Saints Go Marching In Boogie	Imperial 5273	4.00	16.00	53
TRA-LA-LA/Teejim	Decca 48216	5.00	20.00	51
WHO DRANK THE BEER WHILE I WAS IN THE REAR?/ The Rest of My Life	Imperial 5210	8.00	32.00	52
WOULD YOU?/Turn The Lamp Down Low	Imperial 5390	1.50	6.00	56

BARTHOLOMEW, Dave:
see Gross, Leon T. as Archibald
(with Dave Bartholomew's Band)

BASCOMB, Paul

TITLE/FLIP	LABEL & NO.	GOOD TO VERY GOOD	NEAR MINT	YR.
ALLEY B ON 5TH AVENUE/Jumping At The Elcino	Parrot 817	2.50	10.00	54
BLACKOUT/The Blues And The Beat	States S102	1.50	6.00	52
BODY AND SOUL/Mathilda	States S121	1.50	6.00	53
COQUETTE/Got Cool Too Soon	States S110	1.50	6.00	52
JAN, Part 1/Jan, Part 2	Parrot 792	2.50	10.00	53
MUMBLES BLUES/Nona	Mercury 8299	3.00	12.00	52

BASIE, Count & The Deep River Boys:
see Deep River Boys, Count Basie & The

BASIE, Count, Jackie Wilson &

BASIN STREET BOYS, Judy Carol & The

BASIN STREET BOYS, Ormond Wilson & The

BASIN STREET BOYS, The

TITLE/FLIP	LABEL & NO.	GOOD TO VERY GOOD	NEAR MINT	YR.
I SOLD MY HEART TO THE JUNKMAN/ Lost In The Night (by Charles Brown)	Cash 1052	2.00	8.00	57

BASKERVILLE, Hayes & The Five Chestnuts:
see Five Chestnuts, Hayes Baskerville & The

BASKERVILLE, Norven & The Admirations:
see Admirations, Norven Baskerville & The

BASS, Fontella

BASS, Fontella & Bobby McClure

BATES, Lefty Combo, The:
see Luandrew, Albert as Sunnyland Slim
with The Lefty Bates Combo

BAUM, Allen:
see Bunn, Alden as Allen Baum

BAXTER, Annie Lee

BAYOU BOYS, The

TITLE/FLIP	LABEL & NO.	GOOD TO VERY GOOD	NEAR MINT	YR.
DINAH/Jambalaya	Checker 765	7.00	28.00	52

BAYOU, Duke & His Mystic 6:
see Dupree, William Thomas as Duke Bayou

BEACHAM, Rufus

TITLE/FLIP	LABEL & NO.	GOOD TO VERY GOOD	NEAR MINT	YR.
LET ME BE/What Has Happened To Me?	King 4820	1.50	6.00	55
LOVE HAVE MERCY/My Baby And Me	King 4807	1.50	6.00	55
SINCE I FELL FOR YOU/Do You Know How To Boogie-Woogie	Jax 300	5.00	20.00	52

BEALE STREET BOYS, The

TITLE/FLIP	LABEL & NO.	GOOD TO VERY GOOD	NEAR MINT	YR.
NEXT CHRISTMAS/There's Nothing Greater Than A Prayer	Oba 101/102	2.50	10.00	60

BEALE STREET GANG, The

TITLE/FLIP	LABEL & NO.	GOOD TO VERY GOOD	NEAR MINT	YR.
BACK ALLEY BLUES/ Double Crossing Blues (by Little Esther & The Robins) (78)	Savoy 731	3.00	12.00	50

BEASLEY, Good Rockin' Sam

TITLE/FLIP	LABEL & NO.	GOOD TO VERY GOOD	NEAR MINT	YR.
BABY, I'M FOOL PROOF/ Thing-A-Ma-Jig (instrumental by Kid King's Combo)	Excello 2059	2.50	10.00	55
FUNNY FUNNY FEELING/Don't Let Daddy Slow Walk You Down (instrumental by Kid King's Combo)	Excello 2070	2.50	10.00	55
SNEAK, THE/Now Listen, Baby	Excello 2051	3.00	12.00	54

BEASLEY, Good Rockin' Sam as Good Rockin' Beasley

TITLE/FLIP	LABEL & NO.	GOOD TO VERY GOOD	NEAR MINT	YR.
LORD GOODY/Happy To Go Lucky	Excello 2011	7.00	28.00	53

BEASLEY, Jimmy & The Rockers

BEAU BELLS, The (female group)

BEAVERS, The (not a female group)

TITLE/FLIP	LABEL & NO.	GOOD TO VERY GOOD	NEAR MINT	YR.
BIG MOUTH MAMA/I'd Rather Be Wrong Than Blue	Coral 65026	20.00	80.00	50
Recorded in the same session as Coral 56018.				
IF YOU SEE TEARS IN MY EYES/I Gotta Do It	Coral 65018	20.00	80.00	49

BECK, Johnny

TITLE/FLIP	LABEL & NO.	GOOD TO VERY GOOD	NEAR MINT	YR.
LOCKED IN JAIL BLUES/ You've Gotta Lay Down, Mama (78)	Sittin' In With 531	5.00	20.00	50

BEE JAY

TITLE/FLIP	LABEL & NO.	GOOD TO VERY GOOD	NEAR MINT	YR.
I'LL GO ON/There's No One For Me	Clock 1743	2.00	8.00	—

BEES, Honey & The

BEES, The

TITLE/FLIP	LABEL & NO.	GOOD TO VERY GOOD	NEAR MINT	YR.
GET AWAY BABY/I Want To Be Loved	Imperial 5320	5.00	20.00	54
TOY BELL/Snatchin' Back	Imperial 5314	7.00	28.00	54

Chuck Berry

Billy Boy

BEL-AIRES, The

TITLE/FLIP	LABEL & NO.	GOOD TO VERY GOOD	NEAR MINT	YR.
MY YEARBOOK/Rockin' And Strollin'	Decca 30631	2.00	8.00	58

BEL-AIRES, The (with Donald Woods)

TITLE/FLIP	LABEL & NO.	GOOD TO VERY GOOD	NEAR MINT	YR.
THIS PARADISE/Let's Party Awhile (maroon label)	Flip 303	8.00	32.00	54

This record was released on later pressings crediting the group as The Vel-Airs.

TITLE/FLIP	LABEL & NO.	GOOD TO VERY GOOD	NEAR MINT	YR.
WHITE PORT AND LEMON JUICE/This Is Goodbye	Flip 304	7.00	28.00	55

BEL-LARKS, The

TITLE/FLIP	LABEL & NO.	GOOD TO VERY GOOD	NEAR MINT	YR.
GET MARRIED IN JUNE/A Million And One Dreams	Hammer 6313	12.50	50.00	64

The second side of this record is a re-issue of Ransom 5001. The Hammer record was released a year later, but is rarer and in higher demand.

TITLE/FLIP	LABEL & NO.	GOOD TO VERY GOOD	NEAR MINT	YR.
SATISFIED/A Million And One Dreams	Ransom 5001	10.00	40.00	62

BELAIRS, The

TITLE/FLIP	LABEL & NO.	GOOD TO VERY GOOD	NEAR MINT	YR.
OH BABY/(flip by the Decoys)	Times Square 8	1.50	6.00	—
TELL ME WHY/Where Are You?	Times Square 23	1.50	6.00	63

BELGIANS, The

TITLE/FLIP	LABEL & NO.	GOOD TO VERY GOOD	NEAR MINT	YR.
CHANGED/Pray Tell Me	Teek 4824	4.00	16.00	—

BELJEANS, Labrenda Ben & The

BELL HOPS, The

TITLE/FLIP	LABEL & NO.	GOOD TO VERY GOOD	NEAR MINT	YR.
FOR THE REST OF MY LIFE/It Would Take A Million Years	Decca 48208	7.00	28.00	51
I'M ALL YOURS/Where Is Love	Decca 48239	7.00	28.00	51

BELL TONES, The

TITLE/FLIP	LABEL & NO.	GOOD TO VERY GOOD	NEAR MINT	YR.
MY PLEDGE TO YOU/There She Goes	Clock 71889	2.00	8.00	—

BELL TONES, The

TITLE/FLIP	LABEL & NO.	GOOD TO VERY GOOD	NEAR MINT	YR.
HEART TO HEART/The Wedding	Rama 170	10.00	40.00	55

BELL TONES, The:
see Belltones, The

BELL, Archie & The Drells

BELL, Brother

TITLE/FLIP	LABEL & NO.	GOOD TO VERY GOOD	NEAR MINT	YR.
IF YOU FEEL FROGGISH/Whole Heap Of Mamma (78)	Blues & Rhythm 7002	4.00	16.00	51

BELL, Franklin

TITLE/FLIP	LABEL & NO.	GOOD TO VERY GOOD	NEAR MINT	YR.
I DIDN'T KNOW HOW MUCH I LOVED YOU/ Did You Mean What You Said?	Manor 1002	4.00	16.00	—

BELL, Gwenn & The Brown Dots:
see Brown Dots, Gwenn Bell & The

BELL, Madeline

BELL, William

BELL, William, Judy Clay &

BELLS, THE

TITLE/FLIP	LABEL & NO.	GOOD TO VERY GOOD	NEAR MINT	YR.
WHAT CAN I TELL HER NOW/Let Me Love, Love You	Rama 166	30.00	120.00	55

BELLTONES, Lacille Watkins & The

BELLTONES, The

TITLE/FLIP	LABEL & NO.	GOOD TO VERY GOOD	NEAR MINT	YR.
ESTELLE/Promise Love (blue label)	Grand 102	100.00	400.00	54
MERENGUE, THE/I Love You, Darling	J & S 1609/1610	2.00	8.00	58
MERENGUE, THE/I Love You, Darling	Scatt 1609/1610	20.00	80.00	56

The group's name was spelled as two words, Bell Tones, on the Scatt release of The Merengue.

BELTONES, The

TITLE/FLIP	LABEL & NO.	GOOD TO VERY GOOD	NEAR MINT	YR.
I TALK TO MY ECHO/Oof Goof (black label)	Hull 721	5.00	20.00	57
I TALK TO MY ECHO/Oof Goof (red label)	Hull 721	2.50	10.00	57

BELVADERES, The

TITLE/FLIP	LABEL & NO.	GOOD TO VERY GOOD	NEAR MINT	YR.
DON'T LEAVE ME TO CRY/I Love You	Hudson 4	9.00	36.00	—

BELVEDERES, The

TITLE/FLIP	LABEL & NO.	GOOD TO VERY GOOD	NEAR MINT	YR.
COME TO ME BABY/Dear Angels Above (by Jimmy Morris)	Baton 214	1.50	6.00	55
WE TOO/Pepper-Hot Baby	Baton 217	1.50	6.00	55

BELVEDERES, The

TITLE/FLIP	LABEL & NO.	GOOD TO VERY GOOD	NEAR MINT	YR.
WALKIN' IN THE GARDEN/Buena Sera	Jopa 1771	15.00	60.00	59

BELVIN, Andy

BELVIN, Jesse & Marvin Phillips as Jesse & Marvin

Though Belvin's first name is probably Jesse, it appears on some releases on certain labels as "Jessie."

TITLE/FLIP	LABEL & NO.	GOOD TO VERY GOOD	NEAR MINT	YR.
DREAM GIRL/Daddy Loves Baby (red plastic)	Specialty 447	5.00	20.00	53
DREAM GIRL/Daddy Loves Baby	Specialty 447	1.50	6.00	53

BELVIN, Jesse:
see Capris, The
see Chargers, The (featuring Jesse Belvin)
see Cliques, The (featuring Jesse Belvin)
see Sheiks, The
see Three Dots & A Dash (featuring Jesse Belvin)
see Three Dots & A Dash, Jesse Belvin & The

BEN, Labrenda & The Beljeans

BENDER, D. C.:
see Bendy, D. C.
see Tillis, Ellas & D. C. Bendy

BENDY, D. C. as D. C. Bender

TITLE/FLIP	LABEL & NO.	GOOD TO VERY GOOD	NEAR MINT	YR.
WOKE UP THIS MORNING/	Ivory 134	3.00	12.00	—

BENDY, D. C. as D. C. Washington

TITLE/FLIP	LABEL & NO.	GOOD TO VERY GOOD	NEAR MINT	YR.
REBOB BOOGIE/Happy Home Blues (78)	Gold Star 661	4.00	16.00	49

BENDY, D. C.:
see Tillis, Ellas & D. C. Bendy as Big Son Tillis & D. C. Bender

BENITEZ, Marga & The Mello-Tones:
see Mello-Tones, Marga Benitez & The

BENSON-OGLETREE

TITLE/FLIP	LABEL & NO.	GOOD TO VERY GOOD	NEAR MINT	YR.
UPTOWN STOMP (instrumental)/Tell It Like It Is	Parrot 822	2.00	8.00	55

BENSON, George

TITLE/FLIP	LABEL & NO.	GOOD TO VERY GOOD	NEAR MINT	YR.
IT SHOULDA BEEN ME, #2/She Makes Me Mad	Groove 0024	2.50	10.00	54

BENSON, Jo Jo, Peggy Scott &

BENTON, Brook

BENTON, Brook & The Sandmen

TITLE/FLIP	LABEL & NO.	GOOD TO VERY GOOD	NEAR MINT	YR.
KENTUCKIAN SONG, The/Ooh	Okeh 7058	1.50	6.00	55

BENTON, Brook as The Sandmen (featuring Brook Benton)

TITLE/FLIP	LABEL & NO.	GOOD TO VERY GOOD	NEAR MINT	YR.
SOMEBODY TO LOVE/When I Grow Too Old To Dream	Okeh 7052	4.00	16.00	55

BERNAL, Gil

TITLE/FLIP	LABEL & NO.	GOOD TO VERY GOOD	NEAR MINT	YR.
EASYVILLE/The Whip	Spark 102	2.00	8.00	54
KING SOLOMON'S BLUES/Strawberry Stomp	Spark 106	2.00	8.00	54

BERRY CUPS, Terry Clinton & The

TITLE/FLIP	LABEL & NO.	GOOD TO VERY GOOD	NEAR MINT	YR.
HURT BY A LETTER/Dolores Darlin'	Khoury's 710	4.00	16.00	—

BERRY, Chuck

TITLE/FLIP	LABEL & NO.	GOOD TO VERY GOOD	NEAR MINT	YR.
MAYBELLENE/Wee Wee Hours	Chess 1604	2.00	8.00	55
NO MONEY DOWN/Down Bound Train	Chess 1615	2.50	10.00	56
ROLL OVER BEETHOVEN/Drifting Heart	Chess 1626	2.00	8.00	56
THIRTY DAYS/Together	Chess 1610	2.00	8.00	55
TOO MUCH MONKEY BUSINESS/ Brown-eyed Handsome Man	Chess 1635	1.50	6.00	56
YOU CAN'T CATCH ME/Havana Moon	Chess 1645	1.50	6.00	56

BERRY, Richard

TITLE/FLIP	LABEL & NO.	GOOD TO VERY GOOD	NEAR MINT	YR.
BIG BREAK, THE/What You Do To Me	Flair 1055	2.50	10.00	54
DADDY DADDY/Baby Darling	Flair 1058	2.00	8.00	54
GOD GAVE ME YOU/Don't Cha Go	Flair 1068	1.50	6.00	55
I'M STILL IN LOVE WITH YOU/One Little Prayer	Flair 1016	4.00	16.00	53
JELLY ROLL/Together	Flair 1075	1.50	6.00	55
NEXT TIME/Crazy Cover	Flair 1071	1.50	6.00	55
OH, OH! GET OUT OF THE CAR/Please Tell Me	Flair 1064	2.00	8.00	54
PRETTY BROWN EYES/I Am Bewildered	RPM 452	1.50	6.00	56
ROCKING MAN/Big John	RPM 448	1.50	6.00	56
WAIT FOR ME/Good Love	RPM 477	1.50	6.00	56
YAMA YAMA PRETTY MAMA/Angel Of My Life	RPM 465	2.00	8.00	56

Bobby "Blue" Bland

Clarence "Gatemouth" Brown

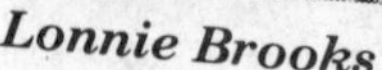

Lonnie Brooks

The Four Buddies

BERRY, Richard:
see Dreamers, Richard Berry & The
see Pharaohs, Richard Berry & The

BERRY, Richard & The Lockettes

BEST, Pat & The Four Tunes

BETHEA & THE CAP-TANS

BETTY JANE & THE TEENETTES (female group)

BIG AMOS (Amos Patton)

BIG BO & THE ARROWS

BIG CHENIER (Morris Chenier)

BIG CHIEF TRIO, The:
see Ellis, Wilbert as The Big Chief Trio

BIG DADDY & THE BOYS

BIG DUKE

TITLE/FLIP	LABEL & NO.	GOOD TO VERY GOOD	NEAR MINT	YR.
BEGGIN' AND PLEADIN'/Baby, Beat It	Flair 1029	4.00	16.00	53
HEY, DR. KINSEY/Hello, Baby	Flair 1018	4.00	16.00	53

BIG ED & HIS COMBO:
see Burns, Eddie as Big Ed & His Combo

BIG JOHN & THE BUZZARDS:
see Buzzards, Big John & The

BIG MACEO:
see Merriweather, Major as Big Maceo

BIG MAYBELLE

TITLE/FLIP	LABEL & NO.	GOOD TO VERY GOOD	NEAR MINT	YR.
GABBIN' BLUES/Rain Down Rain	Okeh 6931	1.50	6.00	52
JIMMY MULE/Send For Me	Okeh 6998	1.50	6.00	53
MY COUNTRY MAN/Maybelle's Blues	Okeh 7009	1.50	6.00	52
WAY BACK HOME/Just Want Your Love	Okeh 6955	1.50	6.00	52
WHOLE LOTTA SHAKIN' GOIN' ON/One Monkey Don't Stop No Show	Okeh 7060	2.00	8.00	55

BIG MIKE:
see Gordon, Big Mike as Big Mike

BIG THREE TRIO, Rosetta Howard & The (with Willie Dixon)

TITLE/FLIP	LABEL & NO.	GOOD TO VERY GOOD	NEAR MINT	YR.
EBONY RHAPSODY/You Made Me Love You (no group)	Columbia 40494	3.00	12.00	55

Both sides recorded in 1947.

BIG THREE TRIO, The (with Willie Dixon)

TITLE/FLIP	LABEL & NO.	GOOD TO VERY GOOD	NEAR MINT	YR.
BLUE BECAUSE OF YOU/Got You On My Mind (78)	Okeh 6863	2.00	8.00	52
CIGARETTES, WHISKEY, AND WILD, WILD WOMEN/Appetite Blues (78)	Delta 208	1.50	6.00	49
COME HERE BABY/Be A Sweetheart (78)	Okeh 6944	2.00	8.00	53
DON'T LET THAT MUSIC DIE/Till The Day I Die (78)	Delta 202	1.50	6.00	49
GET UP THOSE STAIRS, MADEMOISELLE/Lonely Roamin' (78)	Bullet 274	1.50	6.00	—
IT'S ALL OVER NOW/Tell That Woman (78)	Okeh 6842	2.00	8.00	51
LONESOME/Violent Love (instrumental) (78)	Okeh 6807	2.00	8.00	51
SIGNIFYING MONKEY/You Sure Look Good To Me (78)	Bullet 275	1.50	6.00	—
YOU DON'T LOVE ME NO MORE/My Love Will Never Die (78)	Okeh 6901	2.00	8.00	52

BIG TOWN GIRLS, Shirley Matthews & The

BIG WALTER:
see Horton, Walter as Big Walter
see Price, Walter as Big Walter

BIG WILLIE:
see Mabon, Willie as Big Willie

BILLBOARDS, The

TITLE/FLIP	LABEL & NO.	GOOD TO VERY GOOD	NEAR MINT	YR.
WITH ALL MY HEART/Around The World	Vistone 2023	5.00	20.00	61

BILLY & LILLIE (Billy Ford & Lillie)

BILLY BOY:
see Arnold, William as Billy Boy

BINDER, Dennis

TITLE/FLIP	LABEL & NO.	GOOD TO VERY GOOD	NEAR MINT	YR.
I MISS YOU SO/Early Times	Modern 930	3.00	12.00	54

BINDER, Dennis as Long Man Binder & His Thin Men

TITLE/FLIP	LABEL & NO.	GOOD TO VERY GOOD	NEAR MINT	YR.
LONG MAN, THE/I'm A Lover	United 194	2.50	10.00	55

BINGHAMPTON BLUES BOYS, The

TITLE/FLIP	LABEL & NO.	GOOD TO VERY GOOD	NEAR MINT	YR.
CROSS CUT SAW/Slim's Twist	Eastside	10.00	40.00	64
CROSS CUT SAW/Slim's Twist	Ford	10.00	40.00	64
CROSS CUT SAW/Slim's Twist	XL 901	8.00	32.00	64

BINKLEY, Jimmy

TITLE/FLIP	LABEL & NO.	GOOD TO VERY GOOD	NEAR MINT	YR.
HEY, HEY, SUGAR RAY/Midnite Wail	Chance 1134	4.00	16.00	53
NIGHT LIFE/Hot Smoke	Aladdin 3193	4.00	16.00	53
WINE, WINE, WINE/Boogie On The Hour	Checker 789	5.00	20.00	55
YOU MADE A BOO BOO/Messin' Around	Checker 835	2.00	8.00	56

BIRDIES, Robert Byrd & His

TITLE/FLIP	LABEL & NO.	GOOD TO VERY GOOD	NEAR MINT	YR.
BIPPIN' AND BOPPIN' (OVER YOU)/Strawberry Stomp	Jamie 1039	2.00	8.00	—
BIPPIN' AND BOPPIN' (OVER YOU)/Strawberry Stomp	Spark 501	4.00	16.00	—

BIRDLEGS & PAULINE

BIRDS, Bobby Byrd & The

TITLE/FLIP	LABEL & NO.	GOOD TO VERY GOOD	NEAR MINT	YR.
TRUTH HURTS, THE/Let's Live Together As One	Cash 1031	7.00	28.00	56

BIRDS, The (female group)

BIRMINGHAM SAM & HIS MAGIC GUITAR:
see Hooker, John Lee as Birmingham Sam

BISHOPS, The

TITLE/FLIP	LABEL & NO.	GOOD TO VERY GOOD	NEAR MINT	YR.
WEDDING, THE/Pretty	Bridges 1105	5.00	20.00	—

BLACK DIAMOND:
see Butler, James as Black Diamond

BLACK SATIN, Fred Parris &

BLACK, Oscar "Big Blues" & Sue Allen

TITLE/FLIP	LABEL & NO.	GOOD TO VERY GOOD	NEAR MINT	YR.
AIN'T NOBODY HOME BUT ME/Be My Baby	Groove 0102	1.50	6.00	55
BABY, PLEASE DON'T GO/I'll Live My Life Alone	Groove 0115	1.50	6.00	55
I DEDICATE MY HEART/Don't Leave Me Here To Cry	Groove 0037	1.50	6.00	54
I'LL GET BY/Hold Me Baby	Groove 0012	1.50	6.00	54
THINK OF TOMORROW/Set A Wedding Day	Groove 0130	1.50	6.00	55
TROUBLED MIND BLUES/Love, Love, Love	Atlantic 956	4.00	16.00	51

BLACKMAN, Hank & The Killers:
see Killers, Hank Blackman & The

BLACKWELL, Lou

TITLE/FLIP	LABEL & NO.	GOOD TO VERY GOOD	NEAR MINT	YR.
HOW BLUE THE NIGHT/I'm Blue Without You	Chance 1130	5.00	20.00	—

BLAIR, Sunny

TITLE/FLIP	LABEL & NO.	GOOD TO VERY GOOD	NEAR MINT	YR.
FIVE FOOT THREE BLUES/Glad To Be Back Home (78)	RPM 354	5.00	20.00	52
PLEASE SEND MY BABY BACK/Gonna Let You Go	Meteor 5006	20.00	80.00	52

Though both sides of this record are credited to Sunny Blair, the second side is actually by Baby Face Turner.

BLAND, Billy

BLAND, Robert as Bobby Blue Bland

TITLE/FLIP	LABEL & NO.	GOOD TO VERY GOOD	NEAR MINT	YR.
CRYING ALL NIGHT LONG/Dry Up, Baby (78)	Modern 848	2.50	10.00	—
CRYING/A Letter From A Trench In Korea (78)	Chess 1489	2.50	10.00	54
GOOD LOVIN'/Drifting From Town To Town (78)	Modern 868	2.50	10.00	—
I.O.U. BLUES/Lovin' Blues	Duke 105	10.00	40.00	54
IT'S MY LIFE, BABY/Time Out	Duke 141	5.00	20.00	56
NO BLOW NO SHOW/Army Blues	Duke 115	8.00	32.00	54
WOKE UP SCREAMING/You Or None	Duke 146	2.00	8.00	57
YOU GOT BAD INTENTIONS/I Can't Put You Down	Duke 153	1.50	6.00	57

BLANDON, Richard & The Dubs

BLASERS, The

TITLE/FLIP	LABEL & NO.	GOOD TO VERY GOOD	NEAR MINT	YR.
SHE NEEDS TO BE LOVED/Done Got Over	United 191	1.50	6.00	55

BLAYLOCK, Travis as Harmonica Slim

Blaylock is not to be confused with James Moore who recorded both under the names Harmonica Slim and Slim Harpo.

TITLE/FLIP	LABEL & NO.	GOOD TO VERY GOOD	NEAR MINT	YR.
DROP ANCHOR/Do What You Want To Do	*Vita 146*	3.00	12.00	*57*
MARY HELEN/Lonely Hours	*Aladdin 3317*	4.00	16.00	*56*
MY GIRL WON'T QUIT ME/You Better Believe It	*Vita 138*	3.00	12.00	*57*
THOUGHT I DIDN'T LOVE YOU/Going Back Home	*Spry 103*	3.00	12.00	*56*

BLAZER BOY

TITLE/FLIP	LABEL & NO.	GOOD TO VERY GOOD	NEAR MINT	YR.
MORNING TRAIN/Joe's Kid Sister	*Imperial 5199*	8.00	32.00	*52*
SURPRISE BLUES/Waitin' For My Baby	*Imperial 5244*	8.00	32.00	*53*

BLAZERS, Johnny Moore's:

see Moore, Johnny as Johnny Moore's Blazers

BLEDSOE, James as Country Jim

TITLE/FLIP	LABEL & NO.	GOOD TO VERY GOOD	NEAR MINT	YR.
GOOD LOOKING MAMA/Plantation Blues (78)	*Imperial 5091*	5.00	20.00	*50*
OLD RIVER BLUES/I'll Take You Back, Baby (78)	*Imperial 5073*	5.00	20.00	*49*
RAINY MORNING BLUES/Avenue Breakdown (78)	*Imperial 5062*	5.00	20.00	*49*
SAD AND LONELY BLUES/Phillipine Blues (78)	*Imperial 5095*	5.00	20.00	*50*

BLEDSOE, James as Hot Rod Happy

TITLE/FLIP	LABEL & NO.	GOOD TO VERY GOOD	NEAR MINT	YR.
HOT ROD BOOGIE/Worried Blues (78)	*Pacemaker 1014*	10.00	40.00	*50*

BLEND-TONES, The

TITLE/FLIP	LABEL & NO.	GOOD TO VERY GOOD	NEAR MINT	YR.
SHE'S GONE/Lights Please	*Chic-Car 100*	2.00	8.00	*61*
SHE'S GONE/Lights Please	*Don-El 106*	1.50	6.00	*61*

BLENDAIRS, The

TITLE/FLIP	LABEL & NO.	GOOD TO VERY GOOD	NEAR MINT	YR.
MY LOVE IS JUST FOR YOU/Repetition	*Tin Pan Alley 252*	8.00	32.00	—

BLENDERS, Earl Curry & The

TITLE/FLIP	LABEL & NO.	GOOD TO VERY GOOD	NEAR MINT	YR.
LATE RISING MOON/I Want To Be With You	*R & B 1304*	4.00	16.00	*54*

BLENDERS, The (female group)

BLENDERS, The

TITLE/FLIP	LABEL & NO.	GOOD TO VERY GOOD	NEAR MINT	YR.
I WON'T TELL THE WORLD/But I Know	*Paradise 111*	2.50	10.00	*59*

BLENDERS, The

TITLE/FLIP	LABEL & NO.	GOOD TO VERY GOOD	NEAR MINT	YR.
BUSIEST CORNER IN MY HOME TOWN, THE/All I Gotta Do Is Think Of You	*Decca 27587*	10.00	40.00	*51*
COUNT EVERY STAR/ Would I Still Be The One In Your Heart?	*Decca 48158*	15.00	60.00	*50*
DON'T FUCK AROUND WITH LOVE (recorded in 1953)/ I'm Gonna Do That Woman In (by the Sparrows)	*Kelway 101*	1.50	6.00	*71*
DON'T PLAY AROUND WITH LOVE/ You'll Never Be Mine Again	*Jay Dee 780*	5.00	20.00	*53*
GONE/Honeysuckle Rose	*Decca 48156*	15.00	60.00	*50*
I'D BE A FOOL AGAIN/Just A Little Walk With Me	*Decca 28092*	15.00	60.00	*52*
I'M AFRAID THE MASQUERADE IS OVER/ Little Small Town Girl	*Decca 27403*	20.00	80.00	*51*
I'M SO CRAZY FOR LOVE/What About Tonight?	*Decca 48183*	15.00	60.00	*50*
IF THAT'S THE WAY YOU WANT IT, BABY/I Don't Miss You Anymore	*MGM 11488*	25.00	100.00	*53*
MY HEART WILL NEVER FORGET/You Do The Dreamin'	*Decca 48244*	15.00	60.00	*51*
NEVER IN A MILLION YEARS/Memories Of You	*Decca 28241*	15.00	60.00	*52*
PLEASE TAKE ME BACK/Isn't It a Shame?	*MGM 11531*	25.00	100.00	*53*

BLENDORS, The

TITLE/FLIP	LABEL & NO.	GOOD TO VERY GOOD	NEAR MINT	YR.
TELL ME WHAT'S ON YOUR MIND/When I'm Walkin' With My Baby	*Decca 31284*	1.50	6.00	*61*

BLENDTONES, The

BLENTONES, The

TITLE/FLIP	LABEL & NO.	GOOD TO VERY GOOD	NEAR MINT	YR.
LILLY/Military Kick	*MGM 12782*	1.50	6.00	*59*

BLIND WILLIE:

see McTell, Willie Samuel as Blind Willie

BLONDE BOMBER, The

This artist is thought possibly to be Little Red Walter.

TITLE/FLIP	LABEL & NO.	GOOD TO VERY GOOD	NEAR MINT	YR.
STROLLIE BUN/Am I To Blame?	*Hull 737*	2.50	10.00	*61*

BLOSSOMS, The

BLUE ANGELS, The

TITLE/FLIP	LABEL & NO.	GOOD TO VERY GOOD	NEAR MINT	YR.
DESIRIE/Like Heaven	*Edsel 781*	4.00	16.00	*60*
IN THE SUN/Sobbin'	*Palette 5038*	2.00	8.00	*60*

BLUE BEARDS, The

TITLE/FLIP	LABEL & NO.	GOOD TO VERY GOOD	NEAR MINT	YR.
ROMANCE/Crawlin'	*Guide 1002*	1.50	6.00	*58*

BLUE BELLES, Patty La Belle & The

BLUE BELLES, The (female group)

TITLE/FLIP	LABEL & NO.	GOOD TO VERY GOOD	NEAR MINT	YR.
CANCEL THE CALL/The Story Of A Fool	*Atlantic 987*	4.00	16.00	*53*

BLUE BELLES, The (female group) (featuring Patty La Belle)

BLUE CHARLIE

TITLE/FLIP	LABEL & NO.	GOOD TO VERY GOOD	NEAR MINT	YR.
I'M GONNA KILL THAT HEN/Don't Bring No Friend	*Nasco 6002*	7.00	28.00	*57*

BLUE CHIPS, Carlron Lankford & The

BLUE DIAMONDS, The (with Ernie "K-Doe" Kador)

TITLE/FLIP	LABEL & NO.	GOOD TO VERY GOOD	NEAR MINT	YR.
HONEY BABY/No Money	*Savoy 1134*	2.50	10.00	*54*

BLUE DOTS, The

TITLE/FLIP	LABEL & NO.	GOOD TO VERY GOOD	NEAR MINT	YR.
DON'T DO THAT, BABY/You've Got To Live For Yourself	*De Luxe 6052*	5.00	20.00	*54*
DON'T HOLD IT/Street Of Sorrow	*De Luxe 6055*	5.00	20.00	*54*
GOD LOVES YOU, CHILD/Save All Your Love For Me	*De Luxe 6061*	4.00	16.00	*54*
HOLD ME TIGHT/Let Me Know Tonight	*De Luxe 6067*	4.00	16.00	*54*
PLEASE DON'T TELL 'EM/Saturday Night Fish Fry	*Ace 526*	5.00	20.00	*57*

BLUE FLAMERS, The

TITLE/FLIP	LABEL & NO.	GOOD TO VERY GOOD	NEAR MINT	YR.
DRIVING DOWN THE HIGHWAY/Watch On	*Excello 2026*	5.00	20.00	*54*

BLUE FLAMES, The:

see Parker, Herman as Little Junior Parker & The Blue Flames

see Parker, Herman as Little Junior Parker & Bill Johnson's Blue Flames

BLUE JAYS, The

TITLE/FLIP	LABEL & NO.	GOOD TO VERY GOOD	NEAR MINT	YR.
WHITE CLIFFS OF DOVER/Hey, Pappa	*Checker 782*	75.00	300.00	*53*

BLUE JAYS, The (featuring Leon Peels)

TITLE/FLIP	LABEL & NO.	GOOD TO VERY GOOD	NEAR MINT	YR.
LET'S MAKE LOVE/Rock, Rock, Rock	*Milestone 2010*	2.00	8.00	*61*
RIGHT TO LOVE, THE/Rock, Rock, Rock	*Milestone 2012*	1.50	6.00	*62*

BLUE JEANS, Bob B. Soxx & The

BLUE NOTES, Harold Melvin & The

BLUE NOTES, Joe Weaver & The

TITLE/FLIP	LABEL & NO.	GOOD TO VERY GOOD	NEAR MINT	YR.
15-40 SPECIAL/Soft Pillow	*De Luxe 6006*	6.25	25.00	*53*
I'M ON MY MERRY WAY/Loose Caboose	*Fortune 820*	2.50	10.00	*55*
J. B. BOOGIE/Baby, I'm In Love With You	*De Luxe 6021*	6.25	25.00	*54*

BLUE NOTES, The (with Harold Melvin)

TITLE/FLIP	LABEL & NO.	GOOD TO VERY GOOD	NEAR MINT	YR.
MY HERO/A Good Woman	*Value 213*	1.50	6.00	*60*
O HOLY NIGHT/Winter Wonderland	*Value 215*	1.50	6.00	*60*

BLUE NOTES, The (with Joe Weaver)

BLUE NOTES, The (with Todd Randall)

TITLE/FLIP	LABEL & NO.	GOOD TO VERY GOOD	NEAR MINT	YR.
CHARLOTTE AMALIE/Make A Box	*Tico 1083*	1.50	6.00	—
IF YOU LOVE ME/There's Something In Your Eyes, Eloise	*Josie 800*	10.00	40.00	*56*
IF YOU LOVE ME/There's Something In Your Eyes, Eloise	*Port 70021*	2.00	8.00	*61*
IF YOU'LL BE MINE/Too Hot To Handle	*Rama 25*	20.00	80.00	*53*
RETRIBUTION BLUES, THE/Wagon Wheels	*Josie 823*	10.00	40.00	*57*
W-P-L-J/While I'm Away	*3 Sons 103*	1.50	6.00	*62*

BLUE NOTES, Todd Randall & The

TITLE/FLIP	LABEL & NO.	GOOD TO VERY GOOD	NEAR MINT	YR.
WITH THIS PEN/Letters	*Josie 814*	2.50	10.00	*57*

BLUE SMITTY:

see Smith, Clarence as Blue Smitty

BLUE, Little Joe

BLUEBIRDS, Ann Nichols & The

TITLE/FLIP	LABEL & NO.	GOOD TO VERY GOOD	NEAR MINT	YR.
LET ME KNOW/Lost In A Fog Over You (78)	*Sittin' In With 552*	2.50	10.00	*50*
THOSE MAGIC WORDS/I Wonder What it Takes To Make Me Happy? (78)	*Sittin' In With 561*	2.50	10.00	*50*

BLUEBIRDS, The

TITLE/FLIP	LABEL & NO.	GOOD TO VERY GOOD	NEAR MINT	YR.
CAN'T HELP BUT SING THE BLUES/Feel Like Riding On	*Rainbow 199*	40.00	160.00	*53*

TITLE/FLIP	LABEL & NO.	GOOD TO VERY GOOD	NEAR MINT	YR.

BLUEDOTS, The

MY VERY OWN/Mary Had A Rock N' Roll Lamb	Hurricane 104	4.00	16.00	—

BLUES BOY, The:
see Seward, Alec as The Blues Boy

BLUES EXPRESS ORCHESTRA, The

HONKIN' AWAY/Mush	Gem 206	2.50	10.00	53

BLUES KING, The:
see Seward, Alec as The Blues King

BLUES KINGS, Andy Charles & The

LOVE COME BACK/Baby, Don't Go	D 1061	2.50	10.00	59

BLUES RAMBLERS, The:
see Brown, Nature Boy & His Blues Ramblers

BLUES ROCKERS, The

CALLING ALL COWS/Johnnie Mae	Excello 2062	3.00	12.00	55
LITTLE BOY, LITTLE BOY/My Mama's Baby Child (78)	Chess 1483	2.00	8.00	50
TROUBLE IN MY HOME/Times Are Getting Hard (78)	Aristocrat 407	2.50	10.00	50
WHEN TIMES ARE GETTING BETTER/Blues Rocker's Bop (78)	Aristocrat 413	2.50	10.00	50

BLUES TROUBADOR, The:
see Thomas, Jesse (The Blues Troubador)

BLUESMEN, Maggie Hathaway & The

BO DIDDLEY:
see Diddley, Bo

BO, Eddie

DEAREST ONE/Too Much Of A Good Thing	Apollo 509	2.00	8.00	56
I CRY, OH/My Heart Was Meant For You	Apollo 499	2.00	8.00	56
I'M SO TIRED/We Like Mambo	Ace 515	1.50	6.00	57
I'M WISE/Happy Tears	Apollo 486	2.50	10.00	55
INDEED I DO/Every Night, Every Day	Checker 877	1.50	6.00	58
OH-OH/My Dearest Darling	Chess 1698	1.50	6.00	58
PLEASE FORGET ME/I'll Be Satisfied	Apollo 496	2.00	8.00	56
TELL ME WHY/Hey, Bo	Apollo 504	2.00	8.00	56

BO, Eddie as Little Bo

BABY/So Glad	Ace 501	5.00	20.00	55

BO, Mr.

BO, Mr. & His Blues Boys

BOB & EARL

BOBBETTES, The (female group)

BOBBY PINS, The (female group)

BODAFORD, Bill & The Rockets:
see Rockets, Bill Bodaford & The

BOHEMIANS, The

BOINES, Houston

MONKEY MOTION/Superintendent Blues (7-inch 78 rpm)	RPM 364	7.00	28.00	51
MONKEY MOTION/Superintendent Blues (78)	RPM 364	5.00	20.00	51

BOINES, Houston as Houston Baines

GOING HOME/Relation Blues (78)	Blues & Rhythm 7001	7.00	28.00	51

BOLEROS, Carmen Taylor & The

FREDDIE/Ooh !	Atlantic 1041	15.00	60.00	54

BOLLIN, Zu Zu

CRY, CRY, CRY/Stavin' Chain (78)	Torch 6912	2.50	10.00	52
WHY DON'T YOU EAT WHERE YOU SLEPT LAST NIGHT?/ Headlight Blues (78)	Torch 6910	2.50	10.00	52

BOMBERS, The

MALENA/I'll Never Tire Of You	Orpheus 1101	1.50	6.00	55
TWO-TIME HEART/Sentence Of Love	Orpheus 1105	1.50	6.00	56

BOND, Luther & The Emeralds:
see Emeralds, Luther Bond & The

BONDS, Gary "U.S."

BONNER, Weldon as Juke Boy Barner

WELL, BABY/Rock With Me, Baby	Irma 111	15.00	60.00	57

BOOGIE JAKE:
see Jacobs, Matthew as Boogie Jake

BOOGIE MAN, The:
see Hooker, John Lee as The Boogie Man

BOOGIE RAMBLERS, The (featuring Huey Thierry)

CINDY LOU/Such Is Love	Goldband 1130	4.00	16.00	57

Thierry later formed a group recorded as Cookie & His Cupcakes.

BOOKER T. & THE MG'S

BOOKER, Charley

RABBIT BLUES/No Ridin' Blues (7-inch rpm)	Blues & Rhythm 7003	7.00	28.00	51
RABBIT BLUES/No Ridin' Blues (78)	Blues & Rhythm 7003	5.00	20.00	51

BOOKER, Connie Mac:
see McBooker, Connie as Connie Mac Booker

BOOKER, James

BOOKER, John Lee:
see Hooker, John Lee as John Lee Booker

BOOMERANGS, The

BOOTH, Henry & The Midnighters

BOOZE, (Wea) Bea

BOP CHORDS, The

BABY/So Why? (shiny red label)	Holiday 2608	4.00	16.00	57
CASTLE IN THE SKY/My Darling To You (black label)	Holiday 2601	10.00	40.00	57
WHEN I WOKE UP THIS MORNING/I Really Love Her (black label)	Holiday 2603	8.00	32.00	57

BOPTONES, The

BOSS-TONES, The

MOPE-ITTY MOPE/Wings Of An Angel	Boss 401	7.00	28.00	59
MOPETTY MOPE/Wings Of An Angel	V-Tone 208	7.00	28.00	60

TITLE/FLIP	LABEL & NO.	GOOD TO VERY GOOD	NEAR MINT	YR.
BOSTIC, Earl				
I GOT LOADED/Chains Of Love	King 4491	2.50	10.00	51
BOSTICK, Calvin & His Trio				
FOUR ELEVEN BOOGIE/ Christmas Won't Be Christmas Without You	Chess 1530	2.00	8.00	52
FOUR ELEVEN BOOGIE/Bang, Bang, Blues (instrumental)	Chess 1571	1.50	6.00	52
BOULEVARDS, The				
BOUNCE, Reverend				
FLOCK ROCKER/I Guess I'm A Fool (by Memphis Slim & The Vagabonds) (78)	Premium 850	1.50	6.00	50
BOUQUETS, The				
BOUQUETS, Tooti & The				
YOU DONE ME WRONG/The Conqueror	Parkway 887	2.00	8.00	—
BOY FRIENDS, Jeanie & The				
BABY/It's Me Knocking	Warwick 508	1.50	6.00	59
BOYD, Eddie				
FIVE LONG YEARS/Blue Coat Man (black plastic)	J.O.B. 1007	5.00	20.00	52
FIVE LONG YEARS/Blue Coat Man (red plastic)	J.O.B. 1007	5.00	20.00	52
The red plastic pressing of this record is more common than the black, but since more collectors are looking for the red, both have remained of approximate equal value.				
I'M GOIN' DOWNTOWN/Lonesome For My Baby	Herald 406	15.00	60.00	52
IT'S MISERABLE TO BE ALONE/I'm Pleading (78)	J.O.B. 1005	2.00	8.00	52
IT'S MISERABLE TO BE ALONE/I'm Pleading	J.O.B. 1009	6.25	25.00	52
BOYD, Eddie & His Chess Men				
COOL KIND TREATMENT/Rosalee Swing	Chess 1523	7.00	28.00	52
FIVE LONG YEARS/24 Hours Of Fear	Oriole 1316	3.00	12.00	58
HUSH BABY, DON'T YOU CRY/Came Home This Morning	Chess 1573	2.50	10.00	54
I GOT A WOMAN/Hotel Blues	Chess 1660	1.50	6.00	56
I LOVE YOU/Save Her Doctor	J.O.B. 1114	7.00	28.00	58
I'M A PRISONER/I've Been Deceived	Chess 1606	1.50	6.00	56
JUST A FOOL/Four Leaf Clover	Chess 1634	1.50	6.00	54
PICTURE IN THE FRAME/Nothing But Trouble	Chess 1561	2.50	10.00	55
RATTIN' AND RUNNIN' AROUND/Driftin'	Chess 1576	2.00	8.00	54
REAL GOOD FEELING/The Nightmare Is Over	Chess 1595	1.50	6.00	55
STORY OF BILL, THE/Please Help Me	Chess 1582	2.00	8.00	55
THAT'S WHEN I MISS YOU SO/Tortured Soul	Chess 1552	2.50	10.00	53
THIRD DEGREE/Back Beat	Chess 1541	2.50	10.00	53
24 HOURS/The Tickler	Chess 1533	3.00	12.00	52
BOYD, Eddie & The Daylighters				
BOYD, Eddie as Ernie Boyd				
WHY DON'T YOU BE WISE, BABY?/ I Gotta Find My Baby (78)	Regal 3305	2.00	8.00	50
BOYD, Eddie as Little Eddie Boyd & His Boogie Band				
BABY, WHAT'S WRONG WITH YOU?/Eddie's Blues	RCA Victor 22-0002	2.00	8.00	48
WHAT MAKES THESE THINGS HAPPEN TO ME?/ Chicago Is Just That Way (red plastic)	RCA Victor 50-0006	5.00	20.00	48
BOYD, Ernie: see Boyd, Eddie as Ernie Boyd				
BOYD, Robert: see Byrd, Roy as Robert Boyd				
BOYFRIENDS, Wini Brown & The				
BE ANYTHING—BE MINE/Heaven Knows Why	Mercury 8270	10.00	40.00	52
HERE IN MY HEART/Your Happiness Is Mine	Mercury 5870	10.00	40.00	52
BOYS, Big Daddy & The				
BOZE, Calvin				
BEALE STREET ON SATURDAY NIGHT/ Choo Choo Boogieing My Baby Home	Aladdin 3079	5.00	20.00	51
GOOD TIME SUE/Keep Your Nose Out Of My Business	Aladdin 3132	4.00	16.00	52
I'M GONNA STEAM OFF THE STAMP/Fish-tail	Aladdin 3110	4.00	16.00	51
I'VE GOT NEWS FOR YOU/I Can't Stop Crying	Aladdin 3100	5.00	20.00	51
LIZZIE LOU, PART 1/Lizzie Lou, Part 2	Aladdin 3065	6.25	25.00	51
LOOPED/Blow, Man, Blow	Aladdin 3147	4.00	16.00	52
MY FRIEND TOLD ME/Hey Lawdy, Miss Clawdie	Aladdin 3122	4.00	16.00	52
SAFRONIA B/Angel City Blues	Aladdin 3055	10.00	40.00	50
SATISFIED/Working With My Baby (78)	Score 4003	1.50	6.00	—

TITLE/FLIP	LABEL & NO.	GOOD TO VERY GOOD	NEAR MINT	YR.
SHAMROCK/Havin' A Ball	Aladdin 3160	4.00	16.00	52
SLIPPIN' AND SLIDIN'/Baby, You're Tops With Me	Aladdin 3086	5.00	20.00	51
STINKIN' FROM DRINKIN'/Look Out For Tomorrow Today	Aladdin 3072	5.00	20.00	51
WAITING AND DRINKING/If You Ever Had The Blues (78)	Aladdin 3045	1.50	6.00	50
BRADEN, Tommy (Mary Jo) & His Flames				
DO THE DO/Did You Ever See A Monkey?	United 177	2.00	8.00	54
The record label has the words "Mary Jo" in parenthesis after Braden's name, which is a reference to his earlier hit by that name.				
BRADIX, Big Charley				
BOOGIE LIKE YOU WANNA/Dollar Diggin' Woman (78)	Blue Bonnet 153	6.25	25.00	48
BOOGIE LIKE YOU WANNA/Dollar Diggin' Woman (78)	Colonial 108	2.50	10.00	48
NUMBERED DAYS/Wee Wee Hours (78)	Aristocrat 418	6.25	25.00	48
BRADLEY, Jan				
BRADLEY, Sam see Smith, Arthur as Sonny Boy & Sam (with Sam Bradley)				
BRADSHAW, Tiny				
BRADSHAW BOOGIE/Walkin' The Chalk Line	King 4457	5.00	20.00	51
I'M A HIGH BALLIN' DADDY/You Came By	King 4467	5.00	20.00	51
LAY IT ON THE LINE/Rippin' And Runnin'	King 4547	4.00	16.00	52
MAILMAN'S SACK/Newspaper Boy Blues	King 4537	4.00	16.00	52
T.99/Long Time Baby	King 4487	5.00	20.00	51
TRAIN KEPT A ROLLIN', THE/Knockin' Blues	King 4497	7.00	28.00	51
WALK THAT MESS/One, Two, Three, Kick Blues	King 4427	5.00	20.00	50
BRAGG, Johnny & The Marigolds: see Marigolds, Johnny Bragg & The				
BRANTLEY, Charles				
BEGGIN' BLUES/Each Night About This Time	Jax 301	5.00	20.00	—
LOOK AT ME/Think About Me, Baby	King 4640	2.00	8.00	53
MOVIN' ON, NOW/Fog Horn	King 4616	2.50	10.00	53
BRENDA & THE TABULATIONS				
BRENSTON, Jackie				
BLUES GOT ME AGAIN, THE/Starvation	Chess 1532	8.00	32.00	51
COME BACK WHERE YOU BELONG/Rocket "88" (78)	Chess 1458	2.00	8.00	49
IN MY REAL GONE ROCKET/Tuckered Out	Chess 1469	10.00	40.00	49
JUICED/Independent Woman (78)	Chess 1472	2.50	10.00	50
LEO THE LOUSE/Hi-Ho Baby	Chess 1496	8.00	32.00	50
BREWSTER, Ray & The Cadillacs				
BRIM, Grace				
MAN AROUND MY DOOR/Hospitality Blues (78)	J.O.B. 117	5.00	20.00	52
BRIM, Grace as Mrs. John Brim				
GOING DOWN THE LINE/Leaving Blues (78)	Random 202	9.00	36.00	51
BRIM, John				
DARK CLOUDS/Lonesome Man Blues (78)	Random 201	8.00	32.00	51
BRIM, John & His Combo				
STRANGE MAN/Mean Man Blues (78)	Fortune 801	5.00	20.00	50
BRIM, John & His Gary Kings				
GO AWAY/That Ain't Right	Chess 1588	9.00	36.00	55
I WOULD HATE TO SEE YOU GO/ You've Got Me Where You Want Me	Chess 1624	7.00	28.00	56
BRIM, John & His Stompers				
TOUGH TIMES/Gary Stomp (red plastic)	Parrot 799	20.00	80.00	53
TOUGH TIMES/Gary Stomp	Parrot 799	9.00	36.00	53
BRIM, John Trio, The				
DRINKING WOMAN/Woman Trouble (78)		5.00	20.00	54
Though both sides are credited to John Brim, "Woman Trouble" is actually by Albert Luandrew as Sunnyland Slim & His Boys.				
TROUBLE IN THE MORNING/Humming Blues (78)	J.O.B. 110	5.00	20.00	52
BRIM, Mrs. John: see Brim, Grace as Mrs. John Brim				
BRISCOE, Fleming see 5 Blue Notes, The (featuring Fleming Briscoe)				
BRITT, Tina				

BROCHURES, The

TITLE/FLIP	LABEL & NO.	GOOD TO VERY GOOD	NEAR MINT	YR.
THEY LIED/My In-Laws Are Outlaws	*Apollo 757*	2.00	8.00	*61*

BRONZEVILLE, Lewis Five, The

TITLE/FLIP	LABEL & NO.	GOOD TO VERY GOOD	NEAR MINT	YR.
COTTON BLOSSOM BLUES/Laughing At Life (78)	*Bluebird 8433*	5.00	20.00	*40*
COTTON BLOSSOM BLUES/Laughing At Life (78)	*Montgomery Ward 8898*	4.00	16.00	—
IT CAN HAPPEN TO YOU/Oh! Mabel, Oh! (78)	*Bluebird 8480*	5.00	20.00	*40*
IT CAN HAPPEN TO YOU/Oh! Mabel, Oh! (78)	*Montgomery Ward 8901*	4.00	16.00	—
LOW DOWN GAL BLUES/Linda Brown (78)	*Bluebird 8460*	5.00	20.00	*40*
LOW DOWN GAL BLUES/Linda Brown (78)	*Montgomery Ward 8899*	4.00	16.00	—
MISSISSIPPI FIRE BLUES/ Natchez, Mississippi (78)	*Montgomery Ward 8900*	4.00	16.00	—
MISSISSIPPI FIRE BLUES/Natchez, Mississippi (78)	*Bluebird 8445*	5.00	20.00	*40*

BROOKLYN BOYS, The

TITLE/FLIP	LABEL & NO.	GOOD TO VERY GOOD	NEAR MINT	YR.
IF SHE SHOULD CALL/Every Night	*Ferris 902*	2.00	8.00	*56*

BROOKS BROTHERS, The

TITLE/FLIP	LABEL & NO.	GOOD TO VERY GOOD	NEAR MINT	YR.
FOOL THAT I AM/ You're Gonna Make A Wonderful Sweetheart (78)	*Decca 48049*	2.50	10.00	*47*
MICKEY/Is It Too Late? (78)	*Decca 24267*	2.50	10.00	*47*
WHO WERE YOU KISSING?/The Things You Want The Most Of All (78)	*Decca 24287*	2.50	10.00	*48*

BROOKS BROTHERS, The

TITLE/FLIP	LABEL & NO.	GOOD TO VERY GOOD	NEAR MINT	YR.
BABY PLAY IT STRAIGHT/I'm In Love With Two Sweethearts (78)	*Diamond 2005*	2.00	8.00	*46*
ST. LOUIS BLUES/ If Somebody Ever Breaks My Heart (78)	*Diamond 2006*	2.00	8.00	*46*

BROOKS, Billy

TITLE/FLIP	LABEL & NO.	GOOD TO VERY GOOD	NEAR MINT	YR.
I CALLED MY BABY/What Can I Do?	*Peacock 1629*	2.50	10.00	*53*

BROOKS, Dusty:

see Four Tones, Dusty Brooks & The

see Tones, Dusty Brooks & The

BROOKS, Junior

TITLE/FLIP	LABEL & NO.	GOOD TO VERY GOOD	NEAR MINT	YR.
LONE TOWN BLUES/She's The Little Girl For Me (78)	*RPM 343*	5.00	20.00	*51*

BROOKS, Lillian & The Moroccos

BROOKS, Louis

TITLE/FLIP	LABEL & NO.	GOOD TO VERY GOOD	NEAR MINT	YR.
BUS STATION BLUES/Waddle Trot	*Excello 2030*	4.00	16.00	*52*
CAN'T KEEP FROM CRYING'/Baby, Baby, Who's Wrong?	*Excello 2063*	1.50	6.00	*53*
DOUBLE SHOT/Time Out	*Excello 2042*	2.50	10.00	*53*
IT'S LOVE, BABY/Chicken Shuffle	*Excello 2056*	2.00	8.00	*53*

BROOKS, Sonny & The Savoys:

see Savoys, Sonny Brooks & The

BROOKTONES, The

BROONZY, William Lee as Big Bill Broonzy

TITLE/FLIP	LABEL & NO.	GOOD TO VERY GOOD	NEAR MINT	YR.
LITTLE CITY WOMAN/Lonesome	*Chess 1546*	8.00	32.00	*55*

BROTHER BLUES & THE BACK ROOM BOYS:

see Dupree, William Thomas as Brother Blues

BROTHER WOODMAN & THE CHANTERS:

see Chanters, Brother Woodman & The

BROWN DOTS, Deek Watson & The

TITLE/FLIP	LABEL & NO.	GOOD TO VERY GOOD	NEAR MINT	YR.
AS THO YOU DON'T KNOW/Darktown Strutters Ball (78)	*Manor 1166*	1.50	6.00	*49*
BOW-WOW-WOW/At Our Fireplace (78)	*Manor 1170*	1.50	6.00	*49*
FOR SENTIMENTAL REASONS/ It's A Pity To Say Goodnight (78)	*Manor 1041*	1.50	6.00	*46*
HOW CAN YOU SAY I DON'T CARE?/ Long Legged Lizzie (78)	*Manor 1044*	1.50	6.00	*46*
I DON'T KNOW FROM NOTHING, BABY/ Shout, Brother, Shout (78)	*Manor 1057*	1.50	6.00	*47*
IF I CAN'T HAVE YOU/I'm Loving You For You (78)	*Manor 1027*	1.50	6.00	*46*
JUST IN CASE YOU CHANGE YOUR MIND/You're A Heartache To Me (78)	*Manor 1015*	1.50	6.00	*45*
LET'S GIVE LOVE ANOTHER CHANCE/Just In Case You Change Your Mind (78)	*Manor 1163*	1.50	6.00	*49*
LET'S GIVE LOVE ANOTHER CHANCE/Thirty-One Miles For A Nickel (78)	*Manor 1005*	1.50	6.00	*45*
MY BONNIE LIES OVER THE OCEAN/ You Better Think Twice (78)	*Manor 1179*	1.50	6.00	*49*
PATIENCE AND FORTITUDE/Is It Right? (78)	*Manor 1017*	1.50	6.00	*45*
PRAY FOR THE LIGHTS TO GO OUT/I've Got The Situation Well In Hand (78)	*Majestic 1244*	2.00	8.00	*48*
RUMORS ARE FLYING/You Took All My Love (78)	*Manor 1040*	1.50	6.00	*46*
SATCHELMOUTH BABY/Surrender (78)	*Manor 1026*	1.50	6.00	*46*
THAT'S WHAT SHE GETS/Escuchame (78)	*Manor 1016*	1.50	6.00	*45*
THAT'S WHAT SHE GETS/Why You No Knock? (by Benny Davis) (78)	*Manor 1075*	1.50	6.00	*47*
WELL, NATCH!/ Please Give A Broken Heart A Break (78)	*Manor 1032*	1.50	6.00	*46*
YOU'RE HEAVEN SENT/Sentimental Reasons (78)	*Manor 1009*	1.50	6.00	*45*

BROWN DOTS, Gwenn Bell & The

TITLE/FLIP	LABEL & NO.	GOOD TO VERY GOOD	NEAR MINT	YR.
AFTER AWHILE/If I Could Be With You (78)	*Manor 1171*	1.50	6.00	*49*

BROWN, Al as Al Brown's Tunetoppers

BROWN, B.:

see Brown, Buster as B. Brown

BROWN, Buster

TITLE/FLIP	LABEL & NO.	GOOD TO VERY GOOD	NEAR MINT	YR.
FANNIE MAE/Lost In A Dream (78)	*Fire 1008*	6.25	25.00	*60*

Although this record was issued on 45 rpm, it is very common and has little collector value. The rare 78 was one of the last issued in the industry.

BROWN, Buster as B. Brown & His Rockin' McVoots

TITLE/FLIP	LABEL & NO.	GOOD TO VERY GOOD	NEAR MINT	YR.
CANDIED YAMS/Fannie Mae Is Back	*Vest 830*	2.50	10.00	*60*
MY BABY LEFT ME/Hardworking Man	*Vest 827*	2.50	10.00	*60*

BROWN, Charles

TITLE/FLIP	LABEL & NO.	GOOD TO VERY GOOD	NEAR MINT	YR.
ALL MY LIFE/Don't Leave Poor Me	*Aladdin 3200*	2.00	8.00	*53*
BLACK NIGHT/Once There Lived A Fool	*Aladdin 3076*	6.25	25.00	*51*
CRYIN' MERCY/Let's Walk	*Aladdin 3235*	1.50	6.00	*54*
EVENING SHADOWS/Moonrise	*Aladdin 3163*	2.50	10.00	*52*
HARD TIMES/Tender Heart	*Aladdin 3116*	2.50	10.00	*51*
I'LL ALWAYS BE IN LOVE WITH YOU/The Message	*Aladdin 3091*	3.00	12.00	*51*
LONESOME FEELING/I Lost Everything	*Aladdin 3191*	5.00	20.00	*53*
MY LAST AFFAIR/Still Water	*Aladdin 3120*	2.50	10.00	*52*
MY SILENT LOVE/Foolish	*Aladdin 3254*	1.50	6.00	*54*
ROLLIN' LIKE A PEBBLE IN THE SAND/Alley Batting	*Aladdin 3157*	2.50	20.00	*52*
SEVEN LONG DAYS/Don't Fool With My Heart	*Aladdin 3092*	3.00	12.00	*51*
TAKE ME/Sunrise	*Aladdin 3176*	5.00	20.00	*53*
WITHOUT YOUR LOVE/Gee	*Aladdin 3138*	2.50	10.00	*52*

BROWN, Charles:

see Basin Street Boys, The

BROWN, Clarence "Gatemouth"

TITLE/FLIP	LABEL & NO.	GOOD TO VERY GOOD	NEAR MINT	YR.
BOOGIE UPROAR (instrumental)/Hurry Back Good News	*Peacock 1617*	2.50	10.00	*53*
DIRTY WORK AT THE CROSSROADS/You Got Money	*Peacock 1607*	3.00	12.00	*53*
GATE WALKS TO BOARD (instrumental)/ Please Tell Me, Baby	*Peacock 1619*	2.50	10.00	*53*
GATE'S SALTY BLUES/Rock My Blues Away	*Peacock 1653*	2.00	8.00	*56*
GATEMOUTH BOOGIE/After Sunset (78)	*Aladdin 198*	2.00	8.00	*47*
GUITAR IN MY HANDS/Without Me Baby (78)	*Aladdin 199*	2.00	8.00	*47*
I LIVE MY LIFE/Justice Blues (78)	*Peacock 1568*	1.50	6.00	*50*
I'VE BEEN MISTREATED/It Can Never Be That Way (78)	*Peacock 1508*	1.50	6.00	*49*
JUST BEFORE DAWN/Swingin' The Gate	*Peacock 1692*	1.50	6.00	*60*
JUST GOT LUCKY/Baby, Take It Easy (78)	*Peacock 1600*	1.50	6.00	*52*
MERCY ON ME/Didn't Reach My Goal (78)	*Peacock 1500*	1.50	6.00	*49*
MERCY ON ME/Ditch Diggin' Daddy (78)	*Peacock 1501*	1.50	6.00	*49*
MIDNIGHT HOUR/For Now So Long	*Peacock 1633*	2.00	8.00	*54*
MY TIME'S EXPENSIVE/Mary Is Fine (78)	*Peacock 1504*	1.50	6.00	*49*
OKIE DOKIE STOMP (instrumental)/Depression Blues	*Peacock 1637*	2.00	8.00	*54*
PALE DRY BOOGIE, PART 1/Pale Dry Boogie, Part 2 (78)	*Peacock 1575*	1.50	6.00	*52*
SHE WALKS RIGHT IN/Win With Me, Baby (78)	*Peacock 1561*	1.50	6.00	*51*
SHE WINKED HER EYE/Sad Hour (78)	*Peacock 1576*	1.50	6.00	*52*
TOO LATE BABY/Taking My Chance (78)	*Peacock 1586*	1.50	6.00	*52*
TWO O'CLOCK IN THE MORNING/Boogie Rambler (78)	*Peacock 1505*	1.50	6.00	*49*

BROWN, Dusty

TITLE/FLIP	LABEL & NO.	GOOD TO VERY GOOD	NEAR MINT	YR.
PLEASE DON'T GO/Well, You Know	*Bandera 2503*	2.00	8.00	*58*
YES, SHE'S GONE/He Don't Love You	*Parrot 820*	5.00	20.00	*55*

BROWN, Earl

TITLE/FLIP	LABEL & NO.	GOOD TO VERY GOOD	NEAR MINT	YR.
CAT'S WIGGLE, THE/Shake Your Shimmy	*Checker 802*	4.00	16.00	*54*
DUST MY BROOM/Riffle Shuffle	*Swing Time 307*	4.00	16.00	—

BROWN, Gabriel

Some of Brown's Joe Davis recordings were also released on Gennett and Beacon with the same record numbers.

TITLE/FLIP	LABEL & NO.	GOOD TO VERY GOOD	NEAR MINT	YR.
BLACK JACK BLUES/Going My Way (78)	*Joe Davis 5004*	1.50	6.00	*45*
BOOGIE WOOGIE GUITAR/Hold That Train (78)	*Joe Davis 5021*	1.50	6.00	*46*

TITLE/FLIP	LABEL & NO.	GOOD TO VERY GOOD	NEAR MINT	YR.
COLD MAMA/I'm Just Crazy (78)	MGM 11407	1.50	6.00	53
These songs were recorded in 1949.				
DOWN IN THE BOTTOM/Bad Love (78)	Joe Davis 5006	1.50	6.00	45
I CAN'T LAST LONG/Suffer (78)	Coral 65019	1.50	6.00	49
I DON'T FEEL SO GOOD/Stop Jivin' Me (78)	Joe Davis 5016	1.50	6.00	45
I GET EVIL WHEN MY LOVE COMES DOWN/ You Ain't No Good (78)	Joe Davis 5003	1.50	6.00	45
I'LL BE SEEING YOU/It's Time To Move (78)	Joe Davis 5026	1.50	6.00	46
I'VE GOT TO STOP DRINKIN'/Cold Love (78)	Joe Davis 5008	1.50	6.00	45
IT'S GETTING SOFT/Don't Worry About Me (78)	Joe Davis 5020	1.50	6.00	46
NOT NOW, I'LL TELL YOU WHEN/I'm Gonna (78)	Joe Davis 5015	1.50	6.00	45
PLEADING/Mean Old Blues (78)	Joe Davis 5028	1.50	6.00	46
STICK WITH ME/I've Done Stopped Gambling (78)	Joe Davis 5017	1.50	6.00	46
WRAP ME UP TIGHT/I Want A Little Fun (78)	Joe Davis 5025	1.50	6.00	46
YOU HAVE GOT TO BE DIFFERENT/The Jinx Is On Me (78)	Joe Davis 5027	1.50	6.00	46

BROWN, J. T.

TITLE/FLIP	LABEL & NO.	GOOD TO VERY GOOD	NEAR MINT	YR.
BOOGIE BABY/One More Chance (78)	JOB 1103	8.00	32.00	—
BROWN'S BOP BOOGIE/Black Jack Blues (78)	Harlem 1044	2.00	8.00	—
BROWN'S BOP BOOGIE/Black Jack Blues (78)	Harlem 1107	1.50	6.00	—
SAXONY BOOGIE/Dumb Woman Blues	Meteor 5016	5.00	20.00	—
TALKING BABY BLUES/They Call Me Mr. Blues (78)	Harlem 1042	2.00	8.00	—

BROWN, James & The Famous Flames

TITLE/FLIP	LABEL & NO.	GOOD TO VERY GOOD	NEAR MINT	YR.
PLEASE, PLEASE, PLEASE/Why Do You Do Me?	Federal 12258	1.50	6.00	56

BROWN, James "Widemouth"

TITLE/FLIP	LABEL & NO.	GOOD TO VERY GOOD	NEAR MINT	YR.
WEARY SILENT NIGHT, A/ Boogie Woogie Night Hawk (red plastic)	Jax 306	10.00	40.00	51
Henry Hayes vocals.				

BROWN, James, Bobby Byrd &

BROWN, Lee & His Barbeton Boogie Woogie Cats

TITLE/FLIP	LABEL & NO.	GOOD TO VERY GOOD	NEAR MINT	YR.
NEW LITTLE GIRL/Brownie's Boogie (78)	Queen 4157	1.50	6.00	46

BROWN, Lee "The Heartbreaker"

TITLE/FLIP	LABEL & NO.	GOOD TO VERY GOOD	NEAR MINT	YR.
MY LITTLE GIRL BLUE/Bobby Town Boogie (78)	Chicago 104	2.50	10.00	46

BROWN, Little Tommy: see Brown, Tommy

BROWN, Little Willie

Little Willie Brown should not be confused with the Willie Brown who recorded for Decca.

TITLE/FLIP	LABEL & NO.	GOOD TO VERY GOOD	NEAR MINT	YR.
CUT IT OUT/Gonna Make It On Back	Do-Ra-Me 1404	2.50	10.00	61
GOING BACK TO THE COUNTRY/Just Like This	Suntan 1112	7.00	28.00	56

BROWN, Maxine

BROWN, Maxine, Chuck Jackson &

BROWN, Nappy

BROWN, Nappy & The Gibralters

BROWN, Nappy & The Zippers Quartet

BROWN, Nature Boy & His Blues Ramblers

TITLE/FLIP	LABEL & NO.	GOOD TO VERY GOOD	NEAR MINT	YR.
ROCK 'EM/When I Was A Lad	United 106	6.25	25.00	51
STRICKLY GONE (sic)/House Party Groove	United 121	5.00	20.00	52
WINDY CITY BOOGIE/Black Jack Blues	United 103	6.25	25.00	51

BROWN, Piney

TITLE/FLIP	LABEL & NO.	GOOD TO VERY GOOD	NEAR MINT	YR.
WHISPERING BLUES/Walk A Block And Fall	King 4636	2.00	8.00	53
YOU BRING OUT THE WOLF IN ME/Don't Pass Me By	Jubilee 5130	2.00	8.00	54

BROWN, Rayfield

TITLE/FLIP	LABEL & NO.	GOOD TO VERY GOOD	NEAR MINT	YR.
SNATCHING BACK/I'm So Glad, Baby	Dumas 1207	3.00	12.00	64

BROWN, Robert as Washboard Sam

Brown should not be confused with Albert Johnson, who also called himself Washboard Sam, nor should he be confused with the Robert Brown
who used the pseudonym Smokey Babe.

TITLE/FLIP	LABEL & NO.	GOOD TO VERY GOOD	NEAR MINT	YR.
BRIGHT EYES/Diggin' My Potatoes	Chess 1545	10.00	40.00	53
I'M JUST TIRED/Maybe You Love Me (red plastic)	RCA Victor 50-0023	5.00	20.00	49
MOTHERLESS CHILD BLUES/ Gamblin' Man (red plastic)	RCA Victor 50-0090	5.00	20.00	49
YOU SAID YOU LOVED ME/ Market Street Swing (red plastic)	RCA Victor 50-0048	5.00	20.00	49

BROWN, Roy

TITLE/FLIP	LABEL & NO.	GOOD TO VERY GOOD	NEAR MINT	YR.
AIN'T IT A SHAME?/Gal From Kokomo	King 4731	4.00	16.00	54
BAR ROOM BLUES/Good Rockin' Man	DeLuxe 3319	12.50	50.00	50
BOOTLEGGIN' BABY/Trouble At Midnight	King 4704	4.00	16.00	53
DEEP SEA DIVER/Bye, Baby, Bye (78)	Gold Star 636	2.50	10.00	47
DON'T LET IT RAIN/No Love At All	King 4722	4.00	16.00	54
FANNY BROWN GOT MARRIED/Queen Of Diamonds	King 4761	5.00	20.00	54
FOOL IN LOVE, A/Caldonia's Wedding Day	King 4669	4.00	16.00	53
GAMBLIN' MAN/	King 4627	4.00	16.00	52
GOOD ROCKIN' TONIGHT/Lollypop Mama (78)	DeLuxe 1093	2.50	10.00	47
HIP SHAKIN' BABY/Be My Love Tonight	Imperial 5510	5.00	20.00	58
I'VE GOT THE LAST LAUGH NOW/Brown Angel	DeLuxe 3323	8.00	32.00	51
LAUGHING BUT CRYING/Crazy Crazy Woman	King 4654	4.00	16.00	53
LETTER TO BABY/Shake 'Em, Baby	King 4816	4.00	16.00	55
MIDNIGHT LOVER MAN/Letter From Home	King 4684	4.00	16.00	52
MIGHTY MIGHTY MEN/Miss Fanny Brown (78)	DeLuxe 1128	1.50	6.00	47
MONEY CAN'T BUY LOVE/	King 4609	5.00	20.00	52
OLD AGE BOOGIE, PART 1/Old Age Boogie, Part 2	King 4637	4.00	16.00	52
SHE'S GONE TOO LONG/My Little Angel Child	King 4834	4.00	16.00	55
SPECIAL LESSON NR 1/Woman's A Wonderful Thing (78)	DeLuxe 1098	1.50	6.00	47
THIS IS MY LAST GOODBYE/Up Jumped The Devil	King 4715	4.00	16.00	54
TRAVELIN' MAN/Hurry, Hurry Back, Baby (blue plastic)	King 4602	20.00	80.00	52
TRAVELIN' MAN/Hurry, Hurry Back, Baby	King 4602	5.00	20.00	52
WORRIED LIFE BLUES/Black Diamond	King 4743	4.00	16.00	54

BROWN, Ruth

TITLE/FLIP	LABEL & NO.	GOOD TO VERY GOOD	NEAR MINT	YR.
5-10-15 HOURS/Be Anything	Atlantic 962	1.50	6.00	52
GOOD FOR NOTHING JOE/Three Letters	Atlantic 978	1.50	6.00	52
HAVE A GOOD TIME/Daddy, Daddy	Atlantic 973	2.00	8.00	52
I KNOW/I Don't Want Nobody	Atlantic 941	4.00	16.00	50
SHINE ON/Without My Love	Atlantic 948	4.00	16.00	51
TEARDROPS FROM MY EYES/ Am I Making The Same Mistake Again?	Atlantic 919	10.00	40.00	50
WILD WILD YOUNG MEN/Mend Your Ways	Atlantic 993	1.50	6.00	53

BROWN, Skip & The Shantons

BROWN, Skippy

TITLE/FLIP	LABEL & NO.	GOOD TO VERY GOOD	NEAR MINT	YR.
SO MANY DAYS/Tale Of Woe	Chance 1129	5.00	20.00	52

BROWN, Texas Johnny

TITLE/FLIP	LABEL & NO.	GOOD TO VERY GOOD	NEAR MINT	YR.
BLUES ROCK, THE/There Go The Blues (78)	Atlantic 876	2.50	10.00	49

BROWN, Tommy

TITLE/FLIP	LABEL & NO.	GOOD TO VERY GOOD	NEAR MINT	YR.
GOODBYE, I'M GONE/Since You Left Me, Dear	King 4679	2.50	10.00	53
HOW MUCH DO YOU THINK I CAN STAND?/Fore Day Train	King 4658	2.50	10.00	53
REMEMBER ME?/Southern Woman	United 183	6.25	25.00	—
ROCK AWAY MY BLUES/Someday, Somewhere	Imperial 5476	2.00	8.00	56

BROWN, Tommy as Little Tommy Brown

TITLE/FLIP	LABEL & NO.	GOOD TO VERY GOOD	NEAR MINT	YR.
DON'T LEAVE ME/Won't You Forgive Me?	Groove 0132	1.50	6.00	55
GAMBLER'S PRAYER/The Thrill Is Gone	Groove 0143	1.50	6.00	55

BROWN, Wini & The Boyfriends: see Boyfriends, Wini Brown & The

BROWNS, Barbara & The

BRYANT, Beulah

TITLE/FLIP	LABEL & NO.	GOOD TO VERY GOOD	NEAR MINT	YR.
PRIZE FIGHTING PAPA/What Am I Gonna Do?	Excello 2049	5.00	20.00	54

BRYANT, Ray

BUCCANEERS, The

TITLE/FLIP	LABEL & NO.	GOOD TO VERY GOOD	NEAR MINT	YR.
DEAR RUTH/Fine Brown Frame	Rainbow 211	30.00	120.00	53
DEAR RUTH/Fine Brown Frame	Southern 101	60.00	240.00	53
IN THE MISSION OF ST. AUGUSTINE/You Did Me Wrong	Rama 24	75.00	300.00	53
STARS WILL REMEMBER, THE/Come Back My Love	Rama 21	100.00	400.00	53

BUCKEYES, The

TITLE/FLIP	LABEL & NO.	GOOD TO VERY GOOD	NEAR MINT	YR.
DOTTIE BABY/Begging You, Please	De Luxe 6126	4.00	16.00	57
SINCE I FELL FOR YOU/Be Only You	De Luxe 6110	5.00	20.00	57

BUCKNER, Milt

TITLE/FLIP	LABEL & NO.	GOOD TO VERY GOOD	NEAR MINT	YR.
RED RED WINE/Boogie Grunt	Savoy 785	2.50	10.00	52

BUDDIES, Billy Bunn & The

TITLE/FLIP	LABEL & NO.	GOOD TO VERY GOOD	NEAR MINT	YR.
I NEED A SHOULDER TO CRY ON/I'm Afraid	RCA Victor 47-4483	15.00	60.00	51
THAT'S WHEN YOUR HEARTACHES BEGIN/Until The Real Thing Comes Along	RCA Victor 47-4657	12.50	50.00	52

BUDDIES, Carl Ell & The

TITLE/FLIP	LABEL & NO.	GOOD TO VERY GOOD	NEAR MINT	YR.
BOBBY, MY LOVE/Sunshine	Combo 154	4.00	16.00	59

TITLE/FLIP	LABEL & NO.	GOOD TO VERY GOOD	NEAR MINT	YR.
BUDDIES, Little Butchie Saunders & The				
GREAT BIG HEART/I Wanna Holler	Herald 491	2.00	8.00	56
LINDY LOU/Rock 'N' Roll Indian Dance	Herald 485	2.00	8.00	56
BUDDIES, The				
MUST BE TRUE LOVE/Hully Gully Mama	Comet 2143	1.50	6.00	61
BUDDIES, The				
I STOLE YOUR HEART/I Waited	Glory 230	15.00	60.00	55
BUFORD, George as Little Mojo				
PAULA/You Ain't The One	Norman 505	2.50	10.00	62
BUFORD, George as Mojo Buford				
WHOLE LOTTA WOMAN/Messin' With The Kid	Bangar 00622	1.50	6.00	64
BULLARD, John				
MARY LOU/Help Me Find My Right Mind	DeLuxe 6035	10.00	40.00	52
WESTERN UNION BLUES (vocal by Bobby Sands)/ Spoiled Hambone Blues	DeLuxe 6019	10.00	40.00	52
BULLARD, John Quartet, The				
DON'T TALK DEM TRASH/Callin' The Blues	Index 300	4.00	16.00	50
BUNN, Alden: see Lovers, The (with Alden Bunn as Tarheel Slim)				
BUMBLE BEE SLIM: see Easton, Amos as Bumble Bee Slim				
BUNN, Alden as Allen Baum				
MY KINDA WOMAN/Too Much Competition	Red Robin 124	40.00	160.00	53
BUNN, Alden as Allen Bunn				
DISCOURAGED/I Got You Covered	Apollo 439	15.00	60.00	52
SHE'LL BE SORRY/The Guy With The "45"	Apollo 436	1.50	60.00	52
BUNN, Alden as Tarheel Slim				
WILDCAT TAMER/No. 9 Train (maroon label)	Fury 1016	2.50	10.00	59
BUNN, Alden as Tarheel Slim & Little Ann				
BUNN, Allen: see Bunn, Alden as Allen Bunn				
BUNN, Billy & The Buddies: see Buddies, Billy Bunn & The				
BURKE, Soloman				
BURLEY, Dan				
BIG CAT, LITTLE CAT/Three Flights Up (78)	Circle 1021	1.50	6.00	46
DUSTY BOTTOM/South Side Shake (78)	Circle 1020	1.50	6.00	46
SHOTGUN HOUSE RAG/Lake Front Blues (78)	Circle 1022	1.50	6.00	46
BURLEY, Dan & His Skiffle Boys				
CHICKEN SHACK SHUFFLE/Skiffle Blues (78)	Arkay 1001	1.50	6.00	47
BURNETT, Carl & The Hustlers: see Hustlers, Carl Burnett & The				
BURNETT, Chester Arthur as Howlin' Wolf				
Burnett should not be confused with John T. "Howlin' Wolf" Smith who recorded for Vocalion in the 1930s.				
ALL NIGHT BOOGIE/I Love My Baby	Chess 1557	3.00	12.00	53
BABY, HOW LONG?/Evil Is Going On	Chess 1575	2.50	10.00	54
COME TO ME, BABY/Don't Mess With My Baby	Chess 1607	1.50	6.00	55
GETTING OLD AND GREY/Mr. Highway Man	Chess 1510	10.00	40.00	53
HOWLIN' WOLF BOOGIE/The Wolf Is At Your Door (78)	Chess 1497	1.50	6.00	52
I ASKED FOR WATER/So Glad	Chess 1632	1.50	6.00	56
I'LL BE AROUND/Forty Four	Chess 1584	2.50	10.00	55
MOANIN' AT MIDNIGHT/How Many More Tears? (78)	Chess 1479	1.50	6.00	51
MY BABY STOLE OFF/I Want Your Picture	RPM 347	15.00	60.00	51
MY LAST AFFAIR/Oh! Red	Chess 1528	6.25	25.00	52
NO PLACE TO GO/Rockin' Daddy	Chess 1566	2.50	10.00	54
PASSING BY BLUES/Crying At Daybreak (78)	RPM 340	2.50	10.00	51
RIDING IN THE MOONLIGHT/Morning At Midnight (78)	RPM 333	2.50	10.00	51
SADDLE MY PONY/Worried All The Time	Chess 1515	10.00	40.00	52
SMOKE STACK LIGHTNING/You Can't Be Beat	Chess 1618	1.50	6.00	56
WHO WILL BE NEXT?/I Have A Little Girl	Chess 1593	2.00	8.00	55
BURNEY, Mac & The Four Jacks: see Four Jacks, Mac Burney & The				
BURNS, Eddie				
HELLO, MISS JESSIE LEE/Dealing With The Devil	DeLuxe 6024	10.00	40.00	52
TREAT ME LIKE I TREAT YOU/Don't 'Cha Leave Me Baby	Chess 1672	1.50	6.00	57
TREAT ME LIKE I TREAT YOU/Don't 'Cha Leave Me Baby	JVB 82	4.00	16.00	57
BURNS, Eddie as Big Ed & His Combo				
SUPERSTITION/Biscuit Baking Mama	Checker 790	9.00	36.00	54
BURNS, Eddie as Slim Pickens				
PAPA'S BOOGIE/Bad Woman Blues (78)	Holiday 202	8.00	32.00	48
BURNS, Eddie as The Swing Brothers				
PAPA'S BOOGIE/Bad Woman Blues (78)	Palda	10.00	40.00	48
BURRAGE, Harold				
MESSED UP/I Don't Care Who Knows	Cobra 5012	1.50	6.00	56
ONE MORE DANCE/You Eat Too Much	Cobra 5004	1.50	6.00	56
SHE KNOCKS ME OUT/A Heart Filled With Pain	Cobra 5022	1.50	6.00	56
STOP FOR THE RED LIGHT/Satisfied	Cobra 5018	1.50	6.00	56
SWEET BROWN GAL/Way Down Boogie	Aladdin 3194	4.00	16.00	50
BURRAGE, Harold as Harold Barrage				
FEEL SO FINE/You're Gonna Cry	States 144	4.00	16.00	50
BURTON, Ben				
BEE HIVE BOOGIE/Blues And Jim Instrumentals.	Modern 871	3.00	12.00	54
CHEROKEE BOOGIE/Lover's Blues Instrumentals.	Modern 894	2.50	10.00	54
BUSBY, Johnny				
BUTANES, The				
BUTLER, Billy				
BUTLER, Billy & Infinity				
BUTLER, Billy & The Chanters				
BUTLER, Billy & The Enchanters				
BUTLER, Cliff & The Doves: see Doves, Cliff Butler & The				
BUTLER, George (Wild Child)				
BUTLER, James as Black Diamond				
LONESOME BLUES/All My Money Is Gone (by Goldrush)	Jaxyson 6	7.00	28.00	48
T. P. RAILER/Lonesome Blues (78)	Jaxyson 50	7.00	28.00	48
BUTLER, Jerry				
COME BACK MY LOVE (with The Impressions)/ Love Me	Abner 1017	1.50	6.00	58
FOR YOUR PRECIOUS LOVE (with The Impressions)/ Sweet Was The Wine	Abner 1013	1.50	6.00	58
FOR YOUR PRECIOUS LOVE (with The Impressions)/ Sweet Was The Wine	Falcon 1013	2.50	10.00	58
GIFT OF LOVE, THE (with The Impressions)/ At The County Fair	Abner 1023	1.50	6.00	59
HOLD ME, MY DARLING/Rainbow Valley	Abner 1028	1.50	6.00	59
I WAS WRONG/Couldn't Go To Sleep	Abner 1030	1.50	6.00	60
LONELY SOLDIER, A/I Found A Love	Abner 1035	1.50	6.00	60
LOST/One By One	Abner 1024	1.50	6.00	59
BUTLER, Jerry & Brenda Lee Eager				
BUTLER, Jerry & The Impressions: see Impressions, Jerry Butler & The				
BUTTERFLYS, The				
BUZZARDS, Big John & The				
HEY, LITTLE GIRL/Mean Woman	Columbia 40345	1.50	6.00	54
OOP SHOOP/Your Cash Ain't Nothin' But Trash	Okeh 7045	1.50	6.00	54
BUZZARDS, Jake Porter & The				
WINE, WOMEN AND GOLD/The Bop (instrumental)	Combo 91	4.00	16.00	55

BYRD, Bobby

BYRD, Bobby & James Brown

BYRD, Bobby & The Birds:
see Birds, Bobby Byrd & The

BYRD, Robert & His Birdies:
see Birdies, Robert Byrd & His

BYRD, Roland:
see Byrd, Roy as Roland Byrd

BYRD, Roy

TITLE/FLIP	LABEL & NO.	GOOD TO VERY GOOD	NEAR MINT	YR.
K. C. BLUES/Curly Haired Baby (78)	Federal 12061	5.00	20.00	51
ROCKIN' WITH FESS/Gone So Long (78)	Federal 12073	5.00	20.00	51

BYRD, Roy & His Blues Jumpers

TITLE/FLIP	LABEL & NO.	GOOD TO VERY GOOD	NEAR MINT	YR.
HER MIND IS GONE/Hadacol Bounce (78)	Mercury 8184	2.50	10.00	49
HER MIND IS GONE/Oh Well (78)	Mercury 8184	2.50	10.00	49

BYRD, Roy "Bald Head"

TITLE/FLIP	LABEL & NO.	GOOD TO VERY GOOD	NEAR MINT	YR.
MARDI GRAS IN NEW ORLEANS/She Walks Right In (78)	Atlantic 897	6.25	25.00	49

BYRD, Roy as Professor Longhair

TITLE/FLIP	LABEL & NO.	GOOD TO VERY GOOD	NEAR MINT	YR.
CRY PRETTY BABY/No Buts, No Maybes	Ebb 101	5.00	20.00	57
CUTTIN' OUT/If I Only Knew	Ron 326	2.50	10.00	59
GO TO THE MARDI GRAS/Every Day, Every Night	Ron 329	2.50	10.00	59
LOOKA NO HAIR/Baby Let Me Hold Your Hand	Ebb 121	5.00	20.00	57
MISERY/Look What You're Doing To Me	Ebb 106	5.00	20.00	57

BYRD, Roy as Professor Longhair & His Blue Scholars

TITLE/FLIP	LABEL & NO.	GOOD TO VERY GOOD	NEAR MINT	YR.
IN THE NIGHT/Tipitina	Atlantic 1020	6.25	25.00	54

BYRD, Roy as Professor Longhair & His Blues Scholars

TITLE/FLIP	LABEL & NO.	GOOD TO VERY GOOD	NEAR MINT	YR.
WALK YOUR BLUES AWAY/Professor Longhair Blues (78)	Atlantic 906	6.25	25.00	50

BYRD, Roy as Professor Longhair & His Shuffling Hungarians

TITLE/FLIP	LABEL & NO.	GOOD TO VERY GOOD	NEAR MINT	YR.
MARDI GRAS IN NEW ORLEANS/ Professor Longhair's Boogie (78)	Star Talent 808	7.00	28.00	49
SHE AIN'T GOT NO HAIR/Bye Bye Baby (78)	Star Talent 809	7.00	28.00	49

BYRD, Roy as Robert Boyd

TITLE/FLIP	LABEL & NO.	GOOD TO VERY GOOD	NEAR MINT	YR.
EAST ST. LOUIS BABY/Boyd's Bounce (78)	Wasco 201	8.00	32.00	—

BYRD, Roy as Roland Byrd

TITLE/FLIP	LABEL & NO.	GOOD TO VERY GOOD	NEAR MINT	YR.
HEY LITTLE GIRL/Willie Mae (78)	Atlantic 947	6.25	25.00	49

BYSTANDERS, The

C

C & C BOYS, The

C NOTES, Frankie & The

TITLE/FLIP	LABEL & NO.	GOOD TO VERY GOOD	NEAR MINT	YR.
FOREVER AND EVER/Union Hall	Times Square 10	1.50	6.00	63

C TONES, The

TITLE/FLIP	LABEL & NO.	GOOD TO VERY GOOD	NEAR MINT	YR.
ON YOUR MARK/From Now On	Everlast 5005	2.00	8.00	57

C. L. & THE PICTURES:
see Pictues, C. L. & The

C-NOTES, The

C-QUENTS, The

C-QUINS, The

TITLE/FLIP	LABEL & NO.	GOOD TO VERY GOOD	NEAR MINT	YR.
MY ONLY LOVE/You've Been Crying	Ditto 501	1.50	6.00	62

CABINEERS, The

TITLE/FLIP	LABEL & NO.	GOOD TO VERY GOOD	NEAR MINT	YR.
BABY MINE/What's The Matter With You?	Prestige 917	20.00	80.00	52
EACH TIME/Lost	Prestige 904	20.00	80.00	51
MY, MY, MY/Baby, Where'd You Go?	Prestige 902	20.00	80.00	51
TELL ME NOW/How Can I Help It? (78)	Abbey 3001	10.00	40.00	49
WHIRLPOOL/You're Just A Great Big Heartache (78)	Abbey 3003	8.00	32.00	49
WHIRLPOOL/You're Just A Great Big Heartache (78)	Abbey 72	10.00	40.00	49

CADDYS, Jessie Powell & The

CADETS, Aaron Collins & The

CADETS, The

TITLE/FLIP	LABEL & NO.	GOOD TO VERY GOOD	NEAR MINT	YR.
HEARTBREAK HOTEL/Church Bells May Ring	Modern 985	2.00	8.00	56
I CRY/Don't Be Angry	Modern 956	3.00	12.00	55
I CRY/Fine Lookin' Baby	Modern 963	2.50	10.00	55
IF IT IS WRONG/Do You Wanna Rock?	Modern 971	12.50	50.00	55
ROLLIN' STONE/Fine Lookin' Baby	Modern 960	2.50	10.00	55
SO WILL I/Annie Met Henry	Modern 969	2.00	8.00	55

CADETS, Will Jones & The

CADILLACS, Bobby Ray & The

CADILLACS, Ray Brewster & The

CADILLACS, Speedo & The

CADILLACS, The

TITLE/FLIP	LABEL & NO.	GOOD TO VERY GOOD	NEAR MINT	YR.
BETTY MY LOVE/Woe Is Me	Josie 798	1.50	6.00	56
DOWN THE ROAD/Window Lady	Josie 778	11.00	22.00	55
GIRL I LOVE, THE/All I Need	Josie 805	1.50	6.00	56
GLORIA/I Wonder Why?	Josie 765	25.00	100.00	54
MY GIRL FRIEND/Broken Heart	Josie 820	5.00	20.00	57
NO CHANCE/Sympathy	Josie 773	7.00	28.00	55
SHOCK-A-DOO/Rudolph The Red-Nosed Reindeer	Josie 807	1.50	6.00	56
SPEEDO IS BACK/A Looka Here	Josie 836	1.50	6.00	58
SPEEDO/Let Me Explain	Josie 785	1.50	6.00	56
SUGAR-SUGAR/About That Gal Named Lou	Josie 812	1.50	6.00	57
WISHING WELL/I Want To Know About Love	Josie 769	30.00	120.00	54
ZOOM/You Are	Josie 792	1.50	6.00	56

CADILLACS, The:
see Original Cadillacs, The

CAFFERY, Robert

TITLE/FLIP	LABEL & NO.	GOOD TO VERY GOOD	NEAR MINT	YR.
IDA BEE/Blodie's Blues (78)	Chess 1470	4.00	16.00	51

CAIN, Perry

TITLE/FLIP	LABEL & NO.	GOOD TO VERY GOOD	NEAR MINT	YR.
ALL THE WAY FROM TEXAS/Cry, Cry (78)	Gold Star 632	2.50	10.00	48

CALENDARS, Shell Dupont & The

CALENDARS, The

CALHOUN, Charles & The Four Students:
see Four Students, Charles Calhoun & The

CALIFORNIANS, The

TITLE/FLIP	LABEL & NO.	GOOD TO VERY GOOD	NEAR MINT	YR.
MY ANGEL/Heavenly Ruby	Federal 12231	9.00	36.00	55

CALL, Bob

TITLE/FLIP	LABEL & NO.	GOOD TO VERY GOOD	NEAR MINT	YR.
TALKIN' BABY BLUES/Call's Jump (instrumental) (78)	Coral 65009	3.00	12.00	49

CALLOWAY, Baby

TITLE/FLIP	LABEL & NO.	GOOD TO VERY GOOD	NEAR MINT	YR.
MIDNIGHT BLUES/Chuck Wagon	Baytone 106	1.50	6.00	—

CALVAES, The

TITLE/FLIP	LABEL & NO.	GOOD TO VERY GOOD	NEAR MINT	YR.
BORN WITH RHYTHM/Lonely, Lonely Village	Cobra 5014	20.00	80.00	57
FINE GIRL/Mambo Fiesta	Cobra 5003	9.00	36.00	56

CALVANES, The

TITLE/FLIP	LABEL & NO.	GOOD TO VERY GOOD	NEAR MINT	YR.
CRAZY OVER YOU/Don't Take Your Love From Me	Dootone 371	7.00	28.00	55
DREAMWORLD/5, 7 Or 9	Deck 579	7.00	28.00	58
FLORABELLE/One Kiss	Dootone 380	7.00	28.00	56
MY LOVE SONG/Horror Pictures	Deck 580	5.00	20.00	58

CAMEOS, The

TITLE/FLIP	LABEL & NO.	GOOD TO VERY GOOD	NEAR MINT	YR.
CANADIAN SUNSET/Never Before	Matador 1813	1.50	6.00	60
HE/Can You Remember?	Gigi 100	2.50	10.00	63
I REMEMBER WHEN/We'll Still Be Together	Matador 1808	2.00	8.00	—
LOST LOVER/Wait Up	Dean 504	2.00	8.00	60
MERRY CHRISTMAS/New Year's Eve	Cameo 123	10.00	40.00	57
PLEASE LOVE ME/Shanga Langa Ding Dong	Flagship 115	1.50	6.00	—

The Cadillacs

The Cellos

The Channels

TITLE/FLIP	LABEL & NO.	GOOD TO VERY GOOD	NEAR MINT	YR.
CAMEOS, The				
CRAVING/Only For You	Dootone 365	7.00	28.00	55
CAMERSON, G. C.				
CAMP, Bob & His Buddies				
GONNA PITCH A BOOGIE WOOGIE/Blues Mixture (78)	Southern 121	2.00	8.00	45
LONELY/Without Your Love (78)	Southern 130	2.00	8.00	45
READING BLUES/My Little Rose (78)	Decca 48112	1.50	6.00	49
WHEN YOU SURRENDER TO ME/Between You And Me (78)	Decca 48118	1.50	6.00	49
CAMP, Bob & The Nighthawks				
OUT CATTIN'/Pitch A Boogie (78)	Essex 714	1.50	6.00	52
Side one is credited only as The Nighthawks, as an instrumental.				
CAMPBELL, Carl				
BETWEEN MIDNIGHT AND DAWN/Ooh Wee, Baby (78)	Freedom 1521	1.50	6.00	49
CAMPBELL, Carl with Henry Hayes' 4 Kings				
TRAVELING ON/Early Morning Blues (78)	Peacock 1538	1.50	6.00	50
CAMPBELL, Choker				
HAVE YOU SEEN MY BABY?/Jockie Mambo	Atlantic 1038	2.00	8.00	53
LAST CALL FOR WHISKEY/How Could You Do This?	Atlantic 1014	3.00	12.00	53
CAMPBELL, Louis				
GOTTA LOVE YOU, BABY/The Natural Facts	Excello 2035	10.00	40.00	54
CAMPBELL, Louis as The Leapfrogs				
DIRTY BRITCHES/Things Gonna Change	Excello 2014	10.00	40.00	54
CAMPBELL, Milton as Little Milton				
BEGGIN' MY BABY/Somebody Told Me	Sun 194	9.00	36.00	53
IF YOU LOVE ME/Alone And Blue	Sun 200	9.00	36.00	54
LET MY BABY BE/Oh My Little Baby	Meteor 5045	8.00	32.00	57
LET'S BOOGIE, BABY/Love At First Sight	Meteor 5040	6.25	25.00	57
LOOKING FOR MY BABY/Lonesome For My Baby	Sun 220	9.00	36.00	55
CANDIES, The				
CANDLES, Rochell & The				
BIG BOY PETE/A Long Time Ago	Swingin' 652	2.00	8.00	—
EACH NIGHT/Turn Her Down	Challenge 9158	1.50	6.00	62
PEG OF MY HEART/Squat With Me Baby	Swingin' 640	1.50	6.00	—
CANDY & THE KISSES				
CANNA, Little Junior				
DON'T TURN YOUR LOVE ON/I've Got My Eyes On You	Big Star 006	1.50	6.00	—
CAP-TANS, Bethea & The				
CAP-TANS, Paul Chapman & The				
GOODNIGHT MOTHER/Let's Put Our Cards On The Table (78)	D.C. 8064	2.00	8.00	48
YOU'LL ALWAYS BE MY SWEETHEART/Coo-Coo Jug-Jug (78)	D.C. 8054	2.00	8.00	48
CAP-TANS, The				
ASKING/Who Can I Turn To?	Coral 65071	10.00	40.00	51
I'M SO CRAZY FOR LOVE/Crazy About My Honey Dip (78)	Dot 1009	2.00	8.00	50
I'M SO CRAZY FOR LOVE/With All My Love	Dot 15114	5.00	20.00	53
MY, MY, AIN'T SHE PRETTY?/Never Be Lonely	Gotham 233	9.00	36.00	50
WITH ALL MY LOVE/Chief, Turn The Hose On Me (78)	Dot 1018	2.00	8.00	50
YES, I THOUGHT I COULD FORGET/Waiting At The Station	Gotham 268	9.00	36.00	51
CAP-TANS, The (with "Wailing" Harmon Bethea)				
CAP-TANS, Wailing Bethea & The				
CAPERS, The (female group)				
HIGH SCHOOL DIPLOMA/Candy Store Blues	Vee Jay 315	1.50	6.00	59
MISS YOU, MY DEAR/Early One Morning	Vee Jay 297	1.50	6.00	58
CAPISTRANOS, John Littleton & The				
PO MARY/Now Darling (with James Brown, not the artist who records for King)	Duke 179	2.00	8.00	58
CAPITOLS, Mickey Tolliver & The				
MILLIE/Rose-Marie	Cindy 3002	7.00	28.00	57
CAPITOLS, The				
DAY BY DAY/Little Things	Gateway 721	5.00	20.00	—

TITLE/FLIP	LABEL & NO.	GOOD TO VERY GOOD	NEAR MINT	YR.
CAPITOLS, The				
ANGEL OF LOVE/Cause I Love You	Pet 807	4.00	16.00	58
CAPITOLS, The				
WRITE ME A LOVE LETTER/Three O'Clock Rock	Triumph 601	1.50	6.00	59
CAPRIS, The				
MY PROMISE TO YOU/Bop! Bop! Bop!	Sabre 201/202	10.00	40.00	59
CAPRIS, The				
GOD ONLY KNOWS/That's What You're Doing To Me (red label or blue label)	Gotham 304	10.00	40.00	54
GOD ONLY KNOWS/That's What You're Doing To Me (yellow label)	Gotham 304	5.00	20.00	54
IT WAS MOONGLOW/Too Poor To Love	Gotham 306	7.00	28.00	55
IT'S A MIRACLE/Let's Linger Awhile	Gotham 308	7.00	28.00	56
MY WEAKNESS/Yes, My Baby, Please!	20th Century 1201	2.50	10.00	—
OH, MY DARLING/Rock, Pretty Baby	Lifetime 1001/1002	3.00	12.00	—
CAPRIS, The				
ENDLESS LOVE/Beware (with Jesse Belvin)	Tender 518	5.00	20.00	59
This was the second of two records released by the Tender label with the same record number. The second side of this record had been released before on Cash Records (#1056) under the name Jesse Belvin. The group called The Capris on this re-issue was actually a studio group.				
CAPTANS, The				
CARDELLS, The				
HELEN/Lovely Girl	Middle-Tone 011	15.00	60.00	56
CARDINALS, The				
BUMP, THE/She Rocks	Atlantic 972	8.00	32.00	52
DOOR IS STILL OPEN, THE/Misirlou	Atlantic 1054	3.00	12.00	55
END OF THE STORY, THE/I Won't Make You Cry Anymore	Atlantic 1103	1.50	6.00	56
I'LL ALWAYS LOVE YOU/Pretty Baby Blues	Atlantic 952	10.00	40.00	51
NEAR YOU/One Love	Atlantic 1126	1.50	6.00	57
OFF SHORE/Choo Choo	Atlantic 1090	1.50	6.00	56
SHOULDN'T I KNOW?/Please Don't Leave Me	Atlantic 938	125.00	500.00	51
Jellyroll thinks this record exists on 45 r.p.m., but isn't certain. It may have been released only on 78. The price listed is an estimation of the value of a 45.				
THERE GOES MY HEART TO YOU/Lovely Girl	Atlantic 1079	1.50	6.00	55
TWO THINGS I LOVE/Come Back My Love	Atlantic 1067	3.00	12.00	55
UNDER A BLANKET OF BLUE/Please Baby	Atlantic 1025	8.00	32.00	54
WHEEL OF FORTUNE/Kiss Me Baby	Atlantic 958	10.00	40.00	52
YOU ARE MY ONLY LOVE/Lovie Darling	Atlantic 995	8.00	32.00	53
CARIANS, The				
ONLY A DREAM/Girls	Magenta 04	2.50	10.00	61
SHE'S GONE/Snooty Friends	Indigo 136	7.00	28.00	62
CARIBBEANS, George Torrence & The				
CARLTON, Little Carl				
CARLTONS, Andy Mack & The				
CARLTONS, The				
CARNATIONS, The				
ANGELS SENT YOU TO ME, THE/Night Time Is The Right Time	Savoy 1172	2.00	8.00	55
TREE IN THE MEADOW/Clown Of The Masquerade	Derby 789	25.00	100.00	52
CAROL, Judy & The Basin Street Boys				
CAROLINA SLIM: see Harris, Edward as Carolina Slim				
CAROLONS, The				
CAROLS, The				
FIFTY MILLION WOMEN/I Got A Feelin'	Savoy 896	4.00	16.00	53
IF I COULD STEAL YOU FROM SOMEBODY ELSE/I Should Have Thought	Columbia 30217	10.00	40.00	50
PLEASE BELIEVE IN ME/Drink Gin	Columbia 30210	15.00	60.00	50
CARONATORS, The				

TITLE/FLIP	LABEL & NO.	GOOD TO VERY GOOD	NEAR MINT	YR.

CAROUSELS, The

TITLE/FLIP	LABEL & NO.	GOOD TO VERY GOOD	NEAR MINT	YR.
IF YOU WANT TO/Pretty Little Thing	*Gone 5118*	1.50	6.00	*61*

The second of two releases with the same number, but with different first sides.

TITLE/FLIP	LABEL & NO.	GOOD TO VERY GOOD	NEAR MINT	YR.
NEVER LET HIM GO/Dirty Tricks	*Gone 5131*	1.50	6.00	*62*
YOU CAN COME/Pretty Little Thing	*Gone 5118*	1.50	6.00	*61*

CARPETS, The

TITLE/FLIP	LABEL & NO.	GOOD TO VERY GOOD	NEAR MINT	YR.
LONELY ME/Chicken Backs	*Federal 12269*	2.50	10.00	*56*
WHY DO I?/Let Her Go	*Federal 12257*	2.50	10.00	*56*

CARR, Gunter Lee:
see Gant, Cecil as Gunter Lee Carr

CARR, James

CARROLL COUNTY BOYS, The:
see Crayton, Connie Curtiss

CARROLL, Delores & The Four Tops:
see Four Tops, Delores Carroll & The

CARROLL, Earl & The Original Cadillacs:
see Original Cadillacs, Earl Carroll & The

CARSON, Big Blues

CARSON, Mr. Blues

TITLE/FLIP	LABEL & NO.	GOOD TO VERY GOOD	NEAR MINT	YR.
EYE TO EYE/Sittin' By The Window	*Allen 1004*	3.00	12.00	*53*

CARTER BROTHERS, The

CARTER RAYS, Gloria Mann & The

TITLE/FLIP	LABEL & NO.	GOOD TO VERY GOOD	NEAR MINT	YR.
GOODNIGHT, SWEETHEART, GOODNIGHT/Love-Me-Boy	*Jubilee 5142*	1.50	6.00	*54*
GOODNIGHT, SWEETHEART, GOODNIGHT/Love-Me-Boy	*SLS 102*	6.25	25.00	*54*

CARTER RAYS, The

TITLE/FLIP	LABEL & NO.	GOOD TO VERY GOOD	NEAR MINT	YR.
MY SECRET LOVE/Ding Dong Daddy	*Gone 5006*	8.00	32.00	*59*
MY SECRET LOVE/Ding Dong Daddy	*Lyric 2001*	10.00	40.00	—
TAKE EVERYTHING BUT YOU/Cool Whailin' Papa	*Grand 107*	4.00	16.00	*54*

This is the second issue of this record and number. It was first issued as by The Ed Carter Quartet.

CARTER, Ann

TITLE/FLIP	LABEL & NO.	GOOD TO VERY GOOD	NEAR MINT	YR.
YOU OUGHTA QUIT IT/Lovin' Daddy Blues	*Blue Lake 103*	2.50	10.00	*53*

CARTER, Cecil "Count"

TITLE/FLIP	LABEL & NO.	GOOD TO VERY GOOD	NEAR MINT	YR.
I KNOW, I KNOW/Ginger Bread	*Federal 12135*	2.00	8.00	*53*
WHAT'S WRONG WITH ME?/Strange Blues	*Federal 12130*	2.00	8.00	*53*

CARTER, Clarence

CARTER, Ed Quartet, The

TITLE/FLIP	LABEL & NO.	GOOD TO VERY GOOD	NEAR MINT	YR.
TAKE EVERYTHING BUT YOU/Cool Whailin' Papa	*Grand 107*	25.00	100.00	*54*

This record and number was re-issued the same year with the credits as The Carter Rays.

CARTER, Eddie:
see Carter Rays, Gloria Mann & The
see Carter Rays, The
see Carter, Ed Quartet, The
see Carterays, Eddie Carter & The

CARTER, Goree

TITLE/FLIP	LABEL & NO.	GOOD TO VERY GOOD	NEAR MINT	YR.
DRUNK OR SOBER/Lowtop Inn (by Clarence Samuels)	*Bayou 010*	6.25	25.00	*50*
EVERYBODY'S LOVE CRAZY/Let's Rock (78)	*Sittin' In With 556*	1.50	6.00	*50*
I'M YOUR BOOGIE MAN/Please Say You're Mine (78)	*Coral 65064*	3.00	12.00	*50*
I'VE GOT NEWS FOR YOU/Tell Me, Is There Still A Chance? (78)	*Coral 65058*	3.00	12.00	*50*
JUMPIN' AT JEFF'S (credits Goree, but is not by him)/True Love Is Hard To Find (78)	*Sittin' In With 572*	1.50	6.00	*50*
SERENADE/Come On, Let's Boogie (78)	*Freedom 1536*	2.50	10.00	*50*
SWEET OLE WOMAN'S BLUES/Littlefield Boogie (by Little Willie Littlefield) (78)	*Freedom 1502*	3.00	12.00	*49*
YOU'RE MY EVERYTHING/Every Dog Has His Day (78)	*Imperial 5152*	2.00	8.00	*50*

CARTER, Goree & His Hep Cats

TITLE/FLIP	LABEL & NO.	GOOD TO VERY GOOD	NEAR MINT	YR.
BACK HOME BLUES/Rock Awhile (78)	*Freedom 1506*	2.50	10.00	*49*
HOY, HOY/I Just Thought Of You (78)	*Freedom 1516*	2.50	10.00	*49*
I'LL SEND YOU/How Can You Love Me? (78)	*Freedom 1511*	2.50	10.00	*49*
MY LOVE IS COMING DOWN/Workin' With My Baby (by Carter with His Guitar & Rockin' Rhythm Orchestra) (78)	*Freedom 1525*	2.50	10.00	*49*

CARTER, Goree as Gory Carter

TITLE/FLIP	LABEL & NO.	GOOD TO VERY GOOD	NEAR MINT	YR.
SEVEN DAYS/When Night Falls (78)	*Modern 20-819*	1.50	6.00	*51*

CARTER, Goree as Rocky Thompson

TITLE/FLIP	LABEL & NO.	GOOD TO VERY GOOD	NEAR MINT	YR.
BULL CORN BLUES/My Wish (78)	*Jade 207*	1.50	6.00	*51*

CARTER, Goree with His Guitar & Rockin' Rhythm Orchestra

TITLE/FLIP	LABEL & NO.	GOOD TO VERY GOOD	NEAR MINT	YR.
SHE'S JUST OLD FASHIONED/Is It True? (78)	*Freedom 1518*	2.50	10.00	*49*
WHAT A FRIEND WILL DO/She's My Best Bet (78)	*Freedom 1522*	2.50	10.00	*49*
WORKIN' WITH MY BABY/My Love Is Coming Down (by Carter & His Hep Cats) (78)	*Freedom 1525*	2.50	10.00	*49*

CARTER, James & The Sentimentals:
see Sentimentals, James Carter & The

CARTER, Mel

CARTER, Nelson

Possibly a pseudonym for Goree Carter.

TITLE/FLIP	LABEL & NO.	GOOD TO VERY GOOD	NEAR MINT	YR.
MY BABY LEFT ME/Crazy About My Baby (78)	*Sittin' In With 557*	1.50	6.00	*50*

CARTERAYS, Eddie Carter & The

TITLE/FLIP	LABEL & NO.	GOOD TO VERY GOOD	NEAR MINT	YR.
OOH BABY/These Are The Things That Matter	*Sound 105*	2.50	10.00	—

CASALS, The

CASANOVA JR.

TITLE/FLIP	LABEL & NO.	GOOD TO VERY GOOD	NEAR MINT	YR.
SALLY MAE/They Call Me Casanova	*Port 7001*	2.50	10.00	*57*

CASANOVAS, The

TITLE/FLIP	LABEL & NO.	GOOD TO VERY GOOD	NEAR MINT	YR.
GOOD LOOKIN' BABY/You Are My Queen	*Apollo 523*	7.00	28.00	*57*
I DON'T WANT YOU TO GO/Please Be My Love	*Apollo 477*	7.00	28.00	*55*
IT'S BEEN A LONG TIME/Hush-A-Meca	*Apollo 474*	12.50	50.00	*55*
MY BABY'S LOVE/Sleepy Head Mama	*Apollo 483*	12.50	50.00	*55*
PLEASE BE MINE/For You And You Alone	*Apollo 519*	7.00	28.00	*57*
THAT'S ALL/Are You For Real?	*Apollo 471*	7.00	28.00	*55*

CASH, Alvin

CASHMERES, The

TITLE/FLIP	LABEL & NO.	GOOD TO VERY GOOD	NEAR MINT	YR.
DON'T LET IT HAPPEN AGAIN/Boom Mag-Azeno Vip Vay	*Mercury 70617*	7.00	28.00	*55*
LITTLE DREAM GIRL/Do I Upset You?	*Herald 474*	5.00	20.00	*56*
MY SENTIMENTAL HEART/Yes, Yes, Yes	*Mercury 70501*	7.00	28.00	*54*
THERE'S A RUMOR/Second Hand Heart	*Mercury 70679*	7.00	28.00	*55*

CASINOS, THE

TITLE/FLIP	LABEL & NO.	GOOD TO VERY GOOD	NEAR MINT	YR.
I'M FALLING/Speedy	*Maske 803*	1.50	6.00	—

CASTALEERS, The

TITLE/FLIP	LABEL & NO.	GOOD TO VERY GOOD	NEAR MINT	YR.
COME BACK/Hi Fi Baby	*Felsted 8504*	1.50	6.00	*57*
LONELY BOY/My Bull Fightin' Baby	*Felsted 8512*	2.00	8.00	*58*
YOU'RE MY DREAM/I'll Be Around	*Felsted 8585*	6.25	25.00	*59*

CASTELLES, The

TITLE/FLIP	LABEL & NO.	GOOD TO VERY GOOD	NEAR MINT	YR.
DO YOU REMEMBER?/If You Were The Only Girl (blue label)	*Grand 105*	30.00	120.00	*54*
HAPPY AND GAY/Hey, Baby, Baby	*Atco 6069*	4.00	16.00	*56*
HEAVENLY FATHER/My Wedding Day	*Grand 122*	50.00	200.00	*55*
MARCELLA/I'm A Fool To Care	*Grand 114*	50.00	200.00	*54*
MY GIRL AWAITS ME/Sweetness (blue label)	*Grand 101*	25.00	100.00	*53*
OVER A CUP OF COFFEE/Baby, Can't You See?	*Grand 109*	40.00	160.00	*54*
THIS SILVER RING/Wonder Why (blue label)	*Grand 103*	40.00	160.00	*54*

CASTLE-TONES, The

TITLE/FLIP	LABEL & NO.	GOOD TO VERY GOOD	NEAR MINT	YR.
WE MET AT A DANCE/At The Hot Dog Stand	*Rift 504*	6.25	25.00	—

CASTOR, Jimmy

CASTOR, Jimmy Bunch, The

CASTOR, Jimmy:
see Clintonian Cubs, The (with Jimmy Castor)
see Juniors, Jimmy Castor & The

CASTROES, The

TITLE/FLIP	LABEL & NO.	GOOD TO VERY GOOD	NEAR MINT	YR.
DEAREST DARLING/	*Grand 2002*	7.00	28.00	—

The Charms

CASTROS, The

TITLE/FLIP	LABEL & NO.	GOOD TO VERY GOOD	NEAR MINT	YR.
IN MY DREAMS/Is Right?	Lasso 502	25.00	100.00	59
LUCKY ME/Darling, I Fell For You	Lasso 501	25.00	100.00	59

CASUAL TEENS, The

CASUALTONES, The

CATALINAS, The

TITLE/FLIP	LABEL & NO.	GOOD TO VERY GOOD	NEAR MINT	YR.
FRESHMAN QUEEN/	Lesley 1923	3.00	12.00	—

CATS 'N' JAMMER THREE, Bill Samuels & The

TITLE/FLIP	LABEL & NO.	GOOD TO VERY GOOD	NEAR MINT	YR.
FOR YOU/My Baby Didn't Even Say Goodbye (78)	Mercury 8033	2.50	10.00	47
I KNOW WHAT YOU'RE PUTTIN' DOWN/ Lilacs In The Rain (78)	Mercury 8037	2.50	10.00	47
I'M FALLING FOR YOU/ That Chic's Too Young To Fry (78)	Mercury 8006	2.50	10.00	46
IF I HAD ANOTHER CHANCE/One For The Money (78)	Mercury 8064	2.50	10.00	47
JOCKEY BLUES/I Cover The Water-Front (78)	Mercury 2003	2.50	10.00	46
MY BICYCLE TILLIE/I Surrender Dear (78)	Mercury 8021	2.50	10.00	47
ONE HUNDRED YEARS FROM TODAY/I'm Coming Home To Stay (78)	Mercury 2021	2.50	10.00	46
OPEN THE DOOR, RICHARD!/Candy Store Stomp (78)	Mercury 8029	2.50	10.00	47
PORT WINE/Ghost Of A Chance (78)	Mercury 8012	2.50	10.00	47

CATS & THE FIDDLE, The

TITLE/FLIP	LABEL & NO.	GOOD TO VERY GOOD	NEAR MINT	YR.
ANOTHER DAY/Stomp, Stomp (78)	Bluebird 8902	2.50	10.00	42
CHANT OF THE RAIN/ I'd Rather Drink Muddy Water (78)	RCA Victor 20-2795	1.50	6.00	48
CHANT OF THE RAIN/I'd Rather Drink Muddy Water (78)	Bluebird 8402	2.50	10.00	40
CHANT OF THE RAIN/I'd Rather Drink Muddy Water (78)	Montgomery Ward 8521	2.50	10.00	—
CRAWLIN' BLUES/Until I Met You (78)	Bluebird 8705	2.50	10.00	41
DO YOU LOVE ME?/Movin' Out Today (78)	Gotham 239	2.50	10.00	50
GANG BUSTERS/Please Don't Leave Me Now (78)	Bluebird 8248	2.50	10.00	39
GANG BUSTERS/Please Don't Leave Me Now (78)	RCA Victor 20-2794	1.50	6.00	48
GONE/Mister Rhythm Man (78)	Bluebird 8465	2.50	10.00	40
HEP CATS HOLIDAY/In The Midst Of A Dream (78)	Bluebird 8519	2.50	10.00	40
HONEY, HONEY, HONEY/I'm Afraid Of You (78)	Manor 1112	2.00	8.00	47
HUSH-A-BYE LOVE/Swing The Scales (78)	Bluebird 8585	2.50	10.00	40
HUSH-A-BYE LOVE/Swing The Scales (78)	Montgomery Ward 8905	2.50	10.00	—
I DON'T WANT TO SET THE WORLD ON FIRE/ Blue Skies (78)	Bluebird 8847	2.50	10.00	41
I MISS YOU SO/ Dig These Blues (by The Four Clefs) (78)	RCA Victor 20-2072	1.50	6.00	46
I MISS YOU SO/Another Day	RCA Victor 47-4393	15.00	60.00	50
I MISS YOU SO/Dig These Blues (by The Four Clefs) (orange vinyl)	RCA Victor 50-0077	7.00	28.00	50
I MISS YOU SO/My Sugar's Sweet To Me (78)	Manor 6000	2.00	8.00	—
I MISS YOU SO/My Sugar's Sweet To Me (78)	Regis 6000	2.50	10.00	45
I MISS YOU SO/Public Jitterbug No. 1 (78)	Bluebird 8429	2.50	10.00	40
I MISS YOU SO/Public Jitterbug No. 1 (78)	Montgomery Ward 8767	2.50	10.00	—
I'D RATHER DRINK MUDDY WATER/Walkie Talkie (by the Rudy Richardson Trio) (78)	Manor 1045	2.00	8.00	46
I'LL ALWAYS LOVE YOU JUST THE SAME/One Is Never Too Old To Swing (78)	Bluebird 8639	2.50	10.00	41
I'LL NEVER NEVER LET YOU GO/Start Talking, Baby (78)	Gotham 197	2.50	10.00	49
I'M SINGING/My Darling (78)	Bluebird 8685	2.50	10.00	41
IF I DREAM OF YOU/I'm Gonna Pull My Hair (78)	Bluebird 8665	2.50	10.00	41
IF I DREAM OF YOU/I'm Gonna Pull My Hair (78)	RCA Victor 20-3260	1.50	6.00	48
LAWDY-CLAWDY/Sighing And Crying (78)	Bluebird 8870	2.50	10.00	41
LIFE'S TOO SHORT/Part Of Me (78)	Bluebird 8932	2.50	10.00	42
MISTER RHYTHM MAN/Gone (78)	Montgomery Ward 8769	2.50	10.00	—
NEW LOOK BLUES, THE/ That's What I Thought You Said (78)	Manor 1140	2.00	8.00	48
NOTHING/That's All I Mean To You (78)	Bluebird 8535	2.50	10.00	40
NUTS TO YOU/Killin' Jive (78)	Bluebird 8216	3.00	12.00	39
PIG'S IDEA/You're So Fine (78)	Bluebird 8560	2.50	10.00	40
PIG'S IDEA/You're So Fine (78)	Montgomery Ward 8904	2.50	10.00	—
PLEASE DON'T LEAVE ME NOW/Shorty's Got To Go (78)	Manor 1037	2.00	8.00	46
ROMANCE WITHOUT FINANCE/Life's Too Short (78)	Manor 1023	2.00	8.00	45
THAT'S MY DESIRE/ When Elephants Roost In Bamboo Trees (78)	Manor 1064	2.00	8.00	47
THAT'S ON, JACK, THAT'S ON/ Just A Roamer (78)	Montgomery Ward 8770	2.50	10.00	—
THAT'S ON, JACK, THAT'S ON/Just A Roamer (78)	Bluebird 8489	2.50	10.00	40
THEY DON'T UNDERSTAND/I'm Stuck With You (78)	Manor 1067	2.00	8.00	47
THURSDAY EVENING SWING/Killer Diller Man From The South (78)	Bluebird 10484	2.50	10.00	39
THURSDAY EVENING SWING/Killer Diller Man From The South (78)	Montgomery Ward 8519	2.50	10.00	—
WE CATS WILL SWING FOR YOU/ Till The Day I Die (78)	Montgomery Ward 8520	2.50	10.00	—
WE CATS WILL SWING FOR YOU/Till The Day I Die (78)	Bluebird 10547	2.50	10.00	39
WHEN I GROW TOO OLD TO DREAM/Left With The Thought Of You (78)	Bluebird 8443	2.50	10.00	40
WHEN I GROW TOO OLD TO DREAM/Left With The Thought of You (78)	Montgomery Ward 8768	2.50	10.00	—
WHERE ARE YOU?/I'm Gonna Pull My Hair (78)	Manor 1078	2.00	8.00	47
WINE DRINKER/Lover Boy (78)	Decca 48151	2.50	10.00	50
WINE DRINKER/Lover Boy	Decca 48151	15.00	60.00	50
YOU'RE SO FINE/Darling, Can't We Make A Date? (78)	Manor 1086	2.00	8.00	47

CATS, The

TITLE/FLIP	LABEL & NO.	GOOD TO VERY GOOD	NEAR MINT	YR.
I DON'T CARE NO MORE/After I Gave You My Heart	Federal 12238	2.00	8.00	55
YOU'RE SO NICE/Get Gone	Federal 12248	2.00	8.00	55

CAVERLIERS QUARTET, The

TITLE/FLIP	LABEL & NO.	GOOD TO VERY GOOD	NEAR MINT	YR.
YOU THRILL ME SO/Dynaflow	Atlas 1031	10.00	40.00	53

CELLOS, The

TITLE/FLIP	LABEL & NO.	GOOD TO VERY GOOD	NEAR MINT	YR.
BE-BOP MOUSE, THE/Girlie That I Love	Apollo 516	3.00	12.00	57
I BEG FOR YOUR LOVE/What's The Matter For You?	Apollo 524	3.00	12.00	58
UNDER YOUR SPELL/The Juicy Crocodile	Apollo 515	3.00	12.00	57

CELTICS, The

TITLE/FLIP	LABEL & NO.	GOOD TO VERY GOOD	NEAR MINT	YR.
DARLINE, DARLING/Only The Lonely	War Conn 2216	5.00	20.00	—

CENTURIES, The

TITLE/FLIP	LABEL & NO.	GOOD TO VERY GOOD	NEAR MINT	YR.
IN THIS WHOLE WORLD/Mine, All Mine	Life 501	3.00	12.00	61

CENTURYS, The

TITLE/FLIP	LABEL & NO.	GOOD TO VERY GOOD	NEAR MINT	YR.
TAKE MY HAND/Oh, Joe, Joe	Fortune 533	2.50	10.00	59

CEZANNES, The

TITLE/FLIP	LABEL & NO.	GOOD TO VERY GOOD	NEAR MINT	YR.
PARDON ME/	Markay 108	5.00	20.00	—

CHAIRMEN OF THE BOARD, The

CHALLENGERS, The

CHALLENGERS, Walter Ward & The

CHAMBLEE, Eddie

TITLE/FLIP	LABEL & NO.	GOOD TO VERY GOOD	NEAR MINT	YR.
SIX STRING BOOGIE/Wooden Soldiers Swing. Instrumentals.	Coral 65089	2.50	10.00	52
SOUTHERN COMFORT/In A Sentimental Mood. Instrumentals.	Coral 65080	2.50	10.00	52
WALKIN' HOME/Lonesome Road (red plastic). Instrumentals.	United 160	3.00	12.00	53

CHAMPIONS, The

TITLE/FLIP	LABEL & NO.	GOOD TO VERY GOOD	NEAR MINT	YR.
ANNIE MET HENRY/Keep-A-Rockin'	Chart 602	4.00	16.00	54
COME ON/Big Bad Beulah	Chart 631	4.00	16.00	56
I'M SO BLUE/Cute Little Baby	Ace 541	4.00	16.00	58
IT'S LOVE, IT'S LOVE/Mexico Bound	Chart 611	4.00	16.00	56
SAME OLD STORY, THE/Pay Me Some Attention	Chart 620	4.00	16.00	56

CHAMPLAINS, The (with Fred Parris)

TITLE/FLIP	LABEL & NO.	GOOD TO VERY GOOD	NEAR MINT	YR.
DING DONG/Have You Changed Your Mind?	United Artists 346	3.00	12.00	61

CHAMPS, Tony Allen & The:

see Allen, Tony & The Champs

CHANACLAIRS, The

TITLE/FLIP	LABEL & NO.	GOOD TO VERY GOOD	NEAR MINT	YR.
YULETIDE LOVE/See See Rider (78)	Coleman 1056	4.00	16.00	—

CHANCES, The

TITLE/FLIP	LABEL & NO.	GOOD TO VERY GOOD	NEAR MINT	YR.
THROUGH A LONG AND SLEEPLESS NIGHT/What Would You Say?	Roulette 4549	2.00	8.00	64

CHANDELIERS, The

TITLE/FLIP	LABEL & NO.	GOOD TO VERY GOOD	NEAR MINT	YR.
BLUEBERRY SWEET/One More Step	Angle Tone 521	4.00	16.00	58
DOLLY/Dancin' In the Congo	Angle Tone 529	5.00	20.00	53

CHANDLER, Gene

CHANDLER, Gene & Barbara Acklin

CHANIER, Cliston:

see Chenier, Clifton as Cliston Chanier

CHANNELLS, The

TITLE/FLIP	LABEL & NO.	GOOD TO VERY GOOD	NEAR MINT	YR.
IN MY ARMS TO STAY/You Hurt Me	Hit 700	1.50	6.00	63

TITLE/FLIP	LABEL & NO.	GOOD TO VERY GOOD	NEAR MINT	YR.
CHANNELS, Earl Lewis & The				
MY HEART IS SAD/The Girl Next Door	Fire 1001	2.50	10.00	59
CHANNELS, Eddie & The				
CHANNELS, The				
ALTAR OF LOVE/All Alone	Gone 5019	2.50	10.00	58
CLOSER YOU ARE, THE/Now You Know	Whirlin' Disc 100	2.50	10.00	56
Lettering on the label is in a serif print style.				
CLOSER YOU ARE, THE/Now You Know	Whirlin' Disc 100	7.00	28.00	56
Lettering on the label is in a sans serif print style.				
FLAMES IN MY HEART/My Lovin' Baby	Whirlin' Disc 109	4.00	16.00	57
GLEAM IN YOUR EYES, THE/Stars In The Sky	Whirlin' Disc 102	4.00	16.00	56
I REALLY LOVE YOU/What Do You Do?	Whirlin' Disc 107	4.00	16.00	56
MY LOVE WILL NEVER DIE/Bye, Bye, Baby	Fury 1021	2.50	10.00	58
MY LOVE WILL NEVER DIE/Bye, Bye, Baby	Fury 1071	2.50	10.00	—
MY LOVE/Sad Song	Enjoy 2001	1.50	6.00	63
THAT'S MY DESIRE/Stay As You Are	Gone 5012	2.50	10.00	57
CHANTECLAIRS, The				
BELIEVE ME, BELOVED/I've Never Been There	Dot 15404	2.50	10.00	55
SOMEDAY MY LOVE WILL COME MY WAY/Baby, Please	Dot 1227	4.00	16.00	54
CHANTELS, Richard Barrett & The				
COME SOFTLY TO ME/Walking Through Dreamland	Gone 5056	1.50	6.00	59
On some pressings of this record the group's name does not appear, only the name Richard Barrett.				
SUMMER'S LOVE/All Is Forgiven	Gone 5060	2.00	8.00	59
CHANTELS, The				
CHANTELS, The (female group)				
HE'S GONE/The Plea (black label)	End 1001	2.50	10.00	57
MAYBE/Come, My Little Baby (black label)	End 1005	2.00	8.00	57

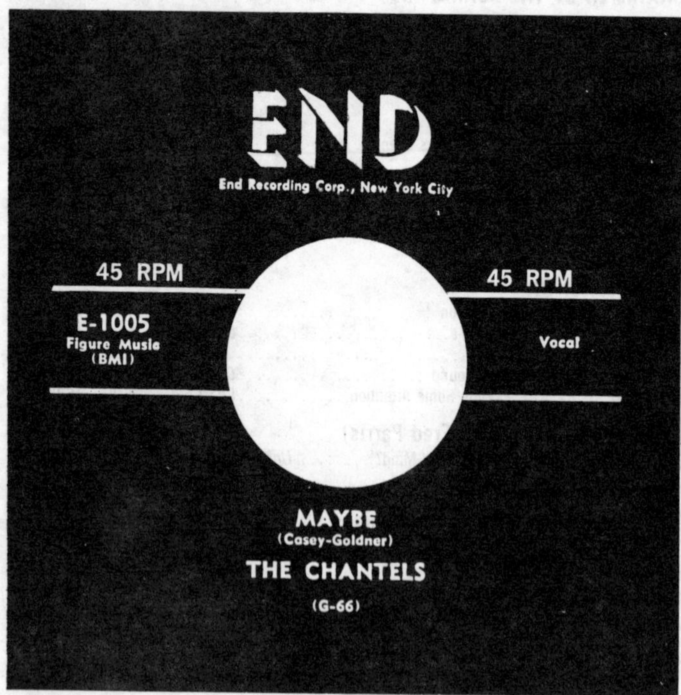

TITLE/FLIP	LABEL & NO.	GOOD TO VERY GOOD	NEAR MINT	YR.
CHANTERS, Billy Butler & The				
CHANTERS, Brother Woodman & The				
WHY?/Watts	Combo 78	8.00	32.00	55
CHANTERS, Bud Johnson & The				
OVER THE RAINBOW/No, No, No	De Luxe 6177	1.50	6.00	58
CHANTERS, The				
FIVE LITTLE KISSES/Angel Darling	De Luxe 6172	2.00	8.00	58
MY MY DARLING/I Need Your Tenderness	De Luxe 6162	2.50	10.00	58
NO, NO, NO/I Make This Pledge	De Luxe 6191	1.50	6.00	61
ROW YOUR BOAT/Stars In The Skies	De Luxe 6166	2.00	8.00	58
CHANTERS, The				
I LOVE YOU/Hot Mamma	Combo 92	8.00	32.00	55
TELL ME, THRILL ME/She Wants To Mambo	RPM 415	10.00	40.00	54
CHANTICLEERS, The				
TO KEEP YOUR LOVE/Daddy Must Be	Lyric 103	2.00	8.00	58
CHANTIERS, Rodney Baker & The				
TEENAGE WEDDING SONG/Graduation	Jan Ell 8	2.00	8.00	61
CHANTS, Jimmy Soul & The				
CHANTS, The				
HEAVEN AND PARADISE/When I'm With You	Nite-Owl 40	3.00	12.00	—
CHANTS, The				
DICK TRACY/Choo Choo	Verve 10244	1.50	6.00	61
CHAPELAIRES, The				
CHAPMAN Paul & The Cap-Tans: see Cap-Tans, Paul Chapman & The				
CHAPTERS, Helen Foster & The				
THEY TELL ME/Somebody, Somewhere	Republic 7037	20.00	80.00	53
CHAPTERS, The				
GOODBYE, MY LOVE/Love You, Love You	Republic 7038	20.00	80.00	53
CHARGERS, The (with Jessie Belvin)				
HERE IN MY HEART/The Counterfeiter	RCA Victor 47-7417	1.50	6.00	58
CHARIOTEERS, Gladys Patrick & The				
SOMEBODY PLEASE/Love Is A Wailing Thing	MGM 55015	7.00	28.00	—
CHARIOTEERS, The				
ALL ALONE AND LONELY/Careless Love (78)	Okeh 6220	1.50	6.00	41
ALL GOD'S CHILLUN GOT SHOES/ Swing Low, Sweet Chariot (78)	Brunswick 8468	3.00	12.00	39
ALONG TOBACCO ROAD/Ridin' Around In The Rain (78)	Decca 420	2.50	10.00	35
BETWEEN FRIENDS/I'll Forget (78)	Columbia 35981	1.50	6.00	41
BRAGGIN'/You Walk By (78)	Columbia 36027	1.50	6.00	41
CALIOPE JANE/ I Should Have Known You Years Ago (78)	Columbia 35779	2.00	8.00	40
CALL OF THE CANYON, THE/We'll Meet Again (78)	Columbia 35811	1.50	6.00	40
CANDLES, THE/I Didn't Mean To Be Mean To You	MGM 12569	4.00	16.00	57
COWBOY SERENADE, THE/Yes, Indeed! (78)	Okeh 6310	1.50	6.00	41
DADDY/Down, Down, Down (78)	Okeh 6247	1.50	6.00	41
DARLING, JE VOUS AIME BEAUCOUP/ Calling Romance (78)	Columbia 35736	2.00	8.00	40
DON'T YOU NOTICE ANYTHING NEW?/It Doesn't Cost You Anything To Dream (78)	Columbia 36792	1.50	6.00	45
ELMER'S TUNE/Hawaiian Sunset (78)	Okeh 6390	1.50	6.00	41
FORGET IF YOU CAN/Sleepy River Moon	Tuxedo 892	5.00	20.00	55
GAUCHO SERENADE, THE/We'll Meet Again (78)	Columbia 37519	1.50	6.00	47
GO DOWN MOSES/Were You There? (78)	Columbia 35718	2.00	8.00	40
GOODNIGHT, MOTHER/My Heart's On Ice (78)	Columbia 35851	1.50	6.00	40
I CAN'T GET STARTED/Sweet Marie (78)	Columbia 37915	1.50	6.00	47
I DON'T WANT TO CRY ANYMORE/Only Forever (78)	Columbia 35765	2.00	8.00	40
I DON'T WANT TO SET THE WORLD ON FIRE/One, Two, Three O'Lairy (78)	Okeh 6332	1.50	6.00	41
I GOT IT BAD, AND THAT AIN'T GOOD/ Cancel The Flowers (78)	Okeh 6509	1.50	6.00	42
I MISS YOU SO/You're Breaking In A New Heart (78)	Columbia 37546	1.50	6.00	47
I UNDERSTAND/A Dream For Sale (78)	Columbia 36094	1.50	6.00	41
I'M IN HIS CARE/All God's Chillun Got Shoes (78)	Columbia 35741	2.00	8.00	40
I'M IN THE MOOD FOR LOVE/Sweet Lorraine (78)	Columbia 37912	1.50	6.00	47
I'VE GOT MY HEART ON MY SLEEVE/Don't Play No Mambo	Josie 787	4.00	16.00	55
IF I COULD BE WITH YOU/ On The Sunny Side Of The Street (78)	Columbia 37914	1.50	6.00	47
IT'S TOO SOON TO KNOW/Until (78)	Columbia 38329	1.50	6.00	48
KISS AND A ROSE, A/A Cottage In Old Donegal (78)	Columbia 38438	1.50	6.00	49
LAUGHING BOY BLUES/Sing, You Sinners (by Fletcher Henderson) (78)	Okeh 4125	1.50	6.00	38
LAUGHING BOY BLUES/Sing, You Sinners (by Fletcher Henderson) (78)	Vocalion 4125	2.00	8.00	38
LET'S HAVE HARMONY/The Man Who Cares (with Penny Wise) (78)	Brunswick 8237	3.00	12.00	38
LITTLE DAVID, PLAY ON YOUR HARP/Snowball (78)	Decca 421	2.50	10.00	35
LOVE'S OLD SWEET SONG/ Silver Threads Among The Gold (78)	Columbia 35749	2.00	8.00	40

TITLE/FLIP	LABEL & NO.	GOOD TO VERY GOOD	NEAR MINT	YR.
MAY I NEVER LOVE AGAIN/Why Is A Good Gal So Hard To Find? (78)	*Columbia 35942*	1.50	6.00	*41*
MY GAL SAL/Forget If You Can (78)	*Okeh 5025*	1.50	6.00	*39*
MY GAL SAL/Forget If You Can (78)	*Vocalion 5025*	2.00	8.00	*39*
NO SOUP/One More Dream (78)	*Columbia 36903*	1.50	6.00	*46*
NOTHIN'/Call It Anything, It's Love (78)	*Okeh 6424*	1.50	6.00	*41*
OLD FOLKS AT HOME/Carry Me Back To Old Virginny (78)	*Columbia 35887*	1.50	6.00	*41*
ON THE BOARDWALK/You Make Me Feel So Young (78)	*Columbia 37074*	1.50	6.00	*46*
OPEN THE DOOR, RICHARD!/You Can't See The Sun When You're Crying (78)	*Columbia 37240*	1.50	6.00	*47*
ROGUE RIVER VALLEY/Bagel And Lox (78)	*Columbia 37195*	1.50	6.00	*46*
RUN, RUN, RUN/The Tourist Trade (78)	*Columbia 38261*	1.50	6.00	*48*
S'POSIN'/I'm The World's Biggest Fool (78)	*Keystone 1416*	1.50	6.00	*52*
SAY NO MORE/Chi-Baba Chi-Baba (78)	*Columbia 37384*	1.50	6.00	*47*
SING A SONG OF SIXPENCE/'Way Down Yonder In New Orleans (78)	*Vocalion 3923*	2.00	8.00	*38*
SLEEPY TIME GAL/My Fate Is In Your Hands (78)	*Columbia 37913*	1.50	6.00	*47*
SO LONG/Ride, Red, Ride (78)	*Columbia 37399*	1.50	6.00	*47*
SO LONG/The Gaucho Serenade (78)	*Columbia 35424*	2.00	8.00	*40*
SONG OF THE VOLGA BOATMEN/Dark Eyes (with Maxine Sullivan) (78)	*Okeh 4015*	1.50	6.00	*38*
SONG OF THE VOLGA BOATMEN/Dark Eyes (with Maxine Sullivan) (78)	*Vocalion 4015*	2.00	8.00	*38*
SPEAK TO ME OF LOVE/A Brown Bird Singing (with Maxine Sullivan) (78)	*Okeh 4068*	1.50	6.00	*38*
SPEAK TO ME OF LOVE/A Brown Bird Singing (with Maxine Sullivan) (78)	*Vocalion 4068*	2.00	8.00	*38*
STEAL AWAY TO JESUS/Jesus Is A Rock In A Weary Land (78)	*Columbia 35787*	1.50	6.00	*40*
STEAL AWAY TO JESUS/Water Boy (78)	*Brunswick 8459*	3.00	12.00	*39*
SYLVIA/I'm Gettin' Sentimental Over You (78)	*Columbia 37518*	1.50	6.00	*47*
SYLVIA/This Side Of Heaven (78)	*Columbia 36730*	1.50	6.00	*44*
THANKS FOR YESTERDAY/I'm A Stranger	*Tuxedo 891*	5.00	20.00	*55*
THIS SIDE OF HEAVEN/Hawaiian Sunset (78)	*Columbia 38602*	1.50	6.00	*49*
TICA-TEE, TICA-TA/The Train Song (78)	*Okeh 6589*	1.50	6.00	*42*
WATER BOY/Swing Low, Sweet Chariot (78)	*Columbia 35693*	2.00	8.00	*40*
WHAT DID HE SAY?/Oooh! Look-A There, Ain't She Pretty? (78)	Columbia 38065	1.50	6.00	*47*
WHEN I GROW TOO OLD TO DREAM/The Last Thing I Want Is Your Pity (78)	*Columbia 38187*	1.50	6.00	*48*
WHY SHOULD I COMPLAIN?/I'm Gettin' Sentimental Over You (78)	*Columbia 35229*	2.00	8.00	*39*
WRAP YOUR TROUBLES IN DREAMS/I Heard Of A City Called Heaven (78)	*Okeh 6292*	1.50	6.00	*41*

CHARLES, Andy & The Blues Kings: see Blues Kings, Andy Charles & The

CHARLES, Jimmy

CHARLES, King: see King Charles

CHARLES, Ray

TITLE/FLIP	LABEL & NO.	GOOD TO VERY GOOD	NEAR MINT	YR.
DON'T YOU KNOW?/Losing Hand	*Atlantic 1037*	1.50	6.00	*53*
FEELIN' SAD/Heartbreaker	*Atlantic 1008*	3.00	12.00	*53*
GREENBACKS/Blackjack	*Atlantic 1076*	1.50	6.00	*54*
I'VE GOT A WOMAN/Come Back, Baby	*Atlantic 1050*	1.50	6.00	*54*
IT SHOULD HAVE BEEN ME/Sinner's Prayer	*Atlantic 1021*	2.00	8.00	*53*
MESS AROUND/Funny, But I Still Love You	*Atlantic 999*	3.00	12.00	*53*
ROLL WITH ME, BABY/The Midnight Hour	*Atlantic 976*	5.00	20.00	*52*
SNOW IS FALLING, THE/Misery In My Heart	*Swingtime 326*	10.00	40.00	*50*
SUN'S GONNA SHINE AGAIN, THE/Jumpin' In The Morning	*Atlantic 984*	6.25	25.00	*52*

CHARMERS, Celestine Stewart & The

TITLE/FLIP	LABEL & NO.	GOOD TO VERY GOOD	NEAR MINT	YR.
WAITIN' FOR THE TRAIN TO COME IN/If I Didn't Have You (78)	*Hub 3006*	2.00	8.00	*46*

CHARMERS, Mark Stevens & The

TITLE/FLIP	LABEL & NO.	GOOD TO VERY GOOD	NEAR MINT	YR.
MAGIC ROSE/Come Back To My Heart	*Allison 921*	4.00	16.00	*62*

CHARMERS, The (female group)

CHARMERS, The

TITLE/FLIP	LABEL & NO.	GOOD TO VERY GOOD	NEAR MINT	YR.
VISITING DAY/Whatever Happened To Baby Jane?	*Terrace 7512*	1.50	6.00	*62*

CHARMERS, The

TITLE/FLIP	LABEL & NO.	GOOD TO VERY GOOD	NEAR MINT	YR.
BEATING OF MY HEART, THE/Why Does It Have To Be Me?	*Central 1002*	40.00	160.00	*54*
CHURCH ON THE HILL, THE/Battle Axe	*Timely 1011*	80.00	320.00	*54*
I WAS WRONG/The Mambo	*Timely 1009*	50.00	200.00	*54*
TONY, MY DARLING/In The Rain	*Central 1006*	75.00	300.00	*54*

CHARMETTES, The (female group)

CHARMS, Otis Williams & The

TITLE/FLIP	LABEL & NO.	GOOD TO VERY GOOD	NEAR MINT	YR.
ROLLING HOME/Do Be You	*De Luxe 6092*	1.50	6.00	*55*
THAT'S YOUR MISTAKE/Too Late I Learned	*De Luxe 6091*	1.50	6.00	*55*

CHARMS, The

TITLE/FLIP	LABEL & NO.	GOOD TO VERY GOOD	NEAR MINT	YR.
BYE-BYE BABY/Please Believe In Me	*De Luxe 6034*	10.00	40.00	*54*
CRAZY, CRAZY LOVE/Mambo Sh-Mambo	*De Luxe 6072*	1.50	6.00	*54*
CRAZY, CRAZY LOVE/Whadaya Want?	*De Luxe 6082*	1.50	6.00	*55*
FIFTY-FIVE SECONDS/Quiet, Please	*De Luxe 6050*	7.00	28.00	*54*
HAPPY ARE WE/What Do You Know About That?	*De Luxe 6014*	15.00	60.00	*53*
HEART OF A ROSE/I Offer You	*Chart 613*	2.50	10.00	*56*
HEARTS OF STONE/Who Knows?	*De Luxe 6062*	2.00	8.00	*54*
HEAVEN ONLY KNOWS/Loving Baby	*De Luxe 6000*	11.00	44.00	*53*
HEAVEN ONLY KNOWS/Loving Baby	*Rockin' 516*	20.00	80.00	*53*
I'LL BE TRUE/Boom Diddy Boom Boom	*Chart 623*	2.50	10.00	*56*
KO KO MO/Whadaya Want?	*De Luxe 6080*	1.50	6.00	*55*
LING, TING, TONG/Bazoom	*De Luxe 6076*	1.50	6.00	*54*
LOVE'S OUR INSPIRATION/Love, Love, Stick Stov	*Chart 608*	2.50	10.00	*55*
MY BABY, DEAREST DARLING/Come To Me Baby	*De Luxe 6056*	5.00	20.00	*54*
ONE FINE DAY/It's You, You, You	*De Luxe 6089*	1.50	6.00	*55*
TWO HEARTS/The First Time We Met	*De Luxe 6065*	2.00	8.00	*54*
WHEN WE GET TOGETHER/Let The Happenings Happen	*De Luxe 6087*	1.50	6.00	*55*

CHARTERS, The

TITLE/FLIP	LABEL & NO.	GOOD TO VERY GOOD	NEAR MINT	YR.
I LOST YOU/My Little Girl	*Alva 1001*	3.00	12.00	*63*
LOST IN A DREAM/This Makes Me Mad	*Merry-Go-Round 103*	5.00	20.00	*63*

CHARTS, The

TITLE/FLIP	LABEL & NO.	GOOD TO VERY GOOD	NEAR MINT	YR.
ALL BECAUSE OF LOVE/I Told You So	*Everlast 5008*	2.50	10.00	*57*
DANCE GIRL/Why Do You Cry?	*Everlast 5002*	2.50	10.00	*57*
DESIREE/Zoop	*Everlast 5001*	2.00	8.00	*57*
DESIREE/Zoop	*Everlast 5026*	1.50	6.00	*63*
MY DIANE/Baby, Be Mine	*Everlast 5010*	2.50	10.00	*57*
YOU'RE THE REASON/I've Been Wondering	*Everlast 5006*	2.50	10.00	*57*

CHATEAUS, The

TITLE/FLIP	LABEL & NO.	GOOD TO VERY GOOD	NEAR MINT	YR.
LADDER OF LOVE/You'll Reap What You Sow	*Warner Brothers 5071*	2.00	8.00	*59*
LET ME TELL YOU, BABY/Darling Je Vous Aime Beaucoup	*Epic 9163*	7.00	28.00	*56*
MASQUERADE IS OVER, THE/If I Didn't Care	*Warner Brothers 5043*	2.00	8.00	*59*
SATISFIED/Brown Eyes	*Warner Brothers 5023*	1.50	6.00	*58*

CHATMAN, Earl

TITLE/FLIP	LABEL & NO.	GOOD TO VERY GOOD	NEAR MINT	YR.
LOVING YOU, BABY/Take Two Steps Back	*Fortune 844*	1.50	6.00	—

CHATMAN, Peter as Memphis Slim & His House Rockers

Chatman should not be confused with Charles "Cow Cow" Davenport, who also used the name Memphis Slim in earlier years.

TITLE/FLIP	LABEL & NO.	GOOD TO VERY GOOD	NEAR MINT	YR.
BACK ALLEY (instrumental)/Living The Life I Love	*United 138*	3.00	12.00	*52*
CALL BEFORE YOU GO HOME/This Is My Lucky Day (red plastic)	*United 166*	5.00	20.00	*53*
CALL BEFORE YOU GO HOME/This Is My Lucky Day	*United 166*	2.50	10.00	*53*
COMEBACK, THE/Five O'Clock Blues (red plastic)	*United 156*	5.00	20.00	*53*
COMEBACK, THE/Five O'Clock Blues	*United 156*	2.50	10.00	*53*
FOUR YEARS OF TORMENT/I Love My Baby	*United 182*	2.50	10.00	*54*
GOT TO FIND MY BABY/Blue And Lonesome	*United 201*	2.50	10.00	*54*
MEMPHIS SLIM U.S.A./Blues All Around My Head	*United 186*	2.50	10.00	*54*
MY COUNTRY GAL/Treat Me Like I Treat You	*Money 212*	2.00	8.00	*54*
SASSY MAE/Wish Me Well	*United 176*	2.50	10.00	*54*
SASSY MEA/Wish Me Well (red plastic)	*United 176*	5.00	20.00	*54*
SHE'S ALRIGHT/Two Of A Kind	*United 189*	2.50	10.00	*54*

CHATMAN, Peter as Memphis Slim & The House Rockers

TITLE/FLIP	LABEL & NO.	GOOD TO VERY GOOD	NEAR MINT	YR.
NO MAIL BLUES/Gonna Need My Help Someday	*Mercury 8266*	2.50	10.00	*51*
QUESTION, THE/Never Let Me Love	*Mercury 8281*	2.50	10.00	*51*
SITTIN' AND THINKIN'/Living Like A King	*Peacock 1602*	2.00	8.00	*51*
TRAIN IS COMIN'/Drivin' Me Mad	*Mercury 70063*	2.50	10.00	*51*
TRAIN TIME/Blue Evening	*Mercury 8251*	2.50	10.00	*51*

CHATMAN, Peter as Memphis Slim: see Vagabonds, Memphis Slim & The

CHAVELLES, The

TITLE/FLIP	LABEL & NO.	GOOD TO VERY GOOD	NEAR MINT	YR.
VALLEY OF LOVE/Red Tape	*Vita 127*	8.00	32.00	*56*

CHAVIS, Wilson as Boozoo Chavis

TITLE/FLIP	LABEL & NO.	GOOD TO VERY GOOD	NEAR MINT	YR.
BOOZOO STOMP (instrumental)/Paper In My Shoe	*Folk Star 1197*	5.00	20.00	*54*
BOOZOO STOMP (instrumental)/Paper In My Shoe	*Imperial 5374*	2.50	10.00	*54*
FORTY ONE DAYS/Bye Bye Catin'	*Folk Star 1201*	4.00	16.00	*54*

CHECKERS, The

TITLE/FLIP	LABEL & NO.	GOOD TO VERY GOOD	NEAR MINT	YR.
FLAME IN MY HEART/Oh, Oh, Oh Baby	*King 4558*	50.00	200.00	*52*

TITLE/FLIP	LABEL & NO.	GOOD TO VERY GOOD	NEAR MINT	YR.
GHOST OF MY BABY/I Wanna Know	King 4626	25.00	100.00	53
HEAVEN ONLY KNOWS/Nine More Miles	King 5156	5.00	20.00	58
HOUSE WITH NO WINDOWS/Don't Stop Dan	King 4710	8.00	32.00	54
I PROMISE YOU/You Never Had It So Good	King 4673	15.00	60.00	54
I WASN'T THINKIN', I WAS DRINKIN'/ Mama's Daughter	King 4751	6.25	25.00	54
MY PRAYER TONIGHT/Love Wasn't There	King 4596	25.00	100.00	53
NIGHT CURTAINS/Let Me Come Back	King 4581	50.00	200.00	52
OVER THE RAINBOW/You've Been Fooling Around	King 4719	6.25	25.00	54
TRYING TO HOLD MY GIRL/Can't Find My Sadie	King 4764	12.50	50.00	55
WHITE CLIFFS OF DOVER/Without A Song	King 4675	10.00	40.00	54
CHECKERS, The				
TEARDROPS ARE FALLING/Rock-A-Locka	King 5199	2.50	10.00	59
This re-issue was originally credited as by the Five Wings on King 4781.				
CHEERIOS, The				
DING DONG HONEYMOON/	Golden Oldies 1	1.50	6.00	—
WHERE ARE YOU TONIGHT?/	Infinity	4.00	16.00	—
CHEERS, The				
CHENIER, Clifton				
BOPPIN' THE ROCK (instrumental)/Ay-Tete-Fee	Specialty 552	2.00	8.00	55
CAT'S DREAMING, THE/ Squeeze Box Boogie (instrumental)	Specialty 568	2.00	8.00	55
COUNTRY BRED/Rockin' The Bop (instrumental)	Post 2010	4.00	16.00	54
TELL ME/Rockin' Hop (instrumental)	Post 2016	4.00	16.00	54
THINK IT OVER/The Things I Did For You	Specialty 556	2.00	8.00	55
CHENIER, Clifton as Cliston Chanier				
LOUISIANA STOMP/Cliston Blues (78)	Elko 920	5.00	20.00	54
LOUISIANA STOMP/Cliston Blues	Imperial 5352	3.00	12.00	54
CHENIER, Morris as Big Chenier				
CHENIER, Morris as Big Chenier & His Night Owls				
CHENIER, Morris as Big Chenier & The R. B. Orchestra				
CHENIER, Rosco				
I BROKE THE YO YO/Born For Bad Luck	Reynaud 1018	2.50	10.00	63
CHEQUES, The				
THOUSAND MILES AWAY, A/Go On, Girl	Sur-Speed 214	2.00	8.00	—
CHEROKEES, Little Mr. Lee & The				
CHEROKEES, Mr. Lee & The				
CHEROKEES, The				
IS SHE REAL?/Drip, Drip, The Coffee Grinder	Peacock 1656	5.00	20.00	55
PLEASE TELL ME SO/Remember When?	Grand 110	20.00	80.00	54
RAINBOW OF LOVE/I Had A Thrill	Grand 106	20.00	80.00	54
CHEROKEES, The (with Fred Parris)				
MY HEAVENLY ANGEL/Bed Bug	United Artists 367	4.00	16.00	61
CHESSMAN, The				
DU-WHOP/I Live For You	Mirasonic 1002	5.00	20.00	—
MR. CUPID/What's To Become Of Me?	Amy 101	1.50	6.00	62
PICK IT UP/Stormy Dreams	Amy 841	1.50	6.00	62
CHESTERFIELDS, The				
I'M IN HEAVEN/All Messed Up	Chess 1559	15.00	60.00	54
CHESTERS, The				
FIRES BURN NO MORE, THE/Life Up Your Head	Apollo 521	2.00	8.00	57
CHESTNUTS, Bill Baker & The				
WON'T YOU TELL ME, MY HEART?/Tell Me Little Darling	Elgin 007/008	2.00	8.00	59
WONDERFUL GIRL/Chit Chat	Elgin 013/014	2.00	8.00	59
CHESTNUTS, The				
THIS IS MY LOVE/Wiggle, Wiggle	Aladdin 3444	1.50	6.00	58
CHESTNUTS, The				
FOREVER I VOW/Brother Ben	Davis 452	4.00	16.00	56
LOVE IS TRUE/It's You I Love	Davis 447	4.00	16.00	56
WHO KNOWS BETTER THAN I?/ Mary, Hear Those Love Bells	Standord 100	7.00	28.00	57
WHO KNOWS BETTER THAN I?/I Feel So Blue	Eldorado 511	2.50	10.00	—

TITLE/FLIP	LABEL & NO.	GOOD TO VERY GOOD	NEAR MINT	YR.
CHESTNUTS, The				
DON'T GO/I Wanna Come Home	Mercury 70489	7.00	28.00	54
CHEV-RONS, The				
DEFENSE RESTS, THE/	Gait 100	4.00	16.00	—
CHEVELLES, The (female group)				
CHEX, Tex & The				
I DO LOVE YOU/My Love	Atlantic 2116	4.00	16.00	61
CHI-LITES, The				
CHIC-LETS, The (female group)				
CHICAGO SUNNY BOY: see Louis, Joe Hill as Chicago Sunny Boy				
CHICKS, Kell Osborne & The				
CHIFFONS, The (female group)				
DO YOU KNOW?/Tonight's The Night	Big Deal 6003	2.00	8.00	60
CHILES, Buddy				
MISTREATED BLUES/Jet Black Woman (78)	Gold Star 660	4.00	16.00	49
CHIMES, Gene Moore & The				
ONLY A DREAM/Reap What You Sow	Combo 43	5.00	20.00	55
CHIMES, The (with Freddy Scott)				
LOVIN' BABY/A Faded Memory	Arrow 726	1.50	6.00	58
PLEASE CALL/The Letter Came This Morning	Arrow 724	2.00	8.00	—
CHIMES, The				
LOVE ME, LOVE ME, LOVE ME/My Heart's Crying For You	Flair 1051	9.00	36.00	55
CHIMES, The				
PRETTY LITTLE GIRL/Chop Chop	Specialty 574	2.00	8.00	56
TEARS ON MY PILLOW/Zindy Lou	Specialty 555	2.50	10.00	55
CHIMES, The				
DEAREST DARLING/A Fool Was I	Royal Roost 577	12.50	50.00	—
CHIMES, Tony Allen & The: see Allen, Tony & The Chimes				
CHIPS, The				
RUBBER BISCUIT/Oh, My Darlin'	Josie 803	5.00	20.00	56

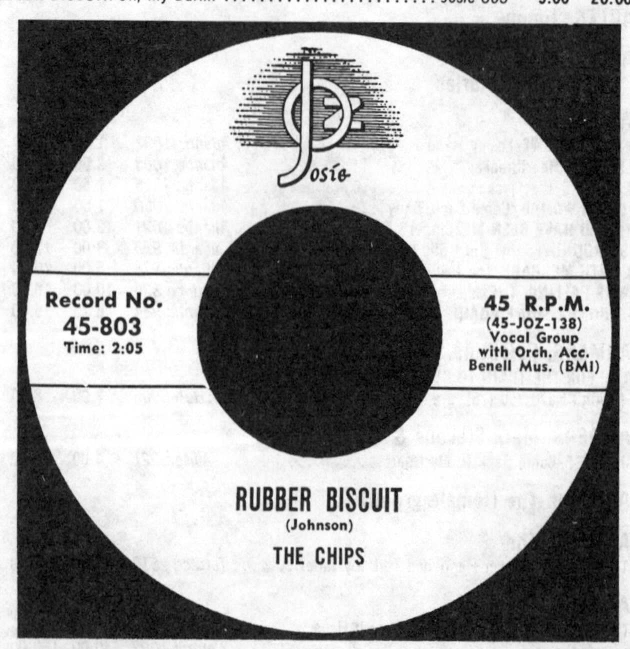

TITLE/FLIP	LABEL & NO.	GOOD TO VERY GOOD	NEAR MINT	YR.
CHIRPS, Marvin & The				
I'LL MISS YOU THIS CHRISTMAS/Sixteen Tons	Tip Top 202	15.00	60.00	—

TITLE/FLIP	LABEL & NO.	GOOD TO VERY GOOD	NEAR MINT	YR.
CHOCOLATEERS, The				
BARTENDER BLUES/Peckin'	*Parrot 781*	4.00	16.00	*54*
CHORALS, The				
IN MY DREAM/Rock And Roll Baby	*Decca 29914*	6.25	25.00	*56*
CHORDCATS, The				
HOLD ME, BABY/A Girl To Love	*Cat 112*	2.50	10.00	*54*
CHORDELLS, The				
HERE'S A HEART FOR YOU/I Started Out	*Onyx 504*	4.00	16.00	*56*
CHORDONES, Leon D. Tarver & The				
I'M A YOUNG ROOSTER/Ooh-Wee, What's Wrong With Me?	*Checker 791*	20.00	80.00	*54*
CHORDS, The				
TEARS IN YOUR EYES/Don't Be A Jumpin' Jack	*Casino 451*	1.50	6.00	—
CHORDS, The				
SH-BOOM/Cross Over The Bridge (first issue)	*Cat 104*	7.00	28.00	*54*
SH-BOOM/Little Maiden (second issue)	*Cat 104*	2.50	10.00	*54*
ZIPPETY ZUM/Bless You	*Cat 109*	2.50	10.00	*54*
CHORDS, The				
IN THE WOODS/Daddy Loves Mommy	*Gem 211*	25.00	100.00	*53*
CHRISTIAN TABERNACLE BAPTIST CHOIR, Reverend Maceo Woods & The				
CHROMATICS, Augie Austin & The				
TOO LATE/My Heart Let Me Be Free	*Brunswick 55080*	3.00	12.00	*58*
CHROMATICS, Eddie Singleton & The				
TOO LATE/Kiss-A-Kiss, Hug-A-Hug	*Amasco 3701*	5.00	20.00	*58*
CHROMATICS, Sherry Washington & The				
HONEY BUG/Wabble Loo	*Million 2016*	1.50	6.00	*56*
CHROMATICS, The				
BELIEVE ME/Who's Fooling Who? (with the Tornadoes)	*Blend 1005*	4.00	16.00	*55*
WILD, MAN, WILD/Devil Blues	*Crest 1011*	4.00	16.00	*57*
CHRYSLERS, Little Nate & The				
CRY BABY CRY/Someone Up There	*Johnson 318*	2.50	10.00	*59*
CHUCK-A-LUCKS, The				
HEAVEN KNOWS/Chuck-A-Luck	*Bow 305*	2.50	10.00	*57*
CHURCH, Eugene & The Fellows				
CHURCHILL, Savannah: see Five Kings, Savannah Churchill & The; see Four Tunes, Savannah Churchill & The; see Striders, Savannah Churchill & The				
CINERAMAS, The				
CRYING FOR YOU/I'm Sorry, Baby	*Rhapsody 71963/71964*	2.50	10.00	*60*
LIFE CAN BE BEAUTIFUL/It Must Be Love	*Champ 103*	2.00	8.00	*59*
CITATIONS, The				
IT HURTS ME/Kiss In The Night	*Don-El 113*	1.50	6.00	—
CLAREMONTS, The				
WHY KEEP ME DREAMING?/Angel of Romance	*Apollo 517*	4.00	16.00	*57*
WHY KEEP ME DREAMING?/Angel of Romance	*Apollo 751*	2.00	8.00	*63*
CLARK, Charles				
ROW YOUR BOAT/Hidden Charms	*Artistic 1500*	2.50	10.00	*58*
CLARK, Claudine & The Spinners				
CLARK, Dee				
GLORIA/Kangaroo Hop	*Falcon 1002*	2.50	10.00	*58*
OH, LITTLE GIRL/	*Falcon 1009*	2.00	8.00	*58*
24 BOY FRIENDS/Seven Nights	*Falcon 1005*	2.00	8.00	*58*
CLARK, Doug & The Nuts				
CLARK, Fred				
WALKIN' AND WONDERIN'/Ground Hog Snooper	*Federal 12136*	2.00	8.00	*53*
CLARKE, James "Beale Street"				
CLARKE, Tony				
CLASSICS, Herb Lance & The				
CLASSICS, The				
CLASSMATES, Ronnie Jones & The				
LITTLE GIRL NEXT DOOR/Teenage Rock	*End 1002*	4.00	16.00	*57*
LONELY BOY/My Baby Cries	*End 1014*	5.00	20.00	*58*
LONELY BOY/Teenage Rock	*End 1125*	1.50	6.00	*64*
CLAUDE & THE HIGHTONES: see Hightones, Claude & The				
CLAY, Judy				
CLAY, Judy & William Bell				
CLAY, Otis				
CLAYTON, Doctor: see Clayton, Peter Joe as Doctor Clayton				
CLAYTON, Merry				
CLAYTON, Peter Joe as Doctor Clayton				
HOLD THAT TRAIN CONDUCTOR/Honey Stealin' Blues	*Groove 4G-5006*	2.50	10.00	*46*
CLEFFTONES, The				
MY DEAREST DARLING/The Masquerade Is Over	*Old Town 1011*	25.00	100.00	*55*
CLEFS, The				
WE THREE/Ride On	*Chess 1521*	7.00	28.00	*52*
CLEFS, The				
I'LL BE WAITING/Please Don't Leave Me	*Peacock 1643*	4.00	16.00	*54*
CLEFTONES, The				
I LIKE YOUR STYLE OF MAKING LOVE/Why Do You Do Me Like You Do?	*Gee 1031*	1.50	6.00	*57*
SEE YOU NEXT YEAR/Ten Pairs Of Shoes	*Gee 1038*	1.50	6.00	*57*
YOU, BABY, YOU/I Was Dreaming	*Gee 1000*	1.50	6.00	*55*
CLEFTS, The				
CLEMENT, Henry				
LATE HOUR BLUES/Trojan Walla	*Spot 1000*	1.50	6.00	*61*
TROJAN WALLA/I'll Be Waiting	*Zynn 1006*	1.50	6.00	*61*
CLEMONS, T. L.				
I'M A TRAVELING MAN/Home Sick Blues	*Combo 167*	2.50	10.00	—
The label lists the artist as just T. Clemons.				
MY BIG MISTAKE/Let's Jerk	*Combo 177*	2.00	8.00	—
CLEO & THE CRYSTALIERS: see Crystaliers, Cleo & The				
CLICK-CLACKS, The				
PRETTY LITTLE PEARLY/Roma Rocka-Rolla	*Apt 25010*	1.50	6.00	*58*
ROCKET ROLL/Kiss Goodbye	*Apt 25032*	1.50	6.00	*59*
CLICKETTES, The (female group)				
CLICKS, The				
COME BACK TO ME/Peace And Contentment	*Josie 780*	15.00	60.00	*55*
CLIFTON, Paul				
ARE YOU ALRIGHT?/Ain't I Cried Enough?	*Flash 127*	1.50	6.00	*57*
CLIMBERS, The				
MY DARLIN' DEAR/Angels In Heaven Know I Love You	*J & S 1652*	5.00	20.00	*57*
CLINTON, Terry & The Berry Cups: see Berry Cups, Terry Clinton & The				
CLINTONIAN CUBS, The (with Jimmy Castor)				
SHE'S JUST MY SIZE/Confusion	*My Brothers 508*	15.00	60.00	—
CLIPS, The				
WISH I DIDN'T LOVE YOU SO/Your Lovin' Moves Me	*Republic 7102*	20.00	80.00	*57*

Dee Clark

Cleftones

TITLE/FLIP	LABEL & NO.	GOOD TO VERY GOOD	NEAR MINT	YR.

CLIQUES, The (with Jesse Belvin)

GIRL IN MY DREAMS, THE/I Wanna Know Why	Modern 987	1.50	6.00	56

CLOUDS, The

I DO/Rock And Roll Boogie	Cobra 5001	15.00	60.00	56

CLOVERMEN, Tippie & The

CLOVERS, THE

BLUE VELVET/If You Love Me	Atlantic 1052	1.50	6.00	54
COMIN' ON/The Feeling Is So Good	Atlantic 1010	2.50	10.00	53
CRAWLIN'/Yes, It's You	Atlantic 989	4.00	16.00	53
DON'T YOU KNOW I LOVE YOU?/Skylark	Atlantic 934	15.00	60.00	51
FOOL, FOOL, FOOL/Needless	Atlantic 944	10.00	40.00	51
GOOD LOVIN'/Here Goes A Fool	Atlantic 1000	6.25	25.00	53
I CONFESS/Alrighty, Oh Sweetie	Atlantic 1046	1.50	6.00	54
I PLAYED THE FOOL/Hey, Miss Fannie	Atlantic 977	9.00	36.00	52
I'VE GOT MY EYES ON YOU/ Your Cash Ain't Nothin' But Trash	Atlantic 1035	1.50	6.00	54
LOVEY DOVEY/Little Mama	Atlantic 1022	2.00	8.00	54
ONE MINT JULEP/Middle Of The Night	Atlantic 963	4.00	16.00	52
TING-A-LING/Wonder Where My Baby's Gone?	Atlantic 969	4.00	16.00	52
YES SIR, THAT'S MY BABY/When You Come Back To Me	Rainbow 122	90.00	360.00	50

CLOVERS, Tippie & The

BOSSA NOVA, BABY (original version of the song that became the Presley hit of '63)/The Bossa Nova	Tiger 201	1.50	6.00	—

CLOWNS, Bobby Marchan & The

CLOWNS, Huey Smith & The: see Smith, Huey "Piano" & The Clowns

CO-EDS, Gwen Edwards & The (female group)

I LOVE AN ANGEL/I'm In Love	Old Town 1033	4.00	16.00	56
LOVE YOU BABY ALL THE TIME/I Beg Your Forgiveness	Old Town 1027	3.00	12.00	56

COASTERS TWO PLUS TWO, The

COASTERS, The

DOWN IN MEXICO/Turtle Dove	Atco 6064	1.50	6.00	56
IDOL WITH THE GOLDEN HEAD/My Baby Comes To Me	Atco 6098	1.50	6.00	57
ONE KISS LED TO ANOTHER/Brazil	Atco 6073	1.50	6.00	56
SEARCHIN'/Young Blood (maroon label)	Atco 6087	3.00	12.00	57
WHAT'S THE SECRET OF YOUR SUCCESS?/ Sweet Georgia Brown	Atco 6104	1.50	6.00	57

COBB, Arnett

FLYING HOME MAMBO/Light Like That	Atlantic 1056	1.50	6.00	55
HORSE LAFF/Mr. Pogo	Atlantic 1042	1.50	6.00	54
NO CHILD, NO MORE/Night	Atlantic 1031	3.00	12.00	54

COBBS, Willie

DON'T SAY GOODBYE/Five Long Years	C & F 300	1.50	6.00	62
TOO SAD/Come On Home	JOB 1127	2.50	10.00	63
YOU DON'T LOVE ME/You're So Hard To Please	Mojo 2168	2.00	8.00	61

COBBS, Willie as Willie C.

WE'LL ALL BE THERE/Slow Down Baby	Ruler 5000	1.50	6.00	63

COBRAS, The

CINDY/I Will Return	Modern 964	15.00	60.00	55

CODAS, Charles Gully & The

COE, Jimmy & His Gay Cats Of Rhythm

AFTER HOURS JOINT/Come Back, Baby (red plastic)	States 118	5.00	20.00	52
AFTER HOURS JOINT/Come Back, Baby	States 118	2.50	10.00	52
HE'S ALRIGHT WITH ME/ Raid On The After Hour Joint (red plastic)	States 129	5.00	20.00	52
HE'S ALRIGHT WITH ME/Raid On The After Hour Joint	States 129	2.50	10.00	52
RUN, JODY, RUN/The Jet	States 155	2.00	8.00	52

COGNACS, The

CHARLENA/Heaven Only Knows	Roulette 4340	1.50	6.00	61

COINS, The

CHEATIN' BABY/Blue Can't Get No Place With You	Gee 10	25.00	100.00	54
LOOK AT ME, GIRL/S. R. Blues	Gee 11	20.00	80.00	54
LOOK AT ME, GIRL/Two Loves Have I (by the Colonials)	Gee 1007	10.00	40.00	56

Both songs recorded in 1954.

COLE, Ann

THOSE LONELY, LONELY NIGHTS/ I Had A Dream	Ace 512	12.50	50.00	53

COLE, Ann & The Suburbans: see Suburbans, Ann Cole & The

COLE, Cozy

COLE, Nat King & The Four Knights

COLE, Nat King as The King Cole Trio

I'M LOST/Pitchin' Up A Boogie (78)	Excelsior 104/105	2.00	8.00	45

COLEMAN BROTHERS, The

GOODNIGHT IRENE/Ooh La La (78)	Regal 3281	2.00	8.00	50

COLEMAN, Honey

TALK ABOUT A GIRL CHILD BEING DOWN/ Daddy, Why Did You Leave Me?	Combo 3	5.00	20.00	52

COLEMANS, The

I AIN'T GOT NOBODY/If You Should Care For Me (78)	Regal 3308	2.00	8.00	50
YOU KNOW I LOVE YOU, BABY/I Don't Mind Being All Alone (78)	Regal 3297	2.00	8.00	50

COLLEGIANS, The

BLUE SOLITUDE/Please Let Me Be The One	Groove 0163	1.50	6.00	56

COLLEGIANS, The

HEAVENLY NIGHT/Let's Go For A Ride	X-Tra 108	4.00	16.00	58

COLLEGIATES, The

I HAD A DREAM/Growing Up	Heritage 105	1.50	6.00	—

COLLIER, Mitty

COLLINS, Aaron & The Cadets

COLLINS, Aaron: see Thor-ables, The

COLLINS, Albert

ALBERT'S ALLEY/Defrost	Great Scott 0007	2.00	8.00	—
COLLINS SHUFFLE/The Freeze	Kangaroo 104	3.00	12.00	—

COLLINS, Big Tom: see McGhee, Walter Brown as Big Tom Collins

COLLINS, Rodger

COLLINS, Tommy & The Paragons: see Paragons, Tommy Collins & The

COLONAIRS, The

CAN'T STAND TO LOSE YOU/Sandy	Ember 1017	3.00	12.00	57

COLONIALS, Bill Gordon & The

TWO LOVES HAVE I/Bring My Baby Back	Gee 12	20.00	80.00	54

COLONIALS, The

TWO LOVES HAVE I/Look At Me Girl (by the Coins)	Gee 1007	10.00	40.00	56

Both songs recorded in 1954.

COLTS, The

ADORABLE/Lips Red As Wine	Mambo 112	10.00	40.00	55
ADORABLE/Lips Red As Wine	Vita 112	5.00	20.00	55
GUIDING ANGEL/Sheik of Araby	Antler 4003/4007	2.50	10.00	59
NEVER NO MORE/Hey You, Shoobebooboo	Vita 130	5.00	20.00	56
NEVER NO MORE/Sheik Of Araby	Antler 4003	2.50	10.00	59
SWEET SIXTEEN/Honey Bun	Vita 121	2.50	10.00	56

COLUMBUS PHARAOHS, The

GIVE ME YOUR LOVE/China Girl	Esta 290	10.00	40.00	58

This record was shortly re-released on Ransom and Paradise Records with the group identified as The Four Pharaohs.

COMBO-NETTES, Jane Porter & The (female group)

I AIN'T GOT TIME/What Kind Of Man Is This?	Combo 118	1.50	6.00	56
IF I HAD MY WISH/Hi-Diddle-Diddle	Combo 74	1.50	6.00	55

The Clovers

The Coasters

Albert Collins

The Contours

TITLE/FLIP	LABEL & NO.	GOOD TO VERY GOOD	NEAR MINT	YR.

COMETS, Herb Kenny & The

ONLY YOU/When The Lights Go On Again	Federal 12083	15.00	60.00	52

COMIC BOOKS, The

MANUEL/Black Magic And Witchcraft	Citation 5001	7.00	28.00	61

COMMANDERS, The

COMPANIONS, The

FALLING/Oh, What A Feeling!	Dove 240	4.00	16.00	—

COMPANIONS, The

IT'S TOO LATE/These Foolish Things	Gina 722	2.00	8.00	—

COMPANY, CLiff Nobles &

CONCEPTS, The

JUNGLE/Whisper	Apache 1515	2.50	10.00	61

CONCORDS, Pearl Reaves & The

YOU CAN'T STAY HERE/I'm Not Ashamed	Harlem 2332	15.00	60.00	55

CONCORDS, The

I'M SATISFIED WITH ROCK 'N' ROLL/I'll Always Say Please	Ember 1007	3.00	12.00	56

CONCORDS, The

CANDLELIGHT/Monticello	Harlem 2328	25.00	100.00	54

CONFINERS, The

HARMONICA BOOGIE/The Toss Bounce	Electro 261	20.00	80.00	61

Instrumentals by Mississippi State Prison inmates.

CONLEY, Arthur

CONNEY'S COMBO WITH L. C. WILLIAMS:
see Williams, L. C.

CONNIE'S COMBO:
see Johnson, Conrad as Connie's Combo
see Williams, L. C. as Connie's Combo

CONQUERORS, The

BILL IS MY BOYFRIEND/Duchess Conquer Duke	Lu Pine 108	6.25	25.00	62

CONROY, Ashton:
see Webster, Katie & Ashton Conroy

CONSTELLATIONS, Jonah Jones, His Orchestra & The

COME SIT BY ME/God Loves You Child	Groove 0140	2.00	8.00	56

CONTINENTALS, The

DEAR LORD/Fine, Fine Frame	Whirlin' Disc 101	4.00	16.00	56
PICTURE OF LOVE/Soft And Sweet	Whirlin' Disc 105	5.00	20.00	56

CONTINENTALS, The

YOU'RE AN ANGEL/Giddy-Up And Ding-Dong (blue label)	Rama 190	40.00	160.00	56
YOU'RE AN ANGEL/Giddy-Up And Ding-Dong (red label)	Rama 190	2.00	8.00	56

CONTOURS, The

FUNNY/The Stretch	Motown 1012	12.50	50.00	61
WHOLE LOTTA WOMAN/Come On And Be Mine	Motown 1008	3.00	12.00	61

COOK, William & The Marshall Brothers:
see Marshall Brothers, William Cook & The

COOKE, Dale:
see Cooke, Sam as Dale Cooke

COOKE, Sam

COOKE, Sam as Dale Cooke

LOVEABLE/Forever	Specialty 596	1.50	6.00	57

COOKER, John Lee:
see Hooker, John Lee as John Lee Cooker

COOKIE & THE CUPCAKES:
see Cupcakes, Cookie & The

COOKIES, The (female group)

DON'T LET GO/All Night Mambo	Lamp 8008	2.00	8.00	54
IN PARADISE/Passing Time	Atlantic 1084	1.50	6.00	56
PRECIOUS LOVE/Later, Later	Atlantic 1061	1.50	6.00	55

COOKIES, Varetta Dillard & The (female group)

COOKS, Donald & His Band

DOLPHIN STREET STOMP/Trouble Making Woman (78)	Jade 202	1.50	6.00	51

COOKS, Donald as Silver Cooks With The Gondoliers

MR. TICKET AGENT/Coming Back Home (78)	Peacock 1510	7.00	28.00	49

COOKS, Silver with The Gondoliers:
see Cooks, Donald as Silver Cooks

COOL GENTS, Deroy Green & The

BEGGAR TO A QUEEN/At The Teen Center	Cee-Jay 584	1.50	6.00	60

COOLBREEZERS, The

GREATEST LOVE OF ALL, THE/Eda Weda Bug	Bale 100/101	2.00	8.00	—
LET CHRISTMAS RING/Hello, Mr. New Year	Bale 102/103	2.00	8.00	—
YOU KNOW I GO FOR YOU/My Brother	ABC 9865	3.00	12.00	57

COOLEY, Eddie & The Dimples

COOLEY, Jack

COULD, BUT I AIN'T/Rain On My Window (red plastic)	States 125	6.25	25.00	53

COOPER, Dolly & The Four Buddies:
see Four Buddies, Dolly Cooper & The

COOPER, Herb

READY, MISS BETTY/Let's Try Again	Okeh 7037	2.00	8.00	54

COOPER, Les

COOPER, Little Sonny as Little Cooper & The Drifters

EVENING TRAIN/Moving Slow	Stevens 105	15.00	60.00	59

COOPER, Rattlesnake

RATTLESNAKE BLUES/Lost Woman (78)	Talent 804	8.00	32.00	49

COPESETICS, The

BELIEVE IN ME/Collegian	Premium 409	10.00	40.00	56

COPYCATS, The

CORALS, The

CORDELLS, The

BELIEVE IN ME/Please Don't Go	Bullseye 1017	5.00	20.00	—

CORDIALS, The

DAWN IS ALMOST HERE/Keep An Eye	7 Arts 707	1.50	6.00	61
ETERNAL LOVE/International Twist	Reville 1066	4.00	16.00	62
MY HEART'S DESIRE/Listen To My Heart	Whip 276	2.00	8.00	—

CORDOVANS, The

MY HEART/Come On, Baby	Johnson 731	1.50	6.00	60

CORONETS, The

HUSH/The Bible Tells Me So	Groove 0116	20.00	80.00	55
I LOVE YOU MORE/Crime Doesn't Pay	Groove 0114	15.00	60.00	55
IT WOULD BE HEAVENLY/Baby's Coming Home (red plastic)	Chess 1553	60.00	240.00	53
IT WOULD BE HEAVENLY/Baby's Coming Home	Chess 1553	30.00	120.00	53
NADINE/I'm All Alone	Chess 1549	20.00	80.00	53

CORONETS, The Bill Reese Quintet & The

DON'T DEPRIVE ME/The Little Boy	Sterling 903	25.00	100.00	55

CORSAIRS, Landy McNeil & The

CORSAIRS, The

CORTEZ, Dave as Baby Cortez

YOU GIVE ME THE HEEBIE JEEBIES/Honey Babe	Okeh 7102	2.50	10.00	54

CORVAIRS, The

Pee Wee Crayton

The Crickets

TITLE/FLIP	LABEL & NO.	GOOD TO VERY GOOD	NEAR MINT	YR.
CORVELLS, The				
WE MADE A VOW/Miss Jones	Lido 509	5.00	20.00	57
CORVELLS, The (female group)				
COSBY, Bill				
COSMIC RAYS, The				
DREAMING/Daddy's Gonna Tell You No Lie	Saturn 401	3.00	12.00	—
COTTON, James				
COMPLETE THE ORDER/Laying In The Weeds	Loma 2042	2.50	10.00	66
COTTON CROP BLUES/Hold Me In Your Arms	Sun 206	40.00	100.00	54
MY BABY/Straighten Up Baby	Sun 199	40.00	100.00	54
COTTON, Little Willie				
GONNA SHAKE IT UP AND GO/A Dream (78)	Swing Time 319	2.50	10.00	52
COTTON, Sylvester				
I TRIED/New Boogie Chillen	Modern 893	7.00	28.00	52
Both sides of this record are credited to John Lee Hooker, but the first side is actually by Sylvester Cotton.				
UGLY WOMAN BLUES/Sak-Relation Blues (78)	Modern 20-655	3.00	12.00	49
UGLY WOMAN BLUES/Sak-Relation Blues (78)	Sensation 7000	5.00	20.00	49
COUNTRY JIM: see Bledsoe, James as Country Jim				
COUNT MORRIS: see Dells, The				
COUNTRY PAUL: see Harris, Edward as Country Paul				
COUNTRY SLIM: see Lewis, Ernest as Country Slim				
COUNTS, The				
DARLING, DEAR/I Need You Always	Dot 1188	5.00	20.00	53
FROM THIS DAY ON/Love And Understanding	Dot 1243	2.50	10.00	55
HEARTBREAKER/To Our Love	Dot 1275	2.50	10.00	56
HOT TAMALES/Baby, Don't You Know?	Dot 1199	2.00	8.00	54
LET ME GO, LOVER/Wailin' Little Mama	Dot 1235	2.00	8.00	54
MY DEAR, MY DARLING/She Won't Say Yes	Dot 1210	6.25	25.00	54
SALLY WALKER/I Need You Tonight	Dot 1265	2.50	10.00	55
WAITIN' AROUND FOR YOU/Baby, I Want You	Dot 1226	5.00	20.00	54
COURTNEY, Lou				
COUSIN LEROY: see Rozier, Leroy as Cousin Leroy				
COVAY, Don & The Goodtimers				
CRAMPTON SISTERS, The (female group)				
CRAWFORD, James as Sugar Boy & His Cane Cutters				
I BOWED ON MY KNEES/No More Heartaches	Checker 795	5.00	20.00	54
I DON'T KNOW WHAT I'LL DO/Overboard	Checker 783	5.00	20.00	53
JOCK-O-MO/You, You, You	Checker 787	5.00	20.00	54
CRAWFORD, James "Sugar Boy"				
HAVE A LITTLE MERCY/I Cried	Ace 625	2.50	10.00	61
CRAYONS, THE				
CRAYTON, Connie Curtis as Homer the Great				
STEPPIN' OUT/Hey Little Dreamboat	Hollywood 1055	3.00	12.00	54
CRAYTON, Connie Curtis as Pee Wee Crayton				
AFTER HOURS BOOGIE (instrumental)/Why Did You Go? (78)	Four Star 1304	2.50	10.00	47
BLUES AFTER HOURS (instrumental)/I'm Still In Love With You (78)	Modern 20-624	1.50	6.00	49
BOUNCE PEE WEE (instrumental)/Old Fashioned Baby (78)	Modern 20-719	1.50	6.00	49
BRAND NEW WOMAN/Long After Hours (instrumental) (78)	Modern 20-707	1.50	6.00	49
CHANGE YOUR WAY OF LOVIN'/Tired of Travelin' (78)	Modern 20-796	1.50	6.00	49
COOL EVENING/Have You Lost Your Love For Me?	Modern 892	4.00	16.00	51
DIZZY (shown as being by The Carroll County Boys)/Central Avenue Blues	Flair 1061	2.50	10.00	—
EV'RY NIGHT 'BOUT THIS TIME/Little Bitty Things	Edco 1009	2.50	10.00	—
GIVE ME ONE MORE CHANCE/Look Up And Live	Fox 10069	2.00	8.00	—
GOOD LITTLE WOMAN/Dedicating The Blues (78)	Modern 20-774	1.50	6.00	50
I LOVE YOU SO/When Darkness Falls (78)	Modern 20-675	1.50	6.00	49
LOUELLA BROWN/ (78)	Modern 20-763	1.50	6.00	49
MONEY TREE/When Darkness Falls	Edco 1010	2.50	10.00	—
PLEASE COME BACK/Rockin' The Blues (instrumental) (78)	Modern 20-732	1.50	6.00	49
POPPA STOPPA/Thinking Of You (78)	Modern 20-816	1.50	6.00	51
ROCK ISLAND BLUES/The Bop Hop (instrumental) (78)	Modern 20-658	1.50	6.00	49
SOME RAINY DAY/Huckle Boogie (instrumental) (78)	Modern 20-742	1.50	6.00	49
TEXAS HOP (instrumental)/Central Avenue Blues (78)	Modern 20-643	1.50	6.00	49
CRAYTON, Connie Curtis as Pee Wee Crayton with The Red Callender Sextet				
BABY PAT THE FLOOR/I'm Your Prisoner	Recorded In Hollywood 426	5.00	20.00	54
DO UNTO OTHERS/Every Dog Has His Day	Imperial 5288	4.00	16.00	54
EYES FULL OF TEARS/Runnin' Wild	Imperial 5345	2.00	8.00	54
FIDDLE DE DEE/Is This The Price I Pay?	Vee Jay 266	1.50	6.00	56
FROSTY NIGHT, A/The Telephone Is Ringing	Vee Jay 214	1.50	6.00	56
I FOUND MY PEACE OF MIND/I Don't Care	Vee Jay 252	1.50	6.00	57
I MUST GO ON/Don't Go	Post 2007	2.00	8.00	55
I NEED YOUR LOVE/You Know-Yeah	Imperial 5321	2.00	8.00	54
MY IDEA ABOUT YOU/I Got News For You	Imperial 5338	2.00	8.00	55
PAPPY'S BLUES/Crying And Walking	Recorded In Hollywood 408	5.00	20.00	54
WIN-O/Hurry, Hurry	Imperial 5297	4.00	16.00	54
YOURS TRULY/Be Faithful	Imperial 5353	2.00	8.00	55
CRAYTON, Connie Curtis as Pee Wee Crayton with The Maxwell Davis Orchestra				
WHEN IT RAINS IT POURS/Daybreak	Aladdin 3112	5.00	20.00	51
CREATIONS, The				
SEVENTEEN/You'll Always Be Mine	Patti-Jo	15.00	60.00	—
CREATIONS, The				
EVERY NIGHT I PRAY/Mommy And Daddy	Tip Top 400	5.00	20.00	56
LADY LUCK/We're In Love	Penny 9022	2.50	10.00	62
LADY LUCK/We're In Love	Take Ten 1501	4.00	16.00	63
THERE GOES THE GIRL I LOVE/You Are My Darling	Lido 501	5.00	20.00	—
THERE GOES THE GIRL I LOVE/You Are My Darling	Tip Top 501	5.00	20.00	56
CREATORS, The				
DO YOU REMEMBER?/There's Going To Be An Angel	Time 1038	1.50	6.00	61
CRENSHAWS, The				
CREOLES, Lil Millet & The				
HOPELESS LOVE/Rich Woman	Specialty 565	2.50	10.00	55
CRESCENDOS, The				
SWEET DREAMS/Finders Keepers	Atlantic 1109	1.50	6.00	56
CRESCENTS, Billy Wells & The				
JULIE/I Love Only You	Reserve 105	15.00	60.00	56
CRESCHENDOS, The				
MY HEART'S DESIRE/Take My Heart	Music City 831	2.50	10.00	60
TEENAGE PRAYER/	Music City 839	2.50	10.00	60
CRESENTS, The				
EVERYBODY KNEW BUT ME/You Have No Heart	Joyce 102	10.00	40.00	57
CRICKETS, Dean Barlow & The				
ARE YOU LOOKING FOR A SWEETHEART?/Never Give Up Hope!	Jay-Dee 789	7.00	28.00	54
BE FAITHFUL/Sleepy Little Cowboy (by The Deep River Boys)	Beacon 104	7.00	28.00	54
BE FAITHFUL/I'm Not The One You Love	Beacon 555	2.00	8.00	63
JUST YOU/My Little Baby's Shoes	Jay-Dee 786	7.00	28.00	54
MAN FROM THE MOON/I'm Going To Live My Life Alone	Jay-Dee 795	7.00	28.00	54
YOUR LOVE/Changing Partners	Jay-Dee 785	7.00	28.00	54
CRICKETS, The				
DREAMS AND WISHES/When I Met You	Jay-Dee 777	7.00	28.00	53
FOR YOU I HAVE EYES/I'll Cry No More	MGM 11507	15.00	60.00	53
I'M NOT THE ONE YOU LOVE/Fine As Wine	Jay-Dee 781	7.00	28.00	53
MAN FROM THE MOON/I'm Going To Live My Life Alone	Davis 459	7.00	28.00	58
YOU'RE MINE/Milk And Gin	MGM 11428	9.00	36.00	53

CROCKETT, G. L.

CROCKETT, G. L. as G. Davy Crockett

TITLE/FLIP	LABEL & NO.	GOOD TO VERY GOOD	NEAR MINT	YR.
LOOK OUT MABEL (this is a different version from the Chief release)/Did You Ever Love Somebody	*Checker 1121*	2.00	8.00	*57*
LOOK OUT MABEL/Did You Ever Love Somebody	*Chief 7010*	3.00	12.00	*57*

CROOK, General

CROOM BROTHERS, The (featuring Dillard Croom, Jr.)

TITLE/FLIP	LABEL & NO.	GOOD TO VERY GOOD	NEAR MINT	YR.
ROCK AND ROLL BOOGIE/It's You I Love	*Vee Jay 283*	8.00	32.00	*58*

CROOM, Dillard, Jr.:
see Croom Brothers, The (featuring Dillard Croom, Jr.)

CROSSE, Gay & His Good Humor Six

TITLE/FLIP	LABEL & NO.	GOOD TO VERY GOOD	NEAR MINT	YR.
IT AIN'T GONNA BE THAT WAY/Swallow Dollow (red plastic)	*RCA Victor 50-0050*	3.00	12.00	*50*
SATURDAY NIGHT FISH FRY/Pelican's Stomp (red plastic)	*RCA Victor 50-0033*	3.00	12.00	*49*

CROTHERS, Scatman

TITLE/FLIP	LABEL & NO.	GOOD TO VERY GOOD	NEAR MINT	YR.
TELEVISION BLUES/I'd Rather Be A Rooster	*London 30081*	2.50	10.00	*50*

CROWLEY, Sheryl

TITLE/FLIP	LABEL & NO.	GOOD TO VERY GOOD	NEAR MINT	YR.
IT AIN'T TO PLAY WITH/My Devotion	*Flash 112*	2.50	10.00	*56*
JUST A NIGHT GIRL/Still Longing For You (by James Curry)	*Flash 107*	2.00	8.00	*56*

CROWNS, Arthur Lee Maye & The

TITLE/FLIP	LABEL & NO.	GOOD TO VERY GOOD	NEAR MINT	YR.
GLORIA/Oh-Rooba-Lee	*Specialty 573*	5.00	20.00	*56*
LOVE ME ALWAYS/Loop De Loop De Loop	*RPM 429*	8.00	32.00	*55*
PLEASE DON'T LEAVE ME/Do The Bop	*RPM 438*	9.00	36.00	*55*
PLEASE SAY YOU LOVE ME/Cool Lovin'	*RPM 420*	8.00	32.00	*55*
SET MY HEART FREE/I Wanna Love	*Modern 944*	15.00	60.00	*54*
TRULY/Oochie Pachie	*RPM 424*	8.00	32.00	*55*

CROWNS, The

TITLE/FLIP	LABEL & NO.	GOOD TO VERY GOOD	NEAR MINT	YR.
KISS AND MAKE UP/I'll Forget About You	*R & B 6901*	1.50	6.00	*58*

CROWS, The

TITLE/FLIP	LABEL & NO.	GOOD TO VERY GOOD	NEAR MINT	YR.
BABY DOLL/Sweet Sue	*Rama 50*	15.00	60.00	*54*
BABY/Untrue	*Rama 29*	15.00	60.00	*54*
CALL A HEARTBREAKER/Heartbreaker	*Rama 10*	25.00	100.00	*53*
GEE/I Love You So (red plastic)	*Rama 5*	20.00	80.00	*53*
GEE/I Love You So	*Rama 5*	6.25	25.00	*53*
MAMBO SHEVITZ/Mambo No. 5 (instrumental)	*Tico 1082*	30.00	120.00	
MISS YOU/I Really Really Love You (red plastic)	*Rama 30*	55.00	220.00	*54*
MISS YOU/I Really Really Love You	*Rama 30*	25.00	100.00	*54*
SEVEN LONELY DAYS/No Help Wanted	*Rama 3*	15.00	60.00	*53*

CROWS, The as The Jewels

TITLE/FLIP	LABEL & NO.	GOOD TO VERY GOOD	NEAR MINT	YR.
CALL A HEARTBREAKER/Heartbreaker (red plastic)	*Rama 10*	75.00	300.00	*53*

This record was also released as by The Crows.

CRUDUP, Arthur as Arthur "Big Boy" Crudup

TITLE/FLIP	LABEL & NO.	GOOD TO VERY GOOD	NEAR MINT	YR.
I LOVE MY BABY/Fall On Your Knees And Pray	*Groove 4G-0011*	3.00	12.00	*53*
IF YOU HAVE EVER BEEN TO GEORGIA/She's Got No Hair	*Groove 4G-0026*	3.00	12.00	*54*
MY WIFE AND WOMEN/The War Is Over	*RCA Victor 47-5563*	3.00	12.00	*53*

CRUDUP, Arthur as Big Boy Crudup

TITLE/FLIP	LABEL & NO.	GOOD TO VERY GOOD	NEAR MINT	YR.
BOY FRIEND BLUES/Katie May (red plastic)	*RCA Victor 50-0001*	5.00	20.00	*46*
COME BACK, BABY/Mercy Blues (red plastic)	*RCA Victor 50-0046*	5.00	20.00	*49*
CRUDUP'S AFTER HOURS/That's All Right (red plastic)	*RCA Victor 50-0000*	8.00	32.00	*46*
CRUDUP'S VICKSBURG BLUES/Shout, Sister, Shout (red plastic)	*RCA Victor 50-0013*	5.00	20.00	*47*
DUST MY BROOM/You Know That I Love You (red plastic)	*RCA Victor 50-0074*	5.00	20.00	*49*
GOIN' BACK TO GEORGIA/Mr. So And So	*RCA Victor 47-4572*	3.00	12.00	*52*
HOODOO LADY BLUES/Tired Of Worry (red plastic)	*RCA Victor 50-0032*	5.00	20.00	*47*
I WONDER/My Baby Boogies All The Time	*Ace 503*	25.00	100.00	*53*
KEEP ON DRINKIN'/Nelvina	*RCA Victor 47-5167*	3.00	12.00	*52*
LONESOME WORLD TO ME/Hand Me Down My Walking Cane (red plastic)	*RCA Victor 50-0100*	5.00	20.00	*47*
LOVE ME, MAMA/Where Did You Stay Last Night?	*RCA Victor 47-4367*	3.00	12.00	*51*
MEAN OLD SANTA FE/ (red plastic)	*RCA Victor 50-0092*	5.00	20.00	*50*
NOBODY WANTS ME/Star Bootlegger	*RCA Victor 50-0117*	4.00	16.00	*50*
PEARLY LEE/Lookin' For My Baby	*RCA Victor 47-5070*	3.00	12.00	*51*
ROBERTA BLUES/Behind Closed Doors	*RCA Victor 50-0126*	4.00	16.00	*47*
SECOND MAN BLUES/Do It If You Want To	*RCA Victor 47-47933*	3.00	12.00	*51*
SHE'S JUST LIKE CALDONIA/ (red plastic)	*RCA Victor 50-0105*	5.00	20.00	*49*
TOO MUCH COMPETITION/I'm Gonna Dig Myself A Hole	*RCA Victor 50-0141*	4.00	16.00	*51*
WORRIED ABOUT YOU, BABY/Late In The Evening	*RCA Victor 47-4753*	3.00	12.00	*52*

CRUDUP, Arthur as Percy Lee Crudup

TITLE/FLIP	LABEL & NO.	GOOD TO VERY GOOD	NEAR MINT	YR.
OPEN YOUR BOOK/Tears In My Eyes (78)	*Checker 754*	2.50	10.00	*52*

CRUDUP, Percy Lee :
see Crudup, Arthur as Percy Lee Crudup

CRUISERS, Herb Johnson & The

TITLE/FLIP	LABEL & NO.	GOOD TO VERY GOOD	NEAR MINT	YR.
GUILTY/Have You Heard?	*Len 1007*	1.50	6.00	—

CRUME BROTHERS, The

CRUSHER, Guitar:
see Guitar Crusher

CRUTCHFIELD, James

CRYSTALIERS, Cleo & The

TITLE/FLIP	LABEL & NO.	GOOD TO VERY GOOD	NEAR MINT	YR.
PLEASE BE MY GUY/Don't Cry	*Cindy 3003*	4.00	16.00	*57*
PLEASE BE MY GUY/Don't Cry	*Johnson 103*	2.50	10.00	—

CRYSTALS, Sam Hawkins & The

CRYSTALS, The

TITLE/FLIP	LABEL & NO.	GOOD TO VERY GOOD	NEAR MINT	YR.
FOUR WOMEN/My Dear	*De Luxe 6013*	20.00	80.00	*53*
HAVE FAITH IN ME/My Love	*De Luxe 6037*	20.00	80.00	*54*
MY GIRL/Don't You Go	*Rockin' 518*	20.00	80.00	*53*
MY GIRL/God Only Knows	*De Luxe 6077*	10.00	40.00	*54*
SQUEEZE ME, BABY/Come To Me, Darling	*Luna 101*	10.00	40.00	—
SQUEEZE ME, BABY/Come To Me, Darling	*Luna 5001*	10.00	40.00	—

CRYSTALS, The (female group)

TITLE/FLIP	LABEL & NO.	GOOD TO VERY GOOD	NEAR MINT	YR.
I LOVE MY BABY/I Do Believe	*Aladdin 3355*	4.00	16.00	*57*

CRYSTALS, The (female group)

TITLE/FLIP	LABEL & NO.	GOOD TO VERY GOOD	NEAR MINT	YR.
HE HIT ME/No One Ever Tells You	*Phillies 105*	2.00	8.00	*62*

CUBANS, The

TITLE/FLIP	LABEL & NO.	GOOD TO VERY GOOD	NEAR MINT	YR.
TELL ME/You've Been Gone So Long	*Flash 133*	4.00	16.00	*58*

CUBS, The

TITLE/FLIP	LABEL & NO.	GOOD TO VERY GOOD	NEAR MINT	YR.
I HEAR WEDDING BELLS/Why Did You Make Me Cry?	*Savoy 1502*	3.00	12.00	*56*

CUES, The

TITLE/FLIP	LABEL & NO.	GOOD TO VERY GOOD	NEAR MINT	YR.
ONLY YOU/I Fell For Your Loving	*Jubilee 5201*	1.50	6.00	*55*
SCOOCHIE SCOOCHIE/Forty 'Leven Dozen Ways	*Lamp 8007*	2.00	8.00	*54*

CUFF LINKS, The

TITLE/FLIP	LABEL & NO.	GOOD TO VERY GOOD	NEAR MINT	YR.
CHANGING MY LOVE/I Don't Want Nobody	*Dooto 474*	2.00	8.00	*63*
FOOL'S FORTUNE, A/Trick Knees	*Dooto 434*	2.50	10.00	*58*
GUIDED MISSLES/My Heart	*Dootone 409*	5.00	20.00	*56*

The Crowns

The Danleers

The Dells

TITLE/FLIP	LABEL & NO.	GOOD TO VERY GOOD	NEAR MINT	YR.
HOW YOU LIED/The Winner	*Dooto 413*	4.00	16.00	*57*
IT'S TOO LATE NOW/Saxophone Rag	*Dooto 422*	7.00	28.00	*57*
LAWFUL WEDDING/Zoom	*Dooto 438*	2.50	10.00	*58*
SO TOUGH/My Love Is With You	*Dooto 433*	2.50	10.00	*58*
TWINKLE/Off Day Blues	*Dooto 414*	4.00	16.00	*57*

CUPCAKES, Cookie & The

TITLE/FLIP	LABEL & NO.	GOOD TO VERY GOOD	NEAR MINT	YR.
BREAKING UP IS HARD TO DO/I Cried	*Lyric 1009*	2.50	10.00	*63*
EVEN THOUGH/Walking Down The Aisle (by Little Alfred)	*Lyric 1016*	2.00	8.00	*64*
GOT YOU ON MY MIND/I've Been So Lonely	*Lyric 1004*	2.50	10.00	*63*
HEY, LITTLE SCHOOLGIRL/Charged With Cheating	*Lyric 1015*	2.00	8.00	*64*
I HEARD THAT STORY BEFORE/All My Lovin' Baby	*Lyric 1008*	2.50	10.00	*63*
LONG TIME AGO/Kissin' Someone Else	*Lyric 1017*	2.00	8.00	*64*
MATILDA/I'm Twisted	*Lyric 1003*	2.50	10.00	*63*
UNTIL THEN/Close Up The Back Door	*Judd 1015*	1.50	6.00	*59*

CUPIDS, The (female group)

TITLE/FLIP	LABEL & NO.	GOOD TO VERY GOOD	NEAR MINT	YR.
MY DOG LIKES YOUR DOG/The Answer To Your Prayer	*Decca 30279*	1.50	6.00	*57*

CUPIDS, The

TITLE/FLIP	LABEL & NO.	GOOD TO VERY GOOD	NEAR MINT	YR.
NOW YOU TELL ME/Lillie Mae	*Aladdin 3404*	1.50	6.00	*58*

CUPIDS, The

TITLE/FLIP	LABEL & NO.	GOOD TO VERY GOOD	NEAR MINT	YR.
I DON'T KNOW/Troubles Not At End	*Chan 107*	3.00	12.00	—

CUPIDS, The

TITLE/FLIP	LABEL & NO.	GOOD TO VERY GOOD	NEAR MINT	YR.
TRUE LOVE, TRUE LOVE/Let's Twist	*UWR 4241/4242*	2.00	8.00	*62*

CURRY, Clifford

CURRY, Dolores & The Original Mustangs

CURRY, Earl

TITLE/FLIP	LABEL & NO.	GOOD TO VERY GOOD	NEAR MINT	YR.
ONE WHOLE YEAR, BABY/I Want Your Lovin'	*RPM 402*	4.00	16.00	*54*

CURRY, Earl & The Blenders:
see Blenders, Earl Curry & The

CURRY, James "King"

TITLE/FLIP	LABEL & NO.	GOOD TO VERY GOOD	NEAR MINT	YR.
MY PROMISE/Please, Baby	*Flash 110*	2.50	10.00	*56*

CURTIS, Cry Baby

TITLE/FLIP	LABEL & NO.	GOOD TO VERY GOOD	NEAR MINT	YR.
DON'T JUST STAND THERE/ There Will Be Some Changes Made	*Trevor 103*	1.50	6.00	—
I WANNA/Did You Think I Care?	*Cash 1062*	3.00	12.00	—
THERE WILL BE SOME CHANGES MADE/ Did You Stay Last Night?	*Romark 110*	1.50	6.00	—

CURTIS, King

TITLE/FLIP	LABEL & NO.	GOOD TO VERY GOOD	NEAR MINT	YR.
KING'S ROCK/Dynamite At Midnight (instrumental)	*Apollo 507*	1.50	6.00	*56*
MOVIN' ON/Rockabye Baby (instrumental)	*Groove 0160*	1.50	6.00	*56*
TENOR IN THE SKY (instrumental)/ No More Crying On My Pillow	*Gem 208*	2.50	10.00	*53*
WINE HEAD/I've Got News For You, Baby	*Monarch 702*	2.50	10.00	*53*

CYCLONES, The

CYMBALS, Lee Williams & The

CYMBALS, The

TITLE/FLIP	LABEL & NO.	GOOD TO VERY GOOD	NEAR MINT	YR.
ONE STEP TOO FAR/Shout Mama Linda	*Amazon 709*	2.00	8.00	—

D

DAHILLS, The

DAIDEMS, The

TITLE/FLIP	LABEL & NO.	GOOD TO VERY GOOD	NEAR MINT	YR.
I'LL DO ANYTHING/Goodnight Theme	*Goldie 715*	1.50	6.00	—
WHAT MORE IS THERE TO SAY?/Ala Vevo	*Lavere 187*	1.50	6.00	*61*
WHY DON'T YOU BELIEVE ME?/	*Star 514*	1.50	6.00	—

DALE & THE DEL-HEARTS

DALE, Larry

TITLE/FLIP	LABEL & NO.	GOOD TO VERY GOOD	NEAR MINT	YR.
FEELIN' ALL RIGHT/No Tellin' What I Do	*Herald 463*	1.50	6.00	*55*
YOU BETTER HEED MY WARNING/Please Tell Me	*Groove 0029*	2.00	8.00	*54*

DALES, The

TITLE/FLIP	LABEL & NO.	GOOD TO VERY GOOD	NEAR MINT	YR.
IF YOU ARE MEANT TO BE/Lonely Women—Lonely Man	*Onyx 509*	1.50	6.00	*57*

DALLAS, Leroy

TITLE/FLIP	LABEL & NO.	GOOD TO VERY GOOD	NEAR MINT	YR.
GOOD MORNING BLUES/I'm Going Away (78)	*Sittin' In With 526*	2.50	10.00	*49*
I'M DOWN NOW, BUT I WON'T BE ALWAYS/Jump, Little Children (78)	*Sittin' In With 522*	2.50	10.00	*49*
YOUR SWEET MAN'S BLUES/Baby Please Don't Go Back To New Orleans (78)	*Jade 707*	1.50	6.00	*49*
YOUR SWEET MAN'S BLUES/Baby Please Don't Go Back To New Orleans (78)	*Sittin' In With 537*	2.50	10.00	*49*

DAMITA JO

DAMITA JO:
see Red Caps, Steve Gibson & The

DANDERLIERS, The

TITLE/FLIP	LABEL & NO.	GOOD TO VERY GOOD	NEAR MINT	YR.
CHOP CHOP BOOM/My Autumn Love (red plastic)	*States 147*	40.00	160.00	*55*
CHOP CHOP BOOM/My Autumn Love	*States 147*	7.00	28.00	*55*
MAY GOD BE WITH YOU/Little Man	*States 152*	5.00	20.00	*56*
MY LOVE/She's Mine	*States 160*	10.00	40.00	*56*
SHU-WOP/My Loving Partner	*States 150*	4.00	16.00	*55*

DANDEVILLES, The

DANDLEERS, The

TITLE/FLIP	LABEL & NO.	GOOD TO VERY GOOD	NEAR MINT	YR.
ONE SUMMER NIGHT/Wheelin' And A-Dealin'	*Amp 3 2115*	2.50	10.00	*58*

DANLEERS, The

TITLE/FLIP	LABEL & NO.	GOOD TO VERY GOOD	NEAR MINT	YR.
I CAN'T SLEEP/Your Love	*Mercury 71441*	1.50	6.00	*59*

DANNY BOY & HIS BLUE GUITAR:
see Thomas, Danny as Danny Boy & His Blue Guitar

DAPPERS, The

TITLE/FLIP	LABEL & NO.	GOOD TO VERY GOOD	NEAR MINT	YR.
UNWANTED LOVE/That's All, That's All, That's All	*Groove 0156*	15.00	60.00	*56*

DAPPERS, The

TITLE/FLIP	LABEL & NO.	GOOD TO VERY GOOD	NEAR MINT	YR.
COME BACK TO ME/Mambo Oongh	*Peacock 1651*	10.00	40.00	*55*

DAPPERS, The

TITLE/FLIP	LABEL & NO.	GOOD TO VERY GOOD	NEAR MINT	YR.
BOP BOP BU/How I Need You, Baby!	*Rainbow 373*	1.50	6.00	—

DAPPS, Hank Ballard & The

DAPPS, Johnnie Mae Matthews & The

DAPPS, The

DAPS, The

TITLE/FLIP	LABEL & NO.	GOOD TO VERY GOOD	NEAR MINT	YR.
WHEN YOU'RE ALONE/Down And Out	*Marterry 5249*	1.50	6.00	*56*

DARLINGS, Jeanne & The (female group)

DARNELL, Larry

TITLE/FLIP	LABEL & NO.	GOOD TO VERY GOOD	NEAR MINT	YR.
BETTER BE ON MY WAY/What's On Your Mind?	*Okeh 6902*	1.50	6.00	*52*
BOOGIE BOOGIE/Darlin'	*Okeh 6869*	2.00	8.00	*52*
CHRISTMAS BLUES/I Am The Sparrow	*Okeh 6926*	1.50	6.00	*52*
SINGIN' MY BLUES/No Time At All	*Okeh 6916*	1.50	6.00	*52*
WORK, BABY, WORK/Left My Baby	*Okeh 6848*	2.00	8.00	*52*

DARNELLS, The (female group)

TITLE/FLIP	LABEL & NO.	GOOD TO VERY GOOD	NEAR MINT	YR.
TOO HURT TO CRY, TOO MUCH IN LOVE TO SAY GOODBYE/Come On Home (instrumental)	*Gordy 7024*	1.50	6.00	*63*

DARNELS, Gus Gordon & The

TITLE/FLIP	LABEL & NO.	GOOD TO VERY GOOD	NEAR MINT	YR.
MY LITTLE HOMIN' PIGEON/In The Valley Of The Roses	*Bana 525*	2.00	8.00	*57*

DARRELLS, The

TITLE/FLIP	LABEL & NO.	GOOD TO VERY GOOD	NEAR MINT	YR.
WITHOUT WARNING/So Tenderly	*Lyco 1003*	3.00	12.00	—

DARTS, Sherman & The

DARTS, The

TITLE/FLIP	LABEL & NO.	GOOD TO VERY GOOD	NEAR MINT	YR.
ON MY MIND/Well Baby	*Apt 25023*	1.50	6.00	*58*

DARVELS, The

TITLE/FLIP	LABEL & NO.	GOOD TO VERY GOOD	NEAR MINT	YR.
DAVE & THE STEREOS: see Stereos, Dave & The				
DAVENPORT, Charles Edward as Cow Cow Davenport				
DAVENPORT, Cow Cow				
DAVID, Geater				
DAVIS, Benny: see Brown Dots, Deek Watson & The				
DAVIS, Billy & The Legends				
DAVIS, Blind John				
DAVIS, Blind Johnny Trio, The				
DAVIS, Eunice				
GO TO WORK, PRETTY DADDY/My Beat Is 125th Street	Atlantic 992	2.50	10.00	53
DAVIS, King				
SOMEDAY YOU'LL UNDERSTAND/Waggin' Your Tail	Hollywood 422	10.00	40.00	54
DAVIS, Larry				
DAVIS, Little Sam				
GOIN' HOME TO MOTHER/1958 Blues	Rockin' 512	12.50	50.00	52
SHE'S SO GOOD TO ME/Goin' To New Orleans	DeLuxe 6025	10.00	40.00	52
SHE'S SO GOOD TO ME/Goin' To New Orleans	Rockin' 519	15.00	60.00	52
DAVIS, Melvin & The Nite Sounds				
DAVIS, Sonny Boy				
RHYTHM BLUES/I Don't Live Here No More (78)	Talent 802	6.25	25.00	49
DAVIS, Tyrone				
DAVIS, Walter				
I JUST CAN'T HELP IT/You Are The One I Love (78)	Bullet 341	1.50	6.00	50
MOVE BACK TO THE WOODS/ You've Got To Reap What You Sow (78)	Bullet 305	1.50	6.00	49
SANTA CLAUS BLUES/Got To See Her Every Night (78)	Bullet 321	1.50	6.00	50
SO LONG, BABY/What May Your Trouble Be?	RCA Victor 47-5168	5.00	20.00	52
STOP THAT TRAIN IN HARLEM/ So Long, Baby (78)	Bullet 326	1.50	6.00	50
WONDER WHAT I'M DOING WRONG?/ I Would Hate To Hate You (78)	Bullet 311	1.50	6.00	49
YOU MADE MY WORLD SO BRIGHT/ Tears Came Rolling Down	RCA Victor 47-5012	5.00	20.00	52
DAVISON, Leo				
HELLO, MAE/It's Never Too Late	Great Scott 0008	2.50	10.00	—
DAWN, Billy Quartet, The				
THIS IS THE REAL THING NOW/Crying For My Baby	Decatur 3001	20.00	80.00	—
DAY, Bobby & The Satelittes				
DAY, Sonny & The Versatiles: see Versatiles, Sonny Day & The				
DAYBREAKERS, The				
I WONDER WHY?/Up, Up And Away	Aladdin 3434	1.50	6.00	58
I WONDER WHY?/Up, Up And Away	Lamp 2016	2.00	8.00	58
DAYDREAMS, Tony & The				
HAND IN HAND/I'll Never Tell	Planet 1055	3.00	12.00	61
WHY DON'T YOU BE NICE?/I'll Never Tell	Planet 1008/1009	4.00	16.00	58
DAYLIGHTERS, Bettie Everett & The				
DAYLIGHTERS, Eddie Boyd & The				
DAYLIGHTERS, The				
MAD HOUSE JUMP/You're Breaking My Heart	Bea & Baby 103	1.50	6.00	59
THIS HEART OF MINE/Bear Mash Stomp	Nike 1011	5.00	20.00	61
TOUGH LOVE/Sweet Rocking Mama	C. J. 614	1.50	6.00	60
DAYLIGHTERS, The (female group)				

TITLE/FLIP	LABEL & NO.	GOOD TO VERY GOOD	NEAR MINT	YR.
DE BERRY, Jimmy				
TAKE A LITTLE CHANCE/Time Has Made A Change	Sun 185	25.00	100.00	53
DE BERRY, Jimmy as Jimmy & Walter (with Walter Horton)				
EASY/Before Long	Sun 180	40.00	160.00	53
DE BONAIRS, The				
LANKY LINDA/Mother's Son	Ping 1000	15.00	60.00	56
SAY A PRAYER FOR ME/Cracker-Jack Daddy	Ping 1001	15.00	60.00	56
DE LOS, The				
DE MILO, Cordella				
AIN'T GONNA HUSH/Lonely Girl	Modern 954	5.00	20.00	—
DE VAURS, The (female group)				
WHERE ARE YOU/Boy In Mexico	Moon 105	2.00	8.00	—
DE VILLES, The				
DO WOP/Kiss Again And Again	Aladdin 3423	3.00	12.00	58
DEAN, David				
STAY HERE WITH ME/Too Fine To Be Mine	Peacock 1645	2.00	8.00	54
DEAN, Johnny see Phillips, Marvin & Johnny Dean as Marvin & Johnny				
DEBONAIRES, The				
THIS MUST BE PARADISE/I Need You Darling	Elmont 1004	2.00	8.00	—
DEBONAIRES, The				
DARLING/Whispering Blues	Herald 509	2.50	10.00	57
EVERY ONCE IN A WHILE/Gert's Skirt	Dore 526	2.50	10.00	59
EVERY ONCE IN A WHILE/Gert's Skirt	Dore 592	1.50	6.00	61
WON'T YOU TELL ME?/I'm Gone	Gee 1008	1.50	6.00	56
DEBONAIRS, The				
BILL COLLECTOR, THE/As Other Lovers Do	Combo 129	4.00	16.00	56
CAUSE OF A BAD ROMANCE/For The Women I Love	Combo 149	4.00	16.00	58
DEBS, The				
SHOO DOO DE DOO/Whadaya Want?	Bruce 129	1.50	6.00	55
DEBS, The (female group)				
JOHNNIE, DARLING/Doom-A-Roca	Keen 34003	1.50	6.00	57
DECEMBER, Bobby				
BYE BYE BABY/Invision	Orchestra 100	4.00	16.00	—
DECOYS, The				
DEE CALS, The				
STARS IN THE BLUE, WHAT SHOULD I DO?/A Wonderful Day	Co-Ed 1960	7.00	28.00	59
STARS IN THE BLUE, WHAT SHOULD I DO?/A Wonderful Day	Mayhams 1960	4.00	16.00	61
DEE-VINES, The				
I BELIEVE/World's Greatest Lover	Lano 2001	2.50	10.00	60
DEEP RIVER BOYS, Count Basie & The				
SOLID AS A ROCK/Mine, Too (not with the group)	RCA Victor 47-3235	2.00	8.00	50
DEEP RIVER BOYS, The				
ALL I NEED IS YOU/Sleepy Little Cowboy	Beacon 9146	4.00	16.00	52
BIRD IN THE HAND, A/You Don't Know Nothin' (78)	Bluebird 10847	2.00	8.00	40
FREE GRACE/ If You Love God, Serve Him (red plastic)	RCA Victor 50-0078	4.00	16.00	50
Both songs recorded in 1947.				
I WAS A FOOL TO LET YOU GO/Bullfrog And The Toad (78)	Bluebird 10676	2.00	8.00	40
I WISH I HAD DIED IN MY CRADLE/Utt Da Zay (78)	Bluebird 11217	2.00	8.00	41
MY HEART AT THY SWEET VOICE/Cherokee (78)	Bluebird 11178	2.00	8.00	41
NO ONE ELSE WILL DO/Truthfully	Jay-Dee 788	2.50	10.00	54
Both songs recorded in 1951.				
NOTHING BUT YOU/Ev'ry Sunday Afternoon (78)	Victor 26533	1.50	6.00	40
OO-SHOO-BE-DO-BE/The Biggest Fool	RCA Victor 47-5268	2.00	8.00	53
SLEEPY LITTLE COWBOY/Be Faithful (by Dean Barlow & The Crickets)	Beacon 104	7.00	28.00	54
TRUTHFULLY/Doesn't Make Sense To Me	Beacon 9143	5.00	20.00	52

TITLE/FLIP	LABEL & NO.	GOOD TO VERY GOOD	NEAR MINT	YR.
DEL CAPRIS, The				
HEY, LITTLE GIRL/Forever My Love	Ronjerdon 39	1.50	6.00	67
DEL COUNTS, The				
LONE STRANGER/Mother Nature	Rose 22/23	4.00	16.00	—
DEL PRIS, The				
WOMP/The Time	Varbee 2003	7.00	28.00	61
DEL RAYS, The				
MY DARLING/The One I Adore	Warner Bros. 5022	4.00	16.00	58
DEL RIOS, Linda & The				
DEL RIOS, The				
ALONE ON A RAINY NITE/Lizzie	Meteor 5038	8.00	32.00	56
DEL RIOS, The				
I'M CRYING/Wait, Wait, Wait	Neptune 108	1.50	6.00	59
DEL ROYALS, The				
WHO WILL BE THE ONE?/She's Gone	Minit 610	1.50	6.00	60
DEL ROYS, The				
DEL VICTORS, The				
DEL VIKINGS, THE				
This group's name was also spelled Dell Vikings on some releases. Both spellings appear with and without a hyphen.				
COME GO WITH ME/How Can I Find True Love?	Fee Bee 205	6.25	25.00	56
DOWN IN BERMUDA/Maggie	Fee Bee 206	6.25	25.00	56
I HEAR BELLS/Don't Get Slick On Me	ABC 10248	1.50	6.00	61
I'LL NEVER STOP CRYING/Bring Back Your Heart	ABC 10208	1.50	6.00	61
I'M SPINNING/You Say You Love Me	Fee Bee 218	6.25	25.00	57
KISS ME/Face The Music	ABC 10278	1.50	6.00	62
PISTOL PACKIN' MAMA/The Sun	Alpine 66	2.50	10.00	60
SOMEWHERE OVER THE RAINBOW/Hey, Senorita	Luniverse 106	3.00	12.00	57
TRUE LOVE/Baby, Let Me Be	Fee Bee 902	5.00	20.00	56
WE THREE/I've Got To Know	Gateway 743	1.50	6.00	64
WHAT MADE MAGGIE RUN?/Down By The Stream	Fee Bee 210	5.00	20.00	56
WHAT MADE MAGGIE RUN?/Uh, Uh, Baby	Fee Bee 210	5.00	20.00	56
WHISPERING BELLS/Don't Be A Fool	Fee Bee 214	6.25	25.00	57
WILLETTE/I Want To Marry You	Fee Bee 221	5.00	20.00	57
WILLETTE/Woke Up This Morning	Fee Bee 221	5.00	20.00	57
DEL-AIRES, The				
ELAINE/Just Wigglin' 'N' Wobblin'	Coral 62370	1.50	6.00	63
DEL-AIRS, The				
I'M LONELY/Why Did He Leave?	Arrawak 1003	1.50	6.00	62
DEL-AIRS, The				
LOST MY JOB/While Walking	M.B.S. 001	2.00	8.00	60

TITLE/FLIP	LABEL & NO.	GOOD TO VERY GOOD	NEAR MINT	YR.
DEL-CHORDS, The				
SAY THAT YOU LOVE ME/Help Me	Jin 126	7.00	28.00	60
DEL-HEARTS, Dale & The				
DEL-KNIGHTS, THE				
DEL-LARDS, Sammy & The				
SLEEPWALK/Little Darling	Stop 101	1.50	6.00	—
DEL-LARKS, Sammy & The				
DEL-LOURDS, The				
ALONE/All Alone	Solar 1001	1.50	6.00	63
GLORIA/All Alone	Solar 1003	1.50	6.00	63
DEL-MARS, The				
THAT'S MY DESIRE/You Know	ABC 10426	1.50	6.00	63
DEL-MINGOS, The				
DEL-PRADOS, The				
OH, BABY/The Skip	Lucky Four 1021	5.00	20.00	—
DEL-RAYS, Detroit, Jr. & The				
DEL-RAYS, The				
DEL-STARS, The				
DELACARDOS, The				
HOLD BACK THE TEARS/Mr. Dillon	United Artists 310	1.50	6.00	61
I GOT IT/Thing-A-Ma-Jig	United Artists 276	1.50	6.00	60
LETTER TO A SCHOOL GIRL/I'll Never Let You Down	Elgey 1001	3.00	12.00	59
DELCOS, The				
THOSE THREE LITTLE WORDS/Arabia	Ebony 01/02	4.00	16.00	62
THOSE THREE LITTLE WORDS/Arabia	Showcase 2501	1.50	6.00	—
DELEGATES, The				
CONVENTION, THE/Jay's Rock (by Big Jay McNeely)	Vee Jay 212	2.00	8.00	56
MOTHER'S SON/I'm Gonna Be Glad	Vee Jay 243	4.00	16.00	57
DELFONICS, The				
DELL VIKINGS, The: see Del Vikings, The				
DELL-O'S, John Shaw & The (same group as The Sensational Dellos)				
WHY DID YOU LEAVE ME?/Why Does It Have To Be Her?	U-C 5002	25.00	100.00	58
DELLAIRS, The				

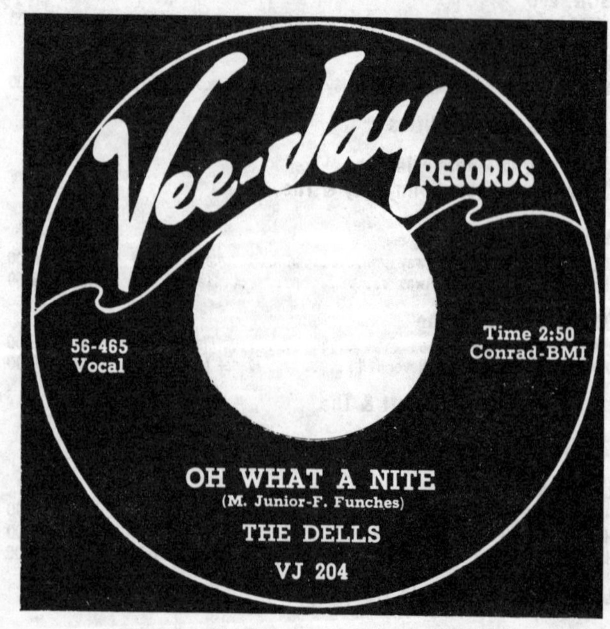

The Diablos

Varetta Dillard

Dominoes

DELLS, The

TITLE/FLIP	LABEL & NO.	GOOD TO VERY GOOD	NEAR MINT	YR.
DISTANT LOVE, A/O-Bop She-Bop	*Vee Jay 251*	2.00	8.00	*57*
DREAMS OF CONTENTMENT/Zing, Zing, Zing	*Vee Jay 166*	10.00	40.00	*55*
DRY YOUR EYES/Baby, Open Up Your Heart	*Vee Jay 324*	1.50	6.00	*59*
I'M CALLING/Jeepers Creepers	*Vee Jay 292*	2.50	10.00	*58*
MOVIN' ON/I Wanna Go Home	*Vee Jay 230*	2.00	8.00	*56*
OH, WHAT A NIGHT/Jo-Jo	*Vee Jay 204*	2.00	8.00	*56*
PAIN IN MY HEART/Time Makes You Change	*Vee Jay 258*	1.50	6.00	*57*
TELL THE WORLD/Blues At Three (by Count Morris) (red plastic)	*Vee Jay 134*	80.00	320.00	*55*
TELL THE WORLD/Blues At Three (by Count Morris)	*Vee Jay 134*	50.00	200.00	*55*
WEDDING DAY/My Best Girl	*Vee Jay 300*	4.00	16.00	*58*
WHY DO YOU HAVE TO GO?/Dance, Dance, Dance	*Vee Jay 236*	1.50	6.00	*57*

DELLTONES, The

DELMONICOS, The

TITLE/FLIP	LABEL & NO.	GOOD TO VERY GOOD	NEAR MINT	YR.
THERE THEY GO/You Can Tell	*Aku (no number)*	2.00	8.00	*63*

DELONGS, The

TITLE/FLIP	LABEL & NO.	GOOD TO VERY GOOD	NEAR MINT	YR.
I WANT YOUR LOVE/You're Never Too Young	*Art Flow 3906*	1.50	6.00	—

DELROYS, The

DELTA JOE:
see Luandrew, Albert as Delta Joe

DELTA RHYTHM BOYS, The

TITLE/FLIP	LABEL & NO.	GOOD TO VERY GOOD	NEAR MINT	YR.
ALL THE THINGS YOU ARE/Lover Come Back To Me	*Mercury 1409*	2.50	10.00	*52*
BLOW OUT THE CANDLE/All The Things You Are	*London 1145*	2.50	10.00	*52*
DON'T ASK ME WHY/Fantastic (78)	*Musicraft 597*	1.50	6.00	*49*
I'LL NEVER GET OUT OF THIS WORLD ALIVE/I'm Used To You	*RCA Victor 47-5094*	2.00	8.00	*52*
I'VE GOT YOU UNDER MY SKIN/The Gypsy In My Soul	*Mercury 1407*	2.50	10.00	*52*
IT'S ALL IN YOUR MIND/Fan Tan Fannie	*Decca 48148*	7.00	28.00	*50*
LAUGH'S ON ME, THE/Sweetheart Of Mine (78)	*Atlantic 889*	2.50	10.00	*49*
LONG GONE BABY/Dancin' With Someone	*RCA Victor 47-5217*	2.00	8.00	*53*
NOBODY KNOWS/If You See Tears In My Eyes (78)	*Atlantic 900*	2.50	10.00	*50*
THEY DIDN'T BELIEVE ME/ On The Sunny Side Of The Street	*Mercury 1408*	2.50	10.00	*52*
YOU ARE CLOSER TO MY HEART/I'd Rather Be Wrong Than Blue	*Decca 48140*	7.00	28.00	*50*
Boxed set of four records:				
(1) **DRY BONES**/September Song	*RCA Victor 47-2826*	2.00	8.00	*49*
(2) **TAKE THE "A" TRAIN**/ East Of The Sun And West Of The Moon	*RCA Victor 47-2827*	2.00	8.00	*49*
(3) **ST. LOUIS BLUES**/ Every Time We Say Goodbye	*RCA Victor 47-2828*	2.00	8.00	*49*
(4) **ONE O'CLOCK JUMP**/ If You Are But A Dream	*RCA Victor 47-2829*	2.00	8.00	*49*
Prices for the complete set, including the box:		9.00	36.00	*49*

DELTAIRS, The (female group)

TITLE/FLIP	LABEL & NO.	GOOD TO VERY GOOD	NEAR MINT	YR.
LULLABY OF THE BELLS/It's Only You, Dear (yellow label)	*Ivy 101*	4.00	16.00	*57*

DELTARS, Pearl & The

TITLE/FLIP	LABEL & NO.	GOOD TO VERY GOOD	NEAR MINT	YR.
TEENAGER'S DREAM/Dance, Dance, Dance	*Fury 1048*	1.50	6.00	*61*

DELTAS, The

TITLE/FLIP	LABEL & NO.	GOOD TO VERY GOOD	NEAR MINT	YR.
LET ME SHARE YOUR DREAM/Lamplight	*Gone 5010*	20.00	80.00	*57*

DELTEENS, The

TITLE/FLIP	LABEL & NO.	GOOD TO VERY GOOD	NEAR MINT	YR.
LISTEN TO THE RAIN/Love Me	*Fortune 541*	5.00	20.00	*61*

DELTONES, Ronnie Baker & The

TITLE/FLIP	LABEL & NO.	GOOD TO VERY GOOD	NEAR MINT	YR.
I WANT TO BE LOVED/My Story	*Laurie 3128*	5.00	20.00	*62*

DEMENS, The

TITLE/FLIP	LABEL & NO.	GOOD TO VERY GOOD	NEAR MINT	YR.
GREATEST OF THEM ALL, THE/Hey, Young Girl	*Teenage 1008*	5.00	20.00	*57*
I'M NOT IN LOVE WITH YOU/Short Daddy	*Teenage 1007*	5.00	20.00	*57*
TAKE ME AS I AM/You Broke My Heart	*Teenage 1006*	5.00	20.00	*57*

DEMIRES, The

TITLE/FLIP	LABEL & NO.	GOOD TO VERY GOOD	NEAR MINT	YR.
WHEELS OF LOVE/The Spiders	*Lunar 519*	2.50	10.00	*59*

DENBY, Junior (of the Swallows)

TITLE/FLIP	LABEL & NO.	GOOD TO VERY GOOD	NEAR MINT	YR.
THIS FOOL HAS LEARNED/If You Only Have Faith In Me	*King 4725*	2.00	8.00	*54*
WITH THIS RING/I'm Still Lonesome	*King 4717*	2.00	8.00	*54*

DENNY & THE LP's:
see LP'S, Denny & The

DERBYS, The

TITLE/FLIP	LABEL & NO.	GOOD TO VERY GOOD	NEAR MINT	YR.
NIGHT AFTER NIGHT/Just Leave Me Alone	*Mercury 71437*	2.50	10.00	*59*

DESANTO, Sugar Pie

DESANTO, Sugar Pie, Etta James &

DESIRES, The

TITLE/FLIP	LABEL & NO.	GOOD TO VERY GOOD	NEAR MINT	YR.
LET IT PLEASE BE YOU/Hey, Lena	*Hull 730*	4.00	16.00	*59*
RENDEZVOUS WITH YOU/Set Me Free	*Hull 733*	5.00	20.00	*60*

DESIRES, The (female group)

TITLE/FLIP	LABEL & NO.	GOOD TO VERY GOOD	NEAR MINT	YR.
BOBBY YOU/Cold Lonely Heart	*Herald 532*	1.50	6.00	*58*

DESTINATIONS, The

DETROIT & THE INTRUDERS

DETROIT COUNT

TITLE/FLIP	LABEL & NO.	GOOD TO VERY GOOD	NEAR MINT	YR.
HASTINGS STREET OPERA, PART 1/Hastings Street Opera, Part 2 (78)	*JVB 75830*	8.00	32.00	*48*
HASTINGS STREET OPERA, PART 1/Hastings Street Opera, Part 2 (78)	*King 4264*	4.00	16.00	*48*
I'M CRAZY ABOUT YOU/Hastings St. Woogie Man (78)	*JVB 75831*	6.25	25.00	*48*
I'M CRAZY ABOUT YOU/Hastings St. Woogie Man (78)	*King 4265*	3.00	12.00	*48*
LITTLE TILLE WILLIE/My Last Call (78)	*King 4279*	2.50	10.00	*48*

DETROIT EMERALDS, The

DETROIT, JR.

DETROIT, Jr., & The Del-Rays

DEVILLES, The

TITLE/FLIP	LABEL & NO.	GOOD TO VERY GOOD	NEAR MINT	YR.
I DO BELIEVE/No Money	*Arrawak 1001*	1.50	6.00	*62*
TELL ME SO/Joan Of Love	*Orbit 540*	1.50	6.00	*59*

DEVINE, Pearl:
see Fabulous Pearl Devines, The

DEVOTIONS, Little Marcus & The

TITLE/FLIP	LABEL & NO.	GOOD TO VERY GOOD	NEAR MINT	YR.
LONE STRANGER WENT MAD/I'll Always Remember	*Gordie 1001*	5.00	20.00	—

DEW DROPS, Little Clem & The

TITLE/FLIP	LABEL & NO.	GOOD TO VERY GOOD	NEAR MINT	YR.
PLEA OF LOVE/Waiting In The Chapel	*Zynn 504*	5.00	20.00	—

DIABLOS, Nolan Strong & The

NOTE: Though Strong was featured on all of the following records, some credited only the group on the label.

TITLE/FLIP	LABEL & NO.	GOOD TO VERY GOOD	NEAR MINT	YR.
BLUE MOON/I Don't Care	*Fortune 544*	1.50	6.00	*62*
CAN'T WE TALK THIS OVER?/The Mambo Of Love	*Fortune 525*	2.00	8.00	*57*
DADDY ROCKIN' STRONG/ Do You Remember What You Did?	*Fortune 516*	2.50	10.00	*55*
GOODBYE, MATILDA/I Am With You	*Fortune 531*	2.50	10.00	*59*
IF I COULD BE WITH YOU/I Wanna Know	*Fortune 532*	2.00	8.00	*59*

TITLE/FLIP	LABEL & NO.	GOOD TO VERY GOOD	NEAR MINT	YR.
IF I, OH I/I Wanna Know	*Fortune 532*	2.00	8.00	*63*
MY HEART WILL ALWAYS BELONG TO YOU/ For Old Time Sake	*Fortune 529*	2.00	8.00	*58*
OLD FASHIONED GIRL, AN/Adios, My Desert Love	*Fortune 509/510*	2.00	8.00	*54*
ROUTE 16/Hold Me Until Eternity	*Fortune 514*	2.50	10.00	*55*
SINCE YOU'RE GONE/Are You Gonna Go?	*Fortune 536*	2.50	10.00	*60*
TRY ME ONE MORE TIME/A Teardrop From Heaven	*Fortune 522*	2.50	10.00	*56*
VILLAGE OF LOVE/Real True Love	*Fortune 563*	1.50	6.00	*64*
WAY YOU DOG ME AROUND, THE/Jump, Shake And Move	*Fortune 518*	2.00	8.00	*55*
WIND, THE/Baby, Be Mine	*Fortune 511*	2.50	10.00	*54*
YOU ARE/You're The Only Girl, Delores	*Fortune 519*	2.00	8.00	*56*

DIABLOS, The

TITLE/FLIP	LABEL & NO.	GOOD TO VERY GOOD	NEAR MINT	YR.
HARRIET/Come Home, Little Girl	*Fortune 841*	2.00	8.00	*58*
MOVIN'/ Movin' (by Andre Williams & The Five Dollars)	*Fortune 851*	1.50	6.00	*60*

DIAMONDS, The

TITLE/FLIP	LABEL & NO.	GOOD TO VERY GOOD	NEAR MINT	YR.
BEGGAR FOR YOUR KISSES, A/Call, Baby, Call	*Atlantic 981*	30.00	120.00	*52*
CHERRY/Romance In The Dark	*Atlantic 1017*	15.00	60.00	*53*
The original first pressing of this record was on thick vinyl only.				
TWO LOVES HAVE I/I'll Live Again	*Atlantic 1003*	20.00	80.00	*53*

DIATONES, The

TITLE/FLIP	LABEL & NO.	GOOD TO VERY GOOD	NEAR MINT	YR.
OH, BABY, COME DANCE WITH ME/Ruby Has Gone	*Bandera 2509*	4.00	16.00	*61*

DIDDLEY, Bo

TITLE/FLIP	LABEL & NO.	GOOD TO VERY GOOD	NEAR MINT	YR.
BO DIDDLEY/I'm A Man	*Checker 814*	2.00	8.00	*55*
DIDDLEY DADDY (with The Moonglows)/ She's Fine, She's Mine	*Checker 819*	2.50	10.00	*55*
DIDDY WAH DIDDY/I'm Looking For A Woman	*Checker 832*	1.50	6.00	*56*
PRETTY THING/Bring It To Jerome	*Checker 827*	1.50	6.00	*55*

DIKES, The (not a female group)

TITLE/FLIP	LABEL & NO.	GOOD TO VERY GOOD	NEAR MINT	YR.
LIGHT ME UP/Don't Leave Poor Me	*Federal 12249*	2.50	10.00	*55*

DILLARD, Varetta

DILLARD, Varetta:

see Cookies, Varetta Dillard & The
see Roamers, Varetta Dillard & The

DILLARD, Varetta & The Four Students

DIMPLES, Eddie Cooley & The

DING DONGS, The

TITLE/FLIP	LABEL & NO.	GOOD TO VERY GOOD	NEAR MINT	YR.
DING DONG/Sweet Thing	*Eldo 109*	1.50	6.00	*60*

DINWIDDIE COLORED QUARTET, The

These are the first black group records ever made. All are one-sided 78s, recorded and released in 1902. The reissues that came out later on the Victor label are somewhat more common and less valuable.

TITLE/FLIP	LABEL & NO.	GOOD TO VERY GOOD	NEAR MINT	YR.
DOWN THE OLD CAMP GROUND	*Monarch 1714*	30.00	120.00	*02*
GABRIEL'S TRUMPET	*Monarch 1725*	25.00	100.00	*02*
MY WAY IS CLOUDY	*Monarch 1724*	25.00	100.00	*02*
POOR MOURNER	*Monarch 1715*	25.00	100.00	*02*
STEAL AWAY	*Monarch 1716*	25.00	100.00	*02*
WE'LL ANCHOR BYE-AND-BYE	*Monarch 1726*	25.00	100.00	*02*

DIPPERS, Georgie Torrence & The

TITLE/FLIP	LABEL & NO.	GOOD TO VERY GOOD	NEAR MINT	YR.
SUCH A FOOL WAS I/Way Over Yonder	*Epic 9453*	1.50	6.00	*61*

DIRTY RED:

see Wilborn, Nelson as Dirty Red

DISCORDS, Willie Loftin & The

TITLE/FLIP	LABEL & NO.	GOOD TO VERY GOOD	NEAR MINT	YR.
BAD HABIT/World Of Make Believe (with Eddie Corner)	*Smoke 101*	1.50	6.00	—

DISTANTS, The

TITLE/FLIP	LABEL & NO.	GOOD TO VERY GOOD	NEAR MINT	YR.
ALWAYS/Come On	*Northern 3732*	3.00	12.00	—
ALWAYS/Come On	*Warwick 546*	2.00	8.00	*60*

DIXIE BLUES BOYS, The

TITLE/FLIP	LABEL & NO.	GOOD TO VERY GOOD	NEAR MINT	YR.
MONTE CARLO/My Baby Left Town	*Flair 1072*	10.00	40.00	*55*

DIXIE CUPS, The (female group)

DIXIEAIRES, The

TITLE/FLIP	LABEL & NO.	GOOD TO VERY GOOD	NEAR MINT	YR.
TRAVELING ALL ALONE/I'm Not Like I Used To Be	*Harlem 2326*	20.00	80.00	*54*

DIXON, Floyd

TITLE/FLIP	LABEL & NO.	GOOD TO VERY GOOD	NEAR MINT	YR.
CALL OPERATOR 210/Wine, Wine, Wine!	*Aladdin 3135*	5.00	20.00	*52*
HARD LIVING ALONE/Please Don't Go (red plastic)	*Specialty 468*	4.00	16.00	*53*
HARD LIVING ALONE/Please Don't Go	*Specialty 468*	2.00	8.00	*53*
HOLE IN THE WALL/Old Memories (red plastic)	*Specialty 477*	4.00	16.00	*53*
HOLE IN THE WALL/Old Memories	*Specialty 477*	2.00	8.00	*53*
OH BABY/Never Can Tell	*Cash 1057*	2.00	8.00	*54*
OOH LITTLE GIRL/What Is Life Without A Home?	*Ebb 105*	2.00	8.00	*54*
OOH-EEE OOH-EE/Nose Trouble (red plastic)	*Specialty 486*	4.00	16.00	*53*
OOH-EEE OOH-EE/Nose Trouble	*Specialty 486*	2.00	8.00	*53*
TIRED, BROKE AND BUSTED/Come Back, Baby	*Aladdin 3151*	5.00	20.00	*52*

DIXON, Floyd & His Band

TITLE/FLIP	LABEL & NO.	GOOD TO VERY GOOD	NEAR MINT	YR.
HEY BARTENDER/Is It True?	*Cat 114*	4.00	16.00	*54*
MOONSHINE/Roll, Baby, Roll	*Cat 106*	2.50	10.00	*54*
RED CHERRIES/The River (red plastic)	*Aladdin 3144*	8.00	32.00	*52*
TIGHT SKIRTS/Wake Up And Live	*Jello 101*	2.00	8.00	*60*

DIXON, Floyd At Frank Bull & Gene Norman's Blues Jubilee

TITLE/FLIP	LABEL & NO.	GOOD TO VERY GOOD	NEAR MINT	YR.
TOO MUCH JELLY ROLL/ Baby, Let's Go Down To The Woods	*Aladdin 3111*	6.25	25.00	*51*

DIXON, Floyd with Johnny Moore's Three Blazers

TITLE/FLIP	LABEL & NO.	GOOD TO VERY GOOD	NEAR MINT	YR.
BAD NEIGHBORHOOD/Blues For Cuba	*Aladdin 3221*	5.00	20.00	*50*
BROKEN HEARTED TRAVELLER/You Played Me For A Fool	*Aladdin 3166*	5.00	20.00	*50*
DO I LOVE YOU?/Time And Place	*Aladdin 3101*	5.00	20.00	*50*
MARRIED WOMAN/Lovin'	*Aladdin 3196*	5.00	20.00	*50*
YOU NEED ME NOW/A Long Time Ago	*Aladdin 3230*	4.00	16.00	*50*

DIXON, Willie

TITLE/FLIP	LABEL & NO.	GOOD TO VERY GOOD	NEAR MINT	YR.
CRAZY FOR MY BABY/I Am The Lover Man	*Checker 828*	1.50	6.00	*55*
TWENTY NINE WAYS/The Pain In My Heart	*Checker 851*	1.50	6.00	*56*
WALKIN' THE BLUES/If You're Mine	*Checker 822*	1.50	6.00	*55*

DIXON, Willie & The All Stars

TITLE/FLIP	LABEL & NO.	GOOD TO VERY GOOD	NEAR MINT	YR.
CRAZY FOR MY BABY/I Am The Lover Man	*Checker 828*	1.50	6.00	*55*
IF YOU'RE MINE/Walkin' The Blues	*Checker 822*	1.50	6.00	*55*
PAIN IN MY HEART, THE/29 Ways	*Checker 851*	1.50	6.00	*56*

DIXON, Willie:

see Big Three Trio, Rosetta Howard & The (with Willie Dixon)
see Big Three Trio, The (with Willie Dixon)
see Five Breezes, The (with Willie Dixon)

DODDS, Malcolm & The Tunedrops

DODGERS, The

TITLE/FLIP	LABEL & NO.	GOOD TO VERY GOOD	NEAR MINT	YR.
CAT HOP/Drip Drop	*Aladdin 3271*	15.00	60.00	*55*
LET'S MAKE A WHOLE LOT OF LOVE/You Make Me Happy	*Aladdin 3259*	8.00	32.00	*54*

DOGGETT, Bill

DOLLARS, Little Eddie & The

TITLE/FLIP	LABEL & NO.	GOOD TO VERY GOOD	NEAR MINT	YR.
YELLOW MOON/My Mamma Said	*Fortune 845*	1.50	6.00	*59*

DOLLS, The:

see Youngtones, The

DOMINEERS, The

TITLE/FLIP	LABEL & NO.	GOOD TO VERY GOOD	NEAR MINT	YR.
NOTHING CAN GO WRONG/Richie, Come On Down	*Roulette 5245*	2.00	8.00	*60*

DOMINO, Fats

TITLE/FLIP	LABEL & NO.	GOOD TO VERY GOOD	NEAR MINT	YR.
AIN'T IT A SHAME?/La-La	*Imperial 5348*	2.00	8.00	*55*
ALL BY MYSELF/Troubles On My Own	*Imperial 5357*	2.00	8.00	*55*
BABY, PLEASE/Where Did You Stay?	*Imperial 5283*	3.00	12.00	*54*
BOOGIE WOOGIE BABY/Little Bee (78)	*Imperial 5065*	2.50	10.00	*50*
BRAND NEW BABY/Hey! La Bas Boogie (78)	*Imperial 5085*	2.50	10.00	*50*
CARELESS LOVE/Rockin' Chair (78)	*Imperial 5145*	1.50	6.00	*51*
DON'T YOU KNOW?/Helping Hand	*Imperial 5340*	2.00	8.00	*55*
DON'T YOU LIE TO ME/Sometimes I Wonder (78)	*Imperial 5123*	2.00	8.00	*51*
FAT MAN, THE/Detroit City Blues (78)	*Imperial 5058*	3.00	12.00	*50*
GOIN' HOME/Reeling And Rocking	*Imperial 5180*	10.00	40.00	*52*
GOING TO THE RIVER/ Mardi Gras In New Orleans (red plastic)	*Imperial 5231*	15.00	60.00	*53*
GOING TO THE RIVER/Mardi Gras In New Orleans	*Imperial 5231*	5.00	20.00	*53*
HOW LONG?/Dreaming (red plastic)	*Imperial 5209*	12.50	50.00	*52*
HOW LONG?/Dreaming	*Imperial 5209*	5.00	20.00	*52*
I KNOW/Thinking Of You	*Imperial 5323*	2.50	10.00	*54*
KOREA BLUES/Every Night About This Time (78)	*Imperial 5099*	2.50	10.00	*50*
LITTLE SCHOOL GIRL/You Done Me Wrong	*Imperial 5272*	3.00	12.00	*54*

TITLE/FLIP	LABEL & NO.	GOOD TO VERY GOOD	NEAR MINT	YR.
LOVE ME/Don't You Hear Me Calling You?	*Imperial 5313*	2.50	10.00	*54*
NOBODY LOVES ME/Cheatin' (red plastic)	*Imperial 5220*	15.00	60.00	*53*
NOBODY LOVES ME/Cheatin'	*Imperial 5220*	5.00	20.00	*53*
PLEASE DON'T LEAVE ME/The Girl I Love	*Imperial 5240*	6.25	25.00	*53*
POOR POOR ME/Trust In Me	*Imperial 5197*	8.00	32.00	*52*
RIGHT FROM WRONG/No, No, Baby (78)	*Imperial 5138*	1.50	6.00	*51*
SHE'S MY BABY/Hide Away Blues (78)	*Imperial 5077*	2.50	10.00	*50*
SOMETHING'S WRONG/Don't Leave Me This Way	*Imperial 5262*	4.00	16.00	*53*
TIRED OF CRYING/What's The Matter, Baby? (78)	*Imperial 5114*	2.00	8.00	*51*
YOU CAN PACK YOUR SUITCASE/I Loved My Life	*Imperial 5301*	2.50	10.00	*54*
YOU KNOW I MISS YOU/I'll Be Gone (78)	*Imperial 5167*	1.50	6.00	*52*
YOU SAID YOU LOVE ME/Rose Mary	*Imperial 5251*	6.25	25.00	*53*

DOMINOES, Billy Ward & The (featuring Jackie Wilson)

TITLE/FLIP	LABEL & NO.	GOOD TO VERY GOOD	NEAR MINT	YR.
ABOVE JACOB'S LADDER/Little Black Train	*Federal 12193*	3.00	12.00	*54*
BOBBY SOX BABY/How Long, How Long Blues	*Federal 12263*	2.00	8.00	*56*
CAN'T DO SIXTY NO MORE/If I Never Get To Heaven	*Federal 12209*	3.00	12.00	*55*
CAVE MAN (recorded in 1953)/ Love Me Now Or Let Me Go	*Federal 12218*	3.00	12.00	*55*
CHRISTMAS IN HEAVEN/Ringing In A Brand New Year	*King 1281*	6.25	25.00	*53*
COME TO ME, BABY/Gimme, Gimme, Gimme	*Jubilee 5163*	1.50	6.00	*54*
HANDWRITING ON THE WALL/One Moment With You	*Federal 12184*	4.00	16.00	*54*
I'D BE SATISFIED/No Room	*Federal 12105*	5.00	20.00	*52*
LEARNIN' THE BLUES/May I Never Love Again	*King 1492*	3.00	12.00	*55*
LITTLE LIE, A/Tenderly	*King 1342*	3.00	12.00	*54*
LITTLE THINGS MEAN A LOT/I Really Don't Want To Know	*King 1368*	3.00	12.00	*54*
MY BABY'S 3-D/Until The Real Thing Comes Along	*Federal 12162*	4.00	16.00	*54*
OVER THE RAINBOW/Give Me You	*King 1502*	4.00	16.00	*55*
PEDAL PUSHIN' PAPA/The Bells	*Federal 12114*	15.00	60.00	*52*
RAGS TO RICHES/Don't Thank Me	*King 1280*	3.00	12.00	*53*
ST. LOUIS BLUES (recorded in 1954)/One Moment With You (recorded in 1953)	*Federal 12301*	1.50	6.00	*57*
SWEETHEARTS ON PARADE/Take Me Back To Heaven	*Jubilee 5213*	1.50	6.00	*55*
THESE FOOLISH THINGS REMIND ME OF YOU/Don't Leave Me This Way	*Federal 12129*	15.00	60.00	*53*

Both songs were recorded in 1951. This was the last "gold top" release on Federal. The gold color on the top half of their labels was replaced with silver after this, and eventually became all green.

TITLE/FLIP	LABEL & NO.	GOOD TO VERY GOOD	NEAR MINT	YR.
THREE COINS IN THE FOUNTAIN/Lonesome Road	*King 1364*	3.00	12.00	*54*
TOOTSIE ROLL/The Outskirts Of Town	*Federal 12178*	4.00	16.00	*54*
WHERE NOW, LITTLE HEART?/You Can't Keep A Good Man Down	*Federal 12139*	4.00	16.00	*53*
YOURS FOREVER/I'm Lonely	*Federal 12106*	5.00	20.00	*52*

DOMINOES, Little Esther (Phillips) & The

TITLE/FLIP	LABEL & NO.	GOOD TO VERY GOOD	NEAR MINT	YR.
DEACON MOVES IN, THE/Other Lips, Other Arms	*Federal 12016*	60.00	240.00	*51*
HEART TO HEART/Lookin' For A Man (no group)	*Federal 12036*	50.00	200.00	*51*

DOMINOES, The (featuring Clyde McPhatter)

TITLE/FLIP	LABEL & NO.	GOOD TO VERY GOOD	NEAR MINT	YR.
DO SOMETHING FOR ME/Chicken Blues	*Federal 12001*	40.00	160.00	*50*
HARBOR LIGHTS/No! Says My Heart	*Federal 12010*	85.00	340.00	*51*
HAVE MERCY, BABY/Deep Sea Blues	*Federal 12068*	15.00	60.00	*52*
HAVE MERCY, BABY/Love, Love, Love	*Federal 12308*	1.50	6.00	*57*
I AM WITH YOU/Weeping Willow Blues	*Federal 12039*	25.00	100.00	*51*
LOVE, LOVE, LOVE/That's What You're Doing To Me	*Federal 12072*	10.00	40.00	*52*
SIXTY MINUTE MAN/I Can't Escape From You	*Federal 12022*	15.00	60.00	*51*
THAT'S WHAT YOU'RE DOING TO ME/When The Swallows Come Back To Capistrano	*Federal 12059*	50.00	200.00	*52*

DON & DEWEY & THE TITANS:
see Titans, Don & Dewey & The

DON CLAIRS, Harold Perkins & The

TITLE/FLIP	LABEL & NO.	GOOD TO VERY GOOD	NEAR MINT	YR.
I LOST MY JOB/Santa Fe	*Amp 3-1001/1002*	3.00	12.00	*58*

DON JUANS, Andre Williams & The

TITLE/FLIP	LABEL & NO.	GOOD TO VERY GOOD	NEAR MINT	YR.
COME ON, BABY/The Greasy Chicken (no group)	*Fortune 839*	1.50	6.00	*57*
IT'S ALL OVER/Bobby Jean	*Fortune 828*	1.50	6.00	*56*
MY LAST DANCE WITH YOU/Hey! Country Girl	*Fortune 842*	1.50	6.00	*58*
PULLING TIME/Going Down To Tia Juana	*Fortune 824*	2.00	8.00	*55*

DON JUANS, Don Lake & The

TITLE/FLIP	LABEL & NO.	GOOD TO VERY GOOD	NEAR MINT	YR.
OOH, OOH, THOSE EYES/Cha-Cha Of Love	*Fortune 520*	4.00	16.00	*56*

DON JUANS, Joe Weaver & The

TITLE/FLIP	LABEL & NO.	GOOD TO VERY GOOD	NEAR MINT	YR.
BABY, I LOVE YOU SO/It Must Be Love (no group)	*Fortune 825*	1.50	6.00	*56*
LOOKA HERE, PRETTY BABY/Baby Child	*Fortune 832*	1.50	6.00	*57*

DON JUANS, Little Eddie & The

TITLE/FLIP	LABEL & NO.	GOOD TO VERY GOOD	NEAR MINT	YR.
THIS IS A MIRACLE/Calypso Beat	*Fortune 836*	2.00	8.00	*57*

DON JUANS, The

TITLE/FLIP	LABEL & NO.	GOOD TO VERY GOOD	NEAR MINT	YR.
GIRL OF MY DREAMS, THE/Dolores	*Onezy 101*	5.00	20.00	—

DONNA, Vic., & The Parakeets:
see Parakeets, Vic. Donna & The

DOOTONES, The

TITLE/FLIP	LABEL & NO.	GOOD TO VERY GOOD	NEAR MINT	YR.
SAILOR BOY/Down The Road	*Dooto 471*	4.00	16.00	*62*
STRANGE LOVE AFFAIR/The Day You Said Goodbye	*Dooto 470*	4.00	16.00	*62*
TELLER OF FORTUNE/Ay, Si, Si	*Dootone 366*	10.00	40.00	*55*

DORSETS, The

DORSEY, Lee

DOTS, The (with Jeanette Baker) (female group)

TITLE/FLIP	LABEL & NO.	GOOD TO VERY GOOD	NEAR MINT	YR.
GOOD LUCK TO YOU/Heartsick And Lonely	*Caddy 111*	2.00	8.00	*57*
I CONFESS/I Wish I Could Meet You	*Caddy 101*	2.50	10.00	*56*
I LOST YOU/Johnny	*Caddy 107*	2.00	8.00	*57*

DOTSON, Big Bill & His Guitar

TITLE/FLIP	LABEL & NO.	GOOD TO VERY GOOD	NEAR MINT	YR.
DARK OLD WORLD/Thinking Life Over (78)	*Blues & Rhythm 7004*	5.00	20.00	*50*

DOTSON, Jimmy

TITLE/FLIP	LABEL & NO.	GOOD TO VERY GOOD	NEAR MINT	YR.
OH BABY/I Need Your Love	*Rocko 516*	1.50	6.00	*60*

DOTSON, Jimmy & The Blues Boys

TITLE/FLIP	LABEL & NO.	GOOD TO VERY GOOD	NEAR MINT	YR.
I WANNA KNOW/Looking For My Baby	*Zynn 511*	1.50	6.00	*62*

DOUGLAS, K. C.

TITLE/FLIP	LABEL & NO.	GOOD TO VERY GOOD	NEAR MINT	YR.
LONELY BLUES/K. C. Boogie	*Hollywood 1040*	5.00	20.00	*54*
LONELY BLUES/K. C. Boogie	*Rhythm 1780*	10.00	40.00	*54*
MERCURY BOOGIE/Eclipse Of The Sun (78)	*Down Town 2004*	4.00	16.00	*48*
MERCURY BOOGIE/Eclipse Of The Sun (78)	*Gilt Edge 5043*	2.50	10.00	*48*

DOUGLAS, Lizzie as Memphis Minnie

TITLE/FLIP	LABEL & NO.	GOOD TO VERY GOOD	NEAR MINT	YR.
WHY DID I MAKE YOU CRY?/Kidman Blues (78)	*Regal 3259*	3.00	12.00	*50*

DOUGLAS, Lizzie as Memphis Minnie & Her Combo

TITLE/FLIP	LABEL & NO.	GOOD TO VERY GOOD	NEAR MINT	YR.
KISSING IN THE DARK/World Of Trouble	*JOB 1101*	25.00	100.00	*54*

DOUGLAS, Lizzie as Memphis Minnie With Little Joe & His Band

TITLE/FLIP	LABEL & NO.	GOOD TO VERY GOOD	NEAR MINT	YR.
BROKEN HEART/Me And My Chauffeur	*Checker 771*	20.00	80.00	*52*

DOUGLAS, Shy Guy:
see Douglas, Thomas as Shy Guy Douglas

DOUGLAS, Thomas as Shy Guy Douglas

TITLE/FLIP	LABEL & NO.	GOOD TO VERY GOOD	NEAR MINT	YR.
DETROIT ARROW/New Memphis Blues	*Excello 2008*	7.00	28.00	*53*
I'M YOUR COUNTRY MAN/Wasted Time	*Excello 2024*	7.00	28.00	*54*
NO PLACE LIKE HOME/She's My Kinda Girl	*Excello 2032*	6.25	25.00	*54*
WHAT'S THIS I HEAR?/Monkey Doin' Woman	*Todd 1092*	1.50	6.00	*66*
YANKEE DOODLE/Harvest Moon	*Chane 517*	1.50	6.00	*54*

DOVERS, Miriam Grate & The

TITLE/FLIP	LABEL & NO.	GOOD TO VERY GOOD	NEAR MINT	YR.
MY ANGEL/Please Squeeze	*Apollo 472*	10.00	40.00	*55*

DOVERS, The

TITLE/FLIP	LABEL & NO.	GOOD TO VERY GOOD	NEAR MINT	YR.
SWEET AS A FLOWER/Boy In My Life	*Davis 465*	1.50	6.00	*59*

DOVES, Cliff Butler & The

TITLE/FLIP	LABEL & NO.	GOOD TO VERY GOOD	NEAR MINT	YR.
WHEN YOU LOVE/People Will Talk	*States 123*	10.00	40.00	*53*

DOWN TOWN TRIO, The

TITLE/FLIP	LABEL & NO.	GOOD TO VERY GOOD	NEAR MINT	YR.
MAKE LOVE TO ME, BABY/Down Town Shuffle (78)	*Down Town 2017*	5.00	20.00	*48*

DOWNBEATS, O. S. Grant & The

TITLE/FLIP	LABEL & NO.	GOOD TO VERY GOOD	NEAR MINT	YR.
FALLING STARS/I Just Can't Understand	*Sarg 197*	4.00	16.00	—
YOU DID ME WRONG/Tanya	*Sarg 200*	2.50	10.00	—

DOWNBEATS, The

TITLE/FLIP	LABEL & NO.	GOOD TO VERY GOOD	NEAR MINT	YR.
COME ON OVER (BABY)/Darling Of Mine	*Sarg 168*	4.00	16.00	—
COME ON OVER/Lady Of The Sea	*Sarg 162*	4.00	16.00	—
I COULDN'T SEE/Oh, Please	*Sarg 186*	4.00	16.00	—
RUN TO ME, BABY/I Need Your Love	*Sarg 173*	4.00	16.00	—

DOWNBEATS, The

TITLE/FLIP	LABEL & NO.	GOOD TO VERY GOOD	NEAR MINT	YR.
LET'S GO STEADY/So Many Tears	*Peacock 1679*	1.50	6.00	*58*
MY GIRL/China Doll	*Gee 1019*	6.25	25.00	*56*
SOMEDAY SHE'LL COME ALONG/You're So Fine	*Peacock 1689*	1.50	6.00	*59*

DOWNING, Big Al

TITLE/FLIP	LABEL & NO.	GOOD TO VERY GOOD	NEAR MINT	YR.
DOWN ON THE FARM/Oh, Babe	*White Rock 1111*	8.00	32.00	*58*
MISS LUCY/Just Around The Corner	*Carlton 489*	2.50	10.00	*58*
MISS LUCY/Just Around The Corner	*White Rock 1113*	8.00	32.00	*58*

The Drifters

The Eldorados

TITLE/FLIP	LABEL & NO.	GOOD TO VERY GOOD	NEAR MINT	YR.

DOZIER BOYS, Andrew Tibbs & The:
see Tibbs, Andrew & The Dozier Boys

DOZIER BOYS, The

TITLE/FLIP	LABEL & NO.	GOOD TO VERY GOOD	NEAR MINT	YR.
BIG TIME BABY/Music Goes 'Round And 'Round (78)	Aristocrat 3002	2.50	10.00	49
EARLY MORNING BLUES/Cold, Cold Rain	United 163	5.00	20.00	53
EARLY MORNING BLUES/Special Kind Of Lovin'	Fraternity 767	4.00	16.00	57
I KEEP THINKING OF YOU/Linger Awhile	United 143	5.00	20.00	53
MY HEART IS YOURS/I Am So	Apt 25014	4.00	16.00	58
SHE ONLY FOOLS WITH ME/St. Louis Blues (78)	Aristocrat 3001	2.50	10.00	49
SHE'S GONE/All I Need Is You (78)	Aristocrat 409	2.50	10.00	50
YOU GOT TO GET IT/Pretty Eyes (78)	Chess 1436	2.50	10.00	50

DRAMATICS, The

DRAPERS, The

TITLE/FLIP	LABEL & NO.	GOOD TO VERY GOOD	NEAR MINT	YR.
BEST LOVE/One More Time	Vest 831	2.00	8.00	—

DREAM GIRLS, Bobbie Smith & The (female group)

DREAM GIRLS, The (female group)

DREAM KINGS, The

TITLE/FLIP	LABEL & NO.	GOOD TO VERY GOOD	NEAR MINT	YR.
M.T.Y.L.T.T./Oh, What A Baby	Checker 858	4.00	16.00	57

DREAM TIMERS, The

DREAMERS, Bubber Johnson & The

TITLE/FLIP	LABEL & NO.	GOOD TO VERY GOOD	NEAR MINT	YR.
FORGET IF YOU CAN/I've Got An Invitation To A Dance	Mercury 8285	5.00	20.00	52

DREAMERS, Richard Berry & The

TITLE/FLIP	LABEL & NO.	GOOD TO VERY GOOD	NEAR MINT	YR.
AT LAST/Bye, Bye	Flair 1052	2.00	8.00	55
DADDY, DADDY/Baby Darling	Flair 1058	2.00	8.00	55
JELLY ROLL/Together	Flair 1075	2.00	8.00	55

DREAMERS, The

TITLE/FLIP	LABEL & NO.	GOOD TO VERY GOOD	NEAR MINT	YR.
DO NOT FORGET/Since You've Been Gone	Flip 319	1.50	6.00	56

DREAMERS, The

TITLE/FLIP	LABEL & NO.	GOOD TO VERY GOOD	NEAR MINT	YR.
NO MAN IS AN ISLAND/Melba	Rollin' 1001	12.50	50.00	—
TEARS IN MY EYES/535	Grand 131	10.00	40.00	55

DREAMERS, The

TITLE/FLIP	LABEL & NO.	GOOD TO VERY GOOD	NEAR MINT	YR.
I'M GONNA HATE MYSELF IN THE MORNING/Ain't Gonna Worry No More	Mercury 5843	15.00	60.00	52
WALKIN' MY BLUES AWAY/Please Don't Leave Me	Mercury 70019	15.00	60.00	52

DREAMLOVERS, The

TITLE/FLIP	LABEL & NO.	GOOD TO VERY GOOD	NEAR MINT	YR.
AMAZONS AND COYOTEES/Together	Casino 1308	1.50	6.00	—
ANNABELLE LEE/Home Is Where The Heart Is	V-Tone 211	1.50	6.00	60
CALLING JO-ANN/You Gave Me Somebody To Love	Mercury 72630	1.50	6.00	66
PRETTY LITTLE GIRL/I'm Thru With You	Columbia 42842	5.00	20.00	63
TIME/May I Kiss The Bride	V-Tone 229	1.50	6.00	61

DREAMS, The

TITLE/FLIP	LABEL & NO.	GOOD TO VERY GOOD	NEAR MINT	YR.
DARLENE/A Letter To My Girl	Savoy 1130	8.00	32.00	54
I'LL BE FAITHFUL/My Little Honeybun	Savoy 1157	2.50	10.00	55
I'M LOSING MY MIND/Under The Willow	Savoy 1140	7.00	28.00	54

DREAMTONES, The

TITLE/FLIP	LABEL & NO.	GOOD TO VERY GOOD	NEAR MINT	YR.
LOVER'S ANSWER, A/Mean Man	Astra 551	1.50	6.00	59
PRAYING FOR A MIRACLE/Jelly Bean	Express 501	8.00	32.00	59
STAND BEHIND ME/Love Me In The Afternoon	Klik 8505	8.00	32.00	—

DRELLS, Archie Bell & The

DREW-VELS, The (with Patti Drew)

DREW, Patti

DRIFTERS, Clyde McPhatter & The

TITLE/FLIP	LABEL & NO.	GOOD TO VERY GOOD	NEAR MINT	YR.
BIP BAM/Someday You'll Want Me To Want You	Atlantic 1043	2.00	8.00	54
HONEY LOVE/Warm Your Heart	Atlantic 1029	5.00	20.00	54
MONEY HONEY/The Way I Feel	Atlantic 1006	6.25	25.00	53
SUCH A NIGHT/Lucille	Atlantic 1019	5.00	20.00	54
WHATCHA GONNA DO?/Gone	Atlantic 1055	1.50	6.00	55
WHITE CHRISTMAS/The Bells Of St. Mary's	Atlantic 1048	2.00	8.00	54

DRIFTERS, The (featuring Johnny Moore)

TITLE/FLIP	LABEL & NO.	GOOD TO VERY GOOD	NEAR MINT	YR.
ADORABLE/Steamboat	Atlantic 1078	1.50	6.00	55
FOOLS FALL IN LOVE/It Was A Tear	Atlantic 1123	1.50	6.00	57
I GOT TO GET MYSELF A WOMAN/Soldier Of Fortune	Atlantic 1101	1.50	6.00	56
RUBY BABY/Your Promise To Be Mine	Atlantic 1089	1.50	6.00	56

DRIFTERS, The

TITLE/FLIP	LABEL & NO.	GOOD TO VERY GOOD	NEAR MINT	YR.
WORLD IS CHANGING, THE/Sacroiliac Swing	Crown 108	15.00	60.00	54

DRIFTERS, The

TITLE/FLIP	LABEL & NO.	GOOD TO VERY GOOD	NEAR MINT	YR.
AND I SHOOK/I Had To Find Out For Myself	Coral 65040	15.00	60.00	50
WINE HEADED WOMAN/I'm The Caring Kind	Coral 65037	20.00	80.00	50

DRIFTIN' SLIM:
see Mickle, Elmon as Driftin' Slim

DRIFTING CHARLES (Charles Tyler)

DRINK SMALL & HIS GUITAR

DRIVERS & THE SPACEMEN, The

TITLE/FLIP	LABEL & NO.	GOOD TO VERY GOOD	NEAR MINT	YR.
DOE DOE/Ho, Ho	Alton 252	2.50	10.00	59

DRIVERS, Leroy & The

DRIVERS, The

TITLE/FLIP	LABEL & NO.	GOOD TO VERY GOOD	NEAR MINT	YR.
MY LONELY PRAYER/Midnight Hours	De Luxe 6104	4.00	16.00	57
OH, MISS NELLIE/Dangerous Lips	De Luxe 6117	4.00	16.00	57
SMOOTH, SLOW AND EASY/Women	De Luxe 6094	4.00	16.00	56

DU DROPPERS, Sunny Gale & The

TITLE/FLIP	LABEL & NO.	GOOD TO VERY GOOD	NEAR MINT	YR.
NOTE IN THE BOTTLE, THE/Mama's Gone, Goodbye	RCA Victor 47-5543	2.00	8.00	53

DU DROPPERS, The

TITLE/FLIP	LABEL & NO.	GOOD TO VERY GOOD	NEAR MINT	YR.
CAN'T DO SIXTY NO MORE/Chain Me, Baby (red plastic)	Red Robin 108	20.00	80.00	52
CAN'T DO SIXTY NO MORE/Chain Me, Baby	Red Robin 108	7.00	28.00	52
COME ON AND LOVE ME, BABY/Go Back	Red Robin 116	5.00	20.00	53
DEAD BROKE/Speed King	Groove 0001	4.00	16.00	54
DON'T PASS ME BY/Get Lost	RCA Victor 47-5504	2.50	10.00	53
I FOUND OUT/Little Girl, Little Girl	RCA Victor 47-5321	2.50	10.00	53
I WANNA KNOW/Laughing Blues	RCA Victor 47-5229	2.50	10.00	53
JUST WHISPER/How Much Longer?	Groove 0013	8.00	32.00	54
LET NATURE TAKE ITS COURSE/Boot 'Em Up	Groove 0036	4.00	16.00	54
TALK THAT TALK/Give Me Some Consideration	Groove 0104	4.00	16.00	55
WHATEVER YOU'RE DOIN'/Somebody Work On My Baby's Mind	RCA Victor 47-5425	2.50	10.00	53
YOU'RE MINE ALREADY/I Wanna Love You	Groove 0120	3.00	12.00	55

DU MAURIERS, The

TITLE/FLIP	LABEL & NO.	GOOD TO VERY GOOD	NEAR MINT	YR.
BABY, I LOVE YOU/All Night Long	Fury 1011	4.00	16.00	57

DUBS, Richard Blandon & The

DUBS, The

TITLE/FLIP	LABEL & NO.	GOOD TO VERY GOOD	NEAR MINT	YR.
BE SURE, MY LOVE/Song In My Heart	Gone 5034	1.50	6.00	58
BESIDE MY LOVE/Gonna Make A Change	Gone 5020	1.50	6.00	58
DON'T ASK ME TO BE LONELY/Darling	Gone 5002	4.00	16.00	57
DON'T ASK ME TO BE LONELY/Darling	Gone 5002	8.00	32.00	57
Some labels were printed with a double image "shadow" and 3-D lettering. These are worth twice the regular issue.				
DON'T ASK ME TO BE LONELY/Darling	Johnson 102	10.00	40.00	57
DON'T LAUGH AT ME/You'll Never Belong To Me	ABC 10100	1.50	6.00	60
DOWN, DOWN, DOWN I GO/Lullaby	ABC 10269	1.50	6.00	61
FOR THE FIRST TIME/Ain't That So?	ABC 10150	1.50	6.00	60
IF I ONLY HAD MAGIC/Joogie Boogie	ABC 10198	1.50	6.00	61
NO ONE/Early In The Evening	ABC 10056	1.50	6.00	59

DUCES OF RHYTHM & The Tempo Toppers, The (featuring Little Richard)

TITLE/FLIP	LABEL & NO.	GOOD TO VERY GOOD	NEAR MINT	YR.
ALWAYS/Rice, Red Beans & Turnip Greens	Peacock 1628	10.00	40.00	54
FOOL AT THE WHEEL, A/Ain't That Good News	Peacock 1616	8.00	32.00	53

DUCHESS, The

TITLE/FLIP	LABEL & NO.	GOOD TO VERY GOOD	NEAR MINT	YR.
MONKEY, THE/The Wang (instrumental by Jake Porter)	Combo 2	5.00	20.00	53

DUCHESSES, The (female group)

TITLE/FLIP	LABEL & NO.	GOOD TO VERY GOOD	NEAR MINT	YR.
EVERY BOY IN TOWN/Will I Ever Make It?	Chief 7023	2.50	10.00	60

DUDADS, The

TITLE/FLIP	LABEL & NO.	GOOD TO VERY GOOD	NEAR MINT	YR.
I HEARD YOU CALL ME DEAR/My Baby Misses Me, Too	De Luxe 6083	7.00	28.00	55

DUDLEY, Bo

TITLE/FLIP	LABEL & NO.	GOOD TO VERY GOOD	NEAR MINT	YR.
SHOTGUN RIDER/Coast To Coast	F-M 745	1.50	6.00	—

DUKAYS, The (with Gene Chandler)

DUKES, The

TITLE/FLIP	LABEL & NO.	GOOD TO VERY GOOD	NEAR MINT	YR.
I LOVE YOU/Leap Year Cha Cha	Flip 345	1.50	6.00	59
LOOKING FOR YOU/Groceries, Sir	Flip 343	1.50	6.00	59

Billy "The Kid" Emerson

The Falcons

The Flairs

TITLE/FLIP	LABEL & NO.	GOOD TO VERY GOOD	NEAR MINT	YR.

DUKES, The

OOH BOP SHE BOP/Oh-Kay	Specialty 543	5.00	20.00	54
TEARDROP EYES/Shimmies And The Shakes	Imperial 5401	9.00	36.00	56
WINI BROWN/Cotton Pickin' Hands	Imperial 5415	7.00	28.00	56

DUNCAN, Cleve & The Penguins

DUNCAN, Cleve & The Radiants

DUNDEES, Carlyle Dundee & The

NEVER/Evil One	Space 201	12.50	50.00	—

DUNHAM, Andrew

SWEET LUCY/Hattie Mae (78)	Sensation 23	7.00	28.00	49

DUNN, Fred & His Barrelhouse Rhythm

BABY, DON'T FEEL LOWDOWN/The Morning After (78)	Signature 1027	1.50	6.00	46
FRED'S BOOGIE WOOGIE/Blues Before Sunrise (78)	Signature 1026	1.50	6.00	46
RAILROAD BLUES/Mountain Blues (78)	Signature 3201	1.50	6.00	46

DUPONT, Shell & The Calendars

DUPONTS, The (featuring Little Anthony Guardine)

PROVE IT TONIGHT/Somebody	Royal Roost 627	5.00	20.00	56
YOU/Must Be Falling In Love	Winley 212	3.00	12.00	56

DUPREE, Champion Jack:
see Dupree, William Thomas as Champion Jack Dupree

DUPREE, William Thomas as Blind Boy Johnson & His Rhythms

MEAN OLD 'FRISCO/When You Ain't Got A Dime (78)	Lenox 511	1.50	6.00	45

DUPREE, William Thomas as Brother Blues & The Back Room Boys

FEATHERWEIGHT MAMA/Day Break (78)	Abbey 3015	2.50	10.00	49

DUPREE, William Thomas as Champion Jack Dupree

HIGHWAY BLUES/Shake, Baby, Shake	Red Robin 112	12.50	50.00	58
RUB A LITTLE BOOGIE/Hard Feeling	King 4706	2.00	8.00	53
SHIM SHAM SHIMMY/Drunk Again	Red Robin 130	12.50	50.00	53
STUMBLIN' BLOCK BLUES/Number Nine Blues	Red Robin 109	12.50	50.00	53
WALKIN' UPSIDE YOUR HEAD/	King 4695	2.00	8.00	53

DUPREE, William Thomas as Champion Jack Dupree & His Country Blues Band

COME BACK, BABY/Chittlins And Rice (78)	Apollo 407	1.50	6.00	49

DUPREE, William Thomas as Champion Jack Dupree & His Combo

DIRTY WOMAN/Just Like A Woman	Vik X-0260	2.00	8.00	57
OLD TIME ROCK & ROLL/Rocky Mountain	Vik X-0279	2.00	8.00	57

DUPREE, William Thomas as Champion Jack Dupree with Big Chief Ellis & His Blues Stars

DEACON'S PARTY/I'm Gonna Find You Someday (78)	Apollo 426	1.50	6.00	50
MY BABY'S COMIN' BACK HOME/Just Plain Tired (78)	Apollo 428	1.50	6.00	50

DUPREE, William Thomas as Duke Bayou & His Mystic 6

RUB A LITTLE BOOGIE/Doomed (78)	Apollo 440	1.50	6.00	50

DUPREE, William Thomas as Jack Dupree & His Band

LONESOME BEDROOM BLUES/Old Woman Blues (78)	Apollo 421	1.50	6.00	49
ONE SWEET LETTER/Mean Mistreatin' Mama	Apollo 413	1.50	6.00	49

DUPREE, William Thomas as Jack Dupree & His Quartet

FIFTH AVENUE BLUES/Highway 51 (78)	Alert 421	1.50	6.00	46

DUPREE, William Thomas as Jack Dupree & Mr. Bear

LONELY ROAD BLUES/When I Got Married	Groove 4G-0171	2.00	8.00	56

DUPREE, William Thomas as Lightnin' Jr. & The Empires

Dupree should not be confused with L. C. Williams, who also recorded as Lightnin' Junior.

RAGGED AND HUNGRY/Somebody Changed The Lock On My Door	Harlem 2334	15.00	60.00	55

DUPREE, William Thomas as Meat Head Johnson

GOIN' BACK TO LOUISIANA/Barrelhouse Mama (78)	Apex 1110	2.00	8.00	50
OLD, OLD WOMAN/Mean Black Woman (78)	Gotham 514	1.50	6.00	50

DUPREE, William Thomas as The Champion Jack Dupree Trio

BIG LEGGED MAMA/I'm A Doctor For Women (78)	Celebrity 2012	1.50	6.00	46
COUNTY JAIL SPECIAL/Fisherman's Blues (78)	Joe Davis 5103	1.50	6.00	46
F. D. R. Blues/God Bless Our New President (78)	Joe Davis 5102	1.50	6.00	46
FORGET IT, MAMA/You've Been Drunk (78)	Joe Davis 5106	1.50	6.00	46
GOING DOWN SLOW/Mean Old Frisco (78)	Continental 6066	1.50	6.00	45
HOW LONG, HOW LONG BLUES/I Think You Need A Shot (78)	Continental 6064	1.50	6.00	45
JOHNSON STREET BOOGIE WOOGIE/I'm Going Down With You (78)	Joe Davis 5101	1.50	6.00	46
LET'S HAVE A BALL/Hard Feeling (78)	Continental 6065	1.50	6.00	45
LOVE STRIKE BLUES/Wet Deck Mama (78)	Joe Davis 5108	1.50	6.00	46
LOVER'S LANE/Black Wolf (78)	Joe Davis 5104	1.50	6.00	46
RUM COLA BLUES/She Makes Good Jelly (78)	Joe Davis 5100	1.50	6.00	46
SANTA CLAUS BLUES/Cin Mill Sal (78)	Joe Davis 5107	1.50	6.00	46
WALKIN' BY MYSELF/Outside Man (78)	Joe Davis 5105	1.50	6.00	46

DUPREE, William Thomas as Willie Jordan & His Swinging Five

CECELIA, CECELIA/Going Down To The Bottom (78)	Alert 207	1.50	6.00	46

DURST, Lavada as L. Durst or Dr. Hepcat

HATTIE GREEN/I Cried (as Dr. Hepcat) (78)	Peacock 1509	2.00	8.00	49

DUVALS, Phil Johnson & The

KISSES LEFT UNKISSED/Three Speed Girl (by The Royal Notes)	Kelit 7032	7.00	28.00	—
WEE SMALL HOURS/You Are My Love (by The Royal Notes)	Kelit 7034	7.00	28.00	—

DUVALS, The:
see Five Crowns, The
see Royal Notes, The

DWELLERS, The

OH, SWEETIE/What's That Thing Called Love?	Oasis 101	7.00	28.00	59
TELL ME WHY/Annie	Howard 503	9.00	36.00	—

DYNAMICS, The

I GUESS YOU DON'T LOVE ME NO MORE/Oh, Night Of Nights	Do-Kay-Lo 101	3.00	12.00	—

DYSON, Ronnie

EAGER, Brenda Lee, Jerry Butler &

EAGER, Jimmy & His Trio:
see Whittaker, Hudson as Jimmy Eager

EAGLES, The

I TOLD MYSELF/What A Crazy Feeling	Mercury 70524	1.50	6.00	54
SUCH A FOOL/Don't You Wanna Be Mine?	Mercury 70464	2.00	8.00	54
TRYIN' TO GET TO YOU/Please, Please	Mercury 70391	1.50	6.00	54

EARTHQUAKES & THE RHYTHM KINGS, The

LOOK WHAT YOU'VE DONE/Baby, Only You	Fortune 549	2.00	8.00	62
THIS IS REALLY REAL/Crazy Bop	Fortune 538	2.00	8.00	60

EARTHQUAKES, The

DARLING, BE MINE/Bashful Guy	Fortune 534	2.00	8.00	59

EASLEY, Benny

YOU SAY YOU LOVE ME/Kiss Tomorrow Goodbye	Worlds 123	2.50	10.00	—

EASTMEN, The

LOVER, COME HOME/Bye, Bye, My Baby	Mercury 71434	1.50	6.00	59

EASTON, Amos & His Orchestra

STRANGE ANGEL/Lonesome Trail Blues (78)	Specialty 410	1.50	6.00	51

EASTON, Amos as Bumble Bee Slim

LONESOME OLD FEELING/Ida Red (78)	Fidelity 3004	1.50	6.00	51

EASTON, Amos as King Bumble Bee Slim & His Pacific Coast Senders

TWO GUITAR'S BATTLE/Twin Beds (78)	Marigold (no number)	2.00	8.00	51

TITLE/FLIP	LABEL & NO.	GOOD TO VERY GOOD	NEAR MINT	YR.
EBB-TONES, Don Grissom & The				
RECESS IN HEAVEN/Just Fall In Love	*Million $ 2011*	6.25	25.00	*56*
EBB-TONES, The				
BABY/What Makes A Man Fool Around?	*Crest 1024*	3.00	12.00	*56*
DUST OFF THE BIBLE/Hum	*Crest 1032*	2.50	10.00	*57*
I WANT YOU ONLY/That's All	*Crest 1016*	3.00	12.00	*56*
EBBONAIRS, Jake Porter & The				
DOODLE DOO DOO/S'posin'	*Combo 110*	1.50	6.00	*55*
ROSETTA/Sioux City Sue	*Combo 126*	1.50	6.00	*56*
YOU/Bring Me A Bluebird	*Combo 111*	1.50	6.00	*55*
EBBTIDES, David Ford & The				
MY CONFESSION/The Sound Of Your Voice	*Specialty 588*	4.00	16.00	*56*
EBBTIDES, The				
LONESOME/Love Doctor	*Jan Lar 101*	2.50	10.00	—
EBBTONES, The				
I'VE GOT A FEELING/Danny's Blues	*Ebb 100*	4.00	16.00	*57*
EBONAIRES, The				
COME IN, MR. BLUES/Bye, Bye, Bye, Bye (78)	*MGM 10361*	2.00	8.00	*49*
SOMEWHERE IN MY HEART/Love Call	*Lena 1001*	2.50	10.00	*59*
SONG OF THE WANDERER/Sleepy Time Gal (78)	*Modern 656*	1.50	6.00	*49*
THAT LUCKY OLD SUN/How Long Can A Heart Go On Loving? (78)	*Modern 711*	1.50	6.00	*49*
THREE O'CLOCK IN THE MORNING/Baby, You're The One	*Aladdin 3211*	5.00	20.00	*53*
VERY BEST LUCK IN THE WORLD, THE/Hey, Baby, Stop	*Money 220*	2.50	10.00	*56*
YOU'RE NOBODY TILL SOMEBODY LOVES YOU/ Lawd, Lawd, Lawd	*Aladdin 3212*	6.25	25.00	*54*
EBONIERS, The				
HAND IN HAND/Shut Your Mouth	*Port 70013*	1.50	6.00	*59*
EBONY MOODS, The				
I'VE GOT NEWS FOR YOU/Grand, Nice, Swell	*Theron 108*	25.00	100.00	*55*
EBONYS, The				
ECHOES, Frankie & The				
ECHOES, The				
DING DONG/My Heart Beats For You	*Gee 1028*	3.00	12.00	*57*
OVER THE RAINBOW/Someone	*Specialty 601*	1.50	6.00	*57*
ECHOES, The				
ALL THAT WINE IS GONE/Please Say You're Mine	*Rockin' 523*	25.00	100.00	*53*
ECKSTINE, Billy				
ECKSTINE, Billy: see Four Blues, The				
ECUADORS, The				
EDDIE & THE CHANNELS				
EDDIE & The Starlites: see Starlites, Eddie & The				
EDDIE BO: see Bo, Eddie				
EDSELS, The				
COULD IT BE/My Whispering Heart	*Dot 16311*	1.50	6.00	*62*
DO YOU LOVE ME?/Rink-A-Din-Ki-Do	*Roulette 4151*	3.00	12.00	*59*
GIRL I LOVE, THE/Got To Find Out About Love	*Tammy 1023*	1.50	6.00	*61*
LAMA RAMA DING DONG/Bells	*Dub 2843*	5.00	20.00	*58*
This is a rare variant label printing of exactly the same record as Rama Lama Ding Dong.				
RAMA LAMA DING DONG/Bells	*Dub 2843*	2.00	8.00	*58*
THREE PRECIOUS WORDS/Let's Go	*Tammy 1014*	1.50	6.00	*61*
WHAT BROUGHT US TOGETHER?/Don't Know What To Do	*Tammy 1010*	1.50	6.00	*60*
EDWARDS, David as Honeyboy Edwards				
BUILD A CAVE/Who May Your Regular Be? (78)	*Artist Record Co. 102*	10.00	40.00	*51*
EDWARDS, Gwen & The Co-Eds: see Co-Eds, Gwen Edwards & The				

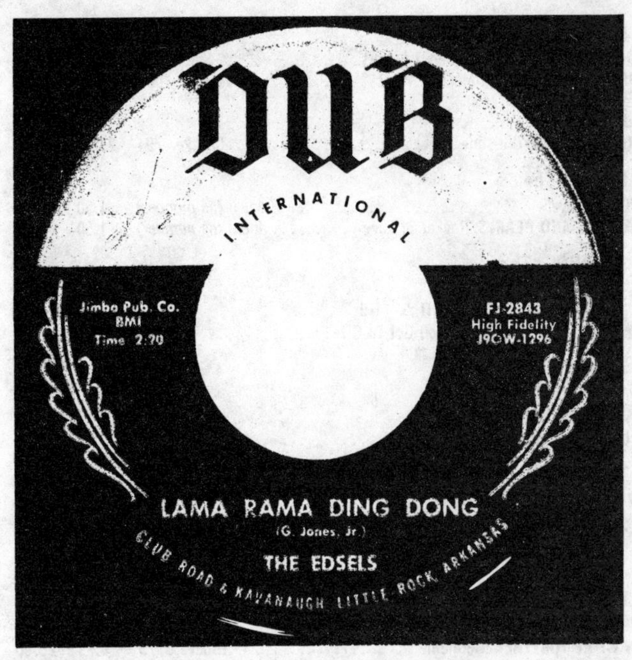

TITLE/FLIP	LABEL & NO.	GOOD TO VERY GOOD	NEAR MINT	YR.
EDWARDS, Honeyboy: see Edwards, David as Honeyboy Edwards				
EDWARDS, J. D.				
CRYIN'/Hobo	*Imperial 5245*	8.00	32.00	*53*
EGANS, Willie				
OH, BABY/Come On	*Mambo 111*	4.00	16.00	—
ROCK AND ROLL FEVER/Chitlins	*Dash 55001*	7.00	28.00	—
SAD, SAD FEELING/Sometimes I Wonder	*Mambo 106*	4.00	16.00	—
TREAT ME RIGHT/You Must Be Fooling	*Mambo 107*	4.00	16.00	—
WHAT A SHAME!/Wow! Wow!	*Mambo 102*	6.25	25.00	—
WILLIE'S BLUES/She's Gone Away, But	*Vita 119*	5.00	20.00	—
EGGLESTON, Cozy				
BIG HEAVY (Alan Freed's theme song)/ Cozy's Beat (red plastic)	*States 133*	8.00	32.00	*53*
BIG HEAVY (Alan Freed's theme song)/ Cozy's Beat	*States 133*	4.00	16.00	*53*
EGYPTIAN KINGS, The				
EL CAPRIS, The				
GIRL OF MINE/These Lonely Nights	*Hi-Q 5006*	1.50	6.00	*57*
KO KO WOP/Oh, But She Did	*Bullseye 102*	3.00	12.00	*56*
YOUR STAR/To Live Again	*Fee Bee 216*	2.00	8.00	—
EL DEENS, The				
EL DOMINGOES, The				
EVENING BELLS/I'm Not Kidding You	*Kappa 206*	4.00	16.00	*58*
EL DOMINGOES, The				
MADE IN HEAVEN/Lucky Me I'm In Love	*Chelsea 1009*	4.00	16.00	*62*
EL DORADOS, The				
ANNIE'S ANSWER (with Hazel McCollum)/Living With Vivian (instrumental) (red plastic)	*Vee Jay 118*	20.00	80.00	*54*
ANNIE'S ANSWER (with Hazel McCollum)/Living With Vivian (instrumental)	*Vee Jay 118*	7.00	28.00	*54*
AT MY FRONT DOOR/What's Buggin' You, Baby?	*Vee Jay 147*	2.00	8.00	*55*
BABY, I NEED YOU/My Loving Baby (red plastic)	*Vee Jay 115*	15.00	60.00	*54*
BABY, I NEED YOU/My Loving Baby	*Vee Jay 115*	2.50	10.00	*54*
BIM BAM BOOM/There In The Night	*Vee Jay 211*	3.00	12.00	*56*
FALLEN TEAR, A/Chop Ling Soon	*Vee Jay 197*	4.00	16.00	*56*
I'LL BE FOREVER LOVIN' YOU/I Began To Realize	*Vee Jay 165*	2.50	10.00	*55*
LIGHTS ARE LOW/Oh, What A Girl	*Vee Jay 302*	7.00	28.00	*58*
NOW THAT YOU'VE GONE/Rock 'N' Roll's For Me	*Vee Jay 180*	2.50	10.00	*56*
ONE MORE CHANCE/Little Miss Love	*Vee Jay 127*	15.00	60.00	*54*
TEARS ON MY PILLOW/A Rose For My Darling	*Vee Jay 250*	2.00	8.00	*57*
3 REASONS WHY/Boom Diddie Boom	*Vee Jay 263*	5.00	20.00	*58*

TITLE/FLIP	LABEL & NO.	GOOD TO VERY GOOD	NEAR MINT	YR.
EL POLLOS, The				
HIGH SCHOOL DANCE/These Four Letters	Studio 999	3.00	12.00	58
SCHOOL GIRL/Why Treat Me This Way?	Neptune 1001	4.00	16.00	—
EL RAYS, The				
DARLING I KNOW/Christine	Checker 794	25.00	100.00	54
EL REYES, The				
BEVERLY/Angalie	Ideal (no number)	1.50	6.00	65
DIAMONDS AND PEARLS/Rocket Of Love	Ideal (no number)	1.50	6.00	64
EL STERROS, The				
EL TEMPOS, Mike Gordon & The				
WHY DON'T YOU DO RIGHT?/You Got To Give	Cat 101	1.50	6.00	54
EL TEMPOS, The				
EL TONES, The				
LOVIN' WITH A BEAT/Like Mattie	Cub 9011	2.00	8.00	58
EL TORROS, The				
DANCE WITH ME/Yellow Hand	Duke 175	1.50	6.00	57
EL TORROS, The				
ALL THE TEARS IS GONE/Love Is Love	Fraternity 811	2.50	10.00	58
EL VENOS, The				
MY HEART BEATS FASTER/You Must Be True	Vik 0305	4.00	16.00	57
NOW WE'RE TOGETHER/Geraldine	Groove 0170	6.25	25.00	56
EL VIREOS, The				
FIRST KISS/Silly Willy	Revello 1002	4.00	12.50	59
ELBERT, Donnie				
ELCHORDS, The				
PEPPERMINT STICK/Gee, I'm In Love	Good 544	4.00	16.00	58
ELDAROS, The				
ROCK-A-BOCK/Please Surrender	Vesta 102	30.00	120.00	—
ELECTRAS, The				
LITTLE GIRL OF MINE/Mary, Mary	Ruby-Doo 2	1.50	6.00	66
ELGINS, Dee Jan				
THAT'S MY GIRL/	Lessie (# unknown)	8.00	32.00	—
ELGINS, Little Tommy & The				
NEVER LOVE AGAIN/I Walk On	ABC 10358	1.50	6.00	62
NEVER LOVE AGAIN/I Walk On	Elmar 1084	2.50	10.00	—
ELGINS, The (female group)				
ELGINS, The				
EXTRA, EXTRA/My Illness	Titan 1724	1.50	6.00	61
HERE IN YOUR ARMS/We're Gonna Have A Good Time	Congress 225	1.50	6.00	64
TIMES WE'VE WASTED, THE/Ritha Mae	Congress 214	1.50	6.00	64
ELGINS, The				
MADEMOISELLE/Picture Of You	MGM 12670	1.50	6.00	58
UNCLE SAM'S MAN/Casey Cop	Flip 353	1.50	6.00	60
ELITES, The				
IN THE LITTLE CHAPEL/Northern Star	Abel 225	2.00	8.00	59
ELL, Carl & The Buddies: see Buddies, Carl Ell & The				
ELLIS, Big Boy & His Rhythm: see Ellis, Wilbert as Big Boy Ellis				
ELLIS, Shirley				
ELLIS, Wilbert as Big Boy Ellis & His Rhythm				
DICES DICES/I Love You Baby (78)	Lenox 521	2.00	8.00	45
ELLIS, Wilbert as Big Chief Ellis: see Dupree, William Thomas as Champion Jack Dupree with Big Chief Ellis & His Blues Stars				
ELLIS, Wilbert as The Big Chief Trio				
BIG CHIEF'S BLUES/She's Gone (78)	Sittin' In With 523	2.00	8.00	45
ELLISON, Lorraine				
ELLISON, Perline				
ELMO, Sunnie & The Minor Chords: see Minor Chords, Sunnie Elmo & The				
ELROY & THE EXCITEMENTS: see Excitements, Elroy & The				
ELTONES, The				
YOU WERE MEANT FOR ME/	Chief 800	25.00	100.00	—
EMANON FOUR, The				
OH! THAT GIRL/Blues For Monday	Flash 106	8.00	32.00	56
EMANONS, The				
BLUE MOON/Wish I Had My Baby	Josie 801	5.00	20.00	56
CHANGE OF TIME/Hindu Baby	Gee 1005	10.00	40.00	56
EMBERS, The				
MY DEAREST DARLING/Please, Mr. Sun	Dot 16162	1.50	6.00	60
PARADISE HILL/Sound Of Love (black label)	Herald 410	15.00	60.00	53
PARADISE HILL/Sound Of Love (red plastic)	Herald 410	15.00	60.00	53
PARADISE HILL/Sound Of Love (yellow label)	Herald 410	7.00	28.00	53
PARADISE HILL/Sound Of Love	Ember 101	8.00	32.00	53
SWEET LIPS/There'll Be No One Else But You	Columbia 40287	1.50	6.00	54
WAIT FOR ME/Couldn't Wait Any Longer	Dot 16101	1.50	6.00	60
EMBERS, Willis Sanders & The				
EMBLEMS, Patty & The (female group)				
EMBLEMS, The				
BANG, BANG, SHOOT 'EM, DADDY/Too Young	Bayfront 108	6.25	25.00	62
WOULD YOU STILL BE MINE?/Poor Humpty Dumpty	Bayfront 107	2.50	10.00	62
EMBRACEABLES, The				
FROM SOMEBODY WHO LOVES YOU/ Gotta Pretty Little Baby	Sandy 1025	6.25	25.00	59
EMERALDS, Luther Bond & The				
HE LOVES YOU, BABY/I Cry	Federal 12279	1.50	6.00	56
I WON'T BELIEVE YOU ANYMORE/It's Written In The Stars	Savoy 1159	1.50	6.00	55
OLD MOTHER NATURE/Six Foot Mule	Federal 12368	1.50	6.00	59
Both songs recorded in 1956.				
SOMEONE TO LOVE ME/Should I Love You So Much?	Showboat 1505	4.00	16.00	60
WHAT IF YOU/See What You Done?	Savoy 1124	2.00	8.00	54
YOU WERE MY LOVE/Starlight, Starbright	Savoy 1131	2.00	8.00	54
EMERALDS, The				
LOVER'S CRY/Rumblin' Tumblin' Baby	Bobbin' 121	4.00	16.00	60
SALLY LOU/Why Must I Wonder?	Allied 10002/10003	2.00	8.00	—
SALLY LOU/Why Must I Wonder?	Kicks 3	10.00	40.00	54
THAT'S THE WAY IT'S GOT TO BE/Maria's Cha Cha	Bobbin' 107	2.50	10.00	59
EMERSON, Billy "The Kid"				
LITTLE FINE HEALTHY THING/Something For Nothing	Sun 233	4.00	16.00	55
NO TEASIN' AROUND/If Lovin' Is Believing	Sun 195	30.00	120.00	54
RED HOT/No Greater Love	Sun 219	8.00	32.00	55
WHEN IT RAINS IT POURS/Move, Baby, Move	Sun 214	8.00	32.00	55
WOODCHUCK, THE/I'm Not Going Home	Sun 203	20.00	80.00	54
EMERSONS, The				
JOANNIE, JOANNIE/Hungry	Newport 7004	2.50	10.00	58
EMOTIONS, The				
EMOTIONS, The (female group)				
EMPERORS, The				
I MAY BE WRONG/Come Back, Come Back	Haven 511	15.00	60.00	—
EMPIRES, Eddie Friend & The				
EMPIRES, Lightnin' Jr. & The see Dupree, William Thomas as Lightnin' Jr.				
RAGGED AND HUNGRY/Somebody Changed The Lock	Harlem 2334	15.00	60.00	55

EMPIRES, The

TITLE/FLIP	LABEL & NO.	GOOD TO VERY GOOD	NEAR MINT	YR.
CORN WISKEY/My Baby, My Baby	Harlem 2325	20.00	80.00	54
I WANT TO KNOW/Shirley	Wing 90023	2.00	8.00	55
IF I'M A FOOL/Zippety Zip	Amp 3 132	10.00	40.00	—
LINDA/Whispering Heart	Whirlin' Disc 104	4.00	16.00	56
MAKE ME OR BREAK ME/Magic Number	Harlem 2333	20.00	80.00	55
MY FIRST DISCOVERY/Don't Touch My Gal	Wing 90080	1.50	6.00	56
TELL ME, PRETTY BABY/By The Riverside	Wing 90050	1.50	6.00	55

EMSLEY, William as Washboard Willie & His Super Suds Of Rhythm

TITLE/FLIP	LABEL & NO.	GOOD TO VERY GOOD	NEAR MINT	YR.
CHERRY RED BLUES/Washboard Shuffle (78)	JVB 59	4.00	16.00	56
FOOL ON A MULE IN THE MIDDLE OF THE ROAD, A/ Hambone	Von 702	1.50	6.00	64
NATURAL BORN LOVER/Wee Baby Blues	Herculon (no number)	2.00	8.00	66
WASHBOARD BLUES, PART 1/Washboard Blues, Part 2	JVB 70	9.00	36.00	56

ENCHANTERS, Billy Butler & The

ENCHANTERS, Garnet Mimms & The

ENCHANTERS, The

TITLE/FLIP	LABEL & NO.	GOOD TO VERY GOOD	NEAR MINT	YR.
BOTTLE UP AND GO/Mambo, Santa, Mambo	Coral 61916	2.50	10.00	57
THERE GOES A PRETTY GIRL/Fan Me, Baby (long version)	Coral 61832	7.00	28.00	57
THERE GOES A PRETTY GIRL/Fan Me, Baby (short version)	Coral 61832	2.50	10.00	57
TRUE LOVE GONE/The Day	Coral 62373	1.50	6.00	63
TRUE LOVE GONE/There Goes A Pretty Girl	Coral 65610	1.50	6.00	67
TRUE LOVE GONE/Wait A Minute, Baby	Coral 61756	2.50	10.00	56

ENCHANTERS, The

TITLE/FLIP	LABEL & NO.	GOOD TO VERY GOOD	NEAR MINT	YR.
WE MAKE MISTAKES/The Decision	Sharp 105	1.50	6.00	60

ENCHORDS, The

TITLE/FLIP	LABEL & NO.	GOOD TO VERY GOOD	NEAR MINT	YR.
ZOOM ZOOM ZOOM/I Need You, Baby	Laurie 3089	2.00	8.00	61

ENCORES, The

TITLE/FLIP	LABEL & NO.	GOOD TO VERY GOOD	NEAR MINT	YR.
WHEN I LOOK AT YOU/Young Girls, Young Girls	Checker 760	120.00	480.00	53

EQUADORS, The

EQUALS, The

ERLENE & THE GIRLFRIENDS

ERMINES, Cornel Gunter & The

TITLE/FLIP	LABEL & NO.	GOOD TO VERY GOOD	NEAR MINT	YR.
I'M SAD/One Thing For Me	Loma 705	4.00	16.00	56
KEEP ME ALIVE/Muchacha, Muchacha	Loma 704	4.00	16.00	56
TRUE LOVE/Peek, Peek-A-Boo	Loma 701	5.00	20.00	55
YOU BROKE MY HEART/I'm So Used To You Now	Loma 703	4.00	16.00	56

ERVIN, Frankie & The Spears:
see Spears, Frankie Ervin & The

ERVIN, Leroy

TITLE/FLIP	LABEL & NO.	GOOD TO VERY GOOD	NEAR MINT	YR.
ROCK ISLAND BLUES/Blue, Black, Evil (78)	Gold Star 628	2.50	10.00	47
ROCK ISLAND BLUES/Blue, Black, Evil (78)	Swing 415	4.00	16.00	47

ERVIN, Odie

TITLE/FLIP	LABEL & NO.	GOOD TO VERY GOOD	NEAR MINT	YR.
SHE'S A BAD, BAD WOMAN/Note Pinned On My Bed	Big Town 111	2.50	10.00	54

ESCORTS, The

TITLE/FLIP	LABEL & NO.	GOOD TO VERY GOOD	NEAR MINT	YR.
I WILL BE HOME AGAIN/Leaky Heart And His Red Go-Kart	Scarlet 4005	8.00	32.00	60

ESCOS, The (originally The Charms)

ESQUIRE, Kenny & The Starlites:
see Starlites, Kenny Esquire & The

ESQUIRES, The

ESSEX, Anita Humes & The

ESSEX, The

ESSQUIRES, The

TITLE/FLIP	LABEL & NO.	GOOD TO VERY GOOD	NEAR MINT	YR.
MISSION BELLS/When I Fall In Love	Meridian (no number)	4.00	16.00	—

ETIQUETTES, Little Nat & The

TITLE/FLIP	LABEL & NO.	GOOD TO VERY GOOD	NEAR MINT	YR.
YOU'RE SO CLOSE/Blah, Blah, Blah	Clock 2001	2.00	8.00	—

ETTA & HARVEY

EVANS, Larry:
see Wayne, James as Larry Evans

EVENTUALS, The

EVERETT, Andrew

EVERETT, Bettie & The Daylighters

EVERGREENS, The

TITLE/FLIP	LABEL & NO.	GOOD TO VERY GOOD	NEAR MINT	YR.
VERY TRULY YOURS/Guitar Player	Chart 605	8.00	32.00	55

EXCELS, The

TITLE/FLIP	LABEL & NO.	GOOD TO VERY GOOD	NEAR MINT	YR.
YOU'RE MINE FOREVER/Baby Doll	Central 2601	2.00	8.00	57

EXCITEMENTS, Elroy & The

TITLE/FLIP	LABEL & NO.	GOOD TO VERY GOOD	NEAR MINT	YR.
MY LOVE WILL NEVER DIE/No One Knows	Alanna 188	1.50	6.00	61

EXCITERS, The (female group)

EXCLUSIVES, The

TITLE/FLIP	LABEL & NO.	GOOD TO VERY GOOD	NEAR MINT	YR.
MY GIRL FRIEND/It's Over	K & C 102/103	3.00	12.00	58

EXOTICS, The

EXPLOITS, Bobby Maxwell & The

TITLE/FLIP	LABEL & NO.	GOOD TO VERY GOOD	NEAR MINT	YR.
STAY WITH ME/You're Laughing At Me	Fargo 1009/1010	1.50	6.00	59

EXPRESSIONS, Johnny & The

EXTENSIONS, The

F

FABULAIRES, The

TITLE/FLIP	LABEL & NO.	GOOD TO VERY GOOD	NEAR MINT	YR.
WHILE WALKING/No, No	East West 103	1.50	6.00	57
WHILE WALKING/No, No	Main Line 103	1.50	6.00	58

FABULEERS, The

TITLE/FLIP	LABEL & NO.	GOOD TO VERY GOOD	NEAR MINT	YR.
IF I HAD ANOTHER CHANCE/I Had A Feeling This Morning	Kenco 5002	1.50	6.00	59

FABULONS, The

FABULOUS CLOVERS, The

FABULOUS DENOS, The

FABULOUS EMBERS, Willis Sanders & The

TITLE/FLIP	LABEL & NO.	GOOD TO VERY GOOD	NEAR MINT	YR.
LOVABLE YOU/Honey Bun	Millionaire 775	2.00	8.00	58

FABULOUS FALCONS, The

FABULOUS FIDELS, The

FABULOUS FIVE FLAMES, The

FABULOUS FLAMES, The

TITLE/FLIP	LABEL & NO.	GOOD TO VERY GOOD	NEAR MINT	YR.
DO YOU REMEMBER?/Get To Stepping	Bay-Tone 102	2.50	10.00	60
LOVER/I'm So All Alone	Bay-Tone 105	2.50	10.00	60

FABULOUS GARDENIAS, The

TITLE/FLIP	LABEL & NO.	GOOD TO VERY GOOD	NEAR MINT	YR.
WHAT'S THE MATTER WITH ME?/It's You, You, You	Liz 1004	1.50	6.00	—

FABULOUS IDOLS, The

TITLE/FLIP	LABEL & NO.	GOOD TO VERY GOOD	NEAR MINT	YR.
BABY/Nellie	Kenco 5011	7.00	28.00	60

FABULOUS MARCELS, The

FABULOUS PEARL DEVINES, The

TITLE/FLIP	LABEL & NO.	GOOD TO VERY GOOD	NEAR MINT	YR.
SO LONELY/You've Been Gone	Alco (no number)	8.00	32.00	63

FABULOUS PEARLS, The

TITLE/FLIP	LABEL & NO.	GOOD TO VERY GOOD	NEAR MINT	YR.
MY HEART'S DESIRE/Jungle Bunny	Dooto 448	1.50	6.00	59

TITLE/FLIP	LABEL & NO.	GOOD TO VERY GOOD	NEAR MINT	YR.

FABULOUS PEPS, The

FABULOUS PERSIANS, The

FABULOUS PLAYBOYS, The

FABULOUS TRENIERS, Skip Trenier & The

FABULOUS TRENIERS, The

FABULOUS TWILIGHTS, Nathaniel Mayer & The

TITLE/FLIP	LABEL & NO.	GOOD TO VERY GOOD	NEAR MINT	YR.
VILLAGE OF LOVE/I Want A Woman	Fortune 545	1.50	6.00	62

FAIRLANES, The

TITLE/FLIP	LABEL & NO.	GOOD TO VERY GOOD	NEAR MINT	YR.
WRITING THIS LETTER/Playboy	Continental 1001	20.00	80.00	—

FAIRMONTS, The

TITLE/FLIP	LABEL & NO.	GOOD TO VERY GOOD	NEAR MINT	YR.
TIMES AND PLACES/Lucky Guy	Planet 053	4.00	16.00	—

FALCONS, Candy Rivers & The

TITLE/FLIP	LABEL & NO.	GOOD TO VERY GOOD	NEAR MINT	YR.
YOU ARE THE ONLY ONE/Mambo Baby Tonight	Flip 302	5.00	20.00	54

FALCONS, The (with Wilson Pickett and Eddie Floyd)

TITLE/FLIP	LABEL & NO.	GOOD TO VERY GOOD	NEAR MINT	YR.
BABY, THAT'S IT/This Day	Mercury 70940	4.00	16.00	56
CAN THIS BE CHRISTMAS?/Sent Up	Silhouette 521	5.00	20.00	57
JUST FOR YOUR LOVE/This Heart Of Mine	Anna 1110	1.50	6.00	60
NOW THAT IT'S OVER/My Only Love	Falcon 1006	4.00	16.00	57
STAY MINE/Du-Bi-A-Do	Flip 301	5.00	20.00	54
TELL ME WHY/I Miss You, Darling	Cash 1002	15.00	60.00	55
THIS HEART OF MINE/Romanita	Kudo 661	2.00	8.00	58
YOU MUST KNOW I LOVE YOU/ That's What I Aim To Do	Flick 008	1.50	6.00	59
YOU'RE SO FINE/Goddess Of Angels	Flick 001	8.00	32.00	59
YOU'RE THE BEATING OF MY HEART/It's You I Miss	Savoy 893	20.00	80.00	53

FAMILY COOKIN,' Limmie & The

FAMILY STONE, Sly & The

FAMOUS FLAMES, James Brown & The:
see Brown, James & The Famous Flames

FANTASTIC FIVE KEYS, The

FANTASTIC FOUR, The

FANTASTIC JOHNNY C.

FANTASTIC VONTASTICS, The

FANTASTICS, The

TITLE/FLIP	LABEL & NO.	GOOD TO VERY GOOD	NEAR MINT	YR.
DANCING DOLL/I Told You Once	United Artists 309	3.00	12.00	61
THERE GOES MY LOVE/ I Wanna Be A Millionaire Hobo	RCA Victor 47-7572	4.00	16.00	59
THIS IS MY WEDDING DAY/I Got A Zero	RCA Victor 47-7664	4.00	16.00	59

FARRAR, Lucien & The Lifesavers:
see Lifesavers, Lucien Farrar & The

FASCINATIONS, The

TITLE/FLIP	LABEL & NO.	GOOD TO VERY GOOD	NEAR MINT	YR.
IT'S MIDNIGHT/Doom Bada Doom	Sure 106	8.00	32.00	60

FASCINATIONS, The (female group)

FASCINATORS, The

TITLE/FLIP	LABEL & NO.	GOOD TO VERY GOOD	NEAR MINT	YR.
CAN'T STOP/Don't Give My Love Away	Blue Lake 112	30.00	120.00	55

FASCINATORS, The

TITLE/FLIP	LABEL & NO.	GOOD TO VERY GOOD	NEAR MINT	YR.
TEARDROP EYES/Shivers And Shakes	Dooto 441	6.25	25.00	—

FASCINATORS, The

TITLE/FLIP	LABEL & NO.	GOOD TO VERY GOOD	NEAR MINT	YR.
CUDDLE UP WITH CAROLYN/Tee Vee	King 5119	5.00	20.00	58

FASCINATORS, The

TITLE/FLIP	LABEL & NO.	GOOD TO VERY GOOD	NEAR MINT	YR.
BELLS OF MY HEART, THE/Sweet Baby	Your Copy 1135	25.00	100.00	—
MY BEAUTY, MY OWN/Don't Give It Away	Your Copy 1136	25.00	100.00	—

FASHIONS, The

TITLE/FLIP	LABEL & NO.	GOOD TO VERY GOOD	NEAR MINT	YR.
I'M DREAMING OF YOU/ Lonesome Road (blue label)	V-Tone 202 (second)	2.50	10.00	59
I'M DREAMING OF YOU/I Love You So (blue label)	V-Tone 202 (first)	2.50	10.00	59

FAT MAN, The

TITLE/FLIP	LABEL & NO.	GOOD TO VERY GOOD	NEAR MINT	YR.
YOU'VE GOT TO STOP THIS MESS/Glad I Don't Worry No More (78)	J.O.B. 103	10.00	40.00	50
YOU'VE GOT TO STOP THIS MESS/Glad I Don't Worry No More (78)	Nashboro 516	7.00	28.00	50

FAWNS, The

TITLE/FLIP	LABEL & NO.	GOOD TO VERY GOOD	NEAR MINT	YR.
UNTIL I DIE/Come On	Apt 25015	1.50	6.00	58

FAYETTES, Hattie Littles & The

FEATHERS, The

TITLE/FLIP	LABEL & NO.	GOOD TO VERY GOOD	NEAR MINT	YR.
I NEED A GIRL/Standin' Right There	Aladdin 3277	10.00	40.00	55
JOHNNY, DARLING/Shake 'Em Up	Aladdin 3267	7.00	28.00	54

There were two issues of this record, both identical in all respects, except that the second side had different "takes" of *Shake 'Em Up*, recorded two weeks apart. Both are of approximate equal value.

TITLE/FLIP	LABEL & NO.	GOOD TO VERY GOOD	NEAR MINT	YR.
LOVE ONLY YOU/Crashing The Party	Show Time 1106	9.00	36.00	55
NONA/Johnny, Darling	Show Time 1104	9.00	36.00	54
WHY DON'T YOU WRITE ME?/Busy As A Bee (by Johnny And Louis Stanton)	Show Time 1105	9.00	36.00	55

FEDERALS, The

TITLE/FLIP	LABEL & NO.	GOOD TO VERY GOOD	NEAR MINT	YR.
COME GO WITH ME/Cold Cash	De Luxe 6112	2.50	10.00	57
DEAR LORAINE/She's My Girl	Fury 1009	3.00	12.00	57
WHILE OUR HEARTS ARE YOUNG/ You're The One I Love	Fury 1005	4.00	16.00	57

FEGAN, Johnny

TITLE/FLIP	LABEL & NO.	GOOD TO VERY GOOD	NEAR MINT	YR.
PROBLEM CHILD/Another Day	Get It 104	3.00	12.00	—

FELLOWS, Eugene Church & The

FERGUSON, H-Bomb

TITLE/FLIP	LABEL & NO.	GOOD TO VERY GOOD	NEAR MINT	YR.
BOOKIE'S BLUES/Big City Blues	Savoy 836	2.50	10.00	52
PREACHIN' THE BLUES/Hot Kisses	Savoy 848	2.00	8.00	52
SLOWLY GOIN' CRAZY/Good Lovin'	Savoy 830	2.50	10.00	52

FERROS, The

FESTIVALS, The

FI-TONES QUINTETTE, The

TITLE/FLIP	LABEL & NO.	GOOD TO VERY GOOD	NEAR MINT	YR.
I BELONG TO YOU/Silly And Sappy	Atlas 1055	7.00	28.00	56
I CALL TO YOU/Love You, Baby	Atlas 1052	6.25	25.00	56
IT WASN'T A LIE/Lots And Lots Of Love	Atlas 1051	5.00	20.00	55
WAITING FOR YOUR CALL/My Tired Feet	Atlas 1056	4.00	16.00	56

FI-TONES, The

TITLE/FLIP	LABEL & NO.	GOOD TO VERY GOOD	NEAR MINT	YR.
DEEP IN MY HEART/Minnie	Angletone 536	2.50	10.00	59
FOOLISH DREAMS/Let's Fall In Love	Atlas 1050	5.00	20.00	55
MY HEART/My Faith	Old Town 1042	6.25	25.00	57
WHAT AM I GOIN' TO DO?/It Wasn't A Lie	Angletone 530	2.50	10.00	58
YOU'LL BE THE LAST/Wake Up	Angletone 525	2.50	10.00	58

FIDELITYS, The

FIELDS, Bobby

TITLE/FLIP	LABEL & NO.	GOOD TO VERY GOOD	NEAR MINT	YR.
PITY POOR ME/Give A Helping Hand	Ace 504	4.00	16.00	53

FIESTAS, The

TITLE/FLIP	LABEL & NO.	GOOD TO VERY GOOD	NEAR MINT	YR.
SHE'S MINE/The Hobo's Prayer	Old Town 1111	1.50	6.00	61

FIFTH DIMENSION, The

FISHER, Tee Bee

FITZGERALD, Ella & Louis Jordan

FITZGERALD, Ella & The Ink Spots:
see Ink Spots, Ella Fitzgerald & The

FIVE ARROWS, Gloria Valdez & The

TITLE/FLIP	LABEL & NO.	GOOD TO VERY GOOD	NEAR MINT	YR.
PRETTY LITTLE THING/You've Got Me Losing My Mind	Parrot 816	12.50	50.00	55

FIVE BARS, The

TITLE/FLIP	LABEL & NO.	GOOD TO VERY GOOD	NEAR MINT	YR.
STORMY WEATHER/Somebody Else's Fool	Money 224	5.00	20.00	57

FIVE BELLS, The

Paul Gayten

H-Bomb Ferguson

Flamingos

FIVE BILLS, The

TITLE/FLIP	LABEL & NO.	GOOD TO VERY GOOD	NEAR MINT	YR.
CAN'T WAIT FOR TOMORROW/ Till I Waltz Again With You	*Brunswick 84002*	10.00	40.00	*53*
TILL DAWN AND TOMORROW/ Waiting, Wanting	*Brunswick 84004*	10.00	40.00	*53*

FIVE BIRDS, Willie Headen & The

TITLE/FLIP	LABEL & NO.	GOOD TO VERY GOOD	NEAR MINT	YR.
BACK HOME AGAIN/I Wanna Know	*Dooto 703*	1.50	6.00	*56*
LET ME CRY/The Skinny Woman Story	*Authentic 410*	2.00	8.00	*57*

FIVE BLAZES, The

TITLE/FLIP	LABEL & NO.	GOOD TO VERY GOOD	NEAR MINT	YR.
ALL MY GEETS ARE GONE/Every Little Dream (78)	*Aristocrat 202*	2.00	8.00	*47*
DEDICATED TO YOU/Chicago Boogie (78)	*Aristocrat 201*	2.00	8.00	*47*

FIVE BLUE FLAMES, Chris Powell & The

TITLE/FLIP	LABEL & NO.	GOOD TO VERY GOOD	NEAR MINT	YR.
BLUE BOY/I Come From Jamaica	*Okeh 6900*	15.00	60.00	*52*
BLUES IN MY HEART/ Dance Til The Break Of Dawn (78)	*Columbia 30216*	1.50	6.00	*50*
COUNTRY GIRL BLUES/ The Man With The Horn	*Columbia 39272*	8.00	32.00	*51*
DOWN IN THE BOTTOM/Hauntin' Pinochle Blues (78)	*Columbia 30205*	1.50	6.00	*50*
IDA RED/Darn That Dream	*Okeh 6875*	8.00	32.00	*52*
LAST SATURDAY NIGHT/Hot Dog (78)	*Columbia 30162*	1.50	6.00	*49*
MASQUERADE IS OVER, THE/Talkin'	*Okeh 6818*	10.00	40.00	*51*
MY LOVE HAS GONE/ In The Cool Of The Evening	*Columbia 39407*	25.00	100.00	*51*
ROCK THE JOINT/ On The Sunny Side Of The Street (78)	*Columbia 30175*	1.50	6.00	*49*
SUNDAY/I've Made A Big Mistake (78)	*Columbia 30169*	1.50	6.00	*49*
SWINGIN' IN THE GROOVE/ I'm Still In Love With You (78)	*Columbia 30180*	1.50	6.00	*50*
TWILIGHT/That's Right!	*Okeh 6850*	8.00	32.00	*51*

5 BLUE NOTES, The (featuring Fleming Briscoe)

TITLE/FLIP	LABEL & NO.	GOOD TO VERY GOOD	NEAR MINT	YR.
BEAT OF OUR HEARTS, THE/You Gotta Go, Baby	*Sabre 108*	100.00	400.00	*54*
MY GAL IS GONE/Ooh, Baby	*Sabre 103*	70.00	280.00	*54*

FIVE BREEZES, The (with Willie Dixon)

TITLE/FLIP	LABEL & NO.	GOOD TO VERY GOOD	NEAR MINT	YR.
LAUNDRY MAN/Just A Jitterbug (78)	*Bluebird 8710*	5.00	20.00	*41*
RETURN GAL O' MINE/My Buddy Blues (78)	*Bluebird 8614*	5.00	20.00	*41*
SWEET LOUISE/Minute And Hour Blues (78)	*Bluebird 8590*	5.00	20.00	*40*
WHAT'S THE MATTER WITH LOVE?/ Swingin' The Blues (78)	*Bluebird 8679*	5.00	20.00	*41*

FIVE BUDDS, The

TITLE/FLIP	LABEL & NO.	GOOD TO VERY GOOD	NEAR MINT	YR.
I GUESS IT'S ALL OVER NOW/I Want Her Back	*Rama 2*	20.00	80.00	*53*
I WAS SUCH A FOOL/Midnight	*Rama 1*	20.00	80.00	*53*

FIVE C'S, The

TITLE/FLIP	LABEL & NO.	GOOD TO VERY GOOD	NEAR MINT	YR.
MY HEART'S GOT THE BLUES/Goody, Goody	*United 180*	25.00	100.00	*55*
TELL ME/Whoo-Wee, Baby	*United 172*	25.00	100.00	*54*

FIVE CAMPBELLS, The

TITLE/FLIP	LABEL & NO.	GOOD TO VERY GOOD	NEAR MINT	YR.
HEY, BABY/Morrine	*Music City 794*	10.00	40.00	*56*

FIVE CHANCELLORS, The

TITLE/FLIP	LABEL & NO.	GOOD TO VERY GOOD	NEAR MINT	YR.
THERE GOES MY GIRL/Tell Me You Love Me	*Port 5000*	4.00	16.00	*58*

FIVE CHANCES, The

TITLE/FLIP	LABEL & NO.	GOOD TO VERY GOOD	NEAR MINT	YR.
ALL I WANT/Shake-A-Link (red plastic)	*Blue Lake 115*	60.00	240.00	*55*
ALL I WANT/Shake-A-Link	*Blue Lake 115*	40.00	160.00	*55*
GLORIA/Sugar Lips	*States 156*	25.00	100.00	*56*
I MAY BE SMALL/Nagasaki	*Chance 1157*	50.00	200.00	*54*
MY DAYS ARE BLUE/Tell My Why	*Federal 12303*	20.00	80.00	*57*

5 CHANELS, The (female group)

FIVE CHESTNUTS, Hayes Baskerville & The

TITLE/FLIP	LABEL & NO.	GOOD TO VERY GOOD	NEAR MINT	YR.
MY ONE AND ONLY LOVE/Billy	*Drum 003/004*	7.00	28.00	*58*

FIVE CHIMES, The

TITLE/FLIP	LABEL & NO.	GOOD TO VERY GOOD	NEAR MINT	YR.
FOOL WAS I, A/Dearest Darling	*Royal Roost 577*	50.00	200.00	*55*
ROSEMARIE/Never Love Another	*Betta 2011*	50.00	200.00	—

FIVE CHORDS, Johnny Jones & The

TITLE/FLIP	LABEL & NO.	GOOD TO VERY GOOD	NEAR MINT	YR.
LOVE IS LIKE MUSIC/Don't Just Stand There	*Jamie 1110*	1.50	6.00	*58*

FIVE CHUMS, The

TITLE/FLIP	LABEL & NO.	GOOD TO VERY GOOD	NEAR MINT	YR.
HIGH SCHOOL AFFAIR/Give Me The Power	*Excello 2123*	2.00	8.00	*58*

FIVE CROWNS, The

TITLE/FLIP	LABEL & NO.	GOOD TO VERY GOOD	NEAR MINT	YR.
ALONE AGAIN/I Don't Have To Hunt No More	*Rainbow 206*	50.00	200.00	*53*
I CAN'T PRETEND/Popcorn Willie	*Caravan 15609*	4.00	16.00	*55*
I CAN'T PRETEND/Popcorn Willie	*Trans-World 717*	5.00	20.00	*55*
KEEP IT A SECRET/Why Don't You Believe Me?	*Rainbow 202*	40.00	160.00	*53*
LULLABY OF THE BELLS/ Later, Later, Baby (red plastic)	*Old Town 792*	100.00	400.00	*53*
STAR, A/You're My Inspiration	*Rainbow 179*	25.00	100.00	*52*
WHO CAN BE TRUE?/$19.50 Bus	*Rainbow 184*	25.00	100.00	*52*
YOU CAME TO ME/Ooh Wee, Baby	*Rainbow 335*	20.00	80.00	*56*
This record was later reissued listing the artists as The Duvals.				
YOU CAME TO ME/Ooh, Wee, Baby	*Riviera 990*	40.00	160.00	*55*
YOU COULD BE MY LOVE/Good Luck, Darlin'	*Old Town 790*	80.00	320.00	*53*

FIVE CROWNS, The

TITLE/FLIP	LABEL & NO.	GOOD TO VERY GOOD	NEAR MINT	YR.
DO YOU REMEMBER?/God Bless You	*Gee 1001*	8.00	32.00	*55*

FIVE CRYSTALS, The

TITLE/FLIP	LABEL & NO.	GOOD TO VERY GOOD	NEAR MINT	YR.
HEY, LANDLORD/Good Looking Out	*Kane 25592*	2.50	10.00	*59*

FIVE DAPS, The

TITLE/FLIP	LABEL & NO.	GOOD TO VERY GOOD	NEAR MINT	YR.
DO WHOP-A-DO/You're So Unfaithful	*Brax (no number)*	15.00	60.00	*58*

FIVE DEBONAIRES, The

TITLE/FLIP	LABEL & NO.	GOOD TO VERY GOOD	NEAR MINT	YR.
WHISPERING BLUES/Darlin'	*Herald 509*	7.00	28.00	*57*

FIVE DELIGHTS, The

TITLE/FLIP	LABEL & NO.	GOOD TO VERY GOOD	NEAR MINT	YR.
THERE'LL BE NO GOODBYE/Okey Dokey, Mama	*Newport 7002*	7.00	28.00	*58*
THERE'LL BE NO GOODBYE/Okey Dokey, Mama	*Unart 2003*	2.50	10.00	*58*

FIVE DIAMONDS, The

TITLE/FLIP	LABEL & NO.	GOOD TO VERY GOOD	NEAR MINT	YR.
TEN COMMANDMENTS OF LOVE/I Cried And Cried	*Treat 501*	20.00	80.00	—

FIVE DIPS, The

TITLE/FLIP	LABEL & NO.	GOOD TO VERY GOOD	NEAR MINT	YR.
TEACH ME TONIGHT/ That's What I Like (by The Allen Trio)	*Original 1005*	40.00	160.00	*55*

FIVE DOLLARS, Andre Williams & The

TITLE/FLIP	LABEL & NO.	GOOD TO VERY GOOD	NEAR MINT	YR.
MOVIN'/Movin' (by The Diablos)	*Fortune 851*	1.50	6.00	*60*

FIVE DOLLARS, The

TITLE/FLIP	LABEL & NO.	GOOD TO VERY GOOD	NEAR MINT	YR.
HARMONY OF LOVE/Doctor Baby	*Fortune 821*	4.00	16.00	*55*
I WILL WAIT/Hard Working Mama	*Fortune 830*	6.25	25.00	*56*
SO STRANGE/You Know I Can't Refuse	*Fortune 826*	2.50	10.00	*56*
THAT'S THE WAY IT GOES/My Baby-O	*Fortune 854*	2.00	8.00	*60*
YOU FOOL/How Do You Do The Bacon Fat?	*Fortune 833*	2.00	8.00	*57*

FIVE DOTS, The

TITLE/FLIP	LABEL & NO.	GOOD TO VERY GOOD	NEAR MINT	YR.
I JUST LOVE THE THINGS SHE DO/Well, Little Baby	*Note 1003*	7.00	28.00	*55*
OTHER NIGHT, THE/Each Night	*Dot 1204*	15.00	60.00	*54*

FIVE DREAMERS, Eddie Banks & The

TITLE/FLIP	LABEL & NO.	GOOD TO VERY GOOD	NEAR MINT	YR.
SUGAR DIABETES/Rock A Bye Blues	*Josie 804*	4.00	16.00	*56*

5 DREAMERS, The

TITLE/FLIP	LABEL & NO.	GOOD TO VERY GOOD	NEAR MINT	YR.
YOU DON'T KNOW/Beverly	*Port 5001*	2.00	8.00	*57*

FIVE DREAMS, The

TITLE/FLIP	LABEL & NO.	GOOD TO VERY GOOD	NEAR MINT	YR.
YOU ARE MY ONLY/Up All Night	*Mercury 71150*	4.00	16.00	*57*

FIVE DU-TONES, The

FIVE DUKES OF RHYTHM, The

TITLE/FLIP	LABEL & NO.	GOOD TO VERY GOOD	NEAR MINT	YR.
SOFT, SWEET AND REALLY FINE/ Everybody's Singing The Blues	*Fortune 812*	10.00	40.00	*54*
SOFT, SWEET AND REALLY FINE/ Everybody's Singing The Blues	*Rendezvous 812*	10.00	40.00	*54*

FIVE DUKES, Bennie Woods & The

TITLE/FLIP	LABEL & NO.	GOOD TO VERY GOOD	NEAR MINT	YR.
I CROSS MY FINGERS/Wheel, Baby, Wheel	*Atlas 1040*	30.00	120.00	*54*

FIVE ECHOES, The

Thought to be the same group as the Five Echos.

TITLE/FLIP	LABEL & NO.	GOOD TO VERY GOOD	NEAR MINT	YR.
BABY, COME BACK TO ME/Lonely Mood	*Sabre 102*	40.00	160.00	*53*
SO LONESOME/Broke	*Sabre 105*	40.00	160.00	*54*

FIVE ECHOS, The

Thought to be the same group as The Five Echoes.

TITLE/FLIP	LABEL & NO.	GOOD TO VERY GOOD	NEAR MINT	YR.
FOOL'S PRAYER/Tastee Freeze	*Vee Jay 156*	10.00	40.00	*55*
TELL ME, BABY/I Really Do	*Vee Jay 129*	15.00	60.00	*54*

FIVE EMBERS, The

TITLE/FLIP	LABEL & NO.	GOOD TO VERY GOOD	NEAR MINT	YR.
PLEASE COME HOME/Love Birds	*Gem 224*	40.00	160.00	*54*

The Five Keys

TITLE/FLIP	LABEL & NO.	GOOD TO VERY GOOD	NEAR MINT	YR.
FIVE EMERALDS, The				
DARLING/Pleasure Me	*S-R-C 107*	40.00	160.00	—
I'LL BEG/Let Me Take You Out Tonight	*S-R-C 106*	30.00	120.00	—
FIVE FABULOUS DEMONS, The				
FIVE FLEETS, The				
CHEER UP/Pitter Patter	*Seville 112*	2.00	8.00	*61*
I BEEN CRYING/Oh, What A Feeling	*Felsted 8513*	2.00	8.00	*58*
SLIGHT CASE OF LOVE/Yo' Good Lovin'	*Felsted 8522*	2.00	8.00	*58*
FIVE FORTUNES, The				
YOU ARE MY ONLY LOVE/	*Ransom*	8.00	32.00	—
FIVE HEARTS, The				
PLEASE, PLEASE, BABY/The Fine One	*Flair 1026*	10.00	40.00	*54*
FIVE HOLLYWOOD BLUEJAYS, The				
PUT A NICKLE IN THE JUKEBOX/ Safronia Ida B. Brown	*Recorded In Hollywood 162*	50.00	200.00	*52*
SO WORRIED/Cloudy And Raining	*Recorded In Hollywood 185*	50.00	200.00	*52*
FIVE J'S, The				
MY DARLING/Calypso Jump	*Fulton 2454*	10.00	40.00	*58*
FIVE JADES, The				
WITHOUT YOUR LOVE/Rock And Roll Molly	*Duke 188*	2.00	8.00	*58*
FIVE JETS, The				
CRAZY CHICKENS/Everybody Do The Chicken	*De Luxe 6064*	5.00	20.00	*54*
DOWN SLOW/Please Love Me, Baby	*De Luxe 6071*	5.00	20.00	*54*
I AM IN LOVE/Not A Hand To Shake	*De Luxe 6018*	7.00	28.00	*53*
I'M STUCK/I Want A Woman	*De Luxe 6053*	5.00	20.00	*54*
TELL ME YOU'RE MINE/Give In	*De Luxe 6058*	20.00	60.00	*54*
FIVE JINKS, The				
CUSHION FOOT/Zazu Swing (78)	*Bluebird 6905*	4.00	16.00	*37*
DIRT-DISHING DAISY/There Goes My Heartache (78)	*Bluebird 6951*	4.00	16.00	*37*
I'M MOANING ALL DAY FOR YOU/ Found A Baby Down Dixie Way (78)	*Bluebird 6857*	4.00	16.00	*37*
FIVE JOHNSON BROTHERS, The				
FIVE JOYS, Juanita Rogers & The				
TEENAGERS'S LETTER OF PROMISES/ I'm So Glad You Love Me	*Pink Clouds 333*	10.00	40.00	—
FIVE KEYS, Rudy West & The				
FIVE KEYS, The				
CAN'T KEEP FROM CRYING/ Come Go My Bail, Louise	*Aladdin 3167*	40.00	160.00	*53*
CLOSE YOUR EYES/Doggone It, You Did It	*Capitol 3032*	2.00	8.00	*55*
DEEP IN MY HEART/ How Do You Expect Me To Get It?	*Aladdin 3245*	40.00	160.00	*54*
DREAM ON/Dancing Senorita	*King 5273*	1.50	6.00	*59*
GEE WHITTAKERS/'Cause You're My Lover	*Capitol 3267*	2.00	8.00	*55*
GLORY OF LOVE, THE/Hucklebuck With Jimmy	*Aladdin 3099*	40.00	160.00	*51*
GONNA BE TOO LATE/Rosetta	*King 5330*	1.50	6.00	*60*
HOW CAN I FORGET YOU?/I Burned Your Letter	*King 5302*	1.50	6.00	*59*
I CRIED FOR YOU/Serve Another Round	*Aladdin 3158*	50.00	200.00	*52*
I DIDN'T KNOW/No Says My Heart	*King 5358*	1.50	6.00	*60*
I DREAMT I DWELT IN HEAVEN/She's The Most	*Capitol 3392*	1.50	6.00	*56*
I HADN'T ANYONE TIL YOU/Hold Me	*Aladdin 3136*	90.00	360.00	*52*
I TOOK YOUR LOVE FOR A TOY/Ziggus	*King 5251*	3.00	12.00	*59*
I WISH I'D NEVER LEARNED TO READ/ Don't You Know Love You?	*Capitol 3185*	3.00	12.00	*55*
I'LL FOLLOW YOU/Lawdy, Miss Mary	*Groove 0031*	250.00	1,000.00	*51*
This record is only known to exist in a disc jockey promo copy. With no documented sales, its value can only be estimated, but there is no doubt it would command a spectacular price in an auction.				
IT'S CHRISTMAS TIME/Old MacDonald	*Aladdin 3113*	45.00	180.00	*51*
LET THERE BE YOU/Tiger Lily	*Capitol 3660*	1.50	6.00	*57*
LING, TING, TONG/I'm Alone	*Capitol 2945*	2.00	8.00	*54*
MISTAKES/How Long?	*Aladdin 3131*	90.00	360.00	*52*
MY LOVE/Why, Oh Why?	*Aladdin 3263*	30.00	120.00	*55*
MY SADDEST HOUR/Oh! Babe!	*Aladdin 3214*	45.00	180.00	*53*
OUT OF SIGHT, OUT OF MIND/That's Right	*Capitol 3502*	1.50	6.00	*56*
PEACE AND LOVE/My Pigeon's Gone	*Capitol 3455*	1.50	6.00	*56*
RED SAILS IN THE SUNSET/ Be Anything, But Be Mine	*Aladdin 3127*	90.00	360.00	*52*
SOMEDAY, SWEETHEART/Love My Loving	*Aladdin 3228*	40.00	160.00	*54*
STOP YOUR CRYING/Do Something For Me	*King 5496*	1.50	6.00	*61*
STORY OF LOVE/Serve Another Round	*Aladdin 3312*	25.00	100.00	*56*
TEARDROPS IN YOUR EYES/I'm So High	*Aladdin 3204*	30.00	120.00	*53*
THERE OUGHT TO BE A LAW/Mama	*Aladdin 3175*	40.00	160.00	*53*
THESE FOOLISH THINGS/Lonesome Old Story	*Aladdin 3190*	100.00	400.00	*53*
VALLEY OF LOVE/Bimbo	*King 5398*	1.50	6.00	*60*
VERDICT, THE/Me Make Um Pow Wow	*Capitol 3127*	2.00	8.00	*55*
WHAT GOES ON?/You Broke The Rules Of Love	*Capitol 3318*	1.50	6.00	*56*
WISDOM OF A FOOL/ Now Don't That Prove I Love You?	*Capitol 3597*	1.50	6.00	*56*
WITH A BROKEN HEART/Too Late	*Aladdin 3085*	50.00	200.00	*51*
YES SIR, THAT'S MY BABY/Old MacDonald	*Aladdin 3118*	45.00	180.00	*52*
YOU BROKE THE ONLY HEART (recorded in 1959)/ That's What You're Doing To Me	*King 5496*	1.50	6.00	*61*
FIVE KINGS, Savannah Churchill & The				
I CAN'T GET UP THE NERVE TO MISS YOU/ Let's Call A Spade A Spade (78)	*Manor 1061*	1.50	6.00	*47*
SINCERELY YOURS/I'm Too Shy (78)	*Manor 1066*	1.50	6.00	*47*
FIVE KINGS, The				
MEET ME AT NO SPECIAL PLACE/ That's How Much I Love You (78)	*Manor 1062*	1.50	6.00	*47*
FIVE KNIGHTS, The				
MIRACLE/Yo Te Amo	*Specialty 675*	2.00	8.00	*59*
FIVE LETTERS, The				
HOLD MY BABY/Your First Love	*Ivy 102*	8.00	32.00	*58*
FIVE LYRICS, The				
I'M TRAVELING LIGHT/My Honey, Sweet Pea	*Music City 799*	9.00	36.00	*56*
FIVE NOTES, Henry Pierce & The				
THRILL ME, BABY/Hey, Fine Mama	*Specialty 461*	20.00	80.00	*52*
FIVE NOTES, The				
PARK YOUR LOVE/Show Me The Way	*Chess 1614*	4.00	16.00	*55*
YOU ARE SO BEAUTIFUL/Broken Hearted Baby	*Jen 4185*	12.50	50.00	*55*
YOU ARE SO BEAUTIFUL/Broken Hearted Baby	*Josie 784*	6.25	25.00	*55*
FIVE OWLS, The				
PLEADING TO YOU/I Like Moonshine	*Vulcan 1025*	20.00	80.00	*55*
FIVE PEARLS, The				
PLEASE LET ME KNOW/Real Humdinger	*Aladdin 3265*	12.50	50.00	*54*
FIVE PENNIES, Big Miller & The				
FIVE PENNIES, The				
MR. MOON/Let It Rain	*Savoy 1182*	1.50	6.00	*55*
MY HEART TREMBLES/Money	*Savoy 1190*	1.50	6.00	*56*
FIVE QUAILS, The				
FIVE RAMBLERS, The				
FIVE REASONS, The				
GO TO SCHOOL/Three O'Clock Rock	*Cub 9006*	3.00	12.00	*58*
FIVE RED CAPS, The				
I MADE A GREAT MISTAKE/ There's A Light On The Hill (78)	*Beacon 116*	1.50	6.00	*43*
I'M THE ONE/Tuscaloosa (78)	*Beacon 115*	1.50	6.00	*43*
MAMA, PUT YOUR BRITCHES ON/Don't Fool With Me (78)	*Beacon 117*	1.50	6.00	*43*
NO FISH TODAY/Grand Central Station (78)	*Beacon 118*	1.50	6.00	*43*
FIVE ROSES, The				
ROMANCE IN THE SPRING/Don't Cry, Della	*Nu Kat 100/101*	1.50	6.00	*59*
FIVE ROVERS, The				
DOWN TO THE SEA/Change Your Mind	*Music City 798*	7.00	28.00	*56*
FIVE ROYALES, The				
BABY, DON'T DO IT/Take All Of Me	*Apollo 443*	3.00	12.00	*52*
COURAGE TO LOVE/You Know I Know	*Apollo 441*	4.00	16.00	*52*
CRY SOME MORE/I Like It Like That	*Apollo 454*	2.50	10.00	*54*
HELP ME, SOMEBODY/Crazy, Crazy, Crazy	*Apollo 446*	3.00	12.00	*53*
I DO/Good Things	*Apollo 452*	1.50	10.00	*54*
I WANT TO THANK YOU/All Righty!	*Apollo 449*	2.50	10.00	*53*
I'M GONNA RUN IT DOWN/Behave Yourself	*King 4740*	1.50	6.00	*54*
LAUNDROMAT BLUES/Too Much Lovin'	*Apollo 448*	4.00	16.00	*53*
TOO MUCH OF A LITTLE BIT/Give Me One More Chance	*Apollo 434*	5.00	20.00	*51*
WHAT'S THAT?/Let Me Come Back Home	*Apollo 458*	2.50	10.00	*54*
WITH ALL YOUR HEART/Six O'Clock In The Morning	*Apollo 467*	2.50	10.00	*55*

FIVE ROYALS, The

FIVE SATINS, The

TITLE/FLIP	LABEL & NO.	GOOD TO VERY GOOD	NEAR MINT	YR.
ALL MINE/Rose Mary	*Standord 100*	15.00	60.00	*56*
CAN I COME OVER TONIGHT?/Golden Earrings	*Cub 9090*	1.50	6.00	*61*
I REMEMBER/Jones Girl	*Standord 200*	25.00	100.00	*56*
I REMEMBER/The Jones Girl	*Ember 1005*	2.00	8.00	*56*
Second issue of Ember 1005.				
IN THE STILL OF THE NITE/The Jones Girl	*Ember 1005*	2.50	10.00	*56*
First issue of Ember 1005.				
MILLION TO ONE, A/Love With No Love In Return	*Ember 1028*	1.50	6.00	*57*
OH, HAPPY DAY/Our Love Is Forever	*Ember 1014*	2.00	8.00	*57*
ON A LOVER'S ISLAND/Till The End	*United Artists 368*	2.50	10.00	*61*
OUR ANNIVERSARY/Pretty Girl	*Ember 1025*	1.50	6.00	*57*
THESE FOOLISH THINGS/A Begger With A Dream	*Cub 9077*	1.50	6.00	*60*
TO THE AISLE/Wish I Had My Baby	*Ember 1019*	1.50	6.00	*57*
WHEN YOUR LOVE COMES ALONG/Skippity Doo	*First 104*	1.50	6.00	*59*
WONDERFUL GIRL/Weeping Willow	*Ember 1008*	2.00	8.00	*56*

FIVE SCALDERS, The

TITLE/FLIP	LABEL & NO.	GOOD TO VERY GOOD	NEAR MINT	YR.
GIRL FRIEND/Willow Blues	*Drummond 3001*	30.00	120.00	—
IF ONLY YOU WERE MINE/There Will Come A Time	*Drummond 3000*	30.00	120.00	—

FIVE SCAMPS, The

TITLE/FLIP	LABEL & NO.	GOOD TO VERY GOOD	NEAR MINT	YR.
CHICKEN SHACK BOOGIE/Gone Home (78)	*Columbia 30157*	1.50	6.00	*49*
WITH ALL MY HEART/Red Hot	*Okeh 7049*	5.00	20.00	*54*

FIVE SHADES, THE

FIVE SHARPS, The

TITLE/FLIP	LABEL & NO.	GOOD TO VERY GOOD	NEAR MINT	YR.
STORMY WEATHER/Sleepy Cowboy (78)	*Jubilee 5104*	1250.00	5000.00	*52*

The storm of controversy continues to surround this record. The only documented sale in recent times—a sale of the only known copy!—brought exactly $3,866.00 in an auction in 1977. That copy was in vg condition. There is no doubt a mint copy would bring more. Even though the price range we've indicated is an estimation and would be the range we feel a second copy of this rare 78 would bring, the real question in most serious collector's minds is: WHAT WOULD "STORMY WEATHER" BE WORTH IF A 45 EVER SURFACES? As far as anyone knows, Jubilee was issuing everything at that time on both 78 r.p.m. and 45 r.p.m. speeds, yet the latter has never been found. Jubilee recorded the song again in 1964 (#5478) by a different group, even though they used the same name of The Five Sharps. It is of minimal value. Should an *authentic* 45 ever turn up, it would tend to temporarily devalue the 78s to some extent. A STANDING OFFER FROM JELLYROLL PRODUCTIONS: if anyone reading this book should ever discover a genuine copy of either the 78 or 45 of "Stormy Weather" that they wished to sell, Jellyroll Productions will act as an agent to auction the item on consignment at *no commission*.

FIVE SHARPS, The:
see Videos, The

FIVE SHILLINGS, The

TITLE/FLIP	LABEL & NO.	GOOD TO VERY GOOD	NEAR MINT	YR.
LETTER TO AN ANGEL/The Snake	*Decca 30722*	7.00	28.00	*58*

FIVE SOUNDS, Russ Riley & The

TITLE/FLIP	LABEL & NO.	GOOD TO VERY GOOD	NEAR MINT	YR.
TONIGHT MUST LIVE ON/Crazy Feeling	*Aljon 115/116*	6.25	25.00	

FIVE SOUNDS, The

TITLE/FLIP	LABEL & NO.	GOOD TO VERY GOOD	NEAR MINT	YR.
THAT'S WHEN I FEEL IN LOVE/Good Time Baby	*Baritone 0940/0941*	4.00	16.00	—

FIVE SPIRITS OF RHYTHM, The

TITLE/FLIP	LABEL & NO.	GOOD TO VERY GOOD	NEAR MINT	YR.
MY OLD MAN/ I'll Be Ready When The Great Day Comes (78)	*Brunswick 6728*	4.00	16.00	*33*

FIVE STAIRSTEPS, The

FIVE STARS, The

TITLE/FLIP	LABEL & NO.	GOOD TO VERY GOOD	NEAR MINT	YR.
LET'S FALL IN LOVE/We Danced In The Moonlight	*Treat 505*	50.00	200.00	—
OOH, SHUCKS/Dead Wrong	*Mark-X 7006*	1.50	6.00	*57*
SO LONELY, BABY/Hey, Juanita	*Blues Boys Kingdom 106*	20.00	80.00	*57*
TAKE FIVE/Humpty Dump	*Atco 6065*	2.50	10.00	*56*
WHERE DID CALEDONIA GO?/ Walkin' An' Talkin'	*Show Time 1102*	7.00	28.00	*54*

FIVE SWANS, The

TITLE/FLIP	LABEL & NO.	GOOD TO VERY GOOD	NEAR MINT	YR.
LI'L GIRL OF MY DREAMS/Li'l Tipa-Tina	*Music City 795*	5.00	20.00	*56*

FIVE THRILLS, The

TITLE/FLIP	LABEL & NO.	GOOD TO VERY GOOD	NEAR MINT	YR.
MY BABY'S GONE/Feel So Good	*Parrot 796*	60.00	240.00	*54*
WEE, WEE BABY/Gloria	*Parrot 800*	75.00	300.00	*54*

FIVE TINOS, The

TITLE/FLIP	LABEL & NO.	GOOD TO VERY GOOD	NEAR MINT	YR.
SITTING BY MY WINDOW/Don't Do That!	*Sun 222*	50.00	200.00	*55*

FIVE TROJANS, Nicky St. Clair & The

TITLE/FLIP	LABEL & NO.	GOOD TO VERY GOOD	NEAR MINT	YR.
I HEAR THOSE BELLS/Creator Of Love	*Edison International 410*	1.50	6.00	*59*

FIVE TROJANS, The

TITLE/FLIP	LABEL & NO.	GOOD TO VERY GOOD	NEAR MINT	YR.
LITTLE DOLL/Lola Lee	*Edison International 412*	1.50	6.00	*59*

FIVE TROJANS, The:
see Trojans, The

FIVE VETS, The

TITLE/FLIP	LABEL & NO.	GOOD TO VERY GOOD	NEAR MINT	YR.
YOU'RE IN LOVE/Right Now	*Allstar 713*	20.00	60.00	—

FIVE WILLOWS, The

TITLE/FLIP	LABEL & NO.	GOOD TO VERY GOOD	NEAR MINT	YR.
BABY, COME A LITTLE CLOSER/ Lay Your Head On My Shoulder	*Herald 433*	12.50	50.00	*54*
DELORES/All Night Long	*Allen 1002*	50.00	200.00	*53*
LOOK ME IN THE EYES/So Help Me	*Herald 442*	9.00	36.00	*55*
LOVE BELLS/Please, Baby	*Pee Dee 290*	30.00	120.00	—
MY DEAR, DEAREST DARLING/Rock, Little Francis	*Allen 1000*	40.00	160.00	*53*
WHITE CLIFFS OF DOVER, THE/With These Hands	*Allen 1003*	60.00	240.00	*53*

FIVE WINGS, Billy Nelson & The

TITLE/FLIP	LABEL & NO.	GOOD TO VERY GOOD	NEAR MINT	YR.
WALK ALONG/Pack - Shack And Stack	*Savoy 1183*	1.50	6.00	*56*

FIVE WINGS, The

TITLE/FLIP	LABEL & NO.	GOOD TO VERY GOOD	NEAR MINT	YR.
JOHNNY HAS GONE/Johnny's Still Singing	*King 4778*	15.00	60.00	*55*
TEARDROPS ARE FALLING/Rock-A-Locka	*King 4781*	9.00	36.00	*55*
This was re-issued on King 5199 as by The Checkers.				

FLACK, Roberta & Donny Hathaway

FLAIRS, Cornel Gunter & The

TITLE/FLIP	LABEL & NO.	GOOD TO VERY GOOD	NEAR MINT	YR.
ALADDIN'S LAMP/Steppin' Out	*ABC 9740*	1.50	6.00	*56*
IN SELF DEFENSE/She Loves To Rock	*ABC 9698*	1.50	6.00	*56*

FLAIRS, Fatso Theus & The

TITLE/FLIP	LABEL & NO.	GOOD TO VERY GOOD	NEAR MINT	YR.
BE COOL, MY HEART/Rock 'N' Roll Drive-In	*Aladdin 3324*	9.00	36.00	*56*

FLAIRS, Shirley Gunter & The

TITLE/FLIP	LABEL & NO.	GOOD TO VERY GOOD	NEAR MINT	YR.
FORTUNE IN LOVE/I Just Got Rid Of A Heartache	*Modern 1001*	1.50	6.00	*56*
HEADIN' HOME/I Want You	*Modern 989*	1.50	6.00	*56*
HOW CAN I TELL YOU?/Ipsy Opsie Ooh	*Flair 1076*	1.50	6.00	*55*

FLAIRS, The

TITLE/FLIP	LABEL & NO.	GOOD TO VERY GOOD	NEAR MINT	YR.
I HAD A LOVE/She Wants To Rock	*Flair 1012*	20.00	60.00	*53*
I'D CLIMB THE HILLS AND MOUNTAINS/ Swing, Pretty Mama	*Antler 4005*	3.00	12.00	*59*
I'LL NEVER LET YOU GO/Hold Me, Thrill Me, Chill Me	*Flair 1056*	7.00	28.00	*55*
LET'S MAKE WITH SOME LOVE/This Is The Night For Love	*Flair 1044*	9.00	36.00	*54*
LOVE ME, GIRL/Gettin' High	*Flair 1028*	7.00	28.00	*54*
MY DARLING, MY SWEET/She Loves To Dance	*Flair 1067*	5.00	20.00	*55*
TELL ME YOU LOVE ME/You Should Care For Me	*Flair 1019*	12.50	50.00	*53*
YOU WERE UNTRUE/Baby Wants	*Flair 1041*	7.00	28.00	*54*

TITLE/FLIP	LABEL & NO.	GOOD TO VERY GOOD	NEAR MINT	YR.

FLAMES, Patty Anne & The

MIDNIGHT/My Heart Is Free Again	Aladdin 3162	6.25	25.00	52

FLAMES, The

CRYIN' FOR MY BABY/Strange Land Blues	Spin 101	15.00	60.00	—
KEEP ON SMILING/Baby, Baby, Baby	7-11 2106	25.00	100.00	53
TOGETHER/Baby, Pretty Baby	7-11 2107	20.00	80.00	53
YOUNG GIRL/Please Tell Me Now (78)	Selective 113	4.00	16.00	50

FLAMING EMBERS, The

FLAMING HEARTS, The

BABY/I Don't Mind	Vulco 1	5.00	20.00	—

FLAMINGOS, The

BLUES IN THE LETTER/Jump, Children	Chance 1162	30.00	120.00	54
CROSS OVER THE BRIDGE/Listen To My Plea	Chance 1154	30.00	120.00	54
DREAM OF A LIFETIME/ On My Merry Way (red plastic)	Parrot 808	50.00	200.00	54
DREAM OF A LIFETIME/On My Merry Way	Parrot 808	30.00	120.00	54

This record was bootlegged in 1961 and contains what was probably an intentional typographical "error" on the label which spells the word, "Bronxville."

DREAM OF A LIFETIME/Whispering Stars	Checker 915	1.50	6.00	59
GOLDEN TEARDROPS/Carried Away (red plastic)	Chance 1145	60.00	240.00	53
GOLDEN TEARDROPS/Carried Away	Chance 1145	40.00	160.00	53
GOODNIGHT SWEETHEART/Does It Really Matter?	Checker 1091	1.50	6.00	64
I REALLY DON'T WANT TO KNOW/Get With It	Parrot 811	75.00	300.00	55
I'LL BE HOME/Need Your Love	Checker 830	5.00	20.00	56
I'M YOURS/Ko Ko Mo (red plastic)	Parrot 812	50.00	200.00	55
I'M YOURS/Ko Ko Mo	Parrot 812	30.00	120.00	55
KISS FROM YOUR LIPS, A/Get With It	Checker 837	2.00	8.00	56
LADDER OF LOVE, THE/Let's Make Up	Decca 30335	1.50	6.00	57
LOVER COME BACK TO ME/Your Little Guy	Checker 1084	1.50	6.00	64
PLAN FOR LOVE/You Ain't Ready	Chance 1149	40.00	160.00	53
PLEASE COME BACK HOME/I Want To Love You	Checker 821	6.25	25.00	55
SOMEDAY, SOMEWAY/ If I Can't Have You (red plastic)	Chance 1133	60.00	240.00	53
SOMEDAY, SOMEWAY/If I Can't Have You	Chance 1133	40.00	160.00	53
THAT'S MY DESIRE/Hurry Home, Baby (red plastic)	Chance 1140	55.00	220.00	53
THAT'S MY DESIRE/Hurry Home, Baby	Chance 1140	30.00	120.00	53
VOW, THE/Shilly Dilly	Checker 846	2.00	8.00	56
WHEN/That's My Baby	Checker 815	4.00	16.00	55
WOULD I BE CRYING?/Just For A Kick	Checker 853	2.00	8.00	56

FLANNELS, The

HEY RUBE/So Shy	Tampa 121	8.00	32.00	56

FLARES, Cookie Jackson & The

FLARES, The

FLASH TERRY:
see Terry, Flash

FLEETONES, The

PLEASE TELL ME/Your Lover Man	Bandera 2511	4.00	16.00	61

FLEMONS, Wade

FLENNOY TRIO, The

CHERRY/Poor Butterfly (78)	Melodisc 103	1.50	6.00	—
DID YOU EVER LOVE A WOMAN? PART 1/ Did You Ever Love A Woman? Part 2 (78)	Excelsior 151	1.50	6.00	—
HEY, LAWDY MAMA/My Honey Chile (78)	Melodisc 101	1.50	6.00	—
I AIN'T MAD AT YOU, PRETTY BABY/ Induction Blues (78)	Excelsior 116/117	1.50	6.00	—
I'M FOR YOU/E-Bob-O-Lee-Bob (78)	Excelsior 130	1.50	6.00	—
IT'S ONLY A PAPER MOON/I'll Be True (78)	Excelsior 139	1.50	6.00	—
MY LOVE/That's The Wrong Gal, Brother (78)	Excelsior 140	1.50	6.00	—
SOMEBODY GOT TO GO, MR. JONES/ Now That You Know (78)	Excelsior 118/119	1.50	6.00	—

FLENNOY TRIO, The (with Joe Turner)

I DON'T DIG IT/I Saw A Star (78)	Excelsior 533	1.50	6.00	—
OOO-UGH STOMP, THE/The T. W. Boogie (78)	Excelsior 534	1.50	6.00	—

FLETCHER, Darrow

FLIPPERS, The

YOU YAKITY YAK TOO MUCH/My Aching Heart	Flip 305	5.00	20.00	55

FLORESCENTS, The

WHAT ARE YOU DOING TONIGHT?/Being In Love	Bethlehem 3079	2.00	8.00	63

FLOYD, Eddie

FLOYD, Eddie:
see Falcons, The (with Eddie Floyd)

FLOYD, Frank

MONKEY LOVE/Rock A Little Baby	F & L 100	30.00	120.00	54

F & L is Floyd's own record label.

FLOYD, Frank as Harmonica Frank

HOWLIN' TOMCAT/She Done Moved (78)	Chess 1494	5.00	20.00	51
ROCKIN' CHAIR DADDY/The Great Medical Menagerist	Sun 205	60.00	240.00	54
SWAMP ROOT/Goin' Away Walkin' (78)	Chess 1475	6.25	25.00	51
SWAMP ROOT/Step It Up And Go (78)	Chess 1475	6.25	25.00	51

FLOYD, King

FLYERS, The

ON BENDED KNEE/My Only Desire	Atco 6088	2.00	8.00	57

FORBES, Wes & The Starlarks:
see Starlarks, Wes Forbes & The

FORD, Billy

Billy Ford sang as part of the duo Billy & Lillie in 1958.

OLD AGE/Confessin'	United 167	2.50	10.00	54
SMOOTH ROCKIN'/You Foxie Thing	United 142	2.50	10.00	53
STOP LYING ON ME/String Of Pearls (instrumental)	Josie 775	2.00	8.00	55

FORD, Billy & The Thunderbirds

FORD, Dave & The Ebbtides:
see Ebbtides, David Ford & The

FORD, Dave & The Hollywood Flames

FORD, Dee Dee, Don Gardner &

FORD, Young Henry & The Gifts

FOREST CITY JOE:
see Pugh, Joe as Forest City Joe

FOREVERS, The

FORREST, Earl

I WRONGED A WOMAN/I Can't Forgive You	Meteor 5005	7.00	28.00	53
LAST NIGHT'S DREAM/Fifty Three	Duke 113	2.50	10.00	53
OUT ON A PARTY/Oh Why?	Duke 121	2.50	10.00	54
ROCK THE BOTTLE/Baby, Baby (78)	Duke 103	2.00	8.00	52
TROUBLE AND ME/Midnight Hours Journey (by Johnny Ace)	Flair 1015	8.00	32.00	53
WHOOPIN' AND HOLLERIN'/Pretty Bessie	Duke 108	3.00	12.00	52
YOUR KIND OF LOVE/Ooh Ooh Wee	Duke 130	2.00	8.00	54

FORREST, Gene & The Four Feathers:
see Four Feathers, Gene Forrest & The

FORREST, Jimmy

NIGHT TRAIN/Bolo Blues (instrumental) (red plastic)	United 113	2.50	10.00	52
NIGHT TRAIN/Bolo Blues (instrumental)	United 110	1.50	6.00	52

FORTESCUE, John Henry as Guitar Shorty

HARD LIFE/Ways Of A Man	Pull 301	3.00	12.00	59
HOW LONG CAN IT LAST?/Love Loves	Pull 302	3.00	12.00	59
YOU DON'T TREAT ME RIGHT/Irma Lee	Cobra 5017	3.00	12.00	57

FORTUNE TELLERS, The

FORTUNE, Jessie

GOOD THINGS/God's Gift To Man	USA 747	2.00	8.00	63
TOO MANY COOKS/Heavy Heart Beat	USA 738	1.50	6.00	63

FORTUNEERS, The

OH, WOH, BABY/Look A There	Skytone 1000	1.50	6.00	—

FORTUNES, The

CONGRATULATIONS/Look At Me, Look At You	Argo 5364	2.00	8.00	60

TITLE/FLIP	LABEL & NO.	GOOD TO VERY GOOD	NEAR MINT	YR.

FORTUNES, The
BELIEVE IN ME/My Baby Is Fine	Checker 818	2.50	10.00	55

FORTUNES, The
HOW CLEVER OF YOU/Trees	Decca 30688	5.00	20.00	58
WHO CARES?/Tarnished Angel	Decca 30541	6.25	25.00	58

FORTUNES, The
STEADY VOWS/In The Night	Top Rank 2019	1.50	6.00	59

FOSTER BROTHERS, The
IF YOU WANT MY HEART/Show Me	Mercury 71360	1.50	6.00	58
REVENGE/Pretty, Fickle Woman	B And F 1333	1.50	6.00	60
TELL ME WHO/I Said She Wouldn't Do	El Bee 161	3.00	12.00	57
TRUST IN ME/Why-Yi-Yi?	Profile 4004	2.00	8.00	59

FOSTER, Cell & The Audios:
see Audios, Cell Foster & The

FOSTER, Helen:
see Chapters, Helen Foster & The
see Rovers, Helen Foster & The

FOSTER, Leroy & Muddy Waters
LOCKED OUT BOOGIE/Shady Grove Blues (78)	Aristocrat 12334	7.00	28.00	49

FOSTER, Leroy as Baby Face
RED HEADED WOMAN/Moonshine Blues (78)	Savoy 1122	2.50	10.00	50

FOSTER, Leroy as Baby Face & The Sunnyland Trio
PET RABBIT/Louella (78)	JOB 1002	12.50	50.00	52

FOSTER, Leroy as Baby Face Leroy
MY HEAD CAN'T REST ANYMORE/Take A Little Walk With Me (78)	Chess 1447	4.00	16.00	50
MY HEAD CAN'T REST ANYMORE/Take A Little Walk With Me (78)	JOB 100	6.25	25.00	50

FOSTER, Leroy as Little Walter
Foster should not be confused with Marion Walter Jacobs, who also recorded as Little Walter, nor with George Smith, who recorded as Little Walter, Jr., nor with a fourth artist who recorded during the 60s as Little Red Walter.

BOLL WEEVIL/Rollin' And Tumblin' (78)	Herald 404	5.00	20.00	50
I JUST KEEP LOVING HER/Moonshine Blues (78)	Parkway 502	12.50	50.00	50
I JUST KEEP LOVING HER/Take A Walk With Me (78)	Herald 403	5.00	20.00	50

FOSTER, Leroy as The Baby Face Leroy Trio
BOLL WEEVIL/Red Headed Woman (78)	Parkway 104	12.50	50.00	50
ROLLIN' AND TUMBLIN', PART 1/Rollin' And Tumblin', Part 2 (78)	Parkway 501	15.00	60.00	50

FOSTER, Lester as Long Tall Lester

FOSTER, Little Willie
CRYING THE BLUES/Little Girl	Cobra 5011	5.00	20.00	57
FALLING RAIN BLUES/Four Day Jump (red plastic)	Blue Lake 113	15.00	60.00	53
FALLING RAIN BLUES/Four Day Jump	Blue Lake 113	10.00	40.00	53
FALLING RAIN BLUES Four Day Jump	Parrot 813	12.50	50.00	53

FOUR ACES, The
Should not be confused with the popular music group which recorded mainly for Decca.

AIN'T IT A CRYING SHAME?/Gumbo (78)	Trilon 180	2.50	10.00	—
I WONDER, I WONDER, I WONDER/I Wonder, I Wonder, I Wonder (instrumental) (78)	Trilon 143	2.50	10.00	—
I'LL NEVER LET YOU GO AGAIN/Cherie (78)	Trilon 178	2.50	10.00	—
I'M CRYING ALL THE TIME/This Little Chick Went To Market (78)	Trilon 179	2.50	10.00	—
RICHARD AIN'T GONNA OPEN THAT DOOR/Richard's Jam (instrumental) (78)	Trilon 153	3.00	12.00	—
THERE'S A RUMOR GOING AROUND/St. Louis Boogie (instrumental) (78)	Trilon 145	2.50	10.00	—

FOUR ACES, The:
see Original Four Aces, The

FOUR AFTER FIVES, The
HELLO, SCHOOL TEACHER!/I Gotta Have Somebody	All Time 9076	2.50	10.00	61

FOUR BARONS, The
LEMON SQUEEZER/Got To Go Back Again (78)	Regent 1026	2.50	10.00	50

FOUR BARS AND A MELODY, The
NEAR YOU/It Shouldn't Happen To A Dream (78)	Savoy 657	1.50	6.00	48

FOUR BARS, Betty Wilson & The

FOUR BARS, Shane Hunter & The

FOUR BARS, The
GRIEF BY DAY, GRIEF BY NIGHT/Hey, Baby	Josie 762	20.00	80.00	54
IF I GIVE MY HEART TO YOU/Stop It! Quit It!	Josie 768	15.00	60.00	54
LET ME LIVE/Why Do You Treat Me This Way?	Josie 783	10.00	40.00	55

FOUR BELLS, The
ONLY A MIRACLE/My Tree	Gem 220	40.00	160.00	54
PLEASE TELL IT TO ME/Long Way To Go	Gem 207	55.00	220.00	53

FOUR BLAZES, The
DO THE DO/Did You Ever See A Monkey Do The Monkey?	United 177	2.50	10.00	54
ELLA LOUISE/Perfect Woman	United 158	2.50	10.00	53
MARY JO/Mood Indigo	United 114	7.00	28.00	52
MY GREAT LOVE AFFAIR/All Night Long	United 168	2.50	10.00	54
NIGHT TRAIN/Rug Cutter	United 125	4.00	16.00	52
NOT ANY MORE TEARS/My Hat's On The Side Of My Head	United 146	2.50	10.00	53
PLEASE SEND HER BACK TO ME/Stop Boogie Woogie	United 127	4.00	16.00	52

FOUR BLUEBIRDS, The
MY BABY DONE TOLD ME/Court Room Blues (by Johnny Otis & Orchestra) (78)	Excelsior 540	5.00	20.00	—

FOUR BLUES, The
AM I ASKING TOO MUCH? (by Lee Richardson)/The Blues Can Jump (78)	De Luxe 3195	2.00	8.00	48
BLUER THAN BLUER THAN BLUE/Honey Chile (78)	Decca 8637	2.50	10.00	42
CHITTLINS AND PIGS FEET/Baby, I Need A Whole Lot Of Everything (78)	De Luxe 1001	2.00	8.00	45
EASY DOES IT/Jitterug Sadie (78)	Decca 8517	2.50	10.00	41
I GOT A DATE WITH RHYTHM (by Billy Eckstine)/I Couldn't Hear Nobody Pray (78)	De Luxe 1003	2.00	8.00	45
I'M GONE/Bell Bottom Trousers (78)	De Luxe 1000	2.00	8.00	45
IT TAKES A LONG TALL BROWNSKINNED GAL/Honey Chile (78)	Apollo 398	2.00	8.00	48
MISSING YOU/As Long As I Live (78)	Apollo 1160	2.00	8.00	50
RE BOP-DE-BOOM/The Vegetable Song (78)	Apollo 1145	2.00	8.00	50
STUDY WAR NO MO'/Noah And The Ark (78)	De Luxe 1005	2.00	8.00	45
THINGS YOU WANT THE MOST OF ALL/Oh Daddy, Please Bring That Suitcase In (78)	De Luxe 1002	2.00	8.00	45
WHEN THE OLD GANG'S BACK ON THE CORNER/The Blues Can Jump (78)	De Luxe 1004	2.00	8.00	45

FOUR BROTHERS & A COUSIN, The
TRUST IN ME/Whistle Stop Blues	Jaguar 3003	30.00	120.00	54
WHISPERING WINDS/Can It Be?	Jaguar 3005	40.00	160.00	54

FOUR BUDDIES, Bobbie James & The
I NEED YOU SO/Baby, I'm Tired	Club 51 104	15.00	60.00	56

FOUR BUDDIES, Dolly Cooper & The
I'D CLIMB THE HIGHEST MOUNTAIN/I Wanna Know	Savoy 891	2.50	10.00	53

FOUR BUDDIES, Rudy Greene & The
YOU MEAN EVERYTHING TO ME/Highway No. 1	Club 51 103	15.00	60.00	56

FOUR BUDDIES, The
DELORES/Look Out (red plastic)	Club 51 105	30.00	120.00	56
DELORES/Look Out	Club 51 105	15.00	60.00	56

FOUR BUDDIES, The
DON'T LEAVE ME NOW/Sweet Slumber	Savoy 779	15.00	60.00	51
HEART AND SOUL/Sin	Savoy 817	12.50	50.00	51
I WILL WAIT/Just To See You Smile Again	Savoy 769	12.50	50.00	50
MY MOTHER'S EYES/Ooh-Ow	Savoy 888	5.00	20.00	53
MY SUMMER'S GONE/Why At A Time Like This?	Savoy 789	15.00	60.00	51
SIMPLY SAY GOODBYE/Window Eyes	Savoy 823	20.00	80.00	51
WHAT'S THE MATTER WITH ME?/Sweet Tooth For My Baby	Savoy 866	9.00	36.00	52
YOU'RE PART OF ME/Story Blues	Savoy 845	8.00	32.00	52

FOUR BUDS, The

FOUR CASTS, The

FOUR CHANELS, Virgil & The

TITLE/FLIP	LABEL & NO.	GOOD TO VERY GOOD	NEAR MINT	YR.
FOUR CHEVELLES, The				
I CAN'T BELIEVE/I Know	Band Box 358	1.50	6.00	64
THIS IS OUR WEDDING DAY/Darling, Forever	Band Box 357	1.50	6.00	64
FOUR CHICADEES, The (female group)				
DING DONG/Teenage Blues	Checker 849	1.50	6.00	56
FOUR CHORDS, The				
AGAIN/You Had The Blues (78)	Sittin' In With 516	2.50	10.00	49
FOUR CLEFS, The				
DIG THESE BLUES/Four Clefs Boogie (78)	RCA Victor 20-4507	2.00	8.00	52
These songs were recorded in 1940 and 1942.				
FOUR CLEFS, The: see Cats & The Fiddle, The				
FOUR CLIPPERS, The				
YOU CAN'T TRUST A WOMAN/Rain	Fox (no number)	7.00	28.00	57
FOUR CLOSURES, The				
FOUR COUNTS, The				
YOUNG HEARTS/I'M Gonna Love You	Dart 1014	2.00	8.00	—
FOUR COUSINS, The				
TIME AND TIME AGAIN/Guaranteed	20th Century 75020	5.00	20.00	58
FOUR CRUISERS, The				
ON ACCOUNT OF YOU/Beale St. Shuffle	Chess 1547	15.00	60.00	53
FOUR DEEP TONES, The				
JUST IN CASE YOU CHANGE YOUR MIND/Castle Rock	Coral 65061	10.00	40.00	51
NIGHT YOU SAID GOODBYE, THE/ When The Saints Go Marching In	Coral 65062	10.00	40.00	51
FOUR DEUCES, The				
DOWN IT WENT/Goose Is Gone	Music City 796	5.00	20.00	56
W-P-L-J/ Here Lies My Love (by Mr. Undertaker) (black label)	Music City 790	4.00	16.00	55
W-P-L-J/ Here Lies My Love (by Mr. Undertaker) (maroon label)	Music City 790	8.00	32.00	55
FOUR DOTS, Jerry Stone & The				
IT'S HEAVEN/My Baby	Freedom 44002	2.50	10.00	58
PLEADING FOR YOUR LOVE/Don't Wake Up The Kids	Freedom 44005	4.00	16.00	58
FOUR DOTS, The				
PEACE OF MIND/Kiss Me, Sugar Plum	Bullseye 104	4.00	16.00	56
RITA/He Man Looking For A She Girl	Bullseye 103	10.00	40.00	56
FOUR DOTS, The				
MY DEAR/You Won't Let Me Go (78)	Dot 1043	5.00	20.00	51
FOUR DUCHESSES, The (female group)				
CRY FOR MY BABY/Queen Without A King	Chief 7014	2.50	10.00	60
FOUR DUKES, The				
CRYING IN THE CHAPEL/I Done Done It	Duke 116	20.00	80.00	53
FOUR ELDORADOS, The				
LONELY BOY, A/Go! Little Susie	Academy 8138	15.00	60.00	58
FOUR FEATHERS, Gene Forrest & The				
WIGGIE/Dubio	Aladdin 3224	2.50	10.00	54
FOUR FELLOWS, Bette McLaurin & The				
GROW OLD ALONG WITH ME/So Will I	Glory 233	2.00	8.00	55
JUST COME A LITTLE BIT CLOSER/ A Love That's True	Glory 237	2.00	8.00	55
FOUR FELLOWS, The				
STOP CRYING/Break My Bones	Tri-Boro 101	8.00	32.00	53
FOUR FELLOWS, The				
ANGELS SAY/In The Rain	Glory 236	2.00	8.00	55
DARLING YOU/Please Don't Deprive Me Of Love	Glory 242	2.50	10.00	56
FALLEN ANGEL/Hold 'Em, Joe	Glory 238	2.00	8.00	56
GIVE ME BACK MY BROKEN HEART/ Loving You, Darling	Glory 250	2.50	10.00	57
I SIT IN MY WINDOW/Please Play My Song	Glory 244	2.50	10.00	56
I TRIED/Bend Of The River	Derby 862	5.00	20.00	54
I WISH I DIDN'T KNOW YOU/I Know Love	Glory 231	4.00	16.00	55
PETTICOAT BABY/ I'm Past Sixteen (with Bette McLaurin)	Glory 241	1.50	6.00	56
SOLDIER BOY/Take Me Back, Baby	Glory 234	1.50	6.00	55
YOU DON'T KNOW ME/You Sweet Girl	Glory 248	2.50	10.00	56
YOU'RE STILL IN MY HEART/ Johnny The Dreamer (with Toni Banks)	Glory 263	1.50	6.00	57
FOUR FLAMES, The				
FOUR GABRIELS, The				
GLORIA/Recess In Heaven (78)	World 2505	2.50	10.00	48
FOUR GENTS, The				
ON BENDED KNEE/Linda	Park 113	15.00	60.00	57
FOUR HAVEN KNIGHTS, The				
IN MY LONELY ROOM/I'm Just A Dreamer	Atlas 1066	7.00	28.00	57
IN MY LONELY ROOM/I'm Just A Dreamer	Josie 824	3.00	12.00	57
WHY GO ON PRETENDING?/Just To Be In Love	Atlas 1092	5.00	20.00	57
FOUR HAWKS, Erskine Hawkins & The: see Hawkins, Erskine & The Four Hawks				
FOUR INTRUDERS, The				
FOUR JACKS, Lil Greenwood & The				
MY LAST HOUR/Monday Morning Blues	Federal 12082	15.00	60.00	52
NEVER AGAIN/Grandpa Can Boogie, Too	Federal 12093	15.00	60.00	52
FOUR JACKS, Mac Burney & The				
LET ME GET NEXT TO YOU/Walking And Crying	Hollywood 1058	15.00	60.00	56
TIRED OF YOUR SEXY WAYS/This Is My Last Affair	Aladdin 3274	7.00	28.00	54
FOUR JACKS, Shirley Haven & The				
TROUBLES OF MY OWN/Stop Foolin' Around	Federal 12092	25.00	100.00	52
FOUR JACKS, The				
I AIN'T COMING BACK ANYMORE (with Cora Williams)/ Sure Cure For The Blues (with Shirley Haven)	Federal 12079	60.00	240.00	52
I'LL BE HOME AGAIN/The Last Of The Good Rocking Men	Federal 12087	25.00	100.00	52
YOU MET A FOOL/Goodbye, Baby	Federal 12075	40.00	160.00	52
FOUR JEWELS, The (female group)				
FOUR JOKERS, The				
WRITTEN IN THE STARS/The Run Around	Sue 703	8.00	32.00	58
FOUR JUMPS OF JIVE, The				
BOO BOO FINE JELLY/ Streamline Woman Blues (78)	Mercury 2015	1.50	6.00	46
SATCHEL MOUTH BABY/It's Just The Blues (78)	Mercury 2001	1.50	6.00	46
FOUR KINGS, The				
DOO-LI-OP/Rose Of Tangier	Fortune 517	5.00	20.00	55
MY HEAD GOES ACTING UP/You Don't Mean Me, Right?	Fortune 811	7.00	28.00	54
FOUR KINGS, The				
YOU NEVER KNEW/Do You Want To Rock?	Jax 323	20.00	80.00	54
FOUR KINGS, Willie Mitchell & The				
TELL IT TO ME, BABY/Walking At Your Will	Stomper Time 1160	4.00	16.00	—
FOUR KITTENS, Fat Man Mathews & The: see Mathews, Fat Man & The Four Kittens				
FOUR KNIGHTS, Nat King Cole & The				
FOUR KNIGHTS, The				
ANNIVERSARY SONG/A Few Kind Words	Capitol 2403	1.50	6.00	53
BABY DOLL/Tennessee Train	Capitol 2517	1.50	6.00	53
CRY/Charmaine	Capitol 1875	2.00	8.00	51
FIVE FOOT TWO, EYES OF BLUE/ Marshmallow Moon	Capitol 1914	1.50	6.00	51
FUNNY HOW YOU GET ALONG WITHOUT ME/ Walkin' With My Shadow (78)	Decca 48014	1.50	6.00	46
HE'LL UNDERSTAND AND SAY WELL DONE/ Lead Me To That Rock	Decca 48018	5.00	20.00	52
I GO CRAZY/Got Her Off My Hands	Capitol 1787	2.00	8.00	51
IN THE CHAPEL IN THE MOONLIGHT/I Want To Say Hello	Capitol 1840	2.00	8.00	51
IT'S A SIN TO TELL A LIE/ I'm The World's Biggest Fool	Capitol 2087	2.00	8.00	52
JUST IN CASE YOU CHANGE YOUR MIND/ Don't Be Ashamed To Say I Love You (78)	Decca 11003	1.50	6.00	46

TITLE/FLIP	LABEL & NO.	GOOD TO VERY GOOD	NEAR MINT	YR.
JUST IN CASE YOU CHANGE YOUR MIND/ Don't Be Ashamed To Say I Love You (78)	*Decca 48026*	1.50	6.00	*47*
LIES/One Way Kisses	*Capitol 2234*	1.50	6.00	*52*
MORE I GO OUT WITH SOMEBODY ELSE, THE/ The Doll With The Sawdust Heart	*Capitol 1998*	2.00	8.00	*52*
OH, BABY MINE/I Couldn't Stay Away From You	*Capitol 2654*	2.00	8.00	*53*

The first side of Capitol 2654 was retitled "I Get So Lonely" on the second pressing.

TITLE/FLIP	LABEL & NO.	GOOD TO VERY GOOD	NEAR MINT	YR.
OH, HAPPY DAY/A Million Tears	*Capitol 2315*	1.50	6.00	*52*
SENTIMENTAL FOOL/I Love The Sunshine Of Your Smile	*Capitol 1587*	2.50	10.00	*51*
SIN/The Glory Of Love	*Capitol 1806*	2.00	8.00	*51*
SO SOON/I'm Falling For You (78)	*Decca 24139*	1.50	6.00	*47*
THAT'S THE WAY IT'S GOING TO BE/Say No More	*Capitol 2195*	1.50	6.00	*52*
WALKIN' IN THE SUNSHINE/ There Are Two Sides To Ev'ry Heart-Ache	*Capitol 1971*	2.00	8.00	*52*
WAY IF FEEL, THE/I Wish I Had A Girl	*Capitol 1930*	2.00	8.00	*52*
WHO AM I?/Walkin' And Whistlin' Blues	*Capitol 1707*	2.00	8.00	*51*
WIN OR LOSE/Doo Wacka Doo	*Capitol 2127*	2.00	8.00	*52*

FOUR MOST, The

TITLE/FLIP	LABEL & NO.	GOOD TO VERY GOOD	NEAR MINT	YR.
BREEZE AND I, THE/I Love You	*Milo 107*	4.00	16.00	—

FOUR NOTES, The

TITLE/FLIP	LABEL & NO.	GOOD TO VERY GOOD	NEAR MINT	YR.
COFFEE FIVE, DOUGHNUTS FIVE/Jungle Twilight (78)	*Premier 29002*	1.50	6.00	—
DEEP RIVER/Eileen (78)	*International 453/454*	1.50	6.00	—
FOOLISHLY YOURS/St. Louis Blues (78)	*International 215/216*	1.50	6.00	
HOUSE I LIVE IN, THE/ Moonlight Bay (78)	*International 455/456*	1.50	6.00	—
MAY IT BE CHRISTMAS/Auld Lang Syne (78)	*Paradise 113*	1.50	6.00	*48*
ROCKIN' CHAIR/Whiffenpoof Song	*Paradise 115*	1.50	6.00	*48*
WHEN DAY IS DONE/Re-Bop (78)	*International 451/452*	1.50	6.00	

FOUR PALMS, The

FOUR PALS, The

TITLE/FLIP	LABEL & NO.	GOOD TO VERY GOOD	NEAR MINT	YR.
IF I CAN'T HAVE THE ONE I LOVE/I Flipped	*Royal Roost 610*	2.00	8.00	*55*
NO ONE EVER LOVED ME/Can't Stand It Any Longer	*Royal Roost 616*	2.00	8.00	*55*

FOUR PENNIES, The

TITLE/FLIP	LABEL & NO.	GOOD TO VERY GOOD	NEAR MINT	YR.
'TIS THE SEASON/Shake A Hand	*Brunswick 55324*	1.50	6.00	*67*

FOUR PHARAOHS, The

TITLE/FLIP	LABEL & NO.	GOOD TO VERY GOOD	NEAR MINT	YR.
GIVE ME YOUR LOVE/China Girl	*Paradise 109*	5.00	20.00	*58*
GIVE ME YOUR LOVE/China Girl	*Ransom 101*	10.00	40.00	*58*
PRAY FOR ME/The Move Around	*Ransom 100*	4.00	16.00	*57*

FOUR PLAID THROATS, The

TITLE/FLIP	LABEL & NO.	GOOD TO VERY GOOD	NEAR MINT	YR.
MY INSPIRATION/The Message	*Mercury 70143*	25.00	100.00	*53*

FOUR ROCKETS, The

TITLE/FLIP	LABEL & NO.	GOOD TO VERY GOOD	NEAR MINT	YR.
LITTLE BROWN JUG/Loch Lomond (78)	*Aladdin 3017*	2.50	10.00	*48*
LITTLE RED WAGON/Travelin' Light (78)	*Aladdin 3007*	2.50	10.00	*48*

FOUR SHADES OF RHYTHM, The

TITLE/FLIP	LABEL & NO.	GOOD TO VERY GOOD	NEAR MINT	YR.
I CAN DREAM/Master Of Me (78)	*Old Swingmaster 23*	1.50	6.00	*49*
MY BLUE WALK/Baby, I'm Gone (78)	*Old Swingmaster 13*	1.50	6.00	*49*

FOUR SHARPS, The

TITLE/FLIP	LABEL & NO.	GOOD TO VERY GOOD	NEAR MINT	YR.
DON'T ASK ME WHY/I Can Hardly Wait (78)	*Atlantic 875*	2.50	10.00	*49*

FOUR SOUNDS, The

TITLE/FLIP	LABEL & NO.	GOOD TO VERY GOOD	NEAR MINT	YR.
AFRAID/Tall Lanky Papa	*Celeste 3010*	15.00	60.00	*57*
YOU STOLE MY HEART/Noisy Clock	*Celeste 3013*	15.00	60.00	*57*

FOUR SPEEDS, The

TITLE/FLIP	LABEL & NO.	GOOD TO VERY GOOD	NEAR MINT	YR.
I NEED YOU, BABY/The Girls Back Home	*De Luxe 6070*	7.00	28.00	*54*

FOUR SPORTSMEN, The

FOUR STUDENTS, Big John Greer & The

TITLE/FLIP	LABEL & NO.	GOOD TO VERY GOOD	NEAR MINT	YR.
MAN AND A WOMAN, A/Blam (instrumental)	*Groove 0131*	1.50	6.00	*55*

FOUR STUDENTS, Charles Calhoun & The

TITLE/FLIP	LABEL & NO.	GOOD TO VERY GOOD	NEAR MINT	YR.
JAMBOREE/My Pigeon's Gone	*Groove 0149*	1.50	6.00	*56*

FOUR STUDENTS, Lil McKenzie & The

TITLE/FLIP	LABEL & NO.	GOOD TO VERY GOOD	NEAR MINT	YR.
RUN ALONG/The Others I Like	*Groove 0113*	4.00	16.00	*55*

FOUR STUDENTS, Sue Allen & The

TITLE/FLIP	LABEL & NO.	GOOD TO VERY GOOD	NEAR MINT	YR.
THINK OF TOMORROW/Set A Wedding Day	*Groove 0130*	2.50	10.00	*55*

FOUR STUDENTS, The

TITLE/FLIP	LABEL & NO.	GOOD TO VERY GOOD	NEAR MINT	YR.
SO NEAR AND YET SO FAR/Hot Rotten Soda Pop	*Groove 0110*	2.50	10.00	*55*

FOUR STUDENTS, Varetta Dillard & The

FOUR STUDENTS, Zilla Mays & The

TITLE/FLIP	LABEL & NO.	GOOD TO VERY GOOD	NEAR MINT	YR.
COME BACK TO ME/Right Now	*Groove 0127*	1.50	6.00	*55*

FOUR TONES, Dusty Brooks & The

TITLE/FLIP	LABEL & NO.	GOOD TO VERY GOOD	NEAR MINT	YR.
CHILI DOGS/You Never Told A Lie (78)	*Dootone 306*	1.50	6.00	*52*
HEAVEN OR FIRE/Tears And Wine	*Sun 182*	60.00	240.00	*53*
I'LL FOLLOW YOU/Do! Do! Baby (78)	*Lamarrs Star 101*	1.50	6.00	*45*
LITTLE CHUM/Play Jackpot (78)	*Lamarrs Star 103*	1.50	6.00	*45*
LITTLE CHUM/Uptown Rhythm (78)	*Memo 1002*	1.50	6.00	*45*
OL' MAN RIVER/Cream Of Wheat (78)	*Majestic 123*	1.50	6.00	*50*
PLAY JACKPOT/Thank You For The Lies (78)	*Memo 1001*	1.50	6.00	*45*
PLEASE DON'T RUSH ME/ Put Your Cards On The Table (78)	*Memo 7001*	1.50	6.00	*48*
PLEASE DON'T RUSH ME/Seclusion (78)	*Memo 1003*	1.50	6.00	*45*
PUT YOUR CARDS ON THE TABLE/Seclusion (78)	*Memo 1005*	1.50	6.00	*45*
SECLUSION/Thank You For The Lies (78)	*Lamarrs Star 102*	1.50	6.00	*45*
SHOO BOOGIE MAMA/Liddy (78)	*Columbia 30230*	1.50	6.00	*50*
SHUFFLE BOARD BOOGIE/I Didn't Cry (78)	*Majestic 127*	1.50	6.00	*50*
SOMEONE OVER HERE LOVES SOMEONE OVER THERE/ Hey, What You Say? (78)	*Preview 666/667*	1.50	6.00	*45*
TWO TEARS MET/Satchelmouth Baby (78)	*Preview 668/669*	1.50	6.00	*45*

FOUR TOPS, Delores Carroll & The

TITLE/FLIP	LABEL & NO.	GOOD TO VERY GOOD	NEAR MINT	YR.
EVERYBODY KNOWS/I Just Can't Keep The Tears From Tumblin' Down	*Chateau 2002*	1.50	6.00	*56*

FOUR TOPS, The

TITLE/FLIP	LABEL & NO.	GOOD TO VERY GOOD	NEAR MINT	YR.
COULD IT BE YOU?/Kiss Me, Baby	*Chess 1623*	5.00	20.00	*56*
PENNIES FROM HEAVEN/Where You Are	*Riverside 4534*	2.50	10.00	*62*

FOUR TUNES, Jimmie Nabbie & The

FOUR TUNES, Juanita Hall & The

Juanita Hall is famous for her portrayal of Bloody Mary in both the original Broadway cast and the motion picture version of South Pacific.

TITLE/FLIP	LABEL & NO.	GOOD TO VERY GOOD	NEAR MINT	YR.
I'M IN THE MOOD FOR LOVE/ Old Bojangles Is Gone	*RCA Victor 47-3149*	5.00	20.00	*50*

FOUR TUNES, Pat Best & The

FOUR TUNES, Savannah Churchill & The

TITLE/FLIP	LABEL & NO.	GOOD TO VERY GOOD	NEAR MINT	YR.
SAVANNAH SINGS THE BLUES/I Want To Be Loved	*Kay-Ron 1000*	1.50	6.00	*56*

FOUR TUNES, The

TITLE/FLIP	LABEL & NO.	GOOD TO VERY GOOD	NEAR MINT	YR.
AM I BLUE?/ There Goes My Heart (red plastic)	*RCA Victor 50-0072*	8.00	32.00	*50*
COME WHAT MAY/The Greatest Song I Ever Heard	*RCA Victor 47-4489*	2.00	8.00	*52*
COOL WATER/How Can You Say That I Don't Care?	*RCA Victor 47-3967*	4.00	16.00	*50*
DO I WORRY?/Say When	*RCA Victor 47-3881*	5.00	20.00	*50*
DON'T GET AROUND MUCH ANYMORE/Water Boy	*RCA Victor 47-5532*	1.50	6.00	*53*
EARLY IN THE MORNING/My Buddy	*RCA Victor 47-4305*	2.50	10.00	*51*
I DON'T WANT TO SET THE WORLD ON FIRE/ Lets Give Love Another Chance	*RCA Victor 47-4968*	4.00	16.00	*52*
I MARRIED AN ANGEL/The Prisoner's Song	*RCA Victor 47-4241*	2.50	10.00	*51*
I UNDERSTAND/Just In Case You Change Your Mind	*Kay-Ron 1005*	2.00	8.00	—
I WONDER/Can I Say Anymore?	*RCA Victor 47-4663*	2.00	8.00	*52*
I'D RATHER BE SAFE THAN SORRY/ I'll Be Waiting For You (78)	*Manor 1049*	1.50	6.00	*46*

This was also released with the artists billed as the Sentimentalists.

TITLE/FLIP	LABEL & NO.	GOOD TO VERY GOOD	NEAR MINT	YR.
I'LL CLOSE MY EYES/Save Me A Dream (78)	*Manor 1047*	1.50	6.00	*46*

This was also released with the artists billed as the Sentimentalists.

TITLE/FLIP	LABEL & NO.	GOOD TO VERY GOOD	NEAR MINT	YR.
I'LL SEE YOU IN MY DREAMS/ Tell Me Why	*RCA Victor 47-4427*	5.00	20.00	*51*
I'M JUST A FOOL IN LOVE/ Lonesome Road (red plastic)	*RCA Victor 50-0042*	8.00	32.00	*49*
MAY THAT DAY NEVER COME/ Carry Me Back To The Lone Prairie (red plastic)	*RCA Victor 50-0131*	7.00	28.00	*51*
MY LAST AFFAIR/I'm The Guy (red plastic)	*RCA Victor 50-0016*	8.00	32.00	*49*
OLD FASHIONED LOVE/Kentucky Babe (red plastic)	*RCA Victor 50-0085*	8.00	32.00	*50*
THEY DON'T UNDERSTAND/ Why Did You Do This To Me?	*RCA Victor 47-4828*	2.00	8.00	*52*
WISHING YOU WERE HERE TONIGHT/ The Last Round-Up	*RCA Victor 47-4102*	5.00	20.00	*51*
YOU'RE HEARTLESS/Careless Love (red plastic)	*RCA Victor 50-0008*	8.00	32.00	*49*

FOUR VAGABONDS, The

TITLE/FLIP	LABEL & NO.	GOOD TO VERY GOOD	NEAR MINT	YR.
DO YOU KNOW WHAT IT MEANS TO MISS NEW ORLEANS?/ The Pleasure's All Mine (78)	*Apollo 1039*	1.50	6.00	*46*
HOE CAKE, HOMINY AND SASSAFRAS TEA/ Kentucky Babe (78)	*Apollo 1030*	1.50	6.00	*46*

TITLE/FLIP	LABEL & NO.	GOOD TO VERY GOOD	NEAR MINT	YR.
I WONDER WHOS KISSING HER NOW?/ Dreams Are A Dime A Dozen (78)	Apollo 1055	1.50	6.00	46
IT CAN'T BE WRONG/ Comin' In On A Wing And A Prayer (78)	Bluebird 30-0815	1.50	6.00	43
LAZY COUNTRY SIDE/Choo-Choo (78)	Apollo 1075	1.50	6.00	47
P.S. I LOVE YOU/Lazy Country Side (78)	Lloyds 102	1.50	6.00	53
P.S. I LOVE YOU/The Freckle Song (78)	Apollo 1057	1.50	6.00	46
ROSIE THE RIVETER/ I Had The Craziest Dream (78)	Bluebird 30-0810	1.50	6.00	43
SLOW AND EASY/Duke Of Dubuque (78)	Bluebird 11519	1.50	6.00	42
TEN LITTLE SOLDIERS/ Rose Ann Of Charing Cross (78)	Bluebird 30-0811	1.50	6.00	43

FOUR WINDS, Sonny Woods & The

TITLE/FLIP	LABEL & NO.	GOOD TO VERY GOOD	NEAR MINT	YR.
I PROMISE/Do You Love Me?	Middle-Tone 008	15.00	60.00	56

FOURMOST, Bobby Moore & The

FOURMOSTS, The

FOX, Eugene

TITLE/FLIP	LABEL & NO.	GOOD TO VERY GOOD	NEAR MINT	YR.
SINNER'S DREAM/Stay At Home	Checker 792	4.00	16.00	54

FOX, Eugene as The Fox

TITLE/FLIP	LABEL & NO.	GOOD TO VERY GOOD	NEAR MINT	YR.
DREAM, THE, PART 1/The Dream, Part 2	RPM 420	7.00	28.00	54

FOX, Eugene as The Sly Fox

TITLE/FLIP	LABEL & NO.	GOOD TO VERY GOOD	NEAR MINT	YR.
HOODOO SAY/I'm Tired Of Beggin'	Spark 108	6.25	25.00	54
MY FOUR WOMEN/Alley Music	Spark 112	6.25	25.00	54

FOX, The:
see Fox, Eugene as The Fox

FOXX, Inez

FOXX, Inez & Charlie as Inez & Charlie Foxx

FRANKIE & THE C NOTES:
see C Notes, Frankie & The

FRANKIE & THE ECHOES

FRANKLIN, Aretha

FRANKLIN, Carolyn

FRANKLIN, Erma

FRANKLIN, Mabel

TITLE/FLIP	LABEL & NO.	GOOD TO VERY GOOD	NEAR MINT	YR.
LET'S DO THE WIGGLE/Dream I Had Last Night	Ritzy 1002	2.00	8.00	65

FRANKLIN, Pete

TITLE/FLIP	LABEL & NO.	GOOD TO VERY GOOD	NEAR MINT	YR.
CASEY BROWN BLUES/Down Behind The Rise (78)	RCA Victor 50-0012	6.25	25.00	47

FRANKLIN, Sonny Boy Orchestra, The

TITLE/FLIP	LABEL & NO.	GOOD TO VERY GOOD	NEAR MINT	YR.
JUMPING THE BLUES/Merry Go Round (78)	Eddie's 1204	2.50	10.00	49

FRAZIER, Calvin

TITLE/FLIP	LABEL & NO.	GOOD TO VERY GOOD	NEAR MINT	YR.
GOT NOBODY TO TELL MY TROUBLES TO/Little Baby Child	Savoy 858	4.00	16.00	52
HAVE BLUES MUST TRAVEL/Lilly Mae	JVB 86	4.00	16.00	58
ROCK HOUSE/We'll Meet Again	JVB 49	5.00	20.00	56

FREDERICK, Tommy & The Hi-Notes

FREEMAN, Bobby

FREEMAN, Ernie

FRENCH, Irlton

TITLE/FLIP	LABEL & NO.	GOOD TO VERY GOOD	NEAR MINT	YR.
MY RUN AROUND BABY/'Bout The Crack O' Dawn	Okeh 6816	4.00	16.00	51

FRIEND, Eddie & The Empires

FRITZ, Joe

TITLE/FLIP	LABEL & NO.	GOOD TO VERY GOOD	NEAR MINT	YR.
CERELLE/If I Didn't Love You So	Peacock 1640	1.50	6.00	51
HONEY, HONEY/Woman I Love	Peacock 1627	1.50	6.00	54

FROST, Frank

FULLER, Johnny

TITLE/FLIP	LABEL & NO.	GOOD TO VERY GOOD	NEAR MINT	YR.
BUDDY/Hard Times	Flair 1054	7.00	28.00	55
FIRST STAGE OF THE BLUES/No More-No More	Irma 110	2.50	10.00	54
FOOL'S PARADISE/Johnny Ace's Last Letter (78)	Rhythm 1767	4.00	16.00	54
I WALK ALL NIGHT/These Young Girls	Money 206	2.50	10.00	55
LOVIN' LOVIN' MAN/Remember (78)	Rhythm 1777	4.00	16.00	55
MEAN OLD WORLD/How Long? (78)	Rhythm 1779	2.00	8.00	55
MEAN OLD WORLD/How Long?	Hollywood 1057	4.00	12.50	55
MY MAMA TOLD ME/Too Late To Change	Hollywood 1077	4.00	16.00	55
ROUGHEST PLACE IN TOWN/Comin' 'Round The Corner	Hollywood 1063	2.50	10.00	55
SUNNY ROAD/I Can't Succeed	Hollywood 1084	4.00	16.00	55
TRAIN, TRAIN BLUES/Bad Luck Overtook Me (78)	Rhythm 1773	2.00	8.00	55
TRAIN, TRAIN BLUES/Bad Luck Overtook Me	Hollywood 1043	3.00	12.00	55

FULLER, Johnny:
see Huff, Willie B. with The Johnny Fuller Orchestra

FULLER, Little Boy:
see Trice, Rich as Little Boy Fuller

FULLER, Playboy:
see Minter, Iverson as Playboy Fuller

FULLER, Rocky:
see Minter, Iverson as Rocky Fuller

FULSON, Lowell

Fulson has also been known as Lowell Fulsom, a spelling of the family name used by his grandfather.

TITLE/FLIP	LABEL & NO.	GOOD TO VERY GOOD	NEAR MINT	YR.
BLACK WIDOW SPIDER/Midnight Showers Of Rain	Swing Time 308	4.00	16.00	51
BLUE SHADOWS/Low Society Blues	Cash 1051	2.00	8.00	50
BLUES NEVER FAIL/You've Got To Reap	Aladdin 3233	3.00	12.00	53
CASH BOX BOOGIE (instrumental)/My Daily Prayer	Swing Time 335	4.00	16.00	53
CHECK YOURSELF/Loving You	Checker 812	1.50	6.00	55
DON'T LEAVE ME, BABY/Chuck With The Boys	Aladdin 3217	3.00	12.00	53
DOUBLE TROUBLE BLUES/Good Woman Blues	Aladdin 3088	8.00	32.00	53
GUITAR SHUFFLE (instrumental)/Mean Old Lonesome Song	Swing Time 295	4.00	16.00	51
HIGHWAY IS MY HOME, THE/(by Lloyd Glenn, piano)	Swing Time 301	4.00	16.00	51
I LOVE MY BABY/Th' Blues Come Rollin' In	Swing Time 330	4.00	16.00	52
I'VE BEEN MISTREATED/ Juke Box Shuffle (instrumental)	Swing Time 338	4.00	16.00	52
I'VE BEEN MISTREATED/Juke Box Shuffle (instrumental) (red plastic)	Parrot 787	12.50	50.00	52
I'VE BEEN MISTREATED/Juke Box Shuffle (instrumental)	Parrot 787	6.25	25.00	52
LET'S LIVE RIGHT/Best Wishes	Swing Time 289	4.00	16.00	51
NIGHT AND DAY/Stormin' And Rainin'	Aladdin 3104	6.25	25.00	53
RAGGEDY DADDY BLUES/Goodbye	Swing Time 315	4.00	16.00	52
RECONSIDER, BABY/I Believe I'll Give It Up	Checker 804	1.50	6.00	54
RIDE UNTIL THE SUN GOES DOWN/Good Party Shuffle (instrumental)	Swing Time 320	4.00	16.00	52
ROCKING AFTER MIDNIGHT/Everyday I Have The Blues	Hollywood 1029	1.50	6.00	50
SCOTTY'S BLUES/ The Train Is Leaving (78)	Scotty's Radio101	1.50	6.00	46
STORMIN' AND RAININ'/Poor Boy (by Ulysses James) (78)	Cavatone 250	4.00	16.00	48
UPSTAIRS/Let Me Ride Your Automobile	Swing Time 325	4.00	16.00	52

FULTON, Sonny & The Mixmasters

FURNESS BROTHERS, The

TITLE/FLIP	LABEL & NO.	GOOD TO VERY GOOD	NEAR MINT	YR.
ONE LITTLE MOMENT WITH YOU/Dukes Place	Rae Cox 104	2.00	8.00	60

FURYS, The

FUZZ, The

G

G-CLEFS, The

TITLE/FLIP	LABEL & NO.	GOOD TO VERY GOOD	NEAR MINT	YR.
CAUSE YOU'RE MINE/Please Write While I'm Away	Pilgrim 720	1.50	6.00	56

GABOR, Szabo & Bobby Womack

GABRIEL & THE ANGELS

TITLE/FLIP	LABEL & NO.	GOOD TO VERY GOOD	NEAR MINT	YR.
GADDY, Bob & His Alley Cats				
I (BELIEVE YOU GOT A SIDEKICK)/Bicycle Boogie (instrumental) (red plastic)	Jackson 2303	20.00	80.00	52
NO HELP WANTED/Little Girl's Boogie (instrumental) (red plastic)	Jax 308	15.00	60.00	52
GADDY, Bob & His Keys				
BLUES HAS WALKED IN MY ROOM/Slow Down, Baby	Harlem 2330	10.00	40.00	52
GAILTONES, The				
GAINES, Roy				
LOUD MOUTH LUCY/I'm Setting You Free	Chart 600	2.50	10.00	55
RIGHT NOW, BABY/De Dat De Dum Dum	Groove 0146	1.50	6.00	56
WORRIED 'BOUT YOU, BABY/All My Life	Groove 0161	1.50	6.00	56
GAINORS, The				
GALE, Billy				
NIGHT HOWLER/My Heart In Your Hands	Flair 1038	5.00	20.00	53
GALE, Billy as Billy Gayles				
DO RIGHT, BABY/No Coming Back	Federal 12282	2.00	8.00	56
I'M TORE UP/If I Never Had Known You	Federal 12265	2.00	8.00	56
JUST ONE MORE TIME/Sad As A Man Can Be	Federal 12287	2.00	8.00	57
TAKE YOUR FINE FRAME HOME/Let's Call It A Day	Federal 12272	2.00	8.00	56
GALE, Sunny & The Du Droppers: see Du Droppers, Sunny Gale & The				
GALES, The				
DARLING PATRICIA/All Is Well, All Is Well	J V B 35	20.00	80.00	55
DARLING PATRICIA/All Is Well, All Is Well	JOB 3001	15.00	60.00	56
DON'T LET THE SUN CATCH YOU CRYING/ My Eyes Keep Me In Trouble	J V B 34	20.00	80.00	55
GALLAHADS, The				
WHY DO FOOLS FALL IN LOVE?/Gone	Rendezvous 153	3.00	12.00	61
GANG, Kool & The				
GANT, Cecil				
GOD BLESS MY DADDY/The Grass Is Gettin' Greener	Decca 48249	2.50	10.00	50
IT'S CHRISTMAS TIME AGAIN/Hello, Santa Claus	Decca 48185	2.50	10.00	50
MY LITTLE BABY/Don't You Worry	Decca 48212	2.50	10.00	51
OWL STEW/Playin' Myself The Blues	Decca 48231	2.50	10.00	50
SHOT GUN BOOGIE/Rock Little Baby	Decca 48200	4.00	16.00	51
TRAIN TIME BLUES NO. 2/It Ain't Gonna Be Like That	Decca 48190	2.50	10.00	50
GANT, Cecil as Gunter Lee Carr				
GOODNIGHT IRENE/My House Fell Down	Decca 48167	2.50	10.00	50
WE'RE GONNA ROCK/Yesterday	Decca 48170	2.50	10.00	50
GANT, Pvt. Cecil "The G.I. Sing-Station"				
HOGAN'S ALLEY/Why? (78)	King 4231	2.50	10.00	47
I WONDER/Cecil's Boogie (instrumental)	Decca 30320	3.00	12.00	52
I WONDER/Cecil's Boogie (instrumental)	Gilt Edge 501	3.00	12.00	52
SOMEDAY YOU'LL BE SORRY, PART 1/Someday You'll Be Sorry, Part 2	Decca 48171	2.50	10.00	50
TRAIN TIME BLUES/Sloppy Joe's	Dot 1121	2.50	10.00	52
GARDENIAS, The				
FLAMING LOVE/My Baby's Tops	Federal 12284	5.00	20.00	56
I'M LAUGHING AT YOU/Houdini	Hi-Q 5005	1.50	6.00	58
GARDNER, Don & Dee Dee Ford				
GARLAND, Willie				
GARLOW, Clarence				
IF I KEEP ON WORRYING/I Called You Up, Daddy	Feature 3005	4.00	16.00	54
NEW BON TON ROULA/Dreaming	Aladdin 3179	6.25	25.00	52
YOU GOT ME CRYING/I'm Hurt	Aladdin 3225	4.00	16.00	52
GARLOW, Clarence & His Accordian				
ZA BELLE/Made Me Cry	Folk Star 1130	4.00	16.00	54
GARLOW, Clarence & His Guitar				
IN A BOOGIE MOOD/Bon Ton Roula (78)	Macy's 5002	1.50	6.00	49
SHE'S SO FINE/Blues As You Like It (78)	Macy's 5001	1.50	6.00	49
GARLOW, Clarence & His Orchestra				
NEW BON TON ROULA/Let Me Be Your Santa (78)	Feature 100	1.50	6.00	51

TITLE/FLIP	LABEL & NO.	GOOD TO VERY GOOD	NEAR MINT	YR.
GARLOW, Clarence "Bon Ton"				
CRAWFISHIN'/Route 90	Flair 1021	6.25	25.00	54
GARLOW, Clarence "Bon Ton", His Guitar & Orchestra				
LOUISIANA BLUES/Watch Your Business (78)	Lyric 100	2.00	8.00	51
WRONG DOING WOMAN/Trouble With My Woman (78)	Lyric 101	2.00	8.00	51
GARLOW, Clarence, His Guitar & Orchestra				
NO, NO BABY/I Feel Like Calling You	Folk Star 1199	2.50	10.00	54
PURTY LITTLE DOOLIE/Sundown	Goldband 1043	1.50	6.00	54
GARNER, Billy				
GARRETT, Robert				
GASSERS, The				
TELL ME/Hum De Dum	Cash 1035	5.00	20.00	56
GATES, The: see Golden Gate Quartet, The as The Gates				
GATOR TAIL: see Jackson, Willis (Gator Tail)				
GATORVETTES, The				
IF IT'S TONIGHT/Midnight	Bocaldun 1001	5.00	20.00	—
IF IT'S TONIGHT/Midnight	Thunder 1001	9.00	36.00	—
GAY CATS OF RHYTHM, Jimmy Coe & His: see Coe, Jimmy & His Gay Cats of Rhythm				
GAY KNIGHTS, The				
ANGEL/The Loudness Of My Heart	Pet 801	3.00	12.00	58
GAY NOTES, The (female group)				
HEAR MY PLEA/Crossroads	Post 2006	2.50	10.00	55
GAY NOTES, The				
FOR ONLY A MOMENT/Pu Pu Pa Doo	Drexel 905	30.00	120.00	55
GAY NOTES, The				
WAITING IN THE CHAPEL/Plea Of Love	Zynn 504	15.00	60.00	58
GAY POPPERS, The				
GOT YOU ON MIND/Don't Go	Dome 502	5.00	20.00	—
THRILL OF ROMANCE/ Wh-y-y Leave Me This Wa-y-y (red plastic)	Timely 1002	50.00	200.00	53
THRILL OF ROMANCE/ Wh-y-y Leave Me This Wa-y-y	Timely 1002	30.00	120.00	53
GAYE, Marvin				
I'M YOURS, YOU'RE MINE/Sandman	Tamla 54055	1.50	6.00	62
I'M YOURS, YOU'RE MINE/Soldier's Plea	Tamla 54063	1.50	6.00	63
LET YOUR CONSCIENCE BE YOUR GUIDE/ Never Let You Go	Tamla 54041	2.00	8.00	61
GAYE, Marvin & Kim Weston				
GAYE, Marvin & Mary Wells				
GAYE, Marvin & Tammi Terrell				
GAYLARKS, The				
TELL ME, DARLING/Whole Lot Of Love (by the Rovers)	Music City 792	4.00	16.00	55
GAYLE, Barbara & The Larks: see Larks, Barbara Gayle & The				
GAYLES, Billy: see Gale, Billy as Billy Gayles				
GAYLORDS, The				

TITLE/FLIP	LABEL & NO.	GOOD TO VERY GOOD	NEAR MINT	YR.
GAYTEN, Paul				
NERVOUS (instrumental)/ Flat Foot Sam (by Oscar Wills with Fats Domino's Band)	Argo 5277	1.50	6.00	57
GAYTUNES, The				
I LOVE YOU/You Left Me	Joyce 101	7.00	28.00	57
GAZELLES, The				
HONEST/Pretty Baby, Baby	Gotham 315	10.00	40.00	56
GEDDINS, Robert as Bob Geddins				
IRMA JEAN/ Re-Enlistment Blues (by Turner Willis) (78)	Big Town 1058	1.50	6.00	45
IRMA JEAN/ Re-Enlistment Blues (by Turner Willis) (78)	Trilon 1058	2.00	8.00	45
GEDDINS, Robert as Bob Geddins & His Cavaliers				
THINKIN' AND THINKIN'/ (by Sherman Louis as Sherman's Trio) (78)	Cavatone 5	2.50	10.00	49
THINKIN' AND THINKIN'/ (by Sherman Louis as Sherman's Trio) (78)	Modern 20-685	2.00	8.00	49
GEDDINS, Robert as Bob Geddins' Cavaliers				
I'M A STRANGER/St. Louis Blues (78)	Cavatone 103	3.00	12.00	49
GEMS, The				
'DEED I DO/Talk About The Weather (red plastic)	Drexel 901	40.00	160.00	54
'DEED I DO/Talk About The Weather	Drexel 901	30.00	120.00	54
I THOUGHT YOU'D CARE/Kitty From New York City	Drexel 903	30.00	120.00	54
ONE WOMAN MAN/The Darkest Night	Drexel 909	35.00	140.00	56
TILL THE DAY I DIE/Monkey Face Baby	Drexel 915	25.00	100.00	57
YOU'RE TIRED OF LOVE/Ol' Man River	Drexel 904	35.00	140.00	54
GEMS, The (female group)				
GEMTONES, Eddie Woods & The				
HEAVEN WAS MINE/Prima Vera	Gem 204	2.50	10.00	53
GENE & JERRY				
GENE & THE JEANETTES				
GENE & WENDELL				
GENIES, The				
CRAZY FEELING/Little Young Girl	Warwick 643	2.00	8.00	61
JUST LIKE THE BLUEBIRD/Twistin' Pneumonia	Warwick 607	2.00	8.00	60
THERE GOES THAT TRAIN/Crazy Love	Warwick 573	1.50	6.00	60
GENT, J. C.				
GENTLEMEN, The				
DON'T LEAVE ME, BABY/Baby, Don't	Apollo 470	12.50	50.00	55
SOMETHING TO REMEMBER YOU BY/Tired Of You	Apollo 464	12.50	50.00	54
GEORGE, Barbara				
GEORGE, Lloyd				
COME ON TRAIN/Frog Hunt	Post 1006	2.50	10.00	63
LUCY LEE/Sing Real Loud	Imperial 5837	2.50	10.00	62
GEORGETTES, The (female group)				
GIBRALTERS, Jimmy Barnes & The				
GIBRALTERS, Nappy Brown and The				
GIBSON, Beverly Ann				
GIBSON, Clifford as Grandpappy Gibson				
IT'S BEST TO KNOW WHO YOU'RE TALKING TO/ I Don't Want No Woman	Bobbin 124	4.00	16.00	60
MONKEY LIKES TO BOOGIE, THE/No Success Blues	Bobbin 127	5.00	20.00	60
GIBSON, Daddyo				
GIBSON, Steve & The Red Caps: see Red Caps, Steve Gibson & The as The Original Red Caps; see Red Caps, Steve Gibson & The				
GIFTS, Little Natalie & Henry & The				

TITLE/FLIP	LABEL & NO.	GOOD TO VERY GOOD	NEAR MINT	YR.
GIFTS, Young Henry Ford & The				
GILLETTES, The				
GILLIAM, Earl				
DON'T MAKE ME LATE, BABY/Nobody's Blues	Sarg 128	1.50	6.00	56
WRONG DOING WOMAN/Petite Baby	Sarg 133	1.50	6.00	56
GILLUM, William McKinley as Jazz Gillum				
GONNA BE SOME SHOOTING/A Lie Is Dangerous (red plastic)	RCA Victor 50-0035	5.00	20.00	47
SIGNIFYING WOMAN/ Take A Little Walk With Me (red plastic)	RCA Victor 50-0004	5.00	20.00	47
TAKE ONE MORE CHANCE WITH ME/Look What You Are Today (red plastic)	RCA Victor 50-0017	5.00	20.00	47
GILMORE, Boyd				
ALL IN MY DREAMS/Take A Little Walk With Me	Modern 872	15.00	60.00	52
RAMBLIN' ON MY MIND/Just An Army Boy	Modern 860	15.00	60.00	52
GIRLFRIENDS, Erlene & The				
GIRLFRIENDS, The (female group)				
GLAD RAGS, The				
MY CHINA DOLL/Just One Love	Excello 2121	2.50	10.00	57
GLADIATORS, The				
GIRL OF MY HEART/My Baby Doll	Dig 135	8.00	32.00	57
GLADIOLAS, The				
I WANTA KNOW/Hey! Little Girl	Excello 2120	1.50	6.00	57
LITTLE DARLIN'/Sweetheart, Please Don't Go	Excello 2101	2.00	8.00	57
RUN, RUN LITTLE JOE/Comin' Home To You	Excello 2110	1.50	6.00	57
SAY YOU'LL BE MINE/Shoop, Shoop	Excello 2136	1.50	6.00	58
GLEAMS, Berlin Perry & The				
TENNESSEE WALTZ/Put That Tear Back	Ribbon 6902	2.00	8.00	59
GLENN, Lloyd: see Fulson, Lowell				
GLENNS, The				
GLIDERS, Lavern Baker & The				
GLOW TONES, The				
GO-TOGETHERS, The				
TRAIN/Time After Time	Coast 100	2.50	10.00	—
GOLDEN GATE QUARTET, The as The Gates				
I'M JUST A DREAMER/ She's Gonna Ruin You, Buddy (78)	Columbia 30149	2.50	10.00	48
GOLDEN TONES, Marie Reynaud & The				
GOLDEN TONES, The (with Joe Simon)				
LITTLE ISLAND GIRL/Doreetha	Hush 101	2.50	10.00	59
YOU LEFT ME HERE TO CRY ALONE/Ocean Of Tears	Hush 102	2.50	10.00	59
GOLDEN, John & The Indexes: see Indexes, John Golden & The				
GOLDENRODS, The				
WISH I WAS BACK IN SCHOOL/Color Cartoons	Vee Jay 307	2.00	8.00	58
GOLDENTONES, The				
MEANING OF LOVE, THE/Run, Pretty Baby	Beacon 560	5.00	20.00	55
MEANING OF LOVE, THE/Run, Pretty Baby	Jay Dee 806	9.00	36.00	55
GOLDRUSH				
ALL MY MONEY IS GONE/ Lonesome Blues (by Black Diamond) (78)	Jaxyson 6	7.00	28.00	48
GONDOLIERS, Johnny Adams & The				
KNOCKED OUT/You Call Everybody Darling	Ric 957	3.00	12.00	59
GOOD HUMOR SIX, The: see Crosse, Gay & His Good Humor Six				

GOOD JELLY BESS

GOOD ROCKIN' SAMMY T.

GOODMAN, George & The Headliners

GOODTIMERS, Don Covay & The

GOOGLES, Barney & The

TITLE/FLIP	LABEL & NO.	GOOD TO VERY GOOD	NEAR MINT	YR.
DOIN' THE SHIMMY/Fall Is Here	Shimmy 1055	7.00	28.00	60

GORDON, Big Mike

TITLE/FLIP	LABEL & NO.	GOOD TO VERY GOOD	NEAR MINT	YR.
WALKIN' SLIPPIN' AND SLIDIN'/ (Ho Ho Ho) You Don't Want Me No More	Baton 219	2.00	8.00	54

GORDON, Big Mike as Big Mike

TITLE/FLIP	LABEL & NO.	GOOD TO VERY GOOD	NEAR MINT	YR.
DOWN IN NEW ORLEANS/Rain Or Shine	Savoy 1152	1.50	6.00	54

GORDON, Bill & The Colonials:
see Colonials, Bill Gordon & The

GORDON, Gus & The Darnels:
see Darnels, Gus Gordon & The

GORDON, Junior

TITLE/FLIP	LABEL & NO.	GOOD TO VERY GOOD	NEAR MINT	YR.
MY LOVE FOR YOU/Blow, Wind, Blow	Ace 522	1.50	6.00	56

GORDON, Lena

TITLE/FLIP	LABEL & NO.	GOOD TO VERY GOOD	NEAR MINT	YR.
MAMA TOOK THE BABY/ Disc Jockey Jamboree (by Sax Kari)	Checker 803	2.00	8.00	54

GORDON, Mike & The El Tempos:
see El Tempos, Mike Gordon & The

GORDON, Roscoe

TITLE/FLIP	LABEL & NO.	GOOD TO VERY GOOD	NEAR MINT	YR.
AIN'T NO USE/Roscoe's Mambo	Duke 114	5.00	20.00	53
BOOTED/Cold, Cold Winter	RPM 344	6.25	25.00	51
BOOTED/I Love You Till The Day I Die	Chess 1487	10.00	40.00	52
CHICKEN, THE/Love For You, Baby	Flip 237	2.00	8.00	56
CHICKEN, THE/Love For You, Baby	Sun 237	8.00	32.00	56
DIME A DOZEN/A New Remedy For Love	RPM 336	8.00	32.00	50
JUST IN FROM TEXAS/I'm In Love	RPM 379	4.00	16.00	52
LUCILLE/Blues For My Baby	RPM 373	4.00	16.00	52
NEW ORLEANS WIMMEN/I Remember Your Kisses	RPM 358	5.00	20.00	51
NO MORE DOGGIN'/Maria	RPM 350	6.25	25.00	51
ONCE, PRETTY BABY/Saddle The Cow	RPM 324	8.00	32.00	50
ROSCOE'S BOOGIE/City Woman	RPM 322	8.00	32.00	50
T-MODEL BOOGIE/New Orleans Boogie	Duke 106	6.25	25.00	53
TELL DADDY/Hey, Fat Girl (78)	Duke 101	2.00	8.00	52
THREE CENT LOVE/You Figure It Out	Duke 129	5.00	20.00	54
TOO MANY WOMEN/Wise You, You Baby	Duke 109	6.25	25.00	53
TRYING/Dream Baby	RPM 369	4.00	16.00	52
WE'RE ALL LOADED/Tomorrow May Be Too Late	RPM 384	4.00	16.00	52
WEEPING BLUES/Just Love Me, Baby	Flip 227	8.00	32.00	55
WEEPING BLUES/Just Love Me, Baby	Sun 227	10.00	40.00	55
WHAT YOU GOT ON YOUR MIND?/Two Kinds Of Woman	RPM 365	4.00	16.00	51

GORDON, Sonny:
see Angels, The (male group)

GORDON, Stomp

TITLE/FLIP	LABEL & NO.	GOOD TO VERY GOOD	NEAR MINT	YR.
DAMP RAG/Fat Mama Blues	Decca 48287	2.50	10.00	52
DEVIL'S DAUGHTER/Hide The Bottle	Decca 48290	2.50	10.00	52
GRIND, THE/Don't Be That Way	Chess 1601	2.00	8.00	54
OOH, YES/Please Don't Pass Me By	Decca 48289	2.50	20.00	52
PENNIES FROM HEAVEN/My Mother's Eyes	Decca 48297	2.00	8.00	52
SLOW DADDY BLUES/Dragnet	Mercury 70223	3.00	12.00	53
WHAT'S HER WHIMSEY, DR. KINSEY?/Juicy Lucy	Mercury 70246	3.00	12.00	53

GOREED, Joseph as Joe Williams

EDITOR'S NOTE: Care should be taken not to confuse Joseph Williams, Joseph Leon Williams and Joe Lee Williams, who recorded under several pseudonyms that we've noted on these pages. None should be mistaken for the legendary Joseph Goreed, the award-winning "Joe Williams," who has achieved worldwide recognition for his urban blues and jazz. The latter has been honored on our cover, as a tribute to his universality, and because of the obvious influence to his music in the genre of rhythm and blues by the great Joe Turner.

TITLE/FLIP	LABEL & NO.	GOOD TO VERY GOOD	NEAR MINT	YR.
EVERY DAY I HAVE THE BLUES/They Didn't Believe Me	Checker 762	2.50	10.00	54
IN THE EVENING/Time For Moving	Blue Lake 102	3.00	12.00	54

GRAND PREES, The

TITLE/FLIP	LABEL & NO.	GOOD TO VERY GOOD	NEAR MINT	YR.
SIT AND CRY/Jungle Fever	Candi 1020	1.50	6.00	—

GRANT, O. S. & The Downbeats:
see Downbeats, O. S. Grant & The

GRATE, Miriam & The Dovers:
see Dovers, Miriam Grate & The

GRAVES, Lee

TITLE/FLIP	LABEL & NO.	GOOD TO VERY GOOD	NEAR MINT	YR.
I'M FROM TEXAS/Sixty Years And A Day	Mercury 8222	1.50	6.00	49
PAPA SAID YES, MAMA SAID NO, NO, NO/ Cloudy Weather Blues	Mercury 8214	1.50	6.00	49

GRAY, Arvella

GRAY, Dobie

GREAVES, R. B.

GREEN, Al

GREEN, Al & The Soul Mates

GREEN, Barbara

GREEN, Boy

TITLE/FLIP	LABEL & NO.	GOOD TO VERY GOOD	NEAR MINT	YR.
A AND B BLUES/Play My Juke Box (78)	Regis 120	9.00	36.00	44

GREEN, Clarence

TITLE/FLIP	LABEL & NO.	GOOD TO VERY GOOD	NEAR MINT	YR.
GREEN'S BOUNCE (instrumental)/Galveston (78)	Eddie's 1207	2.00	8.00	48

GREEN, Clarence as Galveston Green

TITLE/FLIP	LABEL & NO.	GOOD TO VERY GOOD	NEAR MINT	YR.
MY TIME IS YOUR TIME/Bye-Baby-Bye (78)	Essex 701	1.50	6.00	52

GREEN, Deroy & The Cool Gents:
see Cool Gents, Deroy Green & The

GREEN, Fred & The Mellards:
see Mellards, Fred Green & The

GREEN, Galveston:
see Green, Clarence as as Galveston Green

GREEN, Garland

GREEN, George

TITLE/FLIP	LABEL & NO.	GOOD TO VERY GOOD	NEAR MINT	YR.
FINANACE MAN/Brand New Rockin' Chair	Chance 1135	10.00	40.00	53

GREEN, L. C.

TITLE/FLIP	LABEL & NO.	GOOD TO VERY GOOD	NEAR MINT	YR.
GOING DOWN TO THE RIVER BLUES/Ramblin' Around Blues (78)	Von 42	8.00	32.00	52
LITTLE MACHINE/Come Back, Sugar Mama (78)	Dot 1147	4.00	16.00	52
LITTLE SCHOOL GIRL/Remember Way Back? (78)	Dot 1128	4.00	16.00	52
WHEN THE SUN IS SHINING/Hold Me In Your Arms (78)	Dot 1103	4.00	16.00	52

GREEN, Larry (Mr. G.)

GREEN, Lil

TITLE/FLIP	LABEL & NO.	GOOD TO VERY GOOD	NEAR MINT	YR.
EVERY TIME/I've Got That Feeling	Atlantic 951	6.25	28.00	51

GREEN, Madeline & The Three Varieties

GREEN, Norman as Guitar Slim Green

Green should not be confused with Alec Seward nor Eddie Jones, who both recorded as Guitar Slim.

TITLE/FLIP	LABEL & NO.	GOOD TO VERY GOOD	NEAR MINT	YR.
ROCK THE NATION/Movin' Out, Baby	Geenote 907	2.50	10.00	57

GREEN, Norman as R. Green & Turner

Green's recording as R. Green was one of his earliest and, supposedly, Turner was his girlfriend, though her involvement, if any, is unknown to us.

TITLE/FLIP	LABEL & NO.	GOOD TO VERY GOOD	NEAR MINT	YR.
ALLA BLUES/Central Ave. Blues (78)	J & M Fullbright 123	7.00	28.00	48

GREEN, Norman as Slim Green

TITLE/FLIP	LABEL & NO.	GOOD TO VERY GOOD	NEAR MINT	YR.
BABY, I LOVE YOU/Tricky Woman Blues (78)	Murray 501	6.25	25.00	48
MY WOMAN DONE QUIT ME/You Ain't Too Old (with Al Simmons)	Dig 142	4.00	16.00	56
SHAKE 'EM UP/Jerico Alley	Canton 1789	2.50	10.00	57

GREEN, R. & Turner:
see Green, Norman as R. Green

GREEN, Slim:
see Green, Norman as Slim Green
see Simmons, Al with Slim Green & The Cats From Fresno

GREEN, Vernon:
see Medallions, Vernon Green & The
see Phantoms, Vernon Green & The

GREENE, Barbara

TITLE/FLIP	LABEL & NO.	GOOD TO VERY GOOD	NEAR MINT	YR.
LONG TALL SALLY/Slippin' And Slidin'	Atco 6250	2.00	8.00	61

GREENE, Rudy

TITLE/FLIP	LABEL & NO.	GOOD TO VERY GOOD	NEAR MINT	YR.
BUZZARD PIE/Florida Blues (78)	Bullet 266	1.50	6.00	47
EVIL MAN BLUES/ This Happened When I Gave You My Heart (78)	Bullet 260	1.50	6.00	47
GOOD LOVIN' MAMA/My Mumblin' Baby	Excello 2074	2.50	10.00	55
I HAD A FEELING/Meet Me, Baby	Chance 1151	9.00	36.00	52
LETTER, THE/It's You I Love	Chance 1146	9.00	36.00	52
LOVE IS A PAIN/No Need Of Your Crying	Chance 1139	9.00	36.00	52
NO GOOD WOMAN BLUES/Deep In My Heart (78)	Bullet 261	1.50	6.00	47
TEENY WEENY BABY/Queer Feeling	Excello 2090	1.50	6.00	55

GREENE, Rudy & The Four Buddies:
see Four Buddies, Rudy Greene & The

GREENWOOD, Lil & The Four Jacks:
see Four Jacks, Lil Greenwood & The

GREER, Big John

TITLE/FLIP	LABEL & NO.	GOOD TO VERY GOOD	NEAR MINT	YR.
CHEATIN'/It's Better To Be Taken For Granted (red plastic)	RCA Victor 50-0096	5.00	20.00	50
CLAMBAKE BOOGIE/When You Love	RCA Victor 50-0125	3.00	12.00	51
DRINKIN' FOOL/Getting Mighty Lonesome For You	RCA Victor 47-5531	2.00	8.00	53
DRINKIN' WINE SPOO-DEE-O-DEE/ Long Tall Gal (red plastic)	RCA Victor 50-0007	7.00	28.00	49
GOT YOU ON MY MIND/ Woman Is A Five Letter Word	RCA Victor 47-4348	2.00	8.00	51
HAVE ANOTHER DRINK/I'm Savin' All My Love	RCA Victor 47-4293	2.00	8.00	51
I FOUND A DREAM/ If I Told You Once (red plastic)	RCA Victor 50-0029	4.00	16.00	49
I'LL NEVER DO THAT AGAIN/ A Fool Hasn't Got A Chance (red plastic)	RCA Victor 50-0076	5.00	20.00	50
I'M THE FAT MAN/Since You Went Away From Me	RCA Victor 47-5037	1.50	6.00	52
ONCE THERE LIVED A FOOL/I Want Ya, I Need Ya	RCA Victor 50-0108	3.00	12.00	50
RED JUICE/Big John's A-Blowin' (red plastic)	RCA Victor 50-0104	5.00	20.00	50
RIDE PRETTY BABY/Don't Worry 'Bout Me	RCA Victor 47-5259	2.00	8.00	53
ROCKIN' WITH BIG JOHN/How Can You Forget?	RCA Victor 50-0137	3.00	12.00	49
ROCKING JENNY JONES/I've Just Found Love (red plastic)	RCA Victor 50-0051	5.00	20.00	50
STRONG RED WHISKEY/If You Let Me	RCA Victor 47-4484	2.50	10.00	51
WHY DID YOU GO?/Our Wedding Tune	RCA Victor 50-0113	3.00	12.00	50
YOU PLAYED ON MY PIANO/I'll Never Let You Go	RCA Victor 47-5170	1.50	6.00	51

GREER, Big John & The Four Students:
see Four Students, Big John Greer & The

GRIFFIN BROTHERS, The

TITLE/FLIP	LABEL & NO.	GOOD TO VERY GOOD	NEAR MINT	YR.
ACE IN THE HOLE/The Clock Song	Dot 1108	2.50	20.00	52
BLACK BREAD/My Baby's Done Me Wrong	Dot 1145	2.00	8.00	53
COMING HOME/Stay Away From The Horses	Dot 1105	2.50	10.00	52
I WANNA GO BACK/Slow And Mellow	Dot 1117	2.50	10.00	53
I'M GONNA JUMP IN THE RIVER/Stormy Night	Dot 1104	2.50	10.00	52
IT'D SURPRISE YOU/I'll Get A Deal	Dot 1094	3.00	12.00	51
MY STORY/Midnight	Dot 1144	2.00	8.00	53
TEASER, THE/I've Got A New Love	Dot 1095	3.00	12.00	51
WEEPING AND CRYING/Shuffle Bug	Dot 1071	4.00	16.00	51

GRIFFIN, C. C.

TITLE/FLIP	LABEL & NO.	GOOD TO VERY GOOD	NEAR MINT	YR.
I DO BELIEVE/Sitting Here Waiting (yellow plastic)	Allegro 2001	2.50	10.00	63
STORM CLOUDS/I Want To Be With You	Joyce 1001	2.50	10.00	61

GRIFFIN, Little Jimmy

TITLE/FLIP	LABEL & NO.	GOOD TO VERY GOOD	NEAR MINT	YR.
I'M SEARCH'N/If Things Don't Change	R 508	1.50	6.00	62

GRIFFINS, The

TITLE/FLIP	LABEL & NO.	GOOD TO VERY GOOD	NEAR MINT	YR.
BAD LITTLE GIRL/Scheming	Mercury 70650	15.00	60.00	55
FOREVER MORE/Leave It To Me	Wing 90067	9.00	36.00	56
I SWEAR BY ALL THE STARS ABOVE/Sing To Me	Mercury 70558	12.50	50.00	55
MY BABY'S GONE/Why Must You Go?	Mercury 70913	7.00	28.00	56

GRIMES, Tiny

TITLE/FLIP	LABEL & NO.	GOOD TO VERY GOOD	NEAR MINT	YR.
BEGIN THE BEGUINE/The Man I Love	Atlantic 990	2.50	10.00	52
CALL OF THE WILD/Frankie And Johnny Boogie	Gotham 314	1.50	6.00	50
HO-HO-HO/Pert Skirt	Gotham 319	1.50	6.00	50
JUICY FRUIT/Second Floor Rear	Red Robin 123	4.00	16.00	52
ROCKIN' AND SOCKIN'/Howling Blues	Gotham 278	1.50	6.00	49
SOLITUDE/Rockin' The Blues Away	United 109	3.00	12.00	55
TINY'S BOOGIE WOOGIE/Blues Round Up	United 170	2.00	8.00	55

GRINER, Elsie as Miss Peaches

TITLE/FLIP	LABEL & NO.	GOOD TO VERY GOOD	NEAR MINT	YR.
CALLING MOODY FIELD, PART 1/ Calling Moody Field, Part 2	Groove 0009	2.50	10.00	54

GRISSOM, Don & The Ebb-Tones:
see Ebb-Tones, Don Grissom & The

GROOVENEERS, The

TITLE/FLIP	LABEL & NO.	GOOD TO VERY GOOD	NEAR MINT	YR.
I'M NOT THAT WAY ANYMORE/Let Me Rock You Home (by Norma Lee King) (78)	Decca 7883	1.50	6.00	42

GROOVY FIVE, The:
see Johnson, Willie as The Groovy Five

GROOVY TRIO, The:
see Johnson, Willie as the Groovy Trio

GROSS, Felix

GROSS, Leon T. as Archibald (with Dave Bartholomew's Band)

TITLE/FLIP	LABEL & NO.	GOOD TO VERY GOOD	NEAR MINT	YR.
EARLY MORNING BLUES/Great Big Eyes	Imperial 5212	10.00	40.00	52
FRANTIC CHICK/(by Dave Bartholomew) (78)	Imperial 5089	2.50	10.00	50
LITTLE MISS MUFFETT/Crescent City Bounce (78)	Colony 105	4.00	16.00	51
MY GAL/She's Scattered Everywhere (78)	Imperial 5101	2.50	10.00	51
SHAKE, BABY, SHAKE/Ballin' With Archie (78)	Imperial 5082	2.50	10.00	50
STACK-A-LEE, PART 1/Stack-A-Lee, Part 2 (78)	Imperial 5068	2.50	10.00	50
STACK-A-LEE, PART 1/Stack-A-Lee, Part 2	Imperial 5358	4.00	16.00	55
STACK-A-LEE, PART 1/Stack-A-Lee, Part 2	Imperial 5563	3.00	12.00	57

GUARDINE, Little Anthony:
see Little Anthony

GUIDES, The

GUITAR CRUSHER

TITLE/FLIP	LABEL & NO.	GOOD TO VERY GOOD	NEAR MINT	YR.
CUDDLE UP/I've Got To Know	T & S 101	4.00	16.00	
All known copies are reportedly pressed off center.				
GOIN' DOWN SLOW/I Catch Your Tears	Columbia 4-44217	1.50	6.00	67

GUITAR DAVE

GUITAR FRANK

TITLE/FLIP	LABEL & NO.	GOOD TO VERY GOOD	NEAR MINT	YR.
WILD TRACK/Mo-tatoes	Bridges Music Den (no number)	4.00	16.00	60

GUITAR NUBBITT (Alvin Hankerson)

GUITAR SHORTY:
see Fortescue, John Henry as Guitar Shorty

GUITAR SLIM:
see Green, Norman as Guitar Slim Green
see Jones, Eddie as Guitar Slim
see Seward, Alec as Guitar Slim

GUITAR, Sonny

TITLE/FLIP	LABEL & NO.	GOOD TO VERY GOOD	NEAR MINT	YR.
BETTY LOU/Strange Feeling	Yucca 136	1.50	6.00	—

GULLY, Charles & The Codas

GUNTER, Al as Little Al

TITLE/FLIP	LABEL & NO.	GOOD TO VERY GOOD	NEAR MINT	YR.
EVERY DAY BRINGS ABOUT A CHANGE/ Easy Ridin' Buggy	Excello 2128	1.50	6.00	58
LITTLE LEAN WOMAN/No Jive	Excello 2098	2.00	8.00	57

GUNTER, Arthur

TITLE/FLIP	LABEL & NO.	GOOD TO VERY GOOD	NEAR MINT	YR.
BABY LET'S PLAY HOUSE/Blues After Hours	Excello 2047	3.00	12.00	55
HONEY BABE/No Happy Home	Excello 2058	2.00	8.00	55
SHE'S MINE, ALL MINE/You Are Doing Me Wrong	Excello 2053	2.00	8.00	55

GUNTER, Cornel:
see Ermines, Cornel Gunter & The
see Flairs, Cornel Gunter & The

TITLE/FLIP	LABEL & NO.	GOOD TO VERY GOOD	NEAR MINT	YR.

GUNTER, Shirley:
see Flairs, Shirley Gunter & The
see Queens, Shirley Gunter & The

GUY, Browley & The Skyscrapers:
see Skyscrapers, Browley Guy & The

GUY, Buddy:
see Guy, George as Buddy Guy

GUY, George as Buddy Guy & His Band

TITLE/FLIP	LABEL & NO.	GOOD TO VERY GOOD	NEAR MINT	YR.
SIT AND CRY/Try To Quit You Baby	Artistic 1501	1.50	6.00	58
YOU SURE CAN'T DO/This Is The End	Artistic 1503	1.50	6.00	58

GUYTONES, The

TITLE/FLIP	LABEL & NO.	GOOD TO VERY GOOD	NEAR MINT	YR.
BABY, I DON'T CARE/Young Dreamer	De Luxe 6163	3.00	12.00	58
SHE'S MINE/Not Wanted	De Luxe 6152	4.00	16.00	57
TELL ME/Your Heart's Bigger Than Mine	De Luxe 6169	3.00	12.00	58
THIS IS LOVE/Hunky Dory	De Luxe 6159	4.00	16.00	57
YOU WON'T LET ME GO/Ooh Bop Sha Boo	De Luxe 6144	4.00	16.00	57

GYPSIES, Roger & The

TITLE/FLIP	LABEL & NO.	GOOD TO VERY GOOD	NEAR MINT	YR.
PASS THE HATCHET, PART 1/Pass The Hatchet, Part 2	Seven B 7001	2.50	10.00	—

GYPSIES, The (female group)

TITLE/FLIP	LABEL & NO.	GOOD TO VERY GOOD	NEAR MINT	YR.
WHY?/Young Girl To Calypso	Atlas 1073	3.00	12.00	57

H

HAGEN, Sammy & The Viscounts:
see Viscounts, Sammy Hagen & The

HAIRSTON, Brother Will

TITLE/FLIP	LABEL & NO.	GOOD TO VERY GOOD	NEAR MINT	YR.
ALABAMA BUS, PART 1/Alabama Bus, Part 2	JVB 44	12.50	50.00	56

HALL, Bobby & The Kings:
see Kings, Bobby Hall & The

HALL, Freddie

TITLE/FLIP	LABEL & NO.	GOOD TO VERY GOOD	NEAR MINT	YR.
CAN THIS BE MINE?/Playing Hard To Get	Abco 103	2.00	8.00	56
LITTLE BABY ROCK/I'll Be So Glad	C.J. 602	2.00	8.00	56
LOVE AND AFFECTION/She Was My First Love	C.J. 610	1.50	6.00	57
THIS CROOKED WORLD/Knock Me Out	Chance 1159	8.00	32.00	54

HALL, Juanita & The Four Tunes:
see Four Tunes, Juanita Hall & The

HALL, Rene Trio, The

TITLE/FLIP	LABEL & NO.	GOOD TO VERY GOOD	NEAR MINT	YR.
HOW LONG CAN YOU TAKE IT?/Old Soldiers Never Die	Decca 48213	2.50	10.00	51
MY KIND OF ROCKIN'/Summertime Blues	Decca 48217	2.50	10.00	51

HALOS, The

HAMILTON SISTERS, The

TITLE/FLIP	LABEL & NO.	GOOD TO VERY GOOD	NEAR MINT	YR.
OOP SHOOP/Do You Wanna Ride?	Columbia 40319	1.50	6.00	54

HAMILTON, Jimmy

TITLE/FLIP	LABEL & NO.	GOOD TO VERY GOOD	NEAR MINT	YR.
BIG FIFTY/Rockaway Special	States 113	1.50	6.00	52

HAMILTON, Roy

HAMMOND, Stick Horse

TITLE/FLIP	LABEL & NO.	GOOD TO VERY GOOD	NEAR MINT	YR.
GAMBLING MAN/Alberta (78)	J.O.B. 100	6.25	25.00	50
HIGHWAY 51/Too Late, Baby (78)	J.O.B. 105	4.00	16.00	50
HIGHWAY 51/Too Late, Baby (78)	Royalty 906	3.00	12.00	50
LITTLE GIRL/Truck 'Em On Down (78)	Gotham 504	2.50	10.00	50

HAMPTON, Junior

TITLE/FLIP	LABEL & NO.	GOOD TO VERY GOOD	NEAR MINT	YR.
J. H. STOMP/ L. J. Boogie (by Louis Jackson as Brother Jackson) (78)	Murray 500	4.00	16.00	48

HAMPTON, Lionel

TITLE/FLIP	LABEL & NO.	GOOD TO VERY GOOD	NEAR MINT	YR.
WELL, OH WELL/Pink Champagne	Decca 27164	2.00	8.00	50

Sonny Parker vocals.

HANKERSON, Alvin as Guitar Nubbitt

HANLEY, Tye Tongue

TITLE/FLIP	LABEL & NO.	GOOD TO VERY GOOD	NEAR MINT	YR.
YOU GOT MY NOSE WIDE OPEN/I'll Try To Understand	JVB 88	2.50	10.00	57

HANNIBAL & THE ANGELS

HANNIBAL, Mighty

HARDIN BROTHERS, The

TITLE/FLIP	LABEL & NO.	GOOD TO VERY GOOD	NEAR MINT	YR.
I MISS YOU SO!/ Don't You want Me Anymore? (78)	Decca 8511	2.50	10.00	41

HARLEM STARS, The (with Big Mama Thornton)

TITLE/FLIP	LABEL & NO.	GOOD TO VERY GOOD	NEAR MINT	YR.
ALL RIGHT, BABY/Bad Luck Got My Man (78)	E & W 100	3.00	12.00	51

HARLEMAIRES, The

TITLE/FLIP	LABEL & NO.	GOOD TO VERY GOOD	NEAR MINT	YR.
IF YOU MEAN WHAT YOU SAY/ Rose Of The Rio Grande (78)	Atlantic 856	2.50	10.00	48

HARLEMS, Little "D" & The

HARMONAIRES, The

TITLE/FLIP	LABEL & NO.	GOOD TO VERY GOOD	NEAR MINT	YR.
LORRAINE/Come Back	Holiday 2602	3.00	12.00	57

HARMONICA BLUES KING

The artist who used this name should not be confused with George Smith, who recorded as The Harmonica King, nor with Alec Seward, who recorded as The Blues King.

TITLE/FLIP	LABEL & NO.	GOOD TO VERY GOOD	NEAR MINT	YR.
I NEED YOU PRETTY BABY/Blues King Mongo	Ebony 1003	15.00	60.00	56

HARMONICA CAT, The
see Stewart, James (The Harmonica Cat)

HARMONICA FATS

HARMONICA FRANK:
see Floyd, Frank as Harmonica Frank
see Floyd, Frank;

HARMONICA JOE

TITLE/FLIP	LABEL & NO.	GOOD TO VERY GOOD	NEAR MINT	YR.
THAT'S NO BIG DEAL/Look Here, Mama	Skymac 1008	1.50	6.00	64

HARMONICA KING, The:
see Smith, George as The Harmonica King

HARMONICA SLIM:
see Blaylock, Travis as Harmonic Slim

HARMONY GRITS, The

HARPER-BRINSON BAND, The

TITLE/FLIP	LABEL & NO.	GOOD TO VERY GOOD	NEAR MINT	YR.
HARPER'S EXPRESS/Harper's Return	Specialty 593	2.00	8.00	57

Talking vocals with accompaniment.

HARPER, Ben & The Cinco's

HARPER, Bud

TITLE/FLIP	LABEL & NO.	GOOD TO VERY GOOD	NEAR MINT	YR.
DOWN THE AISLE/This Woman I Love	Sarg 196	1.50	6.00	—

HARPER, Sonny

TITLE/FLIP	LABEL & NO.	GOOD TO VERY GOOD	NEAR MINT	YR.
LONELY STRANGER/Going Back Home	Ball 1011	1.50	6.00	62

HARPO, Slim

HARPS, Little David & The

HARPTONES, The

TITLE/FLIP	LABEL & NO.	GOOD TO VERY GOOD	NEAR MINT	YR.
ALL IN YOUR MIND/The Last Dance	Companion 102	1.50	6.00	61
CRY LIKE I CRIED/So Good, So Fine	Gee 1045	1.50	6.00	57
I ALMOST LOST MY MIND/Ou Wee, Baby	Bruce 138	5.00	20.00	55
I DEPENDED ON YOU/Mambo Boogie	Bruce 104	6.25	25.00	54
I'LL NEVER TELL/Honey Love	Essex 364	4.00	16.00	55
LAUGHING ON THE OUTSIDE/I Remember	Warwick 500	1.50	6.00	59
LIFE IS BUT A DREAM/You Know You're Doing Me Wrong	Paradise 101	10.00	40.00	56

The Harptones

Screamin' Jay Hawkins

The Heartbeats

TITLE/FLIP	LABEL & NO.	GOOD TO VERY GOOD	NEAR MINT	YR.
LOVE ME COMPLETELY/Hep Teenager	*Warwick 512*	1.50	6.00	*59*
MASQUERADE IS OVER, THE/On Sunday Afternoon	*Rama 214*	4.00	16.00	*56*
MY MEMORIES OF YOU/High Flyin' Baby	*Tip Top 401*	1.50	6.00	*56*
MY MEMORIES OF YOU/It Was Just For Laughs	*Bruce 102*	6.25	25.00	*54*
MY SUCCESS/I've Got A Notion	*Paradise 103*	9.00	36.00	*56*
NO GREATER MIRACLE/What Kind of Fool	*Warwick 551*	1.50	6.00	*60*
SHRINE OF SAINT CECILIA, THE/Ou Wee, Baby	*Rama 221*	2.00	8.00	*57*
SINCE I FELL FOR YOU/Oobidee-Oobidee-Oo	*Bruce 113*	5.00	20.00	*54*
SUNDAY KIND OF LOVE, A/ I'll Never Tell (maroon label with script writing)	*Bruce 101*	25.00	100.00	*53*
SUNDAY KIND OF LOVE, A/Mambo Boogie	*Raven 8001*	3.00	12.00	*62*
SUNSET/I Gotta Have Your Love	*KT 201*	2.50	10.00	*63*
THREE WISHES/That's The Way It Goes	*Rama 203*	2.00	8.00	*56*
WHAT IS YOUR DECISION?/Gimme Some	*Andrea 100*	3.00	12.00	*56*
WHAT WILL I TELL MY HEART?/Foolish Me	*Companion 103*	4.00	16.00	*61*
WHY SHOULD I LOVE YOU?/Forever Mine	*Bruce 109*	5.00	20.00	*54*

HARRIS, Betty

HARRIS, Bob

TITLE/FLIP	LABEL & NO.	GOOD TO VERY GOOD	NEAR MINT	YR.
BABY, SAY YOU LOVE ME/Drinkin' Little Woman (vocal by Danny Taylor as Little Boy Blue) (78)	*Derby 770*	1.50	6.00	*51*
HEAVYWEIGHT MAMA/Total Stranger (78)	*Par 1304*	1.50	6.00	*52*
UP AND DOWN THE HILL/Doggin' Blues (78)	*Derby 773*	1.50	6.00	*51*

HARRIS, Bob as Little Bobby Harris

TITLE/FLIP	LABEL & NO.	GOOD TO VERY GOOD	NEAR MINT	YR.
LOVE, LOVE, LOVE/Friendly Advice (78)	*Jackson 2301*	2.00	8.00	*52*

HARRIS, Bobby

TITLE/FLIP	LABEL & NO.	GOOD TO VERY GOOD	NEAR MINT	YR.
I FEEL LIKE A STRANGER/You'd Be Glad To Wait	*Moon 203*	2.00	8.00	—
LITTLE GIRL/You'd Be Glad To Wait	*Moon 205*	2.00	8.00	—

HARRIS, Don as Sugarcane & His Violin

TITLE/FLIP	LABEL & NO.	GOOD TO VERY GOOD	NEAR MINT	YR.
THEY SAY YOU NEVER CAN MISS/Elim Stole My Baby	*Eldo 103*	2.50	10.00	*61*

HARRIS, Eddie

HARRIS, Eddie, Les McCann &

HARRIS, Edward as Carolina Slim

Though Harris recorded under various nicknames, he was often called Eddie, and should not be mistaken for the younger rhythm & blues artist, Eddie Harris.

TITLE/FLIP	LABEL & NO.	GOOD TO VERY GOOD	NEAR MINT	YR.
BLUES KNOCKING AT MY DOOR/Worry You Off My Mind (78)	*Acorn 323*	2.00	8.00	*52*
COME BACK, BABY/Pleading Blues (78)	*Acorn 319*	2.00	8.00	*51*
MAMA'S BOOGIE/Black Chariot Blues (78)	*Acorn 3015*	2.00	8.00	*51*
RAG MAMA/I'll Get By Somehow	*Acorn 324*	2.00	8.00	*52*

HARRIS, Edward as Country Paul

TITLE/FLIP	LABEL & NO.	GOOD TO VERY GOOD	NEAR MINT	YR.
I'LL NEVER WALK IN YOUR DOOR/Black Cat Trail	*King 4560*	6.25	25.00	*52*
MOTHER, DEAR MOTHER/Side Walk Boogie	*King 4573*	8.00	32.00	*52*
SINCE I SEEN YOUR SMILING FACE/One More Time	*King 4532*	7.00	28.00	*51*
YOUR PICTURE DONE FADED/Ain't It Sad?	*King 4517*	7.00	28.00	*51*

HARRIS, Edward as Jammin' Jim

TITLE/FLIP	LABEL & NO.	GOOD TO VERY GOOD	NEAR MINT	YR.
SHAKE BOOGIE/Jivin' Woman	*Savoy 1106*	4.00	16.00	*52*

HARRIS, Edward as Lazy Slim Jim

TITLE/FLIP	LABEL & NO.	GOOD TO VERY GOOD	NEAR MINT	YR.
GEORGIA WOMAN/Money Blues	*Savoy 854*	4.00	16.00	*52*
SLO FREIGHT BLUES/Sugaree	*Savoy 868*	4.00	16.00	*52*
WINE HEAD BABY/One More Drink	*Savoy 887*	4.00	16.00	*52*

HARRIS, Erline

TITLE/FLIP	LABEL & NO.	GOOD TO VERY GOOD	NEAR MINT	YR.
ROCK AND ROLL BLUES/Box Car Boogie Baby (78)	*DeLuxe 3220*	2.00	8.00	*49*

HARRIS, Georgia & The Hy-Tones: see Hy-Tones, Georgia Harris & The

HARRIS, James D. as Shakey Jake

TITLE/FLIP	LABEL & NO.	GOOD TO VERY GOOD	NEAR MINT	YR.
ROLL YOUR MONEYMAKER/Call Me If You Need Me	*Artistic 1502*	1.50	6.00	*58*

HARRIS, Peppermint: see Nelson, Harrison as Peppermint Harris

HARRIS, Thurston

HARRIS, Thurston & The Sharps

HARRIS, Willard

TITLE/FLIP	LABEL & NO.	GOOD TO VERY GOOD	NEAR MINT	YR.
STRAIGHTEN UP, BABY/Talking Off The Wall	*Ekko 20001*	8.00	32.00	*55*

HARRIS, Wynonie

TITLE/FLIP	LABEL & NO.	GOOD TO VERY GOOD	NEAR MINT	YR.
ADAM COME AND GET YOUR RIB/Drinking Blues	*King 4565*	6.25	25.00	*52*
ALL SHE WANTS TO DO IS ROCK/ I Want My Fanny Brown (78)	*King 4304*	1.50	6.00	*49*
AROUND THE CLOCK BLUES, PART 1/ Around The Clock Blues, Part 2 (78)	*Philo 103*	2.00	8.00	*45*
BABY, LOOK AT YOU/That's The Stuff You Gotta Watch (78)	*Apollo 361*	1.50	6.00	*45*
BAD NEWS, BABY/Bring It Back	*King 4593*	6.25	25.00	*52*
BATTLE OF THE BLUES, PART 1/ Battle Of The Blues, Part 2 (78)	*Aladdin 3036*	1.50	6.00	*47*
BIG CITY BLUES/Ghost Of A Chance (78)	*Aladdin 196*	1.50	6.00	*47*
BIG OLD COUNTRY FOOL/That's Me Right Now	*King 5050*	1.50	6.00	*57*
BLOODSHOT EYES/Confessin' The Blues	*King 4461*	9.00	36.00	*51*
BLOWIN' TO CALIFORNIA/Bite Again, Bite Again (78)	*King 4252*	1.50	6.00	*47*
CHRISTINA/All She Wants To Do Is Mambo	*King 4763*	4.00	16.00	*54*
COCK-A-DOODLE-DO/Yonder Goes My Baby (78)	*Philo 104*	2.00	8.00	*45*
DEACON DON'T LIKE IT, THE/Song Of The Bayou	*King 4635*	6.25	25.00	*53*
DESTINATION LOVE/Tell A Whale Of A Tale	*Atco 6081*	1.50	6.00	*57*
DIG THIS BOOGIE/Lightning Struck The Poorhouse (78)	*Bullet 251*	2.00	8.00	*46*
DON'T TAKE MY WHISKEY AWAY FROM ME/I Get A Thrill	*King 4724*	6.25	25.00	*54*
DRINKIN' BY MYSELF/My Baby's Barrelhouse (78)	*Bullet 252*	2.00	8.00	*46*
DRINKIN' SHERRY WINE/Git With The Guts	*King 4814*	4.00	16.00	*54*
EVERYBODY BOOGIE/Time To Change Your Tune (78)	*Apollo 378*	1.50	6.00	*46*
GOOD MAMBO TONIGHT/Git To Gittin,' Baby	*King 4774*	4.00	16.00	*54*
GOOD MORNING, CORINNE/In The Evenin' Blues (78)	*Hamp-Tone 103*	1.50	6.00	*45*
GOOD MORNING, MR. JUDGE/Stormy Night Blues (78)	*King 4378*	2.00	8.00	*50*
GOOD ROCKIN' TONIGHT/Good Morning, Mr. Blues	*King 4210*	6.25	25.00	*52*
GRANDMA PLAYS THE NUMBERS/ I Feel That Old Age Comin' On (78)	*King 4276*	1.50	6.00	*48*
HERE COMES THE BLUES/Gone With The Wind (78)	*Apollo 363*	1.50	6.00	*45*
HEY-BA-BA-RE-BOP, PART 1/ Hay-Ba-Ba-Re-Bop, Part 2 (78)	*Hamp-Tone 100*	1.50	6.00	*45*
I GOTTA LYIN' WOMAN/Rebecca's Blues (78)	*Apollo 387*	1.50	6.00	*46*
I LIKE MY BABY'S PUDDING/I Can't Take It No More (78)	*King 4342*	2.50	10.00	*49*
I'LL NEVER GIVE UP/Man, Have I Got Troubles	*King 4468*	6.25	25.00	*51*
KEEP ON CHURNIN'/Married Woman, Stay Married	*King 4526*	10.00	40.00	*52*
LOLLIPOP MAMA/Blow Your Brains Out (78)	*King 4226*	2.00	8.00	*47*
LOVIN' MACHINE/Luscious Woman (blue plastic)	*King 4485*	25.00	100.00	*51*
LOVIN' MACHINE/Luscious Woman	*King 4485*	7.00	28.00	*51*
MR. DOLLAR/Fishtail Blues	*King 4789*	3.00	12.00	*54*
MY PLAYFUL BABY'S GONE/Here Comes The Night	*King 4507*	7.00	28.00	*51*
NIGHT TRAIN/Do It Again, Please	*King 4555*	6.25	25.00	*52*
PLAYFUL BABY/Papa Tree Top (78)	*Apollo 372*	1.50	6.00	*46*
PLEASE, LOUISE/Nearer My Love To Thee	*King 4668*	6.25	25.00	*53*
QUIET WHISKEY/Down, Boy, Down	*King 4685*	6.25	25.00	*53*
ROSE GET YOUR CLOTHES/Wynonie's Boogie (78)	*King 4202*	2.00	8.00	*47*
ROT GUT/Greyhound	*King 4592*	6.25	25.00	*52*
RUGGED ROAD/Come Back, Baby (78)	*Aladdin 172*	1.50	6.00	*46*
SHAKE THAT THING/Keep A-Talking	*King 4716*	6.25	25.00	*54*

TITLE/FLIP	LABEL & NO.	GOOD TO VERY GOOD	NEAR MINT	YR.
SHE JUST WON'T SELL NO MORE/ Drinkin' Wine Spoo-Dee-O-Dee (78)	King 4292	1.50	6.00	48
SHOTGUN WEDDING/I Don't Know Where To Go	King 4839	3.00	12.00	54
SITTIN' ON IT ALL THE TIME/Baby, Shame On You (78)	King 4330	1.50	6.00	49
STRAIGHTEN HIM OUT/Young Man's Blues (78)	Apollo 360	1.50	6.00	45
TAKE ME OUT OF THE RAIN/Young And Wild (78)	Apollo 381	1.50	6.00	46
THERE'S NO SUBSTITUTE FOR LOVE/Tale Of Woe	King 5073	1.50	6.00	57
WASN'T THAT GOOD?/What Shall I Do?	King 4620	6.25	25.00	53
WHISKEY AND JELLY-ROLL BLUES/ Mr. Blues Jumped A Rabbit (78)	Aladdin 171	1.50	6.00	46
WINE, WINE, SWEET WINE/Man's Best Friend	King 4826	4.00	16.00	54
WYNONIE'S BLUES/ Somebody Changed The Lock On My Door (78)	Apollo 362	1.50	6.00	45
YOU GOT TO GET YOURSELF A JOB, GIRL/ Hard Ridin' Mama (78)	Aladdin 208	1.50	6.00	47
YOUR MONEY DON'T MEAN A THING/Love Is Like Rain (78)	King 4217	1.50	6.00	47

HARRISON, Wilbert & The Roamers

HARRISON, Wilbert as Wilburt Harrison

TITLE/FLIP	LABEL & NO.	GOOD TO VERY GOOD	NEAR MINT	YR.
GIN AND COCONUT MILK/Nobody Knows My Trouble	DeLuxe 6031	4.00	16.00	53
THIS WOMAN OF MINE/The Letter	DeLuxe 6002	6.25	25.00	52
THIS WOMAN OF MINE/The Letter	Rockin' 526	10.00	40.00	52

HART, Casey

HART, Haze

TITLE/FLIP	LABEL & NO.	GOOD TO VERY GOOD	NEAR MINT	YR.
LAST TIME/Red River Shuffle	Swingin' 638	1.50	6.00	—

HARVES, Cleo with Lightning Guitar

TITLE/FLIP	LABEL & NO.	GOOD TO VERY GOOD	NEAR MINT	YR.
SKINNY WOMAN BLUES/Crazy With The Blues (78)	O.T. 105	4.00	16.00	49

HARVEY & THE AVERNE DOZEN

HARVEY AND THE SEVEN SOUNDS

HATHAWAY, Donny

HATHAWAY, Donny, Roberta Flack &

HATHAWAY, Maggie & The Bluesmen

HATHAWAY, Maggie:
see Robins, The

HAVEN, Shirley & The Four Jacks:
see Four Jacks
see Four Jacks, Shirley Haven & The

HAWKETTS, The

TITLE/FLIP	LABEL & NO.	GOOD TO VERY GOOD	NEAR MINT	YR.
YOUR TIME'S UP/Mardi Gras Mambo	Chess 1591	8.00	32.00	55

HAWKINS, Edwin Singers, The

HAWKINS, Erskine

TITLE/FLIP	LABEL & NO.	GOOD TO VERY GOOD	NEAR MINT	YR.
DOWN HOME JUMP (instrumental)/ Lost Time (colored plastic)	King 4522	5.00	20.00	52
DOWN HOME JUMP (instrumental)/Lost Time	King 4522	1.50	6.00	52
NEW GIN MILL SPECIAL (instrumental)/Walkin' By The River	King 4574	1.50	6.00	52
STEEL GUITAR RAG (instrumental)/ I Remember My Love (colored plastic)	King 4514	5.00	20.00	52
STEEL GUITAR RAG (instrumental)/ I Remember My Love	King 4514	1.50	6.00	52
WAY YOU LOOK TONIGHT, THE (instrumental)/ Fair Weather Friend	King 4597	1.50	6.00	52

HAWKINS, Erskine & The Four Hawks

TITLE/FLIP	LABEL & NO.	GOOD TO VERY GOOD	NEAR MINT	YR.
DOUBLE SHOT/ Function At The Junction	King 4686	5.00	20.00	53
MY BABY, PLEASE/Down The Alley (instrumental)	King 4671	7.00	28.00	53

HAWKINS, Jalacy

TITLE/FLIP	LABEL & NO.	GOOD TO VERY GOOD	NEAR MINT	YR.
BAPTIZE ME IN WINE/Not Anymore	Timely 1004	10.00	40.00	54
PLEASE TRY TO UNDERSTAND/I Found My Way To Wine	Timely 1005	10.00	40.00	54

HAWKINS, Jalacy as Jay Hawkins

TITLE/FLIP	LABEL & NO.	GOOD TO VERY GOOD	NEAR MINT	YR.
EVEN THOUGH/Talk About Me	Wing 90055	1.50	6.00	56
THIS IS ALL/She Put The Wamee On Me	Mercury 70549	2.50	20.00	55
WELL, I TRIED/All Of My Life	Wing 90005	2.00	8.00	55

HAWKINS, Jalacy as Screamin' Jay Hawkins

TITLE/FLIP	LABEL & NO.	GOOD TO VERY GOOD	NEAR MINT	YR.
ALLIGATOR WINE/There's Something Wrong With You	Okeh 7101	2.00	8.00	57
BAPTIZE ME IN WINE/Not Anymore	Apollo 528	2.00	8.00	57
DARLING, PLEASE FORGIVE ME/You Made Me Love You	Okeh 7084	1.50	6.00	56
FRENZY/Person To Person	Okeh 7087	1.50	6.00	57
I PUT A SPELL ON YOU/Little Demon	Okeh 7072	2.00	8.00	56
NOT ANYMORE/Please Try To Understand	Apollo 506	2.00	8.00	56
TAKE ME BACK/I Is	Grand 135	2.00	8.00	57

HAWKINS, Jay:
see Hawkins, Jalacy as Jay Hawkins

HAWKINS, Jennell

HAWKINS, Roy

TITLE/FLIP	LABEL & NO.	GOOD TO VERY GOOD	NEAR MINT	YR.
BAD LUCK IS FALLING/The Condition I'm In	Modern 898	3.00	12.00	54
CHRISTMAS BLUES/Roy's Boogie (78)	Down Town 2018	2.50	10.00	48
DOIN' ALL RIGHT/The Thrill Hunt	Modern 869	3.00	12.00	52
FORTY JIM/I Don't Know Why (78)	Down Town 2024	2.00	8.00	48
GLOOM AND MISERY ALL AROUND/I Walk Alone	Modern 852	4.00	16.00	51
HIGHWAY 59/Would You?	Modern 859	3.00	12.00	52
I DON'T KNOW JUST WHAT TO DO/You're A Free Little Girl	Modern 853	4.00	16.00	51
I HATE TO BE ALONE/Lonesome Without You	Rhythm 120	5.00	20.00	—
IS IT TOO LATE?/If I Had Listened	RPM 440	2.00	8.00	54
IT'S TOO LATE TO CHANGE/West Express (78)	Down Town 2020	2.50	10.00	48
QUARTER TO ONE/Strange Land (78)	Down Town 2025	2.00	8.00	48
THRILL IS GONE, THE/Trouble Makin' Woman	Modern 826	6.25	25.00	51

HAWKINS, Sam

HAWKINS, Sam & The Crystals:
see Crystals, Sam Hawkins & The

HAWKINS, Screamin' Jay:
see Hawkins, Jalacy as Screamin' Jay Hawkins

HAWKS, The

TITLE/FLIP	LABEL & NO.	GOOD TO VERY GOOD	NEAR MINT	YR.
ALL WOMEN ARE THE SAME/That's What You Are	Imperial 5317	7.00	28.00	54
IT AIN'T THAT WAY/I-Yi	Imperial 5292	7.00	28.00	54
IT'S ALL OVER/Ever Since You Been Gone	Modern 990	4.00	16.00	56
ITS TOO LATE NOW/Can't See For Lookin'	Imperial 5332	7.00	28.00	55
JOE, THE GRINDER/Candy Girl	Imperial 5266	12.50	50.00	54

TITLE/FLIP	LABEL & NO.	GOOD TO VERY GOOD	NEAR MINT	YR.
NOBODY BUT YOU/It Ain't That Way	Imperial 5306	7.00	28.00	54
SHE'S ALL RIGHT/Good News	Imperial 5281	15.00	60.00	54
WHY? OH WHY?/These Blues	Post 2004	9.00	36.00	55

HAYES, Bill:
see Hayes, Henry as Bill Hayes

HAYES, Henry:
see Brown, James "Widemouth"
see Campbell, Carl with Henry Hayes' Four Kings
see Nixon, Elmore with Henry Hayes & His Rhythm Kings

HAYES, Henry

TITLE/FLIP	LABEL & NO.	GOOD TO VERY GOOD	NEAR MINT	YR.
BOWLEGGED ANGELINE/Baby Girl Blues (78)	Gold Star 633	2.00	8.00	48
BOWLEGGED ANGELINE/Baby Girl Blues (78)	Swing 414	1.50	6.00	48

HAYES, Henry as Bill Hayes

TITLE/FLIP	LABEL & NO.	GOOD TO VERY GOOD	NEAR MINT	YR.
I WANT TO CRY/Highway 75 (78)	Sittin' In With 551	1.50	6.00	50
I'M SORRY I WAS RECKLESS/South Texas Blues (78)	Sittin' In With 560	1.50	6.00	50
IF IT'S TRUE WHAT THEY TELL ME/Just (78)	Jade 211	1.50	6.00	50

HAYES, Henry as Henry Hayes Four Kings

TITLE/FLIP	LABEL & NO.	GOOD TO VERY GOOD	NEAR MINT	YR.
ALL ALONE BLUES/Hayes Boogie (78)	Aladdin 157	1.50	6.00	46
ANGEL CHILD BLUES/Kickin' My Love Around (78)	Aladdin 158	1.50	6.00	46

HAYES, Isaac

HAYES, Linda:
see Moore, Johnny as Johnny Moore's Blazers
see Platters, Linda Hayes & The

HAYES, Louis:
see Seward, Alec

HAYNES, Ida:
see Mell-O-Tones, Doug Williams & The

HAYWARD, Leon

HEADEN, Willie:
see Five Birds, Willie Headen & The
see Penguins, The

HEADLINERS, George Goodman & The

HEADLINERS, The

HEART BEATS QUINTET, The:
see Heartbeats, The as The Heart Beats Quintet

HEART-THROBS, The

TITLE/FLIP	LABEL & NO.	GOOD TO VERY GOOD	NEAR MINT	YR.
SO GLAD/All The Way Home	Aladdin 3394	1.50	6.00	57
SO GLAD/All The Way Home	Lamp 2010	1.50	6.00	57

HEARTBEATS, The

TITLE/FLIP	LABEL & NO.	GOOD TO VERY GOOD	NEAR MINT	YR.
CRAZY FOR YOU/ Rockin'-N-Rollin'-N-Rhythm-N-Blues-N- (pink label)	Hull 711	9.00	36.00	55
DARLING, HOW LONG?/Hurry Home, Baby	Hull 713	5.00	20.00	56
EVERYBODY'S SOMEBODY'S FOOL/I Want To Know	Rama 231	1.50	6.00	57
I WON'T BE THE FOOL ANY MORE/Wedding Bells	Rama 222	1.50	6.00	57
ONE MILLION YEARS/Darling, I Want To Get Married	Guyden 2011	1.50	6.00	59
PEOPLE ARE TALKING/Your Way	Hull 716	9.00	36.00	56
THOUSAND MILES AWAY, A/Oh, Baby, Don't (black label)	Hull 720	15.00	60.00	56
THOUSAND MILES AWAY, A/Oh, Baby, Don't (red label)	Hull 720	2.50	10.00	56
THOUSAND MILES AWAY, A/Oh, Baby, Don't	Rama 216	1.50	6.00	56

HEARTBEATS, The as The Heart Beats Quintet

TITLE/FLIP	LABEL & NO.	GOOD TO VERY GOOD	NEAR MINT	YR.
AFTER EVERYBODY'S GONE/Tormented	Network 71200	8.00	32.00	—

HEARTBREAKERS, T. V. Slim & His:
see Wills, Oscar as T. V. Slim & His Heartbreakers.

HEARTBREAKERS, The

TITLE/FLIP	LABEL & NO.	GOOD TO VERY GOOD	NEAR MINT	YR.
HEARTBREAKER/Wanda	RCA Victor 47-4327	35.00	140.00	51
I'M ONLY FOOLING MY HEART/ You're So Necessary To Me	RCA Victor 47-4508	55.00	220.00	51
THERE IS TIME/It's O.K. With Me	RCA Victor 47-4849	25.00	100.00	52
WHY DON'T I?/Rockin Daddy-O	RCA Victor 47-4662	40.00	160.00	52

HEARTBREAKERS, The (female group)

HEARTS OF STONE, The

HEARTS, Billy Austin & The

TITLE/FLIP	LABEL & NO.	GOOD TO VERY GOOD	NEAR MINT	YR.
ANGEL BABY/Night Has Come	Apollo 444	15.00	60.00	53

HEARTS, Lee Andrews & The

TITLE/FLIP	LABEL & NO.	GOOD TO VERY GOOD	NEAR MINT	YR.
BELLS OF ST. MARY/Fairest	Rainbow 259	20.00	80.00	54
BLUEBIRD OF HAPPINESS/Show Me The Merengue	Gotham 318	7.00	28.00	56
JUST SUPPOSE/It's Me	Gotham 321	9.00	36.00	56
LONELY ROOM/Leona	Gotham 320	10.00	40.00	56
LONG, LONELY NIGHTS/The Clock	Main Line 102	8.00	32.00	—
MAYBE YOU'LL BE THERE/Baby, Come Back	Rainbow 252	20.00	80.00	54
MAYBE YOU'LL BE THERE/Baby, Come Back (red plastic)	Rainbow 252	30.00	120.00	54
WHITE CLIFFS OF DOVER/Much Too Much	Rainbow 256	40.00	160.00	54

HEARTS, The

HEARTS, The (mixed group, female lead)

TITLE/FLIP	LABEL & NO.	GOOD TO VERY GOOD	NEAR MINT	YR.
DANCING IN A DREAM WORLD/	J & S 1657	1.50	6.00	57
LIKE, LATER BABY/I Want Your Love Tonite	J & S 1626/1627	1.50	6.00	55
LONELY NIGHTS/Oo-wee	Baton 208	1.50	6.00	55

HEARTSMAN, Johnny

HEBB, Bobby

HEIGHT, Donald

HEMLOCKS, Little Bobby Rivera & The

TITLE/FLIP	LABEL & NO.	GOOD TO VERY GOOD	NEAR MINT	YR.
CORALEE/Joys Of Love	Fury 1004	4.00	16.00	57

HENDERSON, Bertha

TITLE/FLIP	LABEL & NO.	GOOD TO VERY GOOD	NEAR MINT	YR.
ROCK, BERTHA, ROCK/Tears In My Eyes	Chance 1143	7.00	28.00	52

HENDERSON, Fletcher:
see Charioteers, The

HENDERSON, Willie & The Soul Explosions

HENDRICKS, Bobby

HENLEY, John Lee as John Lee

Henley should not be confused with John Arthur Lee, nor with John Lee Hooker, all three having recorded under the name John Lee.

TITLE/FLIP	LABEL & NO.	GOOD TO VERY GOOD	NEAR MINT	YR.
RHYTHM ROCKIN' BOOGIE/Knockin' On Lula Mae's Door	JOB 114	20.00	80.00	52

HENRY, Clarence

HENRY, Robert

TITLE/FLIP	LABEL & NO.	GOOD TO VERY GOOD	NEAR MINT	YR.
MISS ANNA B./Something's Wrong With My Lovin' Machine	King 4624	11.00	44.00	53
OLD BATTLE AX/Early In The Morning	King 4646	12.50	50.00	53

HEPCAT, Dr.:
see Durst, Lavada as Dr. Hepcat

HEPSTERS, The

TITLE/FLIP	LABEL & NO.	GOOD TO VERY GOOD	NEAR MINT	YR.
I GOTTA SING THE BLUES/This-A-Way	Ronel 110	25.00	100.00	56
I HAD TO LET YOU GO/Rockin' 'N Rollin' With Santa Claus	Ronel 107	25.00	100.00	55

HERALDS, The

TITLE/FLIP	LABEL & NO.	GOOD TO VERY GOOD	NEAR MINT	YR.
ETERNAL LOVE/Gonna Love You Everyday	Herald 435	8.00	32.00	54

HERBY JOE

TITLE/FLIP	LABEL & NO.	GOOD TO VERY GOOD	NEAR MINT	YR.
SMOKESTACK LIGHTNING/Dreamed Last Night	Abco 101	3.00	12.00	56

HESITATIONS, The

HI TENSIONS, Leon Peels & The

HI TENSIONS, The

TITLE/FLIP	LABEL & NO.	GOOD TO VERY GOOD	NEAR MINT	YR.
GOT A GOOD FEELING/Ebbing Of The Tide	Milestone 2018	2.50	10.00	63

HI-FI's, The

TITLE/FLIP	LABEL & NO.	GOOD TO VERY GOOD	NEAR MINT	YR.
EACH PASSING DAY/Sally	Devere (# unknown)	30.00	120.00	—
EACH PASSING DAY/Sally	Mark 148	20.00	80.00	60

HI-FIDELITIES, The

TITLE/FLIP	LABEL & NO.	GOOD TO VERY GOOD	NEAR MINT	YR.
STREET OF LONLINESS/Help! Murder! Police!	Fortune 528	4.00	16.00	57

HI-LITES, Ronnie & The

HI-LITES, The

TITLE/FLIP	LABEL & NO.	GOOD TO VERY GOOD	NEAR MINT	YR.
FOR SENTIMENTAL REASONS/For Your Precious Love	Record Fair 501	1.50	6.00	62
I'M FALLING IN LOVE/Walking My Baby Back Home	Record Fair 500	1.50	6.00	61

HI-LITES, The

TITLE/FLIP	LABEL & NO.	GOOD TO VERY GOOD	NEAR MINT	YR.
I FOUND A LOVE/Zanzee	Okeh 7046	15.00	60.00	54

TITLE/FLIP	LABEL & NO.	GOOD TO VERY GOOD	NEAR MINT	YR.

HI-NOTES, Tommy Frederick & The

HICKS, Otis as Lightnin' Slim

TITLE/FLIP	LABEL & NO.	GOOD TO VERY GOOD	NEAR MINT	YR.
BAD FEELING BLUES/Lightnin' Slim Boogie	Ace 505	5.00	20.00	54
BAD LUCK/Rock Me, Mama	Feature 3006	20.00	80.00	54
BUGGER BUGGER BOY/Ethel Mae	Feature 3012	3.00	12.00	54
I CAN'T LIVE HAPPY/New Orleans Bound	Feature 3008	3.00	12.00	54

HIDE-A-WAYS, The

TITLE/FLIP	LABEL & NO.	GOOD TO VERY GOOD	NEAR MINT	YR.
CHERIE/He Make 'Em Powwow	MGM 55004	25.00	100.00	54

HIDEAWAYS, The

TITLE/FLIP	LABEL & NO.	GOOD TO VERY GOOD	NEAR MINT	YR.
CAN'T HELP LOVING THAT GIRL OF MINE/ I'm Coming Home	Ronni 1000	400.00	1600.00	—

HIGGINS, Chuck

Most of the following are instrumentals.

TITLE/FLIP	LABEL & NO.	GOOD TO VERY GOOD	NEAR MINT	YR.
BLUES 'N' MAMBO/Stormy	Combo 17	2.50	10.00	54
BROKE/I'll Be There	Specialty 532	2.00	8.00	52
COTTON PICKER/Iron Head	Combo 14	2.50	10.00	54
FLIP-TOP BOX/Blacksmith Blues	Caddy 108	2.00	8.00	57
GAMBLING WOMAN/The Itch	Dootone 387	1.50	6.00	56
GREASY PIG/Candied Yams	Lucky 45-003	2.50	10.00	53
HERE I'M/Tonky Honk	Dootone 361	1.50	6.00	55
HOUND DOG/Tortas	Combo 25	2.50	10.00	54
LOOKING FOR MY BABY/Eye'ball	Dootone 376	1.50	6.00	56
LOVE ME, BABY/Boyle Heights	Combo 30	2.50	10.00	54
OH YEAH?/I Need Your Love	Dootone 396	1.50	6.00	57
ONE MORE TIME/Oye Ooh Mambo	Specialty 539	2.00	8.00	53
PACHUCO HOP/Motor Head Baby (John Watson vocal)	Combo 12	5.00	20.00	53
PANCHO/Come On And Blow Your Horn	Aladdin 3283	1.50	6.00	53
PAPA CHARLIE/Blue Sax	Combo 67	2.50	10.00	55
ROCK/Chop-Chop	R & B 1314	2.00	8.00	55
WEST SIDE/I'm In Love With You	Combo 48	2.00	8.00	55
WETBACK HOP/Don't You Know I Love You?	Dootone 370	1.50	6.00	55

HIGGINS, Chuck & The Mellomoods:
see Mellomoods, Chuck Higgins & The

HIGGINS, Monk

HIGH KEYS, The

HIGH LITERS, The

TITLE/FLIP	LABEL & NO.	GOOD TO VERY GOOD	NEAR MINT	YR.
HELLO, DEAR/Bobby Sox Baby	Vee Jay 184	20.00	80.00	56

HIGHLANDERS, The

TITLE/FLIP	LABEL & NO.	GOOD TO VERY GOOD	NEAR MINT	YR.
SUNDAY KIND OF LOVE/Beg And Steal	Rays 36	25.00	100.00	57

HIGHTONES, Claude & The

TITLE/FLIP	LABEL & NO.	GOOD TO VERY GOOD	NEAR MINT	YR.
BUCKET HEAD/Doodle Bug	Baytone 113	2.00	8.00	—
MONKEY STUFF/High Sailing	Pammar 614	1.50	6.00	—

HIGHTOWER, Little Donna

TITLE/FLIP	LABEL & NO.	GOOD TO VERY GOOD	NEAR MINT	YR.
FAREWELL BLUES/You Had Better Change Your Ways	Decca 48299	2.00	8.00	52
I FOUND A NEW LOVE/Honest And Truly	Decca 48284	2.00	8.00	52

HIGHTOWER, Willie

HILL, Bunker

HILL, Harvey, Jr. as The Harvey Hill String Band

TITLE/FLIP	LABEL & NO.	GOOD TO VERY GOOD	NEAR MINT	YR.
BOOGIE WOOGIE WOMAN/She Fool Me	SRC 104	20.00	80.00	51

HILL, Henry

TITLE/FLIP	LABEL & NO.	GOOD TO VERY GOOD	NEAR MINT	YR.
HOLD ME, BABY/Since You've Been Gone	Federal 12037	5.00	20.00	51
IF YOU LOVE ME/What's The Matter, Mama?	Federal 12044	5.00	20.00	51
MY BABY'S BACK HOME/Give Me Something Called Love	Federal 12083	5.00	20.00	51
WANDERING BLUES/Sunday Morning Blues	Federal 12030	5.00	20.00	51

HILL, Jessie

HILL, Raymond

TITLE/FLIP	LABEL & NO.	GOOD TO VERY GOOD	NEAR MINT	YR.
SNUGGLE, THE/Bourbon Street Jump	Sun 204	30.00	120.00	54

Instrumentals.

HILL, Z. Z.

HINTON, Joe

HINTON, Otis

TITLE/FLIP	LABEL & NO.	GOOD TO VERY GOOD	NEAR MINT	YR.
WALKIN' DOWN HILL/Emmaline	Timely 1003	20.00	80.00	53

HIPPIES, The

HITS, Tiny Tim & The

TITLE/FLIP	LABEL & NO.	GOOD TO VERY GOOD	NEAR MINT	YR.
WEDDING BELLS/Doll Baby	Roulette 4123	3.00	12.00	58

HODGES, Charlie, Geraldine Hunt &

HOGAN, Carl & The Miracles:
see Miracles, Carl Hogan & The

HOGAN, Cha Cha

TITLE/FLIP	LABEL & NO.	GOOD TO VERY GOOD	NEAR MINT	YR.
MY BABY LOVES ME/My Walking Baby (78)	Star Talent 810	2.50	10.00	50

HOGAN, Silas

HOGG, Andrew

TITLE/FLIP	LABEL & NO.	GOOD TO VERY GOOD	NEAR MINT	YR.
HE KNOWS HOW MUCH WE CAN BEAR/I Don't Want Nobody's Bloodstains On My Hands (78)	Exclusive 89	2.50	10.00	47
I DECLARE/Dark Clouds	Crown 122	5.00	20.00	54

HOGG, Andrew as Smokey (or Smoky) Hogg

Usually considered as the original "Smokey Hogg," Andrew should not be confused with Will Hodges or Willie Hogg, who have both called themselves "Smokey Hogg." The latter may have recorded under this name in the 20s or the 30s.

TITLE/FLIP	LABEL & NO.	GOOD TO VERY GOOD	NEAR MINT	YR.
AIN'T GONNA PLAY SECOND NO MO'/ No More Whiskey	Show Time 1101	6.25	25.00	54
BABY DON'T YOU TEAR MY CLOTHES/Highway 51	Modern 884	4.00	16.00	51
BABY SHAKE YOUR LEG/Fortune Teller Blues (78)	Top Hat 1023	1.50	6.00	52
CAN'T DO NOTHIN'/I Just Can't Help It	Modern 924	3.00	12.00	52
CHANGE YOUR WAYS/Baby, Baby (78)	Macy's 5008	1.50	6.00	49
GONE, GONE, GONE/I Ain't Got Over It Yet	Federal 12127	5.00	20.00	53
HARD TIMES/Goin' Back Home (78)	Bullet 285	2.00	8.00	48
I DECLARE/Dark Clouds	Meteor 5021	5.00	20.00	54
I'VE BEEN HAPPY/I Used To Be Rich	Ray's Record 35	6.25	25.00	52
KEEP A-WALKING/Do It No More	Federal 12109	5.00	20.00	53
MISERY BLUES/You Gotta Go (78)	Independent 300	2.00	8.00	49
MISS GEORGIA/Dirty Mistreater	Mercury 8235	5.00	20.00	51
NEED MY HELP/In This World Alone (78)	Colony C-103	1.50	6.00	50
PENITENTIARY BLUES, PART 1/Penitentiary Blues, Part 2 (78)	Recorded In Hollywood 170	1.50	6.00	52
PENITENTIARY BLUES, PART 1/Penitentiary Blues, Part 2 (78)	Top Hat 1020	2.50	10.00	52
PENITENTIARY BLUES, PART 1/Penitentiary Blues, Part 2	Ray's Record 33	5.00	20.00	52
RESTLESS BED BLUES/My Last Blues (78)	Exclusive 95	1.50	6.00	47
SHE'S ALWAYS ON MY MIND/I'm Looking For Baby	Mercury 8228	5.00	20.00	51
SURE 'NUFF/Good Mornin' Baby	Ebb 127	2.00	8.00	58
TOO LATE, OLD MAN/River Hip Mama	Modern 896	3.00	12.00	51
TRAIN WHISTLE/My Baby's Gone	Imperial 5290	2.50	10.00	53
WHEN I'VE BEEN DRINKING/Tear Me Down	Imperial 5269	3.00	12.00	53
WHY SHOULD I LOVE YOU?/You Won't Stay Home	Sittin' In With 555	5.00	20.00	51
YOUR LITTLE WAGON/Penny Pinchin' Mama	Federal 12117	5.00	20.00	53

HOGG, John

TITLE/FLIP	LABEL & NO.	GOOD TO VERY GOOD	NEAR MINT	YR.
BLACK SNAKE BLUES/ (78)	Octive 705	4.00	16.00	51
GOT A MEAN WOMAN/Why Did You Leave Me? (78)	Mercury 8230	2.50	10.00	51
WEST TEXAS BLUES/Worryin' Blues (78)	Octive 706	4.00	16.00	51

HOGG, Smokey:
see Hogg, Andrew as Smokey (or Smoky) Hogg

HOKE, Billy with James Wayne & The Nighthawks

TITLE/FLIP	LABEL & NO.	GOOD TO VERY GOOD	NEAR MINT	YR.
I WONDER?/I Don't Want No Other Woman	D.W. 101/2	1.50	6.00	65
IN MY OWN SPECIAL WAY/Crying And Wonderin'	D.W. 103	1.50	6.00	65

HOLDEN, Ron

HOLDER, Ace

TITLE/FLIP	LABEL & NO.	GOOD TO VERY GOOD	NEAR MINT	YR.
ENCOURAGE ME, BABY/I'm In Love With You	Lulu 1124	1.50	6.00	64
LEAVE MY WOMAN ALONE/Wabba Suzy-Q	Vanessa 100	2.00	8.00	62
LONESOME HIGHWAY/Homeless Boy	Pioneer 1004	3.00	12.00	61
SORRY I HAD TO LEAVE/The Eatingest Woman	Movin' 142	2.00	8.00	66
WHEN YOU HANG AROUND/Happy Anniversary	Vanessa 102	2.00	8.00	62

HOLIDAY, Jimmy

HOLIDAYS, The

TITLE/FLIP	LABEL & NO.	GOOD TO VERY GOOD	NEAR MINT	YR.
DESPERATELY/The Robin	Melba 112	2.50	10.00	57

HOLIDAYS, The

TITLE/FLIP	LABEL & NO.	GOOD TO VERY GOOD	NEAR MINT	YR.
IRENE/Aw-Aw, Baby	Specialty 533	3.00	12.00	54

TITLE/FLIP	LABEL & NO.	GOOD TO VERY GOOD	NEAR MINT	YR.
HOLLAND, Eddie				
MERRY-GO-ROUND/	Tamla 102	5.00	20.00	59
HOLLER, Dick				
UH, UH, BABY/Living By The Gun	Ace 540	2.50	10.00	58
HOLLINS, Tony				
FISHIN' BLUES/I'll Get A Break	Decca 48300	9.00	36.00	52
WINE-O-WOMAN/Crawlin' King Snake	Decca 48288	9.00	36.00	52
HOLLOWAY, Brenda				
HOLLYWOOD ARIST O KATS, The				
I'LL BE HOME AGAIN/Amazon Beauty	Recorded In Hollywood 406	5.00	20.00	54
HOLLYWOOD BLUEJAYS, The				
CLOUDY AND RAINING/So Worried	Recorded In Hollywood 185	40.00	160.00	52
HOLLYWOOD BLUEJAYS, The				
I HAD A LOVE/Tell Me You Love Me	Recorded In Hollywood 396	25.00	100.00	53
HOLLYWOOD FLAMES, Dave Ford & The				
HOLLYWOOD FLAMES, The				
GO AND GET SOME MORE/ Another Soldier Gone (by The Question Marks)	Swing Time 346	75.00	300.00	54
Though both sides are credited to The Question Marks, the first side of this record is actually by The Hollywood Flames.				
LET'S TALK IT OVER/I Know	Decca 48331	8.00	32.00	55
LET'S TALK IT OVER/I Know	Lucky 009	15.00	60.00	54
LET'S TALK IT OVER/I Know	Swing Time 345	30.00	120.00	53
ONE NIGHT WITH A FOOL/Ride, Helen, Ride	Lucky 001	30.00	120.00	54
PEGGY/Ooh La La	Decca 29285	8.00	32.00	54
PEGGY/Oooh-La La	Lucky 006	25.00	100.00	54
WAGON WHEELS/ It Can't Be True (by The Turks)	Cash 1042	3.00	12.00	56
Though both sides are credited to The Turks, the first side of this record is actually by The Hollywood Flames.				
HOLLYWOOD FOUR FLAMES, The				
I'LL ALWAYS BE A FOOL/ She's Got Something	Recorded In Hollywood 164	25.00	100.00	52
YOUNG GIRL/Baby, Please	Recorded In Hollywood 165	25.00	100.00	52
YOUNG GIRL/The Glory Of Love	Recorded In Hollywood 165	25.00	100.00	52
HOLLYWOOD SAXONS, The				
EVERYDAY'S A HOLIDAY/L. A. Lover	Swingin' 631	1.50	6.00	61
I'M YOUR MAN/It's You	Swingin' 651	1.50	6.00	—
HOLMAN, Eddie				
HOLMES, Groove				
HOLMES, Sonny Boy				
I GOT THEM BLUES/T-N-T Woman (78)	Recorded In Hollywood 225	4.00	16.00	52
WALKING AND CRYING BLUES/I've Got The $64 Question Blues (78)	Recorded In Hollywood 223	3.00	12.00	52
HOLMES, Wright				
ALLEY SPECIAL/Good Road Blues (78)	Miltone 5221	4.00	16.00	47
ALLEY SPECIAL/Quinsella (though credited to Holmes, this side is actually by Sonny Boy Johnson) (78)	Gotham 511	5.00	20.00	47
GOOD ROAD BLUES/Drove From Home Blues (78)	Gotham 508	2.00	8.00	47
HOMER THE GREAT: see Crayton, Connie Curtis as Homer The Great				
HONEY & THE BEES				
HONEY BEARS, The (not a female group)				
I SHALL NOT FAIL/Whoa	Spark 111	10.00	40.00	55
ONE BAD STUD/It's A Miracle	Spark 104	10.00	40.00	54
HONEY BEES, The (female group)				
HONEY BOYS, The				
NEVER LOSE FAITH IN ME/Vippity Vop	Modern 980	5.00	20.00	56
HONEY CONE, The (female group)				
HONEY JUMPERS, Oscar McLollie & The: see McLollie, Oscar & The Honey Jumpers				

TITLE/FLIP	LABEL & NO.	GOOD TO VERY GOOD	NEAR MINT	YR.
HONEYBOY: see Patt, Frank as Honeyboy				
HONEYDRIPPER, The see Sykes, Roosevelt (The Honeydripper)				
HONEYTONES, The				
FALSE ALARM/Honeybun Cha Cha	Wing 90013	4.00	16.00	55
SOMEWHERE, SOMETIME, SOMEDAY/Too Bad	Mercury 70557	1.50	6.00	55
HOOKER, Earl				
BLUES IN D NATURAL/Galloping Horses, A Lazy Mule (by Amos Wells as Junior Wells)	Chief 7016	1.50	6.00	60
RACE TRACK/Blue Guitar Blues (instrumental)	King 4600	12.50	50.00	53
SWEET ANGEL/On The Hook (instrumental) (78)	Rockin' 519	6.25	25.00	52
HOOKER, John Lee				
BLUE MONDAY/Misbelieving Baby	Chart 614	1.50	6.00	53
BLUEBIRD BLUES/Key To The Highway	Modern 886	5.00	20.00	52
BOOGIE RAMBLER/No More Doggin'	JVB 30	5.00	20.00	53
BURNIN' HELL/Miss Sadie Mae (78)	Sensation 21	1.50	6.00	49
CANAL STREET BLUES/Huckle Up, Baby (78)	Sensation 26	1.50	6.00	50
COLD CHILLS ALL OVER ME/Rock Me, Mama	Modern 862	5.00	20.00	52
COOL LITTLE CAR/Bad Boy	Modern 942	2.50	20.00	54
DOWN CHILD/Gotta Boogie	Modern 923	2.50	10.00	53
EVERYBODY'S BLUES/I'm Mad	Specialty 528	2.50	10.00	54
HALF A STRANGER/Shake, Holler And Run	Modern 948	2.50	10.00	54
HOW CAN YOU DO IT?/I'm In The Mood	Modern 835	6.25	25.00	51
HUG AND SQUEEZE/The Syndicator	Modern 966	2.50	10.00	54
I TRIED HARD/Let's Talk It Over	Modern 935	2.50	10.00	53
I WONDER LITTLE DARLING/Jump Me (One More Time)	Modern 931	2.50	10.00	53
IT'S MY OWN FAULT/Women And Money	Chess 1562	4.00	16.00	54
IT'S STORMIN' AND RAININ'/Ride Till I Die	Modern 901	4.00	16.00	52
LET YOUR DADDY RIDE/Goin' On Highway 51 (78)	Sensation 30	1.50	6.00	50
LOOKIN' FOR A WOMAN/I'm Ready	Modern 978	2.50	10.00	54
LOVE MONEY CAN'T BUY/Please Take Me Back	Modern 908	2.50	10.00	53
MISS ELOISE/Boogie Chillen 2 (78)	Sensation 34	1.50	6.00	49
MY BABY'S GOT SOMETHING/Decoration Day Blues (78)	Sensation 33	1.50	6.00	50
NEW BOOGIE CHILLEN/I Tried (though both sides are credited to Hooker, this side is actually by Sylvester Cotton)	Modern 893	7.00	28.00	52
ROCK HOUSE BOOGIE/It's Been A Long Time, Baby	Modern 897	4.00	16.00	52
TOO MUCH BOOGIE/Need Somebody	Modern 916	2.50	10.00	53
WALKIN' THE BOOGIE/Sugar Mama	Chess 1513	8.00	32.00	52
WOBBLING BABY/Goin' South	Chart 609	1.50	6.00	53
YOU RECEIVE ME/Taxi Driver	Modern 958	2.50	10.00	54
HOOKER, John Lee & "Little" Eddie Kirkland				
IT HURTS ME SO/I Got My Eyes On You	Modern 876	5.00	20.00	52
HOOKER, John Lee as Birmingham Sam & His Magic Guitar				
LOW DOWN MIDNITE BOOGIE/Landing Blues (78)	Savoy 5558	1.50	6.00	49
HOOKER, John Lee as Delta John				
HELPLESS BLUES/Goin' Mad Blues (78)	Regent 1001	1.50	6.00	49
HOOKER, John Lee as John L. Booker				
609 BOOGIE/Road Trouble	Chance 1122	15.00	60.00	51
HOOKER, John Lee as John L. Hooker				
GROUND HOG BLUES/Louise	Modern 852	5.00	20.00	51
HOOKER, John Lee as John Lee				
Hooker's recordings as John Lee should not be confused with those by John Arthur Lee nor John Lee Henley. All three recorded as John Lee.				
MEAN OLD TRAIN/Catfish (78)	Gotham 515	1.50	6.00	53
HOOKER, John Lee as John Lee Booker				
BLUE MONDAY/Lovin' Guitar Man	DeLuxe 6004	10.00	40.00	53
GRAVEYARD BLUES/I Love To Boogie	Chance 1110	15.00	60.00	51
MAD MAN BLUES/Boogie Now (78)	Chess 1462	1.50	6.00	51
MAD MAN BLUES/Boogie Now (78)	Gone 60	4.00	16.00	51
MISS LORRAINE/Talkin' Boogie	Chance 1108	15.00	60.00	51
MY BABY DON'T LOVE ME/Real Real Gone	DeLuxe 6046	8.00	32.00	53
POURING DOWN RAIN/Stuttering Blues	DeLuxe 6032	8.00	32.00	53
POURING DOWN RAIN/Stuttering Blues	Rockin' 525	10.00	40.00	53
HOOKER, John Lee as John Lee Cooker				
STOMP BOOGIE/Moaning Blues	King 4504	5.00	20.00	48
HOOKER, John Lee as Johnny Lee				
I CAME TO SEE YOU, BABY/I'm A Boogie Man	DeLuxe 6009	10.00	40.00	52

John Lee Hooker

J.B. Hutto

HOOKER, John Lee as Johnny Williams

Hooker and Robert Warren each recorded as Johnny Williams for the Staff and Swing Time record labels.

TITLE/FLIP	LABEL & NO.	GOOD TO VERY GOOD	NEAR MINT	YR.
LITTLE BOY BLUE/My Daddy Was A Jockey (78)	*Gotham 513*	1.50	6.00	*52*
MISS ROSE MAE/Highway Blues (78)	*Prize 704*	4.00	16.00	*49*
MISS ROSIE MAE/Highway Blues (78)	*Staff 704*	4.00	16.00	*49*
PRISON BOUND/Bumble Bee Blues (78)	*Staff 718*	3.00	12.00	*50*
PRISON BOUND/Bumble Bee Blues (78)	*Swing Time 266*	1.50	6.00	*50*
QUESTIONNAIRE BLUES/Real Gone Gal (78)	*Gotham 509*	1.50	6.00	*52*
WANDERING BLUES/House Rent Boogie (78)	*Gotham 506*	1.50	6.00	*50*
WANDERING BLUES/House Rent Boogie (78)	*Staff 710*	2.50	10.00	*50*

HOOKER, John Lee as Texas Slim

TITLE/FLIP	LABEL & NO.	GOOD TO VERY GOOD	NEAR MINT	YR.
DEVIL'S JUMP/The Number (78)	*King 4315*	1.50	6.00	*49*
HEART TROUBLE BLUES/Slim's Stomp (78)	*King 4329*	1.50	6.00	*49*
LATE LAST NIGHT/Don't You Remember Me? (78)	*King 4366*	1.50	6.00	*49*
MOANING BLUES/Thinking Blues (78)	*King 4377*	1.50	6.00	*50*
NIGHTMARE BLUES/I'm Gonna Kill That Woman (78)	*King 4323*	1.50	6.00	*49*
STOMP BOOGIE/Black Man Blues (78)	*King 4283*	1.50	6.00	*48*
WANDERING BLUES/Don't Go Baby (78)	*King 4334*	1.50	6.00	*49*

HOOKER, John Lee as The Boogie Man

TITLE/FLIP	LABEL & NO.	GOOD TO VERY GOOD	NEAR MINT	YR.
MORNING BLUES/Do The Boogie (78)	*Acorn 308*	1.50	6.00	*50*

HOP, Poppa (or Poppy):
see Wilson, Harding as Poppa (or Poppy) Hop

HOPE, Eddie & The Mannish Boys

TITLE/FLIP	LABEL & NO.	GOOD TO VERY GOOD	NEAR MINT	YR.
FOOL NO MORE, A/Lost Child	*Marlin 804*	10.00	40.00	*56*

HOPKINS, Clyde

HOPKINS, Linda, Jackie Wilson &

HOPKINS, Sam as Lightnin' Hopkins

TITLE/FLIP	LABEL & NO.	GOOD TO VERY GOOD	NEAR MINT	YR.
AIN'T IT A SHAME?/Crazy About My Baby	*Mercury 70081*	4.00	16.00	*52*
ANOTHER FOOL IN TOWN/Candy Kitchen	*RPM 378*	3.00	12.00	*51*
AUTOMOBILE/Zologo (red plastic)	*Jax 318*	20.00	40.00	*49*
AUTOMOBILE/Zologo (78)	*Gold Star 666*	1.50	6.00	*49*
BABY PLEASE DON'T GO/Death Bells (78)	*Gold Star 646*	1.50	6.00	*48*
BEGGIN' YOU TO STAY/Bad Luck And Trouble	*RPM 337*	6.25	25.00	*51*
BLACK CAT/Mistreater Blues	*RPM 388*	3.00	12.00	*51*
BROKEN HEARTED BLUES/Freight Train Blues (red plastic)	*Sittin' In With 658*	9.00	36.00	*51*
COFFEE BLUES/New Short Haired Woman (red plastic)	*Jax 635*	9.00	36.00	*50*
COFFEE BLUES/New Short Haired Woman (red plastic)	*Sittin' In With 635*	9.00	36.00	*50*
CONTRARY MARY/I'm Begging You (red plastic)	*Jax 321*	9.00	36.00	*50*
CONTRARY MARY/I'm Begging You	*Harlem 2321*	7.00	28.00	*50*
DIRTY HOUSE/Bald Headed Woman (red plastic)	*Sittin' In With 647*	9.00	36.00	*51*
DON'T KEEP MY BABY LONG/Last Affair	*RPM 351*	5.00	20.00	*51*
DOWN TO THE RIVER/Gone Again (red plastic)	*Sittin' In With 661*	9.00	36.00	*50*
FAST LIFE/European Blues (78)	*Gold Star 665*	1.50	6.00	*49*
FAST LIFE/Jackstropper Blues	*Harlem 2331*	7.00	28.00	*49*
GIVE ME CENTRAL 209/New York Boogie (red plastic)	*Sittin' In With 621*	9.00	36.00	*50*
GONE WITH THE WIND/She's Almost Dead	*Mercury 8293*	4.00	16.00	*52*
HENNY PENNY BLUES/Jazz Blues (78)	*Gold Star 671*	4.00	16.00	*49*
HIGHWAY BLUES/Cemetary Blues	*Decca 48312*	2.50	10.00	*53*
I'M WILD ABOUT YOU, BABY/Bad Things On My Mind	*Decca 48321*	2.50	10.00	*53*
I'VE BEEN A BAD MAN/I Wonder (red plastic)	*Sittin' In With 660*	9.00	36.00	*51*
IDA MAE/Shining Moon (78)	*Gold Star 613*	1.50	6.00	*47*
JAILHOUSE BLUES/T Model Blues (red plastic)	*Sittin' In With 644*	10.00	40.00	*49*
JAILHOUSE BLUES/T Model Blues (78)	*Gold Star 662*	1.50	6.00	*49*
JAKE HEAD/Lonesome Dog	*RPM 346*	5.00	20.00	*51*
LATE IN THE EVENING/Lightnin's Jump	*TNT 8002*	7.00	28.00	*53*
LEAVIN' BLUES/Moanin' Blues	*TNT 8003*	7.00	28.00	*53*
LIGHTNIN'S BOOGIE/Don't Think 'Cause You're Pretty	*Herald 425*	2.00	8.00	*54*
LIGHTNIN'S BOOGIE/Grievance Blues	*Harlem 2324*	7.00	28.00	*49*
LIGHTNIN'S BOOGIE/Unkind Blues (78)	*Gold Star 664*	1.50	6.00	*49*
LIGHTNIN'S SPECIAL/Life I Used To Live	*Herald 428*	2.00	8.00	*54*
LONESOME HOME/Appetite Blues (78)	*Gold Star 624*	1.50	6.00	*47*
MAD WITH YOU/Airplane Blues (78)	*Gold Star 652*	1.50	6.00	*49*
MERCY/What Can It Be? (78)	*Gold Star 616*	1.50	6.00	*47*
MERRY CHRISTMAS/Happy New Year	*Decca 48306*	2.50	10.00	*53*
MY CALIFORNIA/So Long	*Aladdin 3262*	3.00	12.00	*48*
MY LITTLE KEWPIE DOLL(Wonder What Is Wrong With Me?)/Lightnin' Don't Feel Well (Bad Boogie)	*Ace 516*	1.50	6.00	*54*
MY MAMA TOLD ME/What's The Matter Now?	*Mercury 70191*	4.00	16.00	*52*
NEEDED TIME/One Kind Favor	*RPM 359*	4.00	16.00	*51*
NO GOOD WOMAN/I've Been A Bad Man (red plastic)	*Jax 315*	9.00	36.00	*50*
NO MAIL BLUES/Ain't It A Shame? (78)	*Gold Star 637*	1.50	6.00	*47*
NOTHIN' BUT THE BLUES/Early Mornin' Boogie	*Herald 443*	2.00	8.00	*54*
OLD WOMAN BLUES/Untrue Blues (78)	*Gold Star 669*	1.50	6.00	*49*
OLD WOMAN BLUES/Untrue Blues	*Harlem 2336*	7.00	28.00	*49*
PAPA BONES BOOGIE/Everything Happens To Me (red plastic)	*Sittin' In With 652*	9.00	36.00	*51*
SAD NEWS FROM KOREA/Let Me Fly Your Kite	*Mercury 8274*	4.00	26.00	*52*
SANTA FE/Someday, Baby	*RPM 398*	2.50	10.00	*51*
SHORT HAIRED WOMAN/Big Mama Jump (78)	*Gold Star 3131*	1.50	6.00	*47*
SHOTGUN/Rollin' Blues	*Aladdin 3063*	6.25	25.00	*48*
SICK FEELING BLUES/Moving Out Boogie	*Herald 436*	2.00	8.00	*54*
THEY WONDER WHO I AM/Evil Hearted Woman	*Herald 449*	2.00	8.00	*54*
TIM MOORE'S FARM/You Don't Know (78)	*Gold Star 640*	1.50	6.00	*48*
TREAT ME KIND/Somebody's Got To Go (78)	*Gold Star 641*	1.50	6.00	*48*
UNSUCCESSFUL BLUES/Grievance Blues	*Lightning 104*	4.00	16.00	*49*
UNSUCCESSFUL BLUES/Rollin' Woman Blues (78)	*Gold Star 656*	1.50	6.00	*49*
WALKIN' THE STREETS/Mussy Haired Woman	*Chart 636*	1.50	6.00	*54*
WALKING BLUES/Lightnin' Blues (78)	*Gold Star 634*	1.50	6.00	*47*
WAR IS OVER, THE/Policy Game	*Decca 28841*	2.50	10.00	*53*
YOU ARE NOT GOING TO WORRY MY LIFE ANYMORE/Daddy Will Be Home One Day	*Aladdin 3117*	3.00	12.00	*48*
YOU CAUSED (MY HEART TO WEEP)/Tap Dance Boogie (red plastic)	*Jax 642*	9.00	36.00	*50*
YOU CAUSED (MY HEART TO WEEP)/Tap Dance Boogie (red plastic)	*Sittin' In With 642*	9.00	36.00	*50*

HOPKINS, Sam as Lightnin' Hopkins & Thunder Smith

TITLE/FLIP	LABEL & NO.	GOOD TO VERY GOOD	NEAR MINT	YR.
CAN'T YOU DO LIKE YOU USED TO DO?/West Coast Blues (78)	*Aladdin 165*	1.50	6.00	*46*
FEEL SO BAD/Rocky Mountain Blues (78)	*Aladdin 168*	1.50	6.00	*46*
KATIE MAE BLUES/That Mean Old Twister (78)	*Aladdin 167*	1.50	6.00	*46*

HORNETS, The

TITLE/FLIP	LABEL & NO.	GOOD TO VERY GOOD	NEAR MINT	YR.
CRYING OVER YOU/Tango Moon	*Flash 125*	6.25	25.00	*57*
I CAN'T BELIEVE/Lonesome Baby (red plastic)	*States 127*	45.00	180.00	*53*
STROLLIN'/Slow Dance	*Rev 3515*	1.50	6.00	*58*

HORTON, Bill & The Silhouettes:
see Silhouettes, Bill Horton & The

HORTON, J. D.

TITLE/FLIP	LABEL & NO.	GOOD TO VERY GOOD	NEAR MINT	YR.
CADILLAC BLUES/Why Don't You Let Me Be? (78)	*Bullet 350*	5.00	20.00	*52*

HORTON, Walter as Big Walter & His Combo

Horton should not be confused with Walter Price, who also recorded as Big Walter.

TITLE/FLIP	LABEL & NO.	GOOD TO VERY GOOD	NEAR MINT	YR.
HARD HEARTED WOMAN/Back Home To Mama	*States 145*	8.00	32.00	*54*
HAVE A GOOD TIME/Need My Baby	*Cobra 5002*	5.00	20.00	*54*

HORTON, Walter as Mumbles

TITLE/FLIP	LABEL & NO.	GOOD TO VERY GOOD	NEAR MINT	YR.
BLACK GAL/Jumpin' Blues	*RPM 338*	12.50	50.00	*51*
LITTLE BOY BLUE/Now Tell Me, Baby (78)	*Modern 20-809*	7.00	28.00	*51*

HORTON, Walter:
see De Berry, Jimmy as Jimmy & Walter (with Walter Horton)

HOT ROD HAPPY:
see Bledsoe, James as Hot Rod Happy

HOT SHOT LOVE:
see Love, Hot Shot

HOUSTON, Cissy

HOUSTON, Joe

Most of the following are instrumentals.

TITLE/FLIP	LABEL & NO.	GOOD TO VERY GOOD	NEAR MINT	YR.
ALL NITE LONG/Way Out	*Money 203*	1.50	6.00	*55*
ATOM BOMB/Tough Enough	*Imperial 5213*	3.00	12.00	*53*
BLOWIN' CRAZY/Goin' Crazy	*Modern 917*	1.50	6.00	*52*
DIG IT/Boogie Woogie Woman	*Modern 879*	2.50	10.00	*52*
DOIN' THE LINDY HOP/Sand Storm	*Modern 863*	2.50	10.00	*52*
EARTHQUAKE/Trouble, Trouble, Trouble	*Imperial 5201*	3.00	12.00	*52*
GO, JOE, GO/Joe, Go, Go	*Lucky 45-004*	2.00	8.00	*54*
HAVE A BALL/Houston's Hot House	*Modern 850*	2.50	10.00	*52*
JAY'S BOOGIE/Corn Bread And Cabbage	*Recorded In Hollywood 423*	1.50	6.00	*54*
VINO/MM	*Combo 19*	1.50	6.00	*54*

HOUSTON, Lawyer

TITLE/FLIP	LABEL & NO.	GOOD TO VERY GOOD	NEAR MINT	YR.
DALLAS BE BOP BLUES/Lawyer Houston Blues (78)	*Atlantic 916*	3.00	12.00	*50*

HOUSTON, Lawyer as Soldier Boy Houston

TITLE/FLIP	LABEL & NO.	GOOD TO VERY GOOD	NEAR MINT	YR.
WESTERN RIDER BLUES/Hug Me, Baby	*Atlantic 971*	12.50	50.00	*50*

TITLE/FLIP	LABEL & NO.	GOOD TO VERY GOOD	NEAR MINT	YR.

HOUSTON, Soldier Boy:
see Houston, Lawyer as Soldier Boy Houston

HOWARD, Camille

TITLE/FLIP	LABEL & NO.	GOOD TO VERY GOOD	NEAR MINT	YR.
BACAROLLE BOOGIE/X-Temperaneous Boogie	Specialty 449	2.00	8.00	53
Instrumentals.				
BUSINESS WOMAN/Rock 'N Roll Woman	Vee-Jay 198	1.50	6.00	56
EXCITE ME, DADDY/I'm So Confused	Federal 12125	2.50	10.00	53
HURRY BACK, BABY/I Tried To Tell You	Federal 12134	2.50	10.00	53
OLD BALDY BOOGIE/Song Of India Boogie	Specialty 433	2.50	10.00	53
Instrumentals.				
YOU'RE LOWER THAN A MOLE/Losing Your Mind	Federal 12147	2.50	10.00	53

HOWARD, Johnny

TITLE/FLIP	LABEL & NO.	GOOD TO VERY GOOD	NEAR MINT	YR.
VACATION BLUES/Hastings Street Jump	DeLuxe 6044	12.50	50.00	53

HOWARD, Meredith

TITLE/FLIP	LABEL & NO.	GOOD TO VERY GOOD	NEAR MINT	YR.
COLD POTATO/Home Cookin' Mama (red plastic)	RCA Victor 50-0044	3.00	12.00	49
EASY COME, EASY GO BLUES/ Jelly And Bread (red plastic)	RCA Victor 50-0028	3.00	12.00	49

HOWARD, Rosetta & The Big Three Trio:
see Big Three Trio, Rosetta Howard & The

HOWIE & THE SAPPHIRES:
see Sapphires, Howie & The

HOWLIN' WOLF:
see Burnett, Chester Arthur as Howlin' Wolf

HUDSON, Joe:
see Rockin' Dukes, The (with Joe Hudson)

HUDSON, Pookie & The Spaniels

HUEY, Richard & The Sundown Singers

HUEYS, The (with Huey Smith)

HUFF, Luther

TITLE/FLIP	LABEL & NO.	GOOD TO VERY GOOD	NEAR MINT	YR.
DIRTY DISPOSITION/1951 Blues (78)	Trumpet 132	3.00	12.00	50
ROSALIE BLUES/Bull Dog Blues (78)	Trumpet 141	3.00	12.00	50

HUFF, Willie B. with The Johnny Fuller Orchestra

TITLE/FLIP	LABEL & NO.	GOOD TO VERY GOOD	NEAR MINT	YR.
BEGGAR MAN BLUES/I've Been Thinkin' And Thinkin'	Rhythm 1770	7.00	28.00	53
I LOVE YOU BABY/Operator 209	Big Town 105	5.00	20.00	53

HUGHES, Fred

HUGHES, Jimmy

HUGHES, Pee Wee & The Delta Duo

TITLE/FLIP	LABEL & NO.	GOOD TO VERY GOOD	NEAR MINT	YR.
COUNTRY BOY/Santa Fe Blues (78)	De Luxe 3228	4.00	16.00	49

HUGHES, Rhetta

HUMES, Anita & The Essex

HUMPHRIES, Teddy

HUNT, D. A.

TITLE/FLIP	LABEL & NO.	GOOD TO VERY GOOD	NEAR MINT	YR.
LONESOME OL' JAIL/Greyhound Blues	Sun 183	80.00	320.00	53

HUNT, Geraldine & Charlie Hodges

HUNT, Slim

TITLE/FLIP	LABEL & NO.	GOOD TO VERY GOOD	NEAR MINT	YR.
WELCOME HOME, BABY/Lonesome For My Baby	Excello 2055	10.00	40.00	55

HUNT, Tommy

HUNTER, Fluffy:
see Powell, Jesse

HUNTER, Ivory Joe

TITLE/FLIP	LABEL & NO.	GOOD TO VERY GOOD	NEAR MINT	YR.
I ALMOST LOST MY MIND/If I Give You My Love	MGM 10578	2.00	8.00	49
I ALMOST LOST MY MIND/If I Give You My Love	MGM 8011	3.00	12.00	49

HUNTER, Lee

Lee is the brother of Ivory Joe Hunter.

TITLE/FLIP	LABEL & NO.	GOOD TO VERY GOOD	NEAR MINT	YR.
LEE'S BOOGIE/Back To Santa Fe (78)	Gold Star 651	2.00	8.00	48

HUNTER, Lost John & The Blind Bats

TITLE/FLIP	LABEL & NO.	GOOD TO VERY GOOD	NEAR MINT	YR.
COOL DOWN, MAMA/School Boy (78)	4 Star 1492	3.00	12.00	50
Y-M & V BLUES/Boogie For Me, Baby (78)	4 Star 1511	3.00	12.00	50

HUNTER, Shane & The Four Bars

HUNTER, Ty

HUNTER, Ty & The Voicemasters

HUNTERS, The

TITLE/FLIP	LABEL & NO.	GOOD TO VERY GOOD	NEAR MINT	YR.
DOWN AT HAYDEN'S/Rabbit On A Log	Flair 1017	15.00	60.00	53

HURRICANES, The

TITLE/FLIP	LABEL & NO.	GOOD TO VERY GOOD	NEAR MINT	YR.
DEAR MOTHER/You May Not Know	King 4947	10.00	40.00	56
FALLEN ANGEL/I'll Always Be In Love With You	King 5018	7.00	28.00	57
LITTLE GIRL OF MINE/Your Promise To Me	King 4926	5.00	20.00	56
MAYBE IT'S ALL FOR THE BEST/Yours	King 4867	7.00	28.00	56
POOR LITTLE DANCING GIRL/Pistol Packin' Mama	King 4817	8.00	32.00	55
RAINING IN MY HEART/Tell Me, Baby	King 4898	7.00	28.00	56

HUSTLERS, Carl Burnett & The

TITLE/FLIP	LABEL & NO.	GOOD TO VERY GOOD	NEAR MINT	YR.
SWEET MEMORIES/Jerk, Baby, Jerk	Carmax 102	1.50	6.00	65

HUTTO, J. B. (Joseph Benjamin)

TITLE/FLIP	LABEL & NO.	GOOD TO VERY GOOD	NEAR MINT	YR.
THINGS ARE SO SLOW/Dim Lights	Chance 1165	20.00	80.00	54

HUTTO, J. B. as J. B. & His Hawks

TITLE/FLIP	LABEL & NO.	GOOD TO VERY GOOD	NEAR MINT	YR.
NOW SHE'S GONE/Combination Boogie	Chance 1155	20.00	80.00	54
PET CREAM MAN/Lovin' You	Chance 1160	20.00	80.00	54

HY-TONES, Georgia Harris & The

TITLE/FLIP	LABEL & NO.	GOOD TO VERY GOOD	NEAR MINT	YR.
LET ME HOLD YOUR HAND/I Want To Kiss You	Hy Tone 121	15.00	60.00	58

HY-TONES, The

TITLE/FLIP	LABEL & NO.	GOOD TO VERY GOOD	NEAR MINT	YR.
I'M A FOOL/Chinese Boogie	Hy Tone 120	20.00	80.00	58

HYTONES, The

I

IDEALS, The

TITLE/FLIP	LABEL & NO.	GOOD TO VERY GOOD	NEAR MINT	YR.
MAGIC/Teens	Paso 6402	2.00	8.00	61

IKETTES, The

IMAGINATIONS, The

IMPACTS, The

TITLE/FLIP	LABEL & NO.	GOOD TO VERY GOOD	NEAR MINT	YR.
CANADIAN SUNSET/They Say	RCA Victor 47-7609	5.00	20.00	59
CROC-O-DOLL/Bobby Sox Squaw	RCA Victor 47-7583	2.50	10.00	59
NOW IS THE TIME/Soup	Watts 5599	5.00	20.00	—

IMPALAS, The

IMPERIALS, Anthony & The

IMPERIALS, Little Anthony & The

TITLE/FLIP	LABEL & NO.	GOOD TO VERY GOOD	NEAR MINT	YR.
DIARY, THE/Cha Cha Henry	End 1038	1.50	6.00	59

IMPERIALS, The

TITLE/FLIP	LABEL & NO.	GOOD TO VERY GOOD	NEAR MINT	YR.
LIFE OF EASE/It Won't Be Very Long	Great Lakes 1201	20.00	80.00	54
MY DARLING/You Should Have Told Me	Buzzy 1	1.50	6.00	62
MY DARLING/You Should Have Told Me	Savoy 1104	20.00	80.00	54
WHY DID YOU LEAVE ME?/Hard Workin' Woman	Derby 858	15.00	60.00	54
YOU'LL NEVER WALK ALONE/Ain't Gonna Tell It Right	Great Lakes 1212	20.00	80.00	54

IMPERIALS, The

TITLE/FLIP	LABEL & NO.	GOOD TO VERY GOOD	NEAR MINT	YR.
TEARS ON MY PILLOW/Two People In The World	End 1027	1.50	6.00	58

This record was reissued with artists billed as "Little Anthony & The Imperials".

TITLE/FLIP	LABEL & NO.	GOOD TO VERY GOOD	NEAR MINT	YR.

IMPRESSIONS, Jerry Butler & The

TITLE/FLIP	LABEL & NO.	GOOD TO VERY GOOD	NEAR MINT	YR.
COME BACK, MY LOVE/Love Me	Abner 1017	1.50	6.00	58
FOR YOUR PRECIOUS LOVE/Sweet Was The Wine	Abner 1013	1.50	6.00	58
FOR YOUR PRECIOUS LOVE/Sweet Was The Wine	Falcon 1013	2.50	10.00	58
FOR YOUR PRECIOUS LOVE/Sweet Was The Wine	Vee Jay 280	30.00	120.00	58

IMPRESSIONS, The

TITLE/FLIP	LABEL & NO.	GOOD TO VERY GOOD	NEAR MINT	YR.
LISTEN/Shorty's Got To Go	Bandera 2504	4.00	16.00	59

IMPRESSORS, The

TITLE/FLIP	LABEL & NO.	GOOD TO VERY GOOD	NEAR MINT	YR.
DO YOU LOVE HER?/Loneliness	Cub 9010	2.00	8.00	58
IS IT TOO LATE?/No-No-No	Onyx 514	4.00	16.00	57

INCREDIBLES, The

INDEXES, John Golden & The

TITLE/FLIP	LABEL & NO.	GOOD TO VERY GOOD	NEAR MINT	YR.
TAKE A CHANCE/ You Changed My Mind (with Blanton McFarlin)	Douglas 101	4.00	16.00	—

INDIGOS, The

INDIVIDUALS, The

TITLE/FLIP	LABEL & NO.	GOOD TO VERY GOOD	NEAR MINT	YR.
DEAR ONE/Jungle Superman	Show Time 598	5.00	20.00	59
MET HER AT A DANCE/Jungle Superman	Show Time 595	5.00	20.00	59

INFATUATORS, The

TITLE/FLIP	LABEL & NO.	GOOD TO VERY GOOD	NEAR MINT	YR.
FOUND MY LOVE/Where Are You?	Destiny 504	2.00	8.00	61
FOUND MY LOVE/Where Are You?	Vee Jay 395	1.50	6.00	61

INFINITY, Billy Butler &

INFINITY

INGRAM, Luther

INK SPOTS, Ella Fitzgerald & The

TITLE/FLIP	LABEL & NO.	GOOD TO VERY GOOD	NEAR MINT	YR.
LITTLE SMALL TOWN GIRL/ I Still Feel the Same About You	Decca 27419	1.50	6.00	51

INK SPOTS, The

TITLE/FLIP	LABEL & NO.	GOOD TO VERY GOOD	NEAR MINT	YR.
ALABAMA BARBECUE/With Plenty Of Money And You (78)	Decca 1154	1.50	6.00	37
BLESS YOU/I Don't Want Sympathy, I Want Love (78)	Decca 2841	1.50	6.00	39
BROWN GAL/Pork Chops And Gravy (78)	Decca 2044	1.50	6.00	38
CASTLES IN THE SAND/Tell Me You Love Me	Decca 27464	1.50	6.00	51
CHANGING PARTNERS/Stranger In Paradise	King 1304	4.00	16.00	54
CHRISTOPHER COLUMBUS/Old Joe's Hittin' The Jug (78)	Decca 883	1.50	6.00	36
COMMAND ME/I'll Walk A Country Mile	King 4857	3.00	12.00	55
DO I WORRY?/Java Jive (78)	Decca 3432	1.50	6.00	40
DON'T 'LOW NO SWINGIN' IN HERE/ Swing, Gate, Swing (78)	Victor 24876	7.00	28.00	35
DON'T LAUGH AT ME/Keep It Movin'	King 1512	3.00	12.00	55
DON'T LET OLD AGE CREEP UPON YOU/Yes-suh (78)	Decca 1731	1.50	6.00	37
EBB TIDE/If You Should Say Goodbye	King 1297	4.00	16.00	53
FRIEND OF JOHNNYS, A/If	Decca 27391	1.50	6.00	51
GIVE HER MY LOVE/My Prayer (78)	Decca 2790	1.50	6.00	39
HERE IN MY LONELY ROOM/ Flowers, Mister Florist, Please	King 4670	12.50	50.00	53
HEY, DOC/I Don't Want To Set The World On Fire (78)	Decca 3987	1.50	6.00	41
I WISH YOU THE BEST OF EVERYTHING/ When The Sun Goes Down (78)	Decca 1870	1.50	6.00	38
I'LL NEVER SMILE AGAIN/I Could Make You Care (78)	Decca 3346	1.50	6.00	40
I'M GETTING SENTIMENTAL OVER YOU/Coquette (78)	Decca 3077	1.50	6.00	39
I'M ONLY HUMAN/Puttin' And Takin' (78)	Decca 3468	1.50	6.00	40
I'M STILL WITHOUT A SWEETHEART/So Sorry (78)	Decca 3806	1.50	6.00	41
I'M THROUGH/Memories Of You (78)	Decca 2966	1.50	6.00	39
IF I DIDN'T CARE/Knock Kneed Sal (78)	Decca 2286	1.50	6.00	39
IT'S FUNNY TO EVERYONE BUT ME/Just For A Thrill (78)	Decca 2507	1.50	6.00	39
KEEP COOL, FOOL/Until The Real Thing Comes Along (78)	Decca 3958	1.50	6.00	41
LET'S CALL THE WHOLE THING OFF/Slap That Bass (78)	Decca 1251	1.50	6.00	37
MELODY OF LOVE/Am I Too Late?	King 1336	7.00	28.00	54
MELODY OF LOVE/There Is Something Missing	King 1429	6.25	25.00	54
MY GREATEST MISTAKE/We Three (78)	Decca 3379	1.50	6.00	40
OH, RED/That Cat Is High (78)	Decca 1789	1.50	6.00	38
PLANTING RICE/Yesterdays	King 1378	3.00	12.00	54
RIGHT ABOUT NOW/The Way It Used To Be	Decca 27214	1.50	6.00	50
RING, TELEPHONE RING/ Please Take A Letter, Miss Brown (78)	Decca 3626	1.50	6.00	41
SOMEONE'S ROCKING MY DREAMBOAT/ When You Come To The End Of The Day	King 1425	7.00	28.00	55
SOMETIME/I Was Dancing With Someone	Decca 27102	1.50	6.00	50
STOMPIN' AT THE SAVOY/ Keep Away From My Door Step (78)	Decca 1036	1.50	6.00	36
STOP PRETENDING/ You're Breaking My Heart All Over Again (78)	Decca 3288	1.50	6.00	40
SWING HIGH, SWING LOW/Whoa, Babe (78)	Decca 1236	1.50	6.00	37
SWINGIN' ON THE STRINGS/Your Feet's Too Big (78)	Bluebird 6530	2.50	10.00	36
SWINGIN' ON THE STRINGS/Your Feet's Too Big (78)	Victor 24851	15.00	60.00	35
'TAINT NOBODY'S BIZ-NESS IF I DO/ Your Feet's Too Big (78)	Decca 817	1.50	6.00	36
THAT'S WHEN YOUR HEARTACHES BEGIN/ What Good Would It Do? (78)	Decca 3720	1.50	6.00	41
TIME OUT FOR TEARS/Dream Awhile	Decca 27259	1.50	6.00	50
WE'LL MEET AGAIN/You're Looking For Romance (78)	Decca 3656	1.50	6.00	41
WHAT CAN I DO?/ When The Swallows Come Back To Capistrano (78)	Decca 3195	1.50	6.00	40
WHISPERING GRASS/Maybe (78)	Decca 3258	1.50	6.00	40
YOU BRING ME DOWN/Address Unknown (78)	Decca 2707	1.50	6.00	39

INSPIRATIONS, Andre Williams & The

INSPIRATIONS, The

TITLE/FLIP	LABEL & NO.	GOOD TO VERY GOOD	NEAR MINT	YR.
RAINDROPS/Maggie	Apollo 494	10.00	40.00	56

INSPIRATIONS, The

TITLE/FLIP	LABEL & NO.	GOOD TO VERY GOOD	NEAR MINT	YR.
DON'T CRY/Indian Jane	Lamp 2019	5.00	20.00	58

INSPIRATORS, The

TITLE/FLIP	LABEL & NO.	GOOD TO VERY GOOD	NEAR MINT	YR.
IF LOVING YOU IS WRONG/Three Sixty	Treat 502	15.00	60.00	—
STARLIGHT TONIGHT/Oh, What A Feeling!	Old Town 1053	8.00	32.00	58

INTERIORS, The

TITLE/FLIP	LABEL & NO.	GOOD TO VERY GOOD	NEAR MINT	YR.
DARLING LITTLE ANGEL/Voodoo Doll	Worthy 1008	1.50	6.00	61
ECHOES/Love You Some More	Worthy 1009	1.50	6.00	61

INTERLUDES, The

TITLE/FLIP	LABEL & NO.	GOOD TO VERY GOOD	NEAR MINT	YR.
DARLING, I'LL BE TRUE/Wilted Rose Bud	King 5633	5.00	10.00	62

INTERLUDES, The

TITLE/FLIP	LABEL & NO.	GOOD TO VERY GOOD	NEAR MINT	YR.
I SHED A MILLION TEARS/Oo-wee	RCA Victor 47-7281	1.50	6.00	58

INTERVALS, The

TITLE/FLIP	LABEL & NO.	GOOD TO VERY GOOD	NEAR MINT	YR.
HERE'S THAT RAINY DAY/Wish I Could Change My Mind	Class 304	5.00	20.00	62

INTRUDERS, Detroit & The

INTRUDERS, The

INVICTAS, The

TITLE/FLIP	LABEL & NO.	GOOD TO VERY GOOD	NEAR MINT	YR.
GONE SO LONG/Nellie	Jack Bee 1003	2.50	10.00	59

INVINCIBLES, The

TITLE/FLIP	LABEL & NO.	GOOD TO VERY GOOD	NEAR MINT	YR.
MR. MOONGLOWS/Swayback	Chess 1727	2.00	8.00	59

IRVIN, Curtis & The Sparks:
see Sparks, Curtis Irvin & The

IRWIN, Big Dee:
see Pastels, The (with Big Dee Irwin)

ISLEY BROTHERS, The

TITLE/FLIP	LABEL & NO.	GOOD TO VERY GOOD	NEAR MINT	YR.
ANGELS CRIED/The Cow Jumped Over The Moon	Teenage 1004	4.00	16.00	57
DON'T BE JEALOUS/This Is The End	Cindy 3009	3.00	12.00	58

IVIES, The

TITLE/FLIP	LABEL & NO.	GOOD TO VERY GOOD	NEAR MINT	YR.
SUNSHINE/Come On	Ivy 110	2.50	10.00	58

IVOLEERS, The

TITLE/FLIP	LABEL & NO.	GOOD TO VERY GOOD	NEAR MINT	YR.
LOVER'S QUARREL/Come With Me	Buzz 101	5.00	20.00	59

IVORIES, The

TITLE/FLIP	LABEL & NO.	GOOD TO VERY GOOD	NEAR MINT	YR.
ALONE/Baby, Send A Letter	Jaguar 3019	40.00	160.00	56
ALONE/Baby, Send A Letter	Jaguar 3023	30.00	120.00	56

IVORYTONES, The

IVY LEAGUERS, The

IVY TONES, The

TITLE/FLIP	LABEL & NO.	GOOD TO VERY GOOD	NEAR MINT	YR.
OO WEE, BABY/Each Time (blue label)	Red Top 105	2.50	10.00	58

The Impressions

The Ink Spots

TITLE/FLIP	LABEL & NO.	GOOD TO VERY GOOD	NEAR MINT	YR.

J. B. & HIS BAYOU BOYS:
see Lenoir, J. B. as J. B.

J. B. & HIS HAWKS:
see Hutto, J. B. as J. B.

J. MERCY BABY:
see Mullins, Jimmy as J. Mercy Baby

JAC-O-LACS, The

TITLE/FLIP	LABEL & NO.	GOOD TO VERY GOOD	NEAR MINT	YR.
CINDY LOU/Sha-Ba-Da-Ba-Doo	Tampa 103	7.00	28.00	—

JACKAELS, J. J. Jackson & The

TITLE/FLIP	LABEL & NO.	GOOD TO VERY GOOD	NEAR MINT	YR.
LIFETIME FROM TODAY, A/That Look In Your Eye	Storm 501	1.50	6.00	59

JACKALS, J. J. Jackson & The

JACKIE & THE STARLITES:
see Starlites, Jackie & The

JACKS, The

TITLE/FLIP	LABEL & NO.	GOOD TO VERY GOOD	NEAR MINT	YR.
I'M CONFESSIN'/Since My Baby's Been Gone	RPM 433	5.00	20.00	55
LET'S MAKE UP/Dream A Little Longer	RPM 467	1.50	6.00	56
SO WRONG/How Soon?	RPM 454	4.00	16.00	56
THIS EMPTY HEART/My Clumsy Heart	RPM 444	2.00	8.00	55
WHY DID I FALL IN LOVE?/Sugar Baby	RPM 458	1.50	6.00	56
WHY DON'T YOU WRITE ME?/My Darling	RPM 428	5.00	20.00	55
WHY DON'T YOU WRITE ME?/Smack Dab In The Middle	RPM 428	6.25	25.00	55

JACKSON FIVE, The

JACKSON, Brother:
see Jackson, Louis as Brother Jackson

JACKSON, Bull Moose

TITLE/FLIP	LABEL & NO.	GOOD TO VERY GOOD	NEAR MINT	YR.
BEARCAT BLUES/There Is No Greater Love	King 4551	1.50	6.00	52
BIG TEN INCH RECORD/I Needed You	King 4580	6.25	25.00	52
CHEROKEE BOOGIE/I'm Lucky I Have You	King 4472	2.00	8.00	51
I LOVE YOU, YES I DO/Sneaky Pete	King 4181	2.00	8.00	51
Both songs were originally recorded in 1947.				
I WANT A BOWLEGGED WOMAN/All My Love Belongs To You	King 4189	2.50	10.00	51
Both songs were originally recorded in 1947.				
I'LL BE HOME FOR XMAS/I Never Loved Anyone But You	King 4493	1.50	6.00	51
IF YOU AIN'T LOVIN'/I Wanna Hug You	King 4775	1.50	6.00	55
IF YOU'LL LET ME/Hodge Podge	King 4655	1.50	6.00	53
LET ME LOVE YOU ALL NIGHT/Bootsie	King 4535	1.50	6.00	52
MEET ME WITH YOUR BLACK DRESS ON/ Try To Forget Him, Baby	King 4634	1.50	6.00	53
MUST YOU KEEP ON PRETENDING?/I'm Glad For Your Sake	King 4802	1.50	6.00	56
NOSEY JOE/Sad	King 4524	5.00	20.00	52
TRUST IN ME/Wonder When My Baby's Coming Home?	King 4451	1.50	6.00	51
UNLESS/End This Misery	King 4462	1.50	6.00	51

JACKSON, Chuck

JACKSON, Chuck & Maxine Brown

JACKSON, Cookie & The Flares

JACKSON, George

TITLE/FLIP	LABEL & NO.	GOOD TO VERY GOOD	NEAR MINT	YR.
UH-HUH/I'm Sorry	Atlantic 1024	2.50	10.00	53

JACKSON, Handy

TITLE/FLIP	LABEL & NO.	GOOD TO VERY GOOD	NEAR MINT	YR.
GOT MY APPLICATION, BABY/Trouble	Sun 177	10.00	40.00	53

JACKSON, J. J.

JACKSON, J. J. & The Jackaels:
see Jackaels, J. J. Jackson & The

JACKSON, J. J. & The Jackals

JACKSON, Lee

TITLE/FLIP	LABEL & NO.	GOOD TO VERY GOOD	NEAR MINT	YR.
FISHIN' IN MY POND/I'll Just Keep Walking	Cobra 5007	5.00	20.00	57

JACKSON, Lil' Son:
see Jackson, Melvin as Lil' Son Jackson

JACKSON, Little Son:
see Jackson, Melvin as Little Son Jackson

JACKSON, Louis

TITLE/FLIP	LABEL & NO.	GOOD TO VERY GOOD	NEAR MINT	YR.
TWEEDLE WOOFIN' BOOGIE/Fran's Mood	C-Note 110	2.50	10.00	—

JACKSON, Louis as Brother Jackson

TITLE/FLIP	LABEL & NO.	GOOD TO VERY GOOD	NEAR MINT	YR.
L. J. BOOGIE/J. H. Stomp (by Junior Hampton) (78)	Murray 500	4.00	16.00	48

JACKSON, Louis as Louis & Frosty (William Pyles)

TITLE/FLIP	LABEL & NO.	GOOD TO VERY GOOD	NEAR MINT	YR.
LONESOME AND CONFUSED/Train Time	C-Note 109	2.00	8.00	—

JACKSON, Melvin as Lil' Son Jackson

TITLE/FLIP	LABEL & NO.	GOOD TO VERY GOOD	NEAR MINT	YR.
BLACK AND BROWN/Sad Letter Blues	Imperial 5218	6.25	25.00	52
DIRTY WORK/Little Girl	Imperial 5259	5.00	20.00	53
GET HIGH EVERYBODY/Let Me Down Easy	Imperial 5300	6.25	25.00	52
HOW LONG?/Good Ole Wagon	Imperial 5312	3.00	12.00	53
JOURNEY BACK HOME/Rockin' And Rollin'	Imperial 5204	6.25	25.00	52
LONELY BLUES/Freight Train Blues	Imperial 5229	5.00	20.00	53
LONELY BLUES/No Money	Post 2014	3.00	12.00	53
MOVIN' TO THE COUNTRY/Confession	Imperial 5248	5.00	20.00	53
MY YOUNGER DAYS/I Wish To Go Home	Imperial 5319	3.00	12.00	52
PIGGLY WIGGLY/Big Rat	Imperial 5276	4.00	16.00	53
SPENDING MONEY BLUES/All Alone	Imperial 5237	5.00	20.00	50
SUGAR MAMA/Messin' Up	Imperial 5339	3.00	12.00	54
THRILL ME, BABY/Doctor, Doctor	Imperial 5267	4.00	16.00	53
TROUBLE DON'T LAST ALWAYS/Blues By The Hour	Imperial 5286	4.00	16.00	53

JACKSON, Melvin as Little Son Jackson

TITLE/FLIP	LABEL & NO.	GOOD TO VERY GOOD	NEAR MINT	YR.
CAIRO BLUES/Evil Blues (78)	Gold Star 663	1.50	6.00	49
GAMBLING BLUES/Homeless Blues (78)	Gold Star 668	1.50	6.00	49
GONE WITH THE WIND/No Money, No Love (78)	Gold Star 653	1.50	6.00	49
GROUND HOG BLUES/Bad Whiskey, Bad Women (78)	Gold Star 642	1.50	6.00	48
ROBERTA BLUES/Freedom Train Blues (78)	Gold Star 638	1.50	6.00	48
TALKIN' BOOGIE/Milford Blues (78)	Modern 840	2.50	10.00	49

JACKSON, Michael

JACKSON, Millie

JACKSON, Monroe "Moe"

TITLE/FLIP	LABEL & NO.	GOOD TO VERY GOOD	NEAR MINT	YR.
MOVE IT ON OVER/Go 'Way From My Door (78)	Mercury 8127	7.00	28.00	49

JACKSON, Rudy & The Mel-O-Aires:
see Mel-O-Aires, Rudy Jackson & The

JACKSON, Skip & The Shantons

JACKSON, Walter

JACKSON, Willis (Gator Tail)

All of the following are instrumentals.

TITLE/FLIP	LABEL & NO.	GOOD TO VERY GOOD	NEAR MINT	YR.
GATOR'S GROOVE/Estrelitta	Atlantic 975	3.00	12.00	52
HARLEM NOCTURNE/Street Scene	Atlantic 946	3.00	12.00	51
ROCK, ROCK, ROCK/Here Is My Heart	Atlantic 967	4.00	16.00	52
SHAKE DANCE/Walkin' Home	Atlantic 998	2.50	10.00	53
WINE-O-WINE/Good Gliding	Atlantic 957	5.00	20.00	51

JACKSONS, The

JACOBS, Donnie

JACOBS, Marion Walter as Little Walter

Jacobs should not be confused with Leroy Foster, who also recorded as Little Walter, nor with George Smith, who recorded as Little Walter, Jr., nor with a fourth artist who recorded during the 60s as Little Red Walter.

TITLE/FLIP	LABEL & NO.	GOOD TO VERY GOOD	NEAR MINT	YR.
LIGHTS OUT (instrumental)/You're So Fine	Checker 786	1.50	6.00	54
ORA NELLE BLUES/I Just Keep Loving Her (78)	Ora Nelle 711	5.00	20.00	47
ORA NELLE BLUES/I Just Keep Loving Her	Chance 1116	25.00	100.00	—
ROCKER (instrumental)/Oh, Baby	Checker 793	1.50	6.00	54
YOU'D BETTER WATCH YOURSELF/ Blue Light (instrumental) (red plastic)	Checker 799	10.00	40.00	54
YOU'D BETTER WATCH YOURSELF/Blue Light (instrumental)	Checker 799	1.50	6.00	54

TITLE/FLIP	LABEL & NO.	GOOD TO VERY GOOD	NEAR MINT	YR.

JACOBS, Marion Walter as Little Walter & His Jukes

TITLE/FLIP	LABEL & NO.	GOOD TO VERY GOOD	NEAR MINT	YR.
OFF THE WALL (instrumental)/Tell Me, Mama	Checker 770	2.00	8.00	53
QUARTER TO TWELVE (instrumental)/ Blues With A Feeling	Checker 780	2.00	8.00	54

JACOBS, Marion Walter as Little Walter & His Night Caps

TITLE/FLIP	LABEL & NO.	GOOD TO VERY GOOD	NEAR MINT	YR.
MEAN OLD WORLD/Sad Hours (instrumental)	Checker 764	2.00	8.00	52

JACOBS, Marion Walter as Little Walter & His Night Cats

TITLE/FLIP	LABEL & NO.	GOOD TO VERY GOOD	NEAR MINT	YR.
JUKE (instrumental)/Can't Hold Out Much Longer	Checker 758	2.50	10.00	52

JACOBS, Marion Walter as The Little Walter Trio

TITLE/FLIP	LABEL & NO.	GOOD TO VERY GOOD	NEAR MINT	YR.
MUSKADINE BLUES/Bad Acting Woman (78)	Regal 3296	11.00	44.00	50

JACOBS, Matthew as Boogie Jake

TITLE/FLIP	LABEL & NO.	GOOD TO VERY GOOD	NEAR MINT	YR.
BAD LUCK AND TROUBLE/Early Morning Blues	Minit 601/602	2.50	10.00	59

JACQUET, Illinois

All of the following are instrumentals.

TITLE/FLIP	LABEL & NO.	GOOD TO VERY GOOD	NEAR MINT	YR.
BIG FOOT/B-Yot (red plastic)	RCA Victor 50-0021	2.00	8.00	49
BLACK VELVET/Adam's Alley (red plastic)	RCA Victor 50-0011	2.00	8.00	49
BLUE SATIN/Stay Away (red plastic)	RCA Victor 50-0047	2.00	8.00	49
MY OLD GAL/You Gotta Change (red plastic)	RCA Victor 50-0087	2.00	8.00	49
SLOW DOWN, BABY/Hot Rod (red plastic)	RCA Victor 50-0097	2.50	10.00	49

JADES, The

TITLE/FLIP	LABEL & NO.	GOOD TO VERY GOOD	NEAR MINT	YR.
HOLD BACK THE DAWN/When They Ask About You	Dore 687	1.50	6.00	63
LEAVE HER FOR ME/So Blue	Time 1002	1.50	6.00	58

JAGUARS, The

TITLE/FLIP	LABEL & NO.	GOOD TO VERY GOOD	NEAR MINT	YR.
BE MY SWEETIE/Why Don't You Believe Me?	Aardell 0006	7.00	28.00	55
HOLD ME TIGHT/Picadilly	Ebb 129	1.50	6.00	58
I WANTED YOU/Rock It, Davy, Rock It	Aardell 0003	7.00	28.00	55
ROCK IT, DAVY, ROCK IT/The Big Bear (with Patti Ross)	Aardell 107	4.00	16.00	—
WAY YOU LOOK TONIGHT, THE/ Moonlight And You (red plastic)	R-Dell 11	45.00	180.00	—
WAY YOU LOOK TONIGHT, THE/Moonlight And You	Aardell 0011	1.50	6.00	56
WAY YOU LOOK TONIGHT, THE/Moonlight And You	R-Dell 11	25.00	100.00	—

JAMAL, Ahmad

All of the following are instrumentals.

TITLE/FLIP	LABEL & NO.	GOOD TO VERY GOOD	NEAR MINT	YR.
BUT NOT FOR ME/Sellerltus	Parrot 810	2.00	8.00	54
EXCERPTS FROM THE BLUES/It Could Happen To You	Parrot 818	2.00	8.00	54

JAMECOS, The

JAMES QUINTET, Austin Powell & The

TITLE/FLIP	LABEL & NO.	GOOD TO VERY GOOD	NEAR MINT	YR.
WRONG AGAIN/What More Can I Ask?	Atlantic 968	20.00	80.00	52

JAMES QUINTET, The

TITLE/FLIP	LABEL & NO.	GOOD TO VERY GOOD	NEAR MINT	YR.
DON'T WORRY/Let's Put Our Hearts On The Table (78)	Derby 732	2.50	10.00	50
I COULD MAKE YOU CARE/ Drop A Penny In The Wishing Well	Decca 48237	15.00	60.00	51
I'M JUST A FOOL/Paw's In The Kitchen (78)	Derby 726	2.50	10.00	49
NEIGHBORHOOD AFFAIR, A/ You Make Too Much Noise When We Kiss	Decca 43218	15.00	60.00	51
PLEASING YOU/Bewildered (78)	Coral 60018	2.50	10.00	49
PLEASING YOU/Bewildered (78)	Coral 65002	2.50	10.00	49
TELL ME WHY/Oo Bop Choo Dop (78)	Coral 60022	2.50	10.00	49
TELL ME WHY/Remember When? (78)	Coral 65016	2.50	10.00	49

JAMES, Bobbie & The Four Buddies:
see Four Buddies, Bobbie James & The

JAMES, Elmore

TITLE/FLIP	LABEL & NO.	GOOD TO VERY GOOD	NEAR MINT	YR.
(I BELIEVE) MY TIME AIN'T LONG/ I Wish I Was A Catfish (78)	Trumpet 146	4.00	16.00	53
(I BELIEVE) MY TIME AIN'T LONG/ I Wish I Was A Catfish	Ace 508	15.00	60.00	53
I BELIEVE/I Held My Baby Last Night	Meteor 5000	12.50	50.00	53
SINFUL WOMAN/Baby, What's Wrong?	Meteor 5003	10.00	40.00	53

JAMES, Elmore & His Broomdusters

TITLE/FLIP	LABEL & NO.	GOOD TO VERY GOOD	NEAR MINT	YR.
BLUES BEFORE SUNRISE/Goodbye, Baby	Flair 1079	3.00	12.00	56
CAN'T STOP LOVIN'/Make A Little Love	Flair 1014	5.00	20.00	54
COUNTRY BOOGIE/She Just Won't Do Right	Checker 777	12.50	50.00	55
CRY FOR ME, BABY/Take Me Where You Go	Chief 7006	2.50	10.00	57
CRY FOR ME, BABY/Take Me Where You Go	Vee Jay 269	1.50	6.00	57
DARK AND DREARY/Rock My Baby Right	Flair 1048	4.00	16.00	56
DUST MY BLUES/I Was A Fool	Flair 1074	3.00	12.00	56
EARLY IN THE MORNING/Hawaiian Boogie	Flair 1011	7.00	28.00	54
HAPPY HOME/No Love In My Heart	Flair 1069	3.00	12.00	56
IT HURTS ME, TOO/Elmore's Contribution To Jazz	Chief 7004	2.50	10.00	57
IT HURTS ME, TOO/Elmore's Contribution To Jazz	Vee Jay 259	1.50	6.00	57
LATE HOURS AT MIDNIGHT/The Way You Treat Me	Flair 1062	3.00	12.00	56
MAKE MY DREAMS COME TRUE/Hand In Hand	Flair 1031	5.00	20.00	55
SHO'NUFF, I DO/1839 Blues	Flair 1039	4.00	16.00	55
STANDING AT THE CROSSROADS/Sunnyland	Flair 1057	4.00	16.00	55
STRANGE KINDA FEELING/Please Find My Baby	Flair 1022	5.00	20.00	55
TWELVE YEAR OLD BOY, THE/Coming Home	Chief 7001	2.50	10.00	57
TWELVE YEAR OLD BOY, THE/Coming Home	Vee Jay 249	1.50	6.00	57

JAMES, Elmore:
see Turner, Joe

JAMES, Etta (Miss Peaches)

TITLE/FLIP	LABEL & NO.	GOOD TO VERY GOOD	NEAR MINT	YR.
GOOD ROCKING DADDY/Crazy Feeling	Modern 962	1.50	6.00	55
HEY HENRY/Be Mine	Modern 957	1.50	6.00	55
TOUGH LOVER/Fools We Mortals Be	Modern 998	1.50	6.00	56
WALLFLOWER/Hold Me, Squeeze Me	Modern 947	1.50	6.00	55

JAMES, Etta & Sugar Pie DeSanto

JAMES, Jesse

TITLE/FLIP	LABEL & NO.	GOOD TO VERY GOOD	NEAR MINT	YR.
FORGIVE ME BLUES/Corrina's Boogie (78)	Sittin' In With 569	5.00	20.00	51

Note: This recording and the one by Jesse James as Sunny James are the only two known by this artist. The name Jesse James has been used by other artists.

JAMES, Jesse as Sunny James

TITLE/FLIP	LABEL & NO.	GOOD TO VERY GOOD	NEAR MINT	YR.
PLEASE MAM, FORGIVE ME/Excuse Me, Baby (78)	Down Town 2010	6.25	25.00	48

JAMES, Jessica & The Outlaws

JAMES, Jimmy & The Vagabonds

JAMES, Sunny:
see James, Jesse as Sunny James

JAMES, Ulysses

TITLE/FLIP	LABEL & NO.	GOOD TO VERY GOOD	NEAR MINT	YR.
POOR BOY/Stormin' And Rainin' (by Lowell Fulson) (78)	Cavatone 250	4.00	16.00	48

JAMMIN' JIM:
see Harris, Edward as Jammin' Jim

JAN & THE RADIANTS:
see Radiants, Jan & The

JANUARYS, Little June & The

TITLE/FLIP	LABEL & NO.	GOOD TO VERY GOOD	NEAR MINT	YR.
HELLO/Burgers, Fries & Shakes	Salem 188	10.00	40.00	—
OH, WHAT A FEELING!/Oh, My Love	Profile 4009	4.00	16.00	—

JARMELS, The

JAY & THE TECHNIQUES

JAYHAWKS, Earl Palmer & The

TITLE/FLIP	LABEL & NO.	GOOD TO VERY GOOD	NEAR MINT	YR.
JOHNNY'S HOUSE PARTY, PART 1/ Johnny's House Party, Part 2	Aladdin 3379	1.50	6.00	57

JAYHAWKS, The

TITLE/FLIP	LABEL & NO.	GOOD TO VERY GOOD	NEAR MINT	YR.
COUNTING MY TEARDROPS/The Devil's Cousin	Flash 105	15.00	60.00	56
EVERYONE SHOULD KNOW/The Creature	Aladdin 3393	2.50	10.00	57
LOVE TRAIN/Don't Mind Dyin'	Flash 111	1.50	6.00	56
START THE FIRE/I Wish The World Owed Me A Living	Eastman 792	1.50	6.00	57
STRANDED IN THE JUNGLE/My Only Darling	Flash 109	1.50	6.00	56

JAYNETTS, The

JAYS, Armonda & The

TITLE/FLIP	LABEL & NO.	GOOD TO VERY GOOD	NEAR MINT	YR.
PRESENT OF LOVE/Pony Tails	Apollo 540	4.00	16.00	59

JAYTONES, The

TITLE/FLIP	LABEL & NO.	GOOD TO VERY GOOD	NEAR MINT	YR.
BELLS, THE/Oh, Darling	Timely 1003/1004	8.00	32.00	58
CLOCK, THE/Gasoline	Brunswick 55087	7.00	28.00	58
MY ONLY LOVE/Absolutely Right	Cub 9057	1.50	6.00	59

JEANETTES, Gene & The

JEANIE & THE BOY FRIENDS:
see Boy Friends, Jeanie & The

JEANNE & THE DARLINGS

JEANNIE & THE MILLER SISTERS

JELLY BEANS, The

JELLY BELLY & SLIM SEWARD:
see Seward, Alec & Louis Hayes as Jelly Belly & Slim Seward

JENKINS, Bobo:
see Jenkins, John Pickens as Bobo Jenkins

JENKINS, Gus

TITLE/FLIP	LABEL & NO.	GOOD TO VERY GOOD	NEAR MINT	YR.
I BEEN WORKING/I Miss My Baby	Combo 87	5.00	20.00	54

JENKINS, Gus as Little Temple & His "88"

TITLE/FLIP	LABEL & NO.	GOOD TO VERY GOOD	NEAR MINT	YR.
I ATE THE WRONG PART/Cold Love	Specialty 475	5.00	20.00	54

JENKINS, Gus as The Young Wolf

TITLE/FLIP	LABEL & NO.	GOOD TO VERY GOOD	NEAR MINT	YR.
WORRIES AND TROUBLES/I Tried	Combo 88	4.00	16.00	54

JENKINS, John Pickens as Bobo Jenkins

TITLE/FLIP	LABEL & NO.	GOOD TO VERY GOOD	NEAR MINT	YR.
BABY, DON'T YOU WANT TO GO?/Ten Below Zero (78)	Fortune 838	2.00	8.00	56
DEMOCRAT BLUES/Bad Luck And Trouble	Chess 1565	10.00	40.00	54
NOTHING BUT LOVE/Tell Me Who	Boxer 202	2.50	10.00	55

JENKINS, Robert

TITLE/FLIP	LABEL & NO.	GOOD TO VERY GOOD	NEAR MINT	YR.
STEELIN' BOOGIE, PART 1/Steelin' Boogie, Part 2 (78)	Parkway 103	15.00	60.00	50

JENNINGS, Baby Boy & The Satelites

JERRY O

JESSE & BUZZY

JESSE & MARVIN:
see Belvin, Jesse & Marvin Phillips as Jesse & Marvin

JESTERS, The

TITLE/FLIP	LABEL & NO.	GOOD TO VERY GOOD	NEAR MINT	YR.
I LAUGHED/Now That You're Gone	Cyclone 5011	4.00	16.00	58
PLEA, THE/Oh, Baby	Winley 225	1.50	6.00	58
PLEASE LET ME LOVE YOU/I'm Falling In Love	Winley 221	1.50	6.00	57
SO STRANGE/Love No One But You	Winley 218	4.00	16.00	57

JETS, The

TITLE/FLIP	LABEL & NO.	GOOD TO VERY GOOD	NEAR MINT	YR.
GOT A LITTLE SHADOW/I'll Hide My Tears	Aladdin 3247	15.00	60.00	54
VOLCANO/Gomen Nasai	7-11 2101	25.00	100.00	53

JETS, The

TITLE/FLIP	LABEL & NO.	GOOD TO VERY GOOD	NEAR MINT	YR.
HEAVEN ABOVE ME/Millie Brown	Gee 1020	15.00	60.00	56

JETS, The

TITLE/FLIP	LABEL & NO.	GOOD TO VERY GOOD	NEAR MINT	YR.
LOVERS, THE/Drag It Home, Baby	Rainbow 201	25.00	100.00	53

JEWELS, Billy Abbott & The

JEWELS, The

TITLE/FLIP	LABEL & NO.	GOOD TO VERY GOOD	NEAR MINT	YR.
ANGEL IN MY LIFE/Hearts Can Be Broken	Imperial 5351	2.00	8.00	55
FOOL IN PARADISE, A/Oh Yes, I Know	R & B 1303	9.00	36.00	54
HEARTS OF STONE/Runnin'	R & B 1301	7.00	28.00	54
NATURAL, NATURAL DITTY/Please Return	Imperial 5362	1.50	6.00	55
ROSALIE/Living From Day To Day	R & B 1306	7.00	28.00	55
SHE'S A FLIRT/B-Bomb Baby	RPM 474	2.00	8.00	56

JEWELS, The (female group)

JEWELS, The:
see Crows, The as The Jewels

JILLETTES, The (female group)

JIMMY & WALTER:
see De Berry, Jimmy as Jimmy & Walter (with Walter Horton)

JIMMY LEE:
see Robinson, Jimmy Lee as Jimmy Lee

JIVE BOMBERS, Clarence Palmer & The

TITLE/FLIP	LABEL & NO.	GOOD TO VERY GOOD	NEAR MINT	YR.
BROWN BOY/Pee Wee's Boogie	Citation 1161	5.00	20.00	52
Side one of this release was the original recording of "Bad Boy".				
IT'S SPRING AGAIN/Pork Chop Boogie	Citation 1160	5.00	20.00	52

JIVE BOMBERS, The

JIVE FIVE, The

TITLE/FLIP	LABEL & NO.	GOOD TO VERY GOOD	NEAR MINT	YR.
UNITED/Prove Every Word You Say	Sketch 219	2.50	10.00	64

JIVERS, The

TITLE/FLIP	LABEL & NO.	GOOD TO VERY GOOD	NEAR MINT	YR.
CHERIE/Little Mama	Aladdin 3329	10.00	40.00	56
RAY PEARL/Dear Little One	Aladdin 3347	10.00	40.00	56

JIVING JUNIORS, The

TITLE/FLIP	LABEL & NO.	GOOD TO VERY GOOD	NEAR MINT	YR.
SWEET AS AN ANGEL/Moonlight Lover	Asnes 103	1.50	6.00	—

JO, Damita

JOEY & THE FLIPS

JOEY & THE TEENAGERS:
see Teenagers, Joey & The

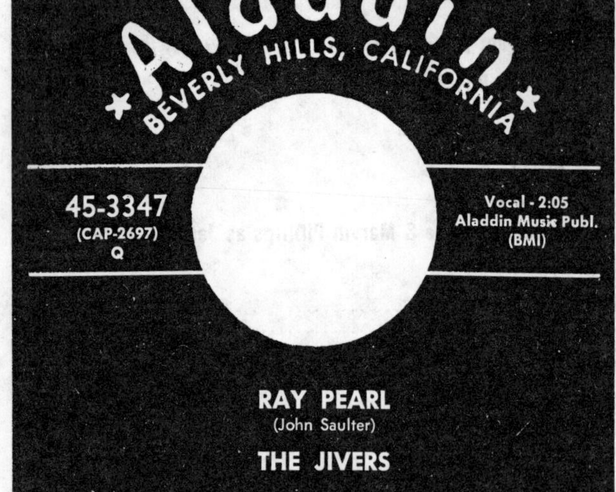

JOHN LEE:
see Henley, John Lee as John Lee
see Hooker, John Lee as John Lee
see Lee, John Arthur as John Lee

JOHN, Little Willie

JOHN, Mable

JOHNNY & THE EXPRESSIONS

JOHNNY LEE:
see Hooker, John Lee as Johnny Lee

JOHNSON, Bill:
see Musical Notes, Bill Johnson & The
see Parker, Herman as Little Junior Parker with Bill Johnson's Blue Flames

JOHNSON, Blind Boy & His Rhythms:
see Dupree, William Thomas as Blind Boy

JOHNSON, Bubber & The Dreamers:
see Dreamers, Bubber Johnson & The

JOHNSON, Bud:
see Chanters, Bud Johnson & The

JOHNSON, Bud & The Voices Five:
see Voices Five, Bud Johnson & The

JOHNSON, Buddy

TITLE/FLIP	LABEL & NO.	GOOD TO VERY GOOD	NEAR MINT	YR.
YOU GOT TO WALK THAT CHALK LINE/Keep Me Close To You	Decca 24996	1.50	6.00	50

JOHNSON, Conrad

TITLE/FLIP	LABEL & NO.	GOOD TO VERY GOOD	NEAR MINT	YR.
HOWLING ON DOWLING/Fisherman Blues (78)	Gold Star 622	2.00	8.00	47

JOHNSON, Conrad as Connie's Combo

Johnson's group should not be confused with another Connie's Combo led by L. C. Williams (or credited as such) on the Eddie's label, even though both recorded during the same period in Houston with some of the same personnel, including Johnson!

TITLE/FLIP	LABEL & NO.	GOOD TO VERY GOOD	NEAR MINT	YR.
UGLY MAE/Shout It Out (78)	Freedom 1508	1.50	6.00	48

JOHNSON, Harry "Slick"

TITLE/FLIP	LABEL & NO.	GOOD TO VERY GOOD	NEAR MINT	YR.
NO ONE CAN TAKE YOUR PLACE/My Baby's Coming Home (78)	Peacock 1560	1.50	6.00	51

JOHNSON, Herb & The Cruisers:
see Cruisers, Herb Johnson & The

JOHNSON, Jimmy

JOHNSON, Joe

JOHNSON, Leroy

TITLE/FLIP	LABEL & NO.	GOOD TO VERY GOOD	NEAR MINT	YR.
NO ONE TO LOVE ME/Loghouse On The Hill (78)	Freedom 1509	4.00	16.00	49
UNLUCKY BLUES/Home Town Woman	Okeh 6813	5.00	20.00	51

JOHNSON, Leslie as Lazy Lester

JOHNSON, Lonnie

TITLE/FLIP	LABEL & NO.	GOOD TO VERY GOOD	NEAR MINT	YR.
DARLIN'/Seven Long Days	King 4503	2.50	10.00	51
DON'T MAKE ME CRY, BABY/My Woman Is Gone (red plastic)	Rama 9	5.00	20.00	56
DON'T MAKE ME CRY, BABY/My Woman Is Gone	Rama 9	2.50	10.00	56
I'M GUILTY/Can't Sleep Any More	King 4553	2.50	10.00	52
IT'S BEEN SO LONG/Vaya Con Dios (red plastic)	Rama 19	5.00	20.00	56
IT'S BEEN SO LONG/Vaya Con Dios	Rama 19	2.50	10.00	56
JUST ANOTHER DAY/You Can't Buy Love	King 4572	2.50	10.00	52
MY MOTHER'S EYES/Me And My Crazy Self	King 4510	2.50	10.00	51
THIS LOVE OF MINE/I Love A Dream (red plastic)	Rama 20	5.00	20.00	56
THIS LOVE OF MINE/I Love A Dream	Rama 20	2.50	10.00	56
TOMORROW NIGHT/Pleasing You	King 4758	1.50	6.00	—
TOMORROW NIGHT/What A Woman	King 4201	3.00	12.00	—
WILL YOU REMEMBER?/Stick With It, Baby (red plastic)	Rama 14	5.00	20.00	56
WILL YOU REMEMBER?/Stick With It, Baby	Rama 14	2.50	10.00	56

JOHNSON, Lonnie:
see Smith, Arthur as Sonny Boy & Lonnie (with Lonnie Johnson)

JOHNSON, Marv

TITLE/FLIP	LABEL & NO.	GOOD TO VERY GOOD	NEAR MINT	YR.
COME TO ME/Whisper	Tamla 101	3.00	12.00	59

JOHNSON, Meat Head:
see Dupree, William Thomas as Meat Head Johnson

JOHNSON, Neal

TITLE/FLIP	LABEL & NO.	GOOD TO VERY GOOD	NEAR MINT	YR.
TRUE TO YOU, BABY/Just Got To Make It	Specialty 688	2.00	8.00	—

JOHNSON, Pete:
see Turner, Joe & Pete Johnson

JOHNSON, Phil & The Duvals:
see Duvals, Phil Johnson & The

JOHNSON, Ray

TITLE/FLIP	LABEL & NO.	GOOD TO VERY GOOD	NEAR MINT	YR.
BOOGIN' THE BLUES/Smilin' Blues	Mercury 70231	2.50	10.00	52
HOUSE OF BLUES/I'll Never Let You Go	Mercury 70203	2.50	10.00	52

JOHNSON, Red

Red Johnson and Ray Johnson are thought to be the same artist.

TITLE/FLIP	LABEL & NO.	GOOD TO VERY GOOD	NEAR MINT	YR.
ON MY WAY TO CALIFORNIA/Mama Does The Boogie	Mercury 70194	2.50	10.00	52
WEST COAST BLUES/Mama Does The Boogie	Mercury 70141	2.50	10.00	52

JOHNSON, Rockheart

TITLE/FLIP	LABEL & NO.	GOOD TO VERY GOOD	NEAR MINT	YR.
BLACK SPIDER/Midnight Rambler	RCA Victor 47-5136	5.00	20.00	52
EVILEST WOMAN IN TOWN/Rockheart's Blues	RCA Victor 47-4967	6.25	25.00	52

JOHNSON, Rozetta

JOHNSON, Ruby

JOHNSON, Sam "Suitcase"

TITLE/FLIP	LABEL & NO.	GOOD TO VERY GOOD	NEAR MINT	YR.
SAM'S COMING HOME/Sam's Boogie (78)	Sittin' In With 608	3.00	12.00	51

JOHNSON, Sherman

TITLE/FLIP	LABEL & NO.	GOOD TO VERY GOOD	NEAR MINT	YR.
BACK ALLEY BOOGIE/Nashville After Midnight (78)	Nashboro 507	3.00	12.00	51

JOHNSON, Sherman & His Clouds Of Joy

TITLE/FLIP	LABEL & NO.	GOOD TO VERY GOOD	NEAR MINT	YR.
HOT FISH/Lost In Korea (78)	Trumpet 190	1.50	6.00	53
PRETTY BABY BLUES/Sugar Mama (78)	Trumpet 189	2.50	6.25	53

JOHNSON, Sonny Boy & His Blue Blazers

TITLE/FLIP	LABEL & NO.	GOOD TO VERY GOOD	NEAR MINT	YR.
COME AND GO WITH ME/Come And Go With Me (78)	Murray 505	7.00	28.00	48

Though both sides of this record are labeled the same, the first side is a different song, the title unknown to us.

TITLE/FLIP	LABEL & NO.	GOOD TO VERY GOOD	NEAR MINT	YR.
I'M DRINKING MY LAST DRINK/Swimming Pool Blues (78)	Murray 507	7.00	28.00	48

TITLE/FLIP	LABEL & NO.	GOOD TO VERY GOOD	NEAR MINT	YR.
JOHNSON, Sonny Boy				
QUINSELLA/Alley Special (by Wright Holmes) (78)	Gotham 511	5.00	20.00	47
Though both sides are credited to Wright Holmes, side one is actually by Sonny Boy Johnson.				
JOHNSON, Syl				
JOHNSON, Willie				
HERE COMES MY BABY/Don't Tell Mama	Savoy 881	1.50	6.00	52
SAMPSON STREET BOOGIE/Got The Boogie Woogie Blues (78)	Sittin' In With 570	1.50	6.00	50
SOMETIMES I WONDER WHY/Love Me Till Dawn	Savoy 894	1.50	6.00	52
THAT NIGHT/Say, Baby	Specialty 493	2.00	8.00	54
JOHNSON, Willie as The Groovy Five				
LOST BABY/Wrong Love Blues (78)	Groovy 103	2.00	8.00	59
JOHNSON, Willie as The Groovy Trio				
TOO LATE, BABY/Squeeze My Baby (78)	Groovy 101	2.00	8.00	49
JOKERS, Ty Stewart & The				
HERE AM I/Young Girl	Amy 828	1.50	6.00	61
JONES BOYS, Jimmy Jones & The				
HEAVEN IN YOUR EYES/The Whistlin' Man	Arrow 717	5.00	20.00	—
JONES BOYS, The				
SONG IS ENDED, THE/ You Make Me Feel Like A Penny Waitin' For Change	S & G 5007	1.50	6.00	—
JONES BROTHERS, The				
HUNDRED YEARS FROM TO-DAY, A/Ain't She Pretty? (78)	Majestic 1038	2.00	8.00	46
THEM THERE EYES/I Wanna Be Loved Like A Baby (78)	Majestic 1039	2.00	8.00	46
JONES, Billy & The Squires: see Squires, Billy Jones & The				
JONES, Billy & The Teenettes				
JONES, Calvert				
TRA LA LA/Two-Timin' Woman	Coral 65056	4.00	16.00	51
JONES, Curtis				
WRONG BLUES/Cool Playing Blues	Parrot 782	10.00	40.00	53
JONES, Eddie & His Playboys				
WOMAN TROUBLES/New Arrival	Imperial 5134	6.25	25.00	51
JONES, Eddie "Guitar Slim"				
FEELIN' SAD/Certainly All	Jim Bullet 603	11.00	44.00	52
JONES, Eddie as Guitar Slim				
Jones should not be confused with Alec Seward, who also recorded as Guitar Slim, nor with Guitar Slim Green.				
NEW ARRIVAL/Standin' At The Station	Imperial 5310	7.00	28.00	51
WOMAN TROUBLES/Cryin' In The Mornin'	Imperial 5278	5.00	20.00	51
JONES, Eddie as Guitar Slim & His Band				
I GOT SUMPIN' FOR YOU/You're Gonna Miss Me	Specialty 551	1.50	6.00	55
LATER FOR YOU, BABY/Trouble Don't Last	Specialty 527	2.00	8.00	56
OUR ONLY CHILD/Stand By Me	Specialty 542	1.50	6.00	55
QUICKSAND/Think It Over	Specialty 557	1.50	6.00	56
STORY OF MY LIFE, THE/A Letter To My Girlfriend	Specialty 490	2.00	8.00	54
SUFFERIN' MIND/Twenty Five Lies	Specialty 536	1.50	6.00	55
SUM'THIN' TO REMEMBER YOU BY/You Give Me Nothin' But The Blues	Specialty 569	1.50	6.00	56
THINGS THAT I USED TO DO, THE/ Well I Done Got Over It	Specialty 482	2.00	8.00	54
JONES, Etta				
JONES, Floyd				
BIG WORLD/Dark Road (78)	JOB 1001	5.00	20.00	52
DARK ROAD/Big World (78)	Chess 1498	4.00	16.00	52
YOU CAN'T LIVE LONG/Early Morning (78)	Chess 1527	7.00	28.00	53
JONES, Floyd & His Trio				
FLOYD'S BLUES/Any Old Lonesome Day (red plastic)	Vee Jay 126	20.00	80.00	55
FLOYD'S BLUES/Any Old Lonesome Day	Vee Jay 126	10.00	40.00	55
SCHOOLDAYS ON MY MIND/Ain't Times Hard? (red plastic)	Vee Jay 111	20.00	80.00	55
SCHOOLDAYS ON MY MIND/Ain't Times Hard?	Vee Jay 111	10.00	40.00	55
SKINNY MAMA/On The Road Again	JOB 1013	10.00	40.00	53

TITLE/FLIP	LABEL & NO.	GOOD TO VERY GOOD	NEAR MINT	YR.
JONES, Floyd: see Pryor, James Edward & Floyd Jones as Snooky & Moody				
JONES, Grant				
CRYING GOOD MORNING BLUES/Piney Brown Blues	Decca 48133	2.00	8.00	49
FOR YOU, MY LOVE/They Call Me Mr. Blues	Decca 48129	2.00	8.00	49
HELLO STRANGER/In The Dark	United 133	2.50	10.00	52
HOSPITALITY BLUES, PART 1/Hospitality Blues, Part 2	Decca 48163	2.00	8.00	50
IT'S BEEN A LONG TIME, BABY/ You Won't Have To Cry No More	Decca 48169	2.00	8.00	50
NIGHT TIME IS THE RIGHT TIME/Michigan Water Blues	Decca 48179	2.00	8.00	50
STORMY MONDAY/Heartache Blues	States 114	3.00	12.00	52
STRANGE MAN/Let's Get High	United 112	4.00	16.00	52
WHEN THE DEAL GOES DOWN/ I'd Rather Drink Muddy Water	Decca 48192	2.00	8.00	50
JONES, Herman & The Kilts: see Kilts, Herman Jones & The				
JONES, Jimmie & The Savoys				
JONES, Jimmy				
JONES, Jimmy & His Trio				
TROUBLE BLUES/Red Beans And Rice (78)	Holiday 702	1.50	6.00	49
JONES, Jimmy: see Jones Boys, Jimmy Jones & The; see Pretenders, Jimmy Jones & The; see Sparks of Rhythm, The (featuring Jimmy Jones)				
JONES, Joe				
ADAM BIT THE APPLE/Will Call	Capitol 2951	2.50	10.00	54
JONES, John as Little Johnny				
BIG TOWN PLAYBOY/Shelby County Blues (78)	Aristocrat 405	8.00	32.00	50
JONES, John as Little Johnny Jones				
HOY, HOY/Doin' The Best I Can	Atlantic 1045	8.00	32.00	54
JONES, John as Little Johnny Jones with The Chicago Hound Dogs				
SWEET LITTLE WOMAN (DIRTY BY THE DOZEN)/ I May Be Wrong	Flair 1010	10.00	40.00	53
JONES, Johnny				
JONES, Johnny & The Five Chords: see Five Chords, Johnny Jones & The				
JONES, Jonah, His Orchestra & The Constellations: see Constellations, Jonah Jones, His Orchestra & The				
JONES, Lee & The Sounds Of Soul				
JONES, Linda				
JONES, Little Johnny: see Jones, John as Little Johnny				
JONES, Little Sonny				
Jones should not be confused with Mac Willis, who recorded as Little Sonny.				
EVERYTHING ALL RIGHT/Do You Really Love Me?	Specialty 443	2.00	8.00	50
I GOT BOOTED/Tend To Your Business Blues	Imperial 5275	4.00	16.00	53
WINEHEAD BABY/Going To The Country	Imperial 5287	4.00	16.00	53
JONES, Mad Man				
JES' ONE MO' TIME/Oh Henry	Mad 1207	1.50	6.00	58
JONES, Mildred				
MR. THRILL/Mis-Used Woman	Peacock 1638	2.00	8.00	54
JONES, Ronnie & The Classmates: see Classmates, Ronnie Jones & The				
JONES, Sunny				
DON'T WANT PRETTY WOMEN/Leaving Home Blues (78)	Orchid 1211	6.25	25.00	—
JONES, Thelma				

JONES, Will & The Cadets

JORDAN, Louis

TITLE/FLIP	LABEL & NO.	GOOD TO VERY GOOD	NEAR MINT	YR.
BLUE LIGHT BOOGIE, PART 1/Blue Light Boogie, Part 2	Decca 27114	2.50	10.00	50
DOLLAR DOWN, A/Hurry Home	Aladdin 3243	2.50	10.00	54
FAT BACK AND CORN LIQUOR/The Dripper	Aladdin 3270	2.00	8.00	54
GAL, YOU NEED A WHIPPIN'/Time Is Passin'	Aladdin 3279	2.00	8.00	54
LET THE GOOD TIMES ROLL/ Ain't Nobody Here But Us Chickens	Decca 23741	2.00	8.00	50
LOUIS' BLUES/If I Had Any Sense	Aladdin 3249	2.00	8.00	54
MESSY BESSIE/I Seen Watcha Done	Aladdin 3246	2.50	10.00	54
OOO-WEE/I'll Die Happy	Aladdin 3227	2.50	10.00	54
PUT SOME MONEY IN THE POT/Yeah, Yeah, Yeah, Baby	Aladdin 3264	2.00	8.00	54
SATURDAY NIGHT FISH FRY, PART 1/ Saturday Night Fish Fry, Part 2	Decca 24725	3.00	12.00	50
SHOW ME HOW/I Want A Roof Over My Head	Decca 27129	2.00	8.00	50
TAMBURITZA BOOGIE/Trouble, Then Satisfaction	Decca 27203	2.00	8.00	50
WHISKEY DO YOUR STUFF/Dad Gum Ya Hide, Boy	Aladdin 3223	2.50	10.00	54

JORDAN, Louis, Ella Fitzgerald &

JORDAN, Willie & His Swinging Five:
see Dupree, William Thomas as Willie Jordan

JOSEPH, Doc Bill

JOSEPH, Margie

JOY, Roddie

JOYETTES, The (female group)

TITLE/FLIP	LABEL & NO.	GOOD TO VERY GOOD	NEAR MINT	YR.
STORY OF LOVE/Boy Next Door	Onyx 502	5.00	20.00	56

JOYLARKS, The

TITLE/FLIP	LABEL & NO.	GOOD TO VERY GOOD	NEAR MINT	YR.
IN THE RAIN/Betty, My Love	Snag 107	6.25	25.00	59

JOYTONES, The (female group)

TITLE/FLIP	LABEL & NO.	GOOD TO VERY GOOD	NEAR MINT	YR.
ALL MY LOVE BELONGS TO YOU/ You Just Won't Treat Me Right	Rama 191	2.50	10.00	56
GEE! WHAT A BOY/Is This Really The End?	Rama 202	2.00	8.00	56
MY FOOLISH HEART/Jimbo Jango	Rama 215	4.00	16.00	56

JUBALAIRES, Johnny Smith & The

TITLE/FLIP	LABEL & NO.	GOOD TO VERY GOOD	NEAR MINT	YR.
HOME, HOME, HOME/I Wish I Had A Sweetheart (78)	Capitol 784	1.50	6.00	49
PAL THAT I LOVED STOLE THE GAL THAT I LOVED, THE/ Blue Ribbon Gal (78)	Capitol 821	1.50	6.00	50

JUBALAIRES, The

TITLE/FLIP	LABEL & NO.	GOOD TO VERY GOOD	NEAR MINT	YR.
DAVID AND GOLIATH/I've Done My Work	Capitol 1888	2.00	8.00	51
I KNOW/Get Together With The Lord (78)	Decca 18782	1.50	6.00	46
LITTLE MR. BIG/Pianola	Capitol 1054	3.00	12.00	50
LIVING IS A LIE/As Summer Turns To Fall	Capitol 1779	3.00	12.00	51
SOMEBODY BROKE MY DOLLY/Mene, Mene, Teckel (78)	Capitol 683	1.50	6.00	49
ST. LOUIS BLUES/ It Ain't What You Want That Does You Good (78)	Capitol 70040	2.00	8.00	49
THAT OLD PIANO ROLL BLUES/ A Dream Is A Wish Your Heart Makes	Capitol 845	3.00	12.00	50
WHEN IT'S ALL OVER BUT THE SHOUTIN'/ Before This Time Another Year (78)	Decca 8666	1.50	6.00	44

JUBALAIRES, The:
see Original Jubalaires, The

JUBILAIRES, The (same group as Johnny Smith & The Jubalaires)

TITLE/FLIP	LABEL & NO.	GOOD TO VERY GOOD	NEAR MINT	YR.
DAY IS MINE, THE/St. Louis Lou (78)	King 4303	2.00	8.00	49
GET LOST/Jean (78)	King 4290	2.00	8.00	49
GOD ALMIGHTY'S GONNA CUT YOU DOWN/ Go Down Moses (78)	Queen 4167	2.00	8.00	47
ICKY, YACKY/ You're Gonna Make A Wonderful Sweetheart (78)	Queen 4172	2.50	10.00	47
JUBES BLUES/I've Waited All My Life For You (78)	Queen 4166	3.00	12.00	47
LET IT RAIN/I've Waited All My Life For You (78)	King 4325	2.00	8.00	49
MY GOD CALLED ME THIS MORNING/ Ring That Golden Bell (78)	Queen 4168	2.00	8.00	47
SUNDAY KIND OF LOVE, A/Pray (78)	Queen 4163	4.00	16.00	47
TWELVE O'CLOCK AND ALL IS WELL/ Chattahoochie Lullabye (78)	King 15040	2.00	8.00	50

JUBILEE FOUR, The

JULIAN, Don & The Larks

JULIAN, Don & The Meadowlarks:
see Meadowlarks, Don Julian & The

JUMPIN' JUDGE, The

TITLE/FLIP	LABEL & NO.	GOOD TO VERY GOOD	NEAR MINT	YR.
TRIAL, THE (novelty break-in)/ Cockroach Run (instrumental by Lafayette Thomas)	Jumping 5000	3.00	12.00	55

JUMPING JACKS, The

TITLE/FLIP	LABEL & NO.	GOOD TO VERY GOOD	NEAR MINT	YR.
DO LET THAT DREAM COME TRUE/Why, Oh, Why?	Lloyds 101	15.00	60.00	53
EMBRACEABLE YOU/Pa-Pa-Ya, Baby	Bruce 115	20.00	80.00	54
MOP-TOP/Let There Be Rockin'	One-O-One 100	20.00	40.00	54

JUNE & DONNIE

JUNIOR BLUES

TITLE/FLIP	LABEL & NO.	GOOD TO VERY GOOD	NEAR MINT	YR.
WHISKEY HEAD WOMAN/Young And Good Lookin' (78)	RPM 320	2.00	8.00	50

JUNIOR GORDON:
see Gordon, Junior

JUNIORS, Jimmy Castor & The

TITLE/FLIP	LABEL & NO.	GOOD TO VERY GOOD	NEAR MINT	YR.
I PROMISE/I Know The Meaning Of Love	Wing 90078	5.00	20.00	56
THIS GIRL OF MINE/Somebody Mentioned Your Name	Atomic 100	8.00	32.00	57

JUVENILES, The

TITLE/FLIP	LABEL & NO.	GOOD TO VERY GOOD	NEAR MINT	YR.
BEAT IN MY HEART/I've Lied	Mode 1	2.50	10.00	58

JYVE FYVE, Eugene Pitt & The

JYVE FYVE, The

K

KADOR, Ernest

TITLE/FLIP	LABEL & NO.	GOOD TO VERY GOOD	NEAR MINT	YR.
ETERNITY/Do, Baby, Do	Specialty 563	2.00	8.00	55

KADOR, Ernest as Ernie K-Doe

KADOR, Ernie "K-Doe":
see Blue Diamonds, The (with Ernie "K-Doe" Kador)

KANSAS CITY TOM CATS, The

TITLE/FLIP	LABEL & NO.	GOOD TO VERY GOOD	NEAR MINT	YR.
DON'T YOU KNOW?/Blues For Josie	Josie 797	1.50	6.00	56
NOBODY KNOWS/Meet Me, Meet Me, Baby	Josie 786	1.50	6.00	55

KARI, Sax

TITLE/FLIP	LABEL & NO.	GOOD TO VERY GOOD	NEAR MINT	YR.
DAUGHTER/Down For Debbie	States 115	2.00	8.00	52
DISC JOCKEY JAMBOREE/ Mama Took The Baby (by Lena Gordon)	Checker 803	2.00	8.00	54
HENRY/You Let My Love Grow Cold	States 117	2.00	8.00	52
TRAIN RIDE/Red Hot Feeling	Great Lakes 1205	2.50	10.00	54

KARI, Sax & The Quailtones:
see Quailtones, Sax Kari & The

KASANDRA

KASHMIRS, The

TITLE/FLIP	LABEL & NO.	GOOD TO VERY GOOD	NEAR MINT	YR.
HEAVEN ONLY KNOWS/Tippi-Tippi-Wang-Wang	Wonder 104	8.00	32.00	58

KELLY, Bob & The Bob Kats

KELTON, Robert & His Trio

TITLE/FLIP	LABEL & NO.	GOOD TO VERY GOOD	NEAR MINT	YR.
MUDDY SHOES/Try Me One More Time (78)	Aladdin 3054	2.00	8.00	50
NO, NO, BABY/Don't Care What You Say	Aladdin 3187	4.00	16.00	50

KENDRICK, Nat & The Swans

KENDRICKS, Eddie

TITLE/FLIP	LABEL & NO.	GOOD TO VERY GOOD	NEAR MINT	YR.

KENNEDY, Tiny

COUNTRY BOY/I Need A Good Woman	Groove 00106	2.50	10.00	55
LADY WITH THE BLACK DRESS ON, THE/ Sister Flat Top	Capitol 840	4.00	16.00	49
STRANGE KIND OF FEELING/It Ain't Right	Groove 00133	2.50	10.00	55

KENNER, Chris

GRANDMA'S HOUSE/ Don't Let Her Pin That Charge On Me	Baton 220	2.50	10.00	55
I HAVE NEWS FOR YOU/Will You Be Mine?	Imperial 5488	1.50	6.00	58
SICK AND TIRED/ Nothing Will Keep Me Away From You	Imperial 5448	1.50	6.00	57

KENNY & MOE—THE BLUES BOYS

CAN'T HELP MYSELF/You're Gonna Miss Me When I'm Gone	DeLuxe 6101	2.00	8.00	56

KENNY, Herb:
see Comets, Herb Kenny & The
see Rockets, Herb Kenny & The

KENT, Al

KENTS, The

I FOUND MY GIRL/With All My Heart And Soul	Argo 5299	2.00	8.00	58
I LOVE YOU SO/Happy Beat	Dome 501	4.00	16.00	—

KETCHUM, Robert

STOCKADE/She's Gone From Me	Peacock 1623	3.00	12.00	53

KEYNOTES, The

I DON'T KNOW/A Star	Apollo 484	5.00	20.00	55
IN THE EVENING/Oh, Yeah, Hm-m-m	Apollo 503	10.00	40.00	56
ONE LITTLE KISS/Now I Know	Apollo 513	7.00	28.00	57
REALLY WISH YOU WERE HERE/Bye, Bye, Baby	Apollo 493	10.00	40.00	56
SUDDENLY/Zenda	Apollo 478	10.00	40.00	55
ZUP, ZUP/Now I Know	Apollo 498	8.00	32.00	56

KEYSTONERS, The

MAGIC KISS/I'd Write About The Blues	G & M 102	10.00	40.00	56
MAGIC KISS, THE/After I Propose	Epic 9187	5.00	20.00	56
SLEEP & DREAM/T. V. Gal	Riff 202	6.25	25.00	—

KEYTONES, The

SEVEN WONDERS OF THE WORLD/A Fool In Love	Old Town 1041	4.00	16.00	57
WONDER OF THE WORLD/A Fool In Love	Old Town 1041	9.00	36.00	57

KID THOMAS:
see Thomas, Kid

KIDD, Kenneth as Prez Kenneth

KIDDS, The

ARE YOU FORGETTING ME?/Drunk, Drunk, Drunk	Imperial 5335	25.00	100.00	55
YOU BROKE MY HEART/I Won't Be Back	Post 2003	50.00	200.00	55

KILGORE, Theola

KILLERS, Hank Blackman & The

EVERYONE HAS SOMEONE/Itchy Koo	Brent 7030	2.00	8.00	62

KILTS, Herman Jones & The

I'LL BE TRUE/Mashed Potatoes	Gaynote 105	1.50	6.00	58

KIMBLE, Quinn Orchestra, The

FEEL MY BROOM/Blue Memories	RPM 400	2.50	10.00	53

KING, B. B.:
see King, Riley as B. B. King

KING BEES, The

CAN'T YOU UNDERSTAND?/Lovely Love	KRC 302	3.00	12.00	57
PUPPY LOVE/Give Me Your Number	Flip 323	1.50	6.00	—

KING BUMBLE BEE SLIM & HIS PACIFIC COAST SENDERS:
see Easton, Amos as King Bumble Bee Slim

KING CHARLES

BOP CAT STOMP/But You Thrill Me	Folk Star 1131	5.00	20.00	54

Vocals by Left Hand Charlie.

KING COBRAS, The

TO HOLD YOUR LOVE/Blue Diamonnd	Irvanne 117	5.00	20.00	59

KING COLE TRIO, The:
see Cole, Nat King as The King Cole Trio

KING CROONERS, The

NOW THAT SHE'S GONE/Won't You Let Me Know?	Excello 2168	5.00	20.00	59

KING IVORY LEE:
see Semien, Lee as King Ivory Lee

KING KROONERS, The (with Little Rico)

MEMOIRS/School Daze	Excello 2187	5.00	20.00	60

KING MOSE ROYAL ROCKERS, The:
see Myers, Sammy with The King Mose Royal Rockers

KING ODOM:
see Odom, King as The King Odum Quartette
see Odom, King Four, The
see Odom, King Quartette, The

KING ODUM QUARTETTE, The:
see Odom, King as The King Odum Quartette

KING PINS, The

KING PLEASURE

MOODY'S MOOD FOR LOVE/ Exclamation Blues (red plastic)	Prestige 924	4.00	16.00	52
MOODY'S MOOD FOR LOVE/Exclamation Blues	Prestige 924	2.00	8.00	52

KING SOLOMAN:
see Soloman, Ellis as King Soloman

KING TOPPERS, The

YOU WERE WAITING FOR ME/Walkin' And Talkin' The Blues	Josie 811	8.00	32.00	57

KING, Al

KING, Albert

BAD LUCK BLUES/Be On Your Merry Way	Parrot 798	10.00	40.00	53

KING, B. B.

KING, Ben E.

KING, Clyde

KING, Earl

EATING AND SLEEPING/No One But Me	Specialty 531	2.50	10.00	54
FUNNY FACE/Sittin' And Wonderin'	Specialty 558	2.50	10.00	55
I'LL NEVER GET TIRED/Well'o Well'o, Baby	Ace 543	2.50	10.00	57
I'M YOUR BEST BET, BABY/A Mother's Prayer	Specialty 495	2.50	10.00	54
THOSE LONELY, LONELY NIGHTS/ Baby, You Can Get Your Gun	Ace 509	3.00	12.00	56
THOSE LONELY, LONELY FEELINGS/ You Can Fly High	Ace 529	2.50	10.00	57

KING, Earl:
see Uniques, The (with Earl King)

KING, Eddie & The Three Queens

SHAKIN' INSIDE/Love You, Baby	JOB 1122	1.50	6.00	60

KING, Freddie as Freddy King

COUNTRY BOY/That's What You Think	El-Bee 157	7.00	28.00	56

KING, Freddie

KING, Jewel

3 x 7 = 21/Don't Marry Too Soon (78)	Imperial 5055	2.00	8.00	49

KING, Johnny

KING, Julius

I WANT A SLICE OF YOUR PUDDING/ If You See My Lover (78)	Tennessee 123	6.25	25.00	52

TITLE/FLIP	LABEL & NO.	GOOD TO VERY GOOD	NEAR MINT	YR.
KING, Kid as Kid King's Combo				
All of the following are instrumentals, except as indicated not by King.				
ARE YOU SURE?/Hob-Nob	*Excello 2109*	2.50	10.00	*56*
BANANA SPLIT/Skip's Boogie	*Excello 2009*	2.00	8.00	*53*
BRASS RAIL, THE/Gimmick	*Excello 2018*	2.00	8.00	*53*
CHOCOLATE SUNDAE/Greasy Feet	*Excello 2025*	2.00	8.00	*53*
DON'T LET DADDY SLOW WALK YOU DOWN/ Funny Funny Feeling (by Good Rockin' Sam Beasley)	*Excello 2070*	2.50	10.00	*55*
DREAMY MOODS/Memories In Melody	*Excello 2037*	1.50	6.00	*53*
FINA/Shaggy Dog	*Excello 2185*	2.50	10.00	*60*
MAMBINE/Strollin' Time	*Excello 2046*	1.50	6.00	*53*
THING-A-MA-JIG/ Baby, I'm Fool Proof (by Good Rockin' Sam Beasley)	*Excello 2059*	2.50	10.00	*55*
KING, Maurice				
I WANT A LAVENDER CADILLAC/Spider's Web	*Okeh 6800*	2.00	8.00	*51*
KING, Norma Lee: see Grooveneers, The				
KING, Richard & His Orchestra				
RIDE, DADDY, RIDE/Banks Of The River (78)	*Khoury's 800*	1.50	6.00	*51*
KING, Riley as B. B. King				
B. B. BLUES/She's Dynamite (78)	*RPM 323*	2.00	8.00	*51*
FINE LOOKING WOMAN/She Don't Love Me No More	*RPM 348*	4.00	16.00	*52*
GOT THE BLUES/Take A Swing With Me (78)	*Bullet 315*	4.00	16.00	*49*
MISS MARTHA KING/When Your Baby Packs Up And Goes (78)	*Bullet 309*	4.00	16.00	*49*
MISTREATED WOMAN/B. B. Boogie (78)	*RPM 304*	2.00	8.00	*50*
MY BABY'S GONE/Don't You Want A Man Like Me? (78)	*RPM 318*	2.00	8.00	*50*
NEIGHBOURHOOD AFFAIR/Please Hurry Home	*RPM 391*	1.50	6.00	*53*
OTHER NIGHT BLUES, THE/Walkin' And Crying' (78)	*RPM 311*	2.00	8.00	*50*
PLEASE LOVE ME/Highway Bound	*RPM 386*	1.50	6.00	*53*
SHAKE IT UP AND GO/My Own Fault, Darling	*RPM 355*	4.00	16.00	*52*
SHE'S A MEAN WOMAN/Hard Working Woman (78)	*RPM 330*	1.50	6.00	*51*
SOMEDAY, SOMEWHERE/Gotta Find My Baby	*RPM 360*	4.00	16.00	*52*
STORY FROM MY HEART AND SOUL/Boogie Woogie Woman	*RPM 374*	2.50	10.00	*53*
3 O'CLOCK BLUES/That Ain't The Way To Do It	*RPM 339*	5.00	20.00	*52*
WHY DID YOU LEAVE ME?/Blind Love	*RPM 395*	1.50	6.00	*53*
WOKE UP THIS MORNING/Don't Have To Cry	*RPM 380*	2.00	8.00	*53*
YOU DIDN'T WANT ME/You Know I Love You	*RPM 363*	3.00	12.00	*52*
KING, Saunders				
MY CLOSE FRIEND/Going Mad	*Flair 1035*	3.00	12.00	*54*
QUIT HANGIN' 'ROUND ME/Long Long Time	*Flair 1045*	2.50	10.00	*54*
KING, Sleepy				
ONE LEG WOMAN/Come Back, Darling	*Sun 704*	1.50	6.00	*58*
KINGLETS, The				
SIX DAYS A WEEK/You Gotta Go	*Calvert 101*	7.00	28.00	*56*
KINGS & THE QUEENS, The (mixed group)				
VOICES OF LOVE/I'm So Lonely	*Everlast 5003*	2.00	8.00	*57*
KINGS MEN, The				
DON'T SAY YOU'RE SORRY/Kicking With My Stallion	*Club 51 108*	25.00	100.00	*57*
KINGS, Bobby Hall & The				
BABY, BE THERE/You Made Me Cry	*Jax 316*	30.00	120.00	*53*
SUNDAY KIND OF LOVE/Love No One (red plastic)	*Jax 320*	30.00	120.00	*53*
WHY? OH, WHY?/I Love You, Baby (red plastic)	*Jax 314*	30.00	120.00	*53*
KINGS, Little Hooks & The				
COUNT YOUR BLESSINGS/How To Start A Romance	*Century 1300*	1.50	6.00	*63*
KINGS, The (with Joe Van Loan)				
LONG LONELY NIGHTS/Let Me Know	*Baton 245*	4.00	16.00	*57*
KINGS, The				
ANGEL/Come On, Little Baby	*Jalo 203*	2.00	8.00	*58*
DON'T GO/Love Is Something From Within	*Gone 5013*	4.00	16.00	*57*
FIRE IN MY HEART/You Never Knew	*Harlem 2322*	20.00	80.00	*54*
GOD MADE YOU MINE/The Good Book	*Gotham 316*	5.00	20.00	*56*
TILL YOU/Elephant Walk	*RCA Victor 47-7419*	1.50	6.00	*58*
YOUR SWEET LOVE/Troubles Don't Last	*RCA Victor 47-7544*	1.50	6.00	*59*
KINGS, The				
WHAT CAN I DO?/Til I Say Well Done	*Specialty 497*	3.00	12.00	*54*

TITLE/FLIP	LABEL & NO.	GOOD TO VERY GOOD	NEAR MINT	YR.
KINGSMEN, The				
GUARDIAN ANGEL/I'm Your Lover Man	*All Star 500*	5.00	20.00	*57*
ONE FOOLISH MISTAKE/Stranded Love	*Neil 102*	6.25	25.00	*56*
KIRK, Roebie				
I DON'T WANT TO PLAY IN THE KITCHEN/ Roebie's Blues (78)	*Queen 4180*	1.50	6.00	*45*
WHERE IS THE GROOVE?/Mix The Boogie (78)	*Queen 4129*	1.50	6.00	*45*
WHERE IS YOUR HUSBAND AT?/Let's Go Upstairs (78)	*Queen 4110*	1.50	6.00	*45*
KIRKLAND, Eddie				
NO SHOES/Time For My Lovin' To Be Done	*King 4659*	6.25	25.00	*53*
PLEASE DON'T THINK I'M NOSEY/Mistreated Woman	*King 4680*	6.25	25.00	*53*
KIRKLAND, Eddie & His House Rockers				
I NEED YOU, BABY/I Must Have Done Somebody Wrong	*Fortune 848*	2.50	10.00	*59*
KIRKLAND, Eddie as Little Eddie Kirkland				
IT'S TIME/That's All Right (7-inch 78)	*RPM 367*	5.00	20.00	*52*
IT'S TIME/That's All Right	*RPM 367*	8.00	32.00	*52*
KIRKLAND, Eddie as Little Eddie Kirkland: see Hooker, John Lee & "Little" Eddie Kirkland				
KISSES, Candy & The				
KITTRELL, Christine				
GOTTA STOP LOVING YOU/Slave To Love	*Republic 7026*	1.50	6.00	*52*
HEARTACHE BLUES/You Ain't Nothin' But Trouble	*Tennessee 133*	2.00	8.00	*52*
I'LL HELP YOU, BABY/L & N Special	*Republic 7044*	1.50	6.00	*53*
LEAVE MY MAN ALONE/Call His Name	*Republic 7109*	1.50	6.00	*52*
PRICE YOU PAY FOR LOVE, THE/ Snake In The Grass	*Republic 7073*	1.50	6.00	*53*
SITTIN' HERE DRINKIN'/I Ain't Nothing But A Fool	*Tennessee 128*	2.00	8.00	*52*
KITTY & THE LA FETS: see La Fets, Kitty & The				
KLIXS, The				
ELAINE/This Is The End Of Love	*Music City 823*	10.00	40.00	—
IT'S ALL OVER/This Is The End Of Love	*Music City 817*	4.00	16.00	—
KNICKERBOCKERS, The				
YOU MUST KNOW/ Somewhere, Somehow, Sweetheart	*It's A Natural 3000*	20.00	80.00	—
KNIGHT BROTHERS, The				
KNIGHT, Gladys & The Pips				

TITLE/FLIP	LABEL & NO.	GOOD TO VERY GOOD	NEAR MINT	YR.
KNIGHT, Jean				
KNIGHT, Marie				
GRASSHOPPER BABY/Look At Me	*Mercury 70969*	2.00	8.00	—
KNIGHT, Robert				
KNIGHT, Sonny				
CONFIDENTIAL/Jail Bird	*Vita 137*	3.00	12.00	*56*
DEAR WONDERFUL/Lonesome Shadows	*Aladdin 3195*	2.50	10.00	*53*
DEDICATED TO YOU/Short Walk	*Starla 1*	1.50	6.00	*57*
WHAT OFFICER?/Baby, Come Back	*Aladdin 3207*	2.50	10.00	*53*
KO KO'S, The (female group)				
FIRST DAY OF SCHOOL, THE/You've Been Cheating	*Combo 141*	4.00	16.00	*57*
KODAKS, The				
DON'T WANT NO TEASING!/Look Up To The Sky	*J & S 1683/1684*	1.50	6.00	*60*
GUARDIAN ANGEL/Run Around Baby	*Fury 1020*	4.00	16.00	*58*
MY BABY AND ME/Kingless Castle	*Fury 1019*	5.00	20.00	*58*
OH, GEE! OH, GOSH!/Make Believe World	*Fury 1015*	2.00	8.00	*57*
TEENAGERS DREAM/Little Boy And Girl	*Fury 1007*	2.00	8.00	*57*

TITLE/FLIP	LABEL & NO.	GOOD TO VERY GOOD	NEAR MINT	YR.
KOLETTES, The (female group)				
KOOL & THE GANG				
KOOL GENTS, The				
THIS IS THE NIGHT/Do Ya Do?	*Vee-Jay 173*	10.00	40.00	*55*
YOU KNOW/I Just Can't Help My Self	*Vee-Jay 207*	10.00	40.00	*56*
KUF-LINX, The				

L

TITLE/FLIP	LABEL & NO.	GOOD TO VERY GOOD	NEAR MINT	YR.
L'CAP-TANS, The				
BELLS RING OUT, THE/Call The Doctor	*Hollywood 1092*	8.00	32.00	*58*
HOMEWORK/Say Yes	*D. C. 0416*	1.50	6.00	*59*
LA BELLE, Patty & The Blue Belles				
LA FETS, Kitty & The				
CHRISTMAS LETTER/Can Can Rock & Roll	*Apollo 520*	10.00	40.00	*57*
LABRADORS, The				
QUEEN OF SWING/When Someone Loves You	*Chief 7009*	7.00	28.00	*58*
LADDERS, The				
COUNTING THE STARS/I Want To Know	*Holiday 2611*	4.00	16.00	*57*
MY LOVE IS GONE/Hey, Pretty Baby	*Vest 826*	2.00	8.00	—
LADDINS, The				
NOW YOU'RE GONE/Did It (black label)	*Central 2602*	7.00	28.00	*57*
NOW YOU'RE GONE/Did It (pink label)	*Central 2602*	1.50	6.00	*57*
LAKE, Don & The Don Juans: see Don Juans, Don Lake & The				
LAMBERT, Rudy & The Mondellos: see Mondellos, Rudy Lambert & The				
LAMP SISTERS, The				
LAMPLIGHTERS, Jimmy Witherspoon & The				
SAD LIFE/Move Me, Baby	*Federal 12156*	5.00	20.00	*53*
24 SAD HOURS/Just For You	*Federal 12173*	5.00	20.00	*53*
LAMPLIGHTERS, The				
DON'T MAKE IT SO GOOD/Hug A Little, Kiss A Little	*Federal 12242*	2.50	10.00	*55*
FIVE MINUTES LONGER/You Hear?	*Federal 12192*	4.00	16.00	*54*
GIVE ME/Be-Bop Wino	*Federal 12152*	7.00	28.00	*53*
I WANNA KNOW/Believe In Me	*Federal 12206*	2.50	10.00	*54*
IT AIN'T RIGHT/Everything's All Right	*Federal 12261*	2.50	10.00	*56*
PART OF ME/Turn Me Loose	*Federal 12149*	12.50	50.00	*53*
ROLL ON/Love, Rock And Thrill	*Federal 12212*	2.50	10.00	*55*
SALTY DOG/Ride, Jockey, Ride	*Federal 12182*	5.00	20.00	*54*
SMOOTCHIE/I Can't Stand It	*Federal 12166*	7.00	28.00	*54*
TELL ME YOU CARE/I Used To Cry Mercy, Mercy	*Federal 12176*	5.00	20.00	*54*
YOU WERE SENT DOWN FROM HEAVEN/Bo Peep	*Federal 12255*	2.50	10.00	*56*
YUM! YUM!/Goody, Good Things	*Federal 12197*	3.00	12.00	*54*
LAMPLIGHTERS, The as The Tenderfoots				
KISSING BUG/Watussi Wussi Wo	*Federal 12214*	5.00	20.00	*55*
MY CONFESSION/Save Me Some Kisses	*Federal 12219*	5.00	20.00	*55*
SINDY/Sugar Ways	*Federal 12228*	6.25	25.00	*55*
THOSE GOLDEN BELLS/I'm Yours, Anyhow	*Federal 12225*	6.25	25.00	*55*
LANCE, Herb				
LANCE, Herb & The Classics				
LANCE, Major				
LANE, Ernest				
WHAT'S WRONG, BABY?/ Little Girl, Little Girl (78)	*Blues & Rhythm 7000*	4.00	16.00	*51*
LANE, Willie (Little Brother)				
HOWLING WOLFE BLUES/Black Cat Rag (78)	*Star Talent 806*	5.00	20.00	*49*
PROWLIN' GROUND HOG/Too Many Women Blues (78)	*Star Talent 805*	5.00	20.00	*49*
LANG, Eddie				
COME ON HOME/I'm All Alone	*RPM 466*	2.00	8.00	*56*
I'M BEGGIN' WITH TEARS/ You Got To Crawl Before You Walk	*RPM 476*	1.50	6.00	*56*

TITLE/FLIP	LABEL & NO.	GOOD TO VERY GOOD	NEAR MINT	YR.

LANGFORD, Billie—"Emperor Of The Blues"

LET ME GREASE YOUR GRIDDLE/Mean And Evil Woman (78)	*Harlem 1102*	1.50	6.00	*46*

LANGFORD, Billy Combo, The

BLUES IN NASHVILLE/Be Bop On The Boogie (78)	*Lenox 504*	1.50	6.00	*45*

LANKFORD, Carlron & The Blue Chips

LAPELS, The

SNEAKIN' AROUND/Sneaky Blues	*Melker 103*	2.50	10.00	*60*

LARADOS, The

NOW THE PARTING BEGINS/Bad, Bad Guitar Man	*Fox (no number)*	5.00	20.00	*57*

LARGOS, The

I WONDER WHY?/Saddle Up	*Dot 16292*	1.50	6.00	*61*

LARK, Claudine

LARKS, Barbara Gayle & The

WHEN YOU'RE NEAR/Who Walks In When I Walk Out?	*Lloyds 111*	2.50	10.00	*54*

LARKS, Don Julian & The

LARKS, The

DARLIN'/Lucy Brown	*Apollo 437*	60.00	240.00	*52*
EYESIGHT TO THE BLIND/ I Ain't Fattenin' Frogs For Snakes	*Apollo 427*	50.00	200.00	*51*
FORGET IT/Os-Ca-Lu-Ski-O	*Lloyds 114*	20.00	80.00	*54*
HOLD ME/I Live True To You	*Apollo 1194*	80.00	320.00	*52*
HONEY FROM THE BEE/No, Mama, No	*Apollo 475*	10.00	40.00	*55*
HOPEFULLY YOURS/When I Leave These Prison Walls	*Apollo 1180*	40.00	160.00	*51*
IF IT'S A CRIME/Tippin' In	*Lloyds 110*	40.00	160.00	*54*
JOHNNY DARLIN'/You're Gonna Lose Your Gal	*Lloyds 115*	20.00	80.00	*54*
LITTLE SIDE CAR/Hey! Little Girl	*Apollo 429*	40.00	160.00	*51*
MARGIE/Rockin' In The Rocket Room	*Lloyds 108*	12.50	50.00	*54*
MY HEART CRIES FOR YOU/ Coffee, Cigarettes And Tears (78)	*Apollo 1177*	5.00	20.00	*51*
MY LOST LOVE/How Long Must I Wait For You?	*Apollo 435*	50.00	200.00	*51*
MY REVERIE/ Let's Say A Prayer (orange-red plastic)	*Apollo 1184*	100.00	400.00	*51*
MY REVERIE/Let's Say A Prayer	*Apollo 1184*	60.00	240.00	*51*
NO OTHER GIRL/The World Is Waiting For The Sunrise	*Lloyds 112*	60.00	240.00	*54*
OOH....IT FEELS SO GOOD/I Don't Believe In Tomorrow	*Apollo 430*	50.00	200.00	*51*
SHADRACK/Honey In The Rock	*Apollo 1189*	50.00	200.00	*52*
STOLEN LOVE/In My Lonely Room	*Apollo 1190*	80.00	320.00	*52*

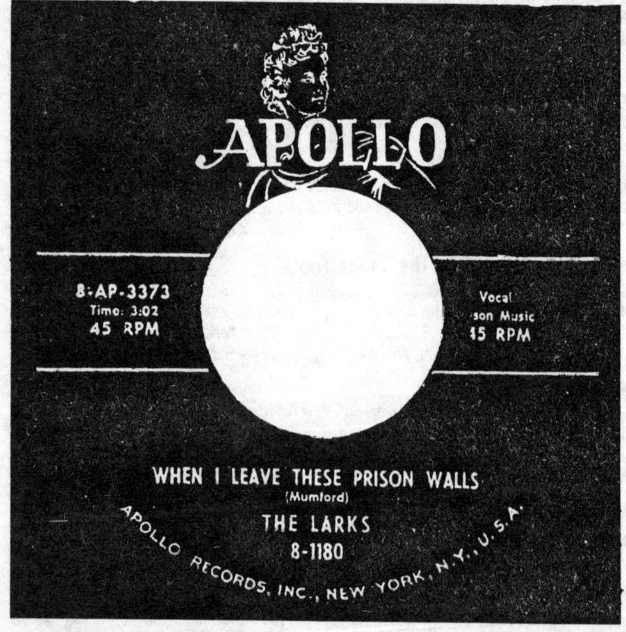

LARKS, The

FABULOUS CARS AND DIAMOND RINGS/ Life Is Sweeter Now	*Cross Fire 74-50/74-59*	1.50	6.00	—

LARKTONES, The

LETTER, THE/Rockin', Swingin' Man	*ABC 9909*	3.00	12.00	*58*

LASALLE, Denise

LATONS, The

LAURELS, Bobby Relf & The

YOURS ALONE/Farewell	*Flair 1063*	15.00	60.00	*55*

LAURELS, The

BABY TALK/You Left Me	*Spring 1112*	2.00	8.00	*60*
This record was the original version of the Jan & Dean hit.				
TRULY, TRULY/'Tis Night	*X 0143*	30.00	120.00	*55*

LAVENDERS, The

ANGEL/Slide	*C R 1003*	1.50	6.00	*61*
BELLS, THE/I Said Look	*Lake 706*	4.00	16.00	*61*

LAVETTE, Betty

LAZY BILL & HIS BLUE RHYTHMS:
see Lucas, William as Lazy Bill

LAZY LESTER

LAZY SLIM JIM:
see Harris, Edward as Lazy Slim Jim

LEACH, Lillian & The Mellows:
see Mellows, Lillian Leach & The

LEADBELLY (Huddie Ledbetter)

LEADERS, The

CAN'T HELP LOVIN' THAT GIRL OF MINE/Lovers	*Glory 243*	6.25	25.00	*56*
DEAREST, BELOVED DARLING/Nobody Loves Me	*Glory 239*	5.00	20.00	*56*
STORMY WEATHER/A Lover Of The Time	*Glory 235*	1.50	6.00	*55*

LEAPFROGS, The:
see Campbell, Louis as The Leapfrogs

LEAVILL, Otis

LEAVY, Calvin

LEDBETTER, Huddie as Leadbelly

LEE & THE LEOPARDS:
see Leopards, Lee & The

LEE, Emma Dell & Trio

HOW MUCH I LOVE YOU/No Good Daddy (78)	*Khoury's 900*	1.50	6.00	*51*

LEE, Jackie

LEE, Jimmy:
see Robinson, Jimmy Lee as Jimmy Lee

LEE, John Arthur as John Lee

Lee should not be confused with John Lee Henley nor John Lee Hooker,
who also recorded as John Lee.

BABY BLUES/Blind's Blues (78)	*Federal 12089*	6.25	25.00	*51*
DOWN AT THE DEPOT/Alabama Boogie (78)	*Federal 12054*	6.25	25.00	*51*

LEE, John:
see Henley, John Lee as John Lee
see Hooker, John Lee as John Lee
see Lee, John Arthur as John Lee

LEE, Johnny:
see Hooker, John Lee as Johnny Lee

LEE, Julia

LAST CALL FOR ALCOHOL/Goin' To Chicago Blues	*Capitol 2203*	2.50	10.00	*52*

LEE, King Ivory:
see Semien, Lee as King Ivory Lee

TITLE/FLIP	LABEL & NO.	GOOD TO VERY GOOD	NEAR MINT	YR.
LEE, Laura				
LEE, Lillian & The Mellows: see Mellows, Lillian Lee & The				
LEE, Nickie				
LEE, Roosevelt				
LAZY PETE/I'm So Sad	*Excello 2022*	5.00	20.00	*54*
LEE, Tommy				
PACKING UP MY BLUES/Highway 80 Blues (78)	*Delta 403*	25.00	100.00	*53*
LEEDS, The				
HEAVEN ONLY KNOWS/Mr. Cool	*Wand 102*	3.00	12.00	*59*
LEGENDS, Billy Davis & The				
LEGENDS, The				
I'LL NEVER FALL IN LOVE AGAIN/The Eyes Of An Angel	*Melba 109*	6.25	25.00	*57*
LEGEND OF LOVE, THE/Now I'm Telling You	*Hull 727*	9.00	36.00	*58*
LENOIR, J. B.				
EISENHOWER BLUES/I'm In Korea	*Parrot 802*	10.00	40.00	*54*
"Eisenhower Blues" was called back shortly after release and was remade into "Tax Paying Blues" with slightly different lyrics.				
FINE GIRLS/I Lost My Baby	*Parrot 821*	5.00	20.00	*55*
MAMA, YOUR DAUGHTER IS GOING TO MISS ME/ What Have I Done?	*Parrot 814*	5.00	20.00	*55*
MAN WATCH YOUR WOMAN/Mama, Talk To Your Daughter	*Parrot 809*	4.00	16.00	*54*
PEOPLE ARE MEDDLIN' IN OUR AFFAIRS/Let's Roll (78)	*JOB 112*	4.00	16.00	*52*
TAX PAYING BLUES/I'm In Korea	*Parrot 802*	12.50	50.00	*54*
LENOIR, J. B. as J. B. & His Bayou Boys				
I'LL DIE TRYING/ I Want My Baby (credited as J. B. Lenore & His Combo)	*JOB 1016*	7.00	28.00	*52*
MOUNTAIN, THE/How Much More	*JOB 1008*	7.00	28.00	*52*
LENOIR, J. B. as J. B. Lenor & His Combo				
MOJO, THE/How Can I Live?	*JOB 1012*	7.00	28.00	*53*
PLAY A LITTLE WHILE/Louise	*JOB 1102*	8.00	32.00	*54*
LENOIR, J. B. as J. B. Lenore				
DON'T TOUCH MY HEAD/I've Been Down So Long	*Checker 856*	1.50	6.00	*56*
LET ME DIE WITH THE ONE I LOVE/ If I Give My Love To You	*Checker 844*	1.50	6.00	*56*
WHAT ABOUT YOUR DAUGHTER?/Five Years	*Checker 874*	1.50	6.00	*57*
LENOIR, J. B. as J. B. Lenore & His Bayou Boys				
DEEP IN DEBT BLUES/Carrie Lee-Oo (78)	*Chess 1463*	3.00	12.00	*51*
MY BABY TOLD ME/Korea Blues (78)	*Chess 1449*	3.00	12.00	*51*
LENOIR, J. B., & His African Hunch Rhythm				
I SING UM THE WAY I FEEL/I Feel So Good	*USA 744*	2.00	8.00	*63*
LENORE, J. B.: see Lenoir, J. B. as J. B. Lenore				
LEO & THE LEOPARDS				
LEOPARDS, Lee & The				
COME INTO MY PALACE/Trying To Make It	*Gordy 7002*	1.50	6.00	*62*
LEOPARDS, Leo & The				
LEROY AND THE DRIVERS				
LESTER, John & The Mello-Queens				
LEWIS, Al & The Modernistics: see Modernistics, Al Lewis & The				
LEWIS, Barbara				
LEWIS, Bobby				
LEWIS, Buddy: see Lewis, Ernest as Buddy Lewis				
LEWIS, Carl as Pete "Guitar" Lewis				
BLAST, THE (instrumental)/ Chocolate Pork Chop Man	*Federal 12112*	5.00	20.00	*52*

TITLE/FLIP	LABEL & NO.	GOOD TO VERY GOOD	NEAR MINT	YR.
GOIN' CRAZY/Back Door Troubles	*Peacock 1624*	4.00	16.00	*52*
HARMONICA BOOGIE (instrumental)/ Raggedy Blues	*Federal 12076*	6.25	25.00	*52*
LOUISIANA HOP (instrumental)/ Crying With The Rising Sun	*Federal 12066*	6.25	25.00	*52*
OOH, MIDNIGHT/Scratchin' Boogie (instrumental)	*Federal 12103*	5.00	20.00	*52*
LEWIS, Clarence, Jr.				
LOST EVERYTHING/Your Heart Must Be Made Of Stone	*Red Robin 136*	5.00	20.00	*55*
LEWIS, Earl & The Channels: see Channels, Earl Lewis & The				
LEWIS, Ernest				
NO MORE LOVIN'/West Coast Blues	*Parrot 791*	12.50	50.00	*53*
LEWIS, Ernest as Buddy Lewis				
LONESOME BEDROOM/You've Got Good Business (78)	*Swing Time 312*	3.00	12.00	*52*
LEWIS, Ernest as Country Slim				
WHAT WRONG HAVE I DONE?/ My Girlish Days (by Miss Country Slim) (78)	*Hollywood 1005*	7.00	28.00	*53*
LEWIS, Ernest as West Texas Slim				
LOU DELLA/Little Mae Belle (78)	*Flame 1007*	8.00	32.00	*53*
LEWIS, Jimmie & The Volumes				
LEWIS, Jimmy				
CHERRY WINE/Dark And Lonely Room	*RCA Victor 47-4899*	3.00	12.00	*52*
LET'S GET TOGETHER AND MAKE SOME LOVE/ I'll Be Faithful To You	*Atlantic 943*	5.00	20.00	*51*
LOVE BROKE MY HEART AGAIN/Last Night	*Cat 103*	1.50	6.00	*54*
LEWIS, Johnny: see Louis, Joe Hill as Johnny Lewis				
LEWIS, Lovey				
ALRIGHT, BABY/Take A Chance With Me	*Duke 126*	2.00	8.00	*53*
LEWIS, Paul & The Swans: see Swans, Paul Lewis & The				
LEWIS, Pete "Guitar": see Lewis, Carl as Pete "Guitar" Lewis				
LEWIS, Ramsey Trio, The				
LEWIS, Richard				
HEY, LITTLE BOY/Call Me, Call Me	*Aladdin 3255*	2.00	8.00	*54*
HEY, LITTLE GIRL/Richard's Bounce (instrumental)	*Aladdin 3238*	2.00	8.00	*54*
LET'S LOVE TONIGHT/Wish You Love	*Aladdin 3239*	2.00	8.00	*54*
STILL DRIFTING/Sweet Dreams	*Aladdin 3261*	1.50	6.00	*54*
LEWIS, Sabby & The Vibra-Tones: see Vibra-Tones, Sabby Lewis & The				
LEWIS, Sammy				
I FEEL SO WORRIED/So Long, Baby, Goodbye	*Sun 218*	4.00	16.00	*54*
LEWIS, Smiley				
BEE'S BOOGIE/My Baby Was Right (78)	*Imperial 5124*	2.50	10.00	*51*
BELLS ARE RINGING, THE/Lilly Mae	*Imperial 5194*	9.00	36.00	*52*
CALDONIA'S PARTY/Oh, Baby	*Imperial 5241*	6.25	25.00	*53*
CAN'T STOP LOVING YOU/That Certain Door	*Imperial 5296*	4.00	16.00	*54*
DOWN THE ROAD/Blue Monday	*Imperial 5268*	5.00	20.00	*54*
DOWN YONDER WE GO BALLIN'/Some Day You'll Want Me	*Imperial 5404*	1.50	6.00	*56*
GUMBO BLUES/It's So Peaceful	*Imperial 5208*	6.25	25.00	*52*
GYPSY BLUES/You're Not The One	*Imperial 5224*	6.25	25.00	*54*
I HEAR YOU KNOCKING/Bumpity Bump	*Imperial 5356*	2.50	10.00	*55*
I LOVE YOU FOR SENTIMENTAL REASONS/The Rocks	*Imperial 5279*	5.00	20.00	*54*
IF YOU EVER LOVED A WOMAN/Dirty People (78)	*Imperial 5102*	2.50	10.00	*51*
JAILBIRD/Farewell	*Imperial 5325*	3.00	12.00	*54*
LITTLE FERNANDEZ/It's Music	*Imperial 5252*	5.00	20.00	*53*
LOOKIN' FOR MY WOMAN/I Wonder?	*Dot 16674*	1.50	6.00	—
ONE NIGHT/Ain't Gonna Do It	*Imperial 5380*	2.00	8.00	*56*
PLAY GIRL/Big Mamou (red plastic)	*Imperial 5234*	12.50	50.00	*53*
PLAY GIRL/Big Mamou	*Imperial 5234*	6.25	25.00	*53*
QUEEN OF HEARTS/Come On	*Imperial 5372*	2.00	8.00	*55*
REAL GONE LOVER/Nobody Knows	*Imperial 5349*	2.50	10.00	*55*

TITLE/FLIP	LABEL & NO.	GOOD TO VERY GOOD	NEAR MINT	YR.
SAD LIFE/Don't Jive Me (78)	Colony 106	4.00	16.00	—
SHAME, SHAME, SHAME/No, No	Imperial 5418	1.50	6.00	56
SHE'S GOT ME HOOK, LINE AND SINKER/ Please Listen To Me	Imperial 5389	2.00	8.00	56
SLIDE ME DOWN/Growing Old (78)	Imperial 5072	3.00	12.00	50
TEE-NAH-NAH/Lowdown (78)	Imperial 5067	3.00	12.00	50
TOO MANY DRIVERS/Ooh La La	Imperial 5316	4.00	16.00	54
TURN YOUR VOLUME ON, BABY/Here Comes Smiley (78)	DeLuxe 3099	5.00	20.00	—
WHERE WERE YOU?/My Baby (78)	Colony 110	4.00	16.00	—

LICK, SLICK & SLIDE

TITLE/FLIP	LABEL & NO.	GOOD TO VERY GOOD	NEAR MINT	YR.
I GOT DRUNK/I Love My Baby	Savoy 1150	8.00	32.00	54

LIFESAVERS, Lucien Farrar & The

TITLE/FLIP	LABEL & NO.	GOOD TO VERY GOOD	NEAR MINT	YR.
DIDN'T YOU KNOW?/Help	Jupiter 45	15.00	60.00	—
TOMORROW NIGHT/	Jupiter 45	15.00	60.00	—

LIGGETT, Larry

TITLE/FLIP	LABEL & NO.	GOOD TO VERY GOOD	NEAR MINT	YR.
THAT MAN IS WALKING/Mama Yo Quiero Mambo	Chess 1578	2.50	10.00	55

LIGGINS, Jimmy

TITLE/FLIP	LABEL & NO.	GOOD TO VERY GOOD	NEAR MINT	YR.
BROWN SKIN BABY/Dark Hour Blues	Specialty 434	2.50	10.00	49
DRUNK/I'll Never Let You Go (red plastic)	Specialty 470	6.25	25.00	53
DRUNK/I'll Never Let You Go	Specialty 470	3.00	12.00	53
GOING AWAY/Come Back Home	Specialty 484	2.50	10.00	54
I AIN'T DRUNK/Talking That Talk	Aladdin 3250	3.00	12.00	54
NO MORE ALCOHOL/Boogie Woogie King	Aladdin 3251	3.00	12.00	54

LIGGINS, Joe

TITLE/FLIP	LABEL & NO.	GOOD TO VERY GOOD	NEAR MINT	YR.
BOOGIE WOOGIE LOU/Rain, Rain, Rain	Specialty 426	2.00	8.00	52
EVERYONE'S DOWN ON ME/The Big Dripper (instrumental)	Specialty 474	2.00	8.00	53
FAREWELL BLUES/Deep Feeling	Specialty 465	2.00	8.00	53
FRANKIE LEE/I Just Can't Help Myself	Specialty 392	2.50	10.00	51
FREIGHT TRAIN BLUES/Blues For Tanya (instrumental)	Specialty 453	2.00	8.00	53
GOIN' BACK TO NEW ORLEANS/Crying Over You	Specialty 441	2.00	8.00	52
HONEY DRIPPER, THE/I've Got A Right To Cry	Specialty 338	2.00	8.00	49
JUSTINA/Go Ahead	Aladdin 3368	1.50	6.00	56
LITTLE JOE'S BOOGIE/Daddy On My Mind	Specialty 379	3.00	12.00	51
LOUISIANA WOMAN/Trying To Lose The Blues	Specialty 409	2.50	10.00	52
SO ALONE/Oh, How I Miss You	Specialty 413	2.00	8.00	52
TANYA/Drippers Boogie (instrumental)	Specialty 430	2.00	8.00	52
WHISKEY, GIN AND WINE/One Sweet Letter	Specialty 402	2.50	10.00	52
WHISKEY, WOMEN AND LOADED DICE/ Do You Love Me, Pretty Baby?	Specialty 529	3.00	12.00	54
YEAH, YEAH, YEAH/They Were Doing The Mambo	Mercury 70440	1.50	6.00	54

LIGHTFOOT, Alexander as Papa Lightfoot

TITLE/FLIP	LABEL & NO.	GOOD TO VERY GOOD	NEAR MINT	YR.
AFTER-WHILE/P. L. Blues (instrumental)	Aladdin 3171	10.00	40.00	52
BLUE LIGHTS/Jumpin' With Jarvis (instrumental)	Aladdin 3304	6.25	25.00	52
WINE, WOMEN, WHISKEY/Mean Old Train	Imperial 5289	9.00	36.00	54

LIGHTNIN' JR.:

see Dupree, William Thomas as Lightnin' Jr.
see Williams, L. C. (Lightnin' Jr.)

LIGHTNIN' LEON:

see Riley, Billy Lee as Lightnin' Leon

LIGHTNIN' SLIM:

see Hicks, Otis as Lightnin' Slim

LIMELIGHTERS, The

TITLE/FLIP	LABEL & NO.	GOOD TO VERY GOOD	NEAR MINT	YR.
CABIN HIDEAWAY/My Sweet Norma Lee	Josie 795	10.00	40.00	56

LIMELITES, Shep & The

TITLE/FLIP	LABEL & NO.	GOOD TO VERY GOOD	NEAR MINT	YR.
I'M SO LONELY/One Week From Today	Apt 25046	2.50	10.00	60
PARTY FOR TWO/You Better Believe	Hull 770	2.50	10.00	65

LIMMIE & THE FAMILY COOKIN'

LINCOLN'S QUINTETT, The

TITLE/FLIP	LABEL & NO.	GOOD TO VERY GOOD	NEAR MINT	YR.
DREAM OF ROMANCE/Tell Me What Is Wrong	Angle Tone 522	7.00	28.00	58

LINCOLNS, The

TITLE/FLIP	LABEL & NO.	GOOD TO VERY GOOD	NEAR MINT	YR.
SOMETIME, SOMEWHERE/Sukiyaki Rocki	Bud 113	1.50	6.00	60

LINCOLNS, The

TITLE/FLIP	LABEL & NO.	GOOD TO VERY GOOD	NEAR MINT	YR.
BABY, PLEASE LET ME LOVE YOU/ Can't You Go For Me?	Mercury 71553	1.50	6.00	59
DON'T LET ME SHED ANY MORE TEARS/ Pleasin' You Pleases Me	Atlas 1100	5.00	20.00	57

LINDA & THE DEL RIOS

LINKS, The

TITLE/FLIP	LABEL & NO.	GOOD TO VERY GOOD	NEAR MINT	YR.
BABY/She's The One	Teenage 1009	9.00	36.00	58

LISA & THE LULLABIES

LITE, Tippo & His All Stars

TITLE/FLIP	LABEL & NO.	GOOD TO VERY GOOD	NEAR MINT	YR.
DARK SKIN WOMAN BLUES/Jumping This Morning (78)	Back Alley 202	3.00	12.00	50

LITTLE "D" & THE HARLEMS

LITTLE "E" & THE MELLO-TONE THREE

LITTLE AL:

see Gunter, Al as Little Al

LITTLE ANTHONY (GUARDINE):

see Duponts, The (featuring Little Anthony Guardine)
see Imperials, The
see Imperials, Little Anthony & The

LITTLE BEATS, The

TITLE/FLIP	LABEL & NO.	GOOD TO VERY GOOD	NEAR MINT	YR.
LOVE IS TRUE/Someone For Me	Mercury 71155	3.00	12.00	57

LITTLE BETTY & THE ANGELS

LITTLE BO:

see Bo, Eddie as Little Bo

LITTLE BOOKER

TITLE/FLIP	LABEL & NO.	GOOD TO VERY GOOD	NEAR MINT	YR.
THINKIN' 'BOUT MY BABY/Doin' The Ham Bone	Imperial 5293	7.00	28.00	54

LITTLE BUBBER

TITLE/FLIP	LABEL & NO.	GOOD TO VERY GOOD	NEAR MINT	YR.
HIGH CLASS WOMAN/Come Back Baby	Imperial 5225	5.00	20.00	53
RUNNIN' 'ROUND/Never Trust A Woman	Imperial 5238	5.00	20.00	53

LITTLE BUTCH & THE VELLS

LITTLE CAESAR

TITLE/FLIP	LABEL & NO.	GOOD TO VERY GOOD	NEAR MINT	YR.
ATOMIC LOVE/You Can't Bring Me Down	Recorded In Hollywood 237	2.50	10.00	53
BIG EYES/Can't Stand It All Alone	Big Town 106	2.50	10.00	—
CHAINS OF LOVE HAVE DISAPPEARED/ Tried To Reason With You, Baby	RPM 393	2.00	8.00	53
GOODBYE BABY/If I Could See My Baby	Recorded In Hollywood 236	2.50	10.00	53
RIVER, THE/Long Time Baby	Recorded In Hollywood 234	2.50	10.00	53
TALKING TO MYSELF/ Don't Mention The Blues To Me	Recorded In Hollywood 235	2.50	10.00	53
WHAT KIND OF FOOL IS HE?/Wonder Why I Am Living?	Big Town 110	2.50	10.00	—

LITTLE CAESAR & THE ROMANS:

see Romans, Little Caesar & The

LITTLE CLEM & THE DEW DROPS:

see Dew Drops, Little Clem & The

LITTLE CLYDE & THE TEENS:

see Teens, Little Clyde & The

LITTLE DAVID

Little David should not be confused with David Wylie, who recorded under the same name for the Regal label. Neither should be mistaken for the Little David who led the rhythm & blues group The Harps.

TITLE/FLIP	LABEL & NO.	GOOD TO VERY GOOD	NEAR MINT	YR.
MACAYO/Crying Blues (7-inch 78)	RPM 371	5.00	20.00	52
MACAYO/Crying Blues (78)	International 104	2.00	8.00	52
MACAYO/Crying Blues (78)	RPM 371	1.50	6.00	52

LITTLE DAVID & THE HARPS

LITTLE DAVID:

see Wylie, David as Little David

LITTLE EDDIE

TITLE/FLIP	LABEL & NO.	GOOD TO VERY GOOD	NEAR MINT	YR.
TEDDY BEAR BLUES/The Skrooch	Reginald 556	1.50	6.00	—

J.B. Lenior

Jimmy Liggins

LITTLE EDDIE:
see Dollars, Little Eddie & The
see Don Juans, Little Eddie & The
see Hooker, John Lee & Little Eddie Kirkland
see Kirkland, Little Eddie

LITTLE ESTHER (Phillips)

TITLE/FLIP	LABEL & NO.	GOOD TO VERY GOOD	NEAR MINT	YR.
AGED AND MELLOW/Bring My Lovin' Back To Me	Federal 12078	6.25	25.00	52
BETTER BEWARE/I'll Be There	Federal 12065	6.25	25.00	52
CHERRY WINE/Love, Oh, Love	Federal 12142	5.00	20.00	53
CRYING AND SIGHING THE BLUES/ Tell Him That I Need Him (78)	Federal 12042	2.00	8.00	51
HE'S A NO GOOD MAN/Sit Back Down	Decca 48314	3.00	12.00	54
HOUND DOG/Sweet Lips	Federal 12126	6.25	25.00	53
I GOTTA GUY/Thursday Night Blues (78)	Modern 715	2.00	8.00	50
I'M A BAD GIRL/Don't Make A Fool Out Of Me (78)	Federal 12023	2.00	8.00	51
LAST LAUGH BLUES/Flesh Blood And Bones	Federal 12108	6.25	25.00	52
Duets with Little Willie Littlefield.				
MEAN OLE GAL/Good Old Blues (78)	Modern 748	2.00	8.00	50
RAMBLIN' BLUES/Somebody New	Federal 12090	6.25	25.00	52
RING-A-DING-DOO/The Crying Blues	Federal 12055	6.25	25.00	51
SATURDAY NIGHT DADDY/Mainliner	Federal 12100	20.00	80.00	52
Featuring The Robins.				
STOP CRYIN'/Please Don't Send Me	Decca 48305	3.00	12.00	54
SUMMERTIME/Dust Storm	Federal 12063	6.25	25.00	52
TALKIN' ALL OUT OF MY HEAD/If You Want Me	Decca 28804	3.00	12.00	54
TURNS THE LAMPS DOWN LOW (duet with Little Willie Littlefield)/ Hollerin' And Screamin'	Federal 12115	6.25	25.00	52
YOU TOOK MY LOVE TOO FAST/Street Lights	Federal 12122	5.00	20.00	52

LITTLE ESTHER & THE DOMINOES:
see Dominoes, Little Esther (Phillips) & The

LITTLE ESTHER (PHILLIPS) & THE ROBINS

TITLE/FLIP	LABEL & NO.	GOOD TO VERY GOOD	NEAR MINT	YR.
DECEIVIN' BLUES/Lost Dream Blues (78)	Savoy 759	3.00	12.00	50
DOUBLE CROSSING BLUES/ Back Alley Blues (by The Beale Street Gang) (78)	Savoy 731	3.00	12.00	50
MISTRUSTIN' BLUES/Misery (78)	Savoy 735	3.00	12.00	50
SATURDAY NIGHT DADDY/Mainliner	Federal 12100	20.00	80.00	52

LITTLE EVA

LITTLE FREDDY & THE ROCKETS:
see Rockets, Little Freddy & The

LITTLE HOOKS & THE KINGS:
see Kings, Little Hooks & The

LITTLE HUDSON'S RED DEVIL TRIO:
see Shower, Hudson as Little Hudson

LITTLE JAN & THE RADIANTS:
see Radiants, Little Jan & The

LITTLE JIMMY:
see Sparrows, Little Jimmy & The
see Tops, Little Jimmy & The

LITTLE JOE:
see Louis, Joe Hill as Little Joe
see Morrocos, Little Joe & The
see Thrillers, Little Joe & The

LITTLE JOE BLUE

LITTLE JOEY & THE FLIPS

LITTLE JOHNNY:
see Jones, John as Little Johnny

LITTLE JUNE & THE JANUARYS:
see Januarys, Little June & The

LITTLE JUNIOR:
see Parker, Herman as Little Junior

LITTLE LARRY

LITTLE LUTHER

TITLE/FLIP	LABEL & NO.	GOOD TO VERY GOOD	NEAR MINT	YR.
STEPPIN' HIGH/Du De Squat	Criss Cross 110	1.50	6.00	—

LITTLE MAC (or LITTLE MACK):
see Simmons, Mack

LITTLE MARCUS & THE DEVOTIONS:
see Devotions, Little Marcus & The

LITTLE MELVIN

TITLE/FLIP	LABEL & NO.	GOOD TO VERY GOOD	NEAR MINT	YR.
LIFE IS MISERABLE/Wabble	AMA 502	2.50	10.00	—

LITTLE MILTON:
see Anderson, Milton as Little Milton
see Campbell, Milton as Little Milton

LITTLE MOJO:
see Buford, George as Little Mojo

LITTLE MR. LEE & THE CHEROKEES

LITTLE NAT & THE ETIQUETTES:
see Etiquettes, Little Nat & The

LITTLE NATALIE & HENRY (FORD) & THE GIFTS

LITTLE NATE & THE CHRYSLERS:
see Chryslers, Little Nate & The

LITTLE PAPA JOE:
see Williams, Joseph Leon as Little Papa Joe

LITTLE RED WALTER

This artist should not be confused with Leroy Foster nor Marion Walter Jacobs, who both recorded as Little Walter, nor with George Smith, who recorded as Little Walter, Jr.

TITLE/FLIP	LABEL & NO.	GOOD TO VERY GOOD	NEAR MINT	YR.
AW SHUCKS, BABY/I'm Mad	Le Sage 711	2.00	8.00	65
PICKIN' COTTON/Ain't Nothing But Gossip	Le Sage 731	2.50	10.00	65

LITTLE RICHARD (Penniman)

TITLE/FLIP	LABEL & NO.	GOOD TO VERY GOOD	NEAR MINT	YR.
AIN'T NOTHIN' HAPPENIN'/Why Did You Leave Me?	RCA Victor 47-4772	15.00	60.00	52
GET RICH QUICK/Thinkin' 'Bout My Mother	RCA Victor 47-4582	15.00	60.00	52
LITTLE RICHARD'S BOOGIE/Directly From My Heart	Peacock 1658	2.50	10.00	53
MAYBE I'M RIGHT/I Love My Baby	Peacock 1673	2.50	10.00	54
PLEASE HAVE MERCY ON ME/I Brought It All On Myself	RCA Victor 47-5025	15.00	60.00	52
TAXI BLUES/Every Hour	RCA Victor 47-4392	15.00	60.00	51

LITTLE RICHARD:
see Duces Of Rhythm & The Tempo Toppers, The (featuring Little Richard)
see Upsetters, The (featuring Little Richard)

LITTLE RICO:
see King Krooners, The (with Little Rico)

LITTLE SAMMY & THE TONES

LITTLE SISTER

LITTLE SONNY:
see Willis, Mac as Little Sonny

LITTLE SYLVIA (Vanderpool)

TITLE/FLIP	LABEL & NO.	GOOD TO VERY GOOD	NEAR MINT	YR.
DRIVE, DADDY, DRIVE/I Went To Your Wedding	Jubilee 5093	3.00	12.00	52
FINE LOVE/Speedy Life	Cat 102	1.50	6.00	53

LITTLE SYLVIA (VANDERPOOL):
see Mickey & Sylvia.

LITTLE T-BONE

TITLE/FLIP	LABEL & NO.	GOOD TO VERY GOOD	NEAR MINT	YR.
LOVE'S A GAMBLE/Christmas Blues (78)	Miltone 5223	4.00	16.00	47

LITTLE TEMPLE:
see Jenkins, Gus as Little Temple

TITLE/FLIP	LABEL & NO.	GOOD TO VERY GOOD	NEAR MINT	YR.

LITTLE TOMMY & THE ELGINS:
see Elgins, Little Tommy & The

LITTLE WALTER, JR.:
see Smith, George as Little Walter, Jr.

LITTLE WALTER:
see Foster, Leroy as Little Walter
see Jacobs, Marion Walter as Little Walter

LITTLE, Lee Roy

TITLE/FLIP	LABEL & NO.	GOOD TO VERY GOOD	NEAR MINT	YR.
I'M A GOOD MAN, BUT A POOR MAN/ Your Evil Thoughts	Cee Jay 578	1.50	6.00	—
LET ME GO HOME, WHISKEY/ Hurry, Baby, Please Come Home	Cee Jay 579	1.50	6.00	—

LITTLEFIELD, Little Willie

TITLE/FLIP	LABEL & NO.	GOOD TO VERY GOOD	NEAR MINT	YR.
CHICAGO BOUND/What's The Use? (78)	Eddie's 1205	3.00	12.00	48
FALLING TEARS/Goofy Dust Blues	Federal 12174	4.00	16.00	53
JIM WILSON'S BOOGIE (instrumental)/ Sitting On The Curbstone (instrumental)	Federal 12221	7.00	28.00	53
K. C. LOVING/Pleading At Midnight	Federal 12110	5.00	20.00	52
LITTLE WILLIE'S BOOGIE (instrumental)/ My Best Wishes (78)	Eddie's 1202	3.00	12.00	48
LITTLEFIELD BOOGIE (instrumental)/ Sweet Ole Woman's Blues (by Goree Carter) (78)	Freedom 1502	3.00	12.00	49
MIDNIGHT HOUR WAS SHINING, THE/ My Best Wishes And Regards	Federal 12137	4.00	16.00	53
MISS K. C.'S FINE/Rock A Bye, Baby	Federal 12148	4.00	16.00	53
PLEASE DON'T GO-O-O-O-OH/ Don't Take My Heart, Little Girl	Federal 12163	4.00	16.00	53
RUBY-RUBY/East Go (instrumental)	Rhythm 108	4.00	16.00	56
STICKING ON YOU, BABY/Blood Is Redder Than Wine	Federal 12101	5.00	20.00	54
SWANEE RIVER (instrumental)/ Boogie Woogie Playgirl (78)	Eddie's 1212	3.00	12.00	49

LITTLES, Hattie & The Fayettes

LITTLETON, John & The Capistranos:
see Capistranos, John Littleton & The

LOAN, Joe Van:
see Van Loan, Joe

LOCKETTES, Richard Berry & The

LOCKETTES, The (female group)

LOCKWOOD, Robert, Jr.

TITLE/FLIP	LABEL & NO.	GOOD TO VERY GOOD	NEAR MINT	YR.
I'M GONNA DIG MYSELF A HOLE/Dust My Broom (78)	Mercury 8260	4.00	16.00	51

LOCKWOOD, Robert, Jr. as Robert Jr. Lockwood

TITLE/FLIP	LABEL & NO.	GOOD TO VERY GOOD	NEAR MINT	YR.
AW, AW BABY/Sweet Woman From Maine	JOB 1107	12.50	50.00	54

LOFTIN, Willie & The Discords:
see Discords, Willie Loftin & The

LOGICS, The

TITLE/FLIP	LABEL & NO.	GOOD TO VERY GOOD	NEAR MINT	YR.
ONE LOVE/Everybody's Doing The Pony	Everlast 5015	1.50	6.00	—

LOLLYPOPS, The

TITLE/FLIP	LABEL & NO.	GOOD TO VERY GOOD	NEAR MINT	YR.
MY LOVE IS REAL/Believe In Me	Holland 7420	8.00	32.00	—

LONDON, Clarence

TITLE/FLIP	LABEL & NO.	GOOD TO VERY GOOD	NEAR MINT	YR.
GOIN' BACK TO MAMA/One Rainy Morning (78)	Fidelity 3009	4.00	16.00	—

LONDON, Mel

TITLE/FLIP	LABEL & NO.	GOOD TO VERY GOOD	NEAR MINT	YR.
DOGGIN' ME AROUND/The Man From The Island	Chief 7000	2.00	8.00	57

LONELY ONES, The

TITLE/FLIP	LABEL & NO.	GOOD TO VERY GOOD	NEAR MINT	YR.
MY WISH/I Want My Girl	Baton 270	1.50	6.00	59

LONESOME LEE:
see Robinson, Jimmy Lee as Lonesome Lee

LONG JOHN

TITLE/FLIP	LABEL & NO.	GOOD TO VERY GOOD	NEAR MINT	YR.
CRAZY GIRL/She Used To Be My Woman	Duke 122	2.50	10.00	53

LONG MAN BINDER & HIS THIN MEN:
see Binder, Dennis as Long Man Binder & His Thin Men

LONG TALL LESTER

LONG TALL MARVIN:
see Phillips, Marvin as Long Tall Marvin

LONG, Shorty

LONNIE THE CAT

TITLE/FLIP	LABEL & NO.	GOOD TO VERY GOOD	NEAR MINT	YR.
I AIN'T DRUNK/The Road I Travel	RPM 410	4.00	16.00	54

LORD LUTHER:
see Modernistics, Al Lewis & The

LOUIS & FROSTY:
see Jackson, Louis as Louis & Frosty (William Pyles)

LOUIS, Joe Hill

TITLE/FLIP	LABEL & NO.	GOOD TO VERY GOOD	NEAR MINT	YR.
BAD WOMAN BLUES/Hydromatic Woman (78)	Big Town 401	12.50	50.00	54
BOOGIE IN THE PARK/Cold Chills (78)	Modern 20-813	2.50	10.00	51
DON'T TRUST YOUR BEST FRIEND/Joe's Jump (78)	Columbia 30221	4.00	16.00	49
DOROTHY MAY/When I'm Gone	Checker 763	25.00	100.00	52
EYESIGHT TO THE BLIND/Goin' Down Slow (78)	Modern 20-828	2.50	10.00	51
GOTTA GO, BABY/Big Legged Woman (78)	Modern 839	2.50	10.00	51
I FEEL LIKE A MILLION/Heartache Baby (78)	Modern 20-795	2.50	10.00	49
PEACE OF MIND/Chocolate Blonde (78)	Modern 856	2.50	10.00	52
RAILROAD BLUES/A Jumpin' And A Shufflin' (78)	Columbia 30182	3.00	12.00	49
WALKIN' TALKIN' BLUES/Street Walkin' Woman (78)	Modern 20-822	2.50	10.00	52
WE ALL GOTTA GO SOMETIME/She May Be Yours (78)	Sun 178	15.00	60.00	53

LOUIS, Joe Hill as Chicago Sunny Boy

TITLE/FLIP	LABEL & NO.	GOOD TO VERY GOOD	NEAR MINT	YR.
JACK POT/Western Union Man	Meteor 5004	20.00	80.00	53
LOVE YOU, BABY/On The Floor	Meteor 5008	40.00	100.00	53

LOUIS, Joe Hill as Johnny Lewis

TITLE/FLIP	LABEL & NO.	GOOD TO VERY GOOD	NEAR MINT	YR.
SHE'S TAKING ALL MY MONEY/Jealous Man (78)	Rockin' 517	8.00	32.00	52

LOUIS, Joe Hill as Little Joe

Louis should not be confused with the rhythm & blues performer Little Joe, who recorded with the groups known as The Thrillers and The Morrocos.

TITLE/FLIP	LABEL & NO.	GOOD TO VERY GOOD	NEAR MINT	YR.
GLAMOUR GIRL/ Keep Your Arms Around Me	House of Sound C & S 500	10.00	40.00	57

LOUIS, Joe Hill as Little Joe:
see Douglas, Lizzie as Memphis Minnie with Little Joe & His Band

LOUIS, Leslie

TITLE/FLIP	LABEL & NO.	GOOD TO VERY GOOD	NEAR MINT	YR.
RIDIN' HOME (instrumental)/ Don't Do It Again	Rockin' 509	20.00	80.00	52

LOUIS, Sherman as Sherman's Trio

TITLE/FLIP	LABEL & NO.	GOOD TO VERY GOOD	NEAR MINT	YR.
JUMPING FOR JULIA/Thinkin' And Thinkin' (by Bob Geddins & His Cavaliers) (78)	Cavatone 5	2.50	10.00	49
JUMPING FOR JULIA/Thinkin' And Thinkin' (by Bob Geddins & His Cavaliers) (78)	Modern 20-685	2.00	8.00	49

LOUIS, Tommy & The Rhythm Rockers

LOUISIANA RED

LOVE BUGS, The (with Preston Love)

TITLE/FLIP	LABEL & NO.	GOOD TO VERY GOOD	NEAR MINT	YR.
BOOM DIDDY WAWA BABY/A Man Goin' Crazy	Federal 12216	5.00	20.00	55

LOVE LETTERS, The

TITLE/FLIP	LABEL & NO.	GOOD TO VERY GOOD	NEAR MINT	YR.
WALKING THE STREETS ALONE/Owee-Nellie	Acme 714	12.50	50.00	57

LOVE NOTES, The

TITLE/FLIP	LABEL & NO.	GOOD TO VERY GOOD	NEAR MINT	YR.
IF I COULD MAKE YOU MINE/Don't Go	Holiday 2607	4.00	16.00	57
UNITED/Tonight	Holiday 2605	4.00	16.00	57

LOVE NOTES, The

TITLE/FLIP	LABEL & NO.	GOOD TO VERY GOOD	NEAR MINT	YR.
I'M SORRY/Sweet Lulu	Rainbow 266	25.00	100.00	54
I'M SORRY/Sweet Lulu	Riviera 970	50.00	200.00	54
SINCE I FELL FOR YOU/Don't Be No Fool	Riviera 975	50.00	200.00	54
SURRENDER YOUR HEART/Get On My Train	Imperial 5254	40.00	160.00	53

LOVE, Billy "Red"

TITLE/FLIP	LABEL & NO.	GOOD TO VERY GOOD	NEAR MINT	YR.
DROP TOP/You're Gonna Cry (78)	Chess 1508	2.50	10.00	52
MY TEDDY BEAR BABY/Just Plain Poor (78)	Chess 1516	2.50	10.00	52

TITLE/FLIP	LABEL & NO.	GOOD TO VERY GOOD	NEAR MINT	YR.
LOVE, Clayton				
CHAINED TO YOUR LOVE/Where I Want To Be	Aladdin 3148	3.00	12.00	52
MARY LOU/Bye Bye Baby	Groove 0161	2.50	10.00	55
WICKED LITTLE BABY/Why Don't You Believe Me?	Modern 929	3.00	12.00	54
LOVE, Hot Shot				
WOLF CALL BOOGIE/Harmonica Jam	Sun 196	30.00	120.00	54
LOVE, Mary				
LOVE, Preston				
LIKE A SHIP AT SEA/Strickly Cash (instrumental)	Federal 12085	3.00	12.00	52
MY LOVE IS DRAGGIN'/Suicide Blues	Federal 12145	2.50	10.00	53
WANGO BLUES/September Song (instrumental)	Federal 12069	3.00	12.00	52
YOU GOT ME DRINKIN'/Stay By My Side	Federal 12132	2.50	10.00	53
LOVE, Preston: see Love Bugs, The (with Preston Love) see Sailor Boy				
LOVE, Ronnie				
LOVE, Willie & His Three Aces				
FEED MY BODY TO THE FISHES/Fallin' Rain (78)	Trumpet 172	1.50	6.00	52
NELSON STREET BLUES/V-8 Ford	Trumpet 175	3.00	12.00	52
SHOUT, BROTHER, SHOUT/Way Back	Trumpet 209	2.50	10.00	53
21 MINUTES TO 9/Shady Lane Blues	Trumpet 174	3.00	12.00	52
VANITY DRESSER BOOGIE/Seventy Four Blues	Trumpet 173	3.00	12.00	52
LOVE, Willie as Willie Love's Three Aces				
EVERYBODY'S FISHING/My Own Boogie (78)	Trumpet 147	1.50	6.00	51
TAKE IT EASY, BABY/Little Car Blues (78)	Trumpet 137	1.50	6.00	51
LOVELARKS, The				
MORE AND MORE/Diddle-Le-Bom	Masons	10.00	40.00	—
LOVELITES, The				
I FOUND ME A LOVER/You Better Stop It	Bandera 2515	2.50	10.00	67
LOVENOTES, The				
LOVE LIKE YOURS, A/Never Look Behind	Premium 411	8.00	32.00	—
LOVERS, The (with Alden Bunn as Tarheel Slim)				
TELL ME/Love Bug Bit Me	Aladdin 3419	1.50	6.00	58
TELL ME/Love Bug Bit Me	Lamp 2018	2.00	8.00	58
LOVETONES, The				
TALK TO AN ANGEL/Take It Easy, Baby	Plus 108	20.00	80.00	—
LOVETTES, The (female group)				
LP'S, Denny & The				
WHY NOT GIVE ME YOUR HEART?/Slide-Cha-Lypso	Rock-It 001	7.00	28.00	—
LUANDREW, Albert as Delta Joe				
4 O'CLOCK BLUES/I Cried (78)	Chance 1115	6.25	25.00	53
GOING BACK TO MEMPHIS/ Devil Is A Busy Man (red plastic)	Blue Lake 105	20.00	80.00	54
GOING BACK TO MEMPHIS/Devil Is A Busy Man	Blue Lake 105	10.00	40.00	54
ROLL, TUMBLE AND SLIP/Train Time (78)	Opera OP-5	7.00	28.00	53
SHAKE IT, BABY/Bassology (red plastic)	Blue Lake 107	20.00	80.00	54
SHAKE IT, BABY/Bassology	Blue Lake 107	10.00	40.00	54
LUANDREW, Albert as Sunnyland Slim & His Boys				
SHAKE IT, BABY/Woman Trouble	JOB 1105	5.00	20.00	54
WOMAN TROUBLE/Drinking Woman (by John Brim) (78)	JOB 1011	5.00	20.00	54
Both sides of this record are credited to John Brim & His Trio, but Sunnyland Slim & His Boys did "Woman Trouble."				
LUANDREW, Albert as Sunnyland Slim & His Playboys				
FOUR DAY BOUNCE/That Woman	JOB 1108	5.00	20.00	54
LUANDREW, Albert as Sunnyland Slim & His Sunny Boys				
5 FOOT 4 GAL/I've Done You Wrong (78)	Hytone 37	2.00	8.00	49
JIVIN' BOOGIE/Brown Skin Woman (78)	Hytone 32	2.00	8.00	49
MISS BESSIE MAE/The Devil Is A Busy Man (78)	Hytone 33	2.00	8.00	49
MUD KICKING WOMAN/Everytime I Got To Drinking (78)	Mercury 8132	1.50	6.00	49
LUANDREW, Albert as Sunnyland Slim & His Sunnyland Boys				
HARD TIMES/School Days (78)	Tempo Tone 1001	12.50	50.00	48
LUANDREW, Albert as Sunnyland Slim & His Trio				
AIN'T NOTHING BUT A CHILD/ Brown Skinned Woman (78)	Mercury 8277	1.50	6.00	51
BACK TO KOREA BLUES/It's All Over Now (78)	Sunny 101	6.25	25.00	50
BAD TIMES/I'm Just A Lonesome Man (78)	Apollo 416	1.50	6.00	50
DOWN HOME CHILD/Sunny Land Special (78)	JOB 102	3.00	12.00	50
HIT THE ROAD AGAIN/Gin Drinkin' Baby (78)	Mercury 8264	1.50	6.00	51
ORPHAN BOY BLUES/When I Was Young (78)	Regal 3327	2.00	8.00	51
LUANDREW, Albert as Sunnyland Slim & Muddy Water				
JOHNSON MACHINE GUN/Fly Right, Little Girl (78)	Aristocrat 1301	4.00	16.00	47
LUANDREW, Albert as Sunnyland Slim & Muddy Waters				
BLUE BABY/I Want My Baby (78)	Tempo Tone 1002	11.00	44.00	48
LUANDREW, Albert as Sunnyland Slim & Muddy Waters' Combo				
SHE AIN'T NOWHERE/My Baby, My Baby (78)	Aristocrat 1304	4.00	16.00	48
LUANDREW, Albert as Sunnyland Slim With The Lefty Bates Combo				
BE MINE ALONE/Sad And Lonesome	Club 51 C-106	7.00	28.00	55
IT'S YOU, BABY/Highway 51	Cobra 5006	4.00	16.00	56
LUANDREW, Albert as The Sunnyland Trio				
LUANDREW, Albert as The Sunnyland Trio: see Foster, Leroy as Baby Face & The Sunnyland Trio				
LEAVING YOUR TOWN/Mary Lee (78)	JOB 1003	2.50	10.00	52
LUCAS, Buddy				
BIG BERTHA/You Belong To Me (instrumental)	Jubilee 5094	2.00	8.00	52
DIANE/Undecided (instrumental)	Jubilee 5070	2.00	8.00	51
EMBRACEABLE YOU/In The Mood (instrumental)	Jubilee 5075	2.00	8.00	52
GREEDY PIG/It Rains	RCA Victor 47-5396	2.00	8.00	53
HIGH LOW JACK/No Dice	Groove 0030	4.00	16.00	54
HUSTLIN' FAMILY BLUES/I'll Never Smile Again (instrumental)	Jubilee 5083	3.00	12.00	52
I GOT DRUNK/My Pinch Hitter	Groove 0003	3.00	12.00	54
I NEED HELP/No Help	Groove 0006	2.50	10.00	54
LET'S GET TO THE PARTY/I Know What I'm Doin'	RCA Victor 47-5508	2.00	8.00	53
WHOPPING BLUES/Sopping Molasses	Jubilee 5058	4.00	16.00	51
LUCAS, William as Lazy Bill & His Blue Rhythms				
SHE GOT ME WALKIN'/I Had A Dream	Chance 1148	20.00	80.00	53
LULLABIES, Lisa & The				
LUMPKIN, Henry				
WE REALLY LOVE EACH OTHER/I've Got A Notion	Motown 1005	1.50	6.00	61
LUTCHER, Joe				
ROCKIN' BOOGIE/Blues For Sale (instrumental)	Specialty 303	5.00	20.00	49
LYMON, Frankie & The Teenagers				
LYMON, Lewis & The Teenchords: see Teenchords, Lewis Lymon & The				
LYNN, Barbara				
LYNN, Blow Top				
COME BACK MY DARLIN'/Home Sick Blues	RCA Victor 47-4328	2.50	10.00	51
RAMPAGING MAMA/Real True Gal	RCA Victor 50-0139	3.00	12.00	51
SCHOOL BOY BLUES/Releasin' Blues	RCA Victor 50-0110	3.00	12.00	51
UP ON THE HILL/Ain't Gonna Tell It Right	RCA Victor 50-0124	3.00	12.00	51
LYNN, Cherri				
BABY I'M GONE/Wait	Apollo 463	2.50	10.00	54
YOUR MONEY AIN'T LONG ENOUGH/ If It Hadn't Been For You	Apollo 456	2.50	10.00	54
LYNN, Smiling Smokey				
LEAVE MY GIRL ALONE/Straighten Up, Pretty Baby (78)	Peacock 1579	1.50	6.00	52
STATE STREET BOOGIE/ Jackson's Blues (instrumental) (78)	Specialty 323	1.50	6.00	49
UNFAITHFUL WOMAN/Goin' Back Home (78)	Peacock 1556	1.50	6.00	51
LYNNE, Gloria				
LYONS, Joe & The Arrows: see Arrows, Joe Lyons & The				

TITLE/FLIP	LABEL & NO.	GOOD TO VERY GOOD	NEAR MINT	YR.
LYONS, Lonnie Combo, The				
FAR AWAY BLUES/Fly Chick Bounce (78)	Freedom 1507	2.00	8.00	49
LONELY HEART BLUES/Barrelhouse Night Cap (78)	Freedom 1504	1.50	6.00	49
NEAT AND SWEET, PART 1/ Neat And Sweet, Part 2 (78)	Freedom 1512	1.50	6.00	49
Instrumentals.				
LYONS, Lonnie, His Piano & Orchestra				
BETRAYED/Sneaky Joe (78)	Freedom 1523	1.50	6.00	49
HELPLESS/Down In The Groovy (78)	Freedom 1519	1.50	6.00	49
LYRES, The				
SHIP OF LOVE/Play Boy	J & G 101	40.00	160.00	53
The same group re-recorded "Ship Of Love" two years later and then called themselves The Nutmegs.				
LYRICS, Ike Perry & The				
I'VE GOT YOU COVERED/You Can Be My Honey	Cowtown 801	4.00	16.00	—
STAIRSTEPS TO HEAVEN/The Love Bug's Got Me	Bridge 110	15.00	60.00	—
LYRICS, The				
I'M IN LOVE/You	Hy-Tone 111	20.00	80.00	—
LYRICS, The				
I WANT TO KNOW/The Beating Of My Heart	Harlem 104	4.00	16.00	59
OH, PLEASE LOVE ME/The Girl I Love	Coral 62322	1.50	6.00	62
OH, PLEASE LOVE ME/The Girl I Love	Wildcat 0028	2.50	10.00	59
LYRICS, The				
COME ON HOME/Why Don't You Stop?	Vee-Jay 285	4.00	16.00	58
CRYING OVER YOU/Down In The Alley	Mid South 1500	2.50	10.00	—

TITLE/FLIP	LABEL & NO.	GOOD TO VERY GOOD	NEAR MINT	YR.
M.V.P.'S, The				
M-M'S & THE PEANUTS				
MABLEY, Moms				
MABON, Willie				
MABON, Willie & His Combo				
I GOT TO GO/Crusin'	Chess 1554	1.50	6.00	53
I'M MAD/Night Latch (instrumental)	Chess 1538	1.50	6.00	53
POISON IVY/Say, Man	Chess 1580	1.50	6.00	54
WORRY BLUES/I Don't Know (red plastic)	Chess 1531	12.50	50.00	53
WORRY BLUES/I Don't Know	Chess 1531	2.00	8.00	53
WOULD YOU, BABY?/Late Again	Chess 1564	1.50	6.00	54
YOU'RE A FOOL/Monday Woman	Chess 1548	1.50	6.00	53
MABON, Willie as Big Willie				
BOGEY MAN/It Keeps Raining (78)	Apollo 450	2.50	10.00	53
MAC, Lou				
ALBERT IS HIM NAME/ I'll Never Let Him Go (red plastic)	Blue Lake 117	6.25	25.00	55
ALBERT IS HIM NAME/I'll Never Let Him Go	Blue Lake 117	3.00	12.00	55
COME BACK, LITTLE DADDY/ Hard To Get Along With (red plastic)	Blue Lake 108	6.25	25.00	54
COME BACK, LITTLE DADDY/Hard To Get Along With	Blue Lake 108	3.00	12.00	54
SLOW DOWN/Baby (red plastic)	Blue Lake 114	6.25	25.00	55
SLOW DOWN/Baby	Blue Lake 114	5.00	20.00	55
TAKE YOUR TROUBLE TO A FRIEND/ Move Me (red plastic)	Blue Lake 119	6.25	25.00	55
TAKE YOUR TROUBLE TO A FRIEND/Move Me	Blue Lake 119	3.00	12.00	55
MACK, Andy & The Carltons				
MACK, Jimmy & The Watts				
MAD LADS, The				

TITLE/FLIP	LABEL & NO.	GOOD TO VERY GOOD	NEAR MINT	YR.
MAE, Daisy & Her Hepcats				
FROSTY'S GROOVE/Hop Scotch	20th Century 1204	1.50	6.00	57
LONESOME PLAYGIRL/Woman Trouble	Gotham 7-317	2.00	8.00	56
MAGHETT, Samuel as Magic Sam				
ALL NIGHT LONG/All My Whole Life	Cobra 5025	2.50	10.00	58
ALL YOUR LOVE/Love Me With A Feeling	Cobra 5013	2.00	8.00	57
EASY, BABY/Twenty One Days In Jail	Cobra 5029	2.00	8.00	58
EVERY NIGHT ABOUT THIS TIME/ Do The Camel Walk (instrumental)	Chief 7026	1.50	6.00	61
EVERYTHING GONNA BE ALRIGHT/Look Watcha Done	Cobra 5021	2.00	8.00	57
MR. CHARLIE/My Love Is Your Love	Chief 7013	1.50	6.00	60
SQUARE DANCE ROCK, PART 1/ Square Dance Rock, Part 2	Chief 7017	1.50	6.00	60
Instrumentals.				
YOU DON'T HAVE TO WORK/Blue Light Boogie	Chief 7033	1.50	6.00	61
MAGIC SAM: see Maghett, Samuel as Magic Sam				
MAGIC TONES, The				
HOW CAN YOU TREAT ME THIS WAY?/Cool, Cool Baby	King 4681	50.00	200.00	53
WHEN I KNEEL DOWN TO PRAY/Good Googa Mooga	King 4665	50.00	200.00	53
MAGNETICS, The				
WHERE ARE YOU?/The Train	Allrite 620	2.00	8.00	62
MAGNIFICENTS, The				
DO YOU MIND?/The Dribble	Kansoma 03	1.50	6.00	62
MAGNIFICENTS, The				
CADDY BO/Hiccup	Vee Jay 208	4.00	16.00	56
DON'T LEAVE ME/Ozeta	Vee Jay 281	6.25	25.00	58
OFF THE MOUNTAIN/Lost Lover	Vee Jay 235	5.00	20.00	56
UP ON THE MOUNTAIN/Why Did She Go?	Vee Jay 183	2.50	10.00	62
MAHARAJAHS, The				
I DO BELIEVE/Why Don't You Answer?	Flip 332	2.00	8.00	58
SWEET LORETTA/Oh, Shirley	Flip 335	2.50	10.00	58
MAIDEN, Sidney: see Simmons, Al with Slim Green & The Cats From Fresno				
MAIDEN, Sidney				
HAND ME DOWN BABY/Old Folks Boogie (by Al Simmons)	Dig 138	5.00	20.00	56
HONEY BEE BLUES/Thinking The Blues	Imperial 5189	9.00	36.00	52
HURRY, HURRY BABY/Everything Is Wrong	Flash 101	7.00	28.00	55
MAIN INGREDIENT, The				
MAJESTICS, The				
GWENDOLYN/Lonely Heart	Chex 1006	2.50	10.00	62
MAJESTICS, The				
NITEY NITE/Cave Man Rock	Marlin 802	40.00	160.00	56
MAJORS, The				
AT LAST/You Ran Away With My Heart	Derby 763	75.00	300.00	51
LAUGHING ON THE OUTSIDE, CRYING ON THE INSIDE/ Come On Up To My Room	Derby 779	50.00	200.00	51
MAKEBA, Miriam				
MALLARD, Sax				
I'M YOURS/Teen Town Strut	Checker 755	3.00	12.00	52
SLOW CABOOSE/Darling, Let's Give Love Another Chance	Checker 750	4.00	16.00	52
MALLETT, Sandra & The Vandellas: see Vandellas, Sandra Mallett & The				
MALONE, Tommie "Blind Tom"				
COW COW SHAKE/Worried Life	Ebony 1055	1.50	6.00	60
MAN YOUNG: see Young, Johnny as Man Young				
MANDELLS, The				
DARLING, I'M HOME/Who, Me?	Chess 1794	1.50	6.00	61
DARLING, I'M HOME/Who, Me?	Smart 323	7.00	28.00	61

TITLE/FLIP	LABEL & NO.	GOOD TO VERY GOOD	NEAR MINT	YR.

MANDERINS, The

GOING AWAY/Let The Bells Ring	Band Box 236	2.00	8.00	60

MANHATTANS, The

MY BIG DREAM/That'll Make It Nice	Dooto 445	4.00	16.00	59

MANN, Gloria & The Carter Rays:
see Carter Rays, Gloria Mann & The

MANN, Scotty & The Masters:
see Masters, Scotty Mann & The

MAPLES, The

I MUST FORGET YOU/99 Guys	Blue Lake 111	40.00	160.00	54

MAR-VELS, The

CHERRY LIPS/Could Be You	Love 5011/5012	2.50	10.00	—

MARATHONS, The

PEANUT BUTTER/Down In New Orleans	Argo 5389	1.50	6.00	61

MARBLES, The

GOLDEN GIRL/Big Wig Walk	Lucky 002	15.00	60.00	54

MARCEL & HIS BAND:
see Morris, Leo with Marcel & His Band

MARCELS, The

ALL RIGHT, OKAY, YOU WIN/Lollipop Baby	Colpix 665	1.50	6.00	62
FLOWERPOT/Hold On	Colpix 640	1.50	6.00	62
FRIENDLY LOANS/Loved Her The Whole Week Through	Colpix 651	1.50	6.00	62
GIVE ME BACK YOUR LOVE/I Wanna Be The Leader	Colpix 687	1.50	6.00	63
ONE LAST KISS/Teeter-Totter Love	Colpix 694	1.50	6.00	63
THAT OLD BLACK MAGIC/Don't Turn Your Back On Me	Colpix 683	1.50	6.00	63

MARCHAN, Bobby

CHICKEE WAH WAH/Don't Take Your Love From Me	Ace 523	1.50	6.00	56
JUST A LITTLE WALK/Have Mercy	Aladdin 3189	4.00	16.00	53

MARCHAN, Bobby & The Clowns

MARCHAN, Bobby & The Tick Tocks

SNOOPIN' AND ACCUSIN'/This Is The Life	Fire 1014	1.50	6.00	60

MARCHAN, Bobby as Bobby Marchon

JUST A LITTLE OL' WINE/You Made A Fool Of Me	Dot 1203	2.50	10.00	54

MARIE & REX

MARIGOLDS, Johnny Bragg & The

FOOLISH ME/Beyond The Clouds	Excello 2078	4.00	16.00	56
IT'S YOU, DARLING, IT'S YOU/Juke Box Rock And Roll	Excello 2091	4.00	16.00	56

MARIGOLDS, The

ROLLIN' STONE/Why Don't You?	Excello 2057	4.00	16.00	55
TWO STRANGERS/Love You, Love You	Excello 2061	3.00	12.00	55

MARKEYS, The

ETERNAL LOVE/You've Got Me On A String	20th Century 1210	4.00	16.00	—

MARKHAM, Pigmeat

MARKTONES, The

HOLD ME CLOSE/Talk It Over	Ember 1022	3.00	12.00	57
YES, SIREE/Hey, Girlee	Ember 1030	3.00	12.00	57

MAROONS, The

MARQUEES, The (with Marvin Gaye)

MARQUEES, The

BELLS, THE/The Rain	Grand 141	20.00	80.00	56

MARQUEES, The

CHRISTMAS IN THE CONGO/Santa Done Got Hip	Warner Brothers 5127	1.50	6.00	59
DON'T BE MEAN, GERALDINE/ Until The Day I Die	Warner Brothers 5139	1.50	6.00	59
LOVE MACHINE/Who Will Be The First One?	Warner Brothers 5072	1.50	6.00	59

MARQUIS, The

HOPE HE'S TRUE/Bohemian Daddy	Onyx 505	25.00	100.00	56

TITLE/FLIP	LABEL & NO.	GOOD TO VERY GOOD	NEAR MINT	YR.

MARQUIS, The

I DON'T WANT YOUR LOVE/Popcorn Willie	Rainbow 358	7.00	28.00	—

MARS, Mitzi

I'M GLAD/Roll 'Em	Checker 773	2.00	8.00	53

MARSHALL BROTHERS, The

WHO'LL BE THE FOOL FROM NOW ON?/Mr. Santa's Boogie	Savoy 825	50.00	200.00	51
WHY MAKE A FOOL OUT OF ME?/Just A Poor Boy In Love	Savoy 833	50.00	200.00	52

MARSHALL BROTHERS, William Cook & The

JUST BECAUSE/A Soldier's Prayer	Savoy 828	2.50	10.00	51

MARSHALL, Frankie

EVERY MINUTE OF THE DAY/Over And Over	Atco 6076	1.50	6.00	56
FANNY LOU/Why, Oh Why?	Atco 6070	1.50	6.00	56
IF IT'S THE LAST THING I DO/Song From My Heart	Atco 6061	1.50	6.00	55
JUST SAY THE WORD/No One Else Will Know	Spark 117	2.00	8.00	55

MARSHALL, Percy

LEAVING TOWN/Give Me My Guitar	Marshall 101	2.50	10.00	—

MARTELL, Linda & The Anglos

MARTELLS, The

FORGOTTEN SPRING/Va Va Boom	Cessna 477	2.50	10.00	61
FORGOTTEN SPRING/Va Va Voom	Bella 45	2.00	8.00	61

MARTELS, The

ROCKIN' SANTA CLAUS/Carol Lee	Bella 20	2.00	8.00	59

MARTHA & THE VANDELLAS

MARTIN, Derek

MARTIN, Kenny

MARTINELS, The

MARVELETTES, The (female group)

MARVELIERS, The

WHEN WE DANCE/Down	Cougar 1868	4.00	16.00	60

MARVELLOS, The

SHE TOLD ME LIES/Salty Sam	Exodus 6214	2.50	10.00	62

MARVELLOS, The

RED HOT MAMA/I Need A Girl	Marvello 5005	25.00	100.00	—
YOU'RE THE DREAM/Calypso Mama	Theron 117	25.00	100.00	55

MARVELLS, The

FOR SENTIMENTAL REASONS/Come Back	Winn 1916	4.00	16.00	61

MARVELOWS, The

MARVELS, The

I WON'T HAVE YOU BREAKING MY HEART/ Jump, Rock And Roll	ABC 9771	20.00	80.00	56

MARVIN & JOHNNY:
see Phillips, Marvin & Johnny Dean as Marvin & Johnny

MARVIN & THE CHIRPS:
see Chirps, Marvin & The

MARYLANDERS, The

FRIED CHICKEN/Good Old 99 (red plastic)	Jubilee 5114	25.00	100.00	53
FRIED CHICKEN/Good Old 99	Jubilee 5114	15.00	60.00	53
I'M A SENTIMENTAL FOOL/Sittin' By The River	Jubilee 5079	40.00	160.00	52
MAKE ME THRILL AGAIN/Please Love Me	Jubilee 5091	40.00	160.00	52

MASCOTS, The

LONELY RAIN/That's The Way I Feel	King 5435	2.50	10.00	60
STORY OF MY HEART, THE/Do The Wiggle	King 5377	2.50	10.00	60

MASEKELA, Hugh

MASK-MEN & THE AGENTS

MASKED MAN & THE AGENTS

MASKMAN & THE AGENTS

MASON, Barbara

MASQUERADES, The

MASQUINS, Tony & The

TITLE/FLIP	LABEL & NO.	GOOD TO VERY GOOD	NEAR MINT	YR.
MY ANGEL EYES/Fugi Womma	Ruthie 1000	10.00	40.00	61

MASTER KEYS, The

TITLE/FLIP	LABEL & NO.	GOOD TO VERY GOOD	NEAR MINT	YR.
I GOT THE BLUES IN THE MORNIN'/ You're Not The Only Apple On The Tree (78)	Jubilee 5004	2.50	10.00	49

MASTERKEYS, The

TITLE/FLIP	LABEL & NO.	GOOD TO VERY GOOD	NEAR MINT	YR.
MR. BLUES/Don't Cry, Darling (78)	Abbey 2017	5.00	20.00	—

MASTERS, Scotty Mann & The

TITLE/FLIP	LABEL & NO.	GOOD TO VERY GOOD	NEAR MINT	YR.
JUST A LITTLE BIT OF LOVING/The Mystery Man	Peacock 1665	2.50	10.00	56

MASTERS, The

TITLE/FLIP	LABEL & NO.	GOOD TO VERY GOOD	NEAR MINT	YR.
LOVELY WAY TO SPEND AN EVENING, A/Dores Blues	Bingo 1008	3.00	12.00	60

MASTERTONES, The

TITLE/FLIP	LABEL & NO.	GOOD TO VERY GOOD	NEAR MINT	YR.
TELL ME/What'll You Do?	Bruce 111	40.00	160.00	54

The valuable first pressing of this release must have "Nu-Way Edgar Publishing" printed on the label.

MATADORS, The

TITLE/FLIP	LABEL & NO.	GOOD TO VERY GOOD	NEAR MINT	YR.
MY FOOLISH HEART/You'd Be Crying	Kieth 6504	2.00	8.00	63

MATADORS, The

TITLE/FLIP	LABEL & NO.	GOOD TO VERY GOOD	NEAR MINT	YR.
BE GOOD TO ME/Have Mercy, Baby	Sue 701	5.00	20.00	58
PENNIES FROM HEAVEN/Vengeance	Sue 700	9.00	36.00	58

MATHEWS, Bill:
see Balladiers, Bill Mathews & The
see Balladeers, Billy Mathews & The

MATHEWS, Fat Man

TITLE/FLIP	LABEL & NO.	GOOD TO VERY GOOD	NEAR MINT	YR.
DOWN THE LINE/You Know It	Imperial 5235	6.25	25.00	52
I'M THANKFUL/Goin' Down	Bayou 016	10.00	40.00	52

MATHEWS, Fat Man & The Four Kittens

TITLE/FLIP	LABEL & NO.	GOOD TO VERY GOOD	NEAR MINT	YR.
WHEN BOY MEETS GIRL/Later, Baby	Imperial 5211	20.00	80.00	52

MATHEWS, Little Arthur

TITLE/FLIP	LABEL & NO.	GOOD TO VERY GOOD	NEAR MINT	YR.
I'M GONNA WHALE ON YOU/Someday, Baby	Federal 12232	2.50	10.00	55

MATHIS, Ralph:
see Ambers, The

MATTHEWS, Carl

TITLE/FLIP	LABEL & NO.	GOOD TO VERY GOOD	NEAR MINT	YR.
BIG MAN/No Man Is Honest	Apollo 453	1.50	6.00	54
CO-OPERATION, PART 1/Co-operation, Part 2	Apollo 459	1.50	6.00	54
I LOVE MY FOLKS/Trouble, Trouble	Apollo 455	1.50	6.00	54
I WAS WRONG/I'm Going Back Home	Apollo 465	1.50	6.00	54

MATTHEWS, Johnnie Mae & The Dapps

MATTHEWS, Shirley & The Big Town Girls

MAURICE & THE RADIANTS

MAXWELL, Bobby & The Exploits:
see Exploits, Bobby Maxwell & The

MAYE, Arthur Lee

TITLE/FLIP	LABEL & NO.	GOOD TO VERY GOOD	NEAR MINT	YR.
'CAUSE YOU'RE MINE ALONE/Hey, Pretty Girl	Flip 330	2.00	8.00	57

MAYE, Arthur Lee & The Crowns:
see Crowns, Arthur Lee Maye & The

MAYER, Nathaniel & The Fabulous Twilights:
see Fabulous Twilights, Nathaniel Mayer & The

MAYFIELD, Curtis

MAYFIELD, Joe

TITLE/FLIP	LABEL & NO.	GOOD TO VERY GOOD	NEAR MINT	YR.
I'M A NATURAL BORN MAN/You're The One I Love	Rocket 501	1.50	6.00	—

MAYFIELD, Percy

TITLE/FLIP	LABEL & NO.	GOOD TO VERY GOOD	NEAR MINT	YR.
BIG QUESTION, THE/The Hunt Is On	Specialty 425	2.50	10.00	52
CRY BABY/Hopeless	Specialty 416	3.00	12.00	52
DOUBLE DEALING/Are You There?	Chess 1599	1.50	6.00	55
HOW DEEP IS THE WELL?/ The Bachelor Blues (red plastic)	Specialty 473	4.00	16.00	54
HOW DEEP IS THE WELL?/ The Bachelor Blues	Specialty 473	2.00	8.00	54
I DARE YOU, BABY/The River's Invitation	Specialty 451	2.00	8.00	54
I NEED LOVE SO BAD/Loose Lips	Specialty 485	2.00	8.00	54
LONELY ONE/Lost Mind (red plastic)	Specialty 460	4.00	16.00	54
LONELY ONE/Lost Mind	Specialty 460	2.00	8.00	54
LOST LOVE/Life Is Suicide	Specialty 390	3.00	12.00	51
LOUISIANA/Two Hearts Are Greater Than One	Specialty 432	2.50	10.00	52
MY BLUES/Prayin' For Your Return	Specialty 408	3.00	12.00	51
MY HEART/Lonesome Highway	Specialty 439	2.50	10.00	53
NIGHTLESS LOVER/What A Fool I Was	Specialty 400	3.00	12.00	51
PLEASE SEND ME SOMEONE TO LOVE/ Strange Things Are Happening	Specialty 375	4.00	16.00	50
VOICE WITHIN, THE/Baby, You're Rich	Specialty 544	1.50	6.00	55
YOU DON'T EXIST NO MORE/Sugar Mama, Peachy Papa	Specialty 499	2.00	8.00	55
YOU WERE LYIN' TO ME/My Heart Is Cryin'	Specialty 537	1.50	6.00	55

MAYS, Zilla & The Four Students:
see Four Students, Zilla Mays & The

MCALLISTER, Red

TITLE/FLIP	LABEL & NO.	GOOD TO VERY GOOD	NEAR MINT	YR.
EGGS AND GRITS/Peacock Blues	King 4598	2.50	10.00	52

MCBOOKER, Connie

TITLE/FLIP	LABEL & NO.	GOOD TO VERY GOOD	NEAR MINT	YR.
SHORT BABY BOOGIE/Rich Woman Blues (78)	Eddie's 1928	2.50	10.00	49

MCBOOKER, Connie as Connie Mack Booker

TITLE/FLIP	LABEL & NO.	GOOD TO VERY GOOD	NEAR MINT	YR.
LOVE ME, PRETTY BABY/All Alone (78)	RPM 401	2.00	8.00	53

MCBOOKER, Connie as The Connie Mac Booker Orchestra

TITLE/FLIP	LABEL & NO.	GOOD TO VERY GOOD	NEAR MINT	YR.
LORETTA/Come Back, Baby (78)	Freedom 1520	2.00	8.00	49

MCCAIN, James "Jack Of All Trades"

TITLE/FLIP	LABEL & NO.	GOOD TO VERY GOOD	NEAR MINT	YR.
GOOD MR. ROOSEVELT/His Spirit Lives On (by Big Joe Williams) (78)	Chicago 103	6.25	25.00	45

MCCAIN, Jerry

TITLE/FLIP	LABEL & NO.	GOOD TO VERY GOOD	NEAR MINT	YR.
SHE'S TOUGH/Steady (instrumental)	Rex 1014	1.50	6.00	61

MCCAIN, Jerry & His Upstarts

TITLE/FLIP	LABEL & NO.	GOOD TO VERY GOOD	NEAR MINT	YR.
BAD CREDIT/Listen, Young Girls	Excello 2111	2.00	8.00	58
COURTIN' IN A CADILLAC/That's What They Want	Excello 2068	2.50	10.00	56
GROOM WITHOUT A BRIDE/The Jig's Up	Excello 2127	1.50	6.00	59
MY NEXT DOOR NEIGHBOR/Trying To Please	Excello 2103	2.00	8.00	58
RUN, UNCLE JOHN, RUN/Things Ain't Right	Excello 2081	2.00	8.00	57
YOU DON'T LOVE ME NO MORE/If It Wasn't For My Baby	Excello 2079	2.00	8.00	57

MCCAIN, Jerry as Jerry "Boogie" McCain

TITLE/FLIP	LABEL & NO.	GOOD TO VERY GOOD	NEAR MINT	YR.
EAST OF THE SUN/Wine-O-Wine	Trumpet 217	4.00	16.00	54
STAY OUT OF AUTOMOBILES/Love To Make Out (78)	Trumpet 231	10.00	40.00	54

MCCALL, Cash

MCCALL, Toussaint

MCCLAM, Pro Orchestra, The

TITLE/FLIP	LABEL & NO.	GOOD TO VERY GOOD	NEAR MINT	YR.
BOOT-UM/Policy Blues (red plastic)	Vee Jay 102	6.25	25.00	53
BOOT-UM/Policy Blues	Vee Jay 102	3.00	12.00	53
CINEMASCOPE BABY/Please Leave Her Alone (red plastic)	Vee Jay 112	6.25	25.00	54
CINEMASCOPE BABY/Please Leave Her Alone	Vee Jay 112	3.00	12.00	54

MCCLAY, Ernest & His Trio

TITLE/FLIP	LABEL & NO.	GOOD TO VERY GOOD	NEAR MINT	YR.
BIG TIMING WOMAN/Night Working Woman (78)	Murray 506	3.00	32.00	48

MCCLAY, Yul & The Mondellos

MCCLURE, Bobby, Fontella Bass &

MCCOLLOUGH, Charles & The Silks

TITLE/FLIP	LABEL & NO.	GOOD TO VERY GOOD	NEAR MINT	YR.
MY GIRL/Zorro	Dooto 462	1.50	6.00	61

MCCOLLUM, Hazel:
see El Dorados, The

MCCOLLUM, Robert as Robert Nighthawk & His Nighthawks Band

TITLE/FLIP	LABEL & NO.	GOOD TO VERY GOOD	NEAR MINT	YR.
MOON IS RISING, THE/Maggie Campbell	States 131	20.00	40.00	53

TITLE/FLIP	LABEL & NO.	GOOD TO VERY GOOD	NEAR MINT	YR.
MCCOLLUM, Robert as Robert Nighthawk				
BLACK ANGEL BLUES/Annie Lee Blues (78)	Aristocrat 2301	5.00	20.00	48
FEEL SO BAD/Take It Easy, Baby (78)	United 105	4.00	16.00	51
KANSAS CITY BLUES/Cryin' Won't Help You (78)	United 102	4.00	16.00	51
MY SWEET LOVIN' WOMAN/Return Mail Blues (78)	Chess 1484	2.50	10.00	48
SIX THREE O/Jackson Town Gal (78)	Aristocrat 413	5.00	20.00	48
MCCOY, Rose Marie				
DIPPIN' IN MY BUSINESS/Down Here	Cat 111	2.00	8.00	55
MCCRACKLIN, Jimmy				
ACHIN' HEART/Street Loafin' Woman (78)	Globe 109	1.50	6.00	45
BLUES BLASTERS BOOGIE (instrumental)/The Panic's On	Modern 926	2.00	8.00	54
DARLIN' SHARE YOUR LOVE/Give My Heart A Break	Modern 934	2.00	8.00	54
FARE YOU WELL/It's All Right	Hollywood 1054	2.00	8.00	55
GONNA TELL YOUR MOTHER/That Ain't Right	Modern 967	1.50	6.00	55
HIGHWAY 101/Baby, Don't You Want To Go? (78)	Globe 104	1.50	6.00	45
JIMMY'S BLUES/ (78)	Cavatone 251	1.50	6.00	47
LOVE FOR YOU/Beer Tavern Girl	Irma 109	1.50	6.00	—
MISS MATTIE LEFT ME/Mean Mistreated Lover (78)	Globe 102	1.50	6.00	45
PLEASE FORGIVE ME, BABY/Couldn't Be A Dream	Modern 951	1.50	6.00	54
RAILROAD BLUES/ (78)	Cavatone 130	1.50	6.00	47
SPECIAL FOR YOU/You Had Your Chance (78)	Courtney 123	1.50	6.00	45
WOBBLE, THE/With Your Love	Mercury 71412	2.00	8.00	59
YOU DECEIVED ME/Blunston's Boogie (78)	Excelsior 182	2.00	8.00	45
MCCRACKLIN, Jimmy & His Blues Blasters				
BAD CONDITION BLUES/ Blues Blasters Shuffle (instrumental) (78)	Down Town 2023	2.00	8.00	48
LOW DOWN MOOD/She's My Baby (78)	Down Town 2027	2.00	8.00	48
PLAYIN' ON ME/Big Foot Mama (78)	Trilon 231	1.50	6.00	49
ROCK AND RYE/Miss Minnie Lee Blues (78)	Trilon 197	1.50	6.00	49
SOUTH SIDE MOOD (instrumental)/ I Can Understand Love (78)	Trilon 244	1.50	6.00	49
WHEN I'M GONE/Listen Woman (78)	Trilon 245	1.50	6.00	49
MCCRACKLIN, Jimmy & His Orchestra				
CHEATER, THE/My Story	Peacock 1639	1.50	6.00	53
END, THE/I Cried	Peacock 1634	1.50	6.00	53
MY DAYS ARE LIMITED/She's Gone	Peacock 1605	2.00	8.00	52
SHARE AND SHARE ALIKE/She Felt Too Good	Peacock 1615	2.00	8.00	53
MCCULLERS, Mickey				
SAME OLD STORY/I'll Cry A Million Tears	Tamla 54064	2.00	8.00	62
MCDANIEL, Willard				
BLUES ON THE DELTA/3 A.M. Boogie	Specialty 415	2.00	8.00	51
Instrumentals.				
CIRIBIRIBIN BOOGIE/Blues For Mimi	Specialty 424	2.00	8.00	51
Instrumentals.				
MCDANIELS, Gene				
MCDUFF, Brother Jack				
McFADDEN, Ruth & The Royaltones				
TWO IN LOVE (With Only One Heart)/ You For Me	Old Town 1020	7.00	28.00	56
The Royaltones are on both sides, but only Ruth McFadden is credited on "You For Me."				
MCFADDEN, Ruth & The Supremes: see Supremes, Ruth McFadden & The				
MCFARLIN, Blanton: see Indexes, John Golden & The				
McGHEE, Brownie: see McGhee, Walter Brown as Brownie McGhee; see Van Walls, Harry as Spider Sam; see Willis, Ralph Featuring Brownie McGhee				
MCGHEE, Granville as Sticks McGhee				
BLUE BARRELHOUSE (instrumental)/ One Monkey Don't Stop No Show (78)	Atlantic 937	1.50	6.00	50
BLUES IN MY HEART/Whiskey, Women And Loaded Dice	King 4628	3.00	12.00	53
DEALIN' FROM THE BOTTOM/Jungle Juice	King 4672	3.00	12.00	53
DOUBLE CROSSIN' LIQUOR/Six To Eight	King 4783	3.00	12.00	55
DRANK UP ALL THAT WINE/Southern Menu (78)	Atlantic 898	2.00	8.00	49
DRINKIN' WINE SPO-DEE-O-DEE/Blues Mixture (78)	Atlantic 873	2.00	8.00	49
GET YOUR MIND OUT OF THE GUTTER/Sad, Bad, Glad	King 4800	3.00	12.00	55
HOUSE WARMIN' BOOGIE/ Tennessee Waltz Boogie (instrumental) (78)	Atlantic 926	1.50	6.00	50
I'M DOIN' ALL THE TIME/The Wiggle Waggle Woo	King 4700	3.00	12.00	53
LET'S DO IT/She's Gone (78)	Atlantic 912	1.50	6.00	50
LITTLE THINGS WE USED TO DO/Head Happy With Wine	King 4610	3.00	12.00	53
LONESOME ROAD BLUES/I'll Always Remember (78)	Atlantic 881	2.00	8.00	49
MY BABY'S COMING BACK/Venus Blues (78)	Atlantic 909	2.00	8.00	49
MCGHEE, Granville as Sticks McGhee & His Buddies				
BLUES MIXTURE/Drinkin' Wine Spo-Dee-O-Dee (78)	Harlem 1018	4.00	16.00	47
DRINKIN' WINE SPO-DEE-O-DEE/Baby, Baby Blues (78)	Decca 48104	3.00	12.00	47
MY LITTLE ROSE/No More Reveille (78)	Essex 709	1.50	6.00	52
NEW FOUND LOVE/Meet You In The Morning	Atlantic 991	5.00	20.00	51
WEE WEE HOURS, PART 1/ Wee Wee Hours, Part 2	Atlantic 955	7.00	28.00	51
MCGHEE, Granville as Sticks McGhee & His Orchestra				
YOU GOTTA HAVE SOMETHING ON THE BALL/ Oh What A Face	London 978	8.00	32.00	51
MCGHEE, Sticks: see McGhee, Granville as Sticks McGhee				
MCGHEE, Walter Brown as Big Tom Collins				
HEART BREAKING WOMAN/Watchin' My Stuff	King 4568	6.25	25.00	51
HEARTACHE BLUES/Real Good Feeling	King 4483	8.00	32.00	51
MCGHEE, Walter Brown as Blind Boy Williams & His Blues Band				
JUST DRIFTING/Yesterday (78)	Sittin' In With 538	2.00	8.00	48
MCGHEE, Walter Brown as Brownie McGhee				
HEART IN SORROW/Operator Long Distance (78)	Par 1301	1.50	6.00	52
I'M GONNA MOVE CROSS THE RIVER/Sleepless Nights (78)	Derby 776	1.50	6.00	51
MY BULLDOG BLUES/Gin Headed Woman (78)	Sittin' In With 517	1.50	6.00	48
WOMAN I LOVE/All Night Party (78)	Derby 783	1.50	6.00	51
MCGHEE, Walter Brown as Brownie McGhee & His Jook Block Busters				
BLUEBIRD/My Confession	Harlem 2329	6.25	25.00	52
CHEATIN' AND LYING/Need Someone To Love Me	Dot 1184	2.00	8.00	53
CHRISTINA/Worrying Over You	Harlem 2323	6.25	25.00	52
DON'T DOG YOUR WOMAN/Daisy	Red Robin 111	15.00	60.00	53
I FEEL SO GOOD/Key To The Highway (red plastic)	Jax 304	8.00	32.00	52
I'M 10,000 YEARS OLD/Cherry Red (red plastic)	Jax 312	8.00	32.00	52
MEET YOU IN THE MORNING/Brownie's Blues (red plastic)	Jax 307	8.00	32.00	52
NEW BAD BLOOD/Pawnshop Blues (red plastic)	Jax 322	8.00	32.00	52
STRANGER'S BLUES/Dissatisfied Woman (red plastic)	Jax 310	8.00	32.00	52
MCGRIFF, Edna				
EDNA'S BLUES/Why, Oh Why? (red plastic)	Jubilee 5109	5.00	20.00	53
EDNA'S BLUES/Why, Oh Why?	Jubilee 5109	2.00	8.00	53
GOOD/Pick-A-Dilly (vocal duet with Sonny Til)	Jubilee 5099	4.00	16.00	52
HEAVENLY FATHER/I Love You	Jubilee 5073	3.00	12.00	52
I'LL BE AROUND/Ooh, Little Daddy	Josie 764	1.50	6.00	54
IN A CHAPEL BY THE SIDE OF THE ROAD/ Pray For A Better World	Jubilee 5089	2.50	10.00	52
IT'S RAINING/Not Now	Jubilee 5087	2.50	10.00	52
NOTE DROPPIN' PAPA/Come Back	Jubilee 5062	3.00	12.00	51
ONCE IN A WHILE/ I Only Have Eyes For You (vocal duet with Sonny Til)	Jubilee 5090	4.00	16.00	52
MCGRIFF, Jimmy				
MCHOUSTON, Big Red: see Baker, Mickey as Big Red McHouston				
MCKENZIE, Lil & The Four Students: see Four Students, Lil McKenzie & The				
MCKINLEY, David Pete				
SHREVEPORT BLUES/Ardelle (78)	Gotham 505	2.50	10.00	52
MCKINLEY, David Pete as Pete McKinley				
BLACK SNAKE BLUES/Crying For My Baby (78)	Fidelity 3008	3.00	12.00	52
MCKINLEY, L. C.				
I'M SO SATISFIED/Lonely	Vee Jay 159	2.50	10.00	55
STRANGE GIRL/She's Five Feet Three	Vee Jay 133	3.00	12.00	55
MCKINLEY, L. C. & His Orchestra				
COMPANION BLUES/Weeping Willow Blues	States 135	7.00	28.00	53

MCKINLEY, Pete:
see McKinley, David Pete as Pete McKinley

MCKINNEY, John & The Premiers:
see Premiers, John McKinney & The

MCLAURIN, Bette:
see Four Fellows, Bette McLaurin & The
see Striders, Bette McLaurin & The

MCLOLLIE, Oscar & The Honey Jumpers

TITLE/FLIP	LABEL & NO.	GOOD TO VERY GOOD	NEAR MINT	YR.
BE COOL, MY HEART/All That Oil In Texas	Modern 915	2.00	8.00	52
CONVICTED/Roll, Hot Rod, Roll	Modern 970	1.50	6.00	55
DIG THAT CRAZY SANTA CLAUS/God Gave Us Christmas	Modern 943	1.50	6.00	54
ETERNAL LOVE/Pagliacci With A Broken Heart	Modern 955	1.50	6.00	55
FALLING IN LOVE WITH YOU/Lolly Pop	Modern 920	2.50	10.00	54
HEY LOLLY, LOLLY/Pretty Girl	Modern 950	1.50	6.00	55
HONEY JUMP, THE, PART I/The Honey Jump, Part 2	Modern 902	5.00	20.00	53
HOT BANANA/Wiggle Toe	Modern 932	1.50	6.00	54
LOVE ME TONIGHT/Take Your Shoes Off, Pop	Modern 940	1.50	6.00	54
MAMA DON'T LIKE/What You Call 'Em, Joe?	Modern 928	2.00	8.00	54

MCMILLAN, Cab & His Fadeaways

TITLE/FLIP	LABEL & NO.	GOOD TO VERY GOOD	NEAR MINT	YR.
I'M YOUNG AND ABLE/Three Women Blues (78)	Macy's 5011	1.50	6.00	50

MCMILLON, Dennis

TITLE/FLIP	LABEL & NO.	GOOD TO VERY GOOD	NEAR MINT	YR.
I WOKE UP ONE MORNING/Paper Wooden Daddy (78)	Regal 3257	3.00	12.00	50
POOR LITTLE ANGEL/Goin' Back Home (78)	Regal 3232	5.00	20.00	50

MCNEELY, Big Jay

All of the following are instrumentals.

TITLE/FLIP	LABEL & NO.	GOOD TO VERY GOOD	NEAR MINT	YR.
BEACHCOMBER/Strip Tease Swing	Federal 12191	1.50	6.00	54
CATASTROPHE/Calamity	Bayou 018	5.00	20.00	53
DEACON'S EXPRESS/Jet Fury	Imperial 5219	2.50	10.00	53
EARTHQUAKE/Penthouse Serenade	Federal 12111	3.00	12.00	52
GOOF, THE/Big Jay Shuffle	Federal 12102	3.00	12.00	52
HOMETOWN JAMBOREE/Teen Age Hop	Bayou 014	5.00	20.00	53
HOT CINDERS/Whipped Cream	Federal 12179	1.50	6.00	54
LET'S SPLIT/Real Crazy Cool	Aladdin 3242	2.00	8.00	54
LET'S WORK/Hard Tack	Federal 12186	1.50	6.00	54
MULE WALK/Ice Water	Federal 12168	1.50	6.00	54
NERVOUS, MAN, NERVOUS/Rock Candy	Federal 12141	1.50	6.00	53
3-D/Texas Turkey	Federal 12151	1.50	6.00	53

MCNEELY, Big Jay:
see Delegates, The

MCNEIL, Landy & The Corsairs

MCPHATTER, Clyde:
see Dominoes, The (featuring Clyde McPhatter)
see Drifters, Clyde McPhatter & The

MCPHERSON, Wyatt (Earp)

MCTELL, Willie Samuel as Barrelhouse Sammy (The Country Boy)

TITLE/FLIP	LABEL & NO.	GOOD TO VERY GOOD	NEAR MINT	YR.
BROKE DOWN ENGINE BLUES/Kill It, Kid (78)	Atlantic 891	6.25	25.00	49

MCTELL, Willie Samuel as Blind Willie

TITLE/FLIP	LABEL & NO.	GOOD TO VERY GOOD	NEAR MINT	YR.
RIVER JORDAN/How About You? (78)	Regal 3260	7.00	28.00	50

MCTELL, Willie Samuel as Blind Willie McTell

TITLE/FLIP	LABEL & NO.	GOOD TO VERY GOOD	NEAR MINT	YR.
IT'S MY DESIRE/Hide Me In Thy Bosom (78)	Regal 3272	5.00	20.00	50

MCTELL, Willie Samuel as The Pig 'N' Whistle Band

TITLE/FLIP	LABEL & NO.	GOOD TO VERY GOOD	NEAR MINT	YR.
LOVE CHANGING BLUES/Talking To You, Mama (78)	Regal 3277	7.00	28.00	50

McVEA, Jack
see Savoys, The
see Sharps, The

MEADOWLARKS, Don Julian & The

TITLE/FLIP	LABEL & NO.	GOOD TO VERY GOOD	NEAR MINT	YR.
ALWAYS AND ALWAYS/I Got Tore Up	Dootone 367	7.00	28.00	55
BLUE MOOD/There's A Girl	Original Sound 12	1.50	6.00	59
BLUE MOON/Big Mama Wants To Rock	Dooto 424	4.00	16.00	57
HEAVEN AND PARADISE/Embarrassing Moments	Dootone 359	5.00	20.00	55
I AM A BELIEVER/Boogie Woogie Teenage	Dootone 405	4.00	16.00	56
PLEASE LOVE A FOOL/Oop Boopy Oop	Dootone 394	5.00	20.00	56
PLEASE/Doin' The Cha Cha Cha	Original Sound 03	1.50	6.00	58
THIS MUST BE PARADISE/Mine All Mine	Dootone 372	5.00	20.00	55

MEADOWLARKS, The

TITLE/FLIP	LABEL & NO.	GOOD TO VERY GOOD	NEAR MINT	YR.
LOVE ONLY YOU/Real Pretty Mamma	RPM 399	15.00	60.00	54
LSMFT BLUES/Pass The Gin	RPM 406	20.00	80.00	54

MEDALLIONAIRES, The

TITLE/FLIP	LABEL & NO.	GOOD TO VERY GOOD	NEAR MINT	YR.
MAGIC MOONLIGHT/Teen-age Caravan	Mercury 71309	7.00	28.00	58

MEDALLIONS, Johnny Twovoice & The

TITLE/FLIP	LABEL & NO.	GOOD TO VERY GOOD	NEAR MINT	YR.
MY PRETTY BABY/I'll Never Love Again	Dootone 373	6.25	25.00	55

MEDALLIONS, The

TITLE/FLIP	LABEL & NO.	GOOD TO VERY GOOD	NEAR MINT	YR.
BEHIND THE DOOR/Rocket Ship	Dooto 454	2.50	10.00	59
DEAR DARLING/Don't Shoot, Baby	Dootone 379	5.00	20.00	55
EDNA/Speedin'	Dootone 364	5.00	20.00	55
59 VOLVO/Magic Mountain	Dooto 446	3.00	12.00	59
I WANT A LOVE/Dance And Swing	Dootone 393	5.00	20.00	56
LETTER, THE/Buick 59	Dootone 347	5.00	20.00	54
LOVER'S PRAYER/Unseen	Dooto 425	5.00	20.00	57
TELEGRAM, THE/Coupe De Ville Baby	Dootone 357	5.00	20.00	55

MEDALLIONS, The

TITLE/FLIP	LABEL & NO.	GOOD TO VERY GOOD	NEAR MINT	YR.
BROKEN HEART, A/Lolo Baby	Singular 1002	3.00	12.00	—

MEDALLIONS, The

TITLE/FLIP	LABEL & NO.	GOOD TO VERY GOOD	NEAR MINT	YR.
I KNOW/Laki-Lani	Essex 901	25.00	100.00	55

MEDALLIONS, Vernon Green & The

TITLE/FLIP	LABEL & NO.	GOOD TO VERY GOOD	NEAR MINT	YR.
DID YOU HAVE FUN?/My Mary Lou	Dootone 407	5.00	20.00	56
FOR BETTER OR FOR WORSE/I Wonder, Wonder, Wonder	Dooto 419	5.00	20.00	57
PUSHBUTTON AUTOMOBILE/Shedding Tears For You	Dootone 400	5.00	20.00	56

MEL & TIM

MEL-O-AIRES, Rudy Jackson & The

TITLE/FLIP	LABEL & NO.	GOOD TO VERY GOOD	NEAR MINT	YR.
I'M CRYING/Enfold Me	R & B 1310	5.00	20.00	55

MEL-O-DOTS, The

TITLE/FLIP	LABEL & NO.	GOOD TO VERY GOOD	NEAR MINT	YR.
ONE MORE TIME/Just How Long?	Apollo 1192	50.00	200.00	52

MELL-O-TONES, Doug Williams & The

TITLE/FLIP	LABEL & NO.	GOOD TO VERY GOOD	NEAR MINT	YR.
SORROW VALLEY/How Many Souls? (with Ida Haynes)	Hy-Tone 103	10.00	40.00	—
SORROW VALLEY/The Battle Of Jericho	Hy-Tone 122	9.00	36.00	59

MELLARDS, Fred Green & The

TITLE/FLIP	LABEL & NO.	GOOD TO VERY GOOD	NEAR MINT	YR.
YOU CAN'T KEEP LOVE IN A BROKEN HEART/ My Sweetheart	Ballad 1012/1013	10.00	40.00	53

MELLO-FELLOWS, The

TITLE/FLIP	LABEL & NO.	GOOD TO VERY GOOD	NEAR MINT	YR.
IDDY BIDDY BABY/My Friend, Charlie	Lamp 8006	2.50	10.00	54

MELLO-HARPS, The

TITLE/FLIP	LABEL & NO.	GOOD TO VERY GOOD	NEAR MINT	YR.
I LOVE ONLY YOU/Ain't Got The Money	Tin Pan Alley 145/146	15.00	60.00	55
LOVE IS A VOW/Valerie	Do-Re-Mi 203	125.00	500.00	—
NO GOOD/Gumma, Gumma	Casino 104	2.50	10.00	58
WHAT GOOD ARE MY DREAMS?/Gone	Tin Pan Alley 157/158	20.00	80.00	56

MELLO-MOODS, The

TITLE/FLIP	LABEL & NO.	GOOD TO VERY GOOD	NEAR MINT	YR.
CALL ON ME/I Tried, Tried And Tried	Prestige 799	50.00	200.00	52
I COULDN'T SLEEP A WINK LAST NIGHT/ And You Just Can't Go Through Life Alone	Red Robin 104	75.00	300.00	52
I'M LOST/When I Woke Up This Morning	Prestige 856	45.00	180.00	53
WHERE ARE YOU?/How Could You?	Red Robin 105	50.00	200.00	51

MELLO-QUEENS, John Lester & The

MELLO-TONE THREE, Little "E" & The

MELLO-TONES, Marga Benitez & The

TITLE/FLIP	LABEL & NO.	GOOD TO VERY GOOD	NEAR MINT	YR.
MAN LOVE WOMAN/Winos On Parade	Decca 48318	20.00	80.00	54

MELLO-TONES, Nat Williams & The

TITLE/FLIP	LABEL & NO.	GOOD TO VERY GOOD	NEAR MINT	YR.
YOU EXCITE ME/A Friend	Aries 1014	2.50	10.00	59

MELLO-TONES, The

TITLE/FLIP	LABEL & NO.	GOOD TO VERY GOOD	NEAR MINT	YR.
I'M JUST ANOTHER ONE IN LOVE WITH YOU/ I'm Gonna Get	Decca 48319	25.00	100.00	54

MELLOMOODS, Chuck Higgins & The

TITLE/FLIP	LABEL & NO.	GOOD TO VERY GOOD	NEAR MINT	YR.
BEAUTIFUL LOVE/Rock & Roll (instrumental)	Money 214	7.00	28.00	56

MELLOMOODS, The

TITLE/FLIP	LABEL & NO.	GOOD TO VERY GOOD	NEAR MINT	YR.
SONG OF LOVE/That Dubonnet Wine	Recorded In Hollywood 396	40.00	160.00	54

Marvin & Johnny

The Marcels

Clyde McPhatter

The Meadowlarks

The Medallions

TITLE/FLIP	LABEL & NO.	GOOD TO VERY GOOD	NEAR MINT	YR.
MELLOW DROPS, The				
WHEN I GROW TOO OLD TO DREAM/The Crazy Song	Imperial 5324	10.00	40.00	54
MELLOW KEYS, The				
LISTEN, BABY/I'm Not A Deceiver	Gee 1014	3.00	12.00	56
MELLOWS, Carl Spencer & The				
FAREWELL, FAREWELL/No More Loneliness	Candlelight 1012	8.00	32.00	—
MELLOWS, Lillian Leach & The				
I WAS A FOOL TO LET YOU GO/I Still Care	Jay Dee 801	4.00	16.00	55
SMOKE FROM YOUR CIGARETTE/ Pretty Baby, What's Your Name?	Jay Dee 797	3.00	12.00	55

TITLE/FLIP	LABEL & NO.	GOOD TO VERY GOOD	NEAR MINT	YR.
YESTERDAY'S MEMORIES/Lovable Lily	Jay Dee 807	6.25	25.00	55
MELLOWS, Lillian Lee & The				
MOON OF SILVER/You've Gone	Candlelight 1011	8.00	32.00	56

TITLE/FLIP	LABEL & NO.	GOOD TO VERY GOOD	NEAR MINT	YR.
MELLOWS, Mack Starr & The				
MELLOWS, The				
HOW SENTIMENTAL CAN I BE?/Nothin' To Do	Jay Dee 793	4.00	16.00	54
I'M YOURS/Sweet Lorraine	Celeste 3004	15.00	60.00	56
MY DARLING/Lucky Guy	Celeste 3002	20.00	80.00	56
MELVIN, Harold				
MELVIN, Harold: see Blue Notes, The (with Harold Melvin)				
MEMORIES, The				
MEMOS, The				
MEMPHIS EDDIE: see Pee, Eddie as Memphis Eddie P.; see Pee, Eddie as Memphis Eddie Pee; see Pee, Eddie as Memphis Eddie				
MEMPHIS MINNIE: see Douglas, Lizzie as Memphis Minnie				
MEMPHIS SLIM: see Chatman, Peter as Memphis Slim; see Vagabonds, Memphis Slim (Peter Chatman) & The				
MERCER, Wally				
LOOPED/Yellow Hornet	Dot 1120	5.00	20.00	—
ROCK AROUND THE CLOCK/Don't Wait Till Tomorrow	Dot 1099	5.00	20.00	—
TOO OLD TO GET MARRIED/ If You Don't Mean Business	Trumpet 227	3.00	12.00	—
MERCY BABY: see Mullins, Jimmy as Mercy Baby				
MERCY DEE: see Walton, Mercy Dee as Mercy Dee				
MERRITT, Daddy: see Merritt, Melvin as Daddy Merritt				
MERRITT, Melvin as The Daddy Merritt Quintet				
KNOCKOUT BLUES/My Daddy Loves It (78)	Monogram 203	1.50	6.00	50
MERRIWEATHER, Major as Big Maceo				
DO YOU REMEMBER?/Big City Blues (78)	Specialty 320	2.00	8.00	49
LEAVIN' BLUES/Have You Heard About It? (78)	Fortune 137	4.00	16.00	52
ONE SUNDAY MORNING/Just Tell Me Baby (78)	Specialty 346	2.00	8.00	49
WORRIED LIFE BLUES, NO. 2/Strange To Me Blues (78)	Fortune 805	4.00	16.00	52
METALLICS, The				
DROP BY/Get Lost	Baronet 14	2.00	8.00	62
LET ME LOVE YOU/	Baronet 16	3.00	12.00	—
METRONOMES, Gene Moore & The				
SHE'S GONE/That's Bad	Specialty 472	20.00	80.00	53
METRONOMES, The				
DEAR DON/How Much I Love You	Cadence 1339	7.00	28.00	57
I LOVE MY GIRL/I'm Gonna' Get Me A Girl Somehow	Cadence 1310	7.00	28.00	57
METRONOMES, The				
MY DEAREST DARLING/The Chickie-Goo	Maureen 1000	3.00	12.00	62
METROPOLITANS, The				
SO MUCH IN LOVE/My Heart Is True	Junior 395	1.50	6.00	58
METROS, The				
METROTONES, The				
PLEASE COME BACK/Skitter, Skatter	Reserve 116	20.00	80.00	57
MEYERS, Louie: see Myers, Louis as Louie Meyers				
MG'S, Booker T. & The				

MICKEY & SYLVIA (Mickey Baker & Little Sylvia Vanderpool)

TITLE/FLIP	LABEL & NO.	GOOD TO VERY GOOD	NEAR MINT	YR.
BECAUSE YOU/Love Drops	*All Platinum 2307*	1.50	6.00	—
FROM THE BEGINNING OF TIME/ Fallin' In Love	*RCA Victor 47-8582*	1.50	6.00	65
I'M SO GLAD/Se De Boom Run Dun	*Rainbow 316*	1.50	6.00	—
RISE, SALLY, RISE/Forever And A Day	*Rainbow 318*	1.50	6.00	—

MICKLE, Elmon

Most of the few songs Mickle recorded under his own name were on his own record labels, E. M. and Elko.

TITLE/FLIP	LABEL & NO.	GOOD TO VERY GOOD	NEAR MINT	YR.
FLATFOOT SAM/I Got To Get Some Money	*Elko 003*	4.00	16.00	59
LONESOME HIGHWAY/Jackson Blues	*E. M. 132*	4.00	16.00	59
LONESOME HIGHWAY/Short 'N' Fat	*E. M. 132*	5.00	20.00	59

MICKLE, Elmon & His Rhythm Aces

TITLE/FLIP	LABEL & NO.	GOOD TO VERY GOOD	NEAR MINT	YR.
INDEPENDENT WALK/Short And Fat	*J Gems 1908*	2.00	8.00	59

MICKLE, Elmon as Driftin' Slim/Drifting Smith

TITLE/FLIP	LABEL & NO.	GOOD TO VERY GOOD	NEAR MINT	YR.
GOOD MORNING, BABY/My Sweet Woman (78)	*RPM 370*	3.00	12.00	52
MY LITTLE MACHINE/Down South Blues (78)	*Modern 849*	4.00	16.00	51

MICKLE, Elmon as Model T Slim

TITLE/FLIP	LABEL & NO.	GOOD TO VERY GOOD	NEAR MINT	YR.
SHAKE YOUR BOOGIE/Good Morning, Little Schoolgirl	*Wonder 15001/2*	3.00	12.00	66

MIDDLETON, Tony & The Willows: see Willows, Tony Middleton & The

MIDNIGHTERS, Hank Ballard & The

MIDNIGHTERS, Henry Booth & The

MIDNIGHTERS, The

TITLE/FLIP	LABEL & NO.	GOOD TO VERY GOOD	NEAR MINT	YR.
ANNIE HAD A BABY/She's The One	*Federal 12195*	2.50	10.00	54
ANNIE'S AUNT FANNY/Crazy Loving	*Federal 12200*	2.50	10.00	54
ASHAMED OF MYSELF/Ring A-Ling, A-Ling	*Federal 12210*	1.50	6.00	55
DON'T CHANGE YOUR PRETTY WAYS/ We'll Never Meet Again	*Federal 12243*	1.50	6.00	55
GIVE IT UP/That Woman	*Federal 12177*	3.00	12.00	54
HENRY'S GOT FLAT FEET/Whatsoever You Do	*Federal 12224*	1.50	6.00	55
IT'S LOVE, BABY/Looka Here	*Federal 12227*	1.50	6.00	55
SEXY WAYS/Don't Say Your Last Goodbye	*Federal 12185*	2.50	10.00	54
SWITCHIE, WITCHIE, TITCHIE/Why Are We Apart?	*Federal 12220*	1.50	6.00	55
TELL THEM/Stingy Little Thing	*Federal 12202*	2.00	8.00	54
THAT HOUSE ON THE HILL/Rock & Roll Wedding	*Federal 12240*	1.50	6.00	55

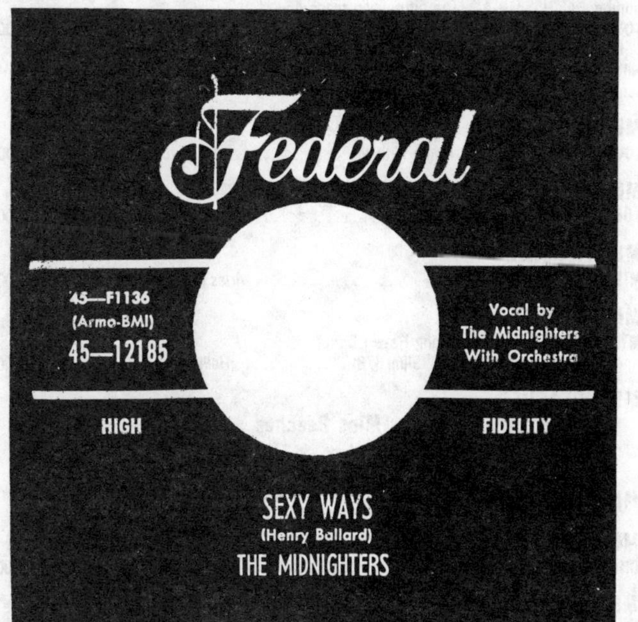

MIDNIGHTERS, The as The Royals

TITLE/FLIP	LABEL & NO.	GOOD TO VERY GOOD	NEAR MINT	YR.
MOONRISE/She's The One	*Federal 12205*	1.50	6.00	54

MIDNIGHTS, The

TITLE/FLIP	LABEL & NO.	GOOD TO VERY GOOD	NEAR MINT	YR.
ANNIE PULLED A HUM-BUG/Hear My Plea	*Music City 746*	4.00	16.00	54
SHE LEFT ME/Cheating On Me	*Music City 762*	5.00	20.00	54

MIGHTY DUKES, The

TITLE/FLIP	LABEL & NO.	GOOD TO VERY GOOD	NEAR MINT	YR.
NO OTHER LOVE/Why Can't I Have You?	*Duke 104*	5.00	20.00	52

MIGHTY FLEA

MIGHTY HANNIBAL

MIGHTY JUPITERS, The

TITLE/FLIP	LABEL & NO.	GOOD TO VERY GOOD	NEAR MINT	YR.
YOUR LOVE/Hy Wocky Toomba	*Warner 1020*	7.00	28.00	—

MIGHTY MARVELOWS, The

MIKE & THE MODIFIERS: see Modifiers, Mike & The

MILBURN, Amos

TITLE/FLIP	LABEL & NO.	GOOD TO VERY GOOD	NEAR MINT	YR.
AFTER MIDNIGHT/Amos' Blues (78)	*Aladdin 159*	2.00	8.00	45
AIN'T NOTHING SHAKING/Just One More Drink	*Aladdin 3093*	5.00	20.00	49
AMOS' BOOGIE (instrumental)/ (78)	*Aladdin 173*	2.00	8.00	46
BAD BAD WHISKEY/I'm Going To Tell My Mama	*Aladdin 3068*	7.00	28.00	49
BOOGIE WOOGIE/She's Gone Again	*Aladdin 3105*	5.00	20.00	49
CHICKEN SHACK BOOGIE/It Took A Long, Long Time	*Aladdin 3014*	10.00	40.00	47
CHICKEN SHACK/Juice, Juice, Juice	*Aladdin 3332*	2.50	10.00	56
DOWN THE ROAD APIECE/Don't Beg Me (78)	*Aladdin 161*	2.00	8.00	45
EVERYBODY CLAP HANDS/That Was Your Last Mistake	*Aladdin 3090*	5.00	20.00	49
FLYING HOME/Put Something In My Hand	*Aladdin 3125*	4.00	16.00	52
GLORY OF LOVE/Baby, You Thrill Me	*Aladdin 3248*	2.00	8.00	49
GOOD GOOD WHISKEY/Let's Have A Party	*Aladdin 3218*	3.00	12.00	53
GREYHOUND/Kiss Me Again	*Aladdin 3150*	3.00	12.00	52
HOUSE PARTY/I Guess I'll Go	*Aladdin 3306*	2.50	10.00	55
JITTERBUG PARADE/Hold Me, Baby (78)	*Aladdin 3023*	1.50	6.00	47
LET ME GO HOME, WHISKEY/Three Times A Fool	*Aladdin 3164*	4.00	16.00	52
LET'S ROCK AWHILE/Tears, Tears, Tears	*Aladdin 3080*	5.00	20.00	49
MILK AND WATER/I'm Still A Fool For You	*Aladdin 3240*	2.50	10.00	54
MONEY HUSTLIN' WOMAN/Real Gone (78)	*Aladdin 191*	2.00	8.00	47
MY BABY'S BOOGIE/Darling, How Long? (78)	*Aladdin 160*	2.00	8.00	45
MY HAPPINESS DEPENDS ON YOU/All Is Well	*Aladdin 3293*	1.50	6.00	55
MY LOVE IS LIMITED/Blues At Sundown (78)	*Aladdin 201*	2.00	8.00	47
ONE SCOTCH, ONE BOURBON, ONE BEER/ What Can I Do?	*Aladdin 3197*	3.00	12.00	53
ONE TWO THREE EVERYBODY/That's It	*Aladdin 3269*	2.00	8.00	54
OPERATION BLUES/Cinch Blues (78)	*Aladdin 174*	2.00	8.00	46
PLEASE, MR. JOHNSON/Long, Long Day	*Aladdin 3168*	3.00	12.00	52
POT LUCK BOOGIE (instrumental)/ In The Middle Of The Night (78)	*Aladdin 3026*	1.50	6.00	47
ROCK, ROCK, ROCK/Boo Hoo	*Aladdin 3159*	4.00	16.00	52
ROCKY MOUNTAIN/How Could You Hurt Me So?	*Aladdin 3226*	3.00	12.00	52
ROLL, MR. JELLY/I Won't Be A Fool Anymore	*Aladdin 3133*	4.00	16.00	52
ROOMIN' HOUSE BOOGIE/Empty Arm Blues (78)	*Aladdin 3032*	1.50	6.00	47
SAD AND BLUES/That's My Chick (78)	*Aladdin 202*	2.00	8.00	47
THINKIN' AND DRINKIN'/Trouble In Mind	*Aladdin 3124*	4.00	16.00	52
VICIOUS VICIOUS VODKA/I Done Done It	*Aladdin 3253*	2.00	8.00	54

MILES, Buddy

MILES, Lenny

MILES, Luke "Long Gone"

TITLE/FLIP	LABEL & NO.	GOOD TO VERY GOOD	NEAR MINT	YR.
LONG GONE/War Time Blues	*Smash 1755*	2.00	8.00	61

MILES, Luke "Long Gone" & The Boys From 25th Street

TITLE/FLIP	LABEL & NO.	GOOD TO VERY GOOD	NEAR MINT	YR.
LENA MAE/38 Pistol	*Two Kings 100*	1.50	6.00	65
LOSING MY MIND/Early One Morning	*Two Kings 101*	1.50	6.00	65

MILLER BROTHERS, The

MILLER SISTERS, Jeannie & The

MILLER SISTERS, The

TITLE/FLIP	LABEL & NO.	GOOD TO VERY GOOD	NEAR MINT	YR.
GUESS WHO?/How Am I To Know?	*Ember 1004*	1.50	6.00	56
LET'S START ANEW/The Flip Skip	*Acme 111*	1.50	6.00	57
MY OWN/Sugar Candy	*Onyx 507*	2.00	8.00	57
PLEASE DON'T LEAVE/Do You Wanna Go?	*Hull 718*	1.50	6.00	—
YOU MADE ME A PROMISE/Crazy Billboard Song	*Acme 717*	1.50	6.00	57

MILLER, Aleck "Rice:" see Williamson, Sonny Boy #2

MILLER, Big & The Five Pennies

MILLER, Tal

TITLE/FLIP — *LABEL & NO.* — GOOD TO VERY GOOD — NEAR MINT — *YR.*

MILLER, Walter & The Yellow Jackets

MILLER, Walter:
see Barons, Walter Miller & The

MILLET, Lil & The Creoles:
see Creoles, Lil Millet & The

MILLET, Lou
JUST YOU AND ME/Whisper Of Doubt .... *Ace 506* 20.00 80.00 *53*

MILLINDER, Lucky
CHEW TOBACCO RAG/Georgia Rose .... *King 4449* 5.00 20.00 *51*
D NATURAL BLUES (instrumental)/
Little Girl Don't Cry (red plastic) .... *RCA Victor 50-0054* 4.00 16.00 *49*
GRAPE VINE, THE/No One Else Could Be .... *King 4476* 4.00 16.00 *51*
I'M WAITING FOR YOU/Bongo Boogie .... *King 4453* 2.00 8.00 *51*
RIGHT KIND OF LOVIN', THE/
It's Been A Long, Long Time (red plastic) .... *King 4496* 6.25 25.00 *51*
RIGHT KIND OF LOVIN', THE/It's Been A Long, Long Time ... *King 4496* 3.00 12.00 *51*

MILLIONAIRES, The
SOMEBODY'S LYIN'/Kansas Kapers .... *Davis 441* 2.50 10.00 *55*

MILLS, Yvonne & The Sensations:
see Sensations, Yvonne Mills & The

MILTON, Buddy & The Twilighters:
see Twilighters, Buddy Milton & The

MILTON, Roy
BELIEVE ME, BABY/Blue Turning Grey Over You......... *Specialty 446* 6.25 25.00 *52*
This record's higher collector value is because of the group harmony.
BIRD IN HAND/Make Me Know It .... *Specialty 489* 1.50 6.00 *54*
DON'T YOU REMEMBER, BABY?/Some Day (red plastic) ... *Specialty 458* 3.00 12.00 *52*
DON'T YOU REMEMBER, BABY?/Some Day .... *Specialty 458* 1.50 6.00 *52*
FLYING SAUCER/As Time Goes By .... *Specialty 436* 1.50 6.00 *52*
GROOVIN' WITH JOE/Blues In My Heart (78) ....*Roy Milton 111* 2.50 10.00 *46*
Released with a special picture label using a cartoon drawing.
I STOOD BY/Baby, Don't You Know? .... *Specialty 480* 1.50 6.00 *54*
IT'S TOO LATE/Gonna Leave You, Baby .... *Specialty 526* 1.50 6.00 *55*
LET ME GIVE YOU ALL MY LOVE/
Early In The Morning (red plastic) .... *Specialty 464* 3.00 12.00 *54*
LET ME GIVE YOU ALL MY LOVE/Early In The Morning.... *Specialty 464* 1.50 6.00 *54*
NIGHT AND DAY/Am I Wasting My Time? .... *Specialty 438* 1.50 6.00 *52*
PACK YOUR SACK, JACK/ (78) .... *Miltone 219* 2.50 10.00 *46*
Released with a special picture label using a cartoon drawing.
SHORT, SWEET AND SNAPPY/Best Wishes .... *Specialty 414* 2.50 10.00 *50*
SO TIRED/Thelma Lou .... *Specialty 429* 2.00 8.00 *51*
TELL IT LIKE IT IS/How Can I Live Without You? .... *Specialty 538* 1.50 6.00 *55*
THEM THERE EYES/Little Boy Blue (78)...............*Roy Milton 207* 2.50 10.00 *46*
Released with a special picture label using a cartoon drawing.
WHAT CAN I DO?/Baby, Don't Do That To Me .... *Specialty 545* 1.50 6.00 *55*

MIMMS, Garnet & The Enchanters

MINOR CHORDS, Sunnie Elmo & The
INDIAN LOVE CALL/Let Me .... *Flick 009* 3.00 12.00 *60*

MINOR CHORDS, The
DON'T LET ME DOWN/I'm Falling In Love With You.......... *Flick 006* 3.00 12.00 *59*

MINORBOPS, The
NEED YOU TONIGHT/I Want You For My Own ....*Lamp 2012* 25.00 100.00 *57*

MINORS, The
JERRY/Where Are You? .... *Celeste 3007* 50.00 200.00 *57*

MINT JULEPS, The
BELLS OF LOVE/Vip-A-Dip .... *Herald 481* 4.00 16.00 *56*

MINTER, Iverson as Louisiana Red

MINTER, Iverson as Playboy Fuller
GONNA PLAY MY GUITAR/Sugar Cane Highway (78).........*Fuller 171* 75.00 300.00 *52*

MINTER, Iverson as Rocky Fuller
SOON ONE MORNING/Come On Baby, Now (78) ....*Checker 753* 6.25 25.00 *52*

MIRACLES, Carl Hogan & The
I LOVE YOU SO/Your Love .... *Fury 1002/1003* 15.00 60.00 *57*

MIRACLES, Smokey Robinson & The
I CARE ABOUT DETROIT (one sided record)..... *Standard Groove 13090* 3.00 12.00 *67*

MINOR CHORDS, The
DON'T LET ME DOWN/I'm Falling In Love With You.......... *Flick 006* 3.00 12.00 *59*

MINORBOPS, The
NEED YOU TONIGHT/I Want You For My Own ....*Lamp 2012* 25.00 100.00 *57*

MINORS, The
JERRY/Where Are You? .... *Celeste 3007* 50.00 200.00 *57*

MINT JULEPS, The
BELLS OF LOVE/Vip-A-Dip .... *Herald 481* 4.00 16.00 *56*

MINTER, Iverson as Louisiana Red

MINTER, Iverson as Playboy Fuller
GONNA PLAY MY GUITAR/Sugar Cane Highway (78).........*Fuller 171* 75.00 300.00 *52*

MINTER, Iverson as Rocky Fuller
SOON ONE MORNING/Come On Baby, Now (78) ....*Checker 753* 6.25 25.00 *52*

MIRACLES, Carl Hogan & The
I LOVE YOU SO/Your Love .... *Fury 1002/1003* 15.00 60.00 *57*

MIRACLES, Smokey Robinson & The
I CARE ABOUT DETROIT (one sided record)..... *Standard Groove 13090* 3.00 12.00 *67*
This unusual record was prepared and released during the 1967 race riots in Detroit, as an effort to help quell the violence. The material, which later appeared on a various artists LP, was written and produced "by permission and co-operation of Motown" records.

MIRACLES, The (featuring Smokey Robinson)
The Tamla releases changed the label credits to Smokey Robinson & The Miracles early in 1967.
BAD GIRL/I Love Your Baby .... *Motown G1* 60.00 240.00 *59*
BAD GIRL/I Love Your Baby .... *Motown TLX 2207* 70.00 280.00 *59*
GOT A JOB/My Mama Done Told Me .... *End 1016* 2.00 8.00 *58*
MONEY/Cry .... *End 1029* 2.00 8.00 *58*
SHOP AROUND (alternate to the hit version/
Who's Lovin' You? .... *Tamla 54034* 7.00 28.00 *60*
Two different recorded versions of "Shop Around" were released with the same number and label. The hit version is of little collector value. The rare "alternate" version can be distinguished from the hit release by the numbers etched in the vinyl, near the label. The rare and valuable issue has the numbers 45-H55518 A-2. The hit version reads 45-L1(3).
YOU CAN DEPEND ON ME/The Feeling Is So Fine.......... *Tamla 54028* 8.00 32.00 *60*
Two different recorded versions of "You Can Depend On Me" were released with the same number and label. Their value and rarity are essentially the same.

MIRACLES, The
LOVERS' CHANT, A/Come Home With Me .... *Baton 210* 7.00 28.00 *55*

MIRACLES, The
YOU'RE AN ANGEL/A Gal Named Jo .... *Cash 1008* 15.00 60.00 *55*

MISFITS, The
MIDNIGHT STAR/I Don't Know.................. *Aries (no number)* 4.00 16.00 —

MISS COUNTRY SLIM
MY GIRLISH DAYS/What Wrong Have I Done?
(by Ernest Lewis as Country Slim) (78) .... *Hollywood 1005* 7.00 28.00 *53*

MISS PEACHES:
see Griner, Elsie as Miss Peaches
see James. Etta

MISSILES, The

MISTAKES, The
CHAPEL BELLS/I Got Fired........................ *Lo-Fi 2311-2312* 3.00 12.00 —

MITCHEL, Lonnie
WATUSI BEAT/Louisiana Slo-Drag .... *Ivory 136/137* 2.00 8.00 *61*

MITCHELL, Billy Group, The

MITCHELL, Billy:
see Morris, Joe & His Orchestra

The Mellow-Tones

The Midnighters

The Moonglows and Moonlighters

Johnny Otis and Junior Ryder

The Paragons

TITLE/FLIP	LABEL & NO.	GOOD TO VERY GOOD	NEAR MINT	YR.
MITCHELL, Bobby				
MITCHELL, Bobby & The Toppers: see Toppers, Bobby Mitchell & The				
MITCHELL, McKinley				
MITCHELL, Rose				
LIVE MY LIFE/Baby, Please Don't Go	Imperial 5260	4.00	16.00	54
SLIPPIN' IN/I'm Searchin'	Imperial 5243	4.00	16.00	54
MITCHELL, Walter				
STOP MESSING AROUND/Pet Milk Blues (78)	JVB 75827	10.00	40.00	48
MITCHELL, Willie				
MITCHELL, Willie & The Four Kings: see Four Kings, Willie Mitchell & The				
MIXERS, The				
LOVE & KISSES/Casanova	Bold 102	20.00	80.00	59
YOU SAID YOU'RE LEAVING ME/Johnny's Got A Girl Friend	Bold 101	20.00	80.00	58
MIXMASTERS, Sonny Fulton & The				
MOBILE STRUGGLERS, The				
MEMPHIS BLUES/Fattenin' Frogs (78)	American Music 104	4.00	16.00	49
MODEL T SLIM: see Mickle, Elmon as Model T Slim				
MODERN RED CAPS, George Tindley & The				
MODERN RED CAPS, The				
MODERNISTICS, Al Lewis & The				
WHAT WILL THE OUTCOME BE?/ Can't Get You Out Of My Mind (by Lord Luther)	Music City 829	2.00	8.00	—
MODIFIERS, Mike & The				
I FOUND MYSELF A BRAND NEW BABY/It's Too Bad	Gordy 7006	1.50	6.00	62
MOHAWKS, Popcorn & The				
SHIMMY GULLY/Custer's Last Man	Motown 1002	1.50	6.00	60
MOHAWKS, The				
MONARCHS, The				
ALWAYS BE FAITHFUL/How Are You?	Neil 103	7.00	28.00	—
PRETTY LITTLE GIRL/In My Younger Days	Neil 101	2.50	10.00	56
MONARCHS, The				
ANGELS IN THE SKY/Wanna Go Home	Wing 90040	8.00	32.00	55
MONDELLOS, Alice Jean & The				
100 YEARS FROM TODAY/Come Back Home	Rhythm 102	20.00	80.00	57
MONDELLOS, Rudy Lambert & The				
MY HEART/That's What I Call Love	Rhythm 114	20.00	80.00	58
MONDELLOS, The				
HARD TO PLEASE/Happiness Street	Rhythm 109	20.00	80.00	57
THAT'S WHAT I CALL LOVE/Daylight Saving Time	Rhythm 106	20.00	80.00	57
MONDELLOS, Yul McClay & The				
MONIQUES, The				
MONITORS, The				
BOY FRIEND'S PRAYER, A/Nita	Circus 219	10.00	40.00	—
MONITORS, The				
OUR SCHOOL DAYS/I've Got A Dream	Specialty 595	5.00	20.00	57
MONOGRAMS, The				
PLEASE, BABY, PLEASE/My Baby, Dearest Darling	Saga 1000	7.00	28.00	—
MONORAYS, The				
MY GUARDIAN ANGEL/Five Minutes To Love You	Tammy 1005	5.00	20.00	59

TITLE/FLIP	LABEL & NO.	GOOD TO VERY GOOD	NEAR MINT	YR.
MONOTONES, The				
BOOK OF LOVE/You Never Loved Me	Mascot 124	15.00	60.00	57
DADDY'S HOME BUT MOMMA'S GONE/Tattletale	Hull 743	1.50	6.00	61
LEGEND OF SLEEPY HOLLOW, THE/Soft Shadows	Argo 5321	1.50	6.00	58
READING THE BOOK OF LOVE/Dream	Hull 735	6.25	25.00	60
TELL IT TO THE JUDGE/Fools Will Be Fools	Argo 5339	1.50	6.00	59
TOM FOOLERY/Zombi	Argo 5301	1.50	6.00	58
MONROE, Vince				
GIVE IT UP/If I Had My Life To Live Over	Excello 2089	2.50	10.00	56
MONTCLAIRS, Mel Williams & The				
MONTCLAIRS, The				
GOLDEN ANGEL/Don Juan	Hi-Q 5001	2.50	10.00	57
MONTCLAIRS, The				
GIVE ME A CHANCE/My Every Dream	Premium 404	10.00	40.00	—
MONTEREYS, Dean Barlow & The				
ANGEL/Tell Me Why	Onyx 517	8.00	32.00	57
DEAREST ONE/Through The Years	Onyx 513	5.00	20.00	57
MONTEREYS, The				
SOMEONE LIKE YOU/Train Whistle Blues	Nestor 15	12.50	50.00	56
SOMEONE LIKE YOU/Train Whistle Blues	Teenage 1001	9.00	36.00	56
MONTRELL, Roy				
EVERYTIME I HEAR THAT MELLOW SAXOPHONE/ Ooh Wow	Specialty 583	2.00	8.00	56
IT AIN'T NOTHIN' BUT A DREAM/How Much Longer?	Specialty 491	2.00	8.00	54
LET IT LAY/I Don't Know Why	Specialty 456	2.00	8.00	54
MY BABY'S GONE AGAIN/I'm Beggin' You, Baby	Specialty 462	2.00	8.00	54
MOOHAH				
ALL SHOOK OUT/Candy	Starmaker 501	5.00	20.00	54
MOONBEEMS, The				
TEEN AGE BABY/Cryin' The Blues	Sapphire 1052	5.00	20.00	58
MOONGLOWS, The				
FOOLISH ME/Slow Down	Chess 1598	2.50	10.00	55
I JUST CAN'T TELL NO LIE/I've Been Your Dog	Champagne 7500	40.00	160.00	52
I WAS WRONG/ Ooh, Rocking Daddy (black and white label)	Chance 1156	30.00	120.00	54
I WAS WRONG/ Ooh, Rocking Daddy (yellow and black label)	Chance 1156	40.00	160.00	54
I'M AFRAID THE MASQUERADE IS OVER/ Don't Say Goodbye	Chess 1651	1.50	6.00	56
IN MY DIARY/Lover, Love Me	Chess 1611	5.00	20.00	55
JUST A LONELY CHRISTMAS/Hey, Santa Claus!	Chance 1150	50.00	200.00	53
MOST OF ALL/She's Gone	Chess 1589	8.00	32.00	54
OVER AND OVER AGAIN (fast version)/ I Knew From The Start	Chess 1646	1.50	6.00	56
OVER AND OVER AGAIN (slow version)/ I Knew From The Start	Chess 1646	1.50	6.00	56
The slow version release of "Over And Over Again" may be identified on the label by the side number 8189A.				
PLEASE SEND ME SOMEONE TO LOVE/Mr. Engineer	Chess 1661	3.00	12.00	57
SECRET LOVE/ Real Gone Mama (blue and silver label)	Chanco 1152	50,00	200.00	54
SECRET LOVE/ Real Gone Mama (yellow and black label)	Chance 1152	40.00	160.00	54
SEE SAW/When I'm With You	Chess 1629	2.50	10.00	56
SINCERELY/Tempting	Chess 1581	6.25	25.00	54
STARLITE/In Love	Chess 1605	4.00	16.00	55
219 TRAIN/My Gal (yellow and black label)	Chance 1161	80.00	240.00	54
219 TRAIN/My Gal (black and white label)	Chance 1161	90.00	280.00	54
WE GO TOGETHER/Chickie Um Bah	Chess 1619	2.00	8.00	56
WHISTLE, MY LOVE/Baby, Please (red plastic)	Chance 1147	100.00	400.00	53
MOONGLOWS, The: see Diddley, Bo				
MOORE, Alexander				
IF I LOSE YOU, WOMAN/Neglected Woman (78)	RPM 326	2.50	10.00	51
MOORE, Bobby & The Fourmost				
MOORE, Bobby & The Rhythm Aces				

TITLE/FLIP	LABEL & NO.	GOOD TO VERY GOOD	NEAR MINT	YR.
MOORE, Gene:				
see Chimes, Gene Moore & The				
see Metronomes, Gene Moore & The				
MOORE, Hank				
RECONSIDER, BABY/Knock-Kneed Rooster	5-4 5425	3.00	12.00	—
SOUR MASH/Part Time	5-4 5426	1.50	6.00	—
MOORE, Jackie				
MOORE, James as Slim Harpo				
MOORE, Johnny as Johnny Moore's Blazers				
CHRISTMAS EVE BABY/Christmas Everyday	Hollywood 1045	2.00	8.00	55
I SEND MY LOVE/Next Time We Meet	Hollywood 1056	2.00	8.00	56
WHY JOHNNY WHY (with Linda Hayes)/Johnny Ace's Last Letter	Hollywood 1031	4.00	16.00	55
MOORE, Johnny as Johnny Moore's Three Blazers				
BOP-A-BYE BABY/What Does It Matter? (red plastic)	RCA Victor 50-0018	2.50	10.00	49
JUMPING JACK/ Someday You'll Need Me (red plastic)	RCA Victor 50-0095	2.50	10.00	50
MISERY BLUES/Rock With It (red plastic)	RCA Victor 50-0073	2.50	10.00	50
MISS MOSEY/Every Time	Blaze 101	1.50	6.00	—
RAIN-CHECK/Melody (red plastic)	RCA Victor 50-0086	2.50	10.00	50
SHUFFLE SHUCK/Cut Off The Fat (red plastic)	RCA Victor 50-0031	2.50	10.00	49
SO LONG/Driftin' Blues (red plastic)	RCA Victor 50-0043	2.50	10.00	49
THIS IS ONE TIME BABY/ A New Shade Of Blues (red plastic)	RCA Victor 50-0009	2.50	10.00	49
WALKIN' BLUES/ You Can Go Feed Yourself (red plastic)	RCA Victor 50-0026	2.50	10.00	49
MOORE, Johnny:				
see Dixon, Floyd with Johnny Moore's Three Blazers				
see Drifters, The (featuring Johnny Moore)				
MOORE, Martha				
BABY, I'M THROUGH/ I Needs A Whole Lot Of Everything	DeLuxe 6049	2.00	8.00	52
I GETS A HARD WAY TO GO/Yo, Yo, Yo	DeLuxe 6038	2.00	8.00	52
MOORE, Ray & The Raytones:				
see Raytones, Rudy Ray Moore as Ray Moore & The				
MOORE, Rudy Ray & The Raytones:				
see Raytones, Rudy Ray Moore & The				
MOORE, Woo Woo				
SOMETHING'S WRONG/Five Long Letters	Mercury 70204	2.50	10.00	53
MOOSE JOHN:				
see Walker, John as Moose John				
MORGANFIELD, McKinley as Muddy Waters				
APPEALING BLUES/Honey Bee (78)	Chess 1468	1.50	6.00	50
BLOW, WIND, BLOW/Mad Love	Chess 1550	4.00	16.00	53
COUNTRY BOY/All Night Long	Chess 1509	7.00	28.00	51
EARLY MORNING BLUES/She Moves Me (78)	Chess 1490	1.50	6.00	50
GYPSY WOMAN/Little Anna Mae (78)	Aristocrat 1302	4.00	16.00	47
I CAN'T BE SATISFIED/I Feel Like Going Home (78)	Aristocrat 1305	4.00	16.00	48
I WANT TO BE LOVED/My Eyes	Chess 1596	1.50	6.00	55
I'M A NATURAL BORN LOVER/Loving Man	Chess 1585	2.00	8.00	54
I'M READY/I Don't Know Why	Chess 1579	2.00	8.00	54
I'M YOUR HOOCHIE COOCHIE MAN/She's So Pretty	Chess 1560	4.00	16.00	53
JUST MAKE LOVE TO ME/Oh, Yeah	Chess 1571	2.50	10.00	54
LITTLE GENEVA/Canary Bird (78)	Aristocrat 1311	3.00	12.00	49
LONG DISTANCE CALL/Too Young To Know (78)	Chess 1452	2.00	8.00	51
LOOKING FOR MY BABY/Please Have Mercy	Chess 1514	7.00	28.00	52
LOUISIANA BLUES/Evan's Shuffle (instrumental) (78)	Chess 1441	2.00	8.00	50
MY FAULT/Still A Fool (78)	Chess 1480	2.00	8.00	51
ROLLIN' AND TUMBLIN', Part 1/ Rollin' And Tumblin', Part 2 (78)	Aristocrat 412	5.00	20.00	50
ROLLIN' STONE/Walkin' Blues (78)	Chess 1426	2.50	10.00	50
SCREAMIN' AND CRYIN'/Where's My Woman Been? (78)	Aristocrat 406	7.00	28.00	50
SHE'S ALL RIGHT/Sad, Sad Day	Chess 1537	6.25	25.00	53
STANDING AROUND CRYING/Gone To Main Street	Chess 1526	7.00	28.00	52
STREAMLINE WOMAN/ Muddy Jumps One (instrumental) (78)	Aristocrat 1310	3.00	12.00	49
TRAIN FARE HOME/Sittin' Here And Drinkin' (78)	Aristocrat 1306	4.00	16.00	48
WHO'S GONNA BE YOUR SWEET MAN?/ Turn The Lamp Down Low	Chess 1542	5.00	20.00	52
YOU'RE GONNA MISS ME/Mean Red Spider (78)	Aristocrat 1307	3.00	12.00	49
YOU'RE GONNA NEED MY HELP, I SAID/Sad Letter Blues (78)	Chess 1434	2.00	8.00	50
MORGANFIELD, McKinley as Muddy Waters:				
see Foster, Leroy & Muddy Waters				
see Luandrew, Albert as Sunnyland Slim & Muddy Waters				
MORISETTE, Johnnie				
MOROCCANS, The				
BELIEVE IN TOMORROW/You Fascinate Me	Salem 1014	15.00	60.00	57
MOROCCOS, Lillian Brooks & The				
MOROCCOS, The				
PARDON MY TEARS/Chicken	United 188	10.00	40.00	55
SAD, SAD HOURS/The Hex	United 207	15.00	60.00	57
SOMEWHERE OVER THE RAINBOW/ Red Hots And Chilli Mac	United 193	8.00	32.00	56
WHAT IS A TEEN-AGER'S PRAYER?/Bang Goes My Heart!	United 204	7.00	28.00	56
MOROCCOS, The:				
see Morrocos, The				
MORRIS, Count:				
see Dells, The				
MORRIS, Jimmy:				
see Belvederes, The				
MORRIS, Joe & His Orchestra				
BALD HEADED WOMAN/Ghost Train (Billy Mitchell vocal)	Atlantic 974	4.00	16.00	52
TRAVELIN' MAN/No, It Can't Be Done (red plastic)	Herald 420	2.50	10.00	53
MORRIS, Joe & His Orchestra:				
see Mr. Stringbean				
see Savage, Al				
see Scruggs, Faye as Faye Adams				
see Scruggs, Faye				
see Tate, Laurie				
MORRIS, Leo With Marcel & His Band				
WANTA KNOW HOW YOU FEEL/I Don't Need You	Ivory 4-1-465	1.50	6.00	61
MORRISON, Dorothy				
MORROCOS, Little Joe & The				
TROUBLE IN THE CANDY SHOP/Bubble Gum	Bumble Bee 500	2.00	8.00	—
MOSES, Johnny				
YOU'RE TORTURING ME/Do You Love Me, Do You?	Imperial 5329	2.00	8.00	55
MOSS, Bill				
MR. BEAR				
I'M GONNA KEEP MY GOOD EYE ON YOU/How Come	Groove 0125	1.50	6.00	55
MR. BEAR COMES TO TOWN/Radar	Groove 0150	1.50	6.00	55
PEEK-A-BOO/The Bear Hug	Groove 0138	1.50	6.00	55
MR. BEAR:				
see Dupree, William Thomas as Jack Dupree & Mr. Bear				
MR. BO				
TIMES ARE HARD/	Northern 3731	1.50	6.00	—
MR. BO & HIS BLUES BOYS				
MR. LEE & THE CHEROKEES				
MR. PERCY				
FULL OF MISERY/Somebody Help Me Out	Dot 1205	4.00	16.00	54
MR. SAD HEAD				
BUTCHER BOY/Mumbles Blues	RCA Victor 47-4938	2.50	10.00	52
HOT WEATHER BLUES/Sad Head Blues	RCA Victor 47-5089	2.50	10.00	52
I'M HIGH/Hard Luck And Traveling	RCA Victor 47-5230	2.50	10.00	53
MAKE HASTE/Black Diamond	RCA Victor 47-5388	2.50	10.00	53

TITLE/FLIP	LABEL & NO.	GOOD TO VERY GOOD	NEAR MINT	YR.
MR. STRINGBEAN (with Joe Morris & His Orchestra)				
PASS THE JUICE, MISS LUCY/ Who's Gonna Cry For Me? (red plastic)	Herald 418	5.00	20.00	53
PASS THE JUICE, MISS LUCY/Who's Gonna Cry For Me?	Herald 418	2.50	10.00	53
MR. UNDERTAKER: see Four Deuces, The				
MUDDY WATERS: see Morganfield, McKinley as Muddy Waters				
MULLINS, Jimmy as J. Mercy Baby				
ROCK AND STOMP, THE/So Lonesome	Mercy Baby 502	1.50	6.00	58
MULLINS, Jimmy as Mercy Baby				
PLEADIN'/Don't Lie To Me	Ric 955	1.50	6.00	57
YOU RAN AWAY/Love's Voodoo	Mercy Baby 501	1.50	6.00	58
MUMBLES: see Horton, Walter as Mumbles				
MUMFORD, Gene & The Serenaders: see Serenaders, Gene Mumford & The				
MURRAY, Mickey				
MUSICAL NOTES, Bill Johnson & The				
DON'T YOU THINK I OUGHTA KNOW?/ Shorty's Got To Go (78)	RCA Victor 20-2225	1.50	6.00	47
HALF A LOVE/Leave It To Fate, Gate (78)	RCA Victor 20-2362	1.50	6.00	47
LET'S BE SWEETHEARTS AGAIN/ Mama, Mama, Mama (78)	RCA Victor 20-2591	1.50	6.00	47
MY BABY LIKES TO BE-BOP/ All Dressed Up With A Broken Heart (78)	RCA Victor 20-2749	1.50	6.00	48
MY BABY'S GIVING ME THE BRUSH/ Elevator Boogie (78)	RCA Victor 20-3108	1.50	6.00	48
MY LITTLE REDHEAD/For Once In Your Life (78)	RCA Victor 20-2427	1.50	6.00	47
PRETTY EYED BABY/ You Didn't Have To Say I Love You (78)	RCA Victor 20-2235	1.50	6.00	47
SAY SOMETHING NICE ABOUT ME/ Believe Me, Beloved (78)	RCA Victor 20-3037	1.50	6.00	48
SO TIRED/I Learned To Cry (78)	RCA Victor 20-2618	1.50	6.00	47
THAT NIGHT WE SAID GOODBYE/ Sharkie's Boogie (78)	RCA Victor 20-2298	1.50	6.00	47
WHEN YOUR HAIR HAS TURNED TO SILVER/ Let's Walk (red plastic)	Tru-Blue 414	7.00	28.00	—
YOU'RE THE DREAM OF A LIFETIME/ Chickasaw Limited (78)	RCA Victor 20-2498	1.50	6.00	47
MUSKATEERS, The				
DEEP IN MY HEART/Love Me Til Your Dying Day	Swing Time 331	40.00	160.00	53
LOVE ME TIL YOUR DYING DAY/Goodbye, My Love	Roxy 801	20.00	80.00	—
MYERS, Louis as Louie Meyers & The Aces				
JUST WAILING/Bluesy Instrumentals.	Abco 104	8.00	32.00	56
MYERS, Sammy				
SAD, SAD LONESOME DAY/You Don't Have To Go	Fury 1035	2.00	8.00	60
MYERS, Sammy With The King Mose Royal Rockers				
MY LOVE IS HERE TO STAY/Sleeping In The Ground	Ace 536	2.50	10.00	57
MYLES, Big Boy & The Shaw-Wees: see Shaw-Wees, Big Boy Myles & The				
MYSTICS, The				
JUST FOR YOUR LOVE/The Jumpin' Bean	King 5735	2.00	8.00	63

TITLE/FLIP	LABEL & NO.	GOOD TO VERY GOOD	NEAR MINT	YR.
NABBIE, Jimmie & The Four Tunes				
NASH, Johnny				
NATIVE BOYS, The				
LAUGHING LOVE/Valley Of Lovers	Combo 119	5.00	20.00	56
NATIVE GIRL/It Won't Take Long	Modern 939	10.00	40.00	54
OH, LET ME DREAM/I've Got A Feeling	Combo 120	7.00	28.00	56
STRANGE LOVE/Cherrlyn	Combo 113	4.00	16.00	55
TEARS/When I Met You	Combo 115	5.00	20.00	—
NATURALS, George Torrence & The				
NATURALS, The				
NELSON, Billy & The Five Wings: see Five Wings, Billy Nelson & The				
NELSON, Earl & The Pelicans: see Pelicans, Earl Nelson & The				
NELSON, Harrison as Peppermint Harris				
BLUES PICK ON ME, THE/Let's Ride (78)	Sittin' In With 597	1.50	6.00	50
BYE, BYE, FARE THEE WELL/Black Cat Bone	Modern 936	4.00	16.00	51
CADILLAC FUNERAL/Treat Me Like I Treat You	Cash 1003	2.50	10.00	54
CADILLAC FUNERAL/Treat Me Like I Treat You	Money 214	2.50	10.00	54
DON'T LEAVE ME ALL ALONE/Wet Rag	Aladdin 3183	4.00	16.00	53
GIMME, GIMME, GIMME/Hey, Sweet Thing (78)	Sittin' In With 576	1.50	6.00	50
GOT A BIG FINE BABY/ I Will Always Think Of You (78)	Sittin' In With 650	1.50	6.00	51
HAVE ANOTHER DRINK AND TALK TO ME/ Middle Of Winter	Aladdin 3107	5.00	20.00	51
I ALWAYS END UP BLUE/I Screamed And I Cried (78)	Sittin' In With 612	1.50	6.00	51
I GOT LOADED/It's You, Yes, It's You	Aladdin 3097	5.00	20.00	51
I NEED YOUR LOVIN'/Just You And Me	"X" 0142	2.50	10.00	55
I NEVER GET ENOUGH OF YOU/Three Sheets In The Wind	Aladdin 3206	3.00	12.00	51
I SURE DO MISS MY BABY/Hey, Little Schoolgirl	Aladdin 3154	4.00	16.00	51
I'M TELLING YOU PEOPLE/How Long Must I Suffer? (78)	Sittin' In With 587	1.50	6.00	51
P. H. BLUES/Let The Back Door Hit You	Aladdin 3108	5.00	20.00	51
PLEASE LET ME COME HOME/ I'm Going Crazy, Baby (78)	Sittin' In With 638	1.50	6.00	51
RAINING IN MY HEART/ My Blues Moved, Rolled Away (78)	Sittin' In With 543	1.50	6.00	50
RECKLESS LOVER/Oo Wee, Baby (78)	Sittin' In With 578	1.50	6.00	50
RIGHT BACK ON/Maggie's Boogie	Aladdin 3130	5.00	20.00	52
SHE'S MY BABY/I Wake Up Screaming (78)	Sittin' In With 623	1.50	6.00	51
TEXARKANA BLUES/Fat Girl Boogie (78)	Sittin' In With 568	1.50	6.00	50
THERE'S A DEAD CAT ON THE LINE/I Cry For My Baby	Aladdin 3141	5.00	20.00	52
THIS IS GOODBYE, BABY/Mabel, Mabel (78)	Sittin' In With 554	1.50	6.00	50
WASTED LOVE/Goodbye Blues	Aladdin 3177	4.00	16.00	51
NELSON, Harrison as Peppermint Nelson				
PEPPERMINT BOOGIE/Houston Blues (78)	Gold Star 626	2.00	8.00	47
NELSON, Jimmy				
FREE AND EASY MIND/Great Big Hunk Of Man	Chess 1587	3.00	12.00	53
MEAN POOR GIRL/Cry Hard Luck	RPM 397	3.00	12.00	53
MEET ME WITH YOUR BLACK DRESS ON/ Married Men Like Sport	RPM 385	3.00	12.00	53
SECOND HAND FOOL/Big Mouth	RPM 389	3.00	12.00	53
NELSON, Peppermint: see Nelson, Harrison as Peppermint Nelson				
NELSON, Vikki & The Sounds				
NEPTUNES, The				
NEVILLE, Aaron				
NEW YORKERS 5, The				
GLORIA, MY DARLING/Cha Cha Baby	Danice 801	25.00	100.00	—

TITLE/FLIP	LABEL & NO.	GOOD TO VERY GOOD	NEAR MINT	YR.

NEW YORKERS, The

TITLE/FLIP	LABEL & NO.	GOOD TO VERY GOOD	NEAR MINT	YR.
TEARS IN MY EYES/A Little Bit	Wall 548	1.50	6.00	61

NIC NACS, The

TITLE/FLIP	LABEL & NO.	GOOD TO VERY GOOD	NEAR MINT	YR.
FOUND ME A SUGAR DADDY/ Gonna Have A Merry Christmas (78)	RPM 313	6.25	25.00	50
FOUND ME A SUGAR DADDY/ Gonna Have A Merry Christmas (78)	RPM 342	4.00	16.00	51
FOUND ME A SUGAR DADDY/You Didn't Want My Love (78)	RPM 316	5.00	20.00	51

NICHOLS, Ann:
see Bluebirds, Ann Nichols & The
see Sentimentals, Ann Nichols & The

NICHOLS, Manny

TITLE/FLIP	LABEL & NO.	GOOD TO VERY GOOD	NEAR MINT	YR.
GET GOING/No One To Love Me (78)	Imperial 5162	5.00	20.00	49
WALKING TALKING BLUES/Tall Skinny Mama Blues (78)	FBC 125	10.00	40.00	49
WORRIED LIFE BLUES/Forgive Me Blues (78)	Imperial 5173	5.00	20.00	49

NICHOLSON, J. D.

TITLE/FLIP	LABEL & NO.	GOOD TO VERY GOOD	NEAR MINT	YR.
ANNIE JO/Tippin' 'N' Shufflin'	IMCO 110	2.00	8.00	—

NIGHT OWLS, The

TITLE/FLIP	LABEL & NO.	GOOD TO VERY GOOD	NEAR MINT	YR.
BELLS RING/Let's Go Again	Bethlehem 3087	1.50	6.00	—

NIGHT RIDERS, The

TITLE/FLIP	LABEL & NO.	GOOD TO VERY GOOD	NEAR MINT	YR.
RAGS/Dr. Velvet	Apollo 466	4.00	16.00	—
WOMEN AND CADILLACS/Say, Hey	Apollo 460	7.00	28.00	54

NIGHTHAWK, Robert:
see McCollum, Robert as Robert Nighthawk

NIGHTHAWKS, The:
see Camp, Bob & The Nighthawks
see Hoke, Billy with James Wayne & The Nighthawks

NIGHTRIDERS, The

TITLE/FLIP	LABEL & NO.	GOOD TO VERY GOOD	NEAR MINT	YR.
NEVER /Tell The Truth	Sound 128	1.50	6.00	—

NITE RIDERS, Doc Starkes & The

TITLE/FLIP	LABEL & NO.	GOOD TO VERY GOOD	NEAR MINT	YR.
APPLE CIDER/Way In The Middle Of A Dream	Teen 114	2.00	8.00	—

NITE RIDERS, Melvin Smith & The

NITE RIDERS, The

TITLE/FLIP	LABEL & NO.	GOOD TO VERY GOOD	NEAR MINT	YR.
GOT ME A SIX BUTTON BENNY/Don't Hang Up The Phone	Teen 118	2.00	8.00	—

NITE SOUNDS, Melvin Davis & The

NITECAPS, The

TITLE/FLIP	LABEL & NO.	GOOD TO VERY GOOD	NEAR MINT	YR.
BAMBOO ROCK AND ROLL/You May Not Know	Groove 0158	5.00	20.00	56
IN EACH CORNER OF MY HEART/Let Me Know Tonight	Groove 0176	8.00	32.00	56
KISS AND A VOW, A/Be My Girl	Groove 0134	5.00	20.00	55
TOUGH MAMA/Sweet Thing	Groove 0147	5.00	20.00	56

NIX, Willie

TITLE/FLIP	LABEL & NO.	GOOD TO VERY GOOD	NEAR MINT	YR.
LONESOME BEDROOM BLUES/Try Me One More Time (78)	RPM 327	7.00	28.00	51
TRUCKIN' LITTLE WOMAN/Just One Mistake (78)	Checker 756	6.25	25.00	52

NIX, Willie & His Combo

TITLE/FLIP	LABEL & NO.	GOOD TO VERY GOOD	NEAR MINT	YR.
JUST CAN'T STAY/All By Myself	Sabre 104	20.00	80.00	53
NERVOUS WRECK/No More Love	Chance 1163	25.00	100.00	53

NIX, Willie—The Memphis Blues Boy

TITLE/FLIP	LABEL & NO.	GOOD TO VERY GOOD	NEAR MINT	YR.
BAKER SHOP BOOGIE/Seems Like A Million Years (78)	Sun 179	25.00	100.00	53

NIXON, Elmore With Henry Hayes & His Rhythm Kings

TITLE/FLIP	LABEL & NO.	GOOD TO VERY GOOD	NEAR MINT	YR.
BROKEN HEART, A/You Left Me	Imperial 5388	2.00	8.00	55
DON'T DO IT/The Women	Post 2008	2.50	10.00	55
ELMORE'S BLUES/Sad And Blue	Savoy 889	1.50	6.00	52
IF YOU'LL BE MY LOVE/Last Nite	Savoy 1105	1.50	6.00	52
OVER HERE, PRETTY BABY/Forgive Me, Baby	Savoy 878	1.50	6.00	52
PLAYBOY BLUES/Million Dollar Blues	Mercury 70061	3.00	12.00	51

NOBELLS, The

TITLE/FLIP	LABEL & NO.	GOOD TO VERY GOOD	NEAR MINT	YR.
SEARCHIN' FOR MY LOVE/Crying Over You	Mar 101	4.00	16.00	62

NOBLES, Cliff & Company

NOBLETONES, The

TITLE/FLIP	LABEL & NO.	GOOD TO VERY GOOD	NEAR MINT	YR.
I LOVE YOU/I'm Really Too Young	C & M 182	2.50	10.00	58
I'M CRYING/Mambo Boogie	C & M 188/189	2.50	10.00	58
WHO CARES ABOUT LOVE?/Cha-lyp-so Baby	C & M 182	2.50	10.00	58

NOLAN

NOLEN, Jimmy

TITLE/FLIP	LABEL & NO.	GOOD TO VERY GOOD	NEAR MINT	YR.
I CAN'T STAND YOU NO MORE/You've Been Goofing	Federal 12246	1.50	6.00	55
SLOW FREIGHT BACK HOME (instrumental)/ Let's Try Again	Imperial 5363	1.50	6.00	55
SLOW FREIGHT BACK HOME (instrumental)/Let's Try Again	Elko 254	5.00	20.00	55
STROLLIN' WITH NOLEN/After Hours	Federal 12252	1.50	6.00	55

Instrumentals.

NOLEN, Jimmy:
see Wilson, Jimmy as Jimmy Nolen

NORMAN, Jimmy

NORMAN, Jimmy & The O'Jays

NORRIS, Charles "Chuck"

TITLE/FLIP	LABEL & NO.	GOOD TO VERY GOOD	NEAR MINT	YR.
MESSIN' UP/Let Me Know	Atlantic 994	3.00	12.00	52

NOTES, The

TITLE/FLIP	LABEL & NO.	GOOD TO VERY GOOD	NEAR MINT	YR.
DON'T LEAVE ME NOW/Cha Jezebel	Capitol 3332	8.00	32.00	56
TRUST IN ME/Round And Round	MGM 12338	15.00	60.00	56

NU PORTS, Tyrone & The

NUBBITT, Guitar (Alvin Hankerson)

NUGGETS, The

NUNN, Bobby & The Robbins:
see Robbins, Bobby Nunn & The

NURSE, Allan as Allan Nurse's Blues Band

TITLE/FLIP	LABEL & NO.	GOOD TO VERY GOOD	NEAR MINT	YR.
BLACK SNAKE BLUES/There's Only One Man (78)	Ebony 1030	2.00	8.00	44
JELLY SHAKIN' BLUES/Bye, Bye, Mary (78)	Southern 123	2.00	8.00	45

NUTMEGS, The

TITLE/FLIP	LABEL & NO.	GOOD TO VERY GOOD	NEAR MINT	YR.
DREAM OF LOVE, A/Someone, Somewhere	Tel 1014	4.00	16.00	60
KEY TO THE KINGDOM/Gift O' Gabbin' Woman	Herald 475	3.00	12.00	56
LOVE SO TRUE, A/Comin' Home	Herald 492	2.50	10.00	56
MY STORY/My Sweet Dream	Herald 538	2.50	10.00	59
RIP VAN WINKLE/Crazy 'Bout You	Herald 574	1.50	6.00	62
SHIP OF LOVE/Rock Me	Herald 459	3.00	12.00	55

In 1953 this same group, then known as The Lyres, recorded "Ship Of Love" for the J & G label.

TITLE/FLIP	LABEL & NO.	GOOD TO VERY GOOD	NEAR MINT	YR.
STORY UNTOLD/Make Me Lose My Mind	Herald 452	2.50	10.00	55
WHISPERING SORROWS/Betty Lou	Herald 466	3.00	12.00	55

TITLE/FLIP	LABEL & NO.	GOOD TO VERY GOOD	NEAR MINT	YR.
NUTONES, The				
BELIEVE/Annie Kicked The Bucket	Hollywood Star 798	75.00	300.00	54
BELIEVE/You're No Barking Dog	Hollywood Star 798	30.00	120.00	55
NUTS, Doug Clark & The				

O

TITLE/FLIP	LABEL & NO.	GOOD TO VERY GOOD	NEAR MINT	YR.
O'JAYS, Jimmy Norman & The				
O'JAYS, The				
CAN'T TAKE IT/Miracles	Apollo 759	1.50	6.00	63
CRACK UP LAUGHING/How Does It Feel?	Little Star 124	1.50	6.00	63
O'KAYSIONS, The				
O'NEAL, Johnny				
JOHNNY FEELS THE BLUES/So Many Hard Times	King 4599	2.00	8.00	52
OCAPELLOS, The				
STARS, THE/Anytime	General (no number)	1.50	6.00	66
ODEN, James as St. Louis Jimmy				
BISCUIT ROLLER/I'm Sorry Now (78)	Miracle 134	2.50	10.00	48
COMING UP FAST/One Doggone Reason (78)	Opera OP-4	2.00	8.00	53
DRINKIN' WOMAN/Why Work?	Duke 110	5.00	20.00	53
FLORIDA HURRICANE/So Nice And Kind (78)	Aristocrat 7001	4.00	16.00	48
GOIN' DOWN SLOW/Murder In The First Degree	Parrot 823	6.25	25.00	55
HARD LUCK BOOGIE/Good Book Blues	Herald 407	10.00	40.00	51
MOTHER'S DAY/Jack L. Cooper (78)	JOB 101	1.50	6.00	49
WHISKEY DRINKIN' WOMAN/Your Evil Ways	Herald 408	10.00	40.00	51
ODOM, King as The King Odum Quartette				
I'M LIVIN' HUMBLE/They Put John On The Island (78)	Musicraft 554	2.00	8.00	—
MOONLIGHT FROST/Who Struck John? (78)	Musicraft 575	2.00	8.00	—
PICKIN' A CHICKEN/I Found A Twinkle (78)	Musicraft 579	2.00	8.00	—
ODOM, King Four, The				
I'M GLAD I MADE YOU CRY/Lover Come Back To Me (78)	Derby 736	2.00	8.00	50
IF HE DIDN'T LOVE ME/Walkin' With My Shadow (78)	Derby 743	2.00	8.00	50
WHAT A WONDERFUL FEELING/My Heart Cries For You (78)	Derby 754	2.00	8.00	51
ODOM, King Quartette, The				
AMAZIN' WILLIE MAYS/Basin Street Blues (78)	Perspective 5001	1.50	6.00	—
OFFITT, Lillian				
OHIO UNTOUCHABLES, The				
OLE SONNY BOY				
BLUES AND MISERY/You Better Change	Excello 2086	3.00	12.00	56
OLYMPICS, The				
ONE STRING SAM				
MY BABY OOO/I Need A Hundred Dollars (78)	J.V.B. 40	12.50	50.00	56
ONTARIOS, The				
MEMORIES OF YOU/Lovers' Mambo	Big Town 121	20.00	80.00	—
OPALS, The				
MY HEART'S DESIRE/Oh, But She Did	Apollo 462	9.00	36.00	54
OPALS, The (female group)				
ORBITS, The				
KNOCK HER DOWN/My Love	Nu Kat 116/117	1.50	6.00	59
MESSAGE OF LOVE/I Really Do	Flair-X 5000	2.00	8.00	56
WHO ARE YOU?/Mr. Hard Luck	Argo 5286	1.50	6.00	57
ORCHIDS, The				
I'VE BEEN A FOOL FROM THE START/ Beginning To Miss You	King 4663	25.00	100.00	53
NEWLY WED/You're Everything To Me	Parrot 815	12.50	50.00	55

TITLE/FLIP	LABEL & NO.	GOOD TO VERY GOOD	NEAR MINT	YR.
OH, WHY?/All Night, Baby	King 4661	25.00	100.00	53
YOU SAID YOU LOVED ME/I Can't Refuse	Parrot 819	10.00	40.00	55
ORIENTALS, The				
GET YOURSELF TO SCHOOL/Please Come Back Home	Kayo 927	2.50	10.00	—
ORIENTS, The				
QUEEN OF ANGELS/Shouldn't I?	Laurie 3232	1.50	6.00	64
ORIGINAL CADILLACS, Earl Carroll & The				
BUZZ-BUZZ-BUZZ/Yea, Yea, Baby	Josie 829	1.50	6.00	58
ORIGINAL CADILLACS, The				
LUCY/Hurry Home	Josie 821	2.00	8.00	57
ORIGINAL CHECKERS, The				
ORIGINAL DRIFTERS, Bill Pinkney & The				
ORIGINAL DRIFTERS, The				
ORIGINAL FOUR ACES, The				
I CAN SEE AN ANGEL/You Were My First Affair	Big Town 118	7.00	28.00	55
ORIGINAL JUBALAIRES, The				
WAITING ALL MY LIFE FOR YOU/ Dreaming Of The Ladies In The Moon	Crown 111	4.00	16.00	—
YOU WON'T LET ME GO/ Little Church Of Capistrano	Crown 118	4.00	16.00	—
ORIGINAL MUSTANGS, Dolores Curry & The				
ORIGINAL RED CAPS, The: see Red Caps, Steve Gibson & The as The Original Red Caps				
ORIGINALS, Bill Pinkney & The				
ORIGINALS, The				
ORIGINALS, Tony Allen & The				
ORIOLES, Sonny Til & The				
ORIOLES, The				

Note: It should be pointed out, as it is explained in the introductory material, that 78s are usually only listed when 45s of the same release are not known to exist. However, such as in the case of early Oriole's records on Jubilee, all had 78 versions, including those listed here only as a 45. It should be noted, though, that all release dates are for first issues. Some of the earliest and most valuable 45s weren't pressed until a year or two after the 78s came out.Also, it is important to know that the 45s listed below are the only ones known, though possibly not the only ones in existence. If, for instance, a copy of Jubilee 5001 were to surface on 45, the price would immediately elevate from the common 78 priced at $10.00 to a conservative $300.00 to $400.00 for the rare 45. See the introduction for further information.

TITLE/FLIP	LABEL & NO.	GOOD TO VERY GOOD	NEAR MINT	YR.
ANGEL/Don't Go To Strangers	Jubilee 5231	4.00	16.00	56
AT NIGHT/Every Dog-gone Time	Jubilee 5025	50.00	200.00	50
BABY, PLEASE DON'T GO/ Don't Tell Her What's Happened To Me (red plastic)	Jubiloe 5065	60.00	240.00	51
BABY, PLEASE DON'T GO/ Don't Tell Her What's Happened To Me	Jubilee 5065	40.00	160.00	51
BAD LITTLE GIRL/Dem Days	Jubilee 5115	15.00	60.00	53
BARFLY/Gettin' Tired, Tired, Tired	Jubilee 5084	30.00	120.00	52
CRYING IN THE CHAPEL/ Don't You Think I Ought To Know?	Jubilee 5122	5.00	20.00	53
DARE TO DREAM/To Be With You (78)	Jubilee 5001	2.50	10.00	48
DON'T CRY, BABY/See See Rider	Jubilee 5092	40.00	160.00	52
FOR ALL WE KNOW/Never Leave Me, Baby	Vee Jay 228	5.00	20.00	56
HAPPY TILL THE LETTER/I Just Got Lucky	Vee Jay 196	4.00	16.00	56
I CHALLENGE YOUR KISS/Donkey Serenade (78)	Jubilee 5008	2.50	10.00	49
I COVER THE WATERFRONT/ One More Time (red plastic)	Jubilee 5120	40.00	160.00	53
I COVER THE WATERFRONT/ One More Time	Jubilee 5120	20.00	80.00	53
I CROSS MY FINGERS/ Can't Seem To Laugh Anymore (78)	Jubilee 5040	2.50	10.00	50
I LOVE YOU MOSTLY/Fair Exchange	Jubilee 5177	6.25	25.00	55
I MISS YOU SO/Till Then (red plastic)	Jubilee 5107	75.00	300.00	53
I MISS YOU SO/Till Then	Jubilee 5107	45.00	180.00	53
I MISS YOU SO/You Are My First Love (red plastic)	Jubilee 5051	75.00	300.00	51
I MISS YOU SO/You Are My First Love	Jubilee 5051	45.00	180.00	51

TITLE/FLIP	LABEL & NO.	GOOD TO VERY GOOD	NEAR MINT	YR.
I NEED YOU SO/Goodnight, Irene	Jubilee 5037	75.00	300.00	50
I NEED YOU, BABY/ That's When The Good Lord Will Smile	Jubilee 5189	6.25	25.00	55
I'D RATHER HAVE YOU UNDER THE MOON/ We're Supposed To Be Through (78)	Jubilee 5031	2.50	10.00	50
I'M JUST A FOOL IN LOVE/ Hold Me, Squeeze Me (78)	Jubilee 5061	2.50	10.00	51
IF YOU BELIEVE/Longing	Jubilee 5161	5.00	20.00	54
IN THE CHAPEL IN THE MOONLIGHT/ Thank The Lord! Thank The Lord!	Jubilee 5154	5.00	20.00	54
IN THE MISSION OF ST. AUGUSTINE/ Write And Tell Me Why	Jubilee 5127	3.00	12.00	53
IT'S OVER BECAUSE WE'RE THROUGH/Waiting	Jubilee 5082	40.00	160.00	52
IT'S TOO SOON TO KNOW/Barbara Lee (78)	It's A Natural 5000	7.00	28.00	48
IT'S TOO SOON TO KNOW/Barbara Lee	Jubilee 5000	80.00	320.00	48
KISS AND A ROSE, A/It's A Cold Summer (78)	Jubilee 5009	2.50	10.00	49
LONELY CHRISTMAS/To Be With You (78)	Jubilee 5001	2.50	10.00	48
MAYBE YOU'LL BE THERE/ Drowning Every Hope I Ever Had	Jubilee 5143	6.25	25.00	54
MOONLIGHT/I Wonder When? (78)	Jubilee 5026	2.50	10.00	50
OH, HOLY NIGHT/The Lord's Prayer	Jubilee 5045	40.00	160.00	50
PAL OF MINE/Happy Go Lucky Local Blues	Jubilee 5055	50.00	200.00	51
PLEASE GIVE MY HEART A BREAK/ It Seems So Long Ago (78)	Jubilee 5002	2.50	10.00	49
PLEASE SING MY BLUES TONIGHT/Moody Over You	Jubilee 5221	5.00	20.00	55
RUNAROUND/ Count Your Blessings Instead Of Sheep	Jubilee 5172	5.00	20.00	54
SECRET LOVE/Don't Go To Strangers	Jubilee 5137	3.00	12.00	54
SO MUCH/Forgive And Forget (78)	Jubilee 5016	2.50	10.00	49
SUGAR GIRL/Didn't I Say?	Vee Jay 244	8.00	32.00	57
TEARDROPS ON MY PILLOW/ Hold Me, Thrill Me, Kiss Me (red plastic)	Jubilee 5108	40.00	160.00	53
TEARDROPS ON MY PILLOW/ Hold Me, Thrill Me, Kiss Me	Jubilee 5108	20.00	80.00	53
TELL ME SO/Deacon Jones	Jubilee 5005	80.00	320.00	49
THERE'S NO ONE BUT YOU/Robe Of Calvary	Jubilee 5134	7.00	28.00	54
TRUST IN ME/Shrimp Boats	Jubilee 5074	40.00	160.00	52
WHAT ARE YOU DOING NEW YEAR'S EVE?/ Lonely Christmas	Jubilee 5017	40.00	160.00	49
WHEN YOU'RE NOT AROUND/How Blind Can You Be?	Jubilee 5071	40.00	160.00	51
WOULD I LOVE YOU?/ When You're A Long, Long Way From Home (78)	Jubilee 5057	2.50	10.00	51
WOULD YOU STILL BE THE ONE IN MY HEART?/ Is My Heart Wasting Time? (78)	Jubilee 5018	2.50	10.00	50
YOU BELONG TO ME/ I Don't Want To Take A Chance	Jubilee 5102	30.00	120.00	52
YOU'RE GONE/ Everything They Said Came True (78)	Jubilee 5028	2.50	10.00	50

ORLANDOS, The

TITLE/FLIP	LABEL & NO.	GOOD TO VERY GOOD	NEAR MINT	YR.
OLD MACDONALD/Cloudburst	Cindy 3006	8.00	32.00	57

ORLONS, The

TITLE/FLIP	LABEL & NO.	GOOD TO VERY GOOD	NEAR MINT	YR.
MR. TWENTY-ONE/Please Let It Be Me	Cameo 211	1.50	6.00	62

OSBORNE, Kell & The Chicks

OSPREYS, The

OTIS & CARLA

OTIS, Johnny

TITLE/FLIP	LABEL & NO.	GOOD TO VERY GOOD	NEAR MINT	YR.
BUTTERBALL/Sandy's Boogie	Peacock 1675	1.50	6.00	52
CALL OPERATOR 210/Baby Baby Blues	Mercury 8289	2.50	10.00	52
COURT ROOM BLUES/My Baby Done Told Me (by The Four Bluebirds) (78)	Excelsior 540	5.00	20.00	—
GOOMP BLUES/One Nighter Boogie Instrumentals.	Mercury 8273	2.50	10.00	51
GYPSY BLUES/The Candle's Burning	Mercury 8295	2.50	10.00	52
LOVE BUG BOOGIE, THE/Brown Skin Butterball	Mercury 70050	2.50	10.00	52
OOPY DOO/Stardust Instrumentals.	Mercury 8263	2.50	10.00	51
ROCK ME, BABY/ Young Girl (with The Peacocks)	Peacock 1625	6.25	25.00	52
SHAKE IT/I Won't Be Your Fool No More	Peacock 1636	2.00	8.00	52
SITTIN' HERE DRINKIN'/You Got Me Crying	Peacock 1648	1.50	6.00	52
WHY DON'T YOU BELIEVE ME?/Wishing Well	Mercury 70038	2.00	10.00	52

OTIS, Johnny & The Peacocks:
see Peacocks, Johnny Otis & The

OUTLAWS, Jessica James & The

OVATIONS, The

OVERBEA, Danny

TITLE/FLIP	LABEL & NO.	GOOD TO VERY GOOD	NEAR MINT	YR.
40 CUPS OF COFFEE/I'll Follow You (red plastic)	Checker 774	5.00	20.00	53
40 CUPS OF COFFEE/I'll Follow You	Checker 774	2.50	10.00	53
HEY, PANCHO/Do You Love Me?	Checker 816	1.50	6.00	55
I COULD, BUT I WON'T/Sorrento	Checker 784	2.00	8.00	54
ROAMIN' MAN/You're Mine	Checker 796	2.00	8.00	54
STOMP AND WHISTLE/Ebony Chant	Checker 788	2.00	8.00	54
TOAST TO LOVERS, A/My Love, My Love	Checker 808	1.50	6.00	55
TRAIN, TRAIN, TRAIN/I'll Wait	Checker 768	2.00	8.00	53

P

PACKARDS, The

TITLE/FLIP	LABEL & NO.	GOOD TO VERY GOOD	NEAR MINT	YR.
DREAM OF LOVE/Ding Dong	Paradise 105	7.00	28.00	56
LADISE/My Doctor Of Love	Pla-Bac 106	40.00	160.00	56

PAGAN, Ralfi

PAGE, Oran "Hot Lips"

TITLE/FLIP	LABEL & NO.	GOOD TO VERY GOOD	NEAR MINT	YR.
CADILLAC SONG, THE/Ain't Nothing Wrong, Baby	King 1404	3.00	12.00	53
CASANOVA CRICKET/The Devil's Kiss	King 15198	2.00	8.00	52
I BONGO YOU/Ruby	King 4594	2.00	8.00	52
I WANT TO RIDE LIKE THE COWBOYS DO/ Strike While The Iron's Hot	RCA Victor 50-0129	4.00	16.00	51
JUNGLE KING/What Shall I Do?	King 4616	3.00	12.00	53
LAST CALL FOR ALCOHOL/Old Paree	King 4584	15.00	60.00	52
THAT'S THE ONE FOR ME/Let Me In	RCA Victor 50-0120	4.00	16.00	51
TIN WHISTLE BLUES/I Tin Whistle You	King 15178	2.00	8.00	52

PAIGE, Hal

TITLE/FLIP	LABEL & NO.	GOOD TO VERY GOOD	NEAR MINT	YR.
BIG FOOT MAY/Please Say You Do	Atlantic 1032	6.25	25.00	53
DRIVE IT HOME/Break Of Day Blues	Atlantic 996	5.00	20.00	52

PAIGE, Hal & The Whalers:
see Whalers, Hal Paige & The

PALISADES, The

TITLE/FLIP	LABEL & NO.	GOOD TO VERY GOOD	NEAR MINT	YR.
CLOSE YOUR EYES/I Can't Quit	Calico 113	1.50	6.00	60

PALMER, Clarence & The Jive Bombers:
see Jive Bombers, Clarence Palmer & The

PALMER, Earl & The Jayhawks:
see Jayhawks, Earl Palmer & The

PALMS, Artie Wilkins & The

TITLE/FLIP	LABEL & NO.	GOOD TO VERY GOOD	NEAR MINT	YR.
DARLING PATRICIA/Please Come Back	States 157	5.00	20.00	56

PALMS, The

TITLE/FLIP	LABEL & NO.	GOOD TO VERY GOOD	NEAR MINT	YR.
EDNA/Teardrops	United 208	7.00	28.00	57

PALS, The

TITLE/FLIP	LABEL & NO.	GOOD TO VERY GOOD	NEAR MINT	YR.
SUMMER IS HERE/My Baby Likes To Rock	Turf 1000/1001	2.00	8.00	58

PARADONS, The

TITLE/FLIP	LABEL & NO.	GOOD TO VERY GOOD	NEAR MINT	YR.
I HAD A DREAM/Never, Never	Milestone 2015	1.50	6.00	—
NEVER AGAIN/	Tuffest 102	4.00	16.00	—

PARAGONS, Mack Starr & The

TITLE/FLIP	LABEL & NO.	GOOD TO VERY GOOD	NEAR MINT	YR.
JUST A MEMORY/Kneel And Pray	Winley 250	1.50	6.00	61

PARAGONS, The

TITLE/FLIP	LABEL & NO.	GOOD TO VERY GOOD	NEAR MINT	YR.
FLORENCE/Hey, Little School Girl	Winley 215	3.00	12.00	57
LET'S START ALL OVER AGAIN/Stick With Me, Baby	Winley 220	3.00	12.00	57
SO YOU WILL KNOW/Doll Baby	Winley 240	1.50	6.00	60
SO YOU WILL KNOW/Don't Cry, Baby	Winley 228	1.50	6.00	58
TWO HEARTS ARE BETTER THAN ONE/Give Me Love	Winley 223	2.00	8.00	57

PARAGONS, Tommy Collins & The

TITLE/FLIP	LABEL & NO.	GOOD TO VERY GOOD	NEAR MINT	YR.
DARLING, I LOVE YOU/Doll Baby	Winley 236	1.50	6.00	59

PARAKEETS QUINTET, The

TITLE/FLIP	LABEL & NO.	GOOD TO VERY GOOD	NEAR MINT	YR.
I HAVE A LOVE/The Rain Starts To Fall	Atlas 1068	10.00	40.00	56
MY HEART TELLS ME/Yvonne	Atlas 1069	7.00	28.00	56

PARAKEETS, Vic. Donna & The

TITLE/FLIP	LABEL & NO.	GOOD TO VERY GOOD	NEAR MINT	YR.
LOVE WAS A STRANGER TO ME/Count The Tears	Atlas 1075	7.00	28.00	57
TEENAGE ROSE/Silly & Sappy	Atlas 1071	4.00	16.00	57

PARAMOUNTS, The

TITLE/FLIP	LABEL & NO.	GOOD TO VERY GOOD	NEAR MINT	YR.
CONGRATULATIONS/Why Do You Have To Go?	Dot 16175	2.50	10.00	60
TAKE MY HEART/Thunderbird Baby	Combo 156	3.00	12.00	59
WHEN YOU DANCE/You're Seventeen	Dot 16201	2.50	10.00	61

PARKER, Herman as Little Junior Parker With Bill Johnson's Blue Flames

TITLE/FLIP	LABEL & NO.	GOOD TO VERY GOOD	NEAR MINT	YR.
DIRTY FRIEND BLUES/Can't Understand	Duke 120	4.00	16.00	54
PLEASE BABY BLUES/Sittin', Drinkin' And Thinkin'	Duke 127	3.00	12.00	54

PARKER, Herman as Little Junior Parker & His Blue Flames

TITLE/FLIP	LABEL & NO.	GOOD TO VERY GOOD	NEAR MINT	YR.
BAD WOMEN, BAD WHISKEY/You're My Angel (78)	Modern 864	4.00	16.00	52

PARKER, Herman as Little Junior Parker & The Blue Flames

TITLE/FLIP	LABEL & NO.	GOOD TO VERY GOOD	NEAR MINT	YR.
BACKTRACKIN'/I Wanna Ramble	Duke 137	2.50	10.00	54

PARKER, Herman as Little Junior's Blue Flames

TITLE/FLIP	LABEL & NO.	GOOD TO VERY GOOD	NEAR MINT	YR.
FEELIN' GOOD/Fussin' And Fightin'	Sun 187	7.00	28.00	53
MYSTERY TRAIN/Love My Baby	Sun 192	7.00	28.00	53

PARKER, Jack "The Bear"

TITLE/FLIP	LABEL & NO.	GOOD TO VERY GOOD	NEAR MINT	YR.
CHEAP OLD WINE AND WHISKEY/I Need You, I Want You	7-11 2100	8.00	32.00	53
ONE MORE KISS/Don't You Stay Away Too Long	7-11 2101	1.50	6.00	53

PARKER, Little Junior:
see Parker, Herman as Little Junior Parker

PARKER, Monister

TITLE/FLIP	LABEL & NO.	GOOD TO VERY GOOD	NEAR MINT	YR.
BLACK SNAKE BLUES/You Gonna Need Me (78)	Nucraft 100	7.00	28.00	51

PARKER, Robert

PARKER, Sonny

TITLE/FLIP	LABEL & NO.	GOOD TO VERY GOOD	NEAR MINT	YR.
DISGUSTED BLUES/My Soul's On Fire	Peacock 1620	2.00	8.00	51
JEALOUS BLUES/I'm Hungry	Brunswick 84025	2.00	8.00	53
MONEY AIN'T EVERYTHING/Worried Life Blues	Peacock 1596	2.50	10.00	51

PARKER, Sonny:
see Hampton, Lionel

PARKER, Willis

PARLIAMENTS, The

TITLE/FLIP	LABEL & NO.	GOOD TO VERY GOOD	NEAR MINT	YR.
LONELY ISLAND/You Make Me Wanna Cry	Flipp 100/101	3.00	12.00	60
PARTY BOYS/Poor Willie	Apt 25036	2.00	8.00	—

PARLIAMENTS, The

TITLE/FLIP	LABEL & NO.	GOOD TO VERY GOOD	NEAR MINT	YR.
DON'T NEED YOU ANYMORE/Honey, Take Me Home With You	Len 101	4.00	16.00	—

PARRIS, Fred & Black Satin

PARRIS, Fred & The Restless Hearts

PARRIS, Fred & The Satins

PARRIS, Fred:
see Champlains, The (with Fred Parris)
see Cherokees, The (with Fred Parris)
see Scarlets, Fred Parris & The

PARROTS, The

TITLE/FLIP	LABEL & NO.	GOOD TO VERY GOOD	NEAR MINT	YR.
PLEASE DON'T LEAVE ME/Weep, Weep, Weep	Checker 772	40.00	160.00	54

PASSIONS, The

TITLE/FLIP	LABEL & NO.	GOOD TO VERY GOOD	NEAR MINT	YR.
JACKIE BROWN/My Aching Heart	Capitol 3963	1.50	6.00	58
JACKIE BROWN/My Aching Heart	Era 1063	2.50	10.00	58

PASTELS, The

TITLE/FLIP	LABEL & NO.	GOOD TO VERY GOOD	NEAR MINT	YR.
PUT YOUR ARMS AROUND ME/Boom De De Boom	United 196	4.00	16.00	56

PASTELS, The (with Big Dee Irwin)

TITLE/FLIP	LABEL & NO.	GOOD TO VERY GOOD	NEAR MINT	YR.
BEEN SO LONG/My One and Only Dream	Argo 5287	1.50	6.00	57
BEEN SO LONG/My One And Only Dream	Mascot 123	10.00	40.00	57
SO FAR AWAY/Don't Knock	Argo 5314	1.50	6.00	58
YOU DON'T LOVE ME ANYMORE/Let's Go To The Rock & Roll Ball	Argo 5297	2.50	10.00	58

PATRICK, Gladys & The Charioteers:
see Charioteers, Gladys Patrick and The

PATT, Frank as Honeyboy

Frank Patt should not be confused with David Edwards, who also used the name Honeyboy.

TITLE/FLIP	LABEL & NO.	GOOD TO VERY GOOD	NEAR MINT	YR.
BLOODSTAINS ON THE WALL/My Time Ain't Long	Specialty 476	5.00	20.00	54

PATT, Frank Orchestra, The

TITLE/FLIP	LABEL & NO.	GOOD TO VERY GOOD	NEAR MINT	YR.
YOU GOING TO PAY FOR IT, BABY/Gonna Hold On	Flash 117	2.00	8.00	57

PATTERSON, Bobby

PATTON, Amos as Big Amos

PATTY & THE EMBLEMS (female group)

PATTY ANNE & THE FLAMES:
see Flames, Patty Anne & The

PAUPERS, The

TITLE/FLIP	LABEL & NO.	GOOD TO VERY GOOD	NEAR MINT	YR.
BLUE SUNDAY MORNING/Prettiest Gal In Town (78)	Melford 258	4.00	16.00	49

PAYNE, Freda

PEACHEROOS, The

TITLE/FLIP	LABEL & NO.	GOOD TO VERY GOOD	NEAR MINT	YR.
BE BOP BABY/Everyday	Excello 2044	15.00	60.00	54

PEACHES & HERB

PEACOCKS, Johnny Otis & The

TITLE/FLIP	LABEL & NO.	GOOD TO VERY GOOD	NEAR MINT	YR.
YOUNG GIRL/Rock Me, Baby	Peacock 1625	6.25	25.00	52

The second side is by Otis without the group.

PEACOCKS, Junior Ryder & The

TITLE/FLIP	LABEL & NO.	GOOD TO VERY GOOD	NEAR MINT	YR.
SAD STORY/Better Stop	Duke 119	4.00	16.00	54

PEANUTS, M-M's & The

PEARL & THE DELTARS:
see Deltars, Pearl & The

PEARLETTES, The

PEARLS, The

TITLE/FLIP	LABEL & NO.	GOOD TO VERY GOOD	NEAR MINT	YR.
BELLS OF LOVE/Come On Home	Atco 6066	5.00	20.00	56
ICE CREAM BABY/Yuz-A-Ma-Tuz	Onyx 511	3.00	12.00	57
LET'S YOU AND I GO STEADY/Zippidy Zippidy Zoom	Onyx 503	3.00	12.00	56
SHADOWS OF LOVE/Yum Yummy	Atco 6057	2.50	10.00	55
TREE IN THE MEADOW/My, Oh My	Onyx 506	7.00	28.00	56
WHEEL OF LOVE, THE/It's Love, Love, Love	Onyx 516	7.00	28.00	57
YOUR CHEATIN' HEART/I Sure Need You	Onyx 510	2.50	10.00	57

PEE, Eddie as Memphis Eddie

TITLE/FLIP	LABEL & NO.	GOOD TO VERY GOOD	NEAR MINT	YR.
GOOD TIME WOMAN/Highway 61 (78)	RPM 310	1.50	6.00	50
I BELIEVE/Mercy Blues (78)	RPM 308	1.50	6.00	50
REAL FINE GIRL/Baby Lou (78)	RPM 315	1.50	6.00	50
VELMA LEE/Lonesome Change (78)	RPM 301	1.50	6.00	50

PEE, Eddie as Memphis Eddie P. & His Trio

TITLE/FLIP	LABEL & NO.	GOOD TO VERY GOOD	NEAR MINT	YR.
TROUBLE BLUES/Hep Chick (78)	Foto 222	2.00	8.00	48

PEE, Eddie as Memphis Eddie Pee

TITLE/FLIP	LABEL & NO.	GOOD TO VERY GOOD	NEAR MINT	YR.
BIG LEG MAMA/My House Fell Down (78)	Globe 108	1.50	6.00	45
MISTREATED ALL THE TIME/Goin' Back to Smokey Mountain (78)	Globe 103	1.50	6.00	45

PEEBLES, Ann

PEELS, Leon & The Hi Tensions

PEELS, Leon:
see Blue Jays, The (featuring Leon Peels)

PEETIE WHEATSTRAW'S BUDDY:
see Harmon, Ray as Peetie Wheatstraw's Buddy

TITLE/FLIP	LABEL & NO.	GOOD TO VERY GOOD	NEAR MINT	YR.

PEJOE, Morris

CAN'T GET ALONG/I'll Plumb Get It	Checker 781	5.00	20.00	54
SCREAMING AND CRYING/Maybe Blues	Abco 106	5.00	20.00	56
SHE WALKED RIGHT IN/You Gone Away	Atomic H-1-410	2.50	10.00	60
TIRED OF CRYING OVER YOU/Gonna Buy Me A Telephone	Checker 766	7.00	28.00	54
YOU GONNA NEED ME/Hurt My Feelings	Vee Jay 148	3.00	12.00	55

PELICANS, Earl Nelson & The

I BOW TO YOU/Oh, Gee, Oh, Golly	Class 209	4.00	16.00	57

PELICANS, The

AURELIA/White Cliffs Of Dover	Parrot 793	80.00	320.00	54
CHIMES/Ain't Gonna Do It	Imperial 5307	60.00	240.00	54

PENGUINS, Cleve Duncan & The

PENGUINS, The

BE MINE OR BE A FOOL/Don't Do It	Mercury 70610	2.00	8.00	55
CHRISTMAS PRAYER/Jingle Jangle	Mercury 70762	4.00	16.00	55
DEALER OF DREAMS/Peace Of Mind	Wing 90076	3.00	12.00	56
DEVIL THAT I SEE/Promises, Promises, Promises	Mercury 70703	3.00	12.00	55
DO NOT PRETEND/If You're Mine	Dooto 435	3.00	12.00	58
EARTH ANGEL/Hey, Senorita	Dootone 348	3.00	12.00	54
EARTH ANGEL/Ice	Mercury 70943	2.00	8.00	56
IT ONLY HAPPENS WITH YOU/Walkin' Down Broadway	Mercury 70654	3.00	12.00	55
KISS A FOOL GOODBYE/Baby, Let's Make Some Love	Dootone 362	4.00	16.00	55
LET ME MAKE UP YOUR MIND/Sweet Love	Dooto 432	3.00	12.00	58
LOVE WILL MAKE YOUR MIND GO WILD/Ookey Ook	Dootone 353	4.00	16.00	54
MY TROUBLES ARE NOT AT AN END/She's Gone, Gone	Mercury 70799	4.00	16.00	56
NO, THERE AIN'T NO NEWS TODAY/When I Am Gone (by D. Williams & Orchestra, vocal by Willie Headen)	Dootone 345	15.00	60.00	54
THAT'S HOW MUCH I NEED YOU/Be My Loving Baby	Dooto 428	3.00	12.00	57
WILL YOU BE MINE?/Cool, Baby, Cool	Mercury 71033	3.00	12.00	57

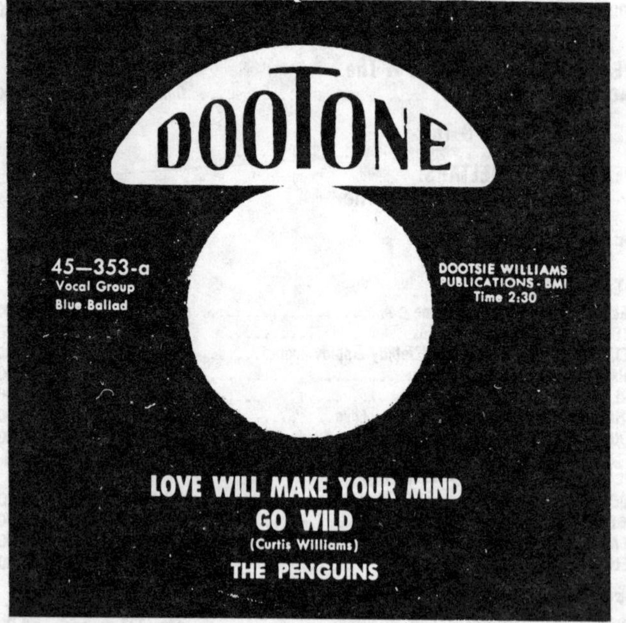

PENIGAR, Eddie "Sugarman"

EASY BABY/Lost And Blues (red plastic)	RCA Victor 50-0020	3.00	12.00	49

PENNIMAN, Richard:
see Duces Of Rhythm & The Tempo Toppers, The (featuring Little Richard)
see Little Richard
see Upsetters, The (featuring Little Richard)

PENTAGONS, The

TO BE LOVED/Down At The Beach	Fleet Int'l 100	2.50	10.00	—

PEPPERMINT HARRIS:
see Nelson, Harrison as Peppermint Harris

PEPPERMINT NELSON:
see Nelson, Harrison as Peppermint Nelson

PEPPERS, The

HOLD ON/Rocking Chair Baby	Chess 1577	15.00	60.00	54

PEPPERS, The

ONE MORE CHANCE/A Place In My Heart	Ensign 1706	7.00	28.00	61

PERFORMERS, The

GIVE ME YOUR HEART/I'll Make You Understand	All Star 714	4.00	16.00	—
GIVE ME YOUR HEART/I'll Make You Understand	Tip Top 402	3.00	12.00	—

PERKINS, Al

PERKINS, George & The Silver Stars

PERKINS, Harold & The Don Clairs:
see Don Clairs, Harold Perkins & The

PERKINS, Jerry & His Blues Blasters

KATHERINE BLUES/Knocking The Boogie (78)	W & W 204	3.00	12.00	50

PERKINS, Jesse & The Bad Boys

PERKINS, Jesse as Jesse & Buzzy

PERRY, Berlin & The Gleams:
see Gleams, Berlin Perry & The

PERRY, Ike & The Lyrics:
see Lyrics, Ike Perry & The

PERRY, King

FAT MAMA/What Now?	Excelsior 4	2.50	10.00	—
KEEP A DOLLAR IN YOUR POCKET/Hold Your Gold	Excelsior 2	2.50	10.00	—

PERRY, King & The Pied Pipers

PERRYMAN, William Lee as Piano Red

Perryman, an albino, was nicknamed "Red" because of his skin pigmentation. His older brother, also an albino, was a boogie pianist called 'Speckled Red." Neither should be confused with pianists Vernon Harrison and Vance Patterson, who also used the name "Piano Red." Still another keyboard man, John Williams, went by the name "Memphis Piano Red."

BABY, WHAT'S WRONG?/ Layin' The Boogie (instrumental)	RCA Victor 50-0130	3.00	12.00	50
BOUNCIN' WITH RED (instrumental)/ Count The Days I'm Gone	RCA Victor 47-4524	2.50	10.00	51
DECATUR STREET BLUES/Big Rock Joe From Kokomo	Groove G-0023	2.00	8.00	54
GET UP MARE/So Worried	Checker 911	1.50	6.00	58
I'M GONNA ROCK SOME MORE/Everybody's Boogie	RCA Victor 47-5101	2.50	10.00	52
I'M GONNA TELL EVERYBODY/She's Dynamite	RCA Victor 47-5224	2.50	10.00	52
I'M NOBODY'S FOOL/That's My Desire	Groove G-0145	1.50	6.00	56
IT MAKES NO DIFFERENCE NOW/ Hey, Good Lookin'	RCA Victor 47-4380	2.50	10.00	51
JUMPIN' THE BOOGIE/Just Right Bounce Instrumentals.	RCA Victor 50-0118	3.00	12.00	50
LET'S HAVE A GOOD TIME/ Diggin' The Boogie (instrumental)	RCA Victor 47-4265	2.50	10.00	50
PAY IT NO MIND/Jump, Man, Jump	Groove G-0101	1.50	6.00	55
RED'S BLUES/Gordy's Rock (instrumental)	Groove G-0126	1.50	6.00	55
RIGHT AND READY/Taxi, Taxi 6963	RCA Victor 47-5544	2.50	10.00	53
ROCKIN' WITH RED/Red's Boogie (red plastic) Instrumentals.	RCA Victor 50-0099	6.25	25.00	50
ROCKIN' WITH RED/Red's Boogie (gray label) Instrumentals.	RCA Victor 50-0099	3.00	12.00	50
SALES TAX BOOGIE, THE/She Walks Right In	RCA Victor 47-4766	2.50	10.00	52
SHE KNOCKS ME OUT/Jumpin' With Daddy	Groove G-0136	1.50	6.00	55
SIX O'CLOCK BOOGIE/Goodbye, Goodbye, Goodbye	Groove G-0118	1.50	6.00	55
VOO DOOPEE DOO/Daybreak	RCA Victor 47-4957	2.50	10.00	52
WRONG YOYO, THE/My Gal Jo	RCA Victor 50-0106	3.00	12.00	50
YOU WERE MINE FOR AWHILE/Woo-ee	Groove G-0169	1.50	6.00	56
YOUR MOUTH'S GOT A HOLE/Decatur Street Boogie	RCA Victor 47-5337	2.50	10.00	53

PERSIANS, The

PERSUADERS, The

PERSUASIONS, The

Junior Parker

Cleve Duncan Lead Singer, The Penguins

The Penguins

TITLE/FLIP	LABEL & NO.	GOOD TO VERY GOOD	NEAR MINT	YR.

PETERSON, Bobby

PETERSON, Lucky Blues Band, The

PETERSON, Pigmeat

TITLE/FLIP	LABEL & NO.	GOOD TO VERY GOOD	NEAR MINT	YR.
EVERYBODY LOVES A FAT MAN/ Loud Mouth Lucy	Federal 12081	6.25	25.00	52

PHANTOMS, Vernon Green & The

TITLE/FLIP	LABEL & NO.	GOOD TO VERY GOOD	NEAR MINT	YR.
SWEET BREEZE/The Old Willow Tree	Specialty 581	4.00	16.00	56

PHARAOHS, Richard Berry & The

TITLE/FLIP	LABEL & NO.	GOOD TO VERY GOOD	NEAR MINT	YR.
LOUIE, LOUIE/Rock, Rock, Rock	Flip 321	1.50	6.00	57
TAKE THE KEY/No Kissin' And A Huggin'	Flip 318	1.50	6.00	56

PHARAOHS, Ricky & The

TITLE/FLIP	LABEL & NO.	GOOD TO VERY GOOD	NEAR MINT	YR.
TEENAGER'S LOVE SONG/Watusi	Class 202	2.00	8.00	57

PHELPS, James

PHILHARMONICS, The

TITLE/FLIP	LABEL & NO.	GOOD TO VERY GOOD	NEAR MINT	YR.
WHY DON'T YOU WRITE ME?/Teen Town Hop	Future 2200	1.50	6.00	58

PHILLIPS, Earl Orchestra, The

TITLE/FLIP	LABEL & NO.	GOOD TO VERY GOOD	NEAR MINT	YR.
OOP DE OOP/Nothing But Love	Vee Jay 158	2.00	8.00	55

PHILLIPS, Marvin

TITLE/FLIP	LABEL & NO.	GOOD TO VERY GOOD	NEAR MINT	YR.
ANNE MARIE/Honey Baby	Parrot 795	4.00	16.00	54
SALTY DOG/Sweetheart Darling	Parrot 786	4.00	16.00	54
SALTY DOG/Sweetheart Darling	Swingtime 339	6.25	25.00	54

PHILLIPS, Marvin:
see Belvin, Jesse & Marvin Phillips as Jesse & Marvin

PHILLIPS, Marvin & Johnny Dean as Marvin & Johnny

TITLE/FLIP	LABEL & NO.	GOOD TO VERY GOOD	NEAR MINT	YR.
BABY DOLL/I'm Not A Fool (red plastic)	Specialty 479	5.00	20.00	53
BABY DOLL/I'm Not A Fool	Specialty 479	2.50	10.00	53
BABY, BABY, BABY/Bye, Bye, Baby	Rays 34	2.00	8.00	54
CHERRY PIE/Tick Tock	Modern 933	2.50	10.00	54
DAY IN, DAY OUT/Flip	Specialty 530	1.50	6.00	53
DING DONG DADDY/Mamo Mamo	Specialty 554	1.50	6.00	53
JO JO/How Long Has She Been Gone?	Specialty 488	2.50	10.00	53
MY DEAR, MY DARLIN'/Hey, Chicken	Aladdin 3335	2.00	8.00	56
SCHOOL OF LOVE/Boy Loves Girl	Specialty 498	2.50	10.00	53

PHILLIPS, Marvin as Long Tall Marvin

TITLE/FLIP	LABEL & NO.	GOOD TO VERY GOOD	NEAR MINT	YR.
HAVE MERCY, MISS PERCY/Tell Me Darling	Modern 993	5.00	20.00	56

PHILLIPS, Phil & The Twilights

TITLE/FLIP	LABEL & NO.	GOOD TO VERY GOOD	NEAR MINT	YR.
SEA OF LOVE/Juella	Khoury's 711	10.00	40.00	59

PIANO RED:
see Perryman, William Lee as Piano Red

PICHON, Walter "Fatz"

PICKETT, Dan

TITLE/FLIP	LABEL & NO.	GOOD TO VERY GOOD	NEAR MINT	YR.
BABY, HOW LONG?/You Got To Do Better (78)	Gotham 242	4.00	16.00	48
LAUGHING RAG/That's Grieving Me (78)	Gotham 201	4.00	16.00	48
LEMON MAN/Number Writer (78)	Gotham 516	3.00	12.00	48
RIDE TO A FUNERAL IN A V-8/ Early One Morning (78)	Gotham 510	3.00	12.00	48
SOMETHING'S GONE WRONG/Chicago Blues (78)	Gotham 512	3.00	12.00	48

PICKETT, Wilson

TITLE/FLIP	LABEL & NO.	GOOD TO VERY GOOD	NEAR MINT	YR.
MY HEART BELONGS TO YOU/Let Me Be Your Boy	Correctone 501	1.50	6.00	—
MY HEART BELONGS TO YOU/Let Me Be Your Boy	Cub 9113	2.00	8.00	62

PICKETT, Wilson:
see Falcons, The (with Wilson Pickett)

PICTURES, C. L. & The

TITLE/FLIP	LABEL & NO.	GOOD TO VERY GOOD	NEAR MINT	YR.
I'M SORRY/That's What's Happening	Dunes 2023	1.50	6.00	63

PIED PIPERS, King Perry & The

PIERCE, Henry & The Five Notes:
see Five Notes, Henry Pierce & The

PIG 'N' WHISTLE BAND, The:
see McTell, Willie Samuel as The Pig 'N' Whistle Band

PINETOP SLIM

TITLE/FLIP	LABEL & NO.	GOOD TO VERY GOOD	NEAR MINT	YR.
APPLEJACK BOOGIE/I'm Gonna Carry On (78)	Colonial 106	5.00	20.00	49

PINKNEY, Bill & The Original Drifters

PINKNEY, Bill & The Originals

PIPES, The

TITLE/FLIP	LABEL & NO.	GOOD TO VERY GOOD	NEAR MINT	YR.
BE FAIR/Let Me Give You Money	Dootone 388	9.00	36.00	56
LOVE THE LIFE I LIVE/You Are An Angel	Dootone 401	7.00	28.00	56

PIPKIN, Jessie

TITLE/FLIP	LABEL & NO.	GOOD TO VERY GOOD	NEAR MINT	YR.
CRY, CRY, CRY/Work With It	Noble 713	2.50	10.00	—

PIPS, The

TITLE/FLIP	LABEL & NO.	GOOD TO VERY GOOD	NEAR MINT	YR.
CHING CHONG/Whistle, My Love	Brunswick 55048	2.50	10.00	58
EVERY BEAT OF MY HEART/Room In Your Heart	Hunton 2510	10.00	40.00	—

PIRATES, The

PITT, Eugene & The Jyve Fyve

PLANTS, The

TITLE/FLIP	LABEL & NO.	GOOD TO VERY GOOD	NEAR MINT	YR.
DEAR, I SWEAR/It's You	J & S 1602	8.00	32.00	57
FROM ME/My Girl	J & S 1617/1618	7.00	28.00	58
I SEARCHED THE SEVEN SEAS/ I Took A Trip Way Over The Sea	J & S 248/249	2.50	10.00	—

PLATTERS '65, The

PLATTERS, Linda Hayes & The

TITLE/FLIP	LABEL & NO.	GOOD TO VERY GOOD	NEAR MINT	YR.
PLEASE HAVE MERCY/Oochi Pachi	King 4773	3.00	12.00	55

PLATTERS, The

TITLE/FLIP	LABEL & NO.	GOOD TO VERY GOOD	NEAR MINT	YR.
GIVE THANKS/Hey, Now	Federal 12153	15.00	60.00	53
GIVE THANKS/I Need You All The Time	Federal 12271	2.50	10.00	56
I NEED YOU ALL THE TIME/I'll Cry When You're Gone	Federal 12164	25.00	100.00	54
MAGGIE DOESN'T WORK HERE ANYMORE/ Take Me Back, Take Me Back	Federal 12204	5.00	20.00	54
ONLY YOU/Bark, Battle and Ball (pink label)	Mercury 70633	4.00	16.00	55
ONLY YOU/You Made Me Cry	Federal 12244	10.00	40.00	55
ROSES OF PICARDY/Beer Barrel Boogie	Federal 12181	15.00	60.00	54
TELL THE WORLD/I Need You All The Time	Federal 12250	4.00	16.00	55
TELL THE WORLD/Love All Night	Federal 12188	4.00	16.00	54
VOO-VEE-AH-BEE/Shake It Up Mambo	Federal 12198	5.00	20.00	54

PLAYBOY FULLER:
see Minter, Iverson as Playboy Fuller

PLAYBOYS, The

TITLE/FLIP	LABEL & NO.	GOOD TO VERY GOOD	NEAR MINT	YR.
ONE QUESTION/So Good	Tetra 4447	5.00	20.00	56

The Planets

The Platters

PLAYBOYS, The

TITLE/FLIP	LABEL & NO.	GOOD TO VERY GOOD	NEAR MINT	YR.
GOOD GOLLY, MISS MOLLY/Honey Bun	*Cat 115*	2.50	10.00	*55*
TELL ME/Rock, Moan and Cry	*Cat 108*	3.00	12.00	*54*

PLAYMATES, The (female group)

PLEASERS, Wilbur Whitfield & The

POETS, The

TITLE/FLIP	LABEL & NO.	GOOD TO VERY GOOD	NEAR MINT	YR.
VOWELS OF LOVE/Dead	*Flash 129*	4.00	16.00	*58*

POINTER SISTERS, The

POLKA DOT SLIM (Monroe Vincent)

POOR BOB (Bob Woodfork)

POOR BOYS, The

TITLE/FLIP	LABEL & NO.	GOOD TO VERY GOOD	NEAR MINT	YR.
DIDN'T WE FOOL THEM?/I'm Not Ashamed	*Apollo 1201*	1.50	6.00	—
WASHBOARD/I'm Going To Spend My Money	*Apollo 1203*	1.50	6.00	—

POPCORN & THE MOHAWKS:
see Mohawks, Popcorn & The

POPPY (or POPPA) HOP:
see Wilson, Harding as Poppy (or Poppa) Hop

POPULAR FIVE, The

TITLE/FLIP	LABEL & NO.	GOOD TO VERY GOOD	NEAR MINT	YR.
TOMORROW NIGHT/Sh-Boom	*Rae Cox 1001*	1.50	6.00	—

PORTER, Jake

TITLE/FLIP	LABEL & NO.	GOOD TO VERY GOOD	NEAR MINT	YR.
WANG, THE (instrumental)/The Monkey (by The Duchess)	*Combo 2*	5.00	20.00	*53*

PORTER, Jake:
see Buzzards, Jake Porter & The
see Ebbonairs, Jake Porter & The

PORTER, Jane & The Combo-Nettes:
see Combo-Nettes, Jane Porter & The

PORTER, Johnny "Schoolboy"

All of the following are instrumentals.

TITLE/FLIP	LABEL & NO.	GOOD TO VERY GOOD	NEAR MINT	YR.
BREAK THROUGH/Junco Partner	*Chance 1119*	4.00	16.00	*58*
FIRE DOME/	*Chance 1117*	4.00	16.00	*58*
KAYRON/Deep Purple	*Chance 1105*	4.00	16.00	*58*
SCHOOLBOY'S BOOGIE/I'll Never Smile Again	*Chance 1101*	4.00	16.00	*58*
SMALL SQUALL/Lonely Walk	*Chance 1132*	4.00	16.00	*58*
SOFT SHOULDER/Rollin' Along	*Chance 1114*	4.00	16.00	*58*
STAIRWAY TO THE STARS/Top Hat	*Chance 1111*	4.00	16.00	*58*
TENNESSEE WALTZ, PART 1/Tennessee Waltz, Part 2	*Chance 1103*	4.00	16.00	*58*
WALK HEAVY/	*Chance 1104*	4.00	16.00	*58*

POSEY, Clarence

TITLE/FLIP	LABEL & NO.	GOOD TO VERY GOOD	NEAR MINT	YR.
ROCKIN' CHAIR BOOGIE (instrumental)/ Dog Me Blues (by Henry Smith) (78)	*Fortune 802*	5.00	20.00	*52*

POWELL, Austin & The James Quintet:
see James Quintet, Austin Powell & The

POWELL, Bobby

POWELL, Chris & The Five Blue Flames:
see Five Blue Flames, Chris Powell & The

POWELL, Jessie

TITLE/FLIP	LABEL & NO.	GOOD TO VERY GOOD	NEAR MINT	YR.
HOT BOX/Leaving Tonight (instrumental)	*Federal 12171*	2.00	8.00	*53*
MOONLIGHT IN VERMONT/Riggin' (instrumental)	*Josie 782*	1.50	6.00	*53*
MY NATCH' MAN/As Long As You're Satisfied Fluffy Hunter vocals.	*Federal 12060*	6.25	25.00	*51*
REAR BUMPER/Love To Spare (instrumental)	*Federal 12159*	2.00	8.00	*53*
WALKIN' BLUES, THE/Love Is A Fortune Fluffy Hunter vocals.	*Federal 12056*	7.00	28.00	*51*

POWELL, Jessie & The Caddys

POWELL, Tiny

POWELL, Vance as Tiny Powell

PRECISIONS, The

PRELUDES, The

TITLE/FLIP	LABEL & NO.	GOOD TO VERY GOOD	NEAR MINT	YR.
VANISHING ANGEL/Kingdom Of Love	*Cub 9005*	8.00	32.00	*58*

PRELUDES, The

TITLE/FLIP	LABEL & NO.	GOOD TO VERY GOOD	NEAR MINT	YR.
DON'T FALL IN LOVE TOO SOON/ I Want Your Arms Around Me	*Empire 103*	3.00	12.00	*56*

PRELUDES, The

TITLE/FLIP	LABEL & NO.	GOOD TO VERY GOOD	NEAR MINT	YR.
LORRAINE/Oh, Please, Genie	*Arliss 1004*	2.00	8.00	—
PLACE FOR YOU, A/That Would Be So Good	*Octavia 8008*	1.50	6.00	*62*

PREMIERS, John McKinney & The

TITLE/FLIP	LABEL & NO.	GOOD TO VERY GOOD	NEAR MINT	YR.
ANGELS IN THE SKY/Gee, How I Love You	*Mad 1009*	5.00	20.00	—

PREMIERS, Julie Stevens & The

TITLE/FLIP	LABEL & NO.	GOOD TO VERY GOOD	NEAR MINT	YR.
BLUE MOOD/Crazy Bells	*Dig 115*	1.50	6.00	*56*
TAKE MY HEART/I Don't Want To Know	*Dig 129*	1.50	6.00	*57*

PREMIERS, The

TITLE/FLIP	LABEL & NO.	GOOD TO VERY GOOD	NEAR MINT	YR.
BABY/New Moon	*Dig 106*	7.00	28.00	*56*
HAVE A HEART/My Darling	*Dig 113*	5.00	20.00	*56*
IS IT A DREAM?/Valerie	*Gone 5009*	12.50	50.00	*57*
WHEN YOU ARE IN LOVE/The Trap Of Love	*Fortune 527*	5.00	20.00	*56*

PREPARATIONS, The

PRESIDENTS, The

PRESTON, Billy

PRESTON, Jimmy

TITLE/FLIP	LABEL & NO.	GOOD TO VERY GOOD	NEAR MINT	YR.
ROCK THE JOINT/Drinkin' Woman (78)	*Gotham 188*	1.50	6.00	*49*

PRESTOS, The

TITLE/FLIP	LABEL & NO.	GOOD TO VERY GOOD	NEAR MINT	YR.
TIL WE MEET AGAIN/Looking For Love	*Mercury 70747*	7.00	28.00	*55*

PRETENDERS, Jimmy Jones & The

TITLE/FLIP	LABEL & NO.	GOOD TO VERY GOOD	NEAR MINT	YR.
LOVER/Plain Old Love	*Rama 207*	10.00	40.00	*56*

PRETENDERS, The

TITLE/FLIP	LABEL & NO.	GOOD TO VERY GOOD	NEAR MINT	YR.
BLUE AND LONELY/Daddy Needs Baby	*Apt 25026*	1.50	6.00	*59*
BLUE AND LONELY/Daddy Needs Baby	*Central 2605*	3.00	12.00	—
CLOSE YOUR EYES/Part Time Sweetheart	*Whirlin' Disc 106*	5.00	20.00	*56*
POSSESSIVE LOVE/I've Got To Have You, Baby	*Rama 198*	3.00	12.00	*56*

PRETENDERS, The

TITLE/FLIP	LABEL & NO.	GOOD TO VERY GOOD	NEAR MINT	YR.
DAY YOU ARE MINE, THE/Ding Dong Bells	*Bethlehem 3050*	2.00	8.00	*62*

PRETTY BOY

TITLE/FLIP	LABEL & NO.	GOOD TO VERY GOOD	NEAR MINT	YR.
I'M BAD/Find My Baby (78) With Johnny Fuller's Band.	*Rhythm 1768*	4.00	16.00	*54*

PREZ KENNETH (Kenneth Kidd)

PRICE, Walter as Big Walter

Price should not be confused with Walter Horton, who also recorded as Big Walter.

TITLE/FLIP	LABEL & NO.	GOOD TO VERY GOOD	NEAR MINT	YR.
HELLO MARIA/Pack Fair And Square	*Peacock 1666*	1.50	6.00	*55*
I GOTTA GO/I'll Cry For You	*Peacock 1674*	1.50	6.00	*55*
JUNIOR JUMPED IN/Calling Margie	*TNT 8005*	7.00	28.00	*55*
JUST LOOKING FOR A HOME/You're The One I Need	*Peacock 1669*	1.50	6.00	*55*
RAMONA/Can't Stand To Lose	*Peacock 1680*	2.50	10.00	*55*
SHIRLEY JEAN/Gamblin' Woman	*Peacock 1661*	1.50	6.00	*55*
SIX WEEKS OF MISERY/Oh No, No Blues	*TNT 8006*	7.00	28.00	*55*
THIS IS ALL/You Make Lovin' So Easy	*TNT 8009*	7.00	28.00	*55*

PRICE, Lloyd

TITLE/FLIP	LABEL & NO.	GOOD TO VERY GOOD	NEAR MINT	YR.
AIN'T IT A SHAME?/Tell Me Pretty Baby (red plastic)	*Specialty 452*	6.25	25.00	*53*
AIN'T IT A SHAME?/Tell Me Pretty Baby	*Specialty 452*	3.00	12.00	*53*
CHEE KOO BABY/Oo Ee Baby With The Dukes	*Specialty 535*	4.00	16.00	*55*
COUNTRY BOY ROCK/Rock 'N' Dance	*Specialty 578*	1.50	6.00	*56*
FORGIVE ME, CLAWDY/I'm Glad Glad	*Specialty 582*	1.50	6.00	*56*
I WISH YOUR PICTURE WAS YOU/Frog Legs	*Specialty 471*	3.00	12.00	*54*
I YI YI GOMEN-A-SAI (I'M SORRY)/Woe Ho Ho	*Specialty 571*	1.50	6.00	*56*
JUST BECAUSE/Why?	*KRC 587/588*	8.00	32.00	*57*
LAWDY, MISS CLAWDY/Mailman Blues	*Specialty 428*	5.00	20.00	*52*
LET ME COME HOME, BABY/Too Late For Tears (red plastic)	*Specialty 483*	6.25	25.00	*54*
LET ME COME HOME, BABY/Too Late For Tears	*Specialty 483*	3.00	12.00	*54*
LORD, LORD, AMEN/Trying To Find Someone To Love	*Specialty 540*	2.00	8.00	*55*
OOH, OOH, OOH/Restless Heart	*Specialty 440*	4.00	16.00	*52*
WALKIN' THE TRACK/Jimmie Lee	*Specialty 494*	2.50	10.00	*54*

TITLE/FLIP	LABEL & NO.	GOOD TO VERY GOOD	NEAR MINT	YR.
WHAT'S THE MATTER NOW?/So Long (red plastic)	Specialty 457	6.25	25.00	53
WHAT'S THE MATTER NOW?/So Long	Specialty 457	3.00	12.00	53
WHERE YOU AT?/ Baby Don't Turn Your Back On Me (red plastic)	Specialty 463	6.25	25.00	53
WHERE YOU AT?/Baby Don't Turn Your Back On Me	Specialty 463	3.00	12.00	53
PRINCE BUSTER				
PRINCE HAROLD				
PRINCE, Al & His Orchestra				
DON'T LOVE A MARRIED WOMAN/Wine (78)	Swing Time 319	3.00	12.00	52
PRINCE, Bobby				
BETTER THINK IT OVER/If You Only Knew	Chance 1158	5.00	20.00	54
TELL ME, WHY? WHY? WHY?/I Want To Hold You	Chance 1128	6.25	25.00	52
TOO MANY KEYS/Please Give Me Your Love	Excello 2039	4.00	16.00	54
PRINCE, Peppy				
AIN'T NOTHING SHAKING/Hey, Miss Harriette	Million 2003	1.50	6.00	54
PRISONAIRES, The				
I KNOW/A Prisoner's Prayer	Sun 191	9.00	36.00	53
JUST WALKIN' IN THE RAIN/Baby, Please	Sun 186	8.00	32.00	53
SOFTLY AND TENDERLY/My God Is Real	Sun 189	12.50	50.00	53
THERE IS LOVE IN YOU/What'll You Do Next?	Sun 207	120.00	480.00	54
PRODIGALS, The				
JUDY/Marsha	Abner 1011	2.00	8.00	—
JUDY/Marsha	Falcon 1011	3.00	12.00	58
WON'T YOU BELIEVE?/Vangie	Abner 1015	5.00	12.50	58
PROFESSOR LONGHAIR: see Byrd, Roy as Professor Longhair				
PRYOR, James Edward & Floyd Jones as Snooky & Moody				
BOOGIE/Telephone Blues (78)	Old Swingmaster 18	7.00	28.00	48
BOOGIE/Telephone Blues (78)	Planet 101/102	15.00	60.00	48
STOCKYARD BLUES/Keep What You Got (78)	Marvel (# unknown)	10.00	40.00	47
STOCKYARD BLUES/Keep What You Got (78)	Old Swingmaster 22	5.00	20.00	47
PRYOR, James Edward as Snooky Pryor				
BOOGY FOOL/Raisin' Sand (78)	JOB 101	8.00	32.00	50
CROSSTOWN BLUES/I Want You For Myself (red plastic)	Parrot 807	25.00	100.00	53
CROSSTOWN BLUES/I Want You For Myself	Parrot 807	12.50	50.00	53
CRYIN' SHAME/Eighty Nine Ten	JOB 1014	15.00	60.00	53
I'M GETTING TIRED/Going Back On The Road (78)	JOB 115	6.25	25.00	52
SOMEONE TO LOVE ME/Judgement Day	Vee Jay 215	3.00	12.00	56
UNCLE SAM, DON'T TAKE MY MAN/Boogie Twist	JOB 1126	5.00	20.00	63
PRYSOCK, Arthur				
PRYSOCK, Red				
All of the following are instrumentals.				
HAMMER/Jackpot	Red Robin 139	4.00	16.00	53
HARD ROCK/Jump For George	Red Robin 117	4.00	16.00	53
Some copies of this label were mis-printed as "Ren" Pryscock.				
WIGGLES/Crying My Heart Out	Red Robin 107	5.00	20.00	53
PRYSOCK, Reo: see Prysock, Red				
PUGH, Joe as Forest City Joe				
MEMORY OF SONNY BOY/A Woman On Every Street (78)	Aristocrat 3101	8.00	32.00	49
PULLUM, Joe				
MY WOMAN, PART 1/My Woman, Part 2 (78) With trio.	Swing Time 267	2.50	10.00	48
PURDIE, Pretty				
PURIFY, James & Bobby as James & Bobby Purify				
PYLES, William: see Jackson, Louis as Louis & Frosty (William Pyles)				
PYRAMIDS, Ruby Whitaker & The				
I DON'T WANT TO SET THE WORLD ON FIRE/ I Get The Feeling	Mark-X 7007	10.00	40.00	57

TITLE/FLIP	LABEL & NO.	GOOD TO VERY GOOD	NEAR MINT	YR.
PYRAMIDS, The				
AT ANY COST/Okay, Baby!	Davis 453	2.00	8.00	56
WHY DID YOU GO?/Before It's Too Late	Davis 457	2.00	8.00	56
PYRAMIDS, The				
DEEP IN MY HEART FOR YOU/And I Need You	Federal 12233	20.00	80.00	55
SOMEDAY/Bow Wow	Hollywood 1047	20.00	80.00	55

TITLE/FLIP	LABEL & NO.	GOOD TO VERY GOOD	NEAR MINT	YR.
QUADRELLS, The				
COME TO ME/What Can The Matter Be?	Whirlin' Disc 103	4.00	16.00	56
QUAILS, Bill Robinson & The				
I KNOW SHE'S GONE/Baby Don't Want Me No More	DeLuxe 6047	15.00	60.00	54
LITTLE BIT OF LOVE, A/Somewhere, Somebody Cares	DeLuxe 6057	15.00	60.00	54
LONELY STAR/Quit Pushin'	DeLuxe 6030	15.00	60.00	54
LOVE OF MY LIFE/Oh, Sugar	DeLuxe 6074	10.00	40.00	55
WHY DO I WAIT?/Heaven Is The Place	DeLuxe 6059	15.00	60.00	54
QUAILS, The				
THINGS SHE USED TO DO, THE/Pretty Huggin' Baby	DeLuxe 6085	7.00	28.00	55
QUAILTONES, Sax Kari & The				
TEARS OF LOVE/Roxana	Josie 779	9.00	36.00	55
QUATTLEBAUM, Doug				
DON'T BE FUNNY, BABY/Lizzie Lou	Gotham 519	7.00	28.00	53
QUEENS, Shirley Gunter & The				
BABY, I LOVE YOU SO/What Difference Does It Make?	Flair 1065	1.50	6.00	55
OOP SHOOP/It's You	Flair 1050	1.50	6.00	54
THAT'S THE WAY I LIKE IT/Gimme, Gimme, Gimme	Flair 1070	1.50	6.00	55
YOU'RE MINE/Why?	Flair 1060	1.50	6.00	55
QUESTION MARKS, The				
ANOTHER SOLDIER GONE/Go and Get Some More	Swing Time 346	75.00	300.00	54
The second side of this record, tho not credited to them, is actually by the Hollywood Flames.				
QUIN-TONES, The				
DOWN THE AISLE OF LOVE/Please Dear	Red Top 108	2.00	8.00	58
OH, HEAVENLY FATHER/I Watch The Stars	Red Top 116	2.50	10.00	—
QUINNS, The				
OH, STARLIGHT/Hong Kong	Cyclone 111	3.00	12.00	—
QUINTONES, Jimmy Witherspoon & The				
STILL IN LOVE/My Girl Ivy	Atco 6084	2.00	8.00	56
QUINTONES, The				
DING DONG/I Try So Hard	Chess 1685	3.00	12.00	58
I'M WILLING/Strange As It Seems	Gee 1009	4.00	16.00	56
SOUTH SEA ISLAND/More Than A Notion	Park 57-111/57-112	8.00	32.00	57

RADARS, The

TITLE/FLIP	LABEL & NO.	GOOD TO VERY GOOD	NEAR MINT	YR.
I WANT A LITTLE GIRL/Too Bad (78)	*Prestige 478*	7.00	28.00	—
YOU BELONG TO ME/I Need You All The Time (78)	*Abbey 3025*	7.00	28.00	—

RADIANTS, Cleve Duncan & The

RADIANTS, Jan & The

TITLE/FLIP	LABEL & NO.	GOOD TO VERY GOOD	NEAR MINT	YR.
IF YOU LOVE ME/Is it True?	*Queen 24007*	1.50	6.00	61
IF YOU LOVE ME/Now Is The Hour	*Goldisc 615*	3.00	12.00	—

RADIANTS, Little Jan & The

TITLE/FLIP	LABEL & NO.	GOOD TO VERY GOOD	NEAR MINT	YR.
IF YOU LOVE ME/Heart and Soul	*Vim 507*	5.00	20.00	60
NOW IS THE HOUR/Is It True?	*Clock 1028*	1.50	6.00	60

RADIANTS, Maurice & The

RADIANTS, The

RAELETS, The (female)

RAINBOWS, The

TITLE/FLIP	LABEL & NO.	GOOD TO VERY GOOD	NEAR MINT	YR.
EVENING/Mary Lee	*Pilgrim 703*	1.50	6.00	56
EVENING/Mary Lee	*Red Robin 134*	10.00	40.00	55
SHIRLEY/Stay	*Argyle 1012*	1.50	6.00	62
SHIRLEY/Stay	*Pilgrim 711*	2.50	10.00	56
THEY SAY/Minnie	*Rama 209*	30.00	120.00	56

RAINDROPS, The

TITLE/FLIP	LABEL & NO.	GOOD TO VERY GOOD	NEAR MINT	YR.
DIM THOSE LIGHTS/Oh, Oh, Baby	*Vega 105*	7.00	28.00	58

RAINEY, Big Memphis Ma with The Onzie Horne Combo

Memphis Ma Rainey (Lilian Glover) is not to be confused with Gertrude Ma Rainey, the legendary blues singer of the 20s and 30s.

TITLE/FLIP	LABEL & NO.	GOOD TO VERY GOOD	NEAR MINT	YR.
CALL ME ANYTHING, BUT CALL ME/Baby, No, No	*Sun 184*	30.00	120.00	53

RAJAHS, The

TITLE/FLIP	LABEL & NO.	GOOD TO VERY GOOD	NEAR MINT	YR.
I FELL IN LOVE/Shifting Sands	*Klik 7805*	7.00	28.00	57

RAMBLERS, The

TITLE/FLIP	LABEL & NO.	GOOD TO VERY GOOD	NEAR MINT	YR.
HEAVEN AND EARTH, THE/Don't You Know?	*Federal 12286*	5.00	20.00	56

RAMBLERS, The

TITLE/FLIP	LABEL & NO.	GOOD TO VERY GOOD	NEAR MINT	YR.
SEARCH MY HEART/50-50 Love	*Jax 319*	20.00	80.00	52

RAMBLERS, The

TITLE/FLIP	LABEL & NO.	GOOD TO VERY GOOD	NEAR MINT	YR.
BAD GIRL/Rickey-Do, Rickey-Do	*MGM 55006*	15.00	60.00	55
VADUNT-LIN-VA-DA SONG/ Please Bring Yourself Back Home	*MGM 11850*	35.00	140.00	54

RAMS, The

TITLE/FLIP	LABEL & NO.	GOOD TO VERY GOOD	NEAR MINT	YR.
SWEET THING/Rock Bottom	*Flair 1066*	5.00	20.00	55

RANDALL, Todd:

see Blue Notes, The (with Todd Randall)
see Blue Notes, Todd Randall & The

RANKIN, R. S. as T-Bone Walker, Jr.

TITLE/FLIP	LABEL & NO.	GOOD TO VERY GOOD	NEAR MINT	YR.
MIDNIGHT BELLS ARE RINGING/Empty Feeling	*Midnite 101*	2.00	8.00	62

RAPIDTONES, The

TITLE/FLIP	LABEL & NO.	GOOD TO VERY GOOD	NEAR MINT	YR.
SUNDAY KIND OF LOVE/Memories Of You	*Rapid 1002*	6.25	25.00	—

RAVELS, The

RAVENETTES, THE (female)

RAVENS, Dinah Washington & The

TITLE/FLIP	LABEL & NO.	GOOD TO VERY GOOD	NEAR MINT	YR.
OUT IN THE COLD AGAIN/Hey, Good Lookin'	*Mercury 8257*	10.00	40.00	51

RAVENS, The

Joe Van Loan appeared as the lead tenor on most Ravens songs from the 1950s.

TITLE/FLIP	LABEL & NO.	GOOD TO VERY GOOD	NEAR MINT	YR.
ALWAYS/Rooster (78)	*National 9064*	2.50	10.00	48
BEGIN THE BEGUINE/Looking For My Baby (pink label)	*Mercury 5800*	9.00	36.00	52
BEGIN THE BEGUINE/Looking For My Baby	*Mercury 5800*	7.00	28.00	52
BYE, BYE, BABY BLUES/Happy Go Lucky Baby	*Jubilee 5184*	3.00	12.00	55
BYE, BYE, BABY BLUES/Once And For All (78)	*Hub 3033*	5.00	20.00	46
BYE, BYE, BABY BLUES/Once And For All (78)	*King 4234*	4.00	16.00	48
CARELESS LOVE/ There's Nothing Like A Woman In Love (78)	*National 9085*	2.50	10.00	49
COME A LITTLE BIT CLOSER/ She's Got To Go (pink label)	*Mercury 70119*	8.00	32.00	53
COME A LITTLE BIT CLOSER/She's Got To Go	*Mercury 70119*	6.25	25.00	53
COUNT EVERY STAR/ I'm Gonna Paper My Walls With Your Love Letters	*National 9111*	100.00	400.00	50
DEEP PURPLE/Leave My Gal Alone (78)	*National 9065*	2.50	10.00	49
DON'T MENTION MY NAME/I'll Be Back	*Mercury 70060*	11.00	44.00	52
FOOL THAT I AM/Be I Bumblebee Or Not (78)	*National 9040*	2.50	10.00	47
FOR YOU/Mahzel (78)	*National 9034*	2.50	10.00	47
GREEN EYES/The Bells Of San Raquel	*Jubilee 5203*	2.50	10.00	55
HONEY/Matinee Hour In New Orleans (instrumental by The Three Clouds) (78)	*King 4272*	4.00	16.00	49
HOUSE I LIVE IN, THE/Ricky's Blues (78)	*National 9073*	2.50	10.00	49
HOW COULD I KNOW?/ I Don't Know Why I Love You Like I Do (78)	*National 9059*	2.50	10.00	48
I DON'T HAVE TO RIDE NO MORE/I've Been A Fool (78)	*National 9101*	2.50	10.00	49
I'LL ALWAYS BE IN LOVE WITH YOU/Boots And Saddles	*Jubilee 5237*	2.50	10.00	56
I'M AFRAID OF YOU/Get Wise, Baby (78)	*National 9098*	2.50	10.00	49
I'M GONNA TAKE TO THE ROAD/ Phantom Stage Couch (78)	*National 9131*	2.50	10.00	50

This record is not known to exist on 45 rpm. Should a copy surface, it would command at least as much as "Count Every Star," a $400 record.

TITLE/FLIP	LABEL & NO.	GOOD TO VERY GOOD	NEAR MINT	YR.
IF YOU DIDN'T MEAN IT/Someday (78)	*National 9089*	2.50	10.00	49
IT'S TOO SOON TO KNOW/Be On Your Merry Way (78)	*National 9056*	2.50	10.00	48
LILACS IN THE RAIN/Time Is Marching On (78)	*National 9148*	2.50	10.00	51

This record is not known to exist on 45 rpm. Should a copy surface, it would command at least as much as "Count Every Star," a $400 record.

TITLE/FLIP	LABEL & NO.	GOOD TO VERY GOOD	NEAR MINT	YR.
LOVE IS NO DREAM/ I've Got You Under My Skin (pink label)	*Mercury 70413*	12.50	50.00	54
LOVE IS NO DREAM/I've Got You Under My Skin	*Mercury 70413*	10.00	40.00	54
LULLABY/Honey (78)	*Hub 3030*	5.00	20.00	46
MAM'SELLE/Calypso Song	*Okeh 6888*	25.00	100.00	52
MY BABY'S GONE/I'm So Crazy For Love (33 single)	*Columbia 1-925*	50.00	200.00	50
MY BABY'S GONE/I'm So Crazy For Love	*Columbia 6-925*	35.00	140.00	50
MY SUGAR IS SO REFINED/ Playing Around (instrumental by The Three Clouds) (78)	*King 4293*	4.00	16.00	49
OL' MAN RIVER/Would You Believe Me? (78)	*National 9035*	2.50	10.00	47
OLD MAN RIVER/Write Me A Letter (pink label)	*Mercury 70554*	9.00	36.00	55
OLD MAN RIVER/Write Me A Letter	*Mercury 70554*	7.00	28.00	55
ON CHAPEL HILL/We'll Raise A Ruckus Tonight	*Jubilee 5217*	2.50	10.00	55
OUT OF A DREAM/Blues In The Clouds (instrumental by The Three Clouds) (78)	*King 4260*	4.00	16.00	48
OUT OF A DREAM/My Sugar Is So Refined (78)	*Hub 3032*	5.00	20.00	46
ROCK ME ALL NIGHT LONG/ Write Me One Sweet Letter (pink label)	*Mercury 8291*	6.25	25.00	54
ROCK ME ALL NIGHT LONG/Write Me One Sweet Letter	*Mercury 8291*	5.00	20.00	52
SEARCHING FOR LOVE/For You (78)	*National 9039*	2.50	10.00	47
SEPTEMBER SONG/Escortin' Or Courtin'	*Mercury 70307*	10.00	40.00	54
SEPTEMBER SONG/Once In A While (78)	*National 9053*	2.50	10.00	48
SILENT NIGHT/White Christmas (78)	*National 9062*	2.50	10.00	48
THAT OLD GANG OF MINE/Everything But You	*Okeh 6843*	60.00	240.00	51
THERE'S NO USE PRETENDING/Wagon Wheels	*Mercury 5764*	20.00	80.00	51
TIME TAKES CARE OF EVERYTHING/ Don't Look Now (33 single)	*Columbia 1-903*	50.00	200.00	50
TIME TAKES CARE OF EVERYTHING/Don't Look Now	*Columbia 6-903*	35.00	140.00	50
TOGETHER/There's No You (78)	*National 9042*	2.50	10.00	48
UNTIL THE REAL THING COMES ALONG/ Send For Me If You Need Me (78)	*National 9045*	2.50	10.00	48
WHITE CHRISTMAS/Silent Night (pink label)	*Mercury 70505*	11.00	44.00	54
WHITE CHRISTMAS/Silent Night	*Mercury 70505*	9.00	36.00	54
WHO'LL BE THE FOOL?/Rough Ridin' (pink label)	*Mercury 70213*	8.00	32.00	53
WHO'LL BE THE FOOL?/Rough Ridin'	*Mercury 70213*	6.25	25.00	53
WHY DID YOU LEAVE ME?/Chloe-e (pink label)	*Mercury 5853*	9.00	36.00	52
WHY DID YOU LEAVE ME?/Chloe-e	*Mercury 5853*	7.00	28.00	52
WIFFENPOOF SONG, THE/ I Get All My Lovin' On A Saturday Night	*Okeh 6825*	60.00	240.00	51
WITHOUT A SONG/Walkin' My Blues Away	*Mercury 70240*	6.25	25.00	53
WITHOUT A SONG/ Walkin' My Blues Away (pink label)	*Mercury 70240*	8.00	32.00	53
WRITE ME A LETTER/Marie (78)	*Rendition 5001*	2.50	10.00	51
WRITE ME A LETTER/Summertime (78)	*National 9038*	2.50	10.00	47

Big Walter Price

The Ravens

TITLE/FLIP	LABEL & NO.	GOOD TO VERY GOOD	NEAR MINT	YR.
YOU DON'T HAVE TO DROP A HEART TO BREAK IT/ Midnight Blues	*Columbia 39112*	30.00	120.00	*50*
YOU FOOLISH THING/Honey, I Don't Want You	*Columbia 39408*	105.00	420.00	*51*
YOU'RE ALWAYS IN MY DREAMS/Gotta Find My Baby	*Columbia 39194*	30.00	120.00	*51*

RAVENS, The

TITLE/FLIP	LABEL & NO.	GOOD TO VERY GOOD	NEAR MINT	YR.
KNEEL AND PRAY/I Can't Believe	*Argo 5255*	4.00	16.00	*56*
SIMPLE PRAYER, A/Water Boy	*Argo 5261*	6.25	25.00	*56*
THAT'LL BE THE DAY/Dear One	*Argo 5276*	2.50	10.00	*57*
THAT'LL BE THE DAY/Dear One	*Checker 871*	1.50	6.00	*57*

RAVENSCROFT, Thur & The Sky Boys:
see Sky Boys, Thur Ravenscroft & The

RAVES, Jimmy Ricks & The

TITLE/FLIP	LABEL & NO.	GOOD TO VERY GOOD	NEAR MINT	YR.
DADDY ROLLIN' STONE/Umgowa	*Festival 25004*	1.50	6.00	*62*

RAVES, The

TITLE/FLIP	LABEL & NO.	GOOD TO VERY GOOD	NEAR MINT	YR.
TELL ME ONE MORE TIME/Billy The Kid	*Swade 104*	3.00	12.00	—

RAVONS, The

TITLE/FLIP	LABEL & NO.	GOOD TO VERY GOOD	NEAR MINT	YR.
WHY DID YOU LEAVE ME?/Everybody's Laughing At Me	*Yucca 142*	3.00	12.00	*62*

RAWLS, Lou

RAY, Bobby & The Cadillacs

RAY, Harmon as Peetie Wheatstraw's Buddy

TITLE/FLIP	LABEL & NO.	GOOD TO VERY GOOD	NEAR MINT	YR.
DOG EATIN' MEN/Miss Irene (78)	*Hy Tone 38*	2.50	10.00	*47*

RAY, Isom:
see Agee, Ray as Isom Ray

RAY, James

RAY, Laverne & The Raytones:
see Raytones, Laverne Ray & The

RAYS, The

TITLE/FLIP	LABEL & NO.	GOOD TO VERY GOOD	NEAR MINT	YR.
ARE YOU HAPPY NOW?/Bright Brown Eyes	*Perri 1004*	1.50	6.00	*62*
HOW LONG MUST I WAIT?/Second Fiddle	*Chess 1678*	1.50	6.00	*57*
MY STEADY GIRL/Nobody Loves You Like I Do	*XYZ 100*	6.25	25.00	*57*
OUETTES/Daddy Cool	*XYZ 102*	5.00	20.00	*57*
TIPPITY TOP/Moo-Goo-Gai-Pan	*Chess 1613*	1.50	6.00	*55*

RAYTONES, Laverne Ray & The

TITLE/FLIP	LABEL & NO.	GOOD TO VERY GOOD	NEAR MINT	YR.
I'VE GOT THAT FEELING/I'm In Love Again	*Okeh 7091*	1.50	6.00	*57*

RAYTONES, Rudy Ray Moore as Ray Moore & The

TITLE/FLIP	LABEL & NO.	GOOD TO VERY GOOD	NEAR MINT	YR.
I'M READY/So Good To Me	*Cash 1060*	2.00	8.00	—

RAYTONES, Rudy Ray Moore as The

TITLE/FLIP	LABEL & NO.	GOOD TO VERY GOOD	NEAR MINT	YR.
MY BABY, PART 1/My Baby, Part 2	*Ball 503*	1.50	6.00	—
UNTIL YOU'RE IN MY ARMS/Ready, Willing And Able	*Cash 1059*	2.00	8.00	—

RE-VELS QUARTETTE, The

TITLE/FLIP	LABEL & NO.	GOOD TO VERY GOOD	NEAR MINT	YR.
MY LOST LOVE/Love Me, Baby	*Atlas 1035*	20.00	80.00	*54*

RE-VELS, The

TITLE/FLIP	LABEL & NO.	GOOD TO VERY GOOD	NEAR MINT	YR.
FALSE ALARM/When You Come Back To Me	*Chess 1708*	10.00	40.00	*58*

RE-VELS, The

TITLE/FLIP	LABEL & NO.	GOOD TO VERY GOOD	NEAR MINT	YR.
DREAM, MY DARLING, DREAM/Cha-Cha-Toni	*Sound 135*	5.00	20.00	*56*
YOU LIED TO ME/Later, Later, Baby	*Sound 129*	5.00	20.00	*56*

READ, Otis

TITLE/FLIP	LABEL & NO.	GOOD TO VERY GOOD	NEAR MINT	YR.
LOVE IS A SERIOUS THING/Come On, Baby	*Nanc 1118/9*	2.50	10.00	*61*

REALISTICS, The

REAVES, Pearl & The Concords:
see Concords, Pearl Reaves & The

RED CAPS, Steve Gibson & The

TITLE/FLIP	LABEL & NO.	GOOD TO VERY GOOD	NEAR MINT	YR.
BLESS YOU/ You Can't See The Sun When You're Crying (78)	*Mercury 5011*	1.50	6.00	*47*
BLUEBERRY HILL/I Love You	*Mercury 8146*	4.00	16.00	*49*
BLUEBERRY HILL/Poor, Poor Me	*Stage 3001*	2.00	8.00	—
BOBBIN'/How I Cry	*RCA Victor 47-6345*	1.50	6.00	*55*
FEELIN' KINDA' HAPPY (with Damita Jo)/ 'Nuff Of That Stuff	*RCA Victor 47-6096*	1.50	6.00	*55*
FOREVER 'N' A DAY/It's Love	*Hi Lo 103*	1.50	6.00	*58*
I WANT TO BE LOVED/I-Bitty-Bitty	*Hi Lo 101*	1.50	6.00	*58*
I'LL NEVER LOVE ANYONE ELSE/ I Want A Roof Over My Head (78)	*Mercury 5380*	1.50	6.00	*50*
IT HURTS ME BUT I LIKE IT/Ouch	*Jay Dee 796*	2.50	10.00	*54*
WEDDING BELLS ARE BREAKING UP THAT OLD GANG OF MINE/ I'd Love To Live A Lifetime For You	*Mercury 8069*	7.00	28.00	*48*
WEDDING BELLS ARE BREAKING UP THAT OLD GANG OF MINE/ Second Hand Romance	*Mercury 70389*	4.00	16.00	*54*
WIN OR LOSE (with Damita Jo)/My Tzatskele	*RCA Victor 47-5987*	1.50	6.00	*55*

RED CAPS, Steve Gibson & The as The Original Red Caps

TITLE/FLIP	LABEL & NO.	GOOD TO VERY GOOD	NEAR MINT	YR.
BIG GAME HUNTER/Do I, Do I, I Do	*RCA Victor 47-5130*	4.00	16.00	*53*
I MAY HATE MYSELF IN THE MORNING/ Two Little Kisses	*RCA Victor 47-4670*	2.50	10.00	*52*
I'M TO BLAME/Sidewalk Shuffle	*RCA Victor 50-0127*	4.00	16.00	*51*
SHAME/Boogie Woogie On A Saturday Night	*RCA Victor 47-4294*	7.00	28.00	*51*
THING, THE/Am I To Blame?	*RCA Victor 47-3986*	8.00	32.00	*50*
THREE DOLLARS AND NINETY-EIGHT CENTS/ D'Ya Eat Yet, Joe?	*RCA Victor 47-4076*	7.00	28.00	*51*
TRUTHFULLY/Why Don't You Love Me?	*RCA Victor 47-5013*	2.50	10.00	*52*
WOULD I MIND?/When You Come Back To Me	*RCA Victor 50-0138*	4.00	16.00	*51*

REDDING, Otis

REED, A. C.

REED, Bob & His Band

REED, James & His Band

TITLE/FLIP	LABEL & NO.	GOOD TO VERY GOOD	NEAR MINT	YR.
DR. BROWN/Better Hold Me	Flair 1042	8.00	32.00	54
OH PEOPLE/My Love Is Real	Money 201	5.00	20.00	54
THIS IS THE END/My Mama Tole Me	Flair 1034	8.00	32.00	54
TIN PAN ALLEY/I Wanna Know (78)	Rhythm 1775	20.00	80.00	54
YOU BETTER HOLD ME/ Things Ain't What They Used To Be	Big Town 117	5.00	20.00	54

REED, Jimmy

TITLE/FLIP	LABEL & NO.	GOOD TO VERY GOOD	NEAR MINT	YR.
HIGH AND LONESOME/Jimmy's Boogie (instrumental)	Chance 1142	15.00	60.00	53
HIGH AND LONESOME/Jimmy's Boogie (instrumental)	Vee Jay 105	4.00	16.00	53
HIGH AND LONESOME/Roll And Rhumba (instrumental)	Vee Jay 100	15.00	60.00	53
I'M GONNA RUIN YOU/Pretty Thing	Vee Jay 132	1.50	6.00	55
SHE DON'T WANT ME NO MORE/I Don't Go For That	Vee Jay 153	1.50	6.00	55
YOU DON'T HAVE TO GO/Boogie In The Dark	Vee Jay 119	1.50	6.00	53

REED, Vivian

REESE, Bill Quintet, The & The Coronets:
see Coronets, The Bill Reese Quintet & The

REESE, Slim

TITLE/FLIP	LABEL & NO.	GOOD TO VERY GOOD	NEAR MINT	YR.
GOT THE WORLD IN A JUG/I'm So Worried (78)	Sittin' In With 581	2.00	8.00	51

REGALS, The

TITLE/FLIP	LABEL & NO.	GOOD TO VERY GOOD	NEAR MINT	YR.
I'M SO LONELY/Got The Water Boiling	Atlantic 1062	2.00	8.00	55
RUN, PRETTY BABY/ May The Good Lord Bless And Keep You	Aladdin 3266	5.00	20.00	54

REID, Clarence

RELF, Bobby & The Laurels:
see Laurels, Bobby Relf & The

REMUS, Eugene

TITLE/FLIP	LABEL & NO.	GOOD TO VERY GOOD	NEAR MINT	YR.
YOU NEVER MISS A GOOD THING/Gotta Have Your Lovin'	Motown 1001	2.00	8.00	61
YOU NEVER MISS A GOOD THING/Hold Me Tight	Motown 1001	2.00	8.00	61

RENE, Googie & His Combo

RESTLESS HEARTS, Fred Parris & The

REVALONS, The

TITLE/FLIP	LABEL & NO.	GOOD TO VERY GOOD	NEAR MINT	YR.
THIS IS THE MOMENT/Dreams Are For Fools	Pet 802	3.00	12.00	58

REVELS, The

REVLONS, The

TITLE/FLIP	LABEL & NO.	GOOD TO VERY GOOD	NEAR MINT	YR.
THIS RESTLESS HEART/I Promise Love	Rae Cox 105	1.50	6.00	61

REYNAUD, Marie & The Golden Tones

REYNOLDS, Big Jack & His Blues Men

REYNOLDS, Teddy

RHODES, Todd

TITLE/FLIP	LABEL & NO.	GOOD TO VERY GOOD	NEAR MINT	YR.
BLUES FOR THE RED BOY/Sportree's Jump (78) Instrumentals.	King 4240	2.50	10.00	48
GIN, GIN, GIN/I Shouldn't Cry	King 4469	6.25	25.00	51
LOST CHILD (Lavern Baker vocal)/ Thunderbolt Boogie (instrumental)	King 4601	2.00	8.00	52
MUST I CRY AGAIN? (Lavern Baker vocal)/ Hog Maw And Cabbage Slaw (instrumental)	King 4583	2.00	8.00	52
PIG LATIN BLUES (Lavern Baker vocal)/ Blue Autumn (instrumental)	King 4566	2.00	8.00	52
ROCKET 69/Possessed (instrumental)	King 4528	6.25	25.00	52
TRYING (Lavern Baker vocal)/Snuff Dipper (instrumental)	King 4556	2.00	8.00	52
YOUR DADDY'S DOGGIN' AROUND/ Red Boy Is Back (colored plastic) Instrumentals.	King 4509	8.00	32.00	51
YOUR DADDY'S DOGGIN' AROUND/Red Boy Is Back Instrumentals.	King 4509	4.00	16.00	51

RHYTHM ACES, Bobby Moore & The

RHYTHM ACES, The

TITLE/FLIP	LABEL & NO.	GOOD TO VERY GOOD	NEAR MINT	YR.
I WONDER WHY?/Get Lost	Vee Jay 124	9.00	36.00	54
ROCK AND ROLL MARCH/Look What You've Done	Ace 518	1.50	6.00	54
THAT'S MY SUGAR/Flippety Flop	Vee Jay 160	15.00	60.00	55
WHISPER TO ME/Olly, Olly, Atsen, Free	Vee Jay 138	15.00	60.00	55

RHYTHM CADETS, The

TITLE/FLIP	LABEL & NO.	GOOD TO VERY GOOD	NEAR MINT	YR.
DEAREST DORYCE/Rocking Jimmy	Vesta 501	50.00	200.00	57

RHYTHM CASTERS, The

TITLE/FLIP	LABEL & NO.	GOOD TO VERY GOOD	NEAR MINT	YR.
LOVE, LOVE, BABY/Oh, My Darling	Excello 2115	2.50	10.00	57

RHYTHM KINGS, The

TITLE/FLIP	LABEL & NO.	GOOD TO VERY GOOD	NEAR MINT	YR.
I SHOULDN'T HAVE PASSED YOUR HOUSE/ Night After Night (78)	Ivory 751	2.50	10.00	—
MERRY CHRISTMAS ONE AND ALL/ Christmas Is Coming At Last (78)	Apollo 1171	2.50	10.00	50
WHY, MY DARLING, WHY?/I Gotta Go Now (78)	Apollo 1181	2.50	10.00	51

RHYTHM KINGS, The Earthquakes & The:
see Earthquakes & The Rhythm Kings, The

RHYTHM WILLIE

TITLE/FLIP	LABEL & NO.	GOOD TO VERY GOOD	NEAR MINT	YR.
WAILIN' WILLIE/I Got Rhythm (78) Instrumentals.	Premium 866	2.50	10.00	50

RHYTHMERES, The

TITLE/FLIP	LABEL & NO.	GOOD TO VERY GOOD	NEAR MINT	YR.
ELAINE/Bow-Legged Baby	Brunswick 55083	5.00	20.00	58

RIBBONS, The (female group)

RICE, Sir Mack

RICHARD BROTHERS, The:
(with Howard Richard)
see Richard, Robert as The Richard Brothers

RICHARD, Robert

TITLE/FLIP	LABEL & NO.	GOOD TO VERY GOOD	NEAR MINT	YR.
CADILLAC WOMAN/ Looking For My Woman (by Joseph Von Battle) (78)	JVB 75828	9.00	36.00	48
WIGWAM WOMAN/Root Hog (78)	King 4274	7.00	28.00	48

RICHARD, Robert as The Richard Brothers (with Howard Richard)

TITLE/FLIP	LABEL & NO.	GOOD TO VERY GOOD	NEAR MINT	YR.
STOLEN PROPERTY/Drunk Driver's Coming	Strate 8-1500	8.00	32.00	56

RICHARDSON, Lee:
see Four Blues, The

RICHARDSON, Rudy Trio, The:
see Cats & The Fiddle, The

RICKATEERS, Jimmy Ricks & The

TITLE/FLIP	LABEL & NO.	GOOD TO VERY GOOD	NEAR MINT	YR.
SHE'S FINE—SHE'S MINE/The Unbeliever	Josie 796	2.00	8.00	56

RICKEY & THE PHARAOHS:
see Pharaohs, Rickey & The

RICKS, Jimmy:
see Raves, Jimmy Ricks & The
see Rickateers, Jimmy Ricks & The
see Suburbans, Jimmy Ricks & The

RIDGLEY, Tommy

TITLE/FLIP	LABEL & NO.	GOOD TO VERY GOOD	NEAR MINT	YR.
BOOGIE WOOGIE MAN/Lonely Man Blues (78)	Imperial 5074	1.50	6.00	49
GOOD TIMES/A Day Is Coming	Imperial 5223	8.00	32.00	49
I LIVE MY LIFE/Lavinia	Imperial 5198	8.00	32.00	49
I'M GONNA CROSS THAT RIVER/Oh, Lawdy, My Baby	Atlantic 1009	4.00	16.00	53
JAM UP/Wish I Had Never	Atlantic 1039	1.50	6.00	54
LOOPED/Junie Mae	Imperial 5203	8.00	32.00	49
MONKEY MAN/Nobody Cares	Imperial 5214	8.00	32.00	49
SHREWSBURY BLUES/Early Dawn Boogie (78)	Imperial 5054	1.50	6.00	49

RILEY, Billy Lee as Lightnin' Leon

TITLE/FLIP	LABEL & NO.	GOOD TO VERY GOOD	NEAR MINT	YR.
DARK MUDDY BOTTOM/Repossession Blues	Rita 1005	1.50	6.00	60

RILEY, Russ & The Five Sounds:
see Five Sounds, Russ Riley & The

Little Richard

A.C. Reed

TITLE/FLIP	LABEL & NO.	GOOD TO VERY GOOD	NEAR MINT	YR.
RIP-CHORDS, The				
I LOVE YOU THE MOST/ Let's Do The Razzle Dazzle	Abco 105	20.00	80.00	56
RIPLEY COTTON CHOPPERS, The				
BLUES WALTZ/Silver Bells (78)	Sun 190	120.00	480.00	53
RIVER ROVERS, The				
BALD-HEADED DADDY/Delta Drag	Apollo 432	10.00	40.00	51
RIVERA, Little Bobby & The Hemlocks: see Hemlocks, Little Bobby Rivera & The				
RIVERS, Candy & The Falcons: see Falcons, Candy Rivers & The				
RIVIERAS, The				
COUNT EVERY STAR/True Love Is Hard To Find	Coed 503	1.50	6.00	58
MOONLIGHT COCKTAILS/Blessing Of Love	Coed 529	1.50	6.00	60
OUR LOVE/True Love Is Hard To Find	Coed 513	1.50	6.00	59

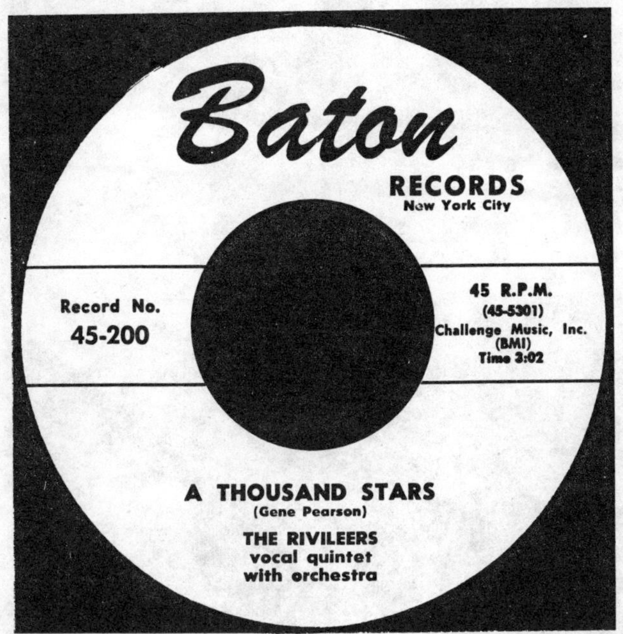

TITLE/FLIP	LABEL & NO.	GOOD TO VERY GOOD	NEAR MINT	YR.
RIVILEERS, The				
CAROLYN/Eternal Love	Baton 205	8.00	32.00	54
DON'T EVER LEAVE ME/Little Girl	Baton 209	5.00	20.00	55
FOR SENTIMENTAL REASONS/I Want To See My Baby	Baton 207	5.00	20.00	54
FOREVER/Darling, Farewell	Baton 201	8.00	32.00	54
THOUSAND STARS, A/Hey, Chiquita	Baton 200	5.00	20.00	54
THOUSAND STARS, A/Who Is The Girl?	Baton 241	3.00	12.00	57
RIVINGTONS, The				
ALL THAT GLITTERS/You Move Me, Baby	A.R.E. American 100	1.50	6.00	64
CHERRY/Little Sally Walker	Liberty 55610	5.00	20.00	63
ROAMERS, The				
I'LL NEVER GET OVER YOU/Deep Freeze	Savoy 1147	1.50	6.00	54
NEVER LET ME GO/Chop, Chop, Ching-A-Ling	Savoy 1156	1.50	6.00	55
ROAMERS, Varetta Dillard & The				
YOU'RE THE ANSWER TO MY PRAYER/ Promise, Mr. Thomas	Savoy 1160	1.50	6.00	55
ROAMERS, Wilbert Harrison & The				
ROBBINS, Bobby Nunn & The				
ROCKIN'/That's What The Good Book Says (78)	Modern 807	5.00	20.00	51
ROBBINS, The				
KEY TO MY HEART/All I Do Is Rock	Crown 120	15.00	60.00	54
ROBERSON, Hubert: see Robinson, Hubert as Hubert Roberson				

TITLE/FLIP	LABEL & NO.	GOOD TO VERY GOOD	NEAR MINT	YR.
ROBERTS, Gip				
NO ONE MONKEY GOIN' TO RUN MY SHOW/Sandman	JVB 29	4.00	16.00	58
ROBERTS, John				
ROBERTSON, Jessie Mae				
ROCK 'EM AND ROLL 'EM, PART 1/ Rock 'Em And Roll 'Em, Part 2	Blaze 111	1.50	6.00	—
ROBERTSON, Walter: see Robinson, Walter as Walter Robertson				
ROBINS, Little Esther & The: see Little Esther (Phillips) & The Robins				
ROBINS, The				
ALL NIGHT BABY/Oh, Why?	RCA Victor 47-5271	20.00	80.00	53
AROUND ABOUT MIDNITE/You Sure Look Good To Me (78)	Score 4010	4.00	16.00	49
DON'T LIKE THE WAY YOU'RE DOING/ Come Back, Baby (78)	Aladdin 3031	8.00	32.00	49
DON'T STOP NOW/Get It Off Your Mind	RCA Victor 47-5564	10.00	40.00	53
FALLING STAR, A/ When Gabriel Blows His Horn (78) Vocals by Maggie Hathaway.	Recorded in Hollywood 121	4.00	16.00	—
FOOL SUCH AS I, A/My Heart's The Biggest Fool	RCA Victor 47-5175	20.00	80.00	53
FRAMED/Loop De Loop Mambo	Spark 107	5.00	20.00	54
I MADE A VOW/Double Crossin' Baby	Crown 106	15.00	60.00	54
I MUST BE DREAMIN'/The Hatchet Man	Spark 116	4.00	16.00	55
I'M THROUGH/You're Fine, But Not My Kind (78)	Savoy 762	2.50	10.00	50
IF IT'S SO, BABY/If I Didn't Love You So (78)	Savoy 726	2.50	10.00	49
IF TEARDROPS WERE KISSES/Whadaya Want?	Spark 110	8.00	32.00	55
LET'S GO TO THE DANCE/How Would You Know?	RCA Victor 47-5434	10.00	40.00	53
MAGIC OF A DREAM/ Mary Lou Loves To Hootchy Kootchy Koo	Lavender 002	1.50	6.00	61
MY BABY DONE TOLD ME/I'll Do It	RCA Victor 47-5486	10.00	40.00	53
ONE KISS/I Love Paris	Spark 113	3.00	12.00	55
OUR ROMANCE IS GONE/There Ain't No Use Beggin' (78)	Savoy 738	2.50	10.00	50
RACE OF MAN/Bayou Baby Blues (78) Vocals by Maggie Hathaway.	Recorded in Hollywood 112	4.00	16.00	—
RIOT IN CELL BLOCK #9/Wrap It Up	Spark 103	5.00	20.00	54
SCHOOL GIRL BLUES/Early Morning Blues	Recorded in Hollywood 150	4.00	16.00	51
SINCE I FIRST MET YOU/That Old Black Magic	Whippit 203	2.50	10.00	56
SMOKEY JOE'S CAFE/Just Like A Fool	Spark 122	10.00	40.00	55
TEN DAYS IN JAIL/Empty Bottles	RCA Victor 47-5489	10.00	40.00	53
THERE'S RAIN IN MY EYES/I'm Living O.K. (78)	Savoy 752	2.50	10.00	50
TURKEY HOP, PART 1/ Turkey Hop, Part 2 (instrumental) (78)	Savoy 732	2.50	10.00	50
WHITE CLIFFS OF DOVER/How Many More Times?	Lavender 001	2.00	8.00	61

The Rivingtons

Fenton Robinson

TITLE/FLIP	LABEL & NO.	GOOD TO VERY GOOD	NEAR MINT	YR.

ROBINSON BROTHERS, The:
see Robinson, L. C. as The Robinson Brothers (with Walter Robinson)

ROBINSON, Bill & The Quails:
see Quails, Bill Robinson & The

ROBINSON, Fention & His Dukes

It's unclear whether Robinson's real first name is Fention or Fenton, the latter used in later recordings.

TITLE/FLIP	LABEL & NO.	GOOD TO VERY GOOD	NEAR MINT	YR.
TENNESSEE WOMAN/Crying Out Loud	Meteor 5041	10.00	40.00	57

ROBINSON, Freddy

ROBINSON, Hubert

TITLE/FLIP	LABEL & NO.	GOOD TO VERY GOOD	NEAR MINT	YR.
ANSWER TO WINTERTIME BLUES/Old Woman Boogie (78)	Macy's 5007	1.50	6.00	50
BAD LUCK AND TROUBLE/Room And Board Boogie (78)	Macy's 5010	1.50	6.00	50
I LOVE YOU, BABY/High Class Woman (78)	Macy's 5015	1.50	6.00	50
WHERE WERE YOU, PRETTY BABY/Boogie The Joint (78)	Macy's 5005	1.50	6.00	50

ROBINSON, Hubert & His Yardbirds

TITLE/FLIP	LABEL & NO.	GOOD TO VERY GOOD	NEAR MINT	YR.
HARD LOVIN' DADDY/Gas Happy Blues (78)	Jade 206	1.50	6.00	51

ROBINSON, Hubert as Hubert Roberson & Orchestra

TITLE/FLIP	LABEL & NO.	GOOD TO VERY GOOD	NEAR MINT	YR.
H. R. JUMPS/Lonely Traveller (78)	Eddie's 1211	2.50	10.00	49

ROBINSON, Hubert:
see Amy, Curtis

ROBINSON, Jimmy Lee

TITLE/FLIP	LABEL & NO.	GOOD TO VERY GOOD	NEAR MINT	YR.
TWIST IT, BABY/Times Is Hard	Bandera 2510	2.00	8.00	62

ROBINSON, Jimmy Lee as Jimmy Lee

TITLE/FLIP	LABEL & NO.	GOOD TO VERY GOOD	NEAR MINT	YR.
ALL OF MY LIFE/Chicago Jump (instrumental)	Bandera 2506	1.50	6.00	60

ROBINSON, Jimmy Lee as Lonesome Lee

TITLE/FLIP	LABEL & NO.	GOOD TO VERY GOOD	NEAR MINT	YR.
LONELY TRAVELLIN'/Cry Over Me	Bandera 2501	4.00	16.00	59

ROBINSON, L. C.

TITLE/FLIP	LABEL & NO.	GOOD TO VERY GOOD	NEAR MINT	YR.
IF I LOSE YOU, BABY/Why Don't You Write To Me? (78)	Rhythm 1772	7.00	28.00	54

ROBINSON, L. C. as The Robinson Brothers (with Walter Robinson)

TITLE/FLIP	LABEL & NO.	GOOD TO VERY GOOD	NEAR MINT	YR.
I GOT TO GO/Come Back To Me, Baby (78)	Black & White 107	4.00	16.00	45
L. C. BOOGIE/Hurry Hurry Baby (78)	Black & White 108	4.00	16.00	45

ROBINSON, Smokey:
see Miracles, Smokey Robinson & The
see Miracles, The (featuring Smokey Robinson)
see Ron & Bill (Ron White & Bill "Smokey" Robinson)

ROBINSON, Walter as Walter Robertson

TITLE/FLIP	LABEL & NO.	GOOD TO VERY GOOD	NEAR MINT	YR.
SPUTTERIN' BLUES/I've Done Everything I Can	Flair 1053	10.00	40.00	54

ROBINSON, Walter:
see Robinson, L. C. as The Robinson Brothers (with Walter Robinson)

ROCHELL & THE CANDLES:
see Candles, Rochell & The

ROCK-A-BYES, Baby Jane & The (female group)

ROCKERS, Jimmy Beasley & The

ROCKERS, Paul Winley & The

TITLE/FLIP	LABEL & NO.	GOOD TO VERY GOOD	NEAR MINT	YR.
MY CONFESSION/Angel Child	Premium 401	4.00	16.00	55

ROCKERS, The

TITLE/FLIP	LABEL & NO.	GOOD TO VERY GOOD	NEAR MINT	YR.
DOWN IN THE BOTTOM/Why Don't You Believe?	Federal 12273	2.50	10.00	56
TELL ME WHY/Count Every Star	Carter 3029	50.00	200.00	—
WHAT AM I TO DO?/I'll Die In Love With You	Federal 12267	2.50	10.00	56

ROCKETEERS, The

TITLE/FLIP	LABEL & NO.	GOOD TO VERY GOOD	NEAR MINT	YR.
FOOLISH ONE/Gonna Feed My Baby Poison	Herald 415	7.00	28.00	53

ROCKETEERS, The

TITLE/FLIP	LABEL & NO.	GOOD TO VERY GOOD	NEAR MINT	YR.
MY RECKLESS HEART/ They Turned The Party Out Down At Bessie's House	M.J.C. 501	50.00	200.00	—

ROCKETONES, The

TITLE/FLIP	LABEL & NO.	GOOD TO VERY GOOD	NEAR MINT	YR.
MEXICO/Dee I	Melba 113	3.00	12.00	57

ROCKETS, Bill Bodaford & The

TITLE/FLIP	LABEL & NO.	GOOD TO VERY GOOD	NEAR MINT	YR.
LITTLE GIRL/Teardrops	Backbeat 507	1.50	6.00	58

ROCKETS, Herb Kenny & The

TITLE/FLIP	LABEL & NO.	GOOD TO VERY GOOD	NEAR MINT	YR.
BUT ALWAYS YOUR FRIEND/Star-Spangled Dawn	MGM 11487	2.50	10.00	53
DO I HAVE TO TELL YOU I'M SORRY?/Don't Take My Word	MGM 11648	2.50	10.00	53
I DON'T CARE/Calling You	MGM 11360	2.50	10.00	52
MY SONG/You Never Heard A Word I Said	MGM 11332	2.50	10.00	52

ROCKETS, Little Freddy & The

TITLE/FLIP	LABEL & NO.	GOOD TO VERY GOOD	NEAR MINT	YR.
ALL MY LOVE/Too Fat	Chief 33	15.00	60.00	—

ROCKETS, The

TITLE/FLIP	LABEL & NO.	GOOD TO VERY GOOD	NEAR MINT	YR.
YOU ARE THE FIRST ONE/Be Lovey Dovey	Modern 992	1.50	6.00	56

ROCKETS, (Harry) Van Walls & The

TITLE/FLIP	LABEL & NO.	GOOD TO VERY GOOD	NEAR MINT	YR.
OPEN THE DOOR/Big Leg Mama	Atlantic 988	7.00	28.00	53

ROCKETTES, The (not a female group)

TITLE/FLIP	LABEL & NO.	GOOD TO VERY GOOD	NEAR MINT	YR.
I CAN'T FORGET/Love Nobody	Parrot 789	60.00	240.00	54

ROCKIN' DUKES, The

TITLE/FLIP	LABEL & NO.	GOOD TO VERY GOOD	NEAR MINT	YR.
ANGEL AND A ROSE/My Baby Left Me	O.J. 1007	30.00	120.00	—

ROCKIN' DUKES, The (with Joe Hudson)

TITLE/FLIP	LABEL & NO.	GOOD TO VERY GOOD	NEAR MINT	YR.
BABY, GIVE ME A CHANCE/Ooh-Wee, Pretty Baby	Excello 2112	3.00	12.00	57

ROCKIN' SYDNEY (or SIDNEY)

ROCKIN' TOWNIES, Bennie Woods & The

TITLE/FLIP	LABEL & NO.	GOOD TO VERY GOOD	NEAR MINT	YR.
I CROSS MY FINGERS/Wheel, Baby, Wheel	Atlas 1040	20.00	80.00	54

ROGER & THE A-TONES:
see Bailon, Roger as Roger & The A-Tones

ROGER & THE GYPSIES:
see Gypsies, Roger & The

ROGERS, Jimmy

Rogers should not be confused with the legendary "Singing Brakeman" Jimmie Rodgers of the 1920s and 1930s, nor with the folk singer for Roulette records, Jimmie Rodgers.

TITLE/FLIP	LABEL & NO.	GOOD TO VERY GOOD	NEAR MINT	YR.
IF IT AIN'T ME/Walking By Myself	Chess 1643	1.50	6.00	56
ONE KISS/I Can't Believe	Chess 1659	1.50	6.00	57

ROGERS, Jimmy & His Rocking Four

TITLE/FLIP	LABEL & NO.	GOOD TO VERY GOOD	NEAR MINT	YR.
BLUES ALL DAY LONG/You're The One	Chess 1616	2.50	10.00	54
CHICAGO BOUND/Sloppy Drunk	Chess 1574	5.00	20.00	54
I USED TO HAVE A WOMAN/Back Door Friend (78)	Chess 1506	2.00	8.00	51
LAST TIME, THE/Out On The Road (78)	Chess 1519	2.00	8.00	52
LEFT ME WITH A BROKEN HEART/Act Like You Love Me	Chess 1543	7.00	28.00	53
MONEY, MARBLES AND CHALK/Chance To Love (78)	Chess 1476	2.00	8.00	51
SHE LOVES ANOTHER MAN/The World Is In A Tangle (78)	Chess 1453	2.00	8.00	51

ROGERS, Jimmy & His Trio

TITLE/FLIP	LABEL & NO.	GOOD TO VERY GOOD	NEAR MINT	YR.
GOING AWAY, BABY/Today, Today Baby (78)	Chess 1442	2.00	8.00	50
THAT'S ALL RIGHT/Ludella (78)	Chess 1435	2.00	8.00	50

ROGERS, Juanita & The Five Joys:
see Five Joys, Juanita Rogers & The

ROGERS, Lee

ROLLERS, The

ROLLETTES, The (female group)

TITLE/FLIP	LABEL & NO.	GOOD TO VERY GOOD	NEAR MINT	YR.
MORE THAN YOU REALIZE/Kiss Me, Benny	Class 203	2.00	8.00	56
SAD FOOL/(instrumental)	Class 201	2.00	8.00	56

ROLLING CREW, The

TITLE/FLIP	LABEL & NO.	GOOD TO VERY GOOD	NEAR MINT	YR.
HOME ON ALCATRAZ/Cryin' Emma	Aladdin 3301	7.00	28.00	55

ROMAINES, The

TITLE/FLIP	LABEL & NO.	GOOD TO VERY GOOD	NEAR MINT	YR.
YOUR KIND OF LOVE/Till The Wee, Wee Morning	Groove 0035	5.00	20.00	54

ROMANCERS, The

TITLE/FLIP	LABEL & NO.	GOOD TO VERY GOOD	NEAR MINT	YR.
I STILL REMEMBER/House Cat	Dootone 381	10.00	40.00	56
THIS IS GOODBYE/Jump And Hop	Dootone 404	10.00	40.00	56
YOU DON'T UNDERSTAND/Baby, I Love You So	Bay Tone 101	2.50	10.00	—

TITLE/FLIP	LABEL & NO.	GOOD TO VERY GOOD	NEAR MINT	YR.
ROMANCERS, The				
NO GREATER LOVE/You'll Never Know	Celebrity 701	1.50	6.00	61
ROMANS, Little Caesar & The				
HULLY GULLY AGAIN/Frankie And Johnny	Del Fi 4164	1.50	6.00	61
ROMANTICS, Ruby & The				
ROMEOS, The				
I BEG YOU, PLEASE/Love Me	Apollo 461	9.00	36.00	54
RAGS/Doctor Velvet	Apollo 466	9.00	36.00	54
ROMEOS, The				
FINE, FINE BABY/Moments To Remember You By	Atco 6107	2.00	8.00	57
GONE, GONE, GET AWAY/Let's Be Partners	Fox (no number)	5.00	20.00	57
MOMENTS TO REMEMBER/Fine, Fine Baby	Fox (no number)	5.00	20.00	57
RON & BILL (Ron White & Bill "Smokey" Robinson of The Miracles)				
IT/Don't Say Bye Bye	Tamla 54025	2.50	10.00	60
RONNIE & THE HI-LITES				
ROSS, Charles as Doctor Ross				
BOOGIE DISEASE, THE/Juke Box Boogie	Sun 212	25.00	100.00	54
COME BACK, BABY/Chicago Breakdown	Sun 193	20.00	80.00	54
INDUSTRIAL BOOGIE/Thirty-Two Twenty	D.I.R. A101	2.00	8.00	58
ROSS, Charles as Dr. Ross & His Jump & Jive Boys				
COUNTRY CLOWN/Dr. Ross Boogie (78)	Chess 1504	5.00	20.00	52
ROSS, Charles as Dr. Ross & His Orbits				
CAT SQUIRREL/The Sunnyland	Fortune 857	1.50	6.00	59
ROSS, Diana				
ROSS, Diana & The Supremes				
ROSS, Diana & The Supremes & The Temptations				
ROSS, Diana: see Supremes, The (featuring Diana Ross)				
ROSS, Doctor: see Ross, Charles as Doctor Ross				
ROSS, Patti: see Jaguars, The				
ROULETTES, The				
I SEE A STAR/Come On, Baby	Champ 102	2.00	8.00	58
WAY YOU CARRY ON, THE/You Don't Care Anymore	Ebb 124	2.50	10.00	57
WOULDN'T BE GOIN' STEADY/Hasten, Jasen	Scepter 1204	8.00	32.00	59
ROVERS, Helen Foster & The				
YOU BELONG TO ME/Oop-Dee-Doo	Republic 7013	10.00	40.00	52
ROVERS, The				
SALUTE TO JOHNNY ACE/Jadda	Music City 780	5.00	20.00	55
WHOLE LOT OF LOVE/ Tell Me, Darling (by The Gaylarks)	Music City 792	4.00	16.00	55
WHY, OH-H?/Ichi-Bon Tami Dachi	Capitol 3078	4.00	16.00	55
WHY, OH-H?/Ichi-Bon Tami Dachi	Music City 750	9.00	36.00	54
ROWLAND, Will				
REEFER BLUES/Don't Lose Your Mind (78)	Gold Star 657	2.50	10.00	47
ROYAL DEBS, The (female group)				
JERRY/I Do	Tifco 826	1.50	6.00	61
ROYAL HALOS, The				
NOBODY BUT ME AND MY GIRL/My Love Is True	Aladdin 3460	1.50	6.00	59
ROYAL HAWK				
ROYAL HAWK (instrumental)/I Wonder Why?	Flair 1013	5.00	20.00	53
ROYAL HOLIDAYS, The				
I'M SORRY/Margaret	Penthouse 9357	2.00	8.00	58
ROYAL JOKERS, The				
DON'T LEAVE ME, FANNY/Rocks In My Pillow	Atco 6062	3.00	12.00	56
RIDE ON, LITTLE GIRL/She's Mine, All Mine	Atco 6077	3.00	12.00	56
SEPTEMBER IN THE RAIN/Spring	Hi-Q 5004	2.50	10.00	57

TITLE/FLIP	LABEL & NO.	GOOD TO VERY GOOD	NEAR MINT	YR.
SWEET LITTLE ANGEL/I Don't Like You That Much	Fortune 840	5.00	20.00	—
YOU TICKLE ME, BABY/Stay Here	Atco 6052	4.00	16.00	55
YOU TICKLE ME, BABY/You Came Along	Fortune 560	2.00	8.00	63
ROYAL NOTES, The				
THREE-SPEED GIRL/ Kisses Left Unkissed (by Phil Johnson & The Duvals)	Kelit 7032	7.00	28.00	—
YOU ARE MY LOVE/ Wee Small Hours (by Phil Johnson & The Duvals)	Kelit 7034	7.00	28.00	—
ROYAL ROBINS, The				
ROYAL SONS QUINTET, The				
BEDSIDE OF A NEIGHBOR/Journey's End (78)	Apollo 253	2.50	10.00	—
COME OVER HERE/Let Nothing Separate Me (78)	Apollo 266	2.50	10.00	—
ROYALETTES, The (female group)				
ROYALS, Chuck Willis & The: see Willis, Chuck & The Royals				
ROYALS, The				
ARE YOU FORGETTING?/What Did I Do?	Federal 12113	45.00	180.00	52
EVERY BEAT OF MY HEART/All Night Long	Federal 12064	45.00	180.00	52
EVERY BEAT OF MY HEART/All Night Long	Federal 12064AA	50.00	200.00	52
GET IT/No, It Ain't	Federal 12133	7.00	28.00	53
GIVE IT UP/That Woman	Federal 12177	5.00	20.00	54
HEY, MISS FINE/I Feel That-A-Way	Federal 12150	5.00	20.00	53
LOVE IN MY HEART, A/I'll Never Let Her Go	Federal 12098	50.00	200.00	52
MOONRISE/Fifth St. Blues	Federal 12088	60.00	240.00	52
SHRINE OF ST. CECILIA, THE/I Feel So Blue	Federal 12121	30.00	120.00	53
STARTING FROM TONIGHT/I Know I Love You So	Federal 12077	80.00	320.00	52
THAT'S IT/Someone Like You	Federal 12160	12.50	50.00	54
WORK WITH ME, ANNIE/Until I Die	Federal 12169	9.00	36.00	54
ROYALS, The				
IF YOU LOVE ME/Dreams Of You	Okeh 6832	50.00	200.00	51
ROYALS, The				
SOMEDAY WE'LL MEET AGAIN/ I Want You To Be My Mambo Baby	Venus 103	10.00	40.00	54
The first side of this record was released three years later on Dawn as by The Scooters.				
ROYALS, The: see Midnighters, The as The Royals				
ROYALTONES, The				
CRAZY LOVE/Never Let Me Go	Old Town 1018	7.00	28.00	56
LATIN LOVE/Hey, Norman!	Old Town 1028	8.00	32.00	56
ROYALTONES, The: see McFadden, Ruth & The Royaltones				
ROZIER, Leroy as Cousin Leroy				
GOIN' BACK HOME/Catfish	Groove 4G-0123	6.25	25.00	55
I'M LONESOME/Up The River	Ember 1023	3.00	12.00	57
WAITING AT THE STATION/Crossroads	Herald 546	2.00	8.00	57
WILL A MATCHBOX HOLD MY CLOTHES?/Highway 41	Ember 1016	6.25	25.00	57
RUBY & THE ROMANTICS				
RUDY & THE WHEELS				
RUFFIN, David				
RUFFIN, David & Jimmy as David & Jimmy Ruffin				
RUFFIN, Jimmy				
RUSH, Bobby				
RUSH, Otis				
ALL YOUR LOVE/My Baby Is A Good-Un	Cobra 5032	1.50	6.00	57
DOUBLE TROUBLE/Keep On Loving Me, Baby	Cobra 5030	1.50	6.00	57
GROANING THE BLUES/If You Were Mine	Cobra 5010	1.50	6.00	57
IT TAKES TIME/Checking On My Baby	Cobra 5027	1.50	6.00	57
LOVE THAT WOMAN/Jump, Sister Bessie	Cobra 5015	1.50	6.00	57
THREE TIMES A FOOL/She's A Good 'Un	Cobra 5023	1.50	6.00	57
RUSH, Otis & His Band				
I CAN'T QUIT YOU, BABY/Sit Down, Baby	Cobra 5000	1.50	6.00	56
VIOLENT LOVE/My Love Will Never Die	Cobra 5005	1.50	6.00	56

The Five Royals

The Scamps

TITLE/FLIP	LABEL & NO.	GOOD TO VERY GOOD	NEAR MINT	YR.
RUSHING, Jimmy				
GO GET SOME MORE, YOU FOOL/That's The Way I Feel	King 4564	2.00	8.00	51
HI-HO SYLVESTER/I'm So Lonely	King 4502	2.00	8.00	51
MR. FIVE BY FIVE/Clothes Pin Blues	Parrot 797	4.00	16.00	53
SHE'S MINE, SHE'S YOURS/ Somebody's Been Spoiling These Women	King 4606	2.00	8.00	52
WHERE WERE YOU?/In The Moonlight	King 4588	2.00	8.00	52
RUSSELL, Al Trio, The				
HOLIDAY BLUES/World War Two Blues (78)	Queen 4162	2.00	8.00	47
RYAN, Cathy: see Admirals, The				
RYDER, Junior & The Peacocks: see Peacocks, Junior Ryder & The				

S

TITLE/FLIP	LABEL & NO.	GOOD TO VERY GOOD	NEAR MINT	YR.
SA-SHAYS, The (female group)				
SABERS, The				
COOL, COOL CHRISTMAS/Always Forever	Cal-West 847	15.00	60.00	—
SABRES, The				
YOU CAN DEPEND ON ME/Calypso Baby	Bullseye 101	7.00	28.00	55
SAD HEAD, Mr.: see Mr. Sad Head				
SADLER, Haskell & His Orchestra				
DO RIGHT, MIND/Gone For Good	Flash 103	7.00	28.00	56
SAIGONS, The				
YOU'RE HEAVENLY/Honey Gee	Dootone 375	10.00	40.00	55
SAILOR BOY				
COUNTRY HOME/(unknown title by Preston Love)	Dig 116	4.00	16.00	56
WHAT HAVE I DONE WRONG?/What Have I Done Wrong?	Dig 126	4.00	16.00	56
Dig 126 shows same title on both sides.				
SAM & BILL				
SAM & DAVE				
SAMMY & THE DEL-LARDS				
SAMMY & THE DEL-LARKS				
SAMUELS, Bill & The Cats 'N' Jammer Three: see Cats 'N' Jammer Three, Bill Samuels & The				
SAMUELS, Clarence				
BOOGIE WOOGIE BLUES/Lollypop Mama (78)	Aristocrat 1001	2.50	10.00	48
CHICKEN HEARTED WOMAN/ Got No Place To Call My Own	Excello 2093	2.00	8.00	56
CRYIN' 'CAUSE I'M TROUBLED/ Charlie, Loan Me 50¢	Sharon (number unknown)	1.50	6.00	66
CRYIN' 'CAUSE I'M TROUBLED/Lightnin' Struck Me	Lamp 8005	2.00	8.00	54
DEEP SEA DIVER/A. C. Boogie Blues (78)	Swing Time 149	1.50	6.00	48
GIMMIE/Jumping At The Jubilee (78)	DeLuxe 3219	1.50	6.00	50
HOUSEHOLD TROUBLES/C. S. Jam (78)	Swing Time 131	1.50	6.00	48
LIFE DON'T MEAN A THING/Crazy With The Heat	Lamp 8004	2.00	8.00	54
LOST MY HEAD/Lowtop Inn (78)	Freedom 1533	2.00	8.00	49
LOWTOP INN/Drunk Or Sober (by Goree Carter)	Bayou 101	6.25	25.00	50
SHE WALK, SHE WALK, SHE WALK, PART 1/ She Walk, She Walk, She Walk, Part 2 (78)	Freedom 1541	2.00	8.00	49
SOMEBODY GOTTA GO/Hey Joe (78)	Freedom 1544	2.00	8.00	49
SANDERS, Willis & The Embers				
SANDERS, Willis & The Fabulous Embers: see Fabulous Embers, Willis Sanders & The				
SANDMEN, Brook Benton & The: see Benton, Brook & The Sandmen				
SANDMEN, Chuck Willis & The: see Willis, Chuck & The Sandmen				
SANDMEN, The: see Benton, Brook as The Sandmen (featuring Brook Benton)				
SANDPEBBLES, The (female group)				
SANDS, Bobby: see Bullard, John				
SAPPHIRES, Howie & The				
MORE THAN THE DAY BEFORE/Rockin' Horse	Okeh 7112	4.00	16.00	59
SAPPHIRES, The (female group)				
SARGENT, Lou as Lou Sargent's Band				
RIDIN' THE BOOGIE/She Really Treats Me Wrong (78)	Chess 1465	2.00	8.00	51
SATELITES, Baby Boy Jennings & The				
SATELITTES, Bobby Day & The				
SATELITTES, The				
HEAVENLY ANGEL/You Ain't Sayin' Nothin'	Class 234	1.50	6.00	58
HEAVENLY ANGEL/You Ain't Sayin' Nothin'	Malynn 234	2.00	8.00	—
SATINS, Fred Parris & The				
SATINTONES, The				
ANGEL/A Love That Can Never Be	Motown 1006	20.00	80.00	61
The third of three issues of Motown 1006. the first two versions of "Tomorrow And Always" were reportedly pulled from the market because of copyright infringement and "Angel" was substituted on the limited third issue. "Angel," ironically, is regarded as one of the finest R&B songs ever recorded for Motown.				
I KNOW HOW IT FEELS/My Kind Of Love	Motown 1010	2.50	10.00	61
MOTOR CITY/Going To The Hop	Tamla 54026	2.00	8.00	60
MY BELOVED (with strings)/Sugar Daddy	Motown 1000	2.50	10.00	60
This issue of "My Beloved" has the number 1000-G3 etched in vinyl, near the label.				
MY BELOVED (without strings)/Sugar Daddy	Motown 1000	3.00	12.00	60
This issue of "My Beloved" has the number MT-12345 etched in the vinyl, near the label.				
TOMORROW AND ALWAYS/A Love That Can Never Be	Motown 1006	2.50	10.00	61
Male leads with strings. This issue of Motown 1006 has the number H-625 etched in the vinyl near the label on the first side.				
TOMORROW AND ALWAYS/A Love That Can Never Be	Motown 1006	3.00	12.00	61
Male/female leads with no strings. This issue of Motown 1006 has the number H-55596 etched in the vinyl near the label on the first side.				
ZING! WENT THE STRINGS OF MY HEART/Faded Letter	Motown 1020	2.00	8.00	61
SAUCERS, The				
FLOSSIE MAE/Hi-Oom	Kick 100	7.00	28.00	—
HELLO, DARLING/Giggle Goo	Lynne 101	5.00	20.00	64
WHY DO I DREAM?/Ch Wailey Routa	Felco 104	5.00	20.00	—
SAUNDERS, Little Butchie & The Buddies: see Buddies, Little Butchie Saunders & The				
SAUNDERS, Slim				
LET'S HAVE SOME FUN/Get Away	Chess 1563	5.00	20.00	54
NO ONE CAN LOVE YOU LIKE I DO/For Me And My Gal	Lamp 2004	2.00	8.00	55
SAUSAGE, Doc				
SAVAGE, Al (with Joe Morris & His Orchestra)				
I HAD A MOTION/Just Your Way, Baby (red plastic)	Herald 417	2.00	8.00	53
LOVE IS A FUNNY THING/Life Begins At 40 (red plastic)	Herald 421	2.00	8.00	54

TITLE/FLIP	LABEL & NO.	GOOD TO VERY GOOD	NEAR MINT	YR.
SAVOY, Ashton & His Combo				
JUKE JOINT/Denga, Denga	Hollywood 1081	3.00	12.00	57
SAVOYS, Jimmie Jones & The				
SAVOYS, Sonny Brooks & The				
HERE I AM/Rocka Rolla Rock	Tip Top 1007	7.00	28.00	—
SWEETHEART DARLING/	Tip Top 1008	7.00	28.00	—
SAVOYS, The				
I LOVE MY BABY/You And I	Bella 18	1.50	6.00	59
SAVOYS, The				
CHOP CHOP BOOM/Nobody In Mind (by Jack McVea)	Combo 90	4.00	16.00	55
DARLING STAY WITH ME/Yacka Hoom Boom	Combo 75	15.00	60.00	55
EVIL WAYS/Loving Man	Combo 81	4.00	16.00	55
LET'S RIDE, RIDE, RIDE/Oh, That'll Be Joyful	Combo 55	20	55	
Both by Jack McVea.				
SAXONS, The				
IS IT TRUE?/Rock And Roll Show	Contender 1313	8.00	32.00	58
MY LOVE IS TRUE/Trying	Tampa 139	2.50	10.00	—
SCALE-TONES, The				
EVERLASTING LOVE/Dreamin' And Dreamin'	Jay Dee 810	5.00	20.00	56
SCALES, Alonzo				
HARD LUCK CHILD/We Just Can't Agree	Wing 90049	5.00	20.00	55
MY BABY LIKES TO SHUFFLE/She's Gone	Wing 90020	5.00	20.00	55
SCALES, Harvey & The Seven Sounds				
SCAMPS, The				
I'LL NEVER SMILE AGAIN/Worry (78)	Modern 561	2.00	8.00	47
I'M FALLING FOR YOU/Sweet Slumber (78)	Modern 521	2.00	8.00	—
MORE THAN YOU KNOW/Don't Cry, Baby (78)	Modern 512	2.00	8.00	—
SOLITUDE/Chica Biddie Boogie (78)	Modern 550	2.00	8.00	47
THAT'S MY DESIRE/I Wonder, I Wonder, I Wonder (78)	Modern 516	2.00	8.00	—
SCAMPS, The				
WATERPROOF/Yes, My Baby	Peacock 1655	4.00	16.00	55
SCARLETS, Fred Parris & The				
SHE'S GONE/The Voice	Klik 7905	4.00	28.00	—
SCARLETS, The				
TRULY YOURS/East Of The Sun	Fury 1036	1.50	6.00	60
SCARLETS, The				
DEAR ONE/I've Lost	Red Robin 128	15.00	60.00	54
KISS ME/Indian Fever	Red Robin 138	25.00	100.00	55
LOVE DOLL/Darling, I'm Yours	Red Robin 133	20.00	80.00	55
TRUE LOVE/Cry Baby	Red Robin 135	20.00	80.00	55
SCHOOLBOY CLEVE: see White, Cleve as Schoolboy Cleve				
SCHOOLBOYS, The				
ANGEL OF LOVE/The Slide	Juanita 103	7.00	28.00	58
CAROL/Pearl	Okeh 7090	1.50	6.00	57
MARY/I Am Old Enough	Okeh 7085	1.50	6.00	—
SHIRLEY/Please Say You Want Me	Okeh 7076	2.00	8.00	56
SCIENTISTS OF SOUL, The				
SCOOTERS, The				
SOMEDAY WE'LL MEET AGAIN/Really	Dawn 224	5.00	20.00	57
The first side of this record was originally released on Venus as by the Royals.				
SCOTT BROTHERS, The				
SCOTT, Beverley & His Trio				
SHAKING THE BOOGIE/Southern California Blues (78)	Murray 503	7.00	28.00	48
SCOTT, Freddy				
SCOTT, Freddy: see Chimes, The (with Freddy Scott)				
SCOTT, Joan				
MIGHTY LONG ROAD/My Wedding Day	Imperial 5328	2.50	10.00	54

TITLE/FLIP	LABEL & NO.	GOOD TO VERY GOOD	NEAR MINT	YR.
SCOTT, Lannie Trio, The: see Scott, Lonnie as The Lannie Scott Trio				
SCOTT, Lonnie as The Lannie Scott Trio				
LANNIE'S BOOGIE WOOGIE /Barrelhouse Boogie (78)	Savoy 614	1.50	6.00	46
Instrumentals.				
SCOTT, Mabel				
FOOL BURRO/Do The Thing	Parrot 794	2.50	10.00	53
MR. FINE/Mabel's Blues (red plastic)	Parrot 780	5.00	20.00	53
SCOTT, Peggy & Jo Jo Benson				
SCRUGGS, Faye (with Joe Morris & His Orchestra)				
I'M GOING TO LEAVE YOU/ That's What Makes My Baby Fat	Atlantic 985	3.00	12.00	52
SCRUGGS, Faye as Faye Adams (with Joe Morris & His Orchestra)				
I'LL BE TRUE/Happiness To My Soul (red plastic)	Herald 419	3.00	12.00	53
I'LL BE TRUE/Happiness To My Soul	Herald 419	1.50	6.00	53
SHAKE A HAND/I've Gotta Leave You (red plastic)	Herald 416	4.00	16.00	53
SHAKE A HAND/I've Gotta Leave You	Herald 416	1.50	6.00	53
SWEET TALK/Watch Out, I Told You	Atlantic 1007	3.00	12.00	53
SEABURY, Levi				
BOOGIE BEAT/Motherless Child	Blues Boy's Kingdom 101	9.00	36.00	57
SELLERS, Johnny				
BLUES, THIS AIN'T NO PLACE FOR YOU/ Mighty Lonesome	Chance 1123	6.25	25.00	52
JOSIE JONES/Rock Me In The Cradle	Chance 1120	6.25	25.00	52
MIRROR BLUES/Newport News	Chance 1138	6.25	25.00	52
SEMIEN, Lee as King Ivory Lee				
ROCKIN' IN THE COCONUT TOP/Fuss Too Much	Trey 1003	2.00	8.00	58
SEMIEN, Sidney as Rockin' Sydney (or as Rockin' Sidney)				
SENDERS, The				
BALLAD OF STAGGER LEE, THE/I Dream Of You	Kent 320	2.00	8.00	59
ONE MORE KISS/Everybody Needs To Know	Kent 324	2.00	8.00	59
SENIORS, The				
WHY DID YOU LEAVE ME?/Sloo Foot Soo	Excello 2130	2.50	10.00	58
SENIORS, The				
EVENING SHADOWS FALLING/I've Got Plenty Of Love	Tetra 4446	10.00	40.00	56
SENORS, The				
SEARCHING FOR OLIVE OIL/May I Have This Dance?	Sue 756	2.00	8.00	62
SENSATIONAL DELLOS, The				
This is the same group as one listed under "Dell-os, John Shaw & The."				
LOST LOVE/So Don't Go	Mida 109	7.00	28.00	—
SO SHY/	Mida 106	7.00	28.00	—
SENSATIONS, The				
MY HEART CRYS FOR YOU/Cry, Baby, Cry	Atco 6075	1.50	6.00	56
YOU MADE A FOOL OF ME/That's What You've Gotta Do	Junior 986	1.50	6.00	—
SENSATIONS, Yvonne Baker (recorded earlier as Yvonne Mills) & The				
SENSATIONS, Yvonne Mills & The				
LITTLE WALLFLOWER/Such A Love	Atco 6083	1.50	6.00	56
PLEASE, MR. DISC JOCKEY/Ain't He Sweet?	Atco 6067	2.00	8.00	56
ROMANCE IN THE DARK/Kiddy Car Love	Atco 6115	1.50	6.00	58
YOU MADE ME LOVE YOU/My Debut To Love	Atco 6090	1.50	6.00	57
SENTIMENTALISTS, The				
SILENT NIGHT/O Come, All Ye Faithful (78)	Manor 8002	1.50	6.00	46
WHITE CHRISTMAS/Ave Maria (78)	Manor 8003	1.50	6.00	46
SENTIMENTALISTS, The: see Four Tunes, The (as The Sentimentalists)				
SENTIMENTALS, Ann Nichols & The				
LOVER, I'M WAITING FOR YOU/I'm Sixteen Years	Tuxedo 926	2.50	10.00	58
SENTIMENTALS, James Carter & The				
I KNOW/Hey, Baby, Hey	Tuxedo 922	5.00	20.00	57

TITLE/FLIP	LABEL & NO.	GOOD TO VERY GOOD	NEAR MINT	YR.
SENTIMENTALS, The				
FOUND A NEW BABY/I'll Miss These Things	Mint 807	1.50	6.00	68
I WANT TO LOVE YOU/Teenie Teenager	Checker 875	1.50	6.00	57
I WANT TO LOVE YOU/Teenie, Teenie, Teenager	Mint 801	4.00	16.00	57
I'M YOUR FOOL, ALWAYS/Rock Me, Mama	Mint 803	1.50	6.00	58
THIS TIME/I Want To Love You	Mint 808	1.50	6.00	72
WEDDING BELLS/A Sunday Kind Of Love	Mint 802	1.50	6.00	57
YOU'RE MINE/Danny Boy	Mint 805	1.50	6.00	59
SEQUINS, The				
WHY CAN'T YOU TREAT ME RIGHT?/Don't Fall In Love	Red Robin 140	10.00	40.00	56
SERENADERS, Gene Mumford & The				
PLEASE GIVE ME ONE MORE CHANCE/When You're Smiling	Whiz 1500	20.00	80.00	—
SERENADERS, The				
DANCE, DARLING, DANCE/Give Me A Girl	MGM 12666	2.50	10.00	58
I'LL CRY TOMORROW/If Your Heart Says Yes	V.I.P. 25002	1.50	6.00	64
NEVER LET ME GO/I Wrote A Letter	Chock Full Of Hits 101/102	6.25	25.00	57
NEVER LET ME GO/I Wrote A Letter	MGM 12623	3.00	12.00	58
SERENADERS, The				
LOVE ME NOW/Gates Of Gold	Teen Life 9	15.00	60.00	58
SERENADERS, The				
IT'S FUNNY/Confession Is Good For The Soul	Coral 60720	25.00	100.00	52
M-A-Y-B-E-L-L/Ain't Goin' To Cry No More	Swingtime 347	25.00	100.00	54
MISERY/But I Forgive You	Coral 65093	25.00	100.00	52
PLEASE, PLEASE FORGIVE ME/Baby	Deluxe 6022	20.00	80.00	53
TOMORROW NIGHT/Why Don't You Do Right?	J.V.B. 2001	15.00	60.00	—
WILL SHE KNOW?/I Want To Love You, Baby	Red Robin 115	20.00	80.00	53
SERENADES, The				
SINNER IN LOVE, A/The Pajama Song	Chief 7002	25.00	100.00	57
SERENADETTS, The (female group)				
SEVEN SOUNDS, Harvey & The				
SEVEN SOUNDS, Harvey Scales & The				
SEVILLES, Richard Barrett & The				
DREAM ON/I Am Yours	Seville 104	1.50	6.00	60
SEVILLES, The				
SEWARD, Alec (with Louis Hayes) as Slim Seward & Fat Boy Hayes				
RAILROAD BLUES/Working Man Blues (78)	MGM 10770	2.00	8.00	47
TRAVELIN' BOY'S BLUES/Christmas Time Blues (78)	MGM 10306	2.00	8.00	47
SEWARD, Alec (with Louis Hayes) as The Back Porch Boys				
BE KIND BLUES/Sweet Woman Blues (78)	Apollo 406	2.00	8.00	47
BIG HIP MAMA/King Kong Blues (78)	Apollo 392	2.00	8.00	47
SEWARD, Alec (with Louis Hayes) as The Blues Boy: Guitar Slim & Jelly Belly				
Seward should not be confused with Eddie Jones, who also recorded as Guitar Slim, nor with Guitar Slim Green.				
BEEN PLOWING BLUES/Don't Leave Me Blues (78)	Tru-Blue 103	2.50	10.00	46
CAROLINA BLUES/Baby Left Me (78)	Tru-Blue 104	2.50	10.00	46
IN LOVE BLUES/Worried Man Blues (78)	Superdisc 1053	2.50	10.00	47
SNOWIN' AND RAININ' BLUES/Smilin' Blues (78)	Tru-Blue 101	2.50	10.00	46
UNGRATEFUL WOMAN BLUES/Keep Straight Blues (78)	Tru-Blue 102	2.50	10.00	46
UP AND DOWN BLUES/Crooked Wife Blues (78)	Tru-Blue 100	2.50	10.00	46
SEWARD, Alec & Louis Hayes as Jelly Belly & Slim Seward				
WATER TROUGH BLUES/Sorry Women Blues (78)	Apollo 412	2.00	8.00	47
SEWARD, Alec as The Blues King (with Louis Hayes)				
ME AND MY BABY/Good Boy (78)	Solo 10-003	3.00	12.00	46
SEWARD, Slim: see Seward, Alex as Slim Seward				
SH-BOOMS, The				
BLUE MOON/Short Skirts	Atlantic 2074	1.50	6.00	60
I DON'T WANT TO SET THE WORLD ON FIRE/Lu Lu	Vik 0295	2.00	8.00	—
PRETTY WILD/Could It Be?	Cat 117	3.00	12.00	55
SHA-WEEZ, The				
NO ONE TO LOVE ME/Early Sunday Morning (78)	Aladdin 3170	100.00	400.00	52
If an authentic original 45 rpm of this record were to turn up, it would command a very high price, as none are known to exist. Collectors do agree, however, that the possibility exists.				
SHADES, The				
DEAR LORI/One Touch Of Heaven	Aladdin 3453	7.00	28.00	59
SHADOWS, The				
BETTER THAN GOLD/Big Mouth Mama	Decca 48322	15.00	60.00	54
COON CAN ANNIE/It's Too Bad (78)	Sittin' In With 627	2.00	8.00	52
DON'T BE LATE/Beans (78)	Sittin' In With 590	2.00	8.00	51
DON'T BLAME MY DREAMS/ I'm Crying 'Cause You're Laughing At Me (78)	Lee 207	2.50	10.00	50
I'D RATHER BE WRONG THAN BLUE/ You Are Closer To My Heart (78)	Lee 202	2.50	10.00	50
I'LL NEVER NEVER LET YOU GO/ Jitterbug Special (78)	Sittin' In With 583	2.00	8.00	50
I'VE BEEN A FOOL/Nobody Knows (78)	Lee 200	2.50	10.00	49
STAY/No Use	Decca 28765	15.00	60.00	53
TELL HER/Don't Be Bashful	Decca 48307	15.00	60.00	53
SHADOWS, The				
UNDER STARS OF LOVE/Jungle Fever	Del-Fi 4109	3.00	12.00	58
SHADOWS, The				
THERE STANDS THE GLASS/Bop-Alena	Delta 1509	7.00	28.00	58
SHAKERS, Shelly Shoop & The				
SHAKEY JAKE: see Harris, James D. as Shakey Jake				
SHAMANS, The				
SOUTHERN CALIFORNIA/I'll Wait Forever	Kayham 3/4	4.00	16.00	59
VALLEY OF TEARS/Shubby Dubby Doo	Kayham 1/2	4.00	16.00	59
SHANTONS, Skip Brown & The				
SHANTONS, Skip Jackson & The				
SHANTONS, The				
CHRISTMAS SONG, THE/ Santa Claus Is Coming To Town	Jay-Mar (no number)	4.00	16.00	60
TO BE IN LOVE WITH YOU/Lucille	Jay Mar (no number)	4.00	16.00	59
TRIANGLE LOVE/Lover's March	Jay Mar (no number)	4.00	16.00	59
SHAPRELS, The (female group)				
SHARMEERS, The (female group)				
SCHOOL GIRL IN LOVE, A/You're My Lover	Red Top 109	3.00	12.00	—
SHARMETTES, The (female group)				
SHARP, Dee Dee				
SHARPEES, The				
SHARPS, The				
ALL MY LOVE/Look What You've Done To Me	Combo 146	4.00	16.00	58
ALL MY LOVE/Look What You've Done To Me	Dot 15806	1.50	6.00	58
COME ON/Sweet Sweetheart	Jamie 1040	1.50	6.00	57
OUR LOVE IS HERE TO STAY/Lock My Heart	Lamp 2007	3.00	12.00	57
SIX MONTHS, THREE WEEKS/Cha Cho Hop (by Jack McVea)	Tag 2200	5.00	20.00	56
6 MONTHS, 3 WEEKS, 2 DAYS, 1 HOUR/ Cha-Cho Hop (by Jack McVea)	Chess 1690	1.50	6.00	58
WHAT WILL I GAIN?/Shufflin'	Aladdin 3401	1.50	6.00	57
SHARPS, Thurston Harris & The				
SHARPTONES, The				
I'LL ALWAYS REMEMBER/Sock Hop	Ace 133	7.00	28.00	—
SHARPTONES, The				
SINCE I FELL FOR YOU/Made To Love	Post 2009	25.00	100.00	55
SHAW-WEES, Big Boy Myles & The				
JUST TO HOLD MY HAND/Hickory Dickory Dock	Specialty 590	2.00	8.00	56
WHO'S BEEN FOOLING YOU?/That's The Girl I Married	Specialty 564	2.00	8.00	55
SHAW, John & The Dell-o's: see Dell-o's, John Shaw & The				

The Shirelles

Shirley and Lee

TITLE/FLIP	LABEL & NO.	GOOD TO VERY GOOD	NEAR MINT	YR.

SHAW, Marlena

SHEFFIELD, Charles

MAD DOG/Clear My Nights Of Misery	Goldband 1045	3.00	12.00	58

SHEFFIELD, Charles as Mad Dog Sheffield

MAD DOG/Nights Of Miserie	Hollywood 1079	2.00	8.00	58

This record is a re-issue of Goldband 1045 by Sheffield, slightly alter-ing the title of the second side, and nicknaming the artist "Mad Dog."

SHEFFIELD, Mad Dog:
see Sheffield, Charles as Mad Dog Sheffield

SHEIKS, The

GIVE ME ANOTHER CHANCE/	Ef-N-De 1000	25.00	100.00	55
SO FINE/Sentimental Heart	Federal 12237	5.00	20.00	55
Vocals by Jesse Belvin.				
SO FINE/Sentimental Heart	Federal 12355	2.50	10.00	59
Vocals by Jesse Belvin.				
WALK THAT WALK/The Kissing Song	Cat 116	2.50	10.00	66

SHELL BROTHERS, The

SHELLS, The

BABY, OH BABY/Angel Eyes	Johnson 104	2.00	8.00	57
BETTER FORGET HIM/Can't Take It	Johnson 109	1.50	6.00	61
IN THE DIM LIGHT OF THE DARK/O-Mi Yum-Mi Yum-Mi	Johnson 110	2.00	8.00	61
ON MY HONOR/My Royal Love	Johnson 127	3.00	12.00	63
PLEADING NO MORE/Don't Say Goodbye	Johnson 106	1.50	6.00	58
PRETTY LITTLE GIRL/Sippin' Soda	End 1022	7.00	28.00	58
PRETTY LITTLE GIRL/Sippin' Soda	Gone 5103	4.00	16.00	61
SHE WASN'T MEANT FOR ME/The Thief	Roulette 4156	1.50	6.00	59
TOAST TO YOUR BIRTHDAY, A/The Drive	Johnson 120	1.50	6.00	63

SHELTON, Roscoe

SHEP & THE LIMELITES:
see Limelites, Shep & The

SHEPPARDS, The

LOVE/Cool Mambo	Theron 112	25.00	100.00	55
SHERRY/Mozelle	United 198	15.00	60.00	56

SHERMAN & THE DARTS

SHERMAN'S TRIO:
see Louis, Sherman as Sherman's Trio

SHERRYS, The (female group)

SHIELDS, The

I'M SORRY NOW/Nature Boy	Tender 518	3.00	12.00	58
PLAY THE GAME FAIR/Fare Thee Well, My Love	Dot 15940	3.00	12.00	59
PLAY THE GAME FAIR/Fare Thee Well, My Love	Tender 521	3.00	12.00	59
YOU CHEATED/That's The Way It's Gonna Be	Tender 513	3.00	12.00	58
YOU'LL BE COMING HOME SOON/ The Girl Around The Corner	Transcontinental 1013	4.00	16.00	—

SHINES, Johnny

EVENING SUN/Brutal Hearted Woman	JOB 1010	25.00	100.00	53
RAMBLIN'/Cool Driver (78)	JOB 116	12.50	50.00	52

SHIRELLES, Shirley & The

SHIRELLES, The (female group)

DEDICATED TO THE ONE I LOVE/Look A Here, Baby	Scepter 1203	2.00	8.00	59
I GOT THE MESSAGE/Stop Me	Decca 30761	1.50	6.00	58
I MET HIM ON A SUNDAY/ I Want You To Be My Boyfriend	Decca 30588	1.50	6.00	58
I MET HIM ON A SUNDAY/I Want You To Be My Boyfriend	Tiara 6112	15.00	60.00	58
MY LOVE IS A CHARM/Slop Time	Decca 30669	1.50	6.00	58
PLEASE BE MY BOYFRIEND/I Saw A Tear	Scepter 1207	1.50	6.00	60
TEARDROP AND A LOLLIPOP, A/Doin' The Ronde	Scepter 1205	1.50	6.00	59
TOMORROW/Boys	Scepter 1211	1.50	6.00	60

SHIRLEY & THE SHIRELLES

SHONDELLES, The (female group)

SHOOP, Shelly & The Shakers

SHOW STOPPERS, The

SHOWER, Hudson as Little Hudson's Red Devil Trio

ROUGH TREATMENT/I'm Looking For A Woman	JOB 1015	15.00	60.00	53

SHOWMEN, The

IT WILL STAND/Country Fool	Minit 632	1.50	6.00	61

SHUFFLERS, The

AIN'T NOTHIN' WRONG WITH THAT/Lovin' On My Mind	Okeh 7040	10.00	40.00	54

SIGLER, Bunny

SILHOUETTES, Bill Horton & The

EVELYN/Never Will Part	Ace 563	1.50	6.00	59

SILHOUETTES, The

BING BONG/Voodoo Eyes	Ember 1037	8.00	32.00	58
GET A JOB/I Am Lonely	Ember 1029	1.50	6.00	57
GET A JOB/I Am Lonely	Junior 391	10.00	40.00	57
HEADIN' FOR THE POORHOUSE/Miss Thing	Ember 1032	1.50	6.00	58
I SOLD MY HEART TO THE JUNKMAN/What Would You Do?	Ace 552	2.00	8.00	58
I SOLD MY HEART TO THE JUNKMAN/What Would You Do?	Junior 396	2.50	10.00	58
YOUR LOVE/Rent Man	Junior 993	1.50	6.00	63

SILKS, Charles McCollough & The:
see McCollough, Charles & The Silks

SILVER COOKS WITH THE GONDOLIERS:
see Cooks, Donald as Silver Cooks

SILVER STARS, George Perkins & The

SIMMON, Mack:
see Simmons, Mack as Mack Simmon

SIMMONS, Al with Slim Green & The Cats From Fresno

OLD FOLKS BOOGIE/Hand Me Down Baby (by Sidney Maiden)	Dig 138	5.00	20.00	56
YOU AIN'T TOO OLD/ My Woman Done Quit Me (by Slim Green)	Dig 142	4.00	16.00	56

SIMMONS, Mack as Little Mack

COME BACK/My Walking Blues	C. J. 606	1.50	6.00	59

SIMMONS, Mack as Little Mack Simmon & His Boys

JUMPING AT THE CADILLAC (instrumental)/I Need You	C. J. 607	1.50	6.00	59

SIMMONS, Mack as Mac Sims

DRIVIN' WHEEL/Broken Hearted	Pacer 1201	1.50	6.00	61

SIMON, Joe

SIMON, Joe:
see Golden Tones, The (with Joe Simon)

SIMONE, Nina

SIMS TWINS, The

SIMS, Frankie Lee

DON'T FORGET ME, BABY/Single Man Blues (78)	Blue Bonnet 148	12.50	50.00	48
HEY, LITTLE GIRL/Walkin' With Frankie	Ace 527	2.50	10.00	57
HOME AGAIN BLUES/Cross Country Blues (78)	Blue Bonnet 147	12.50	50.00	48
I WARNED YOU, BABY/My Talk Didn't Do No Good	Ace 539	2.50	10.00	57
I'M LONG GONE/Yeh, Baby	Specialty 478	2.50	10.00	53
LUCY MAE BLUES/Don't Take It Out On Me	Specialty 459	2.50	10.00	53
RHUMBA MY BOOGIE/I'll Get Along Somehow	Specialty 487	2.50	10.00	53
SHE LIKES TO BOOGIE REAL LOW/ Well, Goodbye, Baby	Vin	3.00	12.00	—
WHAT WILL LUCY DO?/Misery Blues	Ace 524	2.50	10.00	57

SIMS, Mac:
see Simmons, Mack as Mac Sims

SIMS, Marvin L.

SINGING WANDERERS, The

SAY HEY, WILLIE MAYS/Don't Drop It	Decca 29230	4.00	16.00	54
THREE ROSES/The Wrong Party Again	Decca 29298	8.00	32.00	54

SINGLETON, Bebo

Bebo is the brother of artist Jimmy Singleton.

SHRINE OF THE ECHOES/Feeny Jones	Stentor 1001	25.00	100.00	60

Eddie Shaw

The Six Teens

SINGLETON, Eddie & The Chromatics:
see Chromatics, Eddie Singleton & The

SIX TEENS, The

SKOODLE DUM DOO & SHEFFIELD:
see Richard, Seth as Skoodle Dum Doo

SKY BOYS, Thur Ravenscroft & The

TITLE/FLIP	LABEL & NO.	GOOD TO VERY GOOD	NEAR MINT	YR.
NEVER DOUBT MY LOVE/Mad, Baby, Mad	Fabor 4005	2.50	10.00	—

SKYLARKS, The

TITLE/FLIP	LABEL & NO.	GOOD TO VERY GOOD	NEAR MINT	YR.
GLORY OF LOVE, THE/You And I	Decca 48241	30.00	120.00	51

This record was later re-issued with the artists listed as The Starlings.

SKYSCRAPERS, Browley Guy & The

TITLE/FLIP	LABEL & NO.	GOOD TO VERY GOOD	NEAR MINT	YR.
BLUES TRAIN/You Ain't Gonna Worry Me	States 107	4.00	16.00	—
KNOCK ME A ZOMBIE/That Gal Of Mine (78)	Miracle 137	2.00	8.00	59
WATERMELON MAN/You Look Good To Me	Checker 779	15.00	60.00	54

SKYSCRAPERS, The

TITLE/FLIP	LABEL & NO.	GOOD TO VERY GOOD	NEAR MINT	YR.
CERTAIN OTHER SOMEONE/Last Call (78)	Miracle 119	2.00	8.00	—
I THOUGHT YOU'D CARE/Don't Cry	Mercury 70795	7.00	28.00	56

SLAY, Emitt

TITLE/FLIP	LABEL & NO.	GOOD TO VERY GOOD	NEAR MINT	YR.
I'VE LEARNED MY LESSON/ You Told Me That You Loved Me	Savoy 892	1.50	6.00	52
MALE CALL/Be Mine Once More	Savoy 1101	1.50	6.00	52
MY KIND OF WOMAN/Brotherly Love	Savoy 886	1.50	6.00	52

SLEDGE, Percy

SLEEPY JOE'S WASHBOARD BAND:
see Willis, Ralph as Sleepy Joe

SLIM HARPO

SLIM PICKENS:
see Burns, Eddie as Slim Pickens

SLIM, T. V.:
see Wills, Oscar as T. V. Slim
see Wills, Oscar as T. V. Slim & His Heartbreakers
see Wills, Oscar (with Fats Domino's Band)

SLIM, Tarheel (Alden Bunn) & Little Ann

SLY & THE FAMILY STONE

SLY FOX, The:
see Fox, Eugene as The Sly Fox

SMALL, Danny

TITLE/FLIP	LABEL & NO.	GOOD TO VERY GOOD	NEAR MINT	YR.
FREE SUGAR/Don Juan	DeLuxe 6007	1.50	6.00	52

Instrumentals.

SMALL, Drink & His Guitar

SMITH, Al

All of the following are instrumentals.

TITLE/FLIP	LABEL & NO.	GOOD TO VERY GOOD	NEAR MINT	YR.
BEALE STREET STOMP/Sliding Home	Meteor 5013	5.00	20.00	54
SMOKE GETS IN YOUR EYES/Blue Mood	Chance 1124	4.00	16.00	53

SMITH, Arthur as Shorty Smith & His Rhythm

TITLE/FLIP	LABEL & NO.	GOOD TO VERY GOOD	NEAR MINT	YR.
SOUTH WEST PACIFIC BLUES/Wiggle Around Me, Baby (78)	Lenox 510	1.50	6.00	45

SMITH, Arthur as Sonny Boy & Lonnie (with Lonnie Johnson)

TITLE/FLIP	LABEL & NO.	GOOD TO VERY GOOD	NEAR MINT	YR.
I'LL WATER YOU EVERY DAY/Bigheaded Woman (78)	Continental 6054	1.50	6.00	45
MY BABY BLUES/Big Moose Blues (78)	Continental 6053	1.50	6.00	45
SOUTH WEST PACIFIC BLUES/Quincy Avenue Boogie	Continental 6050	1.50	6.00	45
WIDE BOOGIE, THE/Talking Boogie (78)	Continental 6052	1.50	6.00	45

SMITH, Arthur as Sonny Boy & Sam (with Sam Bradley)

TITLE/FLIP	LABEL & NO.	GOOD TO VERY GOOD	NEAR MINT	YR.
I WONDER WHO'S HOLDING YOU?/Mama Blues (78)	Continental 6055	1.50	6.00	45

SMITH, Arthur Trio, The

SMITH, Ben Quartet, The

TITLE/FLIP	LABEL & NO.	GOOD TO VERY GOOD	NEAR MINT	YR.
DON'T WORRY NO MORE/I Ain't Fattenin' Frogs (78)	Abbey 3008	2.50	10.00	—
SHE KNOWS HOW THE DROPS WILL FALL/ You've Got Me Crying My Heart Out (78)	Columbia 30214	2.50	10.00	50
WHERE DID SHE GO?/Leave That Dog Alone (78)	Columbia 30208	2.50	10.00	50
YOU ARE CLOSER TO MY HEART/ Blues Got Me Walking, Talking To Myself (78)	Abbey 3012	2.50	10.00	50

SMITH, Bobbie & The Dream Girls (female group)

SMITH, Bobby & The Spinners

SMITH, Clarence as Blue Smitty & His String Men

TITLE/FLIP	LABEL & NO.	GOOD TO VERY GOOD	NEAR MINT	YR.
CRYING/Sad Story (78)	Chess 1522	6.25	25.00	52

SMITH, Cool Papa & His Orchestsra

TITLE/FLIP	LABEL & NO.	GOOD TO VERY GOOD	NEAR MINT	YR.
YOU BETTER CHANGE YOUR WAYS, WOMAN/ Christmas Blues (78)	Uptown 202	2.50	10.00	49

SMITH, Drifting:
see Mickle, Elmon as Drifting Smith

SMITH, Effie

TITLE/FLIP	LABEL & NO.	GOOD TO VERY GOOD	NEAR MINT	YR.
CHAMPAGNE MIND WITH A SODA WATER INCOME/ Water, Water	Vita 124	2.00	8.00	56
DIAL THAT TELEPONE/Don't Cha Love Me?	Aladdin 3202	2.50	10.00	53
STANDING IN THE DOORWAY/Tropical Seas	Aladdin 3203	2.50	10.00	53

SMITH, Effie:
see Squires, The

SMITH, Floyd

TITLE/FLIP	LABEL & NO.	GOOD TO VERY GOOD	NEAR MINT	YR.
ME AND YOU/After Hours	Decca 28208	2.00	8.00	52

SMITH, Geechie

TITLE/FLIP	LABEL & NO.	GOOD TO VERY GOOD	NEAR MINT	YR.
GENEVA SUE/I Want A Little Girl	Kicks 5	2.50	10.00	54

SMITH, George as George Allen

TITLE/FLIP	LABEL & NO.	GOOD TO VERY GOOD	NEAR MINT	YR.
BROWN MULE/Good Things	Sotoplay S-51	3.00	12.00	65
LOOSE SCREWS/The Time To Go On	Sotoplay 0012	2.50	10.00	57
SOMETIMES YOU WIN WHEN YOU LOSE/ Come On Home	Sotoplay 0021/2	2.50	10.00	57
TIMES WON'T ALWAYS BE HARD/ I Must Be Crazy	Sotoplay 0031/2	2.50	10.00	65
TIMES WON'T BE HARD ALWAYS/Tight Dress	Sotoplay 0010	3.00	12.00	57
YOU CAN'T UNDO WHAT'S BEEN DONE/ Rope That Twist	Sotoplay 0023/4	2.50	10.00	57

SMITH, George as Little Walter, Jr.

Smith should not be confused with Leroy Foster, nor with Marion Walter Jacobs, who both recorded as Little Walter, nor with a fourth artist who recorded during the 60s as Little Red Walter.

TITLE/FLIP	LABEL & NO.	GOOD TO VERY GOOD	NEAR MINT	YR.
MISS O'MALLY'S RALLY/Don't Know	Lapel 100	5.00	20.00	55

SMITH, George as The Harmonica King

TITLE/FLIP	LABEL & NO.	GOOD TO VERY GOOD	NEAR MINT	YR.
ALL LAST NIGHT/Hot Rolls (instrumental)	Lapel 103	5.00	20.00	55

SMITH, Henry

TITLE/FLIP	LABEL & NO.	GOOD TO VERY GOOD	NEAR MINT	YR.
DOG ME BLUES/Rockin' Chair Boogie (instrumental by Clarence Posey) (78)	Fortune 802	5.00	20.00	52
GOOD ROCKING MAMA/Lonesome Blues	Dot 1220	10.00	40.00	54

SMITH, Huey "Piano" & The Clowns

TITLE/FLIP	LABEL & NO.	GOOD TO VERY GOOD	NEAR MINT	YR.
DON'T YOU KNOW YOCKOMO?/ Well I'll Be, John Brown	Ace 553	1.50	6.00	58
FREE, SINGLE AND DISENGAGED/ Just A Lonely Clown	Ace 538	1.50	6.00	57
LITTLE LIZA JANE/Everybody's Wailin'	Ace 521	1.50	6.00	56
ROCKIN' PNEUMONIA AND THE BOOGIE WOOGIE FLU, PART 1/ Rockin' Pneumonia And The Boogie Woogie Flu, Part 2	Ace 530	2.00	8.00	57
TU-BER-CU-LUCAS AND THE SINUS BLUES/Dearest Darling	Ace 571	3.00	12.00	59
YOU MADE ME CRY/You're Down With Me	Savoy 1113	7.00	28.00	52

SMITH, J. L.

TITLE/FLIP	LABEL & NO.	GOOD TO VERY GOOD	NEAR MINT	YR.
HATES TO SEE YOU GO/Do The Mosquito	Friendly Five 741	1.50	6.00	—

SMITH, Jimmy

SMITH, Johnny & The Jubalaires:
see Jubalaires, Johnny Smith & The

SMITH, Lloyd "Fat Man"

TITLE/FLIP	LABEL & NO.	GOOD TO VERY GOOD	NEAR MINT	YR.
MY CLOCK STOPPED/No Better For You	Peacock 1611	2.00	8.00	53
WHY, OH, WHY?/Giddy Up, Giddy Up	Peacock 1593	2.50	10.00	53

SMITH, Melvin

TITLE/FLIP	LABEL & NO.	GOOD TO VERY GOOD	NEAR MINT	YR.
CALIFORNIA BOY/Everybody's Got The Blues	RCA Victor 47-4558	2.50	10.00	52
I DON'T HAVE TO HUNT/Every Pound	RCA Victor 47-5226	2.50	10.00	52
I FEEL LIKE GOING HOME/Letter To My Baby	RCA Victor 47-5578	2.50	10.00	52
I'M OUT OF MY MIND/Baby, I'll Be There	RCA Victor 47-4907	2.50	10.00	52
IT WENT DOWN EASY/ Why Do These Things Have To Be?	RCA Victor 47-5406	2.50	10.00	52
LOOPED/Woman Trainer	RCA Victor 47-4735	2.50	10.00	52
SARAH KELLY FROM PLUMNELLY/Call Me Darling	RCA Victor 47-5058	1.50	6.00	52
YOU CAN'T STAY HERE/No Baby	Groove 0010	2.00	8.00	54

SMITH, Melvin & The Nite Riders

SMITH, Moses as Whispering Smith

SMITH, O. C.

SMITH, Robert T.

TITLE/FLIP	LABEL & NO.	GOOD TO VERY GOOD	NEAR MINT	YR.
WORKIN' AGAIN/Tell Me What In The World	Bobbin 118	2.00	8.00	59

SMITH, Tab

All of the following are instrumentals.

TITLE/FLIP	LABEL & NO.	GOOD TO VERY GOOD	NEAR MINT	YR.
BECAUSE OF YOU/Dee Jay Special (red plastic)	United 104	2.50	10.00	51
ECHO BLUES/Moon Dream	Atlantic 961	2.00	8.00	52
SLOW AND EASY/Love	Chess 1501	2.00	8.00	52

SMITH, Thunder:

see Hopkins, Sam as Lightnin' Hopkins & Thunder Smith
see Smith, Wilson as Thunder Smith

SMITH, Whispering (Moses)

SMITH, Willie "Long Time"

SMITH, Wilson as Thunder Smith

TITLE/FLIP	LABEL & NO.	GOOD TO VERY GOOD	NEAR MINT	YR.
CRUEL HEARTED WOMAN/Big Stars Are Falling (78)	Gold Star 615	2.00	8.00	47
L. A. BLUES/Little Mama Boogie (78)	Aladdin 166	2.50	10.00	46
SANTA FE BLUES/Temptation Blues (78)	Gold Star 644	2.50	10.00	49

SMITH, Wilson as Thunder Smith & Rockie (Luther Stoneham)

TITLE/FLIP	LABEL & NO.	GOOD TO VERY GOOD	NEAR MINT	YR.
LOW DOWN DIRTY WAYS/Water Coast Blues (78)	Down Town 2013	3.00	12.00	48
NEW WORRIED LIFE BLUES/Mable Blues (78)	Down Town 2012	3.00	12.00	48
THUNDER'S UNFINISHED BOOGIE/ The Train Is Leaving (78)	Down Town 2011	3.00	12.00	48

SMITH, Wilson as Thunder Smith:

see Hopkins, Sam as Lightnin' Hopkins & Thunder Smith

SMOOTH-TONES, The

TITLE/FLIP	LABEL & NO.	GOOD TO VERY GOOD	NEAR MINT	YR.
DEAR DIARY/Crazy Baby	Ember 1001	3.00	12.00	56

SMOOTHTONES, The

TITLE/FLIP	LABEL & NO.	GOOD TO VERY GOOD	NEAR MINT	YR.
BRING BACK YOUR LOVE TO ME/No Doubt About It	Jem 412	8.00	32.00	55
DON'T KEEP OUR LOVE HIDDEN IN THE DARK/ Little Cupid	Okeh 7078	2.00	8.00	57

SMOTHERS, (Otis) Smokey

SNAPPERS, The

TITLE/FLIP	LABEL & NO.	GOOD TO VERY GOOD	NEAR MINT	YR.
IF THERE WERE/Big Bull	20th Century Fox 148	1.50	6.00	59

SNOOKY & MOODY:

see Pryor, James Edward & Floyd Jones as Snooky & Moody

SNOW, Valaida

TITLE/FLIP	LABEL & NO.	GOOD TO VERY GOOD	NEAR MINT	YR.
COCONUT HEAD/Chloe (red plastic)	Derby 735	2.50	10.00	50
I AIN'T GONNA TELL/If You Don't Mean It	Chess 1555	2.50	10.00	53

SOFT TONES, The

TITLE/FLIP	LABEL & NO.	GOOD TO VERY GOOD	NEAR MINT	YR.
MY MOTHER'S EYES/A Moth Around A Flame	Samson 103	4.00	16.00	—

SOLDIER BOYS, The

SOLITAIRES, The

TITLE/FLIP	LABEL & NO.	GOOD TO VERY GOOD	NEAR MINT	YR.
BLUE VALENTINE/Wonder Why? (red plastic)	Old Town 1000	40.00	160.00	54
BLUE VALENTINE/Wonder Why?	Old Town 1000	20.00	80.00	54
CHANCES I'VE TAKEN/Lonely	Old Town 1008	15.00	60.00	54
EMBRACEABLE YOU/'Round Goes My Heart	Old Town 1066	1.50	6.00	59
GIVE ME ONE MORE CHANCE/Nothing Like A Little Love	Old Town 1032	7.00	28.00	56
HONEY BABE/The Time Is Here	Old Town 1139	1.50	6.00	63
HONEYMOON, THE/Fine Little Girl	Old Town 1019	4.00	16.00	56
I DON'T STAND A GHOST OF A CHANCE/Girl Of Mine	Old Town 1010	25.00	100.00	55
I REALLY LOVE YOU SO/Thrill Of Love	Old Town 1044	6.25	25.00	57
LIGHT A CANDLE IN THE CHAPEL/Helpless	Old Town 1071	1.50	6.00	59
LONESOME LOVER/Pretty Thing	Old Town 1096	1.50	6.00	61
MAGIC ROSE/Later For You, Baby	Old Town 1015	4.00	16.00	55
PLEASE REMEMBER MY HEART/ South Of The Border	Old Town 1006	15.00	60.00	54
PLEASE REMEMBER MY HEART/ South Of The Border	Old Town 1006/1007	25.00	100.00	54
PLEASE REMEMBER MY HEART/Big Mary's House	Old Town 1059	2.50	10.00	59
WALKIN' AND TALKIN'/No More Sorrows	Old Town 1049	3.00	12.00	58
WALKING ALONG/Please Kiss This Letter	Argo 5316	1.50	6.00	58
WALKING ALONG/Please Kiss This Letter	Old Town 1034	3.00	12.00	57
WEDDING, THE/Don't Fall In Love	Old Town 1014	4.00	16.00	55
WHAT DID SHE SAY?/My Dear	Old Town 1012	15.00	60.00	55
YOU'VE SINNED/The Angels Sang	Old Town 1026	3.00	12.00	56
YOU'VE SINNED/You're Back With Me	Old Town 1026	8.00	32.00	56

SOLOMON, Ellis as King Solomon

TITLE/FLIP	LABEL & NO.	GOOD TO VERY GOOD	NEAR MINT	YR.
MEAN TRAIL/Baby, I'm Cutting Out	Big Town 102	6.25	25.00	53

SOLOTONES, The

TITLE/FLIP	LABEL & NO.	GOOD TO VERY GOOD	NEAR MINT	YR.
PORK AND BEANS/Front Page Blues	Excello 2060	8.00	32.00	55

SONICS, The

TITLE/FLIP	LABEL & NO.	GOOD TO VERY GOOD	NEAR MINT	YR.
AS I LIVE ON/Bumble Bee	Groovo 0112	15.00	60.00	55
THIS BROKEN HEART/You Made Me Cry	Checker 922	1.50	6.00	59
THIS BROKEN HEART/You Made Me Cry	Harvard 801	5.00	20.00	59
THIS BROKEN HEART/You Made Me Cry	Harvard 922	3.00	12.00	59

SONNY BOY & LONNIE:

see Smith, Arthur as Sonny Boy & Lonnie (with Lonnie Johnson)

SONNY BOY & SAM:

see Smith, Arthur as Sonny Boy & Sam (with Sam Bradley)

SONNY GUITAR:

see Guitar, Sonny

SONNY T:

see Terrell, Saunders as Sonny T

SONNY TERRY:

see Terrell, Saunders as Sonny Terry

TITLE/FLIP	LABEL & NO.	GOOD TO VERY GOOD	NEAR MINT	YR.

SONS OF WATTS, The

SOOTHERS, The

TITLE/FLIP	LABEL & NO.	GOOD TO VERY GOOD	NEAR MINT	YR.
LITTLE WHITE CLOUD THAT CRIED, THE/I Believe In You	*Port 70040*	1.50	6.00	*64*

SOPHOMORES, The

TITLE/FLIP	LABEL & NO.	GOOD TO VERY GOOD	NEAR MINT	YR.
CHARADES/What Can I Do?	*Chord 1302*	1.50	6.00	*57*
CHECKERS/Each Time I Hold You	*Dawn 237*	1.50	6.00	—
EVERY NIGHT ABOUT THIS TIME/Cool, Cool Baby	*Dawn 216*	1.50	6.00	*56*
I GET A THRILL/Linda	*Dawn 218*	1.50	6.00	*56*
I JUST CAN'T KEEP THE TEARS FROM TUMBLIN' DOWN/ If I Should Lose Your Love	*Dawn 228*	1.50	6.00	—
IS THERE SOMEONE FOR ME?/Everybody Loves Me	*Dawn 225*	1.50	6.00	*57*
OCEAN BLUE/I Left My Sugar	*Dawn 223*	1.50	6.00	—

SOUL BROTHERS SIX, The

SOUL BROTHERS, The

SOUL EXPLOSIONS, Willie Henderson & The

SOUL MATES, Al Green & The

SOUL SISTERS, The

SOUL, Jimmy

SOUL, Jimmy & The Chants

SOUNDS OF SOUL, Lee Jones & The

SOUNDS, The

TITLE/FLIP	LABEL & NO.	GOOD TO VERY GOOD	NEAR MINT	YR.
SO UNNECESSARY/Cold Chills	*Modern 975*	1.50	6.00	*55*
SWEET SIXTEEN/Anything For You	*Modern 981*	1.50	6.00	*56*

SOUNDS, Vikki Nelson & The

SOUTHERN MALE QUARTET, The

SOUTHERN NEGRO QUARTETTE, The

TITLE/FLIP	LABEL & NO.	GOOD TO VERY GOOD	NEAR MINT	YR.
I'M WILD ABOUT MOONSHINE/Anticipatin' Blues (78)	*Columbia A-3444*	5.00	20.00	*21*
SWEET MAMA/I Ain't Givin' Nothin' Away (78)	*Columbia A-3450*	5.00	20.00	*21*

SOUTHERN QUARTET, The

TITLE/FLIP	LABEL & NO.	GOOD TO VERY GOOD	NEAR MINT	YR.
GONNA RAISE RUKUS TONIGHT/ My Man Rocks Me (78)	*Columbia 14048-D*	5.00	20.00	*24*
HAMPTON ROAD BLUES/Lullaby Blues (78)	*Columbia 14038-D*	5.00	20.00	*24*
HE TOOK IT AWAY FROM ME/ I'll Be Good But I'll Be Lonesome (78)	*Columbia A-3489*	5.00	20.00	*21*
MOANIN' GROANIN' BLUES/Hey! Hey! Hee! Hee! (78)	*Columbia 14043-D*	5.00	20.00	*24*

SOUTHWINDS, The

TITLE/FLIP	LABEL & NO.	GOOD TO VERY GOOD	NEAR MINT	YR.
THEY CALL ME CRAZY/Build Me A Cabin	*Fury 1017*	1.50	6.00	—

SOUVENIRS, The

TITLE/FLIP	LABEL & NO.	GOOD TO VERY GOOD	NEAR MINT	YR.
SO LONG, DADDY/Alene, Sweet Little Texas Queen	*Dooto 412*	2.50	10.00	*57*

SOXX, Bob B. & The Blue Jeans

SPACEMEN, The Drivers & The:
see Drivers & The Spacemen, The

SPANIELS, Pookie Hudson & The

SPANIELS, The

TITLE/FLIP	LABEL & NO.	GOOD TO VERY GOOD	NEAR MINT	YR.
BABY, IT'S YOU/Bounce (red plastic)	*Chance 1141*	50.00	200.00	*53*
BABY, IT'S YOU/Bounce (red plastic)	*Vee Jay 101*	90.00	360.00	*53*
BABY, IT'S YOU/Bounce	*Chance 1141*	35.00	140.00	*53*
BABY, IT'S YOU/Bounce	*Vee Jay 101*	70.00	280.00	*53*
BABY, IT'S YOU/Heart And Soul	*Vee Jay 301*	3.00	12.00	*58*
BELLS RING OUT, THE/House Cleaning (red plastic)	*Vee Jay 103*	60.00	240.00	*53*
BELLS RING OUT, THE/House Cleaning	*Vee Jay 103*	12.50	50.00	*53*
BELLS RING OUT, THE/People Will Say We're In Love	*Vee Jay 342*	1.50	6.00	*59*
DEAR HEART/Why Won't You Dance?	*Vee Jay 189*	8.00	32.00	*56*
DON'CHA GO/Do-Wah	*Vee Jay 131*	5.00	20.00	*55*
EVERYONE'S LAUGHING/I.O.U.	*Vee Jay 246*	3.00	12.00	*57*
FALSE LOVE/Do You Really?	*Vee Jay 178*	8.00	32.00	*56*
GOODNITE, SWEETHEART, GOODNITE/ You Don't Move Me (red plastic)	*Vee Jay 107*	20.00	80.00	*53*
GOODNITE, SWEETHEART, GOODNITE/ You Don't Move Me	*Vee Jay 107*	6.25	25.00	*53*
I KNOW/Bus Fare Home	*Vee Jay 350*	2.00	8.00	*60*
I LOST YOU/Crazee Babee	*Vee Jay 264*	3.00	12.00	*58*
100 YEARS FROM TODAY/These Three Words	*Vee Jay 328*	4.00	16.00	*59*
PAINTED PICTURE/Hey, Sister Lizzie	*Vee Jay 154*	2.50	10.00	*55*

Some later pressings of this record spell their name as "The Spanials."

TITLE/FLIP	LABEL & NO.	GOOD TO VERY GOOD	NEAR MINT	YR.
PLAY IT COOL/Let's Make Up (red plastic)	*Vee Jay 116*	45.00	180.00	*55*
PLAY IT COOL/Let's Make Up	*Vee Jay 116*	9.00	36.00	*55*
SINCE I FELL FOR YOU/Baby, Come Along With Me	*Vee Jay 202*	5.00	20.00	*56*
STORMY WEATHER/Here Is Why I Love You	*Vee Jay 290*	3.00	12.00	*58*
TINA/Great Googley Moo	*Vee Jay 278*	3.00	12.00	*58*
TREES/I Like It Like That	*Vee Jay 310*	2.00	8.00	*59*
YOU GAVE ME PEACE OF MIND/Please Don't Tease	*Vee Jay 229*	3.00	12.00	*56*
YOU PAINTED PICTURES/Hey, Sister Lizzie	*Vee Jay 154*	5.00	20.00	*55*
YOU'RE GONNA CRY/I Need Your Kisses	*Vee Jay 257*	3.00	12.00	*57*

SPANN, Otis

TITLE/FLIP	LABEL & NO.	GOOD TO VERY GOOD	NEAR MINT	YR.
IT MUST HAVE BEEN THE DEVIL/ Five Spot (instrumental)	*Checker 807*	25.00	100.00	*55*

SPANIELS, The

TITLE/FLIP	LABEL & NO.	GOOD TO VERY GOOD	NEAR MINT	YR.
BABY, IT'S YOU/Bounce (red plastic)	*Chance 1141*	50.00	200.00	*53*
BABY, IT'S YOU/Bounce (red plastic)	*Vee Jay 101*	90.00	360.00	*53*
BABY, IT'S YOU/Bounce	*Chance 1141*	35.00	140.00	*53*
BABY, IT'S YOU/Bounce	*Vee Jay 101*	70.00	280.00	*53*
BABY, IT'S YOU/Heart And Soul	*Vee Jay 301*	3.00	12.00	*58*
BELLS RING OUT, THE/House Cleaning (red plastic)	*Vee Jay 103*	60.00	240.00	*53*
BELLS RING OUT, THE/House Cleaning	*Vee Jay 103*	12.50	50.00	*53*
BELLS RING OUT, THE/People Will Say We're In Love	*Vee Jay 342*	1.50	6.00	*59*
DEAR HEART/Why Won't You Dance?	*Vee Jay 189*	8.00	32.00	*56*
DON'CHA GO/Do-Wah	*Vee Jay 131*	5.00	20.00	*55*
EVERYONE'S LAUGHING/I.O.U.	*Vee Jay 246*	3.00	12.00	*57*
FALSE LOVE/Do You Really?	*Vee Jay 178*	8.00	32.00	*56*
GOODNITE, SWEETHEART, GOODNITE/ You Don't Move Me (red plastic)	*Vee Jay 107*	20.00	80.00	*53*
GOODNITE, SWEETHEART, GOODNITE/ You Don't Move Me	*Vee Jay 107*	6.25	25.00	*53*
I KNOW/Bus Fare Home	*Vee Jay 350*	2.00	8.00	*60*
I LOST YOU/Crazee Babee	*Vee Jay 264*	3.00	12.00	*58*
100 YEARS FROM TODAY/These Three Words	*Vee Jay 328*	4.00	16.00	*59*
PAINTED PICTURE/Hey, Sister Lizzie	*Vee Jay 154*	2.50	10.00	*55*

Some later pressings of this record spell their name as "The Spanials."

TITLE/FLIP	LABEL & NO.	GOOD TO VERY GOOD	NEAR MINT	YR.
PLAY IT COOL/Let's Make Up (red plastic)	*Vee Jay 116*	45.00	180.00	*55*
PLAY IT COOL/Let's Make Up	*Vee Jay 116*	9.00	36.00	*55*
SINCE I FELL FOR YOU/Baby, Come Along With Me	*Vee Jay 202*	5.00	20.00	*56*
STORMY WEATHER/Here Is Why I Love You	*Vee Jay 290*	3.00	12.00	*58*
TINA/Great Googley Moo	*Vee Jay 278*	3.00	12.00	*58*
TREES/I Like It Like That	*Vee Jay 310*	2.00	8.00	*59*
YOU GAVE ME PEACE OF MIND/Please Don't Tease	*Vee Jay 229*	3.00	12.00	*56*
YOU PAINTED PICTURES/Hey, Sister Lizzie	*Vee Jay 154*	5.00	20.00	*55*
YOU'RE GONNA CRY/I Need Your Kisses	*Vee Jay 257*	3.00	12.00	*57*

SPANN, Otis

TITLE/FLIP	LABEL & NO.	GOOD TO VERY GOOD	NEAR MINT	YR.
IT MUST HAVE BEEN THE DEVIL/ Five Spot (instrumental)	*Checker 807*	25.00	100.00	*55*

This is a highly-sought-after record with a reputation of having a classic all-star session of blues artists from this period.

SPARKS OF RHYTHM, The (featuring Jimmy Jones)

TITLE/FLIP	LABEL & NO.	GOOD TO VERY GOOD	NEAR MINT	YR.
DON'T LOVE YOU ANYMORE/Woman, Woman, Woman	*Apollo 479*	5.00	20.00	*55*
HANDY MAN/Everybody Rock And Go	*Apollo 541*	4.00	16.00	*60*
STARS ARE IN THE SKY/Hurry Home	*Apollo 481*	5.00	20.00	*55*

SPARKS, Curtis Irvin & The

TITLE/FLIP	LABEL & NO.	GOOD TO VERY GOOD	NEAR MINT	YR.
MAKE A LITTLE LOVE/Cheatin' On Me	*RPM 417*	8.00	32.00	*54*

SPARKS, The

TITLE/FLIP	LABEL & NO.	GOOD TO VERY GOOD	NEAR MINT	YR.
ADREANN/The Finger	*Hull 724*	15.00	60.00	*57*
DANNY BOY/Run, Run, Run	*Hull 723*	15.00	60.00	*57*

SPARROWS, Little Jimmy & The

TITLE/FLIP	LABEL & NO.	GOOD TO VERY GOOD	NEAR MINT	YR.
TWO HEARTS TOGETHER/Snorin'	*Val-ue 101*	5.00	20.00	—

SPARROWS, The

TITLE/FLIP	LABEL & NO.	GOOD TO VERY GOOD	NEAR MINT	YR.
I'LL BE LOVIN' YOU/Hey!	*Jay Dee 790*	10.00	40.00	*54*
I'M GONNA DO THAT WOMAN IN/ Don't Fuck Around With Love (recorded in in 1953)	*Kelway 101*	1.50	6.00	*71*
LOVE ME TENDER/Come Back To Me	*Davis 456*	12.50	50.00	*56*
TELL MY BABY/Why Did You Leave Me?	*Jay Dee 783*	10.00	40.00	*53*

SPEARS, Calvin

TITLE/FLIP	LABEL & NO.	GOOD TO VERY GOOD	NEAR MINT	YR.
COME ON HOME/Doing The Rock And Roll	*Vin 1020*	3.00	12.00	—

The Solitares

The Spaniels

SPEARS, Frankie Ervin & The

TITLE/FLIP	LABEL & NO.	GOOD TO VERY GOOD	NEAR MINT	YR.
WHY DID IT END?/Try To Care	Don 202	10.00	40.00	—

SPEEDO & THE CADILLACS

SPELLMAN, Benny

SPENCER, Carl & The Mellows:
see Mellows, Carl Spencer & The

SPIDER SAM:
see Van Walls, Harry as Spider Sam

SPIDERS, The

TITLE/FLIP	LABEL & NO.	GOOD TO VERY GOOD	NEAR MINT	YR.
AM I THE ONE?/Sukey, Sukey, Sukey	Imperial 5344	4.00	16.00	55
BELLS IN MY HEART/For A Thrill	Imperial 5354	7.00	28.00	55
DEAR MARY/A-1 In My Heart	Imperial 5393	1.50	6.00	56
DON'T PITY ME/How I Feel	Imperial 5376	1.50	6.00	56
GOODBYE/That's The Way To Win My Heart	Imperial 5405	1.50	6.00	56
HONEY BEE/That's My Desire	Imperial 5423	1.50	6.00	56
I DIDN'T WANT TO DO IT/You're The One	Imperial 5265	5.00	20.00	54
I'LL STOP CRYING/Tears Began To Flow	Imperial 5280	7.00	28.00	54
I'M SLIPPIN' IN/I'm Searchin'	Imperial 5291	4.00	16.00	54
REAL THING, THE/Mmm, Mmm, Baby	Imperial 5305	5.00	20.00	54
SHE KEEPS ME WONDERING/21	Imperial 5318	5.00	20.00	54
THAT'S ENOUGH/Lost And Bewildered	Imperial 5331	5.00	20.00	55
WITCHCRAFT/Is It True?	Imperial 5366	2.00	8.00	55

SPINNERS, Bobby Smith & The

SPINNERS, Claudine Clark & The

SPINNERS, Dionne Warwick & The

SPINNERS, The

TITLE/FLIP	LABEL & NO.	GOOD TO VERY GOOD	NEAR MINT	YR.
BIRD WATCHIN'/Richard Pry, Private Eye	End 1045	1.50	6.00	59
GOOFIN'/Love's Prayer	Capitol 3955	2.50	10.00	58
MARVELLA/My Love And Your Love	Rhythm 125	20.00	80.00	58

SPIRES, Arthur as Big Boy Spires

TITLE/FLIP	LABEL & NO.	GOOD TO VERY GOOD	NEAR MINT	YR.
ONE OF THESE DAYS/Murmur Low (78)	Checker 752	5.00	20.00	52

SPIRES, Arthur as Big Boy Spires & His Trio

TITLE/FLIP	LABEL & NO.	GOOD TO VERY GOOD	NEAR MINT	YR.
ABOUT TO LOSE MY MIND/Which One Do I Love?	Chance 1137	20.00	80.00	53

SPIRES, Big Boy:
see Spires, Arthur as Big Boy Spires

SPOTLIGHTERS, The

TITLE/FLIP	LABEL & NO.	GOOD TO VERY GOOD	NEAR MINT	YR.
IT'S COLD/Bam, Jingle, Jingle	Imperial 5342	5.00	20.00	55
PLEASE BE MY GIRLFRIEND/Whisper	Aladdin 3436	10.00	40.00	58
THIS IS MY STORY/Preachin'	Aladdin 3441	5.00	20.00	58

SPRIGGS, Walter

TITLE/FLIP	LABEL & NO.	GOOD TO VERY GOOD	NEAR MINT	YR.
I DON'T WANT YOU/Let Me Love You	Apollo 445	3.00	12.00	53
I PAWNED EVERYTHING/Love You, Love You, Love You	Atco 6079	1.50	6.00	56
I'M NOT YOUR FOOL ANYMORE/Week End Man	Blue Lake 109	5.00	20.00	54

SPUTNICKS, The

TITLE/FLIP	LABEL & NO.	GOOD TO VERY GOOD	NEAR MINT	YR.
MY LOVE IS GONE/Hey, Maryann	Class 217	1.50	6.00	57

SPYDELS, The

SQUIRES, Billy Jones & The

TITLE/FLIP	LABEL & NO.	GOOD TO VERY GOOD	NEAR MINT	YR.
EVERYWORD OF THE SONG/Listen To Your Heart	Deck 478	2.50	10.00	—

SQUIRES, The

TITLE/FLIP	LABEL & NO.	GOOD TO VERY GOOD	NEAR MINT	YR.
DREAMY EYES/Dangling With My Heart	Aladdin 3360	4.00	16.00	57
GUIDING ANGEL/ You Ought To Be Ashamed (with Effie Smith)	Vita 117	7.00	28.00	56
HEAVENLY ANGEL/Sweet Girl	Vita 116	7.00	28.00	56
LUCY LOU/A Dream Come True	Kicks 1	25.00	100.00	54
ME AND MY DEAL/Sweet Girl	Vita 113	7.00	28.00	55
SINDY/Do-Be-Do-Be-Wop-Wop	Mambo 105	9.00	36.00	55
SINDY/Do-Be-Do-Be-Wop-Wop	Vita 105	7.00	28.00	60
VENUS/Breath Of Air	Vita 128	7.00	28.00	56

SQUIRES, The

TITLE/FLIP	LABEL & NO.	GOOD TO VERY GOOD	NEAR MINT	YR.
LET'S GIVE LOVE A TRY/Whop	Combo 35	12.50	50.00	54
OH, DARLING/My Little Girl	Combo 42	12.50	50.00	54

ST. CLAIR, Nicky & The Five Trojans:
see Trojans, Nicky St. Clair & The

ST. LOUIS JIMMY:
see Oden, James as St. Louis Jimmy

STAGS, The

TITLE/FLIP	LABEL & NO.	GOOD TO VERY GOOD	NEAR MINT	YR.
SAILOR BOY/Cool Capri	M & S 502	7.00	28.00	—

STAIRSTEPS,The

STANTON, Johnny & Louis as Johnny & Louis Stanton

TITLE/FLIP	LABEL & NO.	GOOD TO VERY GOOD	NEAR MINT	YR.
BUSY AS A BEE/ Why Don't You Write Me? (by The Feathers)	Show Time 1105	9.00	36.00	55

STAPLES, Mavis

STARGLOWS, The

TITLE/FLIP	LABEL & NO.	GOOD TO VERY GOOD	NEAR MINT	YR.
LET'S BE LOVERS/Walk Softly Away	Atco 6272	1.50	6.00	63

STARKES, Doc & The Nite Riders:
see Nite Riders, Doc Starkes & The

STARLARKS, The

TITLE/FLIP	LABEL & NO.	GOOD TO VERY GOOD	NEAR MINT	YR.
FOUNTAIN OF LOVE/Send Me A Picture, Baby!	Elm (unknown number)	15.00	60.00	57
FOUNTAIN OF LOVE/Send Me A Picture, Baby!	Ember 1013	6.25	25.00	57

STARLARKS, Wes Forbes & The

TITLE/FLIP	LABEL & NO.	GOOD TO VERY GOOD	NEAR MINT	YR.
HEAVENLY FATHER/My Dear	Ancho 102	7.00	28.00	—

STARLETTES, The (female group)

TITLE/FLIP	LABEL & NO.	GOOD TO VERY GOOD	NEAR MINT	YR.
JUNGLE LOVE/Please Ring My Phone	Checker 895	2.00	8.00	58

STARLIGHTERS, Joe Weaver & The

STARLIGHTERS, The

TITLE/FLIP	LABEL & NO.	GOOD TO VERY GOOD	NEAR MINT	YR.
I CRIED/You're The One To Blame	End 1049	2.00	8.00	59
IT'S TWELVE O'CLOCK/The Birdland	End 1031	1.50	6.00	58
STORY OF LOVE, A/Let's Take A Stroll	End 1072	1.50	6.00	60

STARLIGHTERS, The

TITLE/FLIP	LABEL & NO.	GOOD TO VERY GOOD	NEAR MINT	YR.
LOVE CRY/Last Night	Irma 101	20.00	80.00	—
UNTIL YOU RETURN/Whomp, Whomp!	Sun Coast 1001	10.00	40.00	—

STARLINGS, The

TITLE/FLIP	LABEL & NO.	GOOD TO VERY GOOD	NEAR MINT	YR.
A-LOO, A-LOO/I Gotta Go Now	Dawn 213	15.00	60.00	55
I'M JUST A CRYING FOOL/Hokey-Smokey Mama	Dawn 212	15.00	60.00	55
MY PLEA FOR LOVE/Music, Maestro, Please	JOZ 760	25.00	100.00	54

This was the first record by the label that became Josie.

STARLINGS, The:
see Skylarks, The

STARLITERS, The

TITLE/FLIP	LABEL & NO.	GOOD TO VERY GOOD	NEAR MINT	YR.
ARLINE/Sweet Su	Combo 73	4.00	16.00	55

STARLITES, Eddie & The

TITLE/FLIP	LABEL & NO.	GOOD TO VERY GOOD	NEAR MINT	YR.
COME ON HOME/I Need Some Money	Aljon 1260/1261	2.00	8.00	—
TO MAKE A LONG STORY SHORT/Pretty Little Girl	Scepter 1202	2.50	10.00	59

STARLITES, Jackie & The

TITLE/FLIP	LABEL & NO.	GOOD TO VERY GOOD	NEAR MINT	YR.
FOR ALL WE KNOW/I Heard You	Mascot 128	3.00	12.00	62
I FOUND OUT TOO LATE/I'm Coming Home	Fury 1057	1.50	6.00	61
I STILL REMEMBER/I Cried My Heart Out	Hull 760	2.50	10.00	63
I'LL BURN YOUR LETTERS/Walking From School	Mascot 131	7.00	28.00	63
THEY LAUGHED AT ME/You Put One Over On Me	Fire & Fury 1000	8.00	32.00	—
YOU KEEP TELLING ME/	Mascot 130	5.00	20.00	62

STARLITES, Kenny Esquire & The

TITLE/FLIP	LABEL & NO.	GOOD TO VERY GOOD	NEAR MINT	YR.
PRETTY BROWN EYES/They Call Me A Dreamer	Ember 1011	4.00	16.00	57
TEARS ARE JUST FOR FOOLS/Boom Chica Boom	Ember 1021	4.00	16.00	57

STARLITES, The

TITLE/FLIP	LABEL & NO.	GOOD TO VERY GOOD	NEAR MINT	YR.
AIN'T CHA EVER COMING HOME?/Silver Lining	Fury 1045	1.50	6.00	60
SEVEN DAY FOOL/Don't Be Afraid	Sphere Sound 705	2.00	8.00	65
VALERIE/Way Up In The Sky	Fury 1034	1.50	6.00	60

STARR, Edwin

STARR, Mack & The Mellows

STARR, Mack & The Paragons:
see Paragons, Mack Starr & The

STARTONES, The

TITLE/FLIP	LABEL & NO.	GOOD TO VERY GOOD	NEAR MINT	YR.
I LOVE YOU SO DEARLY/Forever My Love	Rainbow 341	2.50	10.00	—

STATON, Candi

STEREOPHONICS, The

STEREOS, Dave & The

TITLE/FLIP	LABEL & NO.	GOOD TO VERY GOOD	NEAR MINT	YR.
THIS MUST BE LOVE/Roamin' Romeo	Pennant 1001	4.00	16.00	61

STEREOS, The

TITLE/FLIP	LABEL & NO.	GOOD TO VERY GOOD	NEAR MINT	YR.
MEMORY LANE/Teenage Kids	Mink 22	3.00	12.00	59

STEVENS, Julie & The Premiers:
see Premiers, Julie Stevens & The

STEVENS, Mark & The Charmers:
see Charmers, Mark Stevens & The

STEWART, Billy

STEWART, Celestine & The Charmers:
see Charmers, Celestine Stewart & The

STEWART, James (The Harmonica Cat)

TITLE/FLIP	LABEL & NO.	GOOD TO VERY GOOD	NEAR MINT	YR.
SWEET WOMAN/Lover Blues	Folk Star 1192	4.00	16.00	54

STEWART, Ty & The Jokers:
see Jokers, Ty Stewart & The

STIDHAM, Arbee

TITLE/FLIP	LABEL & NO.	GOOD TO VERY GOOD	NEAR MINT	YR.
DON'T SET YOUR TRAP FOR ME/I Don't Play	Checker 778	4.00	16.00	52
FEEL LIKE I'M LOSING YOU/Squeeze Me, Baby (red plastic)	RCA Victor 50-0093	4.00	16.00	50
I FOUND OUT FOR MYSELF/My Heart Belongs To You (red plastic)	RCA Victor 50-0003	4.00	16.00	47
I FOUND OUT FOR MYSELF/My Heart Belongs To You	RCA Victor 47-4951	1.50	6.00	47
I'LL ALWAYS REMEMBER/Meet Me Halfway	Abco 100	3.00	12.00	56
LET MY DREAMS COME TRUE/Any Time Ring My Bell (red plastic)	RCA Victor 50-0083	4.00	16.00	50
LOOK ME STRAIGHT IN THE EYE/I Stayed Away Too Long	States 164	4.00	16.00	51
SEND MY REGRETS/Barbecue Lounge (red plastic)	RCA Victor 50-0037	4.00	16.00	49
SOMEONE TO TELL MY TROUBLES TO/Mr. Commissioner	Checker 751	2.00	8.00	52
WHAT THE BLUES WILL DO/Falling Blues (red plastic)	RCA Victor 50-0024	4.00	16.00	49
WHEN I FIND MY BABY/Please Let It Be Me	Abco 107	5.00	20.00	56
YOU'LL BE SORRY/So Tired Of Dreaming (red plastic)	RCA Victor 50-0101	4.00	16.00	49

STONE, Jerry & The Four Dots:
see Four Dots, Jerry Stone & The

STONE, Jesse

TITLE/FLIP	LABEL & NO.	GOOD TO VERY GOOD	NEAR MINT	YR.
DO IT NOW/Cole Slaw (red plastic)	RCA Victor 50-0010	2.50	10.00	49
NIGHT LIFE/Rocket (instrumental)	Atco 6051	1.50	6.00	54
OH, THAT'LL BE JOYFUL/Runaway (instrumental)	Atlantic 1028	2.00	8.00	54

STONEHAM, Luther

TITLE/FLIP	LABEL & NO.	GOOD TO VERY GOOD	NEAR MINT	YR.
SITTIN' AND WONDERIN'/January 11, 1947 Blues (78)	Mercury 8279	4.00	16.00	51

STONEHAM, Luther:
see Smith, Wilson as Thunder Smith & Rockie (Luther Stoneham)

STOREY SISTERS, The

STORM, Billy & The Valiants

TITLE/FLIP	LABEL & NO.	GOOD TO VERY GOOD	NEAR MINT	YR.
WE KNEW/Walkin' Girl	Ensign 4035	1.50	6.00	58

STORMY HERMAN & HIS MIDNIGHT RAMBLERS

TITLE/FLIP	LABEL & NO.	GOOD TO VERY GOOD	NEAR MINT	YR.
JITTERBUG, THE/Bad Luck	Dootone 358	4.00	16.00	55

STRANGERS, The

TITLE/FLIP	LABEL & NO.	GOOD TO VERY GOOD	NEAR MINT	YR.
BLUE FLOWERS/Beg And Steal	King 4709	25.00	100.00	54
DREAMS COME TRUE/How Long Must I Wait?	King 4766	12.50	50.00	55
DROP DOWN TO MY PLACE/Get It One More Time	King 4745	10.00	40.00	54
HOPING YOU'LL UNDERSTAND/Just Don't Care	King 4728	15.00	60.00	54
MY FRIENDS/I've Got Eyes	King 4697	12.50	50.00	54
WITHOUT A FRIEND/Think Again	King 4821	11.00	44.00	55

STREET SINGERS, The

TITLE/FLIP	LABEL & NO.	GOOD TO VERY GOOD	NEAR MINT	YR.
TONIGHT WAS LIKE A DREAM/Caldonia's Mambo	Tuxedo 899	15.00	60.00	56

STRIDERS, Bette McLaurin & The

TITLE/FLIP	LABEL & NO.	GOOD TO VERY GOOD	NEAR MINT	YR.
MY HEART BELONGS TO ONLY YOU/I Won't Tell A Soul I Love You	Derby 804	5.00	20.00	52

STRIDERS, Savannah Churchill & The

TITLE/FLIP	LABEL & NO.	GOOD TO VERY GOOD	NEAR MINT	YR.
WHEN YOU COME BACK TO ME/Once There Lived A Fool (78)	Regal 3309	1.50	6.00	50

STRIDERS, The

TITLE/FLIP	LABEL & NO.	GOOD TO VERY GOOD	NEAR MINT	YR.
5 O'CLOCK BLUES/Cool Saturday Night (78)	Apollo 1159	4.00	16.00	50
HESITATING FOOL/I Wonder	Apollo 480	15.00	60.00	55
PLEASIN' YOU/Somebody Stole My Rose Colored Glasses (78)	Capitol 15306	2.50	10.00	48

STROLLERS, The

TITLE/FLIP	LABEL & NO.	GOOD TO VERY GOOD	NEAR MINT	YR.
COME ON OVER/There's No One But You	Carlton 546	1.50	6.00	61

STROLLERS, The

TITLE/FLIP	LABEL & NO.	GOOD TO VERY GOOD	NEAR MINT	YR.
IN YOUR DREAMS/Go Where Baby Lives	States 163	12.50	50.00	57

STRONG, BARRETT

TITLE/FLIP	LABEL & NO.	GOOD TO VERY GOOD	NEAR MINT	YR.
MONEY (THAT'S WHAT I WANT)/Oh, I Apologize	Tamla 54027	6.25	25.00	60

The first pressing of this early Tamla record can be identified by a series of 17 horizontal lines ruled across the top half of the record label.

STRONG, Nolan & The Diablos:
see Diablos, Nolan Strong & The

STUDENTS, The

TITLE/FLIP	LABEL & NO.	GOOD TO VERY GOOD	NEAR MINT	YR.
I'M SO YOUNG/Every Day Of The Week	Checker 902	1.50	6.00	58
I'M SO YOUNG/Every Day Of The Week	Note 10012	20.00	80.00	58
THAT'S HOW I FEEL/My Vow To You	Checker 1004	1.50	6.00	62
THAT'S HOW I FEEL/My Vow To You	Note 10019	20.00	80.00	58

STUDENTS, The

TITLE/FLIP	LABEL & NO.	GOOD TO VERY GOOD	NEAR MINT	YR.
MY HEART IS AN OPEN DOOR/Mommy & Daddy	Red Top 100	10.00	40.00	—

STYLERS, The

TITLE/FLIP	LABEL & NO.	GOOD TO VERY GOOD	NEAR MINT	YR.
GENTLE AS A TEARDROP/There Were Others	Kicks 2	20.00	80.00	54

STYLISTICS, The

STYLISTS, The

TITLE/FLIP	LABEL & NO.	GOOD TO VERY GOOD	NEAR MINT	YR.
I WONDER/One Room	Rose 16/17	4.00	16.00	—

SUBURBANS, Ann Cole & The

TITLE/FLIP	LABEL & NO.	GOOD TO VERY GOOD	NEAR MINT	YR.
GOT MY MO-JO WORKING/I've Got A Little Boy	Baton 237	1.50	6.00	57
IN THE CHAPEL/Each Day	Baton 232	1.50	6.00	56

SUBURBANS, Jimmy Ricks & The

TITLE/FLIP	LABEL & NO.	GOOD TO VERY GOOD	NEAR MINT	YR.
I'M A FOOL TO WANT YOU/Bad Man Of Missouri	Baton 236	1.50	6.00	57

SUBURBANS, The

TITLE/FLIP	LABEL & NO.	GOOD TO VERY GOOD	NEAR MINT	YR.
I REMEMBER/T.V. Baby	Baton 227	2.00	8.00	56
LEAVE MY GAL ALONE/My First And Last Romance	Baton 240	1.50	6.00	57

SUBURBANS, The

TITLE/FLIP	LABEL & NO.	GOOD TO VERY GOOD	NEAR MINT	YR.
ALPHABET OF LOVE/Sweet Diane Cha Cha	Port 70011	2.00	8.00	59

SUEDES, The

TITLE/FLIP	LABEL & NO.	GOOD TO VERY GOOD	NEAR MINT	YR.
I LOVE YOU SO/Don't Blooper	Money 204	15.00	60.00	54

SUGAR BOY & HIS CANE CUTTERS:
see Crawford, James as Sugar Boy & His Cane Cutters

SUGAR BOY & THE SUGAR LUMPS

SUGAR LUMPS, Sugar Boy & The

SUGAR PIE & HANK (Hank Ballard)

TITLE/FLIP	LABEL & NO.	GOOD TO VERY GOOD	NEAR MINT	YR.
PLEASE BE TRUE/I'm So Lonely	Federal 12217	2.50	10.00	55

SUGAR TONES, The (female group)

SUGARCANE & HIS VIOLIN:
see Harris, Don as Sugarcane

SUGARMAN, The

TITLE/FLIP	LABEL & NO.	GOOD TO VERY GOOD	NEAR MINT	YR.
WHICH WOMAN DO I LOVE?/ She's Gone With The Wind (78)	Sittin' In With 609	4.00	16.00	51

SUGARMINTS, The

TITLE/FLIP	LABEL & NO.	GOOD TO VERY GOOD	NEAR MINT	YR.
YOU'LL HAVE EVRYTHING/I-I-I Could Love You	Brunswick 55042	3.00	12.00	57

SULLIVAN, Maxine:
see Charioteers, The

SULTANS, The

TITLE/FLIP	LABEL & NO.	GOOD TO VERY GOOD	NEAR MINT	YR.
DON'T BE ANGRY/Blues At Dawn	Jubilee 5077	20.00	80.00	52
GOOD THING, BABY/How Deep Is The Ocean?	Duke 125	8.00	32.00	54
I CRIED MY HEART OUT/Baby, Don't Put Me Down	Duke 133	7.00	28.00	54
IF I COULD TELL/My Love Is High	Duke 178	2.50	10.00	57
LEMON SQUEEZING DADDY/You Captured My Heart	Jubilee 5054	15.00	60.00	51
WHAT MAKES ME FEEL THIS WAY?/Boppin' With The Mambo	Duke 135	10.00	40.00	54

SUNBEAMS, The

TITLE/FLIP	LABEL & NO.	GOOD TO VERY GOOD	NEAR MINT	YR.
TELL ME WHY/Come Back, Baby	Herald 451	12.50	50.00	55

SUNDOWN SINGERS, Richard Huey & The

SUNNIE ELMO & THE MINOR CHORDS:
see Minor Chords, Sunnie Elmo & The

SUNNY JAMES:
see James, Jesse as Sunny James

SUNNYLAND SLIM:
see Luandrew, Albert as Sunnyland Slim

SUNNYLAND TRIO, The:
see Foster, Leroy as Baby Face & The Sunnyland Trio
see Luandrew, Albert as The Sunnyland Trio

SUNSETS, The

TITLE/FLIP	LABEL & NO.	GOOD TO VERY GOOD	NEAR MINT	YR.
HOW WILL I REMEMBER?/Sittin' And Cryin'	Rae Cox 102	1.50	6.00	59

SUPERBS, The

SUPERIORS, The

TITLE/FLIP	LABEL & NO.	GOOD TO VERY GOOD	NEAR MINT	YR.
LOST LOVE/Don't Say Goodbye (gray label)	Main Line 104	2.00	8.00	58
LOST LOVE/Don't Say Goodbye	Atco 6106	1.50	6.00	57
LOST LOVE/Don't Say Goodbye	Main Line 104	25.00	100.00	58

SUPREMES & THE FOUR TOPS, The

SUPREMES & THE TEMPTATIONS, Diana Ross & The

SUPREMES FOUR, The

TITLE/FLIP	LABEL & NO.	GOOD TO VERY GOOD	NEAR MINT	YR.
I LOST MY JOB/I Love You, Patricia	Sara 1032	7.00	28.00	61

SUPREMES, Diana Ross & The

SUPREMES, Ruth McFadden & The

TITLE/FLIP	LABEL & NO.	GOOD TO VERY GOOD	NEAR MINT	YR.
DARLING, LISTEN TO THE WORDS OF THIS SONG/ Since My Baby's Been Gone	Old Town 1017	3.00	12.00	56

SUPREMES, The (featuring Diana Ross)

TITLE/FLIP	LABEL & NO.	GOOD TO VERY GOOD	NEAR MINT	YR.
BUTTERED POPCORN/Who's Lovin' You	Tamla 54045	2.50	10.00	61
I WANT A GUY/Never Again	Tamla 54038	2.50	10.00	61

SUPREMES, The

TITLE/FLIP	LABEL & NO.	GOOD TO VERY GOOD	NEAR MINT	YR.
JUST FOR YOU AND I/Don't Leave Me Here To Cry	Ace 534	4.00	16.00	57

SUPREMES, The

TITLE/FLIP	LABEL & NO.	GOOD TO VERY GOOD	NEAR MINT	YR.
TONIGHT/My Babe	Old Town 1024	9.00	36.00	56
TONIGHT/She Don't Want Me No More	Old Town 1024	10.00	40.00	56

SUPREMES, The

TITLE/FLIP	LABEL & NO.	GOOD TO VERY GOOD	NEAR MINT	YR.
COULD THIS BE YOU?/Margie	Kitten 6969	8.00	32.00	56

SWALLOWS, The

Junior Denby, a key member of this group, has records listed under his own name.

TITLE/FLIP	LABEL & NO.	GOOD TO VERY GOOD	NEAR MINT	YR.
BESIDE YOU/You Left Me	King 4525	20.00	80.00	52
ETERNALLY/It Ain't The Meat (blue plastic)	King 4501	60.00	240.00	51
ETERNALLY/It Ain't The Meat	King 4501	50.00	200.00	51
I ONLY HAVE EYES FOR YOU/You Walked In	King 4533	40.00	160.00	52
I'LL BE WAITING/It Feels So Good	King 4676	30.00	120.00	53
LAUGH/Our Love Is Dying	King 4612	15.00	60.00	53
MY BABY/Good Time Girls	After Hours 104	55.00	220.00	54
NOBODY'S LOVIN' ME/Bicycle Tillie	King 4632	20.00	80.00	53
SINCE YOU'VE BEEN AWAY/Wishing For You	King 4466	100.00	400.00	51
TELL ME WHY/Roll, Roll, Pretty Baby	King 4515	50.00	200.00	51
TRUST ME/Pleading Blues	King 4656	20.00	80.00	53
WHERE DO I GO FROM HERE?/Please, Baby, Please	King 4579	25.00	100.00	52
WILL YOU BE MINE?/Dearest	King 4458	75.00	300.00	51

SWALLOWS, The

TITLE/FLIP	LABEL & NO.	GOOD TO VERY GOOD	NEAR MINT	YR.
HOW LONG MUST A FOOL GO ON?/You Must Try	Guyden 2023	2.50	10.00	59

SWALLOWS, The

TITLE/FLIP	LABEL & NO.	GOOD TO VERY GOOD	NEAR MINT	YR.
BESIDE YOU/Laughing Boy	Federal 12329	1.50	6.00	58
ITCHY TWITCHY FEELING/Who Knows, Do You?	Federal 12333	1.50	6.00	58
OH, LONESOME ME/Angel Baby	Federal 12319	1.50	6.00	58
WE WANT TO ROCK/Rock-A-Bye Baby Rock	Federal 12328	1.50	6.00	58

SWAMP DOG

SWANN, Bettye

SWANS, Nat Kendrick & The

SWANS, Paul Lewis & The

TITLE/FLIP	LABEL & NO.	GOOD TO VERY GOOD	NEAR MINT	YR.
LITTLE SENORITA/Wedding Bells, Oh Wedding Bells	Fortune 813	2.00	80.00	—

SWANS, The

TITLE/FLIP	LABEL & NO.	GOOD TO VERY GOOD	NEAR MINT	YR.
BELIEVE IN ME/In The Morning	Steamboat 101	8.00	32.00	—
FOR DREAMS COME TRUE/Happy (78)	Ballad 1000/1001	2.50	10.00	—
HAPPY/Santa Claus Boogie Song (78)	Ballad 1007	2.50	10.00	55
I'LL FOREVER LOVE YOU/Mister Cool Breeze	Fortune 822	15.00	60.00	55
IT'S A MUST/Night Train (78)	Ballad 1003/1006	2.50	10.00	55
MY TRUE LOVE/No More (red plastic)	Rainbow 233	50.00	200.00	—

SWEET INSPIRATIONS, The (female group)

SWEET TEENS, Faith Taylor & The

TITLE/FLIP	LABEL & NO.	GOOD TO VERY GOOD	NEAR MINT	YR.
I LOVE YOU, DARLING/Paper Route Baby	Bea & Baby 105	4.00	16.00	59
I NEED HIM TO LOVE ME/Please Be Mine	Bea & Baby 104	4.00	16.00	59
YOUR CANDY KISSES/Won't Someone Tell Me Why?	Federal 12334	8.00	32.00	58

SWING BROTHERS, The:
see Burns, Eddie as The Swing Brothers

SWINGIN' TIGERS, The

TITLE/FLIP	LABEL & NO.	GOOD TO VERY GOOD	NEAR MINT	YR.
SNAKE WALK, PART 1/Snake Walk, Part 2	Tamla 54024	2.50	10.00	60

Hound Dog Taylor

Koko Taylor

SWINGING OZARKS, Johnny Wick & His:
see Wick, Johnny & His Swinging Ozarks

SWINGING PHILLIES, The

TITLE/FLIP	LABEL & NO.	GOOD TO VERY GOOD	NEAR MINT	YR.
L-O-V-E/Frankenstein's Party	De Luxe 6171	10.00	40.00	58

SYCAMORES, The

TITLE/FLIP	LABEL & NO.	GOOD TO VERY GOOD	NEAR MINT	YR.
I'LL BE WAITING/Darling, Is It True?	Groove 0121	15.00	60.00	55

SYKES, Roosevelt (The Honeydripper)

TITLE/FLIP	LABEL & NO.	GOOD TO VERY GOOD	NEAR MINT	YR.
CANDY MAN BLUES/Why Should I Cry? (78)	Bullet 319	1.50	6.00	47
DRIVIN' WHEEL/West Helena Blues (78)	Regal 3286	2.00	8.00	49
GREEN ONION TOP/Wonderin' Blues (78)	Regal 3324	2.00	8.00	49
I KNOW HOW YOU FEEL/ Stop Her, Poppa (red plastic)	RCA Victor 50-0025	5.00	20.00	47
MAILBOX BLUES/Wintertime Blues (78)	Regal 3306	2.00	8.00	49
ROCK IT/Blues 'n' Boogie (instrumental) (78)	Regal 3269	3.00	8.00	49
SOUTHERN BLUES/My Baby Is Gone (red plastic)	RCA Victor 50-0040	5.00	20.00	48

SYKES, Roosevelt & The Honeydrippers

TITLE/FLIP	LABEL & NO.	GOOD TO VERY GOOD	NEAR MINT	YR.
COME BACK BABY/Tell Me True	United 152	3.00	12.00	54
FOUR O'CLOCK BLUES/To (sic) Hot To Hold (red plastic)	United 139	8.00	32.00	53
FOUR O'CLOCK BLUES/To (sic) Hot To Hold	United 139	4.00	16.00	53
HUSH, OH, HUSH/Crazy Fox	Imperial 5367	2.50	10.00	54
RAINING IN MY HEART/Heavy Heart	United 120	4.00	16.00	52
SHE'S JAIL BAIT/Sputnick	House of Sound 505	4.00	16.00	57
SWEET OLD CHICAGO/Blood Stains	Imperial 5347	3.00	12.00	54
WALKIN' THIS BOOGIE/Security Blues	United 129	4.00	16.00	52

SYLVERS, The

SYNCAPATES, The

SYNCOPATERS, The

TITLE/FLIP	LABEL & NO.	GOOD TO VERY GOOD	NEAR MINT	YR.
MULE TRAIN/ These Are The Things I Want To Share With You (78)	National 9093	4.00	16.00	49
RIVER, STAY AWAY FROM MY DOOR/ These Are The Things I Want To Share With You (78)	National 9095	4.00	16.00	49

T

T. V. SLIM & HIS HEARTBREAKERS:
see Wills, Oscar as T. V. Slim

T-BIRDS, The

TABBY & HIS MELLOW, MELLOW MEN:
see Thomas, Tabby as Tabby

TABBYS, The

TITLE/FLIP	LABEL & NO.	GOOD TO VERY GOOD	NEAR MINT	YR.
MY DARLING/Yes, I Do	Time 1008	1.50	6.00	58

TABS, Joanie Taylor & The

TABS, The

TITLE/FLIP	LABEL & NO.	GOOD TO VERY GOOD	NEAR MINT	YR.
ROCK AND ROLL HOLIDAY/Never Forget	Noble 719	1.50	6.00	59

TABULATIONS, Brenda & The

TADS, The

TITLE/FLIP	LABEL & NO.	GOOD TO VERY GOOD	NEAR MINT	YR.
WOLF CALL/She Is My Dream	Rev 3513	3.00	12.00	58
YOUR REASON/The Pink Panther	Dot 15518	2.50	10.00	56
YOUR REASON/The Pink Panther	Liberty Bell 9010	7.00	28.00	56

TAMPA RED:
see Whittaker, Hudson as Tampa Red

TANGIERS, The

TITLE/FLIP	LABEL & NO.	GOOD TO VERY GOOD	NEAR MINT	YR.
PLEA, THE/The Waddle	A-J 905	2.00	8.00	62

TANNER, Kid

TITLE/FLIP	LABEL & NO.	GOOD TO VERY GOOD	NEAR MINT	YR.
HAVE YOU EVER BEEN IN LOVE?/Wino	Modern 889	2.50	10.00	53

TANTONES, The

TITLE/FLIP	LABEL & NO.	GOOD TO VERY GOOD	NEAR MINT	YR.
NO MATTER/I Love You, Really I Do	Lamp 2002	4.00	16.00	56
SO AFRAID/Tell Me	Lamp 2008	5.00	20.00	57

TARHEEL SLIM (Alden Bunn) & LITTLE ANN

TARHEEL SLIM:
see Bunn, Alden as Tarheel Slim
see Lovers, The (with Alden Bunn as Tarheel Slim)

TARVER, Leon

TITLE/FLIP	LABEL & NO.	GOOD TO VERY GOOD	NEAR MINT	YR.
SOMEBODY HELP ME/Oh Baby, I'm Blue	Blue Lake 118	4.00	16.00	55

TARVER, Leon D. & The Chordones:
see Chordones, Leon D. Tarver & The

TATE, Billy

TITLE/FLIP	LABEL & NO.	GOOD TO VERY GOOD	NEAR MINT	YR.
DON'T CALL MY NAME/Right From Wrong	Peacock 1671	1.50	6.00	56
SINGLE LIFE/You Told Me	Imperial 5337	5.00	20.00	54

TATE, Howard

TATE, Laurie (with Joe Morris & His Orchestra)

TITLE/FLIP	LABEL & NO.	GOOD TO VERY GOOD	NEAR MINT	YR.
ROCK ME DADDY/Can't Stop Me Crying	Atlantic 965	4.00	16.00	52

TAVARES

TAYLOR, Bobby & The Vancouvers

TAYLOR, Carmen

TITLE/FLIP	LABEL & NO.	GOOD TO VERY GOOD	NEAR MINT	YR.
BIG MAMOU DADDY/Mama Me And Johnny Free	Atlantic 1015	2.50	10.00	53
LOVIN' DADDY/Ding Dong	Atlantic 1002	2.50	10.00	53

TAYLOR, Carmen & The Boleros:
see Boleros, Carmen Taylor & The

TAYLOR, Cocoa:
see Taylor, Cora as Koko Taylor

TAYLOR, Cora as Koko Taylor

TITLE/FLIP	LABEL & NO.	GOOD TO VERY GOOD	NEAR MINT	YR.
LIKE HEAVEN TO ME/Honky Tonky	USA 745	1.50	6.00	63

TAYLOR, Danny "Run Joe"

TITLE/FLIP	LABEL & NO.	GOOD TO VERY GOOD	NEAR MINT	YR.
YOU LOOK BAD/'Gator Tail	RCA Victor 47-5558	2.00	8.00	53

TAYLOR, Danny:
see Harris, Bob

TAYLOR, Eddie

TITLE/FLIP	LABEL & NO.	GOOD TO VERY GOOD	NEAR MINT	YR.
BAD BOY/E. T. Blues (instrumental)	Vee Jay 149	5.00	20.00	55
I'M GONNA LOVE YOU/Lookin' For Trouble	Vee Jay 267	2.50	10.00	57
I'M SITTING HERE/Do You Want Me To Cry?	Vivid 104	1.50	6.00	64
RIDE 'EM DOWN/Big Town Playboy	Vee Jay 185	4.00	16.00	55
YOU'LL ALWAYS HAVE A HOME/ Don't Knock At My Door (instrumental)	Vee Jay 206	3.00	12.00	56

TAYLOR, Faith & The Sweet Teens:
see Sweet Teens, Faith Taylor & The

TAYLOR, Felice

TAYLOR, Hound Dog:
see Taylor, Theodore Roosevelt as Hound Dog Taylor

TAYLOR, Joanie & The Tabs

TAYLOR, Johnnie

TAYLOR, Koko:
see Taylor, Cora as Koko Taylor

TAYLOR, Little Johnny

TAYLOR, Ted

TAYLOR, Theodore Roosevelt as Hound Dog Taylor

TITLE/FLIP	LABEL & NO.	GOOD TO VERY GOOD	NEAR MINT	YR.
CHRISTINE/Alley Music (instrumental)	Firma 626	2.00	8.00	62
TAKE FIVE/My Baby's Coming Home	Bea & Baby 112	3.00	12.00	60

TITLE/FLIP	LABEL & NO.	GOOD TO VERY GOOD	NEAR MINT	YR.
TEARDROPS, The				
MY HEART/Ooh, Baby	Josie 771	15.00	60.00	54
STARS ARE OUT TONIGHT, THE/Oh, Stop It!	Josie 766	10.00	40.00	54
STARS ARE OUT TONIGHT, THE/Oh, Stop It!	Port 70019	1.50	6.00	60
TEARDROPS, The				
COME BACK TO ME/Sweet Lovin' Daddy-O	Sampson 634	30.00	120.00	52
TEARS, The (female group)				
NOTHING BUT LOVE/Until The Day I Die	Dig 112	1.50	6.00	56
TEASERS, The				
HOW COULD YOU HURT ME SO?/ I Was A Fool To Love You	Checker 800	40.00	160.00	54
TECHNIQUES, Jay & The				
TEDDY & THE TWILIGHTS				
TEE, Willie				
TEEN QUEENS, The				
TEENAGERS, Frankie Lymon & The				
TEENAGERS, Joey & The				
WHAT'S ON YOUR MIND?/The Draw (with Sherman)	Columbia 42054	3.00	12.00	61
TEENAGERS, The				
LITTLE WISER NOW, A/Can You Tell Me?	End 1076	2.00	8.00	60
MY BROKEN HEART/Momma Wanna Rock	Roulette 4086	1.50	6.00	58
TONIGHT'S THE NIGHT/Crying	End 1071	2.50	10.00	60
TEENAGERS, The (female group)				
TEENCHORDS, Lewis Lymon & The				
DANCE GIRL/Them There Eyes	Juanita 101	3.00	12.00	58
I FOUND OUT WHY/Tell Me, Love	End 1007	3.00	12.00	57
I'M NOT TOO YOUNG TO FALL IN LOVE/Falling In Love	Fury 1006	3.00	12.00	57
I'M SO HAPPY/Lydia	Fury 1000	2.50	10.00	57
TOO YOUNG/I Found Out Why	End 1113	1.50	6.00	62
TOO YOUNG/Your Last Chance	End 1003	4.00	16.00	57
TEENETTES, Betty Jane & The (female group)				
TEENETTES, Billy Jones & The				
TEENETTES, The (female group)				
MY LUCKY STAR/Too Young To Fall In Love	Josie 830	1.50	6.00	58
TEENOS, The				
LOVE ONLY ONE/Alrightee	Dub 2839	2.00	8.00	57
TEENS, Little Clyde & The				
CASUAL LOOK, A/Oh, Me!	RPM 462	3.00	12.00	56
TELLERS, The				
TEARS FELL FROM MY EYES/I Wanna Run To You	Fire 1038	3.00	12.00	61
TEMPLE, Johnny				
BETWEEN MIDNIGHT AND DAY/Sit Right On It (78)	Miracle 156	3.00	12.00	49
YUM, YUM/I Believe I'll Go Downtown (78)	King 4151	2.00	8.00	46
TEMPLE, Little: see Jenkins, Gus as Little Temple				
TEMPO TOPPERS, The: see Duces Of Rhythm & The Tempo Toppers, The (featuring Little Richard)				
TEMPO-MENTALS, The				
BURNING DESIRE/Dearest	Ebb 112	4.00	16.00	57
TEMPO-TONES, The				
COME INTO MY HEART/Somewhere The Is Someone	Acme 718	5.00	20.00	57
GET YOURSELF ANOTHER FOOL/Ride Along	Acme 713	5.00	20.00	57
IN MY DREAMS/My Boy Sleep Pete	Acme 715	5.00	20.00	57
WISHING ALL THE TIME/The Day I Met You	Acme 722	5.00	20.00	57
TEMPOS, The				
PROMISE ME/Never Let Me Go	Rhythm 121	15.00	60.00	58

TITLE/FLIP	LABEL & NO.	GOOD TO VERY GOOD	NEAR MINT	YR.
TEMPTATIONS, The				
CHECK YOURSELF/Your Wonderful Love	Miracle 12	1.50	6.00	62
ROMANCE WITHOUT/Oh, Mother of Mine	Miracle 5	2.00	8.00	61
TEMPTATIONS, The				
STANDING ALONE/Roach's Rock	King 5118	3.00	12.00	58
TEMPTERS, The				
I'LL SEE YOU NEXT FALL/I'm Sorry Now	Empire 105	1.50	6.00	56
TENDERFOOTS, The: see Lamplighters, The as The Tenderfoots				
TERRACETONES, The				
WORDS OF WISDOM/Ride Of Paul Revere	Apt 25016	4.00	16.00	58
TERRELL, Saunders as Sonny "Hootin' " Terry				
I DON'T WORRY/Man Ain't Nothing But A Fool (red plastic)	Jax 305	7.00	28.00	52
TERRELL, Saunders as Sonny "Hootin' " Terry & His Night Owls				
FAST FREIGHT BLUES (instrumental)/ Dangerous Woman	Josie 828	1.50	6.00	56
HARMONICA HOP/Doggin' My Heart Around	Red Robin 110	10.00	40.00	53
HOOTIN' AND JUMPIN'/Hooray, Hooray	RCA Victor 47-5492	3.00	12.00	53
HOOTIN' BLUES NO. 2/Ride And Roll	Groove 0135	2.50	10.00	55
LOST JAWBONE/Louise	Groove 0015	2.50	10.00	54
SONNY IS DRINKING/I'm Gonna Rock My Wig	RCA Victor 47-5577	3.00	12.00	53
THAT WOMAN IS KILLING ME/ Harmonica Train (red plastic)	Jackson 2302	8.00	32.00	52
UNCLE BUD/Climbing On Top Of The Hill	Old Town 1023	1.50	6.00	56
TERRELL, Saunders as Sonny T & His Buckshot Five				
DANGEROUS WOMAN/I Love You, Baby	Harlem 2327	5.00	20.00	52
TERRELL, Saunders as Sonny Terry				
BABY, LET'S HAVE SOME FUN/Four O'Clock Blues	Gotham 517	3.00	12.00	51
HARMONICA RUMBO (instrumental)/Lonesome Room	Gotham 518	3.00	12.00	51
HOOTIN' BLUES/Dangerous Woman (red plastic)	Gramercy 1004	5.00	20.00	52
HOOTIN' BLUES/Dangerous Woman	Gramercy 1004	2.50	10.00	52
TELEPHONE BLUES/Dirty Mistreater	Capitol 931	6.25	25.00	50
TERRELL, Tammi				
TERRELL, Tammi, Marvin Gaye &				
TERRY, Dossie				
DIDN'T SATISFY YOU/Twenty Four Years	RCA Victor 47-4474	2.00	8.00	51
DOROTHEA DOROTHEA BOOGIE/Whiskey Head Woman (78)	Chicago 119	1.50	6.00	45
LOST MY HEAD/Sad, Sad Affair	RCA Victor 47-4864	2.00	8.00	51
THUNDERBIRD/I Got A Watch Dog	King 5072	2.00	8.00	57
WHEN I HIT THE NUMBER/My Love Is Gone	RCA Victor 47-4684	2.00	8.00	51
TERRY, Dossie "Georgia Boy"				
FURLOUGH BLUES/The O.P.A. Blues (78)	Chicago 117	1.50	6.00	45
TERRY, Flash				
HER NAME IS LOU/Cool It	Lavender 5	2.50	10.00	61
ONE THING WE KNOW/On My Way Back Home	Kent 310	6.25	25.00	61
TERRY, Nat				
TAKE IT EASY/I Don't Know Why (78)	Imperial 5150	6.25	25.00	51
TERRY, Sonny: see Terrell, Saunders as Sonny Terry				
TEX & THE CHEX: see Chex, Tex & The				
TEX, Joe				
AIN'T NOBODY'S BUSINESS/I Want To Have A Talk With You	King 5064	1.50	6.00	57
DAVY, YOU UPSET MY HOME/Come In This House	King 4840	1.50	6.00	55
I HAD TO COME BACK TO YOU/She's Mine	King 4911	1.50	6.00	56
MOTHER'S ADVICE, A/You Little Baby Face Thing	Ace 550	5.00	20.00	58
MY BIGGEST MISTAKE/Right Back To My Arms	King 4884	1.50	6.00	56
PNEUMONIA/Get Away Back	King 4980	1.50	6.00	56
TEXAS ALEXANDER: see Alexander, Alger as Texas Alexander				
TEXAS RED				
TURN AROUND/Coming Home	Bullseye 1009	1.50	6.00	56

FRANKIE!

TITLE/FLIP	LABEL & NO.	GOOD TO VERY GOOD	NEAR MINT	YR.
TEXAS SLIM: see Hooker, John Lee as Texas Slim				
THEMES, The				
MAGIC OF YOU, THE/Yes! That's Love	Excello 2152	2.00	8.00	59
THEUS, Fatso & The Flairs: see Flairs, Fatso Theus & The				
THIBADEAUX, R. B.				
R. B. BOOGIE/New Kind Of Loving (78)	Peacock 1513	1.50	6.00	49
THIERRY, Huey: see Boogie Ramblers, The (featuring Huey Thierry); see Cupcakes, Cookie & His (featuring Huey Thierry)				
THOMAS, Alexander "Mudcat"				
12TH STREET RAG (instrumental)/ Step Up And Go	NRC 062	2.00	8.00	60
THOMAS, Andrew				
I LOVE MY BABY/Chicago Blues (78)	Swing With The Stars 1038/39	5.00	20.00	49
THOMAS, Andrew as Andy Thomas				
ANGEL CHILE/My Baby Quit Me Blues (78)	Gold Star 645	4.00	16.00	48
IN LOVE BLUES/Walking And Crying (78)	Gold Star 659	4.00	16.00	49
THOMAS, Burt & His Band				
BOSTON HOP, THE (instrumental)/ Sad Conditions Blues (78)	Jade 205	1.50	6.00	51
THOMAS, Carla				
THOMAS, Danny as Danny Boy & His Blue Guitar				
WILD WOMEN/Kokomo Me Baby	Tifco 824	1.50	6.00	61
THOMAS, Dee & The Versatiles: see Versatiles, Dee Thomas & The				
THOMAS, Irma				
THOMAS, Jesse				
ANOTHER FOOL LIKE ME/Gonna Move To California (78)	Elko 107	7.00	28.00	53
GONNA WRITE YOU A LETTER/Texas Blues (78)	Modern 20-710	2.00	8.00	49
GUESS I'LL WALK ALONE/Let's Have Some Fun (78)	Freedom 1513	2.50	10.00	49
I WONDER WHY?/Another Friend Like Me (78)	Club (no number)	7.00	28.00	48
LONG TIME/Cool Kind Lover	Hollywood 1072	6.25	25.00	51
MELODY IN C/You Are My Dreams (78)	Club (no number)	7.00	28.00	48
NOW'S THE TIME/It's You I'm Thinking Of (78)	Swing Time 241	1.50	6.00	51
WHEN YOU SAY I LOVE YOU/Jack Of Diamonds	Specialty 419	5.00	20.00	51
XMAS CELEBRATION/I Can't Stay Here (78)	Swing Time 240	1.50	6.00	51
THOMAS, Jesse (The Blues Troubador) & His Guitar				
SAME OLD STUFF/Double Due Love You (78)	Miltone 232	6.25	25.00	48
ZEPHER BLUES/Mountain Key Blues (78)	Miltone 233	5.00	20.00	48
THOMAS, Joe				
EVERYBODY LOVES MY BABY/Blue Tango (instrumental)	Mercury 8268	1.50	6.00	52
JUMPIN' JOE/If I Could Be With You	King 4460	1.50	6.00	51
YOU'RE JUST MY KIND/Buttons (instrumental)	King 4474	1.50	6.00	51
THOMAS, Jon				
THOMAS, Kid				
SPELL, THE/The Wolf Pack	Federal 12298	8.00	32.00	57
YOU ARE AN ANGEL/Rockin' This Joint To-Nite	T.R.C. T-1012	6.25	25.00	57
THOMAS, L. J.				
BABY, TAKE A CHANCE WITH ME/Sam's Drag (78)	Chess 1493	5.00	20.00	52
SAM'S DRAG/Baby, Take A Chance With Me (78)	Chess 1493	1.50	6.00	53
THOMAS, Lafayette				
COCKROACH RUN (instrumental)/ The Trial (by The Jumpin' Judge) (novelty break-in)	Jumping 5000	3.00	12.00	55
THOMAS, Marcellus & His Rhythms Of Rockets				
BREATHER BLUES/Haller's 89 Whiskey Boogie	Ajax 104	3.00	12.00	—
THOMAS, Minnie				
WHAT CAN THE MATTER BE?/I Know What I Need	Meteor 5036	4.00	16.00	56

TITLE/FLIP	LABEL & NO.	GOOD TO VERY GOOD	NEAR MINT	YR.
THOMAS, Mule				
TAKE SOME AND LEAVE SOME/ Blow My Baby Back Home	Hollywood 1091	10.00	40.00	52
THOMAS, Playboy				
END OF THE ROAD/Time Will Tell	Swing Time 344	8.00	32.00	53
TOO MUCH PRIDE/No Doubt About It (red plastic)	Parrot 785	15.00	60.00	53
TOO MUCH PRIDE/No Doubt About It	Parrot 785	9.00	36.00	53
TOO MUCH PRIDE/No Doubt About It	Swing Time 340	11.00	44.00	53
THOMAS, Rufus				
BEARCAT/Walkin' In The Rain	Sun 181	12.50	50.00	53
EASY LIVIN' PLAN, THE/I'm Steady Holdin' On	Meteor 5039	6.25	25.00	56
I'LL BE A GOOD BOY/I'm So Worried (78)	Star Talent 807	3.00	12.00	50
JUANITA/Decorate The Counter (78)	Chess 1517	2.50	10.00	52
NIGHT WALKIN' BLUES/Why Did You Dee Gee? (78)	Chess 1466	2.50	10.00	52
NO MORE DOGGIN' AROUND/Crazy 'Bout You, Baby (78)	Chess 1492	2.50	10.00	52
TIGER MAN/Save That Money	Sun 188	20.00	80.00	53
THOMAS, Tabby				
DON'T SAY/Too Late Blues	Rocko 511	1.50	6.00	61
MY BABY'S GOT IT/Tomorrow I'll Be Gone	Zynn 1002	1.50	6.00	61
TOMORROW/Mmmm, I Don't Care	Feature 3007	3.00	12.00	54
THOMAS, Tabby as Tabby & His Mellow, Mellow Men				
THINKING BLUES/Church Member's Ball	Delta 416	7.00	28.00	53
THOMASON, Jimmy				
NOW HEAR THIS/Big Wheel	Vita 143	2.00	8.00	56
THOMPSON, Dickie				
FOOLIN'/If I Hadn't Drunk	Herald 431	1.50	6.00	54
WOMEN AND ONE MAN/I'm Innocent	Herald 424	1.50	6.00	54
THOMPSON, Helen				
ALL BY MYSELF/Going Down To Big Mary's (red plastic)	States 126	5.00	20.00	53
ALL BY MYSELF/Going Down To Big Mary's	States 126	2.50	10.00	53
MY BABY'S LOVE/Troubled Woman	States 138	2.50	10.00	53
THOMPSON, Rocky: see Carter, Goree as Rocky Thompson				
THOMPSON, Sonny				
I'LL DROWN IN MY TEARS/ Clang! Clang! Clang! (instrumental) (78)	King 4527	1.50	6.00	51
MELLOW BLUES, PART 1/Mellow Blues, Part 2 (78) Instrumentals.	King 4488	1.50	6.00	51
THOR-ABLES, The				
MY RECKLESS HEART/Batman And Robin	Titanic 1002	2.50	10.00	—
OUR LOVE SONG/Get That Bread (by Aaron Collins)	Titanic 1001	2.50	10.00	—
THORNE, Del				
FLY CHICKEN BLUES/Goof Train (instrumental)	Excello 2017	5.00	20.00	52
I LET HIM MOVE ME/Down South In Birmingham	Excello 2006	5.00	20.00	52
THORNTON, Big Mama: see Harlem Stars, The (with Big Mama Thornton); see Thornton, Willie Mae "Big Mama"				
THORNTON, Willie Mae "Big Mama"				
COTTON PICKING BLUES/They Call Me Big Mama	Peacock 1621	2.00	8.00	52
FISH, THE/Laugh, Laugh, Laugh	Peacock 1650	1.50	6.00	55
HOUND DOG/Night Mare	Peacock 1612	2.50	10.00	52
HOW COME/Tarzan And The Dignified Monkey	Peacock 1654	1.50	6.00	55
I AIN'T NO FOOL EITHER/The Big Chance	Peacock 1626	2.00	8.00	53
I'VE SEARCHED THE WORLD OVER/I Smell A Rat	Peacock 1632	2.00	8.00	52
MISCHIEVOUS BOOGIE/Everytime I Think Of You	Peacock 1603	3.00	12.00	51
NO JODY FOR ME/Let Your Tears Fall Baby	Peacock 1587	3.00	12.00	52
PARTNERSHIP BLUES/All Fed Up (78)	Peacock 1567	1.50	6.00	51
STOP HOPPIN' ON ME/Story Of My Blues	Peacock 1642	1.50	6.00	53
WALKING BLUES/Rockabye Baby	Peacock 1647	2.00	8.00	52
YOU DID ME WRONG/Big Mama's Blues (instrumental)	Bay Tone 107	2.00	8.00	61
THRASHERS, The				
JEANNIE/Forever, My Love	Masons 0-1	15.00	60.00	—
THREE BARONS, The				
I'D GIVE MY LIFE/Milk Shake Stand (78)	Savoy 527	1.50	6.00	48

TITLE/FLIP	LABEL & NO.	GOOD TO VERY GOOD	NEAR MINT	YR.

THREE BITS OF RHYTHM, The

TITLE/FLIP	LABEL & NO.	GOOD TO VERY GOOD	NEAR MINT	YR.
BRONZEVILLE JUMP/The Old Blues (78)	Decca 8553	1.50	6.00	41
I USED TO WORK IN CHICAGO/ That's The Boogie (78)	Modern Music 118	1.50	6.00	—
I'LL BE TRUE/Yas, Yas, Yas (78)	Modern Music 137	1.50	6.00	—
I'M LONESOME/ This Is The Boogie, The Woogie, The Boogie (78)	Decca 8572	1.50	6.00	41
ROOT BEER SIZZLE, SAZZLE, SIZZLE/ The Man That Comes To My House (78)	Modern 539	1.50	6.00	47
SIGNIFYING MONKEY/Blow My Top (78)	Modern 523	1.50	6.00	47

THREE BLAZERS, Johnny Moore, Floyd Dixon & The

THREE BLAZERS, Johnny Moore's:
see Moore, Johnny as Johnny Moore's Three Blazers

THREE CLOUDS, The:
see Ravens, The

THREE DEGREES, The (female group)

THREE DOTS AND A DASH, Jesse Belvin & The

TITLE/FLIP	LABEL & NO.	GOOD TO VERY GOOD	NEAR MINT	YR.
ALL THAT WINE IS GONE/Don't Cry, Baby	Imperial 5115	15.00	60.00	51

THREE DOTS AND A DASH, The (featuring Jesse Belvin)

TITLE/FLIP	LABEL & NO.	GOOD TO VERY GOOD	NEAR MINT	YR.
I'LL NEVER LOVE AGAIN/Let's Do It	Imperial 5164	15.00	60.00	51

THREE FLAMES, The

THREE FRIENDS, The

THREE KEYS, The

TITLE/FLIP	LABEL & NO.	GOOD TO VERY GOOD	NEAR MINT	YR.
ANYTHING FOR YOU/That Doggone Dog Of Mine (78)	Brunswick 6522	1.50	6.00	33
ANYTHING FOR YOU/That Doggone Dog Of Mine (78)	Vocalion 2755	1.50	6.00	34
BASIN STREET BLUES/Wah-Dee Dah (78)	Vocalion 2744	1.50	6.00	34
BASIN STREET BLUES/Wah-Dee-Dah (78)	Brunswick 6423	1.50	6.00	32
HEEBIE JEEBIES/Song Of The Islands (78)	Vocalion 2523	1.50	6.00	33
I'VE FOUND A NEW BABY/You Can Depend On Me (78)	Vocalion 2569	1.50	6.00	33
JIG TIME/Someone Stole Gabriel's Horn (78)	Brunswick 6388	1.50	6.00	32
JIG TIME/Someone Stole Gabriel's Horn (78)	Vocalion 2730	1.50	6.00	34
MOOD INDIGO/Somebody Loses—Somebody Wins (78)	Columbia 2706	1.50	6.00	32
NAGASAKI/Fit As A Fiddle (78)	Brunswick 6411	1.50	6.00	32
NAGASAKI/Fit As A Fiddle (78)	Vocalion 2732	1.50	6.00	34
RASPUTIN/Oh, By Jingo (78)	Brunswick 6567	1.50	6.00	33
RASPUTIN/Oh, By Jingo (78)	Vocalion 2765	1.50	6.00	34

THREE PEPPERS, The

TITLE/FLIP	LABEL & NO.	GOOD TO VERY GOOD	NEAR MINT	YR.
DOWN BY THE OLD MILL STREAM/Fuzzy, Wuzzy (78)	Decca 2239	1.50	6.00	39
GET THE GOLD/Alexander's Ragtime Band (78)	Variety 523	1.50	6.00	37
GOOD OLD TENNESSEE/Just Because I Do (78)	Decca 48046	1.50	6.00	47
IF I HAD MY WAY/Serenade In The Night (78)	Variety 630	1.50	6.00	37
IT'S A PUZZLE TO ME/Three Foot Skipper Jones (78)	Decca 2609	1.50	6.00	39
LOVE GROWS ON THE WHITE OAK TREE/ Swing Out, Uncle Wilson (78)	Decca 2557	1.50	6.00	39
MARY'S HAD A LITTLE LAMB/ Was That All I Meant To You? (78)	Decca 8508	1.50	6.00	41
ONE POTATO/One Too Many For Me (78)	Gotham 189	1.50	6.00	59
PEPPERISM/Smile Up At The Sun (78)	Decca 2751	1.50	6.00	39
SWING OUT, UNCLE WILSON/ The Duck's Yas, Yas, Yas (78)	Variety 590	1.50	6.00	37
SWING OUT, UNCLE WILSON/ The Duck's Yas, Yas, Yas (78)	Vocalion 3803	1.50	6.00	37
SWINGIN' AT THE COTTON CLUB/ Midnight Ride Of Paul Revere (78)	Variety 650	1.50	6.00	37
SWINGIN' AT THE COTTON CLUB/ Midnight Ride Of Paul Revere (78)	Vocalion 3805	1.50	6.00	37
TOM-TOM SERENADE/Hot Dogs (78)	Decca 3342	1.50	6.00	40
YOURS, ALL YOURS/Smile Up At The Sun (78)	Variety 554	1.50	6.00	37

THREE PLAYMATES, The (female group)

THREE RIFFS, The

TITLE/FLIP	LABEL & NO.	GOOD TO VERY GOOD	NEAR MINT	YR.
BEWILDERED/I'm Glad For Your Sake (78)	Atlantic 867	2.50	10.00	48
DRIFTIN'/Barbecued Ribs (78)	Apollo 1165	1.50	6.00	50
I WISH I DIDN'T LOVE YOU SO/Hard Ridin' Mama (78)	Atlantic 868	2.50	10.00	49
JUMPIN' JACK/Cherry In My Lemon & Lime (78)	Apollo 1164	1.50	6.00	50
PLUTO, YOU DOG/I'll Be There (78)	Atlantic 871	2.50	10.00	49

THREE SHARPS & A FLAT, The

TITLE/FLIP	LABEL & NO.	GOOD TO VERY GOOD	NEAR MINT	YR.
BIG NOISE OF WINNETKA/Sometimes I'm Happy (78)	Tower 1266	1.50	6.00	—
I AIN'T IN LOVE NO MORE/ I Am, I Am, Am, Am (with Ethel Vick) (78)	Decca 7561	1.50	6.00	39
I'M THROUGH/Swinging In The Candy Store (78)	Decca 7569	1.50	6.00	39
POOR LITTLE BUG ON THE WALL/That's No Lie (78)	Decca 7581	1.50	6.00	39
SKINNY-DO/I'm Gettin' Sentimental Over You (78)	Decca 2278	1.50	6.00	39

THREE SHARPS & FLATS, The

TITLE/FLIP	LABEL & NO.	GOOD TO VERY GOOD	NEAR MINT	YR.
CRAZY AND WORRIED BLUES/Rosie In The Garden (78)	Okeh 05857	1.50	6.00	40
HAWAIIAN WAR CHANT/Yes, Yes, Yes (78)	Hamptone 518/519	1.50	6.00	—
THAT'S THAT RHYTHM/Piccolo Stomp (78)	Okeh 05971	1.50	6.00	41

THREE VARIETIES, Madeline Green & The

THRILLERS, Little Joe & The

TITLE/FLIP	LABEL & NO.	GOOD TO VERY GOOD	NEAR MINT	YR.
LET'S DO THE SLOP/This I Know	Okeh 7075	1.50	6.00	54

THRILLERS, The

TITLE/FLIP	LABEL & NO.	GOOD TO VERY GOOD	NEAR MINT	YR.
DRUNKARD, THE/Mattie, Leave Me Alone	Big Town 109	25.00	100.00	53
LIZABETH/Please Talk To Me	Herald 432	15.00	60.00	54

THUNDER, Johnny

THUNDER, Johnny & Ruby Winters

THUNDERBIRDS, Billy Ford & The

THUNDERBIRDS, The

TITLE/FLIP	LABEL & NO.	GOOD TO VERY GOOD	NEAR MINT	YR.
BABY, LET'S PLAY HOUSE/Pledging My Love	De Luxe 6075	9.00	36.00	55
LOVE IS A PROBLEM/Rock Boom Boom	G.G. 518	7.00	28.00	55

THUNDERBIRDS, The

TITLE/FLIP	LABEL & NO.	GOOD TO VERY GOOD	NEAR MINT	YR.
IN MY THUNDERBIRD/Mary	Holiday 2609	4.00	16.00	57

TIBBS, Andrew

TITLE/FLIP	LABEL & NO.	GOOD TO VERY GOOD	NEAR MINT	YR.
BILBO IS DEAD/Union Man Blues (78)	Aristocrat 1101	1.50	6.00	47
GOING DOWN FAST/Same Old Story (78)	Aristocrat 1104	1.50	6.00	47
I FEEL LIKE CRYING/Married Man Blues (78)	Aristocrat 1103	1.50	6.00	47
MOTHER'S LETTER/Rock, Savoy, Rock	Peacock 1597	2.50	10.00	49
TOOTHLESS WOMAN BLUES/Drinking Ink Splink (78)	Aristocrat 1102	1.50	6.00	47

TIBBS, Andrew & The Dozier Boys

TITLE/FLIP	LABEL & NO.	GOOD TO VERY GOOD	NEAR MINT	YR.
HE'S GOT HER AND GONE/In Every Man's Life (78)	Aristocrat 1106	1.50	6.00	48
HOLIDAYS ARE OVER, THE/In A Travelin' Mood (78)	Aristocrat 1105	1.50	6.00	48

TIC TOCS, The

TITLE/FLIP	LABEL & NO.	GOOD TO VERY GOOD	NEAR MINT	YR.
STOP/True By You	Rush 1042	2.00	8.00	—

TICK TOCKS, Bobby Marchan & The:
see Marchan, Bobby & The Tick Tocks

TIDWELL, Harold

TITLE/FLIP	LABEL & NO.	GOOD TO VERY GOOD	NEAR MINT	YR.
SENORITA JUANITA/Sweet Suzie	CJ 605	1.50	6.00	59

TIFANOS, The

TITLE/FLIP	LABEL & NO.	GOOD TO VERY GOOD	NEAR MINT	YR.
IT'S RAINING/Louisiana	Tifco 822	4.00	16.00	60

TITLE/FLIP	LABEL & NO.	GOOD TO VERY GOOD	NEAR MINT	YR.

TIL, Sonny & The Orioles

TIL, Sonny:
see McGriff, Edna

TILLIS, Big Son:
see Tillis, Ellas as Big Son Tillis

TILLIS, Ellas & D. C. Bendy as Big Son Tillis & D. C. Bender

TITLE/FLIP	LABEL & NO.	GOOD TO VERY GOOD	NEAR MINT	YR.
DAYTON STOMP/My Baby Wrote Me A Letter (78)	*Elko 823*	3.00	12.00	*53*
ROCKS IS MY PILLOW/Zetela Blues (78)	*Elko 821*	3.00	12.00	*53*
WHEN I GET IN THIS HOUSE WOMAN/Ten Long Years (78)	*Elko 822*	3.00	12.00	*53*

TIM TAM & THE TURN-ONS

TIMETONES, The

TINDLEY, George

TINDLEY, George & The Modern Red Caps

TINY TIM AND THE HITS:
see Hits, Tiny Tim & The

TINY TIP & THE TIP TOPS:
see Tip Tops, Tiny Tip & The

TIP TOPS, Tiny Tip & The

TITLE/FLIP	LABEL & NO.	GOOD TO VERY GOOD	NEAR MINT	YR.
I SAID A PRAYER/I Found My Love	*Scarlet 4129*	8.00	32.00	—
SAY IT/Matrimony	*Chess 1822*	2.00	8.00	*62*

TIPPIE & THE CLOVERMEN

TIPPIE & THE CLOVERS:
see Clovers, Tippie & The

TISDOM, James

TITLE/FLIP	LABEL & NO.	GOOD TO VERY GOOD	NEAR MINT	YR.
I FEEL SO GOOD/Overhaul Blues (78)	*Universal-Fox 102*	6.25	25.00	*48*
MODEL T BOOGIE/Last Affair Blues (78)	*Universal-Fox 100*	5.00	20.00	*48*
THROW THIS DOG A BONE/Wine Head Swing (78)	*Universal-Fox 101*	6.25	25.00	*48*

TITANS, Don & Dewey & The

TITLE/FLIP	LABEL & NO.	GOOD TO VERY GOOD	NEAR MINT	YR.
JUST A LITTLE LOVIN'/ When The Sun Has Begun To Shine	*Specialty 617*	1.50	6.00	*57*

TITANS, The

TITLE/FLIP	LABEL & NO.	GOOD TO VERY GOOD	NEAR MINT	YR.
ARLENE/Love Is A Wonderful Thing	*Specialty 632*	1.50	6.00	*58*
DON'T YOU JUST KNOW IT?/Can It Be?	*Specialty 625*	1.50	6.00	*57*
EVERYBODY HAPPY/What Have I Done?	*Fidelity 3016*	1.50	6.00	*60*
LOOK WHAT YOU'RE DOING, BABY/G'wan Home Calypso	*Vita 158*	5.00	20.00	*57*
SO HARD TO LAUGH/Rhythm And Blues	*Vita 148*	7.00	28.00	*57*
SWEET PEACH/Free And Easy	*Specialty 614*	2.00	8.00	*57*

TITONES, The

TITLE/FLIP	LABEL & NO.	GOOD TO VERY GOOD	NEAR MINT	YR.
SYMBOL OF LOVE/My Movie Queen	*Wand 105*	1.50	6.00	*60*
SYMBOL OF LOVE/The Movies	*Scepter 1206*	2.00	8.00	*59*

TOKENS, The

TITLE/FLIP	LABEL & NO.	GOOD TO VERY GOOD	NEAR MINT	YR.
COME DANCE WITH ME/Doom-Lang	*Gary 1006*	3.00	12.00	—

TOLBERT, Israel "Popper Stopper"

TOLEDOS, The

TITLE/FLIP	LABEL & NO.	GOOD TO VERY GOOD	NEAR MINT	YR.
THIS IS OUR NIGHT/John Smith's Body	*Down 2003*	1.50	6.00	*61*

TOLIVER, Jimmy & His California Blues Men

TITLE/FLIP	LABEL & NO.	GOOD TO VERY GOOD	NEAR MINT	YR.
BREAKING OUT/Going Home	*T & T 102*	2.00	8.00	*63*

TOLLIVER, Mickey & The Capitols:
see Capitols, Mickey Tolliver & The

TOM & JERRIO

TONES, Dusty Brooks & The

TITLE/FLIP	LABEL & NO.	GOOD TO VERY GOOD	NEAR MINT	YR.
I AIN'T GONNA' WORRY NO MORE/ Shadow Of The Blues (78)	*Columbia 30241*	2.50	10.00	*51*
ONCE THERE LIVED A FOOL/Cryin' To Myself (78)	*Columbia 30236*	2.50	10.00	*51*

TONES, Little Sammy & The

TONES, The

TITLE/FLIP	LABEL & NO.	GOOD TO VERY GOOD	NEAR MINT	YR.
WE/Three Little Loves	*Baton 265*	1.50	6.00	*49*

TONETTES, The (female group)

TONEY, Oscar, Jr.

TONY & THE DAYDREAMS:
see Daydreams, Tony & The

TONY & THE MASQUINS:
see Masquins, Tony & The

TOOTI & THE BOUQUETS:
see Bouquets, Tooti & The

TOP NOTES, The

TOPPERS, Bobby Mitchell & The

TITLE/FLIP	LABEL & NO.	GOOD TO VERY GOOD	NEAR MINT	YR.
ANGEL CHILD/School Boy Blues	*Imperial 5282*	8.00	32.00	*54*
BABY'S GONE/Sister Lucy	*Imperial 5270*	8.00	32.00	*54*
I CRIED/I'm In Love	*Imperial 5346*	4.00	16.00	*55*
I WISH I KNEW/Nothing Sweet As You	*Imperial 5326*	4.00	16.00	*55*
I'M CRYING/Rack'em Back	*Imperial 5236*	15.00	60.00	*53*
I'M YOUNG MAN/She Couldn't Be Found	*Imperial 5309*	8.00	32.00	*54*
ONE FRIDAY MORNING/4 x 11 = 44	*Imperial 5250*	15.00	60.00	*53*
WEDDING BELLS ARE RINGING/Meant For Me	*Imperial 5295*	4.00	16.00	*54*

TOPPERS, The

TITLE/FLIP	LABEL & NO.	GOOD TO VERY GOOD	NEAR MINT	YR.
LET ME BANG YOUR BOX/ You're Laughing 'Cause I'm Crying	*Jubilee 5136*	2.00	8.00	*54*

TOPPS, The

TITLE/FLIP	LABEL & NO.	GOOD TO VERY GOOD	NEAR MINT	YR.
I'VE GOT A FEELING/Won't You Come Home, Baby?	*Red Robin 131*	10.00	40.00	*54*
WHAT DO YOU DO?/Tippin'	*Red Robin 126*	10.00	40.00	*54*

TOPS, Little Jimmy & The

TITLE/FLIP	LABEL & NO.	GOOD TO VERY GOOD	NEAR MINT	YR.
PUPPY LOVE/Say You Love Me	*Len 1011*	2.00	8.00	*61*

TORNADOS, The

TITLE/FLIP	LABEL & NO.	GOOD TO VERY GOOD	NEAR MINT	YR.
LOVE IN YOUR LIFE/Genie In The Jug	*Bumble Bee 503*	2.00	8.00	—

TORNADOS, The:
see Chromatics, The

TORRENCE, George & The Caribbeans

TORRENCE, George & The Naturals

TITLE/FLIP	LABEL & NO.	GOOD TO VERY GOOD	NEAR MINT	YR.

TORRENCE, Georgie & The Dippers:
see Dippers, Georgie Torrence & The

TORRENCE, Johnny

SAD DAY/Bad Habit	Imperial 5230	5.00	20.00	53

TOWNSEND, Ed

TOYS, The (female group)

TRAMMPS, The

TRAMPS, The

YOU'RE A SQUARE/Ride On	Arvee 548	2.00	8.00	59
YOUR LOVE/Midnight Flyer	Arvee 570	2.00	8.00	59

TRAVELERS, The

LENORA/Betty Jean	Atlas 1086	5.00	20.00	57

TREMAINES, The

JINGLE, JINGLE/Moon Shining Bright	Cash 100/101	15.00	60.00	—
JINGLE, JINGLE/Moon Shining Bright	Old Town 1051	5.00	20.00	58

TRENIER TWINS, The

TRENIER, Milt

FLIP YOUR WIGS/You're Killin' Me	RCA Victor 47-5487	1.50	6.00	53
SQUEEZE ME/Rock Bottom	RCA Victor 47-5275	1.50	6.00	53

TRENIER, Skip & The Fabulous Treniers

TRENIERS, The

GO! GO! GO!/Plenty Of Money	Okeh 6804	2.00	8.00	51
HADACOL, THAT'S ALL/Long Distance Blues	Okeh 6876	2.00	8.00	52
HEY, LITTLE GIRL/Old Woman Blues	Okeh 6826	2.00	8.00	51
IT ROCKS! IT ROLLS! IT SWINGS!/Taxi Blues	Okeh 6853	2.00	8.00	51
POON-TANG!/Hi-Yo Silver	Okeh 6932	1.50	6.00	52
POON-TANG!/Hi-Yo Silver	Okeh 6937	1.50	6.00	52
ROCKIN' IS OUR BUSINESS/Sugar-Doo	Okeh 6960	1.50	6.00	52
ROCKIN' ON SUNDAY NIGHT/Cheatin' On Me	Okeh 6904	2.00	8.00	52
THIS IS IT/I'd Do Nothin' But Grieve	Okeh 6984	1.50	6.00	52

TRICE, Rich as Little Boy Fuller

SHAKE YOUR STUFF/Lazy Bug Blues (78)	Savoy 5535	3.00	12.00	47

TRINIDADS, The

ONE LONELY NIGHT/When We're Together	Formal 1006	10.00	40.00	—

TROJANS, The

AS LONG AS I HAVE YOU/I Wanna Make Love To You	RPM 466	10.00	40.00	55
DON'T ASK ME TO BE LONELY/Alone In This World	Tender 516	3.00	12.00	58

On some later pressings the group is listed as the Five Trojans.

TROOPERS, The

MY RESOLUTION/Get Out	Lamp 2009	10.00	40.00	57

TROY, Doris

TRU-TONES, The

TEARS IN MY EYES/Magic	Chart 634	15.00	60.00	57

TRUE LOVES, The

LOVE LIKE YOURS, A/Never Look Behind	Premium 411	8.00	32.00	57

TRUETONES, The

HONEY, HONEY/Whirlwind	Monument 4501	15.00	60.00	58

TUCKER, Monroe

KINFOLKS/Agony	Imperial 5109	10.00	40.00	50

TUGGLE, Bobby

I WONDER/I Know She Loves Me	Checker 840	1.50	6.00	56
64,000 DOLLAR QUESTION/Too Late, Old Man	Checker 823	1.50	6.00	55

TUNE BLENDERS, The

OH, YES, I KNOW/Shoo-Shoo	Federal 12201	5.00	20.00	54

TUNE DROPS, The

TUNE WEAVERS, The

HAPPY, HAPPY BIRTHDAY, BABY/Ol' Man River	Casa Grande 4037	2.50	10.00	57
LITTLE BOY/Look Down That Lonesome Road	Casa Grande 101	2.50	10.00	58
MY CONGRATULATIONS, BABY/This Can't Be Love	Casa Grande 3038	2.50	10.00	60

TUNEDROPS, Malcolm Dodds & The

TUNEDROPS, The

TUNEMASTERS, The

SENDING THIS LETTER/It's All Over	Mark 7002	6.25	25.00	57

TUNEMASTERS, Willie Wilson & The

SENDING YOU THIS LETTER/I've Lied	End 1011	6.25	25.00	58

On some later pressings the label credits were changed to Willie & Arlene & The Tunemasters.

TUNETOPPERS, Al Brown's

TURBANS, The

CONGRATULATIONS/The Wadda-Do	Herald 510	1.50	6.00	57
GOLDEN RINGS/When You Dance	Parkway 820	1.50	6.00	61
I PROMISE YOU LOVE/Curfew Time	Red Top 115	2.00	8.00	—
I'M NOBODY'S/B-I-N-G-O	Herald 478	2.00	8.00	56
IT WAS A NITE LIKE THIS/All Of My Love	Herald 486	2.00	8.00	56
NO, NO, CHERRY/Tick, Tock A-Woo	Money 209	4.00	16.00	55
SISTER SOOKEY/I'll Always Watch Over You	Herald 469	2.00	8.00	55
VALLEY OF LOVE/Bye And Bye	Herald 495	2.50	10.00	57
WHEN I RETURN/Emily (by The Turks)	Money 211	4.00	16.00	55
WHEN YOU DANCE/Let Me Show You	Herald 458	2.00	8.00	55

TURKS, The

EMILY/When I Return (by The Turbans)	Money 211	4.00	16.00	55
FATHERTIME/Okay	Keen 4016	2.00	8.00	58
I'M A FOOL/I've Been Accused	Money 215	4.00	16.00	56
IT CAN'T BE TRUE/Wagon Wheels	Cash 1042	3.00	12.00	56

The second side of this record, "Wagon Wheels," though credited to the Turks is actually by The Hollywood Flames.

THIS HEART OF MINE/Why Did You?	Bally 1017	3.00	12.00	56

TURN-ONS, Tim Tam & The

TURNER, Baby Face

BLUE SERENADE/Gonna Let You Go	Modern 882	15.00	60.00	52
GONNA LET YOU GO/ Please Send My Baby Back (by Sunny Blair)	Meteor 5006	20.00	80.00	52

Both sides of this record are credited to Sunny Blair, but "Gonna Let You Go" is actually by Baby Face Turner.

TURNER, Bonnie:
see Turner, Ike & Bonnie as Ike & Bonnie Turner

TURNER, Ike

BIG QUESTION, THE/Rock-A-Bucket (instrumental)	Federal 12304	1.50	6.00	57
CUBAN GET AWAY/Go To It	Flair 1059	3.00	12.00	52

Instrumentals by Ike Turner's Orchestra.

CUBANO JUMP/Loosely	Flair 1040	3.00	12.00	52

Instrumentals by Ike Turner's Orchestra.

The Tune Weavers

Joe Turner

TITLE/FLIP	LABEL & NO.	GOOD TO VERY GOOD	NEAR MINT	YR.
(I KNOW) DON'T LOVE ME/Down And Out	*Artistic 1504*	1.50	6.00	*58*
HEARTBROKEN AND WORRIED/I'm Lonesome, Baby (78)	*Chess 1459*	2.00	8.00	*51*
SHE MADE MY BLOOD RUN COLD/Do You Mean It?	*Federal 12297*	1.50	6.00	*57*
WALKING DOWN THE AISLE/Box Top (instrumental)	*Cobra 5033*	1.50	6.00	*58*
YOU'RE DRIVING ME INSANE/ Troubles And Heartaches (78)	*RPM 356*	1.50	6.00	*52*
YOU'VE CHANGED MY LOVE/Trail Blazer (instrumental)	*Federal 12307*	1.50	6.00	*57*

TURNER, Ike & Bonnie as Ike & Bonnie Turner

TITLE/FLIP	LABEL & NO.	GOOD TO VERY GOOD	NEAR MINT	YR.
LOOKING FOR A BABY/My Heart Belongs To You (78)	*RPM 362*	1.50	6.00	*52*

TURNER, Ike & Tina as Ike & Tina Turner

TURNER, Joe

TITLE/FLIP	LABEL & NO.	GOOD TO VERY GOOD	NEAR MINT	YR.
ADAM BIT THE APPLE/Still In The Dark (78)	*Freedom 1531*	1.50	6.00	*49*
AFTER A WHILE YOU'LL BE SORRY/Feelin' Happy (78)	*Freedom 1540*	1.50	6.00	*49*
AROUND THE CLOCK BLUES, PART 1/ Around The Clock Blues, Part 2 (78)	*Stag 508*	2.00	8.00	*47*
BACK BREAKING BABY/Empty Pocket Blues (78)	*Aladdin 3070*	1.50	6.00	*50*
BLUES IN THE NIGHT/Cry Baby Blues (78)	*Decca 7885*	1.50	6.00	*42*
BLUES IN THE NIGHT/Cry Baby Blues (78)	*Decca 8606*	1.50	6.00	*42*
BLUES JUMPED A RABBIT, THE/The Sun Is Shining	*Bayou 015*	10.00	40.00	*53*
BLUES ON CENTRAL AVENUE/Sun Risin' Blues (78)	*Coral 65004*	1.50	6.00	*42*
BLUES ON CENTRAL AVENUE/Sun Risin' Blues (78)	*Decca 7889*	1.50	6.00	*42*
BOOGIE WOOGIE BABY/Married Woman Blues (78)	*MGM 10492*	1.50	6.00	*48*
BUMP MISS SUSIE/The Chill Is On	*Atlantic 949*	7.00	28.00	*51*
CARELESS LOVE/Jumpin' Down Blues (78)	*Decca 7827*	1.50	6.00	*41*
CHAINS OF LOVE/After My Laughter	*Atlantic 939*	9.00	36.00	*51*
CHICKEN AND THE HAWK, THE/Morning Noon And Night	*Atlantic 1080*	1.50	6.00	*55*
CHRISTMAS DATE BOOGIE/Tell My Pretty Baby (78)	*Swing Time 153*	1.50	6.00	*48*
CORRINE CORRINA/It's The Same Old Story (78)	*Decca 29924*	1.50	6.00	*44*
DOGGIN' THE DOG/Rainy Day Blues (78)	*Decca 7824*	1.50	6.00	*41*
DON'T YOU CRY/Poor Lover's Blues	*Atlantic 970*	6.25	25.00	*52*
FEELIN' SO SAD/Moody Baby (78)	*MGM 10719*	1.50	6.00	*48*
FLIP, FLOP AND FLY/Ti-Ri-Lee	*Atlantic 1053*	2.00	8.00	*55*
HIDE AND SEEK/Midnight Cannonball	*Atlantic 1069*	2.00	8.00	*55*
HONEY HUSH/Crawdad Hole	*Atlantic 1001*	2.50	10.00	*53*
I DON'T DIG IT/ (78)	*Excelsior OR533*	1.50	6.00	*49*
I DON'T DIG IT/Rainy Weather Blues (78)	*MGM 10397*	1.50	6.00	*48*
I WANT MY BABY/Midnight Is Here Again (78)	*Freedom 1545*	1.50	6.00	*49*
I'VE GOT A GAL FOR EVERY DAY OF THE WEEK/ Piney Brown Blues (78)	*Decca 18121*	1.50	6.00	*40*
I'VE GOT A GAL FOR EVERY DAY OF THE WEEK/ Piney Brown Blues	*Decca 29711*	3.00	12.00	*55*
IT'S A LOW DOWN DIRTY SHAME/Nobody In Mind (78)	*National 9099*	1.50	6.00	*46*
JOHNSON AND TURNER BLUES/Watch That Jive (78)	*National 9011*	1.50	6.00	*45*
JUMPIN' AT THE JUBILEE/Lonely World (78)	*Freedom 1546*	1.50	6.00	*49*
JUST A TRAVELIN' MAN/Life Is Just A Card Game (78)	*Freedom 1537*	1.50	6.00	*49*
LUCILLE/Love My Baby (78)	*Imperial 5093*	1.50	6.00	*50*
MARDI GRAS BOOGIE/My Heart Belongs To You (78)	*MGM 10274*	1.50	6.00	*48*
MESSIN' AROUND/So Many Women Blues (78)	*MGM 10321*	1.50	6.00	*48*
MISS BROWN BLUES/ I'm Sharp When I Hit The Coast (78)	*National 4011*	1.50	6.00	*46*
MORNING GLORY/Low Down Dog (78)	*Aladdin 3013*	1.50	6.00	*49*
MY GAL'S A JOCKEY/I Got Love For Sale (78)	*National 4002*	1.50	6.00	*46*
NOBODY IN MIND/Chewed Up Grass (78)	*Decca 7868*	1.50	6.00	*41*
OLD PINEY BROWN IS GONE/ Baby, Won't You Marry Me? (78)	*Swing Time 154*	1.50	6.00	*48*
OO-OUGH STOMP/ (78)	*Excelsior OR534*	1.50	6.00	*49*
(NEW) OOH WEE BABY BLUES/Hollywood Bed (78)	*National 9100*	1.50	6.00	*46*
PLAY BOY BLUES/Sunday Morning Blues (78)	*Savoy MG 14016*	1.50	6.00	*46*
RADAR BLUES/Trouble Blues (78)	*Swing Time 151*	1.50	6.00	*48*
REBECCA/It's The Same Old Story (78)	*Decca 11001*	1.50	6.00	*44*
RIDING BLUES/Playful Baby (78)	*RPM 345*	1.50	6.00	*52*
ROCKS IN MY BED/Goin' To Chicago Blues (78)	*Decca 4093*	1.50	6.00	*42*
ROCKS IN MY BED/Howlin' Winds (78)	*National 9144*	1.50	6.00	*47*
ROLL 'EM, BOYS/Kansas City Blues (78)	*RPM 331*	1.50	6.00	*52*
S. K. BLUES, PART 1/S. K. Blues, Part 2 (78)	*National 9010*	1.50	6.00	*45*
SALLY ZU-ZAZZ/Rock Of Gibraltar Blues (78)	*National 4016*	1.50	6.00	*46*
SHAKE-RATTLE-AND-ROLL/You Know I Love You	*Atlantic 1026*	2.50	10.00	*54*
SOMEBODY'S GOT TO GO/Ice Man (78)	*Decca 7856*	1.50	6.00	*41*
STILL IN LOVE/I Still Want You	*Atlantic 982*	5.00	20.00	*52*
STILL IN THE DARK/My Gal's A Jockey (78)	*National 9106*	1.50	6.00	*46*
STORY TO TELL/Jumpin' Tonight (78)	*Imperial 5090*	1.50	6.00	*50*
SUNDAY MORNING BLUES/Mad Blues (78)	*National 4009*	1.50	6.00	*46*
SWEET SIXTEEN/I'll Never Stop Loving You	*Atlantic 960*	7.00	28.00	*52*
THAT'S WHEN IT REALLY HURTS/Whistle Stop Blues (78)	*National 4017*	1.50	6.00	*46*
TV-MAMA/Oke-She-Make-She-Pop Featuring Elmore James on guitar.	*Atlantic 1016*	5.00	20.00	*53*
WELL, ALL RIGHT/Married Woman	*Atlantic 1040*	2.00	8.00	*54*
WINE-O-BABY/B & O Blues (78)	*Swing Time 152*	1.50	6.00	*48*

TURNER, Joe & Pete Johnson

TITLE/FLIP	LABEL & NO.	GOOD TO VERY GOOD	NEAR MINT	YR.
ROLL'EM PETE/Goin' Away Blues (78)	*Vocalion 4607*	2.50	10.00	*39*

TURNER, Joe:
see Flennoy Trio, The (with Joe Turner)

TURNER, Odelle

TITLE/FLIP	LABEL & NO.	GOOD TO VERY GOOD	NEAR MINT	YR.
ALARM CLOCK BOOGIE/Draggin' Hours	*Atlantic 964*	3.00	12.00	*52*

TURNER, Pete & His Blues Band

TURNER, Sammy

TURNER, Sammy & The Twisters

TURNER, Spyder

TURNER, Tina

TURNER, Tina:
see Turner, Ike & Tina as Ike & Tina Turner

TURNER, Titus

TITLE/FLIP	LABEL & NO.	GOOD TO VERY GOOD	NEAR MINT	YR.
AROUND THE WORLD/Do You Know?	*Wing 90006*	1.50	6.00	*55*
BE SURE YOU KNOW/	*Okeh 6929*	2.00	8.00	*52*
BIG MARY/Living In Misery	*Okeh 6961*	2.00	8.00	*52*
DON'T TAKE EVERYBODY TO BE YOUR FRIEND/ The Same Old Feeling	*Okeh 6844*	2.00	8.00	*51*
GET ON THE RIGHT TRACK, BABY/I'll Wait Forever	*Wing 90058*	1.50	6.00	*55*
HELLO, STRANGER/Devilish Women	*Okeh 7038*	1.50	6.00	*53*
IT'S TOO LATE NOW/My Plea	*Okeh 6938*	2.00	8.00	*51*
OVER THE RAINBOW/My Lonely Room	*Okeh 7027*	1.50	6.00	*53*
PLEASE, BABY/Jambalaya	*Okeh 6907*	2.00	8.00	*52*
SWEET AND SLOW/Big John	*Wing 90033*	1.50	6.00	*55*
WHAT CHA GONNA DO?/Got So Much Trouble	*Okeh 6883*	2.00	8.00	*51*

TWI-LIGHTERS, The

TITLE/FLIP	LABEL & NO.	GOOD TO VERY GOOD	NEAR MINT	YR.
SITTIN' IN A CORNER/It's A Cold, Cold, Rainy Day	*Groove 0154*	3.00	12.00	*56*

TWIGS, Sonny Woods & The

TITLE/FLIP	LABEL & NO.	GOOD TO VERY GOOD	NEAR MINT	YR.
CHAPEL OF MEMORIES/Song Of India	*Hollywood 1015*	7.00	28.00	*54*
WONDERFUL WORLD/Lover Boy	*Hollywood 1026*	7.00	28.00	*54*

TWILIGHTERS, Buddy Milton & The

TITLE/FLIP	LABEL & NO.	GOOD TO VERY GOOD	NEAR MINT	YR.
O O WAH/I'm The Child	*RPM 419*	4.00	16.00	*54*
PLEASE UNDERSTAND/Say Another Word	*RPM 418*	7.00	28.00	*54*

TWILIGHTERS, The

TITLE/FLIP	LABEL & NO.	GOOD TO VERY GOOD	NEAR MINT	YR.
ETERNALLY/I Believe	*Caddy 103*	4.00	16.00	*56*
ETERNALLY/I Believe	*Dot 15526*	2.00	8.00	*56*
HOW MANY TIMES?/Water-Water	*J-V-B 83*	15.00	60.00	*57*
IT'S TRUE/Wah-Bop-Sh-Wah	*Specialty 548*	7.00	28.00	*55*
LITTLE DID I DREAM/Gotta' Get On The Train	*MGM 55011*	20.00	80.00	*55*
LOVELY LADY/Half Angel	*MGM 55014*	20.00	80.00	*55*
PRIDE AND JOY/Live Like A King	*Ebb 117*	4.00	16.00	*57*

TWILIGHTERS, The

TITLE/FLIP	LABEL & NO.	GOOD TO VERY GOOD	NEAR MINT	YR.
PLEASE TELL ME YOU'RE MINE/Wondering	*Marshall 702*	20.00	80.00	—

TWILIGHTERS, Tony Allen & The:
see Allen, Tony & The Twilighters

TWILIGHTS, Phil Phillips & The:
see Phillips, Phil & The Twilights

TWILIGHTS, Teddy & The

TWILITERS, The

TITLE/FLIP	LABEL & NO.	GOOD TO VERY GOOD	NEAR MINT	YR.
SITTIN' IN A CORNER/It's A Cold, Cold Rainy Day	*Groove 0154*	4.00	16.00	*61*

TWINKLES, The (female group)

TITLE/FLIP	LABEL & NO.	GOOD TO VERY GOOD	NEAR MINT	YR.
BAD MOTORCYCLE/Sweet Daddy	*Peak 5001*	4.00	16.00	*58*

TWISTERS, Sammy Turner & The

TWOVOICE, Johnny & The Medallions:
see Medallions, Johnny Twovoice & The

TYLER, Big T

TITLE/FLIP	LABEL & NO.	GOOD TO VERY GOOD	NEAR MINT	YR.
KING KONG/Sadie Green	*Aladdin 3384*	5.00	20.00	*56*

TITLE/FLIP	LABEL & NO.	GOOD TO VERY GOOD	NEAR MINT	YR.
TYLER, Charles as Drifting Charles				
TYLER, Jimmy				
TAKE IT AWAY/Little Jim (instrumental)	Federal 12080	5.00	20.00	51
TYMES, The				
TYRONE & THE NU PORTS				

TITLE/FLIP	LABEL & NO.	GOOD TO VERY GOOD	NEAR MINT	YR.
UNIFICS, The				
UNIQUE TEENS, The				
JEANNIE/At the Ball	Hanover 4510	2.00	8.00	58
JEANNIE/At the Ball	Ivy 112	3.00	12.00	58
RUN FAST/Whatcha Know New?	Dynamic 110	2.00	8.00	—
UNIQUES, Barbara & The				
UNIQUES, The				
COME MARRY ME/Do You Remember?	Flippin 202	1.50	6.00	59
TELL THE ANGELS/Hey, Little Cupid	End 1012	4.00	16.00	58
UNIQUES, The (with Earl King)				
MYSTERIOUS/Picture Of My Baby	Peacock 1695	1.50	6.00	60
SOMEWHERE/Right Now	Peacock 1677	1.50	6.00	—
UNIVERSALS, The				
AGAIN/Teenage Love	Mark-X 7004	7.00	28.00	57
PICTURE, THE/He's So Right	Cora-Lee 501	4.00	16.00	58
UNIVERSALS, The				
DREAMING/Love Bound	Festival 1601	1.50	6.00	61
UNTOUCHABLES, The				
UPFRONTS, The				
IT TOOK TIME/Benny Lou & The Lion	Lummtone 103	2.00	8.00	60
UPSETTERS, The (featuring Little Richard)				
EVERY NIGHT ABOUT THIS TIME/ Yes, It's Me (I'm In Love Again)	Little Star 123	1.50	6.00	62

TITLE/FLIP	LABEL & NO.	GOOD TO VERY GOOD	NEAR MINT	YR.
V-EIGHTS, The				
VAGABONDS, Jimmy James & The				
VAGABONDS, Memphis Slim (Peter Chatman) & The				
I GUESS I'M A FOOL/ Flock Rocker (by Reverend Bounce) (78)	Premium 850	1.50	6.00	50
VAL-CHORDS, The				
YOU'RE LAUGHING AT ME/Candy Store Love	Gametime 104	3.00	12.00	57
VAL-TONES, The				
TENDER DARLING/Siam Sam	DeLuxe 6084	9.00	36.00	55
VALADIERS, The				
GREETING/Take A Chance	Miracle 6	1.50	6.00	61
VALDEZ, Gloria & The Five Arrows: see Five Arrows, Gloria Valdez & The				

TITLE/FLIP	LABEL & NO.	GOOD TO VERY GOOD	NEAR MINT	YR.
VALENTINE, Billy Trio, The				
FOREVER/She's Fit And Fat And Fine	Decca 48243	1.50	6.00	51
IT'S A SIN TO TELL A LIE/Baby, Please Don't Go	Decca 48261	1.50	6.00	51
ONE COCKTAIL/The Room I'm Sleeping In	Decca 48202	1.50	6.00	51
TEARS, TEARS, TEARS/Clambake Boogie	Decca 48207	1.50	6.00	51
VALENTINE, Floyd				
OFF TIME/Fussing And Loving (red plastic)	Vee Jay 113	5.00	20.00	54
OFF TIME/Fussing And Loving	Vee Jay 113	2.50	10.00	54
VALENTINES, The				
CHRISTMAS PRAYER/K-I-S-S Me	Rama 186	20.00	80.00	55
DON'T SAY GOODNIGHT/I Cried Oh, Oh	Rama 228	6.25	25.00	57
LILY MAEBELLE/Falling For You	Rama 171	7.00	28.00	55
LOVE YOU, DARLING/Hand Me Down Love	Rama 181	9.00	36.00	55
NATURE'S CREATION/My Story Of Love	Rama 208	4.00	16.00	56
TONIGHT, KATHLEEN/Summer Love	Old Town 1009	40.00	160.00	54
TWENTY MINUTES/I'll Never Let You Go	Rama 201	5.00	20.00	56
WOO WOO TRAIN/Why?	Rama 196	7.00	28.00	56

TITLE/FLIP	LABEL & NO.	GOOD TO VERY GOOD	NEAR MINT	YR.
VALENTINOS				
VALENTINOS, The (Womack Brothers, Bobby & Curtis)				
VALIANTS, Billy Storm & The: see Storm, Billy & The Valiants				
VALIANTS, The				
FRIEDA, FRIEDA/Please Wait, My Love	Keen 4026	1.50	6.00	58
THIS IS THE NITE/Good Golly, Miss Molly	Keen 34004	1.50	6.00	57
VALLERY, Joe as Little Joe Blue				
VALQUINS, The				
MY DEAR/Falling Star	Gaity 161/162	5.00	20.00	59
VALTONES, The				
HAVE YOU EVER MET AN ANGEL?/ You Belong to My Heart	Gee 1004	15.00	60.00	56
VALUMES, The				
I LOVE YOU/Dreams	Chex 1000.2	4.00	16.00	62
This record was re-released a month later on Chex with the number changed to 1002 and the artists' names respelled "Volumes."				
VAN DYKES, The				
BELLS ARE RINGING, THE/Meaning of Love	De Luxe 6193	1.50	6.00	61
BELLS ARE RINGING, THE/Meaning of Love	King 5158	5.00	20.00	58
COME ON, BABY/Lambie Baby	Decca 30762	8.00	32.00	58
VAN LOAN, Joe Quartet, The				
TRUST IN ME/Until I fell For You	Carver 1402	15.00	60.00	54

RAMA

45 RPM 45 RPM

Disk Jockey Record RR-201 Kahl Music (BMI) 2:20

NOT FOR SALE Vocal Group Jimmy Wright & his Orch.

TWENTY MINUTES (BEFORE THE HOUR) (Goldner-Barrett)
THE VALENTINES
(RR-3107)

VAN LOAN, Joe:
see Bachelors, The (with Joe Van Loan)
see Kings, The (with Joe Van Loan)
see The Ravens

VAN WALLS & THE ROCKETS:
see Rockets, (Harry) Van Walls & The

VAN WALLS, Harry

TITLE/FLIP	LABEL & NO.	GOOD TO VERY GOOD	NEAR MINT	YR.
AFTER MIDNIGHT/Solid Sender	Atlantic 980	4.00	16.00	50

Instrumentals.

VAN WALLS, Harry as Spider Sam

TITLE/FLIP	LABEL & NO.	GOOD TO VERY GOOD	NEAR MINT	YR.
TEE NAH-NAH/Ain't Gonna Scold You (78)	Atlantic 904	2.00	8.00	50

Vocals by Walter Brown McGhee as Brownie McGhee.

VANCOUVERS, Bobby Taylor & The

VANDELLAS, Martha & The

VANDELLAS, Sandra Mallett & The

TITLE/FLIP	LABEL & NO.	GOOD TO VERY GOOD	NEAR MINT	YR.
IT'S GONNA BE HARD TIMES/Camel Walk	Tamla 54067	5.00	20.00	62

Sandra was the winner in a local Detroit talent contest, the first prize being a chance to have a record released on Motown's Tamla label. She got her prize, Tamla 54067, but the record received no promotion other than a few local copies to radio stations (and to Sandra).

VANDERPOOL, Little Sylvia:
see Little Sylvia (Vanderpool)

VARIETEERS, The

TITLE/FLIP	LABEL & NO.	GOOD TO VERY GOOD	NEAR MINT	YR.
CALL MY GAL MISS JONES/Minnie, Come Home	Hickory 1025	10.00	40.00	54
DEEP BLUES/I've Got A Woman's Love	Hickory 1004	10.00	40.00	53
IF YOU AND I COULD BE SWEETHEARTS/ I Pay With Every Breath	Hickory 1014	25.00	100.00	53
YOU DON'T MOVE ME NO MORE/ I'll Try To Forget I've Loved You	MGM 10888	10.00	40.00	51

VARNELLS, The

TITLE/FLIP	LABEL & NO.	GOOD TO VERY GOOD	NEAR MINT	YR.
DAY IN COURT/All Because	Arnold 1006	1.50	6.00	61
WHO CREATED LOVE?/Strut Time	Arnold 1003	4.00	16.00	61

VAUGHAN, Sarah

VECTORS, The

TITLE/FLIP	LABEL & NO.	GOOD TO VERY GOOD	NEAR MINT	YR.
ONE DAY/Slow, But Sure	Standord 700	4.00	16.00	58

VEL-AIRES, Donald Woods & The

TITLE/FLIP	LABEL & NO.	GOOD TO VERY GOOD	NEAR MINT	YR.
DEATH OF AN ANGEL/Man From Utopia	Flip 306	2.00	8.00	55
HEAVEN IN MY ARMS/Mighty Joe	Flip 312	3.00	12.00	—
STAY WITH ME, ALWAYS/My Very Own	Flip 309	2.00	8.00	55
THIS PARADISE/Let's Party Awhile	Flip 303	7.00	28.00	—

This record was originally released as by The Bel-Airs.

VELLS, Little Butch & The

VELOURS, The

TITLE/FLIP	LABEL & NO.	GOOD TO VERY GOOD	NEAR MINT	YR.
BLUE VELVET/Tired Of Your Rock & Rolling	Cub 9029	1.50	6.00	59
CAN I COME OVER TONIGHT/Where There's A Will	Gone 5092	2.00	8.00	60
CAN I COME OVER TONIGHT?/Where There's A Will	Onyx 512	6.25	25.00	57
I'LL NEVER SMILE AGAIN/Crazy Love	Cub 9014	1.50	6.00	58
LOVER, COME BACK/The Lonely One	End 1090	1.50	6.00	61
MY LOVE COME BACK/Honey Drop	Onyx 501	7.00	28.00	56
REMEMBER?/Can I Walk You Home?	Onyx 520	3.00	12.00	58
REMEMBER?/Can I Walk You Home?	Orbit 9001	2.00	8.00	58
ROMEO/What You Do To Me	Onyx 508	4.00	16.00	57
THIS COULD BE THE NIGHT/Hands Across The Table	Onyx 515	5.00	20.00	57

VELS, The

TITLE/FLIP	LABEL & NO.	GOOD TO VERY GOOD	NEAR MINT	YR.
PLEASE BE MINE/Mysterious Teenage	Trebco 16	4.00	16.00	—

VELVELETTES, The (female group)

VELVETEERS, The

TITLE/FLIP	LABEL & NO.	GOOD TO VERY GOOD	NEAR MINT	YR.
JASIN, GET YOUR BASIN/Fine Like Wine (78)	Manor 1190	2.50	10.00	—
TELL ME YOU'RE MINE/Boo Wacka Boo	Spitfire 15	100.00	400.00	

VELVETIERS, The

TITLE/FLIP	LABEL & NO.	GOOD TO VERY GOOD	NEAR MINT	YR.
OH, BABY/Feelin' Right Saturday Night	Ric 958	15.00	60.00	58

VELVETONES, The

TITLE/FLIP	LABEL & NO.	GOOD TO VERY GOOD	NEAR MINT	YR.
COME BACK/Penalty Of Love	D 1049	5.00	20.00	59
GLORY OF LOVE/I Love Her So	Aladdin 3372	10.00	40.00	57
I FOUND MY LOVE/Melody Of Love	Aladdin 3391	8.00	32.00	57
MY EVERY THOUGHT/Little Girl, I Love You So	Aladdin 3463	5.00	20.00	59
WORRIED OVER YOU/Space Men	D 1072	3.00	12.00	59

VELVETS, The

TITLE/FLIP	LABEL & NO.	GOOD TO VERY GOOD	NEAR MINT	YR.
I CRIED/Tell Her	Red Robin 127	11.00	44.00	54
I/At Last	Red Robin 122	12.50	50.00	53
THEY TRIED/She's Gotta Grin	Red Robin 120	10.00	40.00	53

VELVITONES, The

TITLE/FLIP	LABEL & NO.	GOOD TO VERY GOOD	NEAR MINT	YR.
LITTLE GIRL I LOVE YOU/A Prayer At Gettysburg	Milmart 113	7.00	28.00	59

VENEERS, The (female group)

TITLE/FLIP	LABEL & NO.	GOOD TO VERY GOOD	NEAR MINT	YR.
BELIEVE ME/I	Princeton 102	1.50	6.00	60

VERDICTS, The

TITLE/FLIP	LABEL & NO.	GOOD TO VERY GOOD	NEAR MINT	YR.
MY LIFE'S DESIRE/The Mummy Ball	East Coast 103/104	4.00	16.00	61

VERSATILES, Dee Thomas & The

TITLE/FLIP	LABEL & NO.	GOOD TO VERY GOOD	NEAR MINT	YR.
IN THE GARDEN OF LOVE/Don't Know Where I'm Going	Coaster 800	2.00	8.00	60

VERSATILES, Sonny Day & The

TITLE/FLIP	LABEL & NO.	GOOD TO VERY GOOD	NEAR MINT	YR.
SPEEDILLAC/Half Moon	Checker 886	2.50	10.00	58

VERSATILES, The

TITLE/FLIP	LABEL & NO.	GOOD TO VERY GOOD	NEAR MINT	YR.
CRYING/Passing By	Atlantic 2004	2.00	8.00	58
LUNDEE DUNDEE/Whisper In Your Ear	Ro-Cal 1002	4.00	16.00	60
WHITE CLIFFS OF DOVER, THE/Just Words	Peacock 1910	2.00	8.00	62

VERSATONES, The

TITLE/FLIP	LABEL & NO.	GOOD TO VERY GOOD	NEAR MINT	YR.
TIGHT SKIRT AND SWEATER/Bila	All Star 501	3.00	12.00	58
TIGHT SKIRT/Bila	Fenway 7001	1.50	6.00	60

VESTELLES, The (female group)

TITLE/FLIP	LABEL & NO.	GOOD TO VERY GOOD	NEAR MINT	YR.
COME HOME/Ditta Wa Do	Decca 30733	1.50	6.00	58

VIBES, The

TITLE/FLIP	LABEL & NO.	GOOD TO VERY GOOD	NEAR MINT	YR.
DARLING/Come Back, Baby	ABC Paramount 9810	3.00	12.00	57

VIBES, The

TITLE/FLIP	LABEL & NO.	GOOD TO VERY GOOD	NEAR MINT	YR.
STOP TORTURING ME!/Stop Jibing, Baby	After Hours 105	50.00	200.00	55

VIBES, The

TITLE/FLIP	LABEL & NO.	GOOD TO VERY GOOD	NEAR MINT	YR.
MISUNDERSTOOD/Let The Old Folks Talk	Allied 10007	2.50	10.00	59
WHAT'S HER NAME?/You Are	Allied 10006	2.50	10.00	58

VIBRA-HARPS, The

TITLE/FLIP	LABEL & NO.	GOOD TO VERY GOOD	NEAR MINT	YR.
ONLY LOVE OF MINE, THE/Be My Dancing Pardner	Fury 1022	2.00	8.00	58

TITLE/FLIP	LABEL & NO.	GOOD TO VERY GOOD	NEAR MINT	YR.
VIBRA-TONES, Sabby Lewis & The				
FORGIVE ME, MY LOVE/Regretting	ABC Paramount 9687	4.00	16.00	56
VIBRAHARPS, The				
IT MUST BE MAGIC/Nosey Neighbors	Atco 6134	1.50	6.00	59
WALK BESIDE ME/Cosy With Rosy	Beech 713	5.00	20.00	—
VIBRANAIRES, The				
DOLL FACE/ Ooh, I Feel So Good (red plastic)	After Hours 103	90.00	360.00	54
VIBRATIONS, The				
VICE-ROYS, The				
PLEASE, BABY, PLEASE/I'm Yours As Long As I Live	Aladdin 3273	7.00	28.00	55
VICEROYS, The				
I'M SO SORRY/Uncle Sam Needs You	Little Star 107	1.50	6.00	61
VICEROYS, The				
DREAMY EYES/Ball N' Chain	Original Sound 15	1.50	6.00	61
VICK, Ethel: see Three Sharps & A Flat				
VICTORIALS, The				
I GET THAT FEELING/Prettiest Girl In The World	Imperial 5398	2.50	10.00	56
VICTORIANS, The				
HEARTBREAKING MOON/I'm Rollin'	Saxony 103	5.00	20.00	—
WEDDING BELLS/Please Say You Do	Selma 1002	7.00	28.00	—
VICTORIANS, The				
I GUESS YOU'RE SATISFIED/Don't Break My Heart Again	Specialty 411	20.00	80.00	50
NATURALLY TOO WEAK FOR YOU/Part-Time Sweetheart	Specialty 420	15.00	60.00	51
VIDEOS, The (The Five Sharps)				
LOVE OR INFATUATION/ Shoo-Bee-Doo-Bee Cha Cha Cha	Casino 105	5.00	20.00	58
TRICKLE, TRICKLE/Moonglow, You Know	Casino 102	2.00	8.00	58
VINES, The				
I MUST SEE YOU AGAIN/Love So Sweet	Cee Jay 582	2.00	8.00	61
VINSON, Eddie				
ANXIOUS HEART/Suffer Fool	Mercury 70525	1.50	6.00	54
GOOD BREAD ALLEY/I Need You Tonight	King 4563	3.00	12.00	52
LONESOME TRAIN/Person To Person	King 4582	2.00	8.00	52
OLD MAN BOOGIE/You Can't Have My Love No More	Mercury 70334	1.50	6.00	54
RAIN IN THE FACE/Tomorrow May Never Come	Mercury 70621	1.50	6.00	54
VIRGIL & THE FOUR CHANELS				
VIRGINIA FOUR, The				
DIG MY JELLY ROLL/Moaning The Blues (78)	Decca 7662	7.00	28.00	39
I'D FEEL MUCH BETTER/Queen Street Rag (78)	Decca 7808	7.00	28.00	41
IT'LL SOON BE OVER WITH/Don't Leave Me Behind (78)	Victor 23376	2.50	10.00	33
SINCE I BEEN BORN/Comin' Down The Shiny Way (78)	Victor V38569	2.50	10.00	30
VISCOUNTS, Sammy Hagen & The				
DON'T CRY/Wild Bird	Capitol 3818	1.50	6.00	57
OUT OF YOUR HEART/Smoochie, Poochie	Capitol 3772	4.00	16.00	57
TAIL LIGHT/Snuggle Bunny	Capitol 3885	1.50	6.00	58
VOCAL TONES, The				
WALKIN' WITH MY BABY/Wanna Lee	Juanita 100	4.00	16.00	57
VOCALEERS, The				
ANGEL FACE/Lovin' Baby	Red Robin 132	12.50	50.00	54
BE TRUE/Oh, Where?	Red Robin 113	15.00	60.00	52
I NEED YOUR LOVE SO BAD/ Have You Ever Loved Someone?	Paradise 113	1.50	6.00	59
I WALK ALONE/How Soon?	Red Robin 119	15.00	60.00	53
IS IT A DREAM?/Hurry Home	Red Robin 114	10.00	40.00	52
LOVE YOU/Will You Be True?	Red Robin 125	15.00	60.00	54
NIGHT IS QUIET, THE/Hear My Plea	Vest 832	2.00	8.00	60
VOCALTONES, The				
DARLING/Three Kinds of People	Apollo 492	9.00	36.00	56
HAWAIIAN ROCK 'N ROLL/Walkin' My Baby	Cindy 3004	4.00	16.00	57
MY GIRL/I'm Gonna Get That Girl	Apollo 488	9.00	36.00	55
MY VERSION OF LOVE/I'll Never Let You Go	Apollo 497	10.00	40.00	56

TITLE/FLIP	LABEL & NO.	GOOD TO VERY GOOD	NEAR MINT	YR.
VOICE MASTERS, The				
VOICE MASTERS, Ty Hunter & The				
VOICES FIVE, Bud Johnson & The				
FOR SENTIMENTAL REASONS/All Alone	Craft 116	7.00	28.00	59
VOICES, The				
HEY, NOW/My Love Grows Stronger	Cash 1014	5.00	20.00	55
SANTA CLAUS BOOGIE/Santa Claus Baby	Cash 1016	4.00	16.00	55
TAKES TWO TO MAKE A HOME/I Want To Be Ready	Cash 1015	4.00	16.00	55
TWO THINGS I LOVE/Why?	Cash 1011	4.00	16.00	55
VOLCANOS, The				
VOLUMES, Jimmie Lewis & The				
VOLUMES, Lucille Watkins & The				
YOU LEFT ME LONELY/So Disappointed With Love	Jaguar 3006	10.00	40.00	—
VOLUMES, The				
COME BACK INTO MY HEART/The Bell	Chex 1005	1.50	6.00	62
I LOVE YOU/Dreams	Chex 1002	1.50	6.00	62
This record was released one month earlier on Chex with the number 1000.2 and with the artists' names spelled as "the Valumes."				
OH, MY MOTHER-IN-LAW/Our Song	Jubilee 5454	1.50	6.00	63
VON BATTLE, Joseph				
LOOKING FOR MY WOMAN/ Cadillac Woman (by Robert Richard) (78)	JVB 75828	9.00	36.00	48
VONTASTICS, The				
VOWS, The				

W

TITLE/FLIP	LABEL & NO.	GOOD TO VERY GOOD	NEAR MINT	YR.
WADE, Adam				
WAILERS, The				
HOT LOVE/Stop The Clock	Columbia 40288	12.50	50.00	54
WAILING BETHEA & THE CAP-TANS				
WALKER, Aaron as T-Bone Walker				
ON YOUR WAY BLUES/Go Back To The One You Love	Capitol 799	5.00	20.00	47
WALKER, Aaron as T-Bone Walker & His Band				
BLUE MOOD/Got No Use For You	Imperial 5216	5.00	20.00	52
BYE, BYE, BABY/Wanderin' Heart	Imperial 5284	4.00	16.00	53
HERE IN THE DARK/Party Girl	Imperial 5239	5.00	20.00	52
I GET SO WEARY/Tell Me, What's The Reason?	Post 2002	2.50	10.00	51
I'LL UNDERSTAND/Hard Way	Imperial 5330	3.00	12.00	54
I'M ABOUT TO LOSE MY MIND/I Miss You, Baby	Imperial 5261	5.00	20.00	52
LOVE IS A GAMBLE/High Society	Imperial 5311	4.00	16.00	52
PAPA AIN'T SALTY/T-Bone Shuffle	Atlantic 1065	2.00	8.00	55
RAILROAD STATION BLUES/Long Distance Blues	Imperial 5228	5.00	20.00	52
STREET WALKIN' WOMAN/Blues Is A Woman	Imperial 5202	5.00	20.00	51
TEEN-AGE BABY/Strugglin' Blues	Imperial 5299	4.00	16.00	54
TELL ME WHAT'S THE REASON?/Everytime	Imperial 5247	5.00	20.00	52
VIDA LEE/My Baby Is Now On My Mind	Imperial 5274	4.00	16.00	53
WHEN THE SUN GOES DOWN/Pony Tail	Imperial 5264	5.00	20.00	53
WHY NOT?/Play On, Little Girl	Atlantic 1074	2.00	8.00	55
YOU DON'T UNDERSTAND/Welcome Blues	Imperial 5384	3.00	12.00	54
WALKER, John as Moose John				
WRONG DOIN' WOMAN/Talkin' About Me	Ultra 102	2.00	8.00	55
WALKER, Junior & The All Stars				
WALKER, Lee				
SLIPPING IN/Cold Sand	Clara 110	2.50	10.00	65
WALKER, Mel				
ANOTHER SAD NIGHT/I'd Like To Make You Mine	Mercury 70379	1.50	6.00	54
UNLUCKY MAN/My Baby	Mercury 70276	1.50	6.00	53

TITLE/FLIP	LABEL & NO.	GOOD TO VERY GOOD	NEAR MINT	YR.

WALKER, T-BONE, Jr.:
see Rankin, R. S. as T-Bone Walker, Jr.

WALKER, T-BONE:
see Walker, Aaron as T-Bone Walker

WALKER, Willie & The Alpacas:
see Alpacas, Willie Walker & The

WALLACE, Sippie

WALLS, Van & The Rockets:
see Rockets, (Harry) Van Walls & The

WALTERS, Muddy

WALTON, James as J. Walton

TITLE/FLIP	LABEL & NO.	GOOD TO VERY GOOD	NEAR MINT	YR.
TELL ME WHAT YOU GOT/Shade Grove	Big Star 003	2.00	8.00	64

WALTON, Mercy Dee as Mercy Dee

TITLE/FLIP	LABEL & NO.	GOOD TO VERY GOOD	NEAR MINT	YR.
BABA-DU-LAY FEVER/Lonesome Cabin Blues (78)	Spire 11-001	2.50	10.00	49
BIRDBRAIN BABY/Big Foot Country (78)	Imperial 5110	1.50	6.00	50
COME BACK, MAYBELLENE/True Love	Flair 1077	2.00	8.00	55
DANGER ZONE/Happy Bachelor	Bayou 013	6.25	25.00	50
EMPTY LIFE/Birdbrain Baby (78)	Colony 111	1.50	6.00	50
EVIL AND HANKY/Travellin' Alone Blues (78)	Spire 11-002	2.50	10.00	49
GET TO GETTIN'/Dark Muddy Bottom	Specialty 481	2.50	10.00	54
HAVE YOU EVER?/Stubborn Woman	Flair 1078	2.00	8.00	55
HONEY BABY/Empty Life (78)	Imperial 5104	1.50	6.00	50
OLD FASHIONED WAYS/Pay Off (78)	Colony 107	1.50	6.00	50
ONE ROOM COUNTRY SHACK/ My Woman Knows The Score	Specialty 458	2.50	10.00	53
PLEASE UNDERSTAND/Pay Off	Bayou 003	6.25	25.00	50
RENT MAN BLUES/Fall Guy (red plastic)	Specialty 466	5.00	20.00	53
RENT MAN BLUES/Fall Guy	Specialty 466	2.50	10.00	53
ROAMIN' BLUES/Bought Love (78)	Imperial 5118	1.50	6.00	50
ROMP AND STOMP BLUES/Oh, Oh, Please	Flair 1073	2.00	8.00	55
STRAIGHT AND NARROW/Happy Bachelor (78)	Colony 102	1.50	6.00	50
TRAILING MY BABY/The Main Event (78)	Rhythm 1774	7.00	28.00	54

WALTON, Square

TITLE/FLIP	LABEL & NO.	GOOD TO VERY GOOD	NEAR MINT	YR.
BAD HANGOVER/Fish Tail Blues	RCA Victor 47-5584	6.25	25.00	53
GIMME YOUR BANK ROLL/Pepper Head Woman	RCA Victor 47-5493	6.25	25.00	53

WANDERERS, The

TITLE/FLIP	LABEL & NO.	GOOD TO VERY GOOD	NEAR MINT	YR.
THINKING OF YOU/Great Jumpin' Catfish	Onyx 518	3.00	12.00	57
WE COULD FIND HAPPINESS/Hey, Mae Ethyl	Savoy 1109	5.00	20.00	53

WANDERERS, Tony Allen & The:
see Allen, Tony & The Wanderers

WARD, Billy & The Dominoes:
see Dominoes, Billy Ward & The

WARD, Harold "Thunderhead"

WARD, Singin' Sammy

WARD, Walter & The Challengers

WARE, Eddie & His Band

TITLE/FLIP	LABEL & NO.	GOOD TO VERY GOOD	NEAR MINT	YR.
JEALOUS WOMAN/Give Love Another Chance (78)	Chess 1507	2.00	8.00	51
LIMA BEANS/Wandering Lover (78)	Chess 1461	2.50	10.00	51
THAT'S THE STUFF I LIKE/Lonely Broken Heart	States 130	5.00	20.00	53

WARFIELD, Peter

TITLE/FLIP	LABEL & NO.	GOOD TO VERY GOOD	NEAR MINT	YR.
MORNING TRAIN BLUES/Ragtime Boogie (78)	Miltone 5249	4.00	16.00	47

WARREN, Baby Boy:
see Warren, Robert as Baby Boy Warren

WARREN, Robert as Baby Boy Warren

TITLE/FLIP	LABEL & NO.	GOOD TO VERY GOOD	NEAR MINT	YR.
CHICKEN/Baby Boy Blues (78)	Drummond 3002	6.25	25.00	54
FORGIVE ME, DARLING/ Please Don't Think I'm Nosey (78)	Federal 12008	6.25	25.00	49
FORGIVE ME, DARLING/Please Don't Think I'm Nosey (78)	Staff 709	8.00	32.00	49
MATTIE MAE/Santa Fe (red plastic)	Blue Lake 106	20.00	80.00	54
MY SPECIAL FRIEND BLUES/Nervy Woman Blues (78)	Gotham 507	4.00	16.00	49
MY SPECIAL FRIEND BLUES/Nervy Woman Blues (78)	Staff 706	7.00	28.00	49
SANAFEE/Chuck-A-Luck	Excello 2211	2.00	8.00	53
SANAFEE/Hello Stranger (78)	JVB 26	5.00	20.00	53
SOMEBODY PUT BAD LUCK ON ME/ Stop Breakin' Down (78)	Drummond 3003	6.25	25.00	54
TAXI DRIVER/Bad Lover Blues (78)	Sampson 633	10.00	40.00	54

WARREN, Robert as Baby Boy Warren & His Buddy (Charlie Mills)

TITLE/FLIP	LABEL & NO.	GOOD TO VERY GOOD	NEAR MINT	YR.
LONESOME CABIN BLUES/Don't Want No Skinny Woman (78)	Staff 707	8.00	32.00	49

WARREN, Robert as Johnny Williams

Warren and John Lee Hooker each recorded for Staff and Swing Time as Johnny Williams.

TITLE/FLIP	LABEL & NO.	GOOD TO VERY GOOD	NEAR MINT	YR.
I GOT LUCKY/Let's Renew Our Love (78)	Staff 717	6.25	25.00	50
I GOT LUCKY/Let's Renew Our Love (78)	Swing Time 225	3.00	12.00	50

WARWICK, Dee Dee

WARWICK, Dionne

WARWICK, Dionne & The Spinners

WASHBOARD PETE:
see Willis, Ralph as Washboard Pete

WASHBOARD SAM:
see Brown, Robert as Washboard Sam

WASHBOARD WILLIE & HIS SUPER SUDS OF RHYTHM:
see Emsley William as Washboard Willie

WASHINGTON, Albert & The Kings

WASHINGTON, Baby

WASHINGTON, D. C.:
see Bendy, D. C. as D. C. Washington

WASHINGTON, Dinah

TITLE/FLIP	LABEL & NO.	GOOD TO VERY GOOD	NEAR MINT	YR.
BIG LONG SLIDIN' THING/No You Can't Love Two	Mercury 70392	2.50	10.00	54
DOUBLE DEALING DADDY/Pillow Blues	Mercury 8292	1.50	6.00	52
MY MAN'S AN UNDERTAKER/ Since My Man Has Gone And Went	Mercury 70284	1.50	6.00	53
SHORT JOHN/Feel Like I Wanna Cry	Mercury 70329	1.50	6.00	53
T.V. IS THE THING/Fat Daddy	Mercury 70214	1.50	6.00	53

WASHINGTON, Dinah & The Ravens:
see Ravens, Dinah Washington & The

WASHINGTON, Ella

WASHINGTON, Leroy

TITLE/FLIP	LABEL & NO.	GOOD TO VERY GOOD	NEAR MINT	YR.
WILD CHERRY/Be Kind	Excello 2144	2.00	8.00	58

WASHINGTON, Sherry & The Chromatics:
see Chromatics, Sherry Washington & The

WATERFORD, Charles as Crown Prince Waterford

TITLE/FLIP	LABEL & NO.	GOOD TO VERY GOOD	NEAR MINT	YR.
DRIFTWOOD BLUES/I'm Gonna Do Right	Excello 2065	2.00	8.00	56
EATIN' WATERMELON/Love Awhile (78)	Torch 6911	1.50	6.00	50

WATERFORD, Crown Prince:
see Waterford, Charles as Crown Prince Waterford

WATERS, Muddy:
see Morganfield, McKinley as Muddy Waters

WATKINS, Katie

WATKINS, Lucille as Lacille Watkins & The Belltones

WATKINS, Lucille & The Volumes:
see Volumes, Lucille Watkins & The

WATKINS, Viola

TITLE/FLIP	LABEL & NO.	GOOD TO VERY GOOD	NEAR MINT	YR.
REAL FINE MAN/Grunt Your Last Time, Daddy	Rama 8	2.50	10.00	52

WATSON, Alabama

WATSON, Deek & The Brown Dots:
see Brown Dots, Deek Watson & The

The Five Willows

Muddy Waters

TITLE/FLIP	LABEL & NO.	GOOD TO VERY GOOD	NEAR MINT	YR.

WATSON, John:
see Higgins, Chuck

WATSON, Johnny, Larry Williams &

WATSON, Johnny "Guitar"

TITLE/FLIP	LABEL & NO.	GOOD TO VERY GOOD	NEAR MINT	YR.
DEANA BABY/Honey	*Keen 4023*	1.50	6.00	*57*
GANGSTER OF LOVE/One Room Country Shack	*Keen 4005*	1.50	6.00	*57*
HOT LITTLE MAMA/I Love To Love You	*RPM 423*	2.50	10.00	*55*
OH, BABY/Give A Little	*RPM 447*	2.00	8.00	*55*
SHE MOVES ME/Love Me, Baby	*RPM 471*	1.50	6.00	*56*
THOSE LONELY, LONELY NIGHTS/Someone Cares For Me	*RPM 436*	2.00	8.00	*55*
THREE HOURS PAST MIDNIGHT/Ruben	*RPM 455*	1.50	6.00	*56*
TOO TIRED/Don't Touch Me	*RPM 431*	2.00	8.00	*55*

WATSON, Johnny "Guitar" as Young John Watson

TITLE/FLIP	LABEL & NO.	GOOD TO VERY GOOD	NEAR MINT	YR.
GETTIN' DRUNK/You Can't Take It With You	*Federal 12183*	5.00	20.00	*54*
HALF PINT OF WHISKEY/Space Guitar (instrumental)	*Federal 12175*	5.00	20.00	*54*
HIGHWAY 60/No I Can't	*Federal 12120*	9.00	36.00	*53*
I GOT EYES/Walkin' To My Baby	*Federal 12143*	5.00	20.00	*53*
MOTOR HEAD BABY/Sad Fool	*Federal 12131*	9.00	36.00	*53*
WHAT'S GOING ON?/Thinking	*Federal 12157*	5.00	20.00	*53*

WATSON, K. C. "Mo Jo"

TITLE/FLIP	LABEL & NO.	GOOD TO VERY GOOD	NEAR MINT	YR.
LOVE BLOODHOUND/I Keep On Trying	*Nanc 003*	3.00	12.00	*61*
YOU KNOW YOU DON'T WANT ME/All Alone	*Atlas 1080*	4.00	16.00	*57*

WATTS, Jimmy Mack & The

WAYNE, James

TITLE/FLIP	LABEL & NO.	GOOD TO VERY GOOD	NEAR MINT	YR.
CRYING IN VAIN/Lonely Room	*Aladdin 3234*	3.00	12.00	*54*
I'M IN LOVE WITH YOU/Sweet Little Woman	*Imperial 5258*	5.00	20.00	*51*
JUNCO'S RETURN/Gotta Good Girl	*Million 2009*	2.50	10.00	*54*

WAYNE, James as Larry Evans

TITLE/FLIP	LABEL & NO.	GOOD TO VERY GOOD	NEAR MINT	YR.
HENPECKED/Crazy 'Bout My Baby	*Fabor 400*	2.00	8.00	—
JUNCO RETURNS/What About Me?	*Fabor 4009*	2.50	10.00	—

WAYNE, James as Wee Willie Wayne

TITLE/FLIP	LABEL & NO.	GOOD TO VERY GOOD	NEAR MINT	YR.
GOOD NEWS/Kinfolks	*Imperial 5368*	1.50	6.00	*55*
TRAVELIN' MOOD/I Remember	*Imperial 5355*	2.00	8.00	*55*

WAYNE, James:
see Hoke, Billy with James Wayne & The Nighthawks

WAYNE, Wee Willie:
see Wayne, James as Wee Willie Wayne

WEATHERS, Oscar

WEAVER, Curley

TITLE/FLIP	LABEL & NO.	GOOD TO VERY GOOD	NEAR MINT	YR.
MY BABY'S GONE/Ticket Agent (78)	*Sittin' In With 547*	4.00	16.00	*50*

WEAVER, Curley & His Guitar

TITLE/FLIP	LABEL & NO.	GOOD TO VERY GOOD	NEAR MINT	YR.
SOME RAINY DAY/Trixie (78)	*Sittin' In With 646*	4.00	16.00	*50*

WEAVER, Joe

TITLE/FLIP	LABEL & NO.	GOOD TO VERY GOOD	NEAR MINT	YR.
15:40 SPECIAL/Soft Pillow (instrumental)	*DeLuxe 6006*	3.00	12.00	*53*
J. B. BOOGIE/Baby, I'm In Love With You	*DeLuxe 6021*	3.00	12.00	*53*

WEAVER, Joe & The Starlighters

WEAVER, JOE:
see Blue Notes (with Joe Weaver)
see Blue Notes, Joe Weaver & The
see Don Juans, Joe Weaver & The

WEBB, Bobby

TITLE/FLIP	LABEL & NO.	GOOD TO VERY GOOD	NEAR MINT	YR.
SOMEBODY ELSE IS TAKING MY PLACE/ Hear Me	*Ace 542*	2.50	10.00	*58*

WEBB, Boogie Bill

TITLE/FLIP	LABEL & NO.	GOOD TO VERY GOOD	NEAR MINT	YR.
I AIN'T FOR IT/Bad Dog	*Imperial 5257*	12.50	50.00	*53*

WEBSTER, Katie

TITLE/FLIP	LABEL & NO.	GOOD TO VERY GOOD	NEAR MINT	YR.
OPEN ARMS/On The Sunny Side Of Love	*Rocko 503*	1.50	6.00	*61*
SEA OF LOVE/I Feel So Low	*Decca 30945*	1.50	6.00	*61*

WEBSTER, Katie & Ashton Conroy

TITLE/FLIP	LABEL & NO.	GOOD TO VERY GOOD	NEAR MINT	YR.
BABY, BABY/I Want You To Love Me	*Kry 100*	2.00	8.00	*58*

WEBTONES, The

TITLE/FLIP	LABEL & NO.	GOOD TO VERY GOOD	NEAR MINT	YR.
MY LOST LOVE/Walk, Talk And Kiss	*MGM 12724*	2.00	8.00	*58*

WEE WILLIE WAYNE:
see Wayne, James as Wee Willie Wayne

WELCH, Lenny

WELLS, Amos as Junior Wells & His Eagle Rockers

TITLE/FLIP	LABEL & NO.	GOOD TO VERY GOOD	NEAR MINT	YR.
'BOUT THE BREAK OF DAY/Lawdy! Lawdy! (red plastic)	*States 139*	10.00	40.00	*53*
CUT THAT OUT/ Eagle Rock (instrumental) (red plastic)	*States 122*	10.00	40.00	*53*
GALLOPING HORSES, A LAZY MULE/ Blues in D Natural (by Earl Hooker)	*Chief 7016*	1.50	6.00	*60*
HODO MAN/Junior's Wail (instrumental) (red plastic)	*States 134*	10.00	40.00	*53*

Side one of this release appeared in various pressings (with the same label number) as "Hodo Man," "Hoodoo Man," and "Somebody Hoodooed The Hoodoo Man."

TITLE/FLIP	LABEL & NO.	GOOD TO VERY GOOD	NEAR MINT	YR.
IT HURTS ME, TOO/Cha Cha Cha In Blues	*Chief 7035*	1.50	6.00	*62*
MESSIN' WITH THE KID/Universal Rock (instrumental)	*Chief 7021*	1.50	6.00	*61*
SO ALL ALONE/Tomorrow Night (red plastic)	*States 143*	10.00	40.00	*53*
SO TIRED/Love Me	*Chief 7037*	1.50	6.00	*62*
TWO-HEADED WOMAN/Lovey Dovey Lovely One	*Chief 7005*	2.00	8.00	*57*
YOU SURE LOOK GOOD TO ME/Lovey Dovey Lovely One	*Chief 7034*	1.50	6.00	*62*

WELLS, Billy & The Crescents:
see Crescents, Billy Wells & The

WELLS, Jean

WELLS, Junior
see Wells, Amos as Junior Wells

WELLS, Mary

TITLE/FLIP	LABEL & NO.	GOOD TO VERY GOOD	NEAR MINT	YR.
BYE BYE BABY/Please Forgive Me	*Motown 1003*	1.50	6.00	*61*
I DON'T WANT TO TAKE A CHANCE/I'm So Sorry	*Motown 1011*	1.50	6.00	*61*

The first issue of this record was the last Motown release on the old pink label. It was also the first Motown single released with a picture sleeve (price shown does not include the sleeve).

WELLS, Mary, Marvin Gaye &

WEST TEXAS SLIM:
see Lewis, Ernest as West Texas Slim

WEST, Rudy & The Five Keys

WESTBROOK, Walter J. & His Phantom Five

TITLE/FLIP	LABEL & NO.	GOOD TO VERY GOOD	NEAR MINT	YR.
MIDNIGHT JUMP/Bring Your Clothes Back, Baby	*Bobbin 106*	2.50	10.00	*59*
WHY DID SHE LEAVE ME?/Darling, I Cried All Night Long	*Bobbin 115*	2.50	10.00	*59*

WESTON, Kim

WESTON, Kim, Marvin Gaye &

WHALERS, Hal Paige & The

TITLE/FLIP	LABEL & NO.	GOOD TO VERY GOOD	NEAR MINT	YR.
DON'T HAVE TO CRY NO MORE/Pour The Corn	*Checker 873*	1.50	6.00	*58*
DON'T HAVE TO CRY NO MORE/Pour The Corn	*Fury 1002*	3.00	12.00	*57*
THUNDERBIRD/Sugar Babe	*J&S 1601*	2.50	10.00	—

WHEATON, Little David

WHEATSTRAW, Peetie

WHEATSTRAW, Peetie's Buddy:
see Harmon, Ray as Peetie Wheatstraw's Buddy

WHEELERS, The

TITLE/FLIP	LABEL & NO.	GOOD TO VERY GOOD	NEAR MINT	YR.
ONCE I HAD A GIRL/Shine 'Em On	*Cenco 107*	8.00	32.00	—

WHEELS, Rudy & The

WHEELS, The

TITLE/FLIP	LABEL & NO.	GOOD TO VERY GOOD	NEAR MINT	YR.
I CAN'T FORGET/How Could I Ever Leave You?	*Premium 410*	5.00	20.00	*57*
MY HEART'S DESIRE/Let's Have A Ball	*Premium 405*	2.00	8.00	*56*
TEASIN' HEART/Loco	*Premium 408*	2.50	10.00	*56*

WHIPS, The

TITLE/FLIP	LABEL & NO.	GOOD TO VERY GOOD	NEAR MINT	YR.
PLEADIN' HEART/She Done Me Wrong	*Flair 1025*	15.00	60.00	—

Jimmy Wright

Jackie Wilson

TITLE/FLIP	LABEL & NO.	GOOD TO VERY GOOD	NEAR MINT	YR.
WHIRLERS, The				
MAGIC MIRROR/Tonight And Forever	Whirlin' Disc 108	4.00	16.00	57
WHISPERS, The				
ARE YOU SORRY?/We're Getting Married	Gotham 312	15.00	60.00	53
DON'T FOOL WITH LIZZIE/Fool Heart	Gotham 309	7.00	28.00	53
WHISPERS, The (female group)				
WHITAKER, Ruby & The Pyramids: See Pyramids, Ruby Whitaker & The				
WHITE, Booker T. Washington as Bukka White				
WHITE, Bukka				
WHITE, Cleve as Schoolboy Cleve				
SHE'S GONE/Strange Letter Blues	Feature 3013	6.25	25.00	54
WHITFIELD, Smoki				
DON'T SHOOT/Behind Those Swingin' Doors	Crest 1023	1.50	6.00	58
TAKE THE HINT/Function At The Junction (red plastic)	Crest 1010	3.00	12.00	58
TAKE THE HINT/Function At The Junction	Crest 1010	1.50	6.00	58
WHITFIELD, Wilbur & The Pleasers				
WHITNEY, Marva				
WHITTAKER, Hudson as Jimmy Eager & His Trio				
PLEASE, MR. DOCTOR/I Should Have Loved Her More	Sabre 100	12.50	50.00	53
WHITTAKER, Hudson as Tampa Red				
BOOGIE WOOGIE WOMAN/I Won't Let Her Do It	RCA Victor 47-4275	4.00	16.00	51
COME ON, IF YOU'RE COMING/ When Things Go Wrong With You (red plastic)	RCA Victor 50-0019	6.25	25.00	49
DON'T BLAME SHORTY FOR THAT/ Sweet Little Angel	RCA Victor 50-0107	5.00	20.00	50
I'LL NEVER LET YOU GO/ Got A Mind To Leave This Town	RCA Victor 47-5273	3.00	12.00	52
I'M GONNA PUT YOU DOWN/But I Forgive You	RCA Victor 47-4722	3.00	12.00	52
IF SHE DON'T COME BACK/Big Stars Falling Blues	RCA Victor 47-5594	4.00	16.00	53
IT'S A BRAND NEW BOOGEY/Put Your Money Where Your Mouth Is (red plastic)	RCA Victor 50-0027	6.25	25.00	49
IT'S GOOD LIKE THAT/New Deal Blues (red plastic)	RCA Victor 50-0094	6.25	25.00	50
LOOK A THERE, LOOK A THERE/True Love	RCA Victor 47-4898	3.00	12.00	52
MIDNIGHT BOOGIE/I Miss My Lovin' Blues	RCA Victor 50-0112	5.00	20.00	50
1950 BLUES/Love Her With A Feelin' (red plastic)	RCA Victor 50-0084	6.25	25.00	50
PLEASE TRY TO SEE IT MY WAY/ It's Too Late Now (red plastic)	RCA Victor 50-0056	6.25	25.00	49
SHE'S A COOL OPERATOR/Green And Lucky Blues	RCA Victor 47-4399	4.00	16.00	51
SHE'S DYNAMITE/Early In The Morninng	RCA Victor 50-0123	5.00	20.00	51
SINCE MY BABY'S BEEN GONE/ Pretty Baby Blues	RCA Victor 50-0136	5.00	20.00	51
SO CRAZY ABOUT YOU, BABY/So Much Trouble	RCA Victor 47-5523	3.00	12.00	53
THAT'S HER OWN BUSINESS/ I'll Find My Way (red plastic)	RCA Victor 50-0041	6.25	25.00	49
TOO LATE TOO LONG/All Mixed Up Over You	RCA Victor 47-5134	3.00	12.00	52
WICK, Johnny & His Swinging Ozarks				
GLASGOW, KY BLUES/Blue Dawn	United 126	1.50	6.00	52
JOCKEY JACK BOOGIE/Big Horn Blues (instrumental)	United 116	1.50	6.00	52
WIGGINS, Spencer				
WILBORN, Nelson as Dirty Red				
HOTEL BOOGIE/You Done Me Wrong (78)	Aladdin 207	2.00	8.00	47
MOTHER FUYER/Home Last Night (78)	Aladdin 194	3.00	12.00	47
WILCOX, Eddie				
WHEEL OF FORTUNE/You Showed Me The Way	Derby 787	1.50	6.00	51
WILDWOODS, The				
WHEN THE SWALLOWS COME BACK TO CAPISTRANO/ Heart Of Mine	Caprice 101/102	10.00	40.00	61
WILEY, Arnold				
WILEY, Arnold as Doc Wiley				
WILEY, Doc (Arnold Wiley)				

TITLE/FLIP	LABEL & NO.	GOOD TO VERY GOOD	NEAR MINT	YR.
WILEY, Ed				
BLUES AFTER HOURS (instrumental)/ Cry, Cry Baby (78)	Sittin' In With 545	10.00	40.00	50
SO GLAD I'M FREE/Deep Moanin' Blues	Atlantic 959	3.00	12.00	51
WILEY, Irene				
WILKINS, Artie & The Palms: see Palms, Artie Wilkins & The				
WILLAMS, Jeanette				
WILLIAMS, Andre & The Don Juans: see Don Juans, Andre Williams & The				
WILLIAMS, Andre & The Five Dollars: see Five Dollars, Andre Williams & The				
WILLIAMS, Andre & The Inspirations				
WILLIAMS, B.—His Guitar & Trio				
YOU'RE SO NEAR TO ME/Mortgaged Love (78)	Top Tunes 101	5.00	20.00	50
WILLIAMS, Billy Quartet, The				
WILLIAMS, Blind Boy: see McGhee, Walter Brown as Blind Boy Williams				
WILLIAMS, Cootie				
SHOTGUN BOOGIE/Divorce Me C.O.D. Blues	Derby 756	5.00	20.00	50
WILLIAMS, Cora: see Four Jacks, The				
WILLIAMS, Dee Sextet, The				
BONGO BLUES/ Dee's Boogie (instrumental) (78)	Savoy 684	2.50	10.00	48
WILLIAMS, Dickie				
WHAT MAKES YOU THINK YOU'RE IN LOVE?/ Tee-Na-Na	Vin 1021	3.00	12.00	—
WILLIAMS, Donnie				
WILLIAMS, Doug & The Mell-O-Tones: see Mell-O-Tones, Doug Williams & The				
WILLIAMS, Eddie				
WILLIAMS, Eddie & The Brown Buddies				
WILLIAMS, Emery, Jr. as Detroit Jr.				
WILLIAMS, Enoch as The Sunny Williams Trio Often referred to as "Sonny Boy" Williams (rather than "Sunny"), he shouldn't be confused with any of the three artists known as "Sonny Boy" Williamson.				
BOOGIE MAN, THE/Reverse The Charges (78)	Super Disc 1030	2.00	8.00	47
JUMP IT, DON'T BUMP IT/You'll Never Cry Again (78)	Super Disc 1058	2.00	8.00	47
WILLIAMS, Jo Jo: see Williams, Joseph as Jo Jo Williams				
WILLIAMS, Jody: see Williams, Joseph Leon as Jody Williams				
WILLIAMS, Joe (Lee) Joe (Lee) Williams should not be confused with Joseph Goreed, who records under the name Joe Williams.				
HIS SPIRIT LIVES ON/ Good Mr. Roosevelt (by James McCain) (78)	Chicago 103	6.25	25.00	45
JIVIN' WOMAN/She's A Married Woman (78)	Bullet 337	25.00	100.00	49
WILLIAMS, Joe (Lee) as Po' Joe Williams				
GOING BACK HOME/Baby Left Town	Vee Jay 227	4.00	16.00	56
WILLIAMS, Joe: see Goreed, Joseph as Joe Williams				

WILLIAMS, Johnny:
see Hooker, John Lee as Johnny Williams
see Warren, Robert as Johnny Williams

WILLIAMS, Joseph as Jo Jo Williams
Joseph Williams should not be confused with Joseph Leon Williams.

TITLE/FLIP	LABEL & NO.	GOOD TO VERY GOOD	NEAR MINT	YR.
ALL PRETTY WIMMINS/Rock 'n' Roll Boogie	Atomic H (no number)	5.00	20.00	59

WILLIAMS, Joseph Leon as Jody Williams

TITLE/FLIP	LABEL & NO.	GOOD TO VERY GOOD	NEAR MINT	YR.
HIDEOUT/Moaning For Molasses Instrumentals.	Smash 1081	1.50	6.00	62
LONELY WITHOUT YOU/Moaning For Molasses (instrumental)	Nike 1013	2.00	8.00	62
TIME FOR A CHANGE/Lonely Without You	Yulando 8665	1.50	6.00	62
YOU MAY/Lucky Lou (instrumental)	Argo 5274	2.50	10.00	57

WILLIAMS, Joseph Leon as Little Papa Joe

TITLE/FLIP	LABEL & NO.	GOOD TO VERY GOOD	NEAR MINT	YR.
LOOKING FOR MY BABY/Easy Lovin'	Blues Lake 116	8.00	32.00	55

WILLIAMS, Joseph Leon as Sugar Boy Williams

TITLE/FLIP	LABEL & NO.	GOOD TO VERY GOOD	NEAR MINT	YR.
FIVE LONG YEARS/Little Girl	Herald 555	2.00	8.00	60
LITTLE GIRL TAKE YOUR TIME/Someday Darling	Raines 2906	1.50	6.00	65

WILLIAMS, L. C.

TITLE/FLIP	LABEL & NO.	GOOD TO VERY GOOD	NEAR MINT	YR.
ALL THROUGH MY DREAMS/Mean And Evil Blues (78)	Freedom 1529	2.00	8.00	49
ALL THROUGH MY DREAMS/Mean And Evil Blues (78)	Imperial 5195	1.50	6.00	49
DON'T WANT NO WOMAN/Louise (78)	Mercury 8276	1.50	6.00	51
HOLE IN THE WALL/Boogie All The Time (78)	Gold Star 623	2.50	10.00	48
LAZY J, THE/Fannie Mae (78)	Jax 648	2.00	8.00	51
LAZY J, THE/Fannie Mae (78)	Sittin' In With 648	2.00	8.00	51
MY DARKEST HOUR/Want My Baby Back	Bayou 008	6.25	25.00	49
SO SORRY/Baby Child (78)	Jax 640	2.00	8.00	51
SO SORRY/Baby Child (78)	Sittin' In With 640	2.00	8.00	51
STRIKE BLUES/You Can't Take It With You, Baby (78)	Gold Star 667	2.50	10.00	48

WILLIAMS, L. C. (Lightnin' Jr.)
Williams should not be confused with William Thomas Dupree, who also recorded as Lightnin' Junior.

TITLE/FLIP	LABEL & NO.	GOOD TO VERY GOOD	NEAR MINT	YR.
TRYING, TRYING/You'll Never Miss The Water (78)	Gold Star 614	2.50	10.00	47

WILLIAMS, L. C. as Conney's Combo With L. C. Williams

TITLE/FLIP	LABEL & NO.	GOOD TO VERY GOOD	NEAR MINT	YR.
THAT'S ALRIGHT/Gonna Change My Love (78)	Freedom 1510	2.00	8.00	49

WILLIAMS, L. C. as Connie's Combo
Williams' group should not be confused with the Connie's Combo led by Conrad Johnson. The two groups recorded in Houston during the same period, however, and had some of the same personnel, including Johnson. The same record as below was also issued on the Freedom label as by The L. C. Williams Orchestra.

TITLE/FLIP	LABEL & NO.	GOOD TO VERY GOOD	NEAR MINT	YR.
WHY DON'T YOU COME BACK?/I Don't Want Your Baby (78)	Eddie's 1203	2.50	10.00	48

WILLIAMS, L. C. as Lightnin' Jr. Williams

TITLE/FLIP	LABEL & NO.	GOOD TO VERY GOOD	NEAR MINT	YR.
BLACK WOMAN/I Won't Be Here Long (78)	Gold Star 648	2.50	10.00	48

WILLIAMS, L. C. Orchestra, The

TITLE/FLIP	LABEL & NO.	GOOD TO VERY GOOD	NEAR MINT	YR.
WHY DON'T YOU COME BACK?/ I Don't Want Your Baby (78)	Freedom 1501	2.00	8.00	48

WILLIAMS, L. C. With J. C. Conney's Combo

TITLE/FLIP	LABEL & NO.	GOOD TO VERY GOOD	NEAR MINT	YR.
JELLY ROLL/Louisiana Boogie (78)	Freedom 1524	2.00	8.00	49
SHOUT, BABY, SHOUT/Ethel Mae (78)	Freedom 1517	2.00	8.00	49

WILLIAMS, Larry

WILLIAMS, Larry & Johnny Guitar Watson

WILLIAMS, Lee & The Cymbals

WILLIAMS, Lester

TITLE/FLIP	LABEL & NO.	GOOD TO VERY GOOD	NEAR MINT	YR.
ALL I NEED IS YOU/I Know That Chick (78)	Macy's 5004	1.50	6.00	49
BRAND NEW BABY/If You Knew How Much I Love You	Specialty 450	4.00	16.00	52
CRAZY 'BOUT MY BABY/ Don't Ever Take Your Love From Me	Duke 131	2.00	8.00	54
DOWLING STREET HOP/Don't Treat Me So Low Down (78)	Macy's 5006	1.50	6.00	49
HEY, JACK/The Folks Around The Corner (78)	Macy's 5016	1.50	6.00	50
I CAN'T LOSE WITH THE STUFF I USE/ My Home Ain't Here	Specialty 422	5.00	20.00	51
LET ME TELL YOU A THING OR TWO/ Tryin' To Forget	Specialty 431	4.00	16.00	51
LET'S DO IT/Good Loving Baby	Duke 123	2.00	8.00	54
MCDONALD'S DAUGHTER/Daddy Loves You	Imperial 5402	2.50	10.00	56
SWEET LOVIN' DADDY/Lost Gal	Specialty 437	4.00	16.00	51
TEXAS TOWN/Mary Lou (78)	Macy's 5009	1.50	6.00	50
WINTER TIME BLUES/ I'm So Glad I Could Jump And Shout (78)	Macy's 5000	1.50	6.00	49

WILLIAMS, Lightnin' Jr.:
see Williams, L. C. as Lightnin' Jr. Williams

WILLIAMS, Little Jerry

WILLIAMS, Lonnie

TITLE/FLIP	LABEL & NO.	GOOD TO VERY GOOD	NEAR MINT	YR.
TEARS IN MY HEART/New Road Blues (78)	Sittin' In With 567	3.00	12.00	51
WAVIN' SEA BLUES/ I'm Tired Of Running Around (78)	Sittin' In With 593	3.00	12.00	51

WILLIAMS, Maurice & The Zodiacs

WILLIAMS, Mel & The Montclairs

WILLIAMS, Mike

WILLIAMS, Nat & The Mello-Tones:
see Mello-Tones, Nat Williams & The

WILLIAMS, Otis & The Charms:
see Charms, Otis Williams & The

WILLIAMS, Paul

TITLE/FLIP	LABEL & NO.	GOOD TO VERY GOOD	NEAR MINT	YR.
HELLO/Rock It, Davy Crockett	Capitol 3205	1.50	6.00	55
ONCE UPON A TIME/Suggie Duggie Baby	Josie 806	1.50	6.00	56
THIN MAN/Shame, Shame, Shame (red plastic)	Jax 313	5.00	20.00	54
WOMEN ARE THE ROOT OF ALL EVIL/Spread Joy	Groove 0014	2.00	8.00	54

WILLIAMS, Po' Joe:
see Williams, Joe (Lee) as Po' Joe Williams

WILLIAMS, Sugar Boy:
see Williams, Joseph Leon as Sugar Boy Williams

WILLIAMS, Sunny Trio, The:
see Williams, Enoch as The Sunny Williams Trio

WILLIAMSON, James & His Trio

TITLE/FLIP	LABEL & NO.	GOOD TO VERY GOOD	NEAR MINT	YR.
HOMESICK/The Woman I Love	Chance 1131	20.00	80.00	53
LONESOME OLE TRAIN/Farmer's Blues (78)	Chance 1121	12.50	50.00	52

WILLIAMSON, James as Homesick James

TITLE/FLIP	LABEL & NO.	GOOD TO VERY GOOD	NEAR MINT	YR.
CAN'T AFFORD TO DO IT/Set A Date	Colt 632	3.00	12.00	62
CROSSROADS/My Baby's Sweet	USA 746	4.00	16.00	62

WILLIAMSON, John Lee:
see Williamson, Sonny Boy #1

WILLIAMSON, Sonny Boy #1
EDITOR'S NOTE: There are three different artists named SONNY BOY WILLIAMSON. These singers are usually designated as Sonny Boy Number 1, 2, or 3. For that reason, we have numbered them accordingly. For clarity we also have listed them together here, rather than under their real names.

#1's real name is John Lee Williamson.

TITLE/FLIP	LABEL & NO.	GOOD TO VERY GOOD	NEAR MINT	YR.
I LOVE YOU FOR MYSELF/ Southern Dream (red plastic)	RCA Victor 50 0030	6.25	25.00	47
LITTLE GIRL/Bring Another Half Pint (red plastic)	RCA Victor 50-0005	6.25	25.00	47

WILLIAMSON, Sonny Boy #2
#2's real name is Aleck or "Rice" Miller.

TITLE/FLIP	LABEL & NO.	GOOD TO VERY GOOD	NEAR MINT	YR.
BOPPIN' WITH SONNY/No Nights By Myself	Ace 511	5.00	20.00	54
DON'T START ME TO TALKIN'/All My Love In Vain	Checker 824	1.50	6.00	55
EMPTY BEDROOM/From The Bottom	Trumpet 228	4.00	16.00	54
I CROSS MY HEART/West Memphis Blues	Trumpet 144	7.00	28.00	51
KEEP IT TO YOURSELF/The Key To Your Door	Checker 847	1.50	6.00	55
LET ME EXPLAIN/Your Imagination	Checker 834	1.50	6.00	55
MIGHTY LONG TIME/Nine Below Zero	Trumpet 166	5.00	20.00	52
RED HOT KISSES/Going In Your Direction	Trumpet 216	3.00	12.00	53
SHE BROUGHT LIFE BACK TO THE DEAD/ Gettin' Out Of Town	Trumpet 215	3.00	12.00	52
SONNY BOY'S CHRISTMAS BLUES/Pontiac Blues (78)	Trumpet 145	1.50	6.00	51
STOP NOW, BABY/Mr. Down Child	Trumpet 168	4.00	16.00	52
TOO CLOSE TOGETHER/Cat Hop	Trumpet 212	3.00	12.00	52

WILLIAMSON, Sonny Boy #3

TITLE/FLIP	LABEL & NO.	GOOD TO VERY GOOD	NEAR MINT	YR.
PRETTY LI'L THING/Mailman, Mailman	Ram 2501	2.50	10.00	60

TITLE/FLIP	LABEL & NO.	GOOD TO VERY GOOD	NEAR MINT	YR.

WILLIE & ARLENE & THE TUNEMASTERS:
see Tunemasters, Willie Wilson & The

WILLIE C.:
see Cobbs, Willie as Willie C.

WILLIS, Aaron as Little Sonny

TITLE/FLIP	LABEL & NO.	GOOD TO VERY GOOD	NEAR MINT	YR.
LOVE SHOCK/I'll Love You, Baby	JVB 5001	2.50	10.00	58

WILLIS, Chuck

TITLE/FLIP	LABEL & NO.	GOOD TO VERY GOOD	NEAR MINT	YR.
CAN'T YOU SEE?/It Ain't Right To Treat Me Wrong	Columbia 30238	5.00	20.00	51
COME ON HOME/It Were You	Epic 7067	1.50	6.00	54
DON'T DECEIVE ME/I've Been Treated Wrong	Okeh 6985	2.50	10.00	52
GOING TO THE RIVER/Baby, Have Left Me Again?	Okeh 6952	2.00	8.00	53
I CAN TELL/One More Break	Epic 7055	1.50	6.00	54
I FEEL SO BAD/Need One More Change	Okeh 7029	2.00	8.00	53
I RULE MY HOUSE/I Tried	Okeh 6810	2.50	10.00	51
I'VE BEEN AWAY TOO LONG/Give And Take	Okeh 7048	1.50	6.00	54
LAWDY, MISS MARY/Lovestruck	Epic 7051	1.50	6.00	54
LET'S JUMP TONIGHT/It's Too Late, Baby	Okeh 6841	2.50	10.00	51
LOUD MOUTH LUCY/Here I Come	Okeh 6873	2.50	10.00	52
MY BABY'S COMING HOME/When My Day Is Over	Okeh 7004	2.00	8.00	52
MY HEART'S BEEN BROKEN AGAIN/Change My Mind	Epic 7041	1.50	6.00	54
MY STORY/Caldonia	Okeh 6905	2.00	8.00	52
SEARCH MY HEART/Bing Bong Doo	Epic 7062	1.50	6.00	54
TWO SPOONS OF TEARS/Charged With Cheating	Epic 7070	1.50	6.00	54
WRONG LAKE TO CATCH A FISH/Salty Tears	Okeh 6930	2.00	8.00	52
YOU'RE STILL MY BABY/What's Your Name?	Okeh 7015	1.50	6.00	53

WILLIS, Chuck & The Royals

TITLE/FLIP	LABEL & NO.	GOOD TO VERY GOOD	NEAR MINT	YR.
I'VE BEEN TREATED WRONG TOO LONG/Don't Deceive Me	Okeh 6985	4.00	16.00	53

WILLIS, Chuck & The Sandmen

TITLE/FLIP	LABEL & NO.	GOOD TO VERY GOOD	NEAR MINT	YR.
I CAN TELL/One More Break	Okeh 7055	1.50	6.00	55

WILLIS, Little Son:
see Willis, Mac as Little Son Willis

WILLIS, Mac

TITLE/FLIP	LABEL & NO.	GOOD TO VERY GOOD	NEAR MINT	YR.
PRETTY WOMAN/Howling Woman	Elko 254	5.00	20.00	50

WILLIS, Mac as Little Son Willis

TITLE/FLIP	LABEL & NO.	GOOD TO VERY GOOD	NEAR MINT	YR.
BAD LUCK AND TROUBLE/Operator Blues	Swing Time 304	7.00	28.00	52
HARLEM BLUES/I Love You Just The Same	Swing Time 305	7.00	28.00	52
NOTHING BUT THE BLUES/Skin And Bones	Swing Time 306	7.00	28.00	52
ROLL ME OVER SLOW/Baby, Come Back Home	Swing Time 341	7.00	28.00	53

WILLIS, Milton Combo, The

TITLE/FLIP	LABEL & NO.	GOOD TO VERY GOOD	NEAR MINT	YR.
LITTLE JOE'S BOOGIE/Three O'Clock Boogie (78)	Lucky 7 5001	2.50	6.25	49

WILLIS, Ralph

TITLE/FLIP	LABEL & NO.	GOOD TO VERY GOOD	NEAR MINT	YR.
COOL THAT THING/Sportin' Life (78)	Abbey 3002	2.50	10.00	49
JUST A NOTE/Church Bells (78)	Signature 32016	2.50	10.00	46
TROUBLE DON'T LAST/Shake That Thing (78)	Signature 32012	2.50	10.00	46

WILLIS, Ralph ('Bama)

TITLE/FLIP	LABEL & NO.	GOOD TO VERY GOOD	NEAR MINT	YR.
WORRIED BLUES/Comb Your Kitty Kat (78)	Regis 118	3.00	12.00	44

WILLIS, Ralph & His Alabama Trio

TITLE/FLIP	LABEL & NO.	GOOD TO VERY GOOD	NEAR MINT	YR.
NEW GOIN' DOWN SLOW/Goin' To Chattanooga (78)	20th Century 20-11	2.50	10.00	46
SO MANY DAYS/That Gal's No Good (78)	20th Century 20-09	2.50	10.00	46
STEEL MILL BLUES/I Will Never Love Again	20th Century 20-12	3.00	12.00	46

WILLIS, Ralph as Alabama Slim

TITLE/FLIP	LABEL & NO.	GOOD TO VERY GOOD	NEAR MINT	YR.
BOAR HOG BLUES/Eloise (78)	Savoy 5553	1.50	6.00	47

WILLIS, Ralph as Sleepy Joe's Washboard Band

TITLE/FLIP	LABEL & NO.	GOOD TO VERY GOOD	NEAR MINT	YR.
AMEN BLUES/Mama, Mama Blues (78)	Savoy 753	1.50	6.00	48

WILLIS, Ralph as Washboard Pete

TITLE/FLIP	LABEL & NO.	GOOD TO VERY GOOD	NEAR MINT	YR.
CHRISTMAS BLUES/Neighbourhood Blues (78)	Savoy 5556	2.00	8.00	47

WILLIS, Ralph Country Boys, The

TITLE/FLIP	LABEL & NO.	GOOD TO VERY GOOD	NEAR MINT	YR.
COLD CHILLS/Amen (78)	Prestige 923	2.00	8.00	52
GONNA HOP ON DOWN THE LINE/Door Bell Blues	King 4631	5.00	20.00	53
IT'S TOO LATE/I'll Never Love Again (78)	Par 1306	2.50	10.00	52
WHY'D YOU DO IT?/Do Right	King 4611	5.00	20.00	53

WILLIS, Ralph Featuring Brownie McGhee

TITLE/FLIP	LABEL & NO.	GOOD TO VERY GOOD	NEAR MINT	YR.
CHURCH BELL BLUES/Tell Me, Pretty Baby (78)	Prestige 907	1.50	6.00	51
CHURCH BELL BLUES/Tell Me, Pretty Baby (78)	Signature 1006	2.50	10.00	51
EVERYDAY I WEEP AND MOAN/I Got A Letter (78)	Jubilee 5044	1.50	6.00	50
GOODBYE BLUES/Lazy Woman Blues (78)	Prestige 906	1.50	6.00	51
GOODBYE BLUES/Lazy Woman Blues (78)	Signature 1007	2.50	10.00	51
INCOME TAX BLUES/Bed Tick Blues (78)	Jubilee 5078	1.50	6.00	51
OLD HOME BLUES/Salty Dog (78)	Prestige 919	1.50	6.00	51
SOMEBODY'S GOT TO GO/Blues, Blues, Blues (78)	Jubilee 5034	1.50	6.00	50

WILLIS, Slim

Slim Willis should not be confused with Ralph Willis, who recorded as Alabama Slim.

TITLE/FLIP	LABEL & NO.	GOOD TO VERY GOOD	NEAR MINT	YR.
RUNNING AROUND/No Feeling For You	C.J. 627	1.50	6.00	61
STRANGE FEELING/I Love To Play	C.J. 622	1.50	6.00	61
YOU'RE THE SWEETEST GIRL I KNOW/From Now On	C.J. 635	1.50	6.00	62

WILLIS, Turner

TITLE/FLIP	LABEL & NO.	GOOD TO VERY GOOD	NEAR MINT	YR.
RE-ENLISTMENT BLUES/ Irma Jean (by Bob Geddins) (78)	Big Town 1058	1.50	6.00	45
RE-ENLISTMENT BLUES/Irma Jean (by Bob Geddins) (78)	Trilon 1058	2.00	8.00	45

WILLOWS, The

TITLE/FLIP	LABEL & NO.	GOOD TO VERY GOOD	NEAR MINT	YR.
CHURCH BELLS ARE RINGING/Baby Tell Me	Melba 102	10.00	40.00	56
CHURCH BELLS MAY RING/Baby Tell Me	Melba 102	1.50	6.00	56
DO YOU LOVE ME?/My Angel	Melba 106	3.00	12.00	56
LITTLE DARLIN'/My Angel	Melba 115	3.00	12.00	57

WILLOWS, Tony Middleton & The

TITLE/FLIP	LABEL & NO.	GOOD TO VERY GOOD	NEAR MINT	YR.
FIRST TASTE OF LOVE, THE/Only My Heart	Eldorado 508	1.50	6.00	57
LET'S FALL IN LOVE/Say Yeah	Gone 5015	2.50	10.00	58

WILLS, Oscar (with Fat's Domino's Band)

TITLE/FLIP	LABEL & NO.	GOOD TO VERY GOOD	NEAR MINT	YR.
FLAT FOOT SAM/Nervous (instrumental by Paul Gayten)	Argo 5277	1.50	6.00	57

WILLS, Oscar as T. V. Slim

TITLE/FLIP	LABEL & NO.	GOOD TO VERY GOOD	NEAR MINT	YR.
GOING TO CALIFORNIA, AIN'T GOT BUT 15 CENTS/ (No flip)	Speed (number unknown)	6.25	25.00	57

WILLS, Oscar as T. V. Slim & His Heartbreakers

TITLE/FLIP	LABEL & NO.	GOOD TO VERY GOOD	NEAR MINT	YR.
FLAT FOOT SAM/Darling, Remember?	Checker 870	1.50	6.00	57
FLAT FOOT SAM/Darling, Remember?	Cliff 103	5.00	20.00	57
TO PROVE MY LOVE/You Can't Buy A Woman	Speed 6865	4.00	16.00	58

WILSON, Al

WILSON, Betty & The Four Bars

WILSON, Harding as Hop Wilson & His Two Buddies

TITLE/FLIP	LABEL & NO.	GOOD TO VERY GOOD	NEAR MINT	YR.
BROKE AND HUNGRY/Always Be In Love With You	Goldband 1078	1.50	6.00	59
CHICKEN STUFF/That Wouldn't Satisfy	Goldband 1071	2.50	10.00	58

WILSON, Harding as Poppa Hop

TITLE/FLIP	LABEL & NO.	GOOD TO VERY GOOD	NEAR MINT	YR.
I'M A STRANGER/My Woman Has A Black Cat Bone	Ivory 127	2.00	8.00	60

WILSON, Harding as Poppy Hop

TITLE/FLIP	LABEL & NO.	GOOD TO VERY GOOD	NEAR MINT	YR.
GOOD WOMAN IS HARD TO FIND, A/I Met A Strange Woman	Ivory 133	2.00	8.00	61
MERRY CHRISTMAS, DARLING/ Be Careful With The Blues	Ivory 134/135	2.00	8.00	61

WILSON, Hop:
see Wilson, Harding as Hop Wilson

WILSON, Jackie

WILSON, Jackie & Count Basie

WILSON, Jackie & Lavern Baker

WILSON, Jackie & Linda Hopkins

WILSON, Jackie:
see Ward, Billy & The Dominoes (featuring Jackie Wilson)

WILSON, Jimmy & His All Stars

TITLE/FLIP	LABEL & NO.	GOOD TO VERY GOOD	NEAR MINT	YR.
BABY DON'T WANT NOBODY BUT ME/ Crying Like A Baby Child	7-11 2105	10.00	40.00	53
ETHEL LEE/Tell Me	7-11 2104	8.00	32.00	53
HONEY BEE/Please Believe In Me (78)	Aladdin 3087	5.00	20.00	51
I'VE FOUND OUT/Oh, Red	Big Town 123	3.00	12.00	55
INSTRUMENTAL JUMP (instrumental)/ Call Me A Hound Dog	Big Town 103	3.00	12.00	53
IT'S TIME TO CHANGE/Any Man's A Fool	Aladdin 3241	3.00	12.00	52
MISTAKE IN LIFE/It's A Sin To Tell A Lie	Aladdin 3140	4.00	16.00	51
STRANGEST BLUES/I Used To Love A Woman (78)	Rhythm 1765	4.00	16.00	54
TEARDROPS ON MY PILLOW/Mountain Climber	Big Town 113	3.00	12.00	54
TIN PAN ALLEY/Big Town Jump (instrumental)	Big Town 101	2.50	10.00	53
TROUBLE IN MY HOUSE/Jumping From Six To Six	Big Town 115	3.00	12.00	54
WOMAN IS TO BLAME, A/Blues At Sundown	Big Town 107	3.00	12.00	53

WILSON, Jimmy & The Blues Blasters Band

TITLE/FLIP	LABEL & NO.	GOOD TO VERY GOOD	NEAR MINT	YR.
BLUES IN THE ALLEY/Oh, Red	Irma 107	2.50	10.00	55
LOUISE/Alley Blues	Chart 610	4.00	16.00	56
SEND ME THE KEY/Poor Poor Lover	Chart 629	3.00	12.00	56

WILSON, Jimmy as Jimmy Nolen

TITLE/FLIP	LABEL & NO.	GOOD TO VERY GOOD	NEAR MINT	YR.
STRANGEST BLUES/I Used To Love A Woman (78)	Elko 915	3.00	12.00	54

WILSON, Nancy

WILSON, Ormond & The Basin Street Boys

WILSON, Willie & The Tunemasters:
see Tunemasters, Willie Wilson & The

WINLEY, Paul & The Rockers:
see Rockers, Paul Winley & The

WINNERS, The

TITLE/FLIP	LABEL & NO.	GOOD TO VERY GOOD	NEAR MINT	YR.
CAN THIS BE LOVE?/Rockin' And Rollin'	Rainbow 331	2.00	8.00	56

WINTERS, Eddie "Doodie Pickle"

TITLE/FLIP	LABEL & NO.	GOOD TO VERY GOOD	NEAR MINT	YR.
DON'T YOU KNOW?/1601 Stomp (instrumental)	Grand 104	2.00	8.00	53

WINTERS, Ruby

WINTERS, Ruby, Johnny Thunder &

WISE, Penny:
see Charioteers, The

WITHERS, Bill

WITHERSPOON, Jimmy

TITLE/FLIP	LABEL & NO.	GOOD TO VERY GOOD	NEAR MINT	YR.
BABY, BABY/Slow Your Speed	Modern 895	3.00	12.00	53
BACK DOOR BLUES/The Last Mile	Federal 12138	3.00	12.00	53
CORN WHISKEY/Don't Tell Me How	Federal 12107	5.00	20.00	52
DADDY PINOCCHIO/Love My Baby	Modern 877	3.00	12.00	53
EACH SLIP OF THE WAY/Let Jesus Fix It For You	Modern 903	1.50	6.00	51
FAST WOMAN—SLOW GIN/Miss Miss Mistreater	Federal 12155	3.00	12.00	53
I DONE TOLD YOU/Oh, Boy	Federal 12189	2.50	10.00	53
I'LL BE RIGHT ON DOWN/Oh Mother, Dear Mother	Modern 909	2.50	10.00	51
IT AIN'T NO SECRET/Why Did I Love You Like I Do?	Checker 826	1.50	6.00	55
IT/Highway To Happiness	Federal 12180	2.50	10.00	53
JAY'S BLUES, PART 1/Jay's Blues, Part 2	Federal 12118	4.00	16.00	52
LUCILLE/Blues In Trouble	Federal 12099	4.00	16.00	52
ONE FINE GAL/Back Home	Federal 12128	3.00	12.00	52
TIME BRINGS ABOUT A CHANGE/Waitin' For Your Return	Checker 810	1.50	6.00	54
TWO LITTLE GIRLS/Foolish Prayer	Federal 12095	4.00	16.00	52
WHEN THE LIGHTS GO OUT/Big Daddy	Checker 798	2.00	8.00	54

WITHERSPOON, Jimmy:
see Lamplighters, Jimmy Witherspoon & The
see Quintones, Jimmy Witherspoon & The

WOMACK BROTHERS, The (Bobby & Curtis)

WOMACK BROTHERS, The (Bobby & Curtis) as The Valentinos

WOMACK, Bobby

WOMACK, Bobby, Szabo Gabor &

WONDERS, The

TITLE/FLIP	LABEL & NO.	GOOD TO VERY GOOD	NEAR MINT	YR.
BY MY LOVE, BE MY LOVE/Tell Me	Forward 601	3.00	12.00	—
BY MY LOVE, BE MY LOVE/Tell Me	Tampa 157	1.50	6.00	58

WONDERS, Tony Allen & The

WOOD, Brenton

WOODFORK, Bob as Poor Bob

WOODS, Bennie:
see Five Dukes, Bennie Woods & The
see Rockin' Townies, Bennie Woods & The

WOODS, Donald:
see Bel-Aires, The (with Donald Woods)
see Vel-Aires, Donald Woods & The

WOODS, Eddie & The Gemtones:
see Gemtones, Eddie Woods & The

WOODS, Reverend Maceo & The Christian Tabernacle Baptist Choir

WOODS, Sonny:
see Four Winds, Sonny Woods & The
see Twigs, Sonny Woods & The

WRENS, The

TITLE/FLIP	LABEL & NO.	GOOD TO VERY GOOD	NEAR MINT	YR.
BETTY JEAN/Everything	Rama 175	20.00	80.00	55
C'EST LA VIE/C'est La Vie (instrumental by Jimmy Wright)	Rama 194	20.00	80.00	56
COME BACK MY LOVE/Beggin' For Love	Rama 65	10.00	40.00	55
ELEVEN ROSES/Come Back My Love	Rama 65	20.00	80.00	55
ELEVEN ROSES/Love's Something That's Made For Two	Rama 110	25.00	100.00	55
HEY, GIRL/Love's Something That's Made For Two	Rama 174	20.00	80.00	55
I WON'T COME TO YOUR WEDDING/What Makes You Do?	Rama 184	20.00	80.00	55
LOVE'S SOMETHING THAT'S MADE FOR TWO/Beggin' For Love	Rama 53	20.00	80.00	55
SERENADE OF THE BELLS/Hey, Girl	Rama 174	20.00	80.00	55

WRIGHT, Arthur

WRIGHT, Berry

WRIGHT, Billy

TITLE/FLIP	LABEL & NO.	GOOD TO VERY GOOD	NEAR MINT	YR.
DRINKIN' AND THINKIN'/Keep Your Lamp Down Low	Savoy 827	2.50	10.00	52
GOIN' DOWN SLOW/If I Didn't Love You	Savoy 870	1.50	6.00	52
MEAN OLD WINE/Keep Your Hands On Your Heart	Savoy 776	4.00	16.00	51

WRIGHT, Jimmy Orchestra, The

All of the following are instrumentals.

TITLE/FLIP	LABEL & NO.	GOOD TO VERY GOOD	NEAR MINT	YR.
I'M IN THE MOOD TO BE LOVED/Slow Down, Baby	Meteor 5011	3.00	12.00	—
PORKEY PINE/Scotch Mist	Meteor 5007	3.00	12.00	—

WRIGHT, Jimmy Orchestra, The:
see Wrens, The

WRIGHT, Johnny

TITLE/FLIP	LABEL & NO.	GOOD TO VERY GOOD	NEAR MINT	YR.
I STAYED DOWN/I Was In St. Louis	DeLuxe 6029	3.00	12.00	54
SUFFOCATE/The World Is Yours	RPM 443	2.50	10.00	55

WRIGHT, O. V.

WRIGHT, Ruben

TITLE/FLIP	LABEL & NO.	GOOD TO VERY GOOD	NEAR MINT	YR.

WYLIE, David as Little David

Wylie should not be confused with the Little David who recorded for International and RPM record labels. Neither should be mistaken in this guide for the Little David who led The Harps, a rhythm & blues group.

TITLE/FLIP	LABEL & NO.	GOOD TO VERY GOOD	NEAR MINT	YR.
SHACKLES 'ROUND MY BODY/ You're Gonna Weep And Moan (78)	Regal 3271	4.00	16.00	50

WYLIE, Popcorn

YELLOW JACKETS, Walter Miller & The

YOUNG JESSIE

TITLE/FLIP	LABEL & NO.	GOOD TO VERY GOOD	NEAR MINT	YR.
BROWN EYES/Make Me Feel A Little Good	Vanessa 101	1.50	6.00	—
HIT, GIT AND SPLIT/Don't Happen No More	Modern 1002	1.50	6.00	56
I SMELL A RAT/Lonesome Desert	Modern 921	3.00	12.00	54
MARY LOU/Don't Think I Will	Modern 961	2.00	8.00	55
NOTHING SEEMS RIGHT/Do You Love Me?	Modern 973	1.50	6.00	55

YOUNG LADS, The

TITLE/FLIP	LABEL & NO.	GOOD TO VERY GOOD	NEAR MINT	YR.
MOONLIGHT/I'm In Love	Neil 100	5.00	20.00	56

YOUNG WOLF, The:
see Jenkins, Gus as The Young Wolf

YOUNG-HOLT UNLIMITED

YOUNG, Johnny

TITLE/FLIP	LABEL & NO.	GOOD TO VERY GOOD	NEAR MINT	YR.
WORRIED MAN BLUES/Money Takin' Woman (78)	Ora Nelle 712	4.00	16.00	47

YOUNG, Johnny as Man Young

TITLE/FLIP	LABEL & NO.	GOOD TO VERY GOOD	NEAR MINT	YR.
MY BABY WALKED OUT ON ME/ Let Me Ride Your Mule (78)	Old Swingmaster 19	6.25	25.00	48
MY BABY WALKED OUT ON ME/ Let Me Ride Your Mule (78)	Planet 103/104	10.00	40.00	48

YOUNG, Man:
see Young, Johnny as Man Young

YOUNG, Mighty Joe

YOUNGSTERS, The

TITLE/FLIP	LABEL & NO.	GOOD TO VERY GOOD	NEAR MINT	YR.
COUNTERFEIT HEART/You're An Angel	Empire 107	2.50	10.00	56
DREAMY EYES/Christmas In Jail	Empire 109	3.00	12.00	56
DREAMY EYES/I'm Sorry Now	Empire 109	2.50	10.00	56
SHATTERED DREAMS/Rock'n Roll'n Cowboy	Empire 104	3.00	12.00	56

YOUNGTONES, The

TITLE/FLIP	LABEL & NO.	GOOD TO VERY GOOD	NEAR MINT	YR.
O, TELL ME/Come On, Baby	Brunswick 55089	3.00	12.00	58
PATRICIA/By The Candleglow (with The Dolls)	X-Tra 110	3.00	12.00	58
YOU I ADORE/It's Over Now	X-Tra 104	3.00	12.00	58

ZEBULONS, The

TITLE/FLIP	LABEL & NO.	GOOD TO VERY GOOD	NEAR MINT	YR.
FALLING WATER/Wo-Ho-La-Tee-Da	Cub 9069	3.00	12.00	60

ZEPHERS, Benn Zeppa & The

TITLE/FLIP	LABEL & NO.	GOOD TO VERY GOOD	NEAR MINT	YR.
BABY, I NEED/A Foolish Fool	Specialty 577	5.00	20.00	56

ZEPPA, Benn & The Zephers:
see Zephers, Benn Zeppa & The

ZIP & THE ZIPPERS (female group)

ZIPPERS QUARTET, Nappy Brown & The

ZIPPERS, Zip & The (female group)

ZIRCONS, The

ZODIACS, Maurice Williams &

ZODIACS, The

TITLE/FLIP	LABEL & NO.	GOOD TO VERY GOOD	NEAR MINT	YR.
ANYTHING/Little Sally Walker	Soma 1418	1.50	6.00	64
GOLLY GEE/"T" Town	Cole 100	3.00	12.00	63
LITA/Another Little Darling	Soma 1410	1.50	6.00	—
LOVER/She's Mine	Cole 101	2.00	8.00	—

WHOLESALE PRICE LIST

FOR
RECORD SLEEVES

SIZES	NUMBERS OF SLEEVES PER CARTON	WEIGHT PER CTN	YOUR COST PER CARTON
7" White Sleeves	2,500/ctn	20 lbs	$28.75/ctn
7" Green Sleeves	1,000/ctn	15 lbs	$25.00/ctn
10" Green Sleeves	750/ctn	27 lbs	$41.25/ctn
12" Green Sleeves	500/ctn	28 lbs	$32.00/ctn
12" White Sleeves	1,000/ctn	27 lbs	$28.25/ctn
12" White Polylined Sleeves	600/ctn	30 lbs	$45.00/ctn

MINIMUM ORDER 2 CARTONS ANY SIZE

TERMS AND CONDITIONS

FULL PAYMENT WITH ORDER. Checks must clear before sleeves are shipped. Please allow sufficient time for delivery.

FREIGHT — NOTE CAREFULLY

ALL SHIPMENTS WILL BE SENT VIA UPS COLLECT (Cash Only).
Over 100 lbs. will be sent via truck, freight collect.
Please include Street Address and Telephone Number.

BILL COLE

P.O. BOX 60, DEPT. LP-9
WOLLASTON, MA 02170 TEL. (617) 963-5510

Prices subject to change without notice.

Starfire Records

For Collectors Only

THE SERENADERS: Night Owl/I'm Gonna Love You (unreleased 1958 R&B on red wax)

RAL DONNER: Rip It Up/Don't Leave Me Now (black wax)

THE LUCKY CHARMS: Who Do You Love/Potential So And So (unreleased R&B on red wax)

A TINT OF DARKNESS: Sixty Minute Man/Farewell My Love (R&B on splash wax, accapella)

THE VIBES: Beat Of My Heart/Oh Darlin' (unreleased 1957 R&B)

THE LUCKY CHARMS: You're The Girl For Me/Born To Be Lonely (unreleased 1957 R&B)

A TINT OF DARKNESS: You Send Me/Steal Away (R&B accapella, marble wax)

THE VIBES: Tell Me I'm Your Love/Up On The Mountain (unreleased 1957 R&B, on blue wax)

$10 each

Includes Scotty Moore, D. J. Fontana & the Jordanaires.

ALL STARFIRE SINGLES, EXCEPT THE PICTURE DISC SHOWN ABOVE, ARE ONLY $3.00 EACH.

Rip Lay
STARFIRE RECORDS
Box 342
Concord, CA 94522

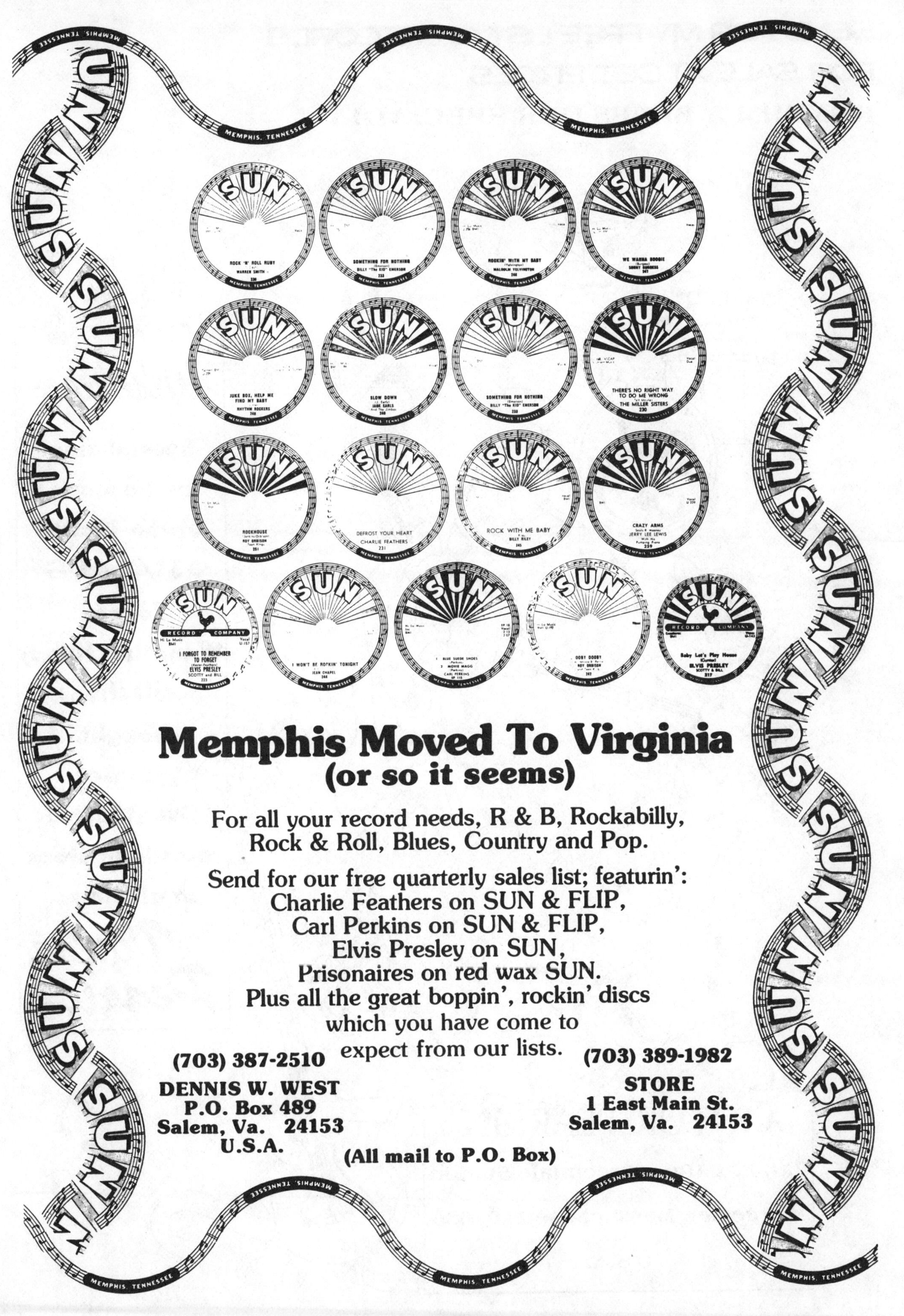

Memphis Moved To Virginia
(or so it seems)
For all your record needs, R & B, Rockabilly,
Rock & Roll, Blues, Country and Pop.
Send for our free quarterly sales list; featurin':
Charlie Feathers on SUN & FLIP,
Carl Perkins on SUN & FLIP,
Elvis Presley on SUN,
Prisonaires on red wax SUN.
Plus all the great boppin', rockin' discs
which you have come to
expect from our lists.
(703) 387-2510
DENNIS W. WEST
P.O. Box 489
Salem, Va. 24153
U.S.A.
(703) 389-1982
STORE
1 East Main St.
Salem, Va. 24153
(All mail to P.O. Box)

Joel Whitburn's Latest Release!

The Complete History of Billboard's "Hot 100" Charts!

From ABBA to ZAPPA, Each Page Packed With Information About Every Artist & Single to Hit Any of Billboard's Pop Charts From January, '55 Through December, '78!
Over 3600 Artists & 14,000 Singles Listed!

Plus Much More...

- **Complete Title Section** with: • All titles cross-referenced alphabetically • Highest position record reached • Year of peak popularity • Title • Artist • Various versions of same title ranked according to popularity
- **Chronological Listing of All #1 Records**
- **Photographs of the Top 100 Artists**
- **Top Artist Achievement Section** listing artists with: • The most charted records • The most #1 records • The most weeks in the #1 position • The most Top 10 records • The most consecutive Top 10 records • The most Top 40 records • The longest chart span
- **Records of Longevity** (30 or more weeks charted)
- **Top 10 Hit Creators Section** listing: • Top labels • Top songwriters • Top producers • Top arrangers • Top publishers
- Full-color cover • Over 660 pages

Record Research

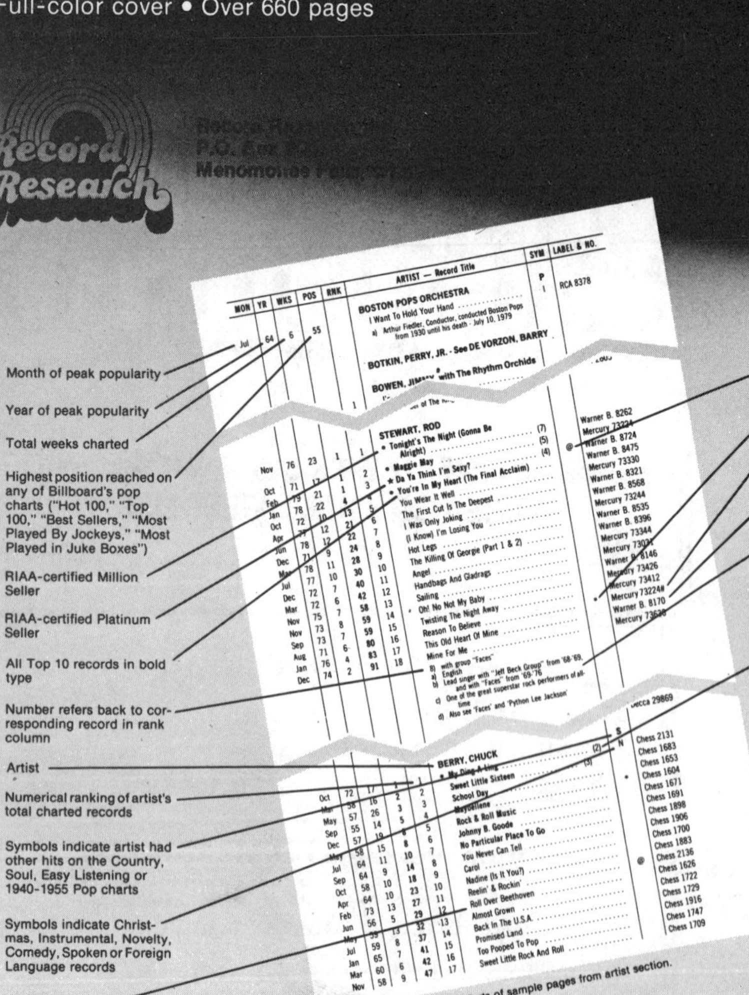

Parts of sample pages from artist section.

Terms & Conditions

Check or money order for full amount in U.S. dollars must accompany order. U.S. orders add $1.25 for postage and handling. Overseas orders add $5.00 per book and $1.00 per supplement. All Canadian orders add 15% to total (unless paid in U.S. dollars).

Please send me _____ **hardcover** edition(s) of Joel Whitburn's **Top Pop Artists & Singles 1955-1978** at $60.00 each.

Please send me _____ **softcover** edition(s) of Joel Whitburn's **Top Pop Artists & Singles 1955-1978** at $50.00 each.

In addition, I'd like to complete my Record Research collection with the following books and supplements:

Books

- ☐ Pop Annual '55-'77 (Hardcover)† ... $50
- ☐ Pop Annual '55-'77† ... $40
- ☐ Top Pop '40-'55 ... $20
- ☐ Top LPs '45-'72 ... $30
- ☐ Top Country Singles '49-'71 ... $25
- ☐ Top Soul Singles '49-'71 ... $25
- ☐ Top Easy Listening Singles '61-'74 .. $25

†Year-by-year history of Billboard's "Hot 100" charts

Supplements ... **$10 each**

	'78	'77	'76	'75	'74	'73	'72-'73
Pop*	☐						
LPs	☐	☐	☐	☐	☐	☐	
Country**	☐	☐	☐	☐	☐		☐
Soul**	☐	☐	☐	☐	☐		☐
Easy Listening	☐	☐	☐	☐			

*Supplement to both Pop Annual and Top Pop Records
**'78 supplement covers both singles and LPs charts

NAME ____________________
ADDRESS ____________________
CITY ____________________
STATE ____________________ ZIP ____________________

Mail to: Record Research Inc./P.O. Box 200/Menomonee Falls, WI 53051

All books and supplements compiled by Joel Whitburn with exclusive rights as licensed between Billboard Publications, Inc. and Record Research Inc. Published and sold exclusively by Record Research Inc.